Judges, Transition, and Human Rights

GW00994209

Judges, Transition, and Human Rights

Edited by
JOHN MORISON
KIERAN McEVOY
and
GORDON ANTHONY

OXFORD
UNIVERSITY PRESS

OXFORD
UNIVERSITY PRESS

Great Clarendon Street, Oxford OX2 6DP

Oxford University Press is a department of the University of Oxford.
It furthers the University's objective of excellence in research, scholarship,
and education by publishing worldwide in

Oxford New York

Auckland Cape Town Dar es Salaam Hong Kong Karachi
Kuala Lumpur Madrid Melbourne Mexico City Nairobi
New Delhi Shanghai Taipei Toronto

With offices in

Argentina Austria Brazil Chile Czech Republic France Greece
Guatemala Hungary Italy Japan Poland Portugal Singapore
South Korea Switzerland Thailand Turkey Ukraine Vietnam

Oxford is a registered trade mark of Oxford University Press
in the UK and in certain other countries

Published in the United States
by Oxford University Press Inc., New York

British Library Cataloguing in Publication Data

Data available

Library of Congress Cataloging-in-Publication Data

Judges, transition, and human rights / edited by John Morison, Kieran McEvoy,
and Gordon Anthony
     p. cm.
  Includes bibliographical references and index.
  ISBN 978–0–19–920493–9 (alk. paper)—ISBN 978–0–19–920494–6 (alk. paper)
1. Human rights.   2. Judicial power.   3. Due process of law.   4. Political violence.
5. Terrorism.   6. Human rights—Europe.   7. Human rights—Northern Ireland.
8. Political violence—Northern Ireland.   I. Morison, John.   II. McEvoy, Kieran.
III. Anthony, Gordon.
  K3240. J833 2007
  341.4'8—dc22

                                                             2007003105

Typeset by Newgen Imaging Systems (P) Ltd., Chennai, India
Printed in Great Britain
on acid-free paper by
Biddles Ltd, King's Lynn

ISBN 978–0–19–920493–9
ISBN 978–0–19–920494–6 (Pbk.)

1 3 5 7 9 10 8 6 4 2

Preface

Stephen Livingstone was a new breed of lawyer in Northern Ireland, engaging and engaged. Not for him the delicate discussions in the ivy-covered common rooms of the Malone Road on the *ratio decidendi* of the latest case from the House of Lords. I remember him from the time I first met him as a human rights activist and a public intellectual intent on teasing out legal rules in favour of the citizen.

His was an involvement in a public project of the most pleasing kind. Everything he did pushed him into matters of urgent relevance to pressing debates in the real world. He brought to these current concerns the scholar's virtues of thoroughness, commitment and reflection. His was a world of uncompromising intellectual and moral integrity.

Seriousness of purpose combined with extraordinary courage and a sense of justice made his contribution irresistible. His greatest virtue was to ensure that people recognized how the law worked, either for or against them, and how Protestants or Catholics should be able to reach out for legal remedies.

His involvement at Queen's University Belfast in non-governmental organizations and his appointment to public office reflected his life-view, an abiding belief in a non-sectarian approach to life.

For many of us, he was a pilot who helped us to navigate the very treacherous waters of the often uncharted area of civil liberties in Northern Ireland. He has handed to us a lively, committed, and passionate approach to public life. These essays do justice to his memory and his life.

Kader Asmal
Professor in the University of the Western Cape
Former Minister of Education, South Africa

Acknowledgements

This collection has been written in memory of Professor Stephen Livingstone, whose life was sadly cut short in 2004. The editors would like to thank each of the contributors for their willingness to participate both in an earlier conference in Stephen's memory in Belfast on 7–8 October 2005 (at which many of the chapters were first presented) and in working the book through to completion. Their affection and respect for Stephen was apparent throughout and they all remained (fairly) disciplined and enthusiastic and took all of our editorial poking and prodding in good spirit. We would in similar vein express our appreciation to Professor Kadar Asmal for his warm and touching tribute to Stephen.

We would also like to thank our colleague Dr Alison Mawhinney for her assistance and goodwill in preparing the manuscript. John Louth, Rebecca Smith, and Hugh Logue at OUP too were characteristically professional, encouraging and patient during the book's different stages of gestation and production.

Our thanks are due too, for all their support and encouragement, to Stephen's partner Karen; to his parents Max and Flo; and to his sister Alison.

It is to Stephen Livingstone's memory that we dedicate the book.

John Morison
Kieran McEvoy
Gordon Anthony
December 2006

Contents

PART III: HUMAN RIGHTS

List of Contributors

Gordon Anthony Senior Lecturer in Law, The Queen's University Belfast.

Maggie Beirne Director of the Committee on the Administration of Justice, Belfast.

Christine Bell Professor of Public International Law and Director of the Transitional Justice Institute, University of Ulster.

Kevin Boyle Professor of Law and Director, Human Rights Centre, University of Essex.

Colm Campbell Professor of Public International Law and Associate Director of the Transitional Justice Institute, University of Ulster.

Hugh Corder Dean and Professor of Law, University of Cape Town.

Brice Dickson Professor of International and Comparative Law, The Queen's University Belfast and former Chief Commissioner, Northern Ireland Human Rights Commission.

David Feldman Rouse Ball Professor of English Law and Fellow of Downing College, The University of Cambridge and Judge of the Constitutional Court of Bosnia and Herzegovina.

Martin S. Flaherty Professor and Co-Director, Joseph R. Crowley Program in International Human Rights, Fordham Law School; Visiting Professor, Woodrow Wilson School of Public and International Affairs, Princeton University.

Tom Hadden Professor Emeritus, The Queen's University Belfast.

Robert Harmsen Senior Lecturer, School of Politics, International Studies and Philosophy, The Queen's University Belfast.

David Harris Professor Emeritus and Co-Director, Human Rights Law Centre, University of Nottingham.

Colin Harvey Professor of Human Rights Law and Director of the Human Rights Centre, The Queen's University Belfast.

Angela Hegarty Senior Lecturer in Law, University of Ulster.

Murray Hunt Barrister at Law, and Legal Advisor to the Joint Committee on Human Rights, UK Parliament.

Laura Lundy Reader in Education, The Queen's University Belfast.

Marie Lynch PhD Candidate, School of Law, The Queen's University Belfast.

Christopher McCrudden Professor of Human Rights Law and Fellow of Lincoln College, The University of Oxford.

Kieran McEvoy Professor of Law and Transitional Justice, and Director of the Institute of Criminology and Criminal Justice, The Queen's University Belfast.

Lesley McEvoy Lecturer in Education, The Queen's University Belfast.

Paul Mageean Solicitor and former Legal Officer with the Committee on the Administration of Justice, Belfast. Currently an inspector with the Criminal Justice Inspection Northern Ireland.

Elizabeth Meehan Professor Emerita and former Director of the Institute of Governance, Public Policy and Social Research, The Queen's University Belfast.

John Morison Professor of Jurisprudence and Head of the School of Law, The Queen's University Belfast.

Thérèse Murphy Professor of Law and Critical Theory, The University of Nottingham.

Rachel Murray Professor of Law, The University of Bristol.

Fionnuala Ní Aoláin Professor of Law and Associate Director of the Transitional Justice Institute, University of Ulster, and Dorsey and Whitney Chair in Law at the University of Minnesota Law School.

Gerard Quinn Professor of Law, National University of Ireland, Galway.

Rachel Rebouche Clerk, Constitutional Court of South Africa.

William Schabas Professor of Human Rights Law, National University of Ireland, Galway and Director, Irish Centre for Human Rights.

Sally Wheeler Professor of Law, Business and Society, The Queen's University Belfast.

Noel Whitty Professor of Human Rights Law, University of Strathclyde.

Tom Zwart Dean of International Relations, Faculty of Law, University of Utrecht, The Netherlands.

Tables of Cases

United States

Zimbabwe

Tables of Legislation

Table of Treaties and Conventions

1

Judges, Transition, and Human Rights: Essays in Memory of Stephen Livingstone

John Morison, Kieran McEvoys, and Gordon Anthony (eds)

Choosing titles for edited books is usually no easy task. The title for this book, however, was something of an exception as it largely chose itself. Professor Stephen Livingstone, whose life was sadly cut short in 2004 and to whose memory the book is dedicated, was a scholar of international standing who wrote on each of the themes of judges, transition, and human rights.[1] Stephen, perhaps ahead of many of his colleagues, appreciated that these themes overlapped with each other and, moreover, deserved the shared attention of lawyers, criminologists, and social and political scientists. The chapters in this book have thus been written by individuals from within and across those disciplines who knew Stephen either personally or professionally and who have extensive experience of working on one or more of these themes. The book, in that sense, represents a collective attempt to further debates in areas of interest to Stephen, and to complement his own highly influential contributions.

The book of course thereby also makes its own unique contribution to existing literature on judges, transition, and human rights. Although the words 'judges', 'transition', and 'human rights' can be read disjunctively, literature has increasingly started to examine the overlap between these themes and to view them as parts of an interlocking whole.[2] This shift has perhaps been most pronounced in the area of transitional justice scholarship as lawyers, political scientists, sociologists and others have come to examine the relationship between legal formations

---

[1] See 'Tribute to Stephen Livingstone' (2004) 55 Northern Ireland Legal Quarterly 209–13.

[2] eg, Mark Osiel, *Mass Atrocity, Collective Memory, and the Law* (1999); David Dyzenhaus, *Judging the Judges. Judging Ourselves: Truth. Reconciliation and the Apartheid Legal Order* (1998); Jiří Přibáň, Pauline Roberts and James Young (eds), *Systems of Justice in Transition: Central European Experiences Since 1989* (2003); Renáta Uitz, *Constitutions, Courts And History: Historical Narratives in Constitutional Adjudication* (2005).

and social and political change in societies emerging from conflict.[3] One prominent variant of transitional justice scholarship entails the exploration of legal
methods for dealing with the past; ranging from local amnesties, truth recovery or
prosecutorial mechanisms, through to more international manifestations such as
the international indictment of suspected war criminals and individuals charged
with crimes against humanity.[4] Although many of these processes are essentially
political initiatives, the corresponding role of human rights law, as mediated by
judges, raises important questions about how 'rights' and 'judges' facilitate or frustrate wider processes of social and political transformation.[5] Transitional justice
scholars have, in that context, started to engage with the discourse of 'law' and of
'rights' in order to assess their transformative impact.

Identifying the links between judging, transition, and human rights is also a
familiar feature of legal and political science accounts of the role of, most typically,
constitutional courts. The frenzy of constitution-making and guaranteeing rights
that have characterized the last decade or so is bedding down and this process puts
judges centre stage in a way that has not been paralleled in history—at least
for many years. Judges in a variety of jurisdictions across the world are involved
in processes of translating various powerful 'constitutional moments' of far-reaching
change into ways of living together and they are attracting increased attention as
they perform this role.[6] This attention is a consequence not just of the content and
implications of their judgments, but also of the political and democratic ramifica-
tions of entrusting so much of importance to such a group. As the judges are mediating the social changes that new structures and mechanisms of government bring,
and are working through how a new vocabulary of rights should condition a whole
range of new and existing practices, academic attention has therefore focused both
on what they are doing and on the legitimacy of their role in doing so. Literature has
also started to focus on judges' self-perceptions of their role and how far—if at all—
they attempt to 'join up' what they are doing with wider currents and trends.

---

[3] eg, A. James MacAdams (ed.), *Transitional Justice and the Rule of Law in New Democracies*
(1997); Ruti Teitel, *Transitional Justice* (2001); John Elster, *Closing the Books: Transitional Justice in
Historical Perspective* (2004).

[4] Priscilla Hayner, *Unspeakable Truths: Facing the Challenge of Truth Commissions* (2002); Teresa
Godwin Phelps, *Shattered Voices: Language, Violence, and the Work of Truth Commissions* (2004);
Richard Wilson, *The Politics of Truth and Reconciliation in South Africa: Legitimizing the Post-
apartheid State* (2001); Kieran McEvoy, *Making Peace with the Past: Truth Recovery in Northern
Ireland* (2007); Dominic McGoldrick, Peter Rowe and Eric Donnelly, *The Permanent International
Criminal Court: Legal and Policy Issues* (2003); William Schabas, *The UN International Criminal
Tribunals: The Former Yugoslavia, Rwanda and Sierra Leone* (2006).

[5] Colin Harvey (ed.), *Human Rights, Equality and Democratic Renewal in Northern Ireland* (2001);
Shale Horowitz, and Albrecht Schnabel (eds), *Human Rights and Societies in Transition: Causes, Consequences,
Responses* (2004).

[6] Robert Stevens, *The English Judges: Their Role in the Changing Constitution* (2002); Carlo Guarnieri
and Patrizia Pederzoli, *The Power of Judges* (2003); Andrew Le Sueur (ed.), *Building the UK's New
Supreme Court: National and Comparative Perspectives* (2004); Wojciech Sadurski, *Rights Before Courts:
A Study of Constitutional Courts in Postcommunist States of Central and Eastern Europe* (2005) and Kate
Malleson and Peter H Russell (eds), *Appointing Judges in an Age of Judicial Power: Critical Perspectives
from Around the World* (2006).

The corresponding points of emphasis in human rights literature have increasingly been placed on questions of the practical effectiveness of human rights standards; that is, the extent to which they truly foster change in society and to the benefit of that society.[7] Such lines of enquiry, of course, pre-suppose normative arguments in favour of rights and of their corresponding content and hierarchical value, and there are strong counter-arguments to the effect that rights can promote anti-democratic tendencies, particularly when their protection is entrusted to judges.[8] However, an alternative vision of rights protection holds that judges/lawyers are only one of the actors involved in making rights meaningful in practice, and that the role played by other actors at the national and international levels—legislatures/politicians, rights institutions such as human rights commissions, and civil society—is also key. No set template for rights as agents for change exists (there will in any event sometimes be limits to the relevance of rights), although it is understood that rights are at their most vibrant and transformative when these actors engage with each other.[9] The quest in the literature is therefore to identify instances of change being led by rights, or certainly instances where rights influence a transformative agenda.

These issues run through the various essays in this collection and link in, to varying degrees, with Stephen's contributions and interests. One of the essays (Morison and Lynch) reports on work that Stephen and these authors had started through an ESRC-funded project on judicial constitutionalism in Northern Ireland. Another essay by McEvoy and Rebouche draws upon fieldwork conducted in South Africa, Canada, the US, and elsewhere concerning the ways in which lawyers contribute to, and cope with, profound moments of legal and constitutional change. Murray's essay also draws upon fieldwork that Stephen was involved with, which looked at the effectiveness of national human rights institutions as vehicles for ensuring the protection of human rights, and the ways in which such bodies co-exist with and relate to national parliaments.

Other essays pick up on themes that were of particular interest to Stephen. The domestication of human rights in the UK through the Human Rights Act 1998 was an important landmark for Stephen as a human rights activist, based in Northern Ireland. The significance of the Human Rights Act 1998 as a step along a much longer journey to justice and reconciliation is considered in the essay by Dickson, which looks at the impact of the Act in Northern Ireland. The essay by Beirne and Hegarty picks up on Stephen's role as an activist in and former Chairman of the Belfast-based human rights organization, the Committee on

---

[7] Michael Ignatieff, *Human Rights as Politics and Idolatry* (2001); David Chandler (ed.), *Rethinking Human Rights: Critical Approaches to International Politics* (2002); A. Belden Fields, *Rethinking Human Rights for the New Millennium* (2003); Conor Gearty, *Can Human Rights Survive?* (2006).

[8] Robert Martin, *The Most Dangerous Branch: How the Supreme Court of Canada Has Undermined Our Law and Our Democracy* (2005) and Adam Tomkins, *Our Republican Constitution* (2005). For more general critiques see Tom Campbell, Keith Ewing and Adam Tomkin (eds), *Sceptical Essays on Human Rights* (2001).

[9] Colin Harvey (ed.), *Human Rights in the Community: Human Rights as Agents of Change* (2005).

the Administration of Justice, as it provides an account of how lessons learned from the conflict in Northern Ireland might be of relevance in the new war on terror. McCrudden's account of the Northern Ireland Human Rights Commission's efforts to utilize the Council of Europe Framework Convention on National Minorities as part of its work on the unfinished Bill of Rights for Northern Ireland process also develops a particular interest which was held by Stephen. McCrudden's argument, that the experience here demonstrates the limitations of resorting to international human rights concepts in a complex domestic context, and the difficulties of national institutions which are perceived to be 'shopping' for bespoke human rights frameworks to suit particular political circumstances, would certainly have been of import to Stephen in his role in public life in Northern Ireland in the parallel Equality Commission.

The role of the European Convention and the Court of Human Rights was also central to Stephen's scholarship and this is reflected in a number of the essays. Anthony and Mageean consider how the demands of Article 2 of the European Convention on Human Rights (ECHR) have been given effect in post-conflict Northern Ireland and link that to wider themes of transparency and accountability that are taken as key to any meaningful process of transition. The scope of Article 6 ECHR rights to a fair trial, and the issue of how far these apply in non-criminal cases (viz those concerned with 'civil' rights under the ECHR), is reviewed by Harris. Harmsen considers the European Court of Human Rights, the claim that it might be a constitutional court, and what that might mean for a wider constitutional order in Europe and beyond.

But just as Stephen's interest in rights went beyond an immediate focus on courts and judges, so too the chapters address some of the wider questions. The theme of the limiting influence of the doctrine of parliamentary sovereignty provides the starting point for Hunt's contribution, which considers the role that Westminster's Joint Committee on Human Rights might play in facilitating a shift away from more traditional conceptions of constitutionalism in the UK. Hunt argues that the UK needs to develop a 'culture of justification' whereby all exercises of power which impinge upon fundamental rights require public justification, and he suggests that the work of Joint Committee is to the fore in developing such a culture. And then there are two essays directly on the tensions between human rights and democracy. Feldman asks searching questions about whether constitutionalism, deliberative democracy or human rights should be accepted as fundamental to legal orders. Feldman's central point is that 'good' constitutions draw their legitimacy from a number of normative sources—which include democracy, human rights, the rule of law, public safety, etc—and that none of these sources is necessarily superior to the other. Human rights, within this framework, do not therefore define the constitution, although they are an important part of it and are crucially affected by the constitution's corresponding models of constitutionalism and democracy. Harvey's essay reminds us that human rights law should have an express and declared purpose, and that this must be less about the origins of rights or the doctrinal coherence of rights norms, and more closely linked to addressing the needs of vulnerable and marginalized individuals and groups. Boyle's essay examines how human rights connect with other important concepts such as the environment, development and security. Hadden argues that the close yet difficult relationship between human rights and conflict resolution would be resolved best if different rights were attached at various stages during a process of dealing with conflict. Bell, Campbell, and Ní Aoláin provide an exploration of the notion of transitional justice as a more ambitious project than dealing with the legacy of past human rights violations. They explore some of the theoretical tensions between the traditional emphases on the rule of law in transitional justice discourses and the undermining of law's credibility by the US-led 'war on terror'.

The particular issue of how women's movements have used international human rights standards in pursuit of better representation at the domestic or regional levels is explored by Meehan. Wheeler also picks up on an interest that Stephen was developing towards the end of his life by examining the role (or otherwise) of rights in regulating corporations. Highlighting some of the limitations of human rights norms in this context, Wheeler prefers the language of 'political responsibility' as she considers that it speaks to the fact that social injustice is wrong and is to be challenged. Thus, she deconstructs corporations by describing them as mere 'instruments of the will of the wider public in which they are situated' and concludes that it is individual awareness of, and reaction to, the strategies of multi-national enterprises that will bring change.

Expanding on an involvement that Stephen had through a Rowntree-funded project in the 1990s, McEvoy and Lundy consider the role of schools in educating children in the values of civic participation, democracy, and rights. They argue that a co-ordinated approach which harnesses the normative and enforcing capacity of law to the persuasive potential of education is the most effective means of securing and sustaining the much-vaunted notion of a human rights culture. Murphy and Whitty's essay, likewise, acknowledges both Stephen's enduring interest in prisons and prisoners' rights and his openness to interdisciplinary research. Using Scottish prisons as their primary site of analysis, they explore the respective legal discourses of human rights in prison governance and criminological accounts of risk theory as perhaps the two key penological frameworks of the contemporary era.

Many of the essays range across jurisdictions and particular examples that interested Stephen especially, thus drawing widely on comparative experiences in South Africa, Canada, the US, Britain, Ireland, Israel/Palestine, the Balkans, Bosnia and Herzegovina (and, historically, in the Weimar Republic in Germany and the Irish Free State). Corder's account of how the South African judiciary have engaged with the complexity of the transformative agenda in the Constitution, in their treatment of national legislation and policy, picks up on a country and an issue that held a deep fascination for Stephen. The drama of judicial politics in the US was also a special interest for Stephen, perhaps dating back to his time as LL.M candidate at Harvard Law School. Flaherty's essay picks up on this theme as he locates the judicial role within a globalizing trend whereby domestic judges in the US and elsewhere increasingly rely on international and foreign legal materials in the interpretation of domestic constitutional law. Within this context, Flaherty critically examines the boundaries of the judicial decision-making framework, and in particular how ideas of separation of powers can be factored in. With Zwart's contribution the emphasis is again on how the changing judicial role can be understood. Looking at public law cases across a number of jurisdictions, Zwart considers the circumstances where judges feel encouraged (or otherwise) to intervene through reviewing executive actions and measures, and sets these examples against traditional ideas of the separation of powers. Quinn draws a series of parallels between the dismantling of the Irish Free State Constitution by Éamon De Valera (and its replacement by the more 'Republican' Constitution of 1937) with the 'tactic of legality' used by Hitler to destroy the Weimar Constitution. Quinn argues that both constitutional processes offer insights into the ways in which constitutions may be employed as spring boards for the emergence of very different styles of transition. The essay by Schabas traces the contribution of the Irish State as a nascent democracy to the development of the European Convention of Human Rights in 1949 and 1950. Through extensive archival work, Schabas traces this history through the particular leadership of the then Foreign Minister Seán MacBride. For Schabas, MacBride, a former IRA leader and ultimate Nobel Peace Prize winner, personifies the ways in which human rights discourses may become central in a process of personal and political transition.

Beyond these jurisdictions, many of the chapters cover constitutional issues that have emerged in the particular context of Northern Ireland but which resonate elsewhere. This is appropriate for a book that seeks to honour an outstanding scholar from Northern Ireland who combined his interest in the issues of judges, transition, and human rights in his place of birth, with recognition that knowledge should not be constrained by geographical boundaries and that international best practice should be the standard. That international perspective is evident from the list of contributors to the book—which includes some of the most prominent scholars in Ireland, the UK, and beyond—and the resulting chapters are testimony both to Stephen's intellectual powers and to the excellence of his scholarship.

For the sake of structure we have organized the essays into the three sections of judges, transition, and human rights. However, we are conscious that, as with much of Stephen's work, a number could have fitted in one or other, or indeed all of these categories. This book should therefore be regarded as evidence not only of the dynamism of Stephen Livingstone's work and his capacity to suggest an agenda for research that will take many years to develop fully; it should also, and much more importantly, be taken as a sign of the deep affection in which he was held by so many of his colleagues, mentors, former students, and friends now scattered across the world.

John Morison
Kieran McEvoy
Gordon Anthony

PART I

JUDGES

2

Separation of Powers in a Global Context

Martin S. Flaherty*

Introduction

'In the United States, torture was recognised to be prohibited by the law of
nations even before the Torture Convention was made: Filartiga v Peña-Irala
630 F 2d 876 (1980). Earlier still, it had been said to be 'unthinkable that a
statement obtained by torture or by other conduct belonging only in a police state
should be admitted at the government's behest in order to bolster its case':
LaFrance v Bohlinger 499 F 2d 29 (1974), para 6.

Lord Bingham of Cornhill, A (FC) and others (FC) v
Secretary of State for the Home Department[1]

'It is my opinion that modern foreign legal material can never be relevant to any
interpretation of, that is to say, to the meaning of, the U.S. Constitution'.'

Antonin Scalia, speech, American Society of
International Law, April 2, 2004[2]

Alexander Hamilton, among the United States' most cosmopolitan founders,
famously declared, 'The truth is, after all the declamations we have heard, that
the Constitution is itself, in every rational sense, and to every useful purpose, a
Bill of Rights.'[3] Among other things, Hamilton had in mind a separation of
powers, including, and especially, an independent judiciary armed with judicial
review. As Hamilton's then alter-ego, James Madison, even more famously
declared, 'The accumulation of all powers, legislative, executive, and judiciary, in the same hands ... may justly be pronounced the very definition of
tyranny.'[4]

* My thanks to Deborah Hoehne and Ian Davie for research assistance.
[1] [2005] UKHL 71, para 38 (interpreting UK statutory and common law).
[2] Quoted in Anne Gearan, 'Foreign Rulings Not Relevant to High Court, Scalia Says', The
Washington Post (3 April 2004) at A7.
[3] Alexander Hamilton in Clinton Rossiter (ed.), The Federalist (No. 84, 1961) 515.
[4] James Madison in Clinton Rossiter (ed.), The Federalist (No. 47, 196) 301.

Then as now, this insight has global implications. In the eighteenth century, Hamilton and his peers looked at the doctrine's likely effects on foreign affairs. An enhanced Congress would regulate international trade; a strong executive would protect national security; and an independent judiciary would help enforce the law of nations and so keep the republic at peace. Two hundred years later, the doctrine no longer simply has effects beyond US borders, but transcends borders altogether. As Anne-Marie Slaughter has documented, executives, legislatures, and judiciaries around the world bolster their institutional counterparts though direct interaction.[5] Northern Ireland has long been a leading example of the process. The UK and US executives have shared security information, training, and techniques, and Members of Parliament and Congress have visited one another to undertake fact-finding, co-ordinate policy, or simply to lobby. Last and perhaps still least, judges from both jurisdictions meet, and sometimes cite, one another. The critical question, as yet unaddressed and unanswered, is whether this institutional form of globalization sustains or undermines the fundamental rights-protecting balance that separation of powers aims to preserve.

Exactly this inquiry, I shall argue, yields a novel and powerful justification for that aspect of intergovernmental relations that remains the most controversial in the United States—what Slaughter terms 'judicial globalization'.[6] This is not to say that Americans object to US judges meeting with their foreign counterparts, or even taking advantage of international sojourns; for example, Justice O'Connor has participated as a lecturer in the summer program at Queen's University Belfast. Using international and comparative sources to interpret US law, however, is something else again. Against this practice, moreover, some of the most strident condemnations come from the American judiciary itself, with no less than Justice Scalia typically leading the charge.

To a non-American audience, opposition to such judicial borrowing might appear mystifying. Outside the US, judicial globalization of this sort is all but taken for granted. A random list of national courts that cite to outside law includes: India, Canada, Zimbabwe, and Hong Kong. Some nations, most notably South Africa, constitutionally require reference to international and comparative law for domestic interpretation. Last and here not least, the Irish Supreme Court and the House of Lords frequently cite to outside sources for domestic purposes, including US Supreme Court case law.[7]

The US Supreme Court has not returned the favor until very recently. Or, in the longer view, the Justices for over a century relied on international and at least outside common law sources extensively before entering an isolationist phase which it only lately appears to be leaving.[8] Even then, the Court's new embrace of non-US materials remains tentative and contentious. Widely noted have been

[5] Anne-Marie Slaughter, *A New World Order* (2004).   [6] ibid, 66.
[7] See generally Martin S. Flaherty, 'Aim Globally' (2000) 17 Const. Commentary 285.
[8] See Sarah H. Cleveland, 'Our International Constitution' (2006) 31 Yale Journal of International Law 12.

recent allusions to outside sources in important decisions on privacy,[9] affirmative action,[10] and the death penalty.[11]

Wide, too, has been the opposition. As noted, some dissents have come from within the judiciary itself. Other dissents have come from more expected quarters such as the academy, the executive, and the legislature; in the case of the latter, even to the point of a Congressional Bill to prohibit reliance on foreign law. These dissents have put forth various rationales, ranging from the ease with which unfamiliar sources can be manipulated, to concern that looking abroad may diminish certain fundamental rights at home. But by far the greatest source of hostility flows from a potent mix of US exceptionalism and democratic theory. The Constitution of the United States, and the laws made pursuant thereto, derive their force from the positive consent of the American people. Interpreting US law with reference to international and comparative standards empowers an unelected judiciary to privilege the views of outsiders at the expense of the American people, and so is inconsistent with our fundamental conceptions of self-government. Nowhere does this inconsistency become more insufferable than where unelected judges apply a Constitution ordained by 'We the People of the United States' to invalidate laws enacted by US representatives based upon legal materials in whole or in part foreign to American democracy. Put in European terms, the practice suffers from a near total 'democratic deficit'.

This essay, part of a larger project, argues that such democratic objections to US participation in judicial globalization have it exactly wrong. The first part examines the US Supreme Court's recent embrace of foreign legal sources, the hostility that these have prompted, and various possible responses. The second part offers separation of powers as the most promising reply, both in general and in terms of democratic self-government. Toward this end, it considers how globalization systemically favors domestic executives at the expense of other governmental departments. It then considers how judicial globalization can restore the balance that separation of powers serves to protect and so safeguard rather than undermine democratic self-government—even in the US.

Judicial Globalization in the United States

The British are Coming! (Along with the Rest of the World)

The US Supreme Court has cited to 'foreign law' with gusto from the early days of the Republic. The overseas materials on which it has relied include international law, whether treaties or custom, as well as comparative sources such as the

[9] *Lawrence v Texas* 539 U.S. 558 (2003).
[10] *Grutter v Bollinger* 539 U.S. 306, 344 (2003) (opinion of Ginsburg, J., concurring).
[11] *Roper v Simmons* No. 03-663, 1, 21–24 (2005) (slip.op.); *Atkins v Virgina* 536 U.S. 304, 316–17, n. 21 (2002).

jurisprudence of other national courts, and common law jurisdictions especially. Often the US Supreme Court's invocation of foreign law has been tightly cabined, as in cases that turned on 'the law of nations', or demanded the application of other nations' jurisprudence on conflict of laws grounds. Yet, to a surprising degree, the Federal courts also relied on foreign law when applying purely domestic standards. What all this meant, to what extent it has continued, and its relevance to current practices are questions to which scholars are only now turning.[12]

Nonetheless, for the past several generations the conventional wisdom has been that the Supreme Court has been parochial, or at least a net exporter of legal ideas rather than a receptive importer.[13] Until recently over the past several years, US justices and judges have begun to 'borrow' foreign law in a series of high-profile cases that have required interpretation of the Constitution on many of the most controversial issues of the day. Not surprisingly, the combination of what appears to be a new practice with the adjudication of hot button controversies has drawn strident opposition.

Among the most telling early examples occurred when Justice Stevens made the barest reference to global practice (or non-practice) in *Atkins v Virginia*, where he observed: 'within the world community, the imposition of the death penalty for crimes committed by mentally retarded offenders is overwhelmingly disapproved'.[14] That passing comment drew the extended wrath of Chief Justice Rehnquist and Justice Scalia, jurists who acknowledge the use of domestic tradition, however grudgingly. Justice Scalia in particular put his contempt on full display: 'But the Prize for the Court's Most Feeble Effort to fabricate "national consensus" must go to its appeal (deservedly relegated to a footnote) to the views of . . . members of the so-called "world community". . . . [I]rrelevant are the practices of the "world community", whose notions of justice are (thankfully) not always those of our people.'[15]

Yet 'judicial globalization'—domestic courts relying in some way on international and comparative law—has continued to infiltrate the US nonetheless.[16] To great fanfare the Court, or at least individual Justices, have cited international and comparative law sources in a number of cases. In *Lawrence v Texas*, the Court relied in part on the jurisprudence of the European Court of Human Rights when declaring unconstituitonal state law criminalizing sodomy.[17] For Justice Ginsburg, international human rights treaties mattered in deciding to uphold law

---

[12] See Cleveland, 'Our International Constitution' (n 8 above).

[13] See Flaherty, 'Aim Globally', (n 7 above), 206–7.

[14] *Atkins v Virginia* 536 U.S. at 304 (2002).

[15] ibid, 337, 347–48 (Scalia J., dissenting). In less flamboyant fashion, the Chief Justice agreed, stating: 'For if it is evidence of a *national* consensus for which we are looking, then the viewpoints of other countries are simply not relevant'. ibid at 312, 325 (Rehnquist, C.J., dissenting).

[16] The term was coined by Anne-Marie Slaughter. See Anne-Marie Slaughter, 'Judicial Globalization' (2000) 40 Virginia Journal of International Law 1103; see also Harold Hongju Koh, 'Bringing International Law Home' (1998) 35 Houston Law Review 623 (noting and advocating the phenomenon).   [17] *Lawrence v Texas* 539 U.S. at 558 (2002).

school affirmative action programs.[18] As noted, the Court, however fleetingly, referred to comparative law in voiding the death penalty for the mentally challenged.[19] Though less noted, Justice Breyer looked to European Union practice in seeking, unsuccessfully, to justify Federal 'commandeering' of local officials.[20]

As with globalization in general, the phenomenon—and the reactions to it—promise only to continue. This past term, in *Roper v Simmons*, the Court not only declared that the execution of prisoners convicted of a capital crime committed as a minor violated the Eighth Amendment's prohibition on 'cruel and unusual punishment',[21] Justice Kennedy's majority opinion also did so, with a discrete section devoted to both international human rights instruments and comparative practice, including discussion of the International Covenant on Civil and Political Rights and the Convention on the Rights of the Child, as well as a global survey of State practice.[22] On cue, sharp disagreement and defence followed both within and outside the Court. Justice Scalia's dissent reserved special contempt on the majorities overseas reliance, declaring:

'[t]hough the views of our own citizens are essentially irrelevant to the Court's decision today, the views of other countries and the so-called international community take center stage,[23] that American law should conform to the laws of the rest of the world—ought to be rejected out of hand'.[24]

Outside the Court the debate continued as Justices Scalia and Breyer joined the issue in a debate at the US Association of Constitutional Law.[25] As will be discussed, so too did American scholars and not for the first time, did the Congress, which more than once ominously considered a bill that would have prohibited the Federal judiciary from committing similar sins in future.[26] Perhaps most important of all, the legitimacy of judicial globalization arose during the hearings for the now Chief Justice Roberts, who himself appeared to betray a degree of Scalia-like skepticism.[27]

---

[18] *Grutter v Bollinger* 539 U.S. at 342 (2003) (Ginsburg J. concurring).

[19] *Atkins v Virginia* 536 U.S. at 304 (2002).

[20] *Printz v United States* 521 U.S. 898, 976, 976–78 (1997) (Breyer J., dissenting).

[21] *Roper* (n 11 above), at 6. [22] ibid, 21–23. [23] *Roper* (n 11 above) at 16.

[24] ibid, 18.

[25] The debate took place on 13 January 2005 and is available at: http://www.freerepublic.com/focus/f-news/1352357/posts.

[26] In response to *Roper*, resolutions were introduced in the House and Senate indicating that US judges should not rely on foreign legal materials in interpreting the US Constitution, unless these reflect the Constitution's 'original understanding', H. Res. 97, 109th Cong., 1st Sess. (15 February 2005); S. Res. 92, 109th Cong., 1st Sess. (20 March 2005). A year before a similar resolution had been introduced in the House. H. Res. 568, 108th Cong., 2nd Sess. (17 March 2004). None of these resolutions, however, passed.

[27] Roberts mentioned two concerns with regard to reliance on foreign precedents to interpret the US Constitution: first, 'democratic theory', suggesting that only the views of those who participate in American democratic processes should count; second, the concern that 'relying on foreign precedent doesn't confine judges' to the extent that domestic precedent does. Testimony of John Roberts before the Senate Judiciary Committee (13 September 2005) (responding to a question from Senator Jon Kyl).

Dissents: Democratic and Otherwise

American objections to judicial globalization have been as varied as they have been strong. For present purposes, they may, however, be broadly divided into concerns about foreign legal materials themselves and even greater concerns about democratic self-government.

Worries about foreign legal materials begin with their ostensibly unique susceptibility for selective reading and similar abuse. As both Justice Scalia and then Judge Roberts intimated, seeking an international consensus is all but an invitation to selective and idiosyncratic 'cherry picking' among scores of national and transnational jurisdictions. Scalia made the point with particular brio in his *Roper* dissent: 'To invoke alien law when it agrees with one's own thinking, and ignore it otherwise, is not reasoned decision-making, but sophistry.'[28] Better, then, to simply have a prophylactic rule barring this inherently misleading material to begin with.

Prominent American scholars echo this theme. Professor Ernest Young chides internationalists, arguing, 'We might well compare foreign citation to the classic quip about legislative history: it is like "looking over a crowd and picking out your friends".'[29] Young, along with such commentators as Professors Kenneth Kersch, John McGinnis, and Michael Ramsey, further assert that US judges have not done very well when they have borrowed from foreign legal materials in any case. The conclusion follows that they should refrain from doing so, at the very least pending the advent of better training, a more coherent framework for borrowing, or both.[30]

But by far the more strident opposition stems from idea of democratic self-government. This objection in some fashion argues that the people of a nation state make their own laws, that courts should only rely on domestic sources to be faithful to the will of the people, and that national court invalidation of home-grown laws ostensibly on the basis of the domestic constitution—but in reality on the grounds of foreign materials—represents the worst kind of judicial usurpation of power, especially where judges are not elected. Justice Scalia notably made the stakes clear in his *Atkins* dissent, quoting himself in an even earlier foreign law skirmish:

'We must never forget that it is a Constitution for the United States of America that we are expounding . . . [W]here there is not first a settled consensus among our own people, the

---

    [28] *Roper* (n 11 above) 84 (Scalia J., dissenting).
    [29] Ernest A. Young, '*Foreign Law and the Denominator Problem*' (2005) 119 Harvard Law Review 148, 167 (citation omitted).
    [30] ibid, 167–68; Kenneth I. Kersch, 'The New Legal Transnationalism, the Globalized Judiciary, and the Rule of Law' (2005) 4 Washington University Global Studies Law Review 345, 369; Michael D. Ramsey, 'International Materials and Domestic Rights: Reflections on *Atkins* and *Lawrence*'

views of other nations, however enlightened the Justices of this Court may think them to be, cannot be imposed upon Americans through the Constitution.'[31]

Lest the rhetoric appear unique to the inimitable Justice, Professor Kersch sounds a similar alarm, declaring judicial globalization to be an 'elite-driven, politically motivated worldwide trend toward judicial governance which is antithetical to democratic self rule, if not the rule of law itself.'[32]

These and other critics see no shortage of related deficiencies. Not only do comparative and international legal materials lack a democratic approval by US institutions—absent ratification in the case of treaties—these materials often lack a democratic pedigree on their own terms: comparative materials to the extent they are opinions by unelected judges; customary international law norms because they lack a specific vote up or down; multi-lateral treaties because they are distant 'top-down' even when ratified.[33] Judicial globalization, moreover, has the effect of undermining democratic processes, not to mention national pride, both in the US and abroad, by diminishing the power of elected institutions.[34] As if this were not enough, foreign legal materials are undemocratic because they are simply too alien to American values, even those from Western Europe.[35]

Defences: Democratic and Otherwise

The foregoing indictment notwithstanding judicial globalization ultimately prevails even, and especially, on democratic terms. Yet democratic self-government offers but one of several possible normative justifications for the practice. Of these others, principles of justice and international peace have commonly been put forward as the more promising justifications for judicial cosmopolitanism. As with other aspects of global judicial practice, at least briefly considering these alternative justifications helps clarify the normative stakes. Doing so will explain why seeking to legitimize judicial globalization in terms of self-government presents the greater challenge and, likely, the greater rewards.

(2004) 98 American Journal of International Law 69; John O. McGinnis, 'Foreign to Our Constitution' (2006) 100 Northwestern University Law Review.

[31] *Atkins* (n 11 above) 347–48 (Scalia J., dissenting) (quoting *Thompson v Oklahoma* 487 U.S. 815, 868–69 (1988) (Scalia J., dissenting)).

[32] Kersch, 'The New Legal Transnationalism, the Globalized Judiciary, and the Rule of Law' (n 30 above) 346. Former Judge Bork has made the related assertion that the undemocratic power lust of US judges is now spreading to other countries such as Canada and Israel. Robert H. Bork, *Coercing Virtue: The Worldwise Rule of Judges* (2002). See also Kenneth Anderson, 'Foreign Law and the U.S. Constitution' (2005, June–July) Policy Review 33, 47–49 (arguing that *Roper's* use of foreign authorities undermines the democratic basis of American constitutional jurisprudence).

[33] See McGinnis, 'Foreign to Our Constitution' (n 30 above).

[34] Kersch, 'The New Legal Transnationalism, the Globalized Judiciary, and the Rule of Law' (n 30 above) 372–75; see McGinnis, 'Foreign to Our Constitution' (n 30 above).

[35] See Young, 'Foreign Law and the Denominator Problem' (n 29 above) 161; Jed Rubenfeld, 'Unilateralism and Constitutionalism' (2004) 79 New York University Law Review 1971, 1999.

Non-Democratic Justifications

Concerns about international peace, stability, and the rule of law offer another basis for justifying deference to international law. Here the basic argument holds that courts should as much as possible conform domestic practice to international rules because doing so at a minimum will reduce the pretexts that foreign nations might have for intruding upon the nation's affairs, and at a potential maximum will promote orderly relations among nations in general. Whatever its other features, this approach relates more distinctively to international law more than any other. In part, for this reason, it has a distinguished historical pedigree dating to the earliest days of the republic.[36]

Consider, next, reliance on international human rights standards in the name of justice. On the assumption that courts are properly charged with making this type of determination, the argument runs, there is every reason domestic judges should look to foreign materials. In this regard such sources operate less as binding rules than as relevant information, much like reliance on the views of thinkers with no special connection to the domestic legal regime. This approach appears best to characterize the use of external legal rules the foreign courts commonly make.[37] This understanding perhaps most accurately describes what Justice Kennedy was up to in *Lawrence*[38] when he invoked European law to refute the position in *Bowers*[39] that the Court had taken on whether the scope of privacy extended to consensual sexual relations between adults. This approach likewise characterizes his follow-up performance in *Roper*, invoking foreign legal materials to 'confirm' the determination that the Court had reached about the execution of minor offenders.[40]

The normative case for this approach would appear just about impossible to refute. Among other things, making the best judgment on fundamental questions of justice, rights, or even institutional arrangements and procedures, will depend upon the persuasiveness of arguments advanced, intuitions based upon human experience, and consequences evident from applications of earlier judgments. None of these bases varies *a priori* in light of national borders. The extent that such variations may occur, moreover, may justify discounting the weight of external materials, but hardly a per se prohibition.[41] Anne-Marie Slaughter dismissed

[36] See text below accompanying notes 47–57.
[37] eg *Catholic Common for Justice and Peace in Zimb. v Attorney Gen.*, No. S.C. 73/93 (Zimb. 1993), reported in 14 Hum. Rts. L. J. 323, 329 (1993).   [38] *Lawrence* (n 9 above) 558.
[39] *Bowers v Hardwick* 478 U.S. 186 (1986).   [40] *Roper* (n 11 above) 21.
[41] Though my interest centers on fundamental rights, the point applies more generally. To take a recent example, *Printz v United States* 521 U.S. 898 (1997), 95–1478 featured a pointed exchange between Justices Scalia and Breyer on the question of whether it followed that Federal government lacked the power to 'commandeer' State officials because the US features two levels of 'sovereign' government. Justice Scalia argued that this conclusion did follow (*Printz*, 521 U.S. 918–22). Justice Breyer rejected this position, indicating that it was not only possible to imagine a system in which the central sovereign government commandeered officers of the constituent sovereigns, but that this was exactly how the European Union—a system comprised of genuine sovereign States—operated

arguments to the contrary pretty much with the respect they deserve when she noted that a good idea is still a good idea, even if it comes from France.

It is against such assertions that critics respond with the selectivity argument. Against this two near conclusive rejoinders may be advanced. First, to the extent the foreign source is either a widely ratified treaty or customary international law, then by definition the rule commands a high degree of generality. More generally, the charge of selectivity attaches to *any* set of complex and wide-ranging legal materials. One damning, comparison must suffice to make the point. Many critics who advance the selectivity objection also tend to view reliance on the Constitutional's original understanding as a method to constrain judicial choice. Yet few sources are or have been more prone to ambiguity, manipulation, or selectivity than the thousands of primary source pages, and hundreds of historical monographs, written on the Founding. It follows that if such historical sources can be held out as a means of precise guidance, foreign law sources can at least be admitted for consideration. In fact the most vociferous opponents of international law do not really deny the point. Instead, critics such as Justice Scalia consistently, and now Chief Justice Roberts, object based upon the threat international law poses to self-government.[42]

Democratic Justifications

Debating international law in terms of self-government tends to raise the stakes in terms of reward and challenge. Greater reward, at least as a practical matter, comes from the apparently greater commitment American legal culture has to self-government theories than to its rivals.[43] At least in constitutional theory, theories premised on self-government attract a more widespread following than their competitors.[44] Democratic, or self-government, theories currently appear to resonate

---

(ibid 976, 976–77 (Breyer, J., dissenting)). Justice Scalia summarily rejected this example on the apparently irrelevant ground that it was 'foreign' (ibid 921, n 11 (opinion of the Court)). For a discussion, see Martin S. Flaherty, 'Are We To Be A Nation?: Federal Power vs. "States' Rights" in Foreign Affairs' (1999) 70 Colombia Law Review 1277, 1288–89.

[42] See text above accompanying notes 25–27.

[43] This is not to say, as Jed Rubenfeld argues, that US legal culture is distinctively democratic compared to other systems, such as those that comprise the European Union. Jed Rubenfeld, 'Two World Orders' (2003) 27 Wilson Quarterly 22. For analyses that are more rigorous, see Anne-Marie Slaughter, *Leading Through Law* (2003) 27 Wilson Quarterly 37; Andrew Moravcsik, 'In Defence of the "Democratic Deficit": Reassessing Legitimacy in the European Union' (2002) 40 JCMS 603, 613–14.

[44] For now, this is a nakedly impressionistic claim. To give one basis for that impression, Randy Barnett recently surveyed constitutional literature to proclaim, with what I believe is only mild overstatement, that the most rigid type of self-government theory has carried the day when he asserted that 'originalism is now the prevailing approach to the Constitution' (Randy E. Barnett, 'An Originalism for Nonoriginalists' (1999) 45 Loyola Law Review 611, 613). For another, in his recent book, *Constitutional Self-Government*, Chris Eisgruber acknowledges a shift from premising his constitutional theory on a direct consideration of justice, to according greater weight to pursuing justice within a self-conscious framework of self-government (Christopher Eisgruber, *Constitutional Self-Government* (2001) 46–78).

more deeply as well.[45] Carry the day on these grounds, in other words, and in current American legal culture one has gone a long way towards carrying the day in general. Conversely, the greater reward comes with greater difficulty. Even formal, transparent, and democratically approved international law norms, such as treaties, appear remote from popular processes when compared with most types of domestic law-making. Precisely for this reason, the term 'democratic deficit' dogs international law-making more than virtually any other current criticism.[46]

Although separation of powers ultimately offers the most promising democratic justification, it is by no means the only one. Others, worth noting briefly, include originalism, as well as an idea of transborder commonality that may be described as 'the global mirror'.[47]

Originalism

Perhaps the strongest possibility for a democratic justification for domestic judges looking abroad arises from the possibility that the Founding generation expected this practice to take place and be approved. As noted, the Supreme Court itself has never weighed in on the matter from an originalist perspective or otherwise. An early case, emanating from a jurist who was present at the creation, is nonetheless tantalizing. In the celebrated *Schooner Charming Betsy v Murray* case, Chief Justice John Marshall declared generally that 'an act of Congress ought *never* to be construed to violate the law of nations *if any other possible construction obtains*'.[48] In a somewhat softer version, the '*Charming Betsy* canon' has remained part of US foreign relations law ever since.[49] Marshall's opinion did not elaborate the basis for the canon that bears its name. Yet Marshall's very authorship suggests an originalist foundation. A young but significant member of the Virginia Ratifying Convention, Marshall commonly articulated mainstream Federalist defences of the new Constitution.[50]

Applying the *Charming Betsy* canon to the Constitution, however, is not the same thing as applying it to statutes. Professor Curtis Bradley has explained why, through focusing upon separation of powers. An internationalist presumption applied to statutes is subject to a formally democratic check by the President

---

[45] Another impressionistic claim, based in part on the stridency of ostensibly democratic rhetoric.

[46] cf Moravcsik, 'In Defence of the "Democratic Deficit": Reassessing Legitimacy in the European Union' (n 43 above).

[47] Preliminary attempts to develop other democratic justifications—as well as these at greater length—are available in an unpublished version as Martin S. Flaherty, 'Judicial Globalization in the Service of Self-Government', (2004) Princeton Law and Public Affairs Paper No. 04-017; Fordham Law Legal Studies Research Paper No. 58. Available at http://ssrn.com/abstract=600677.

[48] *Murray v Schooner Charming Betsy* 6 U.S. (2 Cranch) 64, 118 (1804) (emphasis added).

[49] See RESTATEMENT THIRD, at sec. 114 ('Where fairly possible, a United States statute should be construed so as not to conflict with international law or with an international agreement of the United States').

[50] cf Martin S. Flaherty, 'John Marshall, *McCulloch v. Maryland*, and We the People: Revisions in Need of Revising' (2002) 43 William & Mary Law Review 1339.

and Congress, who can make clear an intent to depart from international law by passing a statute that clearly does so. In this way, the 'so-called' political branches remain free to determine that, in certain instances, violation of international law may better promote justice or, more likely, further US interest in a stable world. As with any statutory presumption, the canon's accommodation of other concerns ultimately bows to the demands of self-government in a fairly straightforward and transparent fashion.[51]

The balance shifts in the constitutional context. The lack of democratic checks in this setting weakens the case of an internationalist presumption from a self-government perspective. It does not mean, however, that the canon cannot be sustained. Dissatisfaction at the polls could always lead to the election of a President and Senate who will approve a less internationally inclined judiciary.[52] Then there is the difficult option of constitutional amendment. But at least for some—and among them the greatest opponents of judicial globalization—a theoretically more powerful justification comes not from the availability of attenuated democratic checks; rather, and especially for the likes of Justice Scalia and Judge Bork, the better democratic defence would come from an originalist authorization of the canon by 'We the People of the United States'.[53]

There is reason to suppose that 'We the People' did just that. Relevant sources suggest that, for the American Founders, discerning the law of nations complemented the project of constitutional thought, that American thinkers were particularly open to the influence of the law of nations, and that an important stream in Founding thought supported the idea that, where possible, interpretation of the Constitution should conform to international law. For starters, the Founding generation embraced the ideas of great contemporary international jurists such as Vattel, Burlamaqui, Puffendorf, and Grotius, with nearly the same fervor as they did the works of Locke, Montesquieu, and Blackstone.[54] Independence deepened this theoretic commitment to international law not least because the revolutionary act of the American people assuming 'among the Powers of the Earth, the separate and Equal Station to which the Laws of Nature and Nature's God entitle them'[55] of necessity reoriented thinking about the direct applications of international law from questions of how constituent units fit within an Empire, to the place of the new republic itself within the law of nations. Here the fledging US discovered what many newly independent nations would learn in recognizing the utility of international law as a safeguard for peace and security. In part for this

---

[51] Curtis A. Bradley, 'The *Charming Betsy* Canon and Separation of Powers: Rethinking the Interpretive Role of International Law' (1998) 86 Georgetown Law Journal 479.

[52] cf Eisgruber, *Constitutional Self-Government* (n 44 above) 64–66.

[53] In this regard Judge Bork is especially vulnerable. He has written the classic, if flawed, modern defence of originalism. Robert H. Bork, *The Tempting of America: The Political Seduction of the Law* (1990).

[54] Berhard Bailyn, *The Ideological Origins of the American Revolution* (1967) 27.

[55] Declaration of Independence, para 1.

reason, the new Constitution would adopt a monist position, proclaiming that treaties would be part of the 'supreme Law of the Land'.[56]

Converting this working hypothesis into a reliable historical interpretation, however, would require substantial research, which at a minimum would require a broad survey of primary and secondary sources, as well as a broad conception of the relevant context. As to sources, the question implicates the standard plethora of eighteenth-century constitutional materials, yet could not enjoy anything like the scholarly work that exists on the domestic side. As to the context, the most basic framework would require considering; first, the general influence of the law of nations on eighteenth-century Anglophone political thought; second, the international law implications of independence, the Revolution, and the so-called 'Critical Period'; and only then, what (if anything) the Founders believed to be the relation between their new Constitution, international law, and the role of the judiciary as evidenced in the Federal Convention, the document it produced, the ratification debates, and early practice.[57] Though the focus of a related yet separate project, an initial inquiry along the lines suggested at least indicates that such research is worth pursuing, and at most promises substantial problems for those who would at once claim adherence to originalism yet oppose reliance on foreign materials in the name of democratic self-government.

A Global Mirror

One further democratic justification at first glance appears counter-intuitive. Critics of international borrowing commonly assume, as Justice Scalia stated, that foreign judgments either have no bearing on US views or frequently diverge from them. As Professor Young blandly assumes, even 'when we look to "other nations that share our Anglo-American heritage, and . . . the leading members of the Western European community", we see divergence rather than convergence on many aspects of values and political culture'.[58] More likely, however, where a clearly dominant position exists, foreign legal materials presumptively reflect commitments that are widely held domestically as well as internationally—at least with regard to a discrete list of fundamental rights. Moreover, judges are at least as well placed to determine the content and extent of popular rights-based judgments made transnationally, and indeed are likely to be better situated than the executive and the legislature, the so-called 'political branches'.

To be clear, the key inquiry is not whether turning to foreign legal materials aids the effort of determining whether there is widespread global support for a particular right, but whether a particular interpretation of a right contained in the US Constitution has a significant, popular, American grounding. Skeptics answer

[56] US Constitution, art VI, cl. 2. See Martin S. Flaherty, 'History Right? Historical Scholarship, Original Understanding and Treaties as "Supreme Law of the Land"' (1999) Columbia Law Review 2095.   [57] cf Flaherty, ibid.

[58] Young, '*Foreign Law and the Denominator Problem*', (n 29 above) 161 (citing *Thompson*, 487 U.S. at 830).

obviously not. For them, judicial globalization misfires to begin with because self-government implies direct, positivist, usually majoritarian (or supermajoritarian) procedures, and neither the courts' indirect democratic pedigree nor reliance on popular sentiment expressed outside these procedures suffices. Even if they did, there would remain the simple problem of borders. It appears counter-intuitive, to say the least, to try to discover American values by looking outside America. For both sets of reasons, Young, Kersch, and others question reliance on foreign legal materials insofar as the practice reflects an undemocratic judicial elite teaming up with undemocratic foreign legal elites to override the democratic wishes of the domestic citizenry.[59]

There are, nonetheless, reasons to believe that looking abroad in this context does help clarify popular sentiment at home. The first, and likely most controversial, arises from an assumption of commonality among constitutional cultures with regard to fundamental rights. In colloquial terms, we look abroad not because *we* can learn from *them*, but because *they are* like *us*, and so can confirm what appear to be our own commitments or can tip the scales where those commitments appear conflicting. Especially in the context of international human rights law, which itself builds widespread national recognition of rights, this assumption runs in the face of philosophical, anthropological, and cultural objections that emphasize difference.[60] Assuming commonality in this instance, however, is a far cry from such cases as western human rights activists making similar assumptions when ostensibly imposing their alien standards on indigenous cultures.

By comparison, judicial reliance on international and related comparative standards takes place in a context in which relevant differences are modest. To begin with, those domestic rights with international law analogues are those that tend to command overlapping consensus across substantially different cultures. Suggestive here is Richard Rorty's speculation that non-rational human sentiment points to such an overlap, even if rational philosophy cannot.[61] More concretely, and contrary to a frequent caricature, the effort to hammer out the foundational Universal Declaration of Human Rights rested on a conscious cross-cultural effort, including an important UNESCO report attempting to set out various overlaps.[62] Moreover, the specific cultures in play here are essentially the constitutional culture of the US and the parallel cultures of other nations that generate international human rights law, a process in which the US has played a substantial,

[59] See Young, ibid; cf Kersch, 'The New Legal Transnationalism, the Globalized Judiciary, and the Rule of Law' (n 30 above).

[60] See eg Richard A. Schweder, 'When Cultures Collide: Which Rights? Whose Tradition of Values?': A Critique of the Global Anti-FGM Campaign, in Christopher Eisgruber and Andra Sajo (eds), *Global Justice and the Bulwarks of Localism: Human Rights in Context* (2005).

[61] Richard Rorty, 'Human Rights, Rationality, and Sentimentality' in Stephen Schute and Susan Hurley (eds), *On Human Rights: The Oxford Amnesty Lectures 1993* (1993) 111.

[62] Mary Ann Glendon, *A World Made New: Eleanor Roosevelt and the Universal Declaration of Human Rights* (2001) 73–78, 222–23.

if uneven, part. Ironically, the usual relativist critique of human rights tends to emphasize this particular overlapping consensus by juxtaposing generally local or regional conceptions against imperialist human rights norms advanced by liberal States, the North, the West, or more directly, the United States and its allies.

To the extent that such an assumption about commonality in this context holds, it follows that international, or even much foreign constitutional law, reflects not simply basic commitments of other nations, but commitments that have a sufficient grounding within the US to form the requisite basis for judicial judgments. At the end of the day, of course, all this turns on empirical inquiry, not to mention further definition of what counts as a sufficient popular grounding. In any particular instance, moreover, an assumption about commonality could be rebutted; arguably, the US conception of a right to own guns.[63]

A second set of reasons to look above to international law as a reflection of popular domestic commitments below has to do with democratic process. As any comparativist would indicate, liberal democracies vary significantly in the mechanisms they employ to register popular sentiment, including and especially for the purposes of treaties and customary international law.[64] International human rights standards commanding general global assent, have therefore not only survived the hurdles of international law-making rules, but have also navigated differing domestic systems that do not necessarily channel democratic preference in similar ways. The diversity of national mechanisms—parliamentary, presidentialist, unicameral, bicameral—theoretically filter in only those norms that genuinely command broad cross-border agreement. On this theory, formal outlier States may still be just that, nations in which popular sentiment has roundly rejected a proposed standard. Yet this view points to the possibility that an outlier result may be a function of a particularly idiosyncratic domestic mechanism.[65]

Turning from task to institution, the judiciary enjoys as good or better an advantage in this setting as it does in exercising foreign affairs authority. From the earliest days of the republic, courts have assumed a broad expertise in formally discerning rules established in foreign legal materials. At least through the early twentieth century, moreover, a staple of domestic common law jurisprudence involved reliance on English common law decisions.[66] More closely on this point, domestic courts throughout our history have surveyed foreign legal sources to make the kind of judgments about international law that parallel constitutional and Federal common law questions. In the Supreme Court itself, this tradition extends at least as far back as *Ware v Hylton*,[67] and continues through *Roper*.[68] Beyond this, face-to-face discussion among judges of different jurisdictions has

---

[63] Michael Bellesisles, *Arming America: The Origins of a National Gun Culture* (2000) to the extent that his central thesis appears to have survived the controversy.

[64] cf Vicki C. Jackson and Mark Tushnet, *Comparative Constitutional Law* (1999).

[65] cf Moravcsik, 'In Defence of the "Democratic Deficit": Reassessing Legitimacy in the European Union' (n 43 above).   [66] See Cleveland, 'Our International Constitution' (n 8 above).

[67] 3 U.S. (3 Dall.) 199 (1796).   [68] *Roper* (n 11 above) 21–23.

added a new and important informal mechanism of aiding courts in discerning international judgments. Reliance on international and comparative legal materials, as a general matter, has always been central to the judicial function. Nor has it been one in which even the executive or legislature has presumed to assert superior expertise.

Not only are courts comparatively suited to interpreting international law, they are likewise well-fitted for determining when national tradition offers so little support for a global norm that it cannot support an equivalent judgment domestically. Among other things, judicial practice limits the potential role of foreign legal materials in at least two ways. First, the American judiciary long ago established the practice of concluding when tradition or other indicators of popular commitment are so slim that they cannot sustain a particular constitutional judgment.[69] In such an instance, contrary foreign sources would indicate national divergence rather than allegiance with the international position. Second, on the *Charming Betsy* model, it also has traditionally fallen to the judiciary to decide when domestic legal materials taken together remain sufficiently indeterminate to permit reliance on international law in the first place.

Global Separation of Powers

These and other justifications for judicial globalization each merit further exploration. The balance of this essay, however, offers one more defence which is at once more original and potentially the most powerful. Call this separation of powers in a global context—or 'global separation of powers' for short. The premise is straightforward. It assumes, first, that globalization generally has resulted in a net gain in power not for judiciaries, but for the 'political' branches—and above all for executives—*within* domestic legal systems. In other words, the growth of globalized transnational government networks has yielded an imbalance among the three (to four) major branches of government in separation of powers terms. Such an imbalance, among other things, poses a significant and growing threat for the protection of individual rights by domestic courts, whether on the basis of international *or* national norms.

Yet if separation of powers analysis helps identify the problem, it also suggests the solution. If globalization has comparatively empowered executives in particular, it follows that fostering—rather than prohibiting—judicial globalization provides a parallel approach to help restore the balance. In this way, judicial separation of powers justifies judicial borrowing on both *democratic and non-democratic grounds*. From a non-democratic perspective, transnational

---

[69] With regard to the role tradition plays in due process, see *Poe v Ullman* 367 U.S. 497 (1961) (Harlan J., dissenting); *Roe* 410 U.S. at 113 (1973); *Bowers*, 478 U.S. 186 (1986); *Lawrence*, 539 U.S. at 1102. For the Eighth Amendment, see *Trop v Dulles* 356 U.S. 86 (1958).

judicial dialogue with reference to international law and parallel comparative questions gives national judiciaries a unique expertise on one aspect of foreign affairs, and so is a further exception to the usual presumption that the judiciary is the least qualified branch of government for the purposes of foreign affairs. More important, from a democratic point of view, restoring the balance that separation of powers seeks promotes self-government to the extent that separation of powers is itself seen as a predicate for any well-ordered form of democratic self-government.

Globalization and Imbalance

Globalization, and the corollary erosion of sovereignty, may not yet be clichés, but they are hardly news. As any human rights lawyer would be quick to point out, the post-World War II emergence of international human rights law represents one of the most profound assaults on the notion that State sovereigns are the irreducible, impermeable building blocks of foreign affairs.[70] But the nation State model has been eroding no less profoundly in less formal ways. Central here is the insight that governments today no longer simply interact State-to-State, through heads of State, foreign ministers, ambassadors and consuls. Increasing, if not already dominant, in significance is the interaction which takes place through global networks in which sub-units of governments directly deal with one another. In separation of powers terms, executive branches at all levels interact less as the representative of the nation, than as a partner education ministry, intelligence agency, or on health and education initiatives. Likewise, though lagging, legislators and committees from different jurisdictions meet to share approaches and discuss common ways forward. Last, and least powerful if not dangerous, judges from different nations share approaches in conferences, teaching abroad programs, and of course, formally citing to one another in their opinions. Only recently has pioneering work by Anne-Marie Slaughter, among others, given a comprehensive picture of this facet of globalization.[71] That work, in turn, suggests that among the results of this process have been a net shift of domestic power in any given State toward the executive and away from the judiciary and the protection of fundamental rights.

Executive Globalization

Where international human rights lawyers seek directly to pierce the veil of State sovereignty, international relations experts have chronicled the no less significant desegregation of State sovereignty through the emergence of sub-governmental networks. Nowhere has this process been more greatly marked than with regard to

---

[70] cf Harold Hongju Koh, 'Complementarity on Human Rights Organisatons in International Human Rights/The Rise of Transnational Networks as the "Third Globalization"' (2000) 21 Human Rights Law Journal 307.
[71] Slaughter has developed her previous writings on the subject in *A New World Order* (n 5 above).

the interaction of various levels of regulators within the executive branches—in parliamentary systems, the governments—of individual nations. Starting with pioneering work by Robert Koehane and Joseph Nye,[72] and more recently enhanced and consolidated by Slaughter, current scholarship offers a multifaceted picture of what may be termed 'executive globalization'. That said, much work remains to be done on how the 'Global War on Terror' post 9/11 has accelerated this process with regard to security agencies. Nor, on a more general level, has significant work been done as to what the net effects of executive networking has been in separation of powers terms. The following reviews what has been done and suggests the likely answers to the questions that in turn arise.

Slaughter, somewhat consciously overstating, terms government regulators who associate with their counterparts abroad 'the new diplomats'. This characterization immediately raises the question of who they are and in what contexts they operate. Perhaps ironically, desegregation begins at the top. When presidents, prime ministers and heads of State gather in settings such as the G-8, they act not as representatives of their State, but as chief executives with common problems, which may include dealing with other branches of their respective governments. Moving down the ladder come an array of different specialists who meet across borders with one another both formally and informally: central bankers, finance ministers, environmental regulators, health officials, government educators, prosecutors, and today perhaps most importantly, military, security, and intelligence officials. The frameworks in which these horizontal groups associate are various. One type of setting might be transnational organizations under the aegis of the UN, the EU, NATO, or the WTO. Another framework can be networks that meet within the framework of executive agreements, such as the Transatlantic Economic Partnership of 1998. Others meet outside governmental frameworks, at least to begin with, with examples ranging from the Basel Committee to the Financial Crime Enforcement Network.[73]

As important as identifying which executive officials currently cross borders, is the question of what they actually do. The activities that make up 'executive transgovernmentalism' may be sliced in various ways. One breakdown divides the phenomenon into: (a) information networks; (b) harmonization networks; and (c) enforcement networks. An obvious yet vital activity of many government regulatory networks is to interact simply to exchange relevant information and expertise. Such exchanges include simple brainstorming on common problems, sharing information on identified challenges, banding together to collect new information, and reviewing the performance of others' agencies.[74] Harmonization networks, which usually arise in settings such as the EU or NAFTA, entail relevant

---

[72] See eg Robert O. Keohane and Joseph Nye, Jr, 'Transgovernmental Relations and International Organizatons' 39 World Politics 27.   [73] Slaughter, *A New World Order* (n 5 above) 36–64.
[74] See Kal Raustiala, 'The Architecture of International Cooperation: Transgovernmental Frameworks and the Future of International Law' (2002) Virginia Journal of Transnational Law 1.

administrators working together to fulfill the mandate of common regulations pursuant to the relevant international instrument.[75]

For present purposes, however, enforcement networks most greatly implicate separation of powers concerns, precisely because they generally involve police and security agencies sharing intelligence in specific cases and, more generally, in capacity building and training. In the Northern Ireland context, the Royal Ulster Constabulary (RUC) maintained, 'numerous links with other police services, particularly with those in Britain, but also with North American agencies and others elsewhere in the world . . . [including] the Federal Bureau of Investigation'.[76] In a relatively benign vain, the Independent Police Commission charged with reforming the RUC recommended further international contact, in part because, 'the globalisation of crime requires police services around the world to collaborate with each other more effectively and also because the exchange of best practice ideas between police services will help the effectiveness of domestic policing'.[77]

It is exactly at this point, moreover, that 9/11 era concerns render this aspect of executive globalization ever more salient, and often more ominous. To take one example, consider the shadowy practice of 'extraordinary renditions', that is, the security forces of one country capture a person and send him or her to another where rough interrogation practices are likely to take place—all this outside the usual mechanisms of extradition.[78] To this extent, transnational executive co-operation moves from general mutual bolster to the expansion of one another's jurisdiction in the most direct and concrete fashion possible.

All this, in turn, suggests a profound shift in power to the executives in any given nation State. At least in the US, the conventional wisdom holds that the Executive Branch has grown in power relative to Congress or the Courts, not even counting the rise of administrative and regulatory agencies—all this in purely domestic terms.[79] Add to the specter of enlarged executives worldwide enhancing one another's power through information and enforcement networks in particular, and the conclusion becomes presumptive. Furthermore, the co-operation of executives in light of 9/11 and the pro-executive implications of government globalization become more troubling still.

Legislative Globalization

This pro-executive conclusion becomes even harder to resist given the slowness with which national legislators have been interacting with their counterparts.

---

[75] See Sydney A. Shapiro, 'International Trade Agreements, Regulatory Protection, and Public Accountabiity' (2002) 54 Administrative Law Review 435.

[76] The Independent Commission for Policing in Northern Ireland, *A New Beginning: Policing in Northern Ireland* (1999) 101.   [77] ibid.

[78] For a discussion of the practice with regard to international human rights law, see Association of the Bar and the City of New York & Center for Human Rights and Global Justice, NYU School of Law, 'Torture by Proxy: International and Domestic Law Applicable to "Extraordinary Renditions"' (2005) 60 The Record of the Association of the Bar of the City of New York 13.

[79] See Martin S. Flaherty, 'The Most Dangerous Branch' (1996) 105 Yale Law Journal 1725.

Several factors account for the slower pace of legislative globalization. Membership in a legislature almost by definition entails not just representation, but representation keyed to national and subnational units. The turnover among legislators typically outpaces executive officials and, for that matter, judges. In further contrast to legislators, regulators need to be specialists, and specialization facilitates cross-border interaction if only because it is easier to identify counterparts and focus upon common problems challenges.[80]

Transnational legislative networks exist nonetheless, and are growing. To take one example, national legislators have begun to work with one another in the context of such international organizations as NATO, OSCE, and ASEAN. To take another, independent legislative networks have begun to emerge, such as the Inter-Parliamentary Union and Parliamentarians for Global Action.[81]

Yet even were national legislators to 'catch up' to their executive counterparts in any meaningful way, the result would not necessarily be a more robust or adequate protection of fundamental rights in times of perceived danger or the protection of minority rights at any time. Human rights organizations around the world are all too familiar with the democratic pathology of draconian statutes hastily enacted in response to actual attacks or perceived threats, including the Prevention of Terrorism Act in the UK, the USA Patriot Act in the US, and the Internal Security Act in Malaysia. It is for this reason that the essential players in the matter of rights protection must remain the courts.

General Judicial Globalization

Several years ago, Justice Sandra Day O'Connor visited Queen's University Belfast to participate in a summer academic program that also involved universities from the Republic of Ireland and the US. During the course of her visit, she was able to meet with local leaders of the bench and bar, exchange experiences, compare notes, and talk shop with her UK and Irish counterparts.

This is but one facet of what Slaughter calls the 'construction of a global legal system' through both formal and informal transnational judicial networks.[82] Such judicial globalization, broadly conceived, occurs in several ways. The most mundane yet potentially transformative are the increasing number of face-to-face meetings through teaching, conferences, and more formal exchanges. Next, and directly tied to classic economic globalization, courts of different nations have transformed the idea of simple comity to co-ordination in tackling complex multi-national commercial litigation. Of immense regional importance, the dialogue between the European Court of Justice and national courts constitutes a more formal, horizontal aspect of direct interaction among judiciaries.[83]

---

[80] Slaughter, *A New World Order* (n 5 above) 104–6.   [81] ibid 104–30.
[82] ibid, 65. Slaughter earlier has written about this phenomenon extensively, see Slaughter, *Judicial Globalization* (n 16 above); and Anne-Marie Slaughter, 'Court to Court' (1998) 92 American Journal of International Law 708.   [83] Slaughter, *A New World Order* (n 5 above) 82–99.

For the purposes of present analysis, however, by far the most important aspects of judicial globalization involve national courts use of comparative materials and international law—above all international human rights law. Ostensibly new and controversial in the US, these aspects of globalization are familiar in most other jurisdictions. As noted, national, supreme, and appellate courts have with apparent frequency cited comparable case law in other jurisdictions as at least persuasive authority to resolve domestic constitutional issues.[84] Likewise, such courts also cite with increasing frequency the human rights jurisprudence of such transnational tribunals as the European Court of Human Rights and its Inter-American counterpart.[85] In spectacular fashion, the House of Lords has recently been doing both.[86] Likewise, the still-recent South African Constitution famously requires judges interpreting its Bill of Rights to consult international law, while expressly allowing them to consult 'foreign', ie comparative law.[87] So marked is the phenomenon that several comparative constitutional law casebooks that highlight such borrowing have carved out a significant market niche, even in the US.[88]

It follows that in all these ways the global interaction of judges strengthens their hands within their respective countries. In both theory and in the substance of these interactions, the bolstering of judiciaries generally works toward a greater protection of individual and minority rights. But while leading authorities view judicial globalization as outpacing its legislative counterpart, so too do they describe a world in which executive and regulatory interaction outpaces them all.

To this extent, judicial globalization helps identify a problem, yet also suggests a solution. The problem, simply, is that transgovernmental globalization taken as a whole draws power to national executive branches and away from rights-protecting judiciaries. Against this problem, the solution becomes fostering the judicial side of the phenomenon, particularly with regard to the use of comparative and international materials.

Restoring the Balance

Return, now, to the US. Judicial globalization has made it to the shores, but the practice has yet to be securely planted on dry land. As noted, some of the resistance comes from intuitions that sound in democratic theory, and some that do not. This section will suggest how a global conception of separation of powers

---

[84] See eg *Catholic Commission for Justice and Peace in Zimbabwe v Attorney-General*, Judgment No. S.C. 73/93, (1993) 14 Human Rights Law Journal 323 (surveying comparative and international law in interpreting the Zimbabwean Constitution regarding delay in application of the death penalty).

[85] See eg *HKSAR v Ng Kung Siu* [1999] 2 HKC 10 (opinion of the Court of Appeal of Hong Kong).

[86] See eg *A (FC) and others (FC) v Secretary of State for the Home Department* [2005] UKHL 71.

[87] Constitution of the Republic of South Africa (1996), Art. 39(1) b and c (1996).

[88] See eg Jackson and Tushnet, *Comparative Constitutional Law* (n 64 above); Norman Dorsen, Michel Rosenfeld, Andras Sajo, and Susanne Baer, *Comparative Constitutionalism* (2003).

goes beyond the descriptive task of identifying concerns that globalization yields, but in the normative task of providing justifications for judicial borrowing that addresses each set of concerns. Once applied, an intriguing counter-intuitive result emerges. Non-democratic aspects of separation of powers theory suggest unappreciated grounds for using foreign legal materials as persuasive authority. Yet the democratic aspects of the theory suggest, if anything, a stronger basis for defending judicial borrowing as dispositive authority, at least when domestic sources fail to yield any clear answer.

Persuasive Authority

A global conception of separation of powers offers an additional and powerful argument for domestic judicial reliance on foreign legal materials as persuasive authority. Of course, the previously noted defence for the practice would seem justification enough. More knowledge is generally better than less knowledge, even for lawyers. Absent some claim that foreign legal materials are so exceptionally prone to selectivity, manipulation, and misuse that they require a prophylactic ban, and consultation of comparative and international law to shed insight on a comparable domestic issue appears unassailable. Although most imply, and a few claim, just that, the arguments put forward thus far appear unconvincing.[89] Given the legal profession's problematic record of using history,[90] judicial abuse of foreign legal materials would have to be abysmally uninformed and selective to be demonstrably worse. That demonstration has yet to be offered. To the contrary, foreign materials that nonetheless remain within the discipline of law should be theoretically less susceptible either to professional ignorance or unchecked manipulation precisely because they are legal. This point applies notwithstanding the US judiciary's provincialism, which itself appears to be of apparently recent vintage.[91]

Whether needed or not, global separation of powers makes the informational argument even more compelling. The key has to do precisely with the enhanced understanding of foreign legal norms that the phenomenon yields. While the emphasis of this essay has been on separation of powers as a means to safeguarding democratic protection of rights, the doctrine is conventionally understood to promise another non-democratic benefit of nearly equal weight. That benefit is specialization and efficiency.[92] To the extent that foreign legal materials have by definition dealt with the law, courts have always had a theoretical advantage in mastering them. At least in the US, however, that mastery may always have been

---

[89] On this point Professor Young has gone furthest, seriously asserting that judicial use of history is generally acceptable while parallel use of foreign legal materials fails to pass muster. Young, 'Foreign Law and the Denominator Problem' (n 29 above) 166–67.

[90] See Martin S. Flaherty, 'History "Lite" in Modern American Constitutionalism' (1995) 95 Columbia Law Review 523.　　　　　　　　　　　　[91] See text above accompanying notes 7–10.

[92] Flaherty, 'The Most Dangerous Branch' (n 79 above) 1768–70. See Charles C. Thach, *The Creation of the Presidency 1775–1789: A Study in Constitutional History* (1969) 51–52.

more apparent than real, to the extent that international and comparative law has for several generations not loomed large in American legal training. Conversely, the Legal Advisor to the State Department, an executive office, by its remit possessed international expertise that likely surpassed that of most judges. Judicial globalization makes this less true. To the contrary, the interaction among judges has put a premium on understanding foreign legal material and will continue to do so. For the American judiciary, the result can only be an expertise in foreign law that will parallel its domestic knowledge.

In this way, judicial globalization realizes courts' theoretic expertise in foreign law, and so their primacy in this discrete area of foreign relations. As such, the process provides a strong rejoinder to a running theme in American jurisprudence that the judiciary is bound to defer to the executive in foreign affairs on the basis of institutional capacity. In so doing, the process also provides further justification for leaving to legal experts the task of making transnational legal comparisons for the purpose of invoking persuasive authority.

Dispositive Authority

The true potency of global separation of powers analysis, however, lies elsewhere. To its critics, the one test that judicial globalization cannot pass is that of democratic self-government. Worse, the more that judges use foreign law as an authoritative, rather than merely persuasive, source, the greater and more flagrant the failure is to meet the mandate of democratic first principles. Yet global separation of powers suggests that the critics have it exactly backward. The substantial recent international relations scholarship describes the emergences of transgovermental networks on a global scale. This work suggests, though has yet to explore, the comparative institutional results in any given State. The overwhelming evidence nonetheless suggests that the primary comparative beneficiary of the modern disaggregated State has been the executive.

Given this development, transgovernmental globalization violates the core tenets of separation of powers doctrine in any given country. These tenets have long made separation of powers in some form a predicate for properly functioning democratic self-government. First and foremost, separation of powers theory promises balance among the major branches of government to prevent a tyrannical accretion of power in any one. In the US, the Founding generation prized this facet of the doctrine above all else, and though they viewed the 'most dangerous branch' as the legislature, subsequent history has clearly established the executive as the greatest threat to the type of balance that separation of powers presupposes.[93] Beyond this, the American Founders also believed that separation of powers could facilitate democracy not simply by preserving liberty, but by widely

---

[93] James Madison in Clinton Rossiter (ed.), *The Federalist* (No. 48, 1961) 309; Flaherty, 'The Most Dangerous Branch' (n 79 above) 1810–39.

dispersing democratic accountability.[94] For this reason they ensured that all three branches of government had a direct or indirect democratic provenance: the House of Representatives through direct elections; the Senate initially through election by the State legislatures; the President through the Electoral College; and not least, the judiciary through presidential appointment and senatorial approval.[95] Of course not all liberal democracies, especially in the parliamentary mode, follow the US model in these and other specifics. At a more general and no less relevant level, they nonetheless do, especially in the idea that an independent judiciary, itself at least indirectly accountable, serves as a check on behalf of individual rights against too great a concentration of power in the legislature and executive in the service of energetic government. Not only is this idea commonly evident in democratic constitutions, it is also expressed in various international human rights instruments.[96]

It is precisely on the grounds of rights and self-government, therefore, that the judicial facet of globalization ought to be encouraged rather than attacked—and not just in the US. At least in a US setting, the strongest case would arise in a constitutional setting that echoed a *Charming Betsy* situation with statues, ie where conventional domestic materials fail to yield a clear answer to a constitutional question, a court should select among rival interpretations the one that best comports with either an applicable international law norm or a prevailing comparative consensus. Of course, many devils lurk in the details. Not least among these would be: what counts as a 'clear' answer from domestic materials; how much weight the foreign materials should be given; and whether the application of the canon should differ in the constitutional setting. That said, at least preliminary answers to these and other matters in the first instance would come from the Court's existing *Charming Betsy* jurisprudence with regard to statutes. Further answers, ironically, might well come from how the judiciaries of other nations, from the House of Lords to the South African Constitutional court, grapple with foreign materials in domestic interpretation. For present purposes, what matters is not resolving any of these questions, but establishing the threshold principle.

Whether encouraging a *Charming Betsy* canon of constitutional borrowing, or the resulting practice itself, will suffice to redress the imbalance may be an open question. But to paraphrase Justice Jackson in *Youngstown*, those concerned with self-government should be the last, not the first, to oppose it.[97]

[94] Flaherty, ibid 1767–68, 1821–26; see Peter M. Shane, 'Political Accountability in a System of Checks and Balances: The Case of Presidential Review of Rulemaking' (1995) Arkansas Law Review 161, 212.   [95] US Constitution, art. I, secs. 2 & 3; art. II, secs. 1 & 2.

[96] See eg Universal Declaration of Human Rights, art. 21.

[97] In *Youngstown*, Justice Jackson famously declared, 'With all its defects, delays, and inconveniences, men have discovered no technique for long preserving free government except that the Executive be under the rule of law, and that the law be made by parliamentary deliberations. Such institutions may be destined to pass away. But it is the duty of the Court to be last, not first, to give them up.' *Youngstown Sheet & Tube Company v Sawyer* 543 U.S. 579, 634, 655 (1952) (Jackson J., concurring).

Conclusion

Democratically based resistance to judicial borrowing may be simply the latest manifestation of American exceptionalism to both the creation of a global legal system and to the development of international human rights. If so, it is perhaps appropriate that there may exist distinctive American defences such as original understanding. Yet other defences transcend borders. Of these, a global conception of separation of powers appears by far the most promising. As such, it may serve to bolster the practice in States in which it thrives, and protect it in States where, like the US, it subsists but has yet to flourish.

3

The European Court of Human Rights as a 'Constitutional Court': Definitional Debates and the Dynamics of Reform

*Robert Harmsen**

Introduction

It has become something of a commonplace to speak of the European Court of Human Rights (the Court) as facing a crisis. Over the course of the past decade, the Court has had to confront a series of unprecedented quantitative and qualitative challenges. Quantitatively, its caseload has continued to grow exponentially. The Strasbourg institutions, in the last years of the 1980s, were receiving an average of fewer than 5,000 petitions per year. By the late 1990s, that number had jumped to over 20,000 petitions annually, reaching 30,000 in the early years of the current decade, and breaking the 40,000 mark in 2004. Put in still starker terms, the Court now receives, every year, almost the equivalent of the total number of petitions which had been filed with the Strasbourg institutions during their first three decades of existence.

Qualitatively, the Court has also been faced with dramatically changed circumstances, largely flowing from the expansion of the Council of Europe to encompass virtually all of the post-Communist successor States of Central and Eastern Europe. This expansion of the Council's membership, and with it the reach of the European Convention on Human Rights (ECHR), has presented the Court with a far broader range of human rights problems than had previously been the case in the more limited West European context. The Court has increasingly had to deal with structural or systemic problems of human rights protection, associated with ongoing processes of democratic transition and, in more dramatic circumstances, with the manifest failures of such transitions. At the limit,

* The present essay largely draws on research completed while the author was, successively, a Fellow in the Institute of Governance, Public Policy and Social Research of The Queen's University of Belfast and a Visiting Researcher in the Faculty of Humanities of the University of Amsterdam. I am grateful to both institutions for the invaluable support which they provided.

the Court has been called upon to adjudicate questions of State responsibility in situations where the effective exercise of sovereignty, let alone the operation of the rule of law, is fundamentally in doubt.[1]

The growth of these challenges has been accompanied by an almost permanent process of institutional reform. Protocol 11 to the ECHR, effecting a major structural reform of the Convention institutions (merging the previous part-time Commission and Court into a single full-time Court), was opened for signature in 1994 and entered into force in 1998. Only two years after the entry into force of this major reform, however, formal discussions opened concerning the need for a still further reform of the Convention system. This ultimately gave rise to Protocol 14 to the ECHR, a more modest package of changes largely intended to enhance the efficiency of the system's operation. This later Protocol was opened for signature in 2004 and is currently still in the process of national ratification. Yet, even before Protocol 14 has been ratified, a start has been given to a third round of reform. The Council of Europe's Warsaw summit of May 2005 decided, at the behest of the Court, to set up a 'Group of wise persons' charged with drawing up 'a comprehensive strategy to secure the effectiveness of the [Convention] system in the longer term'.[2]

It is unsurprising, given such dramatic circumstances, that there has been a firmament of more general debate surrounding the very nature and purpose of the Strasbourg system. The accumulation of pressures and reforms has led to significant 'existential' discussions, which have engaged the relevant scholarly and practitioner communities, as well as members of the Court themselves. It is these discussions which form the starting point of this essay, focusing in the first instance on the animated debates which have emerged around the question of whether the Court is best conceived as a 'constitutional court'. While on the surface an apparently rather arcane definitional question, this debate nonetheless goes to the core of the choices which the institution must face in adapting to its dramatically changed environment. The broad terms of this debate are then, in a subsequent section, given more tangible form through an examination of recent jurisprudential developments. This section focuses attention on the Court's innovative responses to the structural problems which have assumed an increasingly prominent place on its docket. These two strands of analysis, concerned abstractly with the Court's 'constitutional vocation' and more concretely with its handling of systemic violations, are brought together in the conclusion, which further turns its attention to related questions of institutional reform.

---

[1] See notably *Assanidze v Georgia*, judgment of 8 April 2004 on application no. 71503/01 and *Ilaşcu and Others v Moldova and Russia*, judgment of 8 July 2004 on application no. 48787/99.

[2] Warsaw Declaration of the Heads of State and Government of the Council of Europe, 16–17 May 2005. Document available at: http://www.coe.int/t/dcr/summit/20050517_decl_varsovie_en.asp.

A 'Constitutional Court'?

The broad contours of recent discussions concerning the reform of the Strasbourg system have, as noted in the introduction, been significantly shaped by the question of whether the Court should more resolutely move towards the model of a 'constitutional court'.[3] The term 'constitutional court' is an inherently ambiguous one, which has, over the years, figured in multiple and different guises in connection with the Court. From the 1990s onwards, the Court itself came increasingly to adopt a discourse of 'constitutionalism', affirming its place at the heart of a now well-established legal system which had given rise to an extensive body of jurisprudence.[4] At the same time, within the academic literature, studies focused on the extent to which the Court could be likened to a national 'constitutional court'— raising, most importantly, questions concerned with the general (*erga omnes*) effects of the Court's decisions beyond the particular cases under consideration.[5]

In current discussions, however, the advocacy of a more 'constitutional' role for the Court is clearly identified with one of two competing visions concerning the future direction of the institution. 'Constitutionalists', in essence, argue that the principal function of the Court is that of acting as a pan-European standard setter in the field of human rights. In this vision, the extent to which the Court provides

---

[3] The wider 'constitutional' debate has further been more specifically centred on the question of whether a new admissibility criterion should be introduced into the Convention, allowing the Court to exercise a degree of discretion regarding the cases which it hears. A new criterion of this type was ultimately included in Protocol 14 (Art. 12, amending Art. 35/3 ECHR), though in a highly qualified form relative to the aspirations of those who sought to give the Court an expansive instrument of control over its own docket. Under the new criterion, a case is to be declared inadmissible where the applicant has suffered no 'significant disadvantage', provided that the case has been 'duly considered by a domestic tribunal' and that it raises no issue of more general importance as regards 'respect for human rights as defined in the Convention and the Protocols thereto'. While one can only speculate at present as to the use which may eventually be made by the Court of this provision, it has been suggested that the complex set of interlocking 'tests' which it establishes are unlikely to make it particularly attractive as a jurisprudential tool of general scope, capable (as intended) of significantly subsuming the existing admissibility criteria in a more efficient manner. See notably Marie-Aude Beernaert, 'Protocol 14 and New Strasbourg Procedures: Towards Greater Efficiency? And at What Price?' (2004) 9 European Human Rights Law Review 544, 551–54 and Roeland Böcker, 'Protocol nr 14 bij het EVRM: Hervorming van de hervorming' (2004) 79 Nederlands Juristenblad 1840, 1842.

[4] For eg, in its opinion of 7 September 1992 on the then Draft Protocol 11, the Court referred to its role as that of an 'international Court responsible for a "European Human Rights Constitution"'. Reprinted in (1993) 14 Human Rights Law Journal 47, 48. See also Rolv Ryssdal, 'On the Road to a European Constitutional Court', *Collected Courses of the Academy of European Law Vol. 2, Book 2* (1993) 7–20.

[5] See particularly Jean-François Flauss, 'La Cour européenne est-elle une Cour constitutionnelle?', in Jean-François Flauss and Michel de Salvia (eds), *La Convention européenne des droits de l'homme: Développements récents et nouveaux défis* (1997) 69–92. Also reprinted as 'La Cour européenne des droits de l'homme est-elle une Cour constitutionnelle?' (1999) No. 36 Revue française de Droit constitutionnel 711.

remedies in individual cases is seen to be of secondary importance. The specific cases which come before the Court are, in effect, the 'raw material' out of which more general principles of human rights law are shaped; it is the policy role itself which must be seen as the institution's *raison d'être*.

The articulation of this 'constitutionalist' vision of the Court's future has given rise to a vigorous and open discussion, both within the Court itself and in the wider human rights community. In opposition to the constitutionalists, a strong line of argument has emerged stressing the centrality of individual remedy. For proponents of this 'individual rights' position, the Court's function and legitimacy must remain centrally defined by its ability, in each individual case, to provide for the adequate redress of human rights violations where national remedies have been found wanting. Clearly, in dealing with individual cases, the Court will be called upon to enunciate general principles of human rights law— the 'great decisions' or '*grands arrêts*' which define the jurisprudential canon. Yet, for those holding to the 'individual rights' position, this policy role cannot be divorced from—and certainly should not be privileged at the expense of—a continued emphasis on the provision of an effective remedy at the level of the individual victim.

The constitutionalist case has been forcefully and repeatedly made by the President of the Court, Luzius Wildhaber. For President Wildhaber, the exponential growth in the number of cases coming to the Court risks 'asphyxiating' the institution.[6] The sheer quantity of complaints arriving in Strasbourg is overloading the institution, increasingly preventing the Court, despite its best efforts, from giving due and full attention to the limited number of cases which either raise serious issues of legal principle or point to more general, structural failings in the legal orders of one or more of the contracting States. Following this analysis, a clear change of institutional direction is thus required. The Court should be given the means to focus on major issues of policy, by curtailing, if not eliminating, the need to deal with certain categories of minor or repetitive violations at the European level. Although recognizing the understandable anxiety which such a change of tack might create both amongst some of his fellow justices and in the wider human rights community, President Wildhaber has nevertheless insisted on the need for a 'realism' as to what the Court, as an international institution with inevitably limited resources, may accomplish. The trade-off is that between the maintenance of an increasingly illusory generalized right of individual petition and a clear focus on a more limited number of cases where a clearly articulated European jurisprudence may be expected to resonate more widely. As President Wildhaber himself puts it:

'Will we really be able to claim that with say 30,000 cases a year, full, effective access can be guaranteed? Is it not better to take a more realistic approach to the problem and preserve

---

[6] See eg the speech delivered by President Wildhaber to mark the opening of the judicial year on 22 January 2004. Available at http://www.echr.coe.int/Eng/Speeches/Wildhaberspeech.htm.

the essence of the system, in conformity with its fundamental objective, with the individual application being seen as a means to an end itself, as the magnifying glass which reveals the imperfections in national legal systems, as the thermometer which tests the democratic temperature of States? Is it not better for there to be far fewer judgments, but promptly delivered and extensively reasoned ones which establish the jurisprudential principles with a compelling clarity that will render them de facto binding erga omnes, while at the same time revealing the structural problems which undermine democracy and the rule of law in parts of Europe?'[7]

The Registrar of the Court, Paul Mahoney, has developed a similar line of analysis. Mahoney stresses that reform discussions must be guided by the need to maintain the quality of the Court's jurisprudence. Ultimately, it is only through preserving the force and consistency of its reasoning that the Court will be able to maintain the confidence of its national counterparts, and with it the wider credibility of the European human rights system. In this optic, the right of individual petition thus clearly remains an 'indissoluble' part of the functioning of the system, but must not become its exclusive focus. Indeed, in sharply critical language, Mahoney warns against reducing the Court to a pan-European 'small claims court'—'a court for adjudicating on every alleged interference with a guaranteed right in a Convention country and then awarding carefully assessed relief for every single instance of violation shown to exist, whether or not the case involves what one might call a wider public-policy issue of human rights protection in Europe'.[8] For Mahoney, such a conception of the Court's role runs the continued risk of perhaps fatally clogging up the international machinery of human rights protection, while at the same time fundamentally failing to respect the principle of subsidiarity and the paramount national-level responsibility for the provision of adequate remedies in individual cases.

Within the academic community, the balance of opinion had tended towards sounding a sceptical, if not resolutely critical note as regards the constitutionalist case, insofar as it has become principally associated with the potentially significant restriction of the right of individual petition. Nevertheless, voices have been raised within the academic literature to support a move in this direction. For example, Professor Rick Lawson has argued that discussions surrounding the reform of the Court must not be restricted by what he terms 'the myth of necessity'[9]—referring to the position whereby any reform must, necessarily, respect an unrestricted right of individual petition. For Lawson, this is to misconceive the core function of the Court, which is not that of providing redress to individuals, but rather that of ensuring State compliance with the Convention. In other words, the basis of any

---

[7] Luzius Wildhaber, 'A Constitutional Future for the European Court of Human Rights?' (2002) 23 Human Rights Law Journal 161, 164.

[8] Paul Mahoney, 'An Insider's View of the Reform Debate (How to Maintain the Effectiveness of the European Court of Human Rights)' (2004) 29 NJCM-Bulletin 170, 175.

[9] Rick Lawson, 'De mythe van het moeten: Het Europees Hof voor de Rechten van de Mens en 800 miljoen klagers' (2003) 28 NJCM-Bulletin 120.

reform should be that of seeking to ensure that the Court system effectively brings to light State violations of the Convention and, in so doing, creates the conditions whereby general remedial measures are adopted, as appropriate, at the national level. Lawson illustrates his argument with reference to the seminal case of *Kalashnikov v Russia*,[10] in which the Court found Russian prison conditions to constitute a form of 'inhuman' treatment under the terms of Article 3 ECHR. The question, however, then arises as to what the most appropriate course of action is to follow up such a decision, which concerns an underlying, structural problem. Is it that of indefinitely multiplying the number of individual complaints—and findings of violations—in similar cases from across the country? Or, alternatively, would the interests of both detainees and the wider human rights system be better served by a follow-up mechanism which, on the basis of a single landmark decision, brought national authorities to the table within the wider Council of Europe system to deal with the general problem? Lawson's model clearly points us in the direction of the second option—focusing our attention on the wider problem of State compliance, even if this has the effect of restricting individual access to the European Court. As he provocatively makes the point, 'the Court must not seek to rescue every drowning person'. Rather, its mission is 'to oversee that, in every member state, the ship of state is seaworthy and makes adequate provision for lifeboats'.[11]

On the other side of the argument, the right of individual petition has found perhaps its most notable defence from within the Court in a brief submitted by four justices—Françoise Tulkens (Belgium), Marc Fischbach (Luxembourg), Josep Casadevall (Andorra), and Wilhelmina Thomassen (The Netherlands).[12] The four judges recognize the growing problems which confront the Court on account of its expanding caseload, but argue that this does not, in itself, necessitate a reconceptualization of its role. They stress that the Court must continue to improve and adapt its working techniques, so as, for example, to deal more expeditiously with repetitive violations. Yet, this should not be allowed to lead to an erosion of the principle of a generalized right of individual petition. The Court should not, in particular, place itself in the position of denying access to the victims of violations of Convention rights on the grounds that the violation in question is too 'minor' to warrant attention at the European level. For the four judges, a selective jurisprudence of this type, in which the Court dealt only with what it deemed to be the more serious issues arising under the Convention, would risk losing the 'credibility' and the 'authority' which the institution had built up over its 50-year life. Such a move, in more general terms, could only be read as a regression relative to the level of protection already achieved by the Strasbourg

---

[10] Judgment of 15 July 2002 on application no. 47095/99.

[11] Lawson, 'De mythe van het moeten: Het Europees Hof voor de Recheten van de Mens en 800 miljoen klagers', n 9 above, 130.

[12] 'Pour le droit de recours individuel', reprinted as Annex 3 in Gérard Cohen-Jonathan and Christophe Pettiti (eds), *La réforme de la Cour européenne des droits de l'homme* (2003) 171–75.

system—running contrary to the broader development of international human rights law and potentially sending a signal of decreased vigilance to the contracting parties.

Both Judge Tulkens and Judge Thomassen have further separately intervened in defence of the right of individual petition. Judge Tulkens, in particular, is concerned that current discussions appear to be taking place in a climate of 'moral panic', whereby a singular focus on the numbers of both current and potential cases has obscured a deeper analysis of the underlying trends which they represent.[13] Without such a deeper analysis, she argues, one should not proceed blindly to restructure the system, in the name of a misguided hope to 'turn off the tap' so as to restrict the volume of future cases coming forward. This is all the more true as the right of individual petition stands at the 'heart of the Convention system', conferring upon it a 'unique and original character'.[14] Any restriction on this right would seriously diminish this exemplary quality, sending an invidious message of reduced concern for human rights to both European and wider international audiences.

Judge Thomassen argues in comparably strong terms that, 'Reforms intended to maintain the efficiency of the system must not be allowed to lead to an elitist constitutional system which will discourage ordinary people from calling upon it.'[15] In her view, it is the right of individual petition which defines the legitimacy of the Court as it deals with failings in national legal systems. Moves towards a 'pick and choose' system, in which the Court would selectively determine which cases it will hear, must thus be opposed. She further argues that an international court is ill placed to make selective determinations as to the relative importance of particular issues, given that this would necessarily be informed by specific national contexts. Moreover, in making such determinations, the Court would also risk an overt politicization of its function—which issues it did or did not *choose* to take up in the case of individual countries could not help but attract criticisms of institutional bias.

Similar criticisms of the Court's possible move in a more 'constitutional' direction have also found robust expression in the academic community. Writing in this vein, Professor Florence Benoît-Rohmer acknowledges the 'seductive' character of a strategy by which the Court would seek to 'boost its prestige' by concentrating on 'decisions of a constitutional character'.[16] Yet, in her estimation, such a narrowing of the Court's docket could only come at the expense of the overall

---

[13] Françoise Tulkens, 'Les réformes à droit constant' (2002) 14 Revue universelle des Droits de l'homme 265. See also Judge Tulkens' report in Cohen-Jonathan and Pettiti, *La réforme de la Cour européenne des droits de l'homme* (n 12 above) 53–62.

[14] Tulkens, 'Les réformes à droit constant' (n 13 above) 273.

[15] Wilhelmina Thomassen, 'Het individuele klachtrecht moet behouden blijven: Over het Europees Hof voor de Rechten van de Mens en zijn toekomst' (2003) 28 NJCM-Bulletin 11, 13.

[16] Florence Benoît-Rohmer, 'Il faut sauver le recours individuel...' (2003) No. 38 *Recueil Dalloz* 2584. See also Florence Benoît-Rohmer, 'Les perspectives de réforme à long terme de la CourEDH: «*certiorari*» versus renvoi préjudiciel' (2002) 14 Revue universelle des Droits de l'homme 313.

credibility of the European human rights system. Professor Benoît-Rohmer is particularly concerned to dispel a possible tendency towards the transplantation of an American-style logic of *certiorari* to the European human rights system. Under such a system, only a very small proportion of the cases brought before the Court would be heard by it, with the remainder being dispatched with no reasoned opinion provided. Following Benoît-Rohmer's analysis, this practice cannot be transplanted to the European context, as it lacks the shared cultural understandings, clear hierarchy of courts, and established logic of precedent which allow for its operation in the American case. In the absence of such factors, a more selective judicial role would risk being perceived as an arbitrary exercise of judicial power. This line of analysis stresses that the Court is called upon to play a broadly defined pedagogical role across a heterogonous community of States. To do this, wide rights of access to the Court must be maintained, with clearly defined and explicitly articulated admissibility criteria applied in each case.

The implications of a more restrictive access regime for the Court's legitimacy also concern Tom Barkhuysen and Michiel van Emmerick, in a direct rebuttal to Rick Lawson's support for such a move. As discussed above, Lawson supports such a restrictive approach on the grounds that the core task of the Court is one of ensuring state compliance with the ECHR, rather than necessarily providing redress to individual victims. For Barkhuysen and van Emmerick, this is to misunderstand the 'greatest achievement of the ECHR supervisory mechanism', that of 'breaking through the sovereignty of the contracting states as regards the protection of individual rights'.[17] The essence of the Strasbourg system's achievement, in other words, is that of placing the individual at the centre of an international legal order, protecting his or her rights and interests against the arbitrary actions of national authorities (including the possible shortcomings of national courts). Any movement which seeks to restrict the right of individual access to the Court is thus seen as striking at the heart of the system, undermining the individual's newfound centrality in a legal order extending beyond the State. This core problem is, moreover, further compounded by the perverse 'bonus' potentially accorded to States in the case of repetitive violations. In effect, the individual victims of systemic violations of human rights at the national level might find the route to Strasbourg blocked by the fact that the violation in question had already been the subject of a 'constitutional decision' by the Court—even if remedial action had not (yet) followed.

Overall, the debates surrounding the Court's 'constitutional' vocation thus appear to flow from clear philosophical differences concerning the underlying purpose of the institution itself. Those who see the Court as principally concerned with the maintenance of the broad principles of the European human rights system are opposed by those who, conversely, see the defining function of the Court

---

[17] Tom Barkhuysen and Michiel L. van Emmerick, 'De Toekomst van het EHRM: Meer middelen voor effectievere rechtsbescherming' (2003) 28 NJCM-Bulletin 298, 299.

as that of providing a final recourse for individual victims of human rights violations who have failed to find redress at the national level. These philosophical differences may, in turn, be linked to differing strategic visions as to the Court's future development. For the constitutionalists, the maintenance of the right of individual petition in its present form will inevitably have the effect of pushing the system as a whole beyond the breaking point; the right of individual petition, if left unchecked, will in effect become meaningless. By way of contrast, proponents of the individual rights approach argue that the Court's wider 'constitutional' function cannot be divorced from its role as a pan-European guardian of individual rights; a Court which 'picks and chooses' its cases, rather than systematically dealing with all violations, would risk losing the very legitimacy that has allowed it to assume the role of 'the constitutional instrument of the European public order'.[18]

Yet, although the terms of the debate have been sharply cast, one must be careful not to exaggerate the extent of the divisions which exist within either the Court or the wider human rights community. The question, in practice, is essentially that of where to strike the balance between the competing demands inevitably placed on the institution. Proponents of both positions would agree that the redress of individual violations and the enunciation of broad principles of law are, ultimately, two faces of the same coin—but disagree as to the relative emphasis to be placed on each of these two, intertwined functions. The broader philosophical differences thus resolve themselves into more concrete issues, concerning the working methods and judicial policy choices of the Court, as well the Court's place within the wider architecture of the European human rights system. It is against this background that the following section examines what is presently termed a 'systemic turn' in Strasbourg jurisprudence, analysing the manner in which the Court has sought to strike new balances between the provision of remedies to individual applicants and its wider standard-setting function.

A 'Systemic Turn' in Strasbourg Jurisprudence

A 'systemic turn' in the jurisprudence of the Court is undoubtedly one of the most significant developments of recent years in the overall institutional evolution of the Convention system. This systemic turn most obviously refers to a trend within Strasbourg jurisprudence whereby increasingly explicit attention is being paid to underlying or systemic problems of human rights protection. The Court has, in significant instances, no longer contented itself with the repeated finding of violations in individual cases stemming from the same root cause. Rather, departing from a predominant 'case-by-case' jurisprudential methodology, the Court has

---

[18] The phrase is that of the Court in *Loizidou v Turkey* (Preliminary Objections), judgment of 23 February 1995 on application no. 15318/89, para 75.

made use of appropriate individual cases as a means to highlight more general structural problems in domestic legal orders and further required, as part of its decision in the individual case, that the more general problem also be addressed by the respondent State. By dealing with repetitive cases in such a manner, the Court is clearly seeking to deal with its workload problem, while at the same time ensuring for the adequate provision of remedies at the domestic level.

This shift, however, further calls forth a second 'systemic turn', insofar as the development of a jurisprudence of this type necessarily has an impact on the balance of roles within the wider Convention system concerning the implementation of decisions. As the Court shifts attention from individual violations to structural problems, more demands are correspondingly placed on the Committee of Ministers in its oversight function as regards the execution of Court decisions. Court decisions cast in general terms place a correspondingly general obligation on the Committee to engage in potentially wide-ranging dialogues with respondent States concerning the reform of domestic legislation and practice. National authorities are also, as a consequence, placed more squarely before their general obligations as regards the respect of Convention rights. The adoption of a more systemic approach to violations by the Court has, in other words, the institutional consequence of rebalancing the wider pattern of institutional relationships within the Convention system—placing a more direct onus on both the Committee of Ministers and national authorities to fulfil their Convention obligations, while repositioning the Court as the pivotal institution in a broader institutional architecture of shared responsibility.

The implications of this systemic turn are detailed below with reference to two sets of developments, dealing, respectively, with the reaffirmation of the principle of subsidiarity through Article 13 ECHR and the first use of a newly adopted 'pilot judgment' procedure.

The *Kudla* Case and the Reaffirmation of Subsidiarity

In *Kudla v Poland*, the Court explicitly reversed its established jurisprudence concerning the relationship of Articles 6(1) and 13 of the Convention.[19] The Strasbourg institutions had previously treated the Convention right to a trial within a reasonable period as a form of *lex specialis*, which therefore absorbed the more general right to an effective remedy contained in Article 13.[20] As a consequence, where a violation had been found of Article 6(1), no further consideration was given to the existence of a possible separate violation of Article 13. With *Kudla*, however, the Court pointedly chose to break with this precedent. Having found Poland in violation of Article 6(1) as regards the undue length of proceedings, the Court nevertheless then further proceeded to find a separate violation of

---

[19] Judgment of 26 October 2000, application no. 30210/96.
[20] See eg the Court's judgment of 2 February 1993 in the case of *Pizzetti v Italy*, application no. 12444/86.

Article 13, insofar as no adequate domestic remedy was deemed to exist by which the applicant could have sought relief for such forms of unreasonable delay.

The *Kudla* decision was clearly influenced by broad considerations of judicial policy. In coming to its decision, the Court noted the large numbers of cases dealing with the undue length of proceedings which made their way on to its docket. Here, it stressed that, were this flow of cases not to be stemmed, 'In the long term the effective functioning, on both the national and the international level, of the scheme of human rights protection set up by the Convention is likely to be weakened.'[21] The Court thus explicitly noted, as part of the basis of its decision, considerations to do with the expansion of its own workload and the need for its interpretation of Convention rights to be consonant with the requirements of the overall functioning of the Strasbourg system. This practical concern, however, finds a further principled basis in the Court's strong reaffirmation of the primary responsibility of national authorities for the provision of effective remedies under the ECHR. On this wider canvas, Article 13, long confined to the relative margins of Strasbourg jurisprudence, appears set to assume a more prominent place as an embodiment of a wider principle of subsidiarity. Beyond the immediate circumstance, the Court's underlying intent is clearly that of seeking to 'restore the balance' between the national and the European roles in the operation of the Convention system.[22]

Critics of the Court's fundamental change of tack in *Kudla* have raised both issues of principle and problems of practice. In his (lone) dissenting opinion, Justice Josep Casadevall was sharply critical of the majority's citation of the growing backlog of length of procedure cases as itself providing a basis for a major jurisprudential reversal. For Judge Casadevall, such workload considerations were of 'no legal interest' and should not form part of the basis of the Court's reasoning. His dissent further went on to argue that the separate invocation of Article 13 was not amenable to solving the underlying problem which the Court sought to address and, indeed, was more likely to lead to an accumulation of further problems over time. In terms which have found a broader resonance in later legal commentaries,[23] the dissenting opinion stressed that, in effect, the Court was potentially opening a significant new vein of litigation concerned with Article 13 itself. Following this line of argument, the Strasbourg docket could ultimately (and almost *ad absurdum*) be further crowded by claims concerning the adequacy of the remedies put in place at the national level to deal with undue delays in judicial proceedings.

---

[21] *Kudla* (n 19, above) para. 155.

[22] Tom Barkhuysen, in his case note on *Kudla*, characterizes the decision as fitting within a more generalized—and, in his view, potentially worrying—trend of 'decentralization' in the operation of the Convention system. See Tom Barkhuysen, 'Effectieve nationale rechtsbescherming bij overschrijding van de redelijke termijn vereist op grond van Artikel 6 en Artikel 13' (2001) 26 NJCM-Bulletin 71.

[23] See notably the case commentary by Jean-François Flauss in (2002) 13 Revue trimestrielle des Droits de l'Homme 169.

The practical problems raised by critics of the *Kudla* jurisprudence cannot be ignored, but do not call into question the underlying logic of the decision. At its core, the Court sought, with *Kudla*, to shift the basis of its supervisory role from a position in which it is concerned with providing remedies in individual cases to one in which it is primarily concerned with assessing the adequacy of the system of remedies put in place at the national level. A renewed emphasis is consequently placed on the need for a dialogue to be established with national authorities concerning the adoption of appropriate domestic reforms, which would obviate the need for large numbers of individual applicants to seek redress for their claims at the European level. The logic—and the limits—of this approach may be illustrated with reference to related Italian developments.

Italy has been, by far, the most frequent offender as regards violations of Article 6(1) concerning the length of proceedings. Indeed, the Court, in its 1999 *Bottazzi v Italy* judgment, drew attention to the systemic character of the problem, finding 'an accumulation of breaches' which itself 'constitutes a practice that is incompatible with the Convention'.[24] It was with a view to resolving this ongoing structural problem that the Italian authorities introduced legislation providing applicants with a means to seek both pecuniary and non-pecuniary damages before national courts where their right to trial within a reasonable time had not been respected. This legislation, the so-called 'Pinto Act', was adopted on 24 March 2001. The procedure created by the Pinto Act was rapidly recognized by the Court as a domestic remedy which must be exhausted under the terms of Article 35(1)—and this, exceptionally, with retrospective effect.[25] Nevertheless, in assessing the application of the Pinto Act, the Court found, in the *Scordino v Italy (No.1)* case, that the applicant concerned had not been 'properly and adequately compensated' by the domestic court.[26] At the time of writing, the matter has been referred to the Grand Chamber, and, at the request of the Italian government, proceedings in all similar cases (more than 800) have been suspended pending the Grand Chamber decision.

The experience with the Italian cases thus, in part, would seem to bear out the criticisms which have been levelled at *Kudla*. Clearly, as illustrated by the *Scordino* case, the Court has opened a secondary vein of litigation concerned with the adequacy of the domestic remedies provided for Article 6(1) violations. Yet, at the same time, the Italian developments may also be seen as entirely consistent with the underlying intentions of the *Kudla* jurisprudence. Essentially, the Court

---

[24] Judgment of 28 July 1999, application no. 34884/97, para. 22.

[25] See notably *Brusco v Italy*, admissibility decision of 6 September 2001 on application no. 69789/01.

[26] Judgment of 29 July 2004, application no. 36813/97, para. 67. The Chamber judgment on the merits confirmed, in this respect, the earlier finding of a committee of the Court at the admissibility stage. In its decision on admissibility of 27 March 2003, the committee had already held that the amount of damages awarded by the regional court of appeal in the present case 'does not bear a reasonable relationship' to the amounts awarded by the Court in comparable cases and therefore 'cannot be regarded as adequate and hence capable of making good the alleged violation'.

is now engaged, on a systemic basis, with the question of the adequacy of the remedies provided at the domestic level. *Scordino* has emerged as a 'test case'[27] which will allow the Court to pronounce upon the general requirements which must be met by the relevant domestic legislation, thus engaging, as intended, in a form of dialogue with national authorities. At least as regards the framing of the issue, the Court has successfully repositioned itself so as to deal with the general, structural problem in a manner which both addresses its practical workload concerns as regards Article 6(1) litigation and strongly reaffirms a broader principle of subsidiarity in the overall operation of the Convention system.

The *Broniowski* Case and the Development of a 'Pilot Judgment' Procedure

The development of a so-called 'pilot judgment' procedure within the framework of the Convention system must be situated relative to the broader reform discussions which accompanied the drafting of Protocol 14. The Court had sought, as part of this reform process, to secure the adoption of such a mechanism within the Convention system. As detailed below, the Court was partially successful in this regard. While the Member States proved unwilling to support the inclusion of a pilot judgment procedure in the text of the Convention itself, they nevertheless have, by way of a resolution and a recommendation of the Committee of Ministers, given a formal institutional basis to the mechanism. The *Broniowski* case, as further detailed below, marks the first instance in which the Court has made use of this new procedure.

The initial proposal to vest the European Court of Human Rights with an explicit jurisdiction to hand down 'pilot judgments' was made by the Court in its September 2003 Position Paper, submitted as part of the drafting process for Protocol 14. In this paper, the Court advocated consideration of a new procedure for handling situations in which it had identified structural shortcomings in the protection of human rights.[28] Specifically, a 'pilot judgment' would be delivered where the Court deemed that its finding of a violation in an individual case pointed to an instance of wider, systemic problems in the domestic legal order of the respondent State. This finding of a systemic problem would be communicated to both the Committee of Ministers and to the State concerned, triggering an 'accelerated execution process'. The respondent State would be obliged, under this process, to introduce a general remedy of retroactive effect. The pilot judgment

---

[27] The term 'test case' was explicitly used by the Registrar of the Court with reference to *Scordino* in his press release of 18 January 2005, announcing the suspension of proceedings in all comparable cases. See ' "Pinto" cases adjourned pending decision on test case', available at http://www.echr.coe.int/eng/press/2005/jan/pintocasessuspended.htm.

[28] Document CDDH-GDR (2003) 024, Position Paper of the European Court of Human Rights, 12 September 2003, 12–13. I am grateful to the Library of the European Court of Human Rights for supplying me with a copy of this document.

would also have the effect of suspending proceedings before the Court as regards all other cases against the respondent State dealing with the same issue. Once the Court had satisfied itself that appropriate domestic remedies had been put in place, the remaining cases dealing with the same issue could then be removed from the Strasbourg docket and referred back to the appropriate national channels. The clear intention of the Court was thus to find a means whereby it could deal more effectively with the 'repetitive' or 'clone' cases (those dealing, repeatedly, with the same violation of the Convention by the same State) that account for approximately two-thirds of all admissible cases under the Convention system. In essence, following the same logic seen in its *Kudla* jurisprudence, the Court here too sought to place itself in the position of adjudicating the general, remedial measures adopted by a contracting State where systemic problems had been identified, rather than dealing on a case-by-case basis with the individual violations of Convention rights that stem from such instances of dysfunction. The Court left open, at this stage, the question of whether the adoption of such a mechanism would necessitate an amendment of the Convention.

The Steering Committee for Human Rights (CDDH)[29] was broadly sympathetic to the Court's proposal, but resistant as regards the creation of an obligation on States to provide for general, retroactive remedies. Although recognizing the 'usefulness' of such a solution for dealing with repetitive cases 'wherever the domestic legal order allows it', the CDDH nevertheless felt it best to maintain a degree of flexibility.[30] It thus put paid to any possible move in the direction of formal Convention amendment, insisting instead that the basis for a pilot judgment procedure should be set out by way of a (non-binding) recommendation of the Committee of Ministers. The Steering Committee's finding reflected a strong undercurrent of political resistance. Substantial opposition was expressed within Council of Europe governmental circles to providing an explicit Convention basis whereby the Court might require general and retroactive measures to be taken by the contracting States. While such a requirement could arguably be said to flow from the existing Article 46 ECHR, there was little sustained political will to clarify such ambiguities as might continue to surround the precise scope of State obligation.

The Court, faced with this reticence, came out strongly for a Convention-based mechanism in its February 2004 response to the ongoing drafting work of the CDDH. In this later document, it stressed that 'a pilot-judgment procedure with

---

[29] The Steering Committee for Human Rights (usually known by its French acronym, CDDH) is the expert, intergovernmental body within the Council of Europe charged with overseeing the functioning and development of the organization's human rights activities. As such, it plays a pivotal role in the process of amending the Convention.

[30] Document CDDH (2003) 026 Addendum I Final, 26 November 2003, para. 20. This document, together with most of the relevant documentation concerned with the drafting of Protocol 14, is available via a dedicated web page on 'The Reform of the European Court of Human Rights', which may be accessed at http://www.coe.int/T/E/Human_rights/ECHRReform.asp.

enhanced execution, enshrined in the Convention, is necessary to deal with the phenomenon of repetitive cases'.[31] The Member State governments were not, however, to be swayed. Provision was made for a pilot judgment procedure, but on a non-Treaty basis. The mechanism is included in the parallel package of measures adopted at the same time as Protocol 14, in the form, as previously noted, of a recommendation and a resolution of the Committee of Ministers.

The relevant recommendation deals generally with the improvement of domestic remedies.[32] Here, States are called upon to review and, where necessary, to reform existing domestic remedies where Court judgments have pointed to 'structural or general deficiencies in national law or practice'. The corresponding resolution of the Committee of Ministers sets out a more detailed institutional road map as to how such cases are to be handled.[33] Specifically, the document invites the Court 'as far as possible, to identify, in its judgments finding a violation of the Convention, what it considers to be an underlying systemic problem and the source of this problem'. The Court should, in so doing, seek to assist the State concerned and the Committee of Ministers in finding an appropriate solution for the identified problem. The implication is thus that its decision should, with due respect for the principle of subsidiarity, provide guidance as to the remedial measures to be taken. The Court is further called upon to notify such pilot judgments not only to the respondent State and to the Committee of Ministers, but also to the Parliamentary Assembly, the Secretary General of the Council of Europe, and the Council of Europe Human Rights Commissioner.

Although the measures adopted by the Committee of Ministers fell short of the Treaty base finally advocated by the Court, a door had nonetheless been opened. The Court was, indeed, quick to seize on the opportunity, delivering its first pilot judgment on 22 June 2004 in the case of *Broniowski v Poland*.[34] *Broniowksi* concerned a compensation claim for the loss of property in the territories east of the Bug River which Poland had ceded to the then Soviet Union at the end of the Second World War. The petitioner claimed that the compensation which he had received for the loss of his late mother's property in the former Polish territory was inadequate under the terms of Article 1 of the First Protocol to the ECHR. In particular, the petition contended that the system of 'credits' which the Polish government had established, allowing those who had lost property east of the Bug River to bid for State assets, had proved to be of little or no worth as the relevant assets had largely been withdrawn from the bidding process. The Court, in the instant case, found for the petitioner. While stressing the wide margin of appreciation which must be accorded to a national government in dealing with so complex and politically sensitive an issue, the Court nonetheless equally emphasized

---

[31] Response of the European Court of Human Rights, 2 February 2004, para. 37(b). This document is available as at n 30 above.   [32] Recommendation Rec (2004) 6, adopted 12 May 2004.
[33] Resolution Res (2004) 3, adopted 12 May 2004.
[34] *Broniowski v Poland* (Merits and Just Satisfaction), judgment of 22 June 2004, application no. 31443/96.

that this margin cannot be unlimited. Drawing on an earlier decision of the Polish Constitutional Court, the Court noted the extent to which the authorities' handling of the present issue appeared to have fostered a climate of legal uncertainty, at variance with 'the imperative of maintaining citizens' legitimate confidence in the State'.[35] More specifically, the Court held that the successive imposition of limitations on the use of the State credits awarded had, in effect, rendered the right to compensation 'illusory' and 'destroyed its very essence'.[36] As such, the petitioner had been obliged 'to bear a disproportionate and excessive burden'[37] relative to the general public interest pursued by the authorities.

The Court then moved beyond the specific case to a consideration of the wider problem of which it forms a part. Explicitly citing the Committee of Ministers' recommendation and resolution of 12 May 2004,[38] the decision noted the large numbers of actual and potential applicants concerned with the same issue. By the Court's estimate, 167 further applications were already on its docket concerned with the same question, while the settlement of the Bug River claims more generally concerns nearly 80,000 people. Given the scope of the problem, the Court held that its finding of a violation in the present case 'originated in a systemic problem connected with the malfunctioning of domestic legislation and practice' and further held that the respondent State must, in consequence, adopt appropriate measures so as to secure an adequate right of compensation or equivalent redress to all those concerned by the Bug River claims. Pending the satisfactory adoption of such measures of general effect, the Court postponed consideration of the question of compensation (just satisfaction) in the immediate case and, on 6 July 2004, adjourned proceedings in all other cases concerned with the same cause.[39]

The *Broniowski* case itself was resolved by means of a friendly settlement between the parties signed on 6 September 2005.[40] The terms of this settlement must, however, be highlighted. Innovatively, the agreement moved beyond a simple settlement of the individual case to incorporate a broader set of remedial measures, so as to deal with the underlying or systemic problems identified by the Court in its pilot judgment. Specifically, beyond providing for the payment of both material and non-material damages to the applicant in the instant case, the friendly settlement agreement further encompassed a declaration by the Polish government which affirmed its overarching commitment to ensure the proper

---

[35] ibid, para 184.   [36] ibid, para 185.   [37] ibid, para 187.

[38] This citation of the Committee of Ministers' measures prompted a separate, concurring opinion from Judge Zupančič. While the Slovene judge 'wholeheartedly and unequivocally' supported the 'principled essence' of the Court's decision, he disagreed with his colleagues' rationale. In his view, the legal basis for identifying general, remedial measures could and should be drawn only from Articles 41 and 46 of the Convention itself.

[39] See '"*Bug River*" cases adjourned', Press Release issued by the Registrar, 31 August 2004, available at http://www.echr.coe.int/Eng/Press/2004/Aug/Broniowskibugrivercasesadjourned.htm.

[40] See *Broniowski v Poland* (Friendly Settlement), judgment of 28 September 2005, application no. 31443/96.

implementation of all relevant measures in domestic law and practice, while also listing more specific measures adopted in this regard. This latter list included: the establishment of a Compensation Fund for those applicants who did not wish to avail themselves of the 'right to credit' established by the original scheme; a raising of the statutory ceiling for compensation from 15 to 20 per cent of the assessed value of the property concerned; and a declaration by the Government acknowledging the basis within the national Civil Code by which claims for non-material damages could be brought before the domestic courts in connection with the present cases.

In turn, the Court, in its judgment taking note of the settlement, carefully examined the question of the extent to which the systemic problems found in its initial judgment had been addressed. The Court stressed its obligation to ensure that any friendly settlement between the parties 'has been reached on the basis of respect for human rights as defined in the Convention and the Protocols thereto'[41]—an obligation which, after the delivery of a pilot judgment, 'necessarily extends beyond the sole interests of the individual applicant and requires the Court to examine the case also from the point of view of "relevant general measures"'.[42] With respect to the present case, the Court took note of 'the active commitment' which had been displayed by the Polish authorities in resolving the systemic problems identified in its initial verdict.[43] It further concluded, in deciding to strike the case from the list, that it 'cannot but rely on the respondent's government's actual and promised remedial action as a positive factor going to the issue of '"respect for human rights" as defined in the Convention and the Protocols thereto'.[44] The Court did, however, also emphasize the continued responsibility of the Committee of Ministers, under Article 46 ECHR, to evaluate the general measures taken by the respondent government as regards their compliance with the Court's principal judgment.[45]

The first use of the pilot judgment mechanism appears, at least in broad procedural terms, to have been a noteworthy success. Clearly, the Court has been able to engage the relevant national authorities in a quite extensive remedial dialogue, using the verdict in the individual case to prompt a substantial process of domestic reform. Questions do, of course, remain. As regards the Bug River cases themselves, for example, the Court was careful not to pronounce on the adequacy of the level of compensation available under the revised scheme—leaving the door open for further litigation.[46] More generally, one may also question the range of

---

[41] As set out in Rule 62 § 3 of the Rules of Court.

[42] *Broniowski* (Friendly Settlement) (n 40 above), para 36.   [43] ibid, para 42.   [44] ibid.

[45] ibid. The Committee of Ministers had previously adopted an Interim Resolution on 5 July 2005 taking note of the relevant legislative reforms then being prepared by the Polish government to deal with the question, but also expressing its 'concern' that, pending the adoption of such reforms, the potentially large number of *Bug River* claimants had effectively been left without recourse. See ResDH(2005)58.

[46] The Court explicitly noted, with reference to the individual settlement reached by the Polish authorities with Mr Broniowski, that 'there is nothing to prevent a future challenge of [the] 20%

circumstances in which such a pilot judgment procedure may effectively be deployed.[47] Nevertheless, after this initial, positive experience, it is likely that the Court will recur to the mechanism with increasing frequency. A number of Chamber judgments have, since the initial June 2004 *Broniowski* verdict, already set in motion similar processes by identifying, in the operative part of the relevant judgments, the need to remedy underlying or systemic problems.[48] Moreover, in his December 2005 report on the reform of the Court's working methods, Lord Woolf strongly encouraged the use of this mechanism as a 'vital' means to deal with the problem of repetitive cases—recommending that priority treatment be given to pilot judgments in the management of the Court's docket.[49] The pilot judgment mechanism thus appears set to become a potentially important tool in the Court's arsenal as it seeks to deal with its workload problem and, in so doing, addresses wider questions of institutional balance within the Convention system as a whole.

Conclusion

Faced with a host of new quantitative and qualitative challenges, the core purpose of the Court has become the subject of high-profile debate, both within the Court itself and in the wider human rights community. Most strikingly, a clear division has emerged between 'constitutionalist' and 'individual rights' visions of the Court's role. The terms of this debate bear emphasis. In effect, the institutional roles focused on by each of the two principal positions in this debate—the enunciation of general human rights standards and the provision of remedies in individual cases—have long, *implicitly*, represented the two principal functions of the Court. The increased pressures placed on the Court have, however, seen these

ceiling before either the Polish Constitutional Court or ultimately this Court'. *Broniowski* (Friendly Settlement) (n 40 above) para 43.

[47] The Council of Europe's Director General of Human Rights, Pierre-Henri Imbert, has interestingly suggested that a distinction should be drawn between repetitive cases which raise 'specific' problems and those which raise 'structural' problems. In Imbert's view, while a specific problem concerning a large number of applicants may lend itself to a relatively rapid resolution (as in *Broniowksi*), a problem which is 'really systemic', in the sense of pointing to a broad dysfunction in human rights protection, requires the development of a longer-term reform strategy and, consequently, a distinctive implementation framework. Imbert's remarks are reproduced in *Reform of the European Human Rights System: Proceedings of the High-level Seminar, Oslo, 18 October 2004* (Strasbourg: Council of Europe, 2004), 33–43. The full text of the publication is available online at: http://www.coe.int/T/E/Human_rights/reformeurhrsystem_e.pdf.

[48] See, notably, the cases of: *Sejdovic v Italy*, Chamber judgment of 10 November 2004, application no. 56581/00 (referred to the Grand Chamber); *Hutten-Czapska v Poland*, Chamber judgment of 22 February 2005, application no. 35014/97(referred to the Grand Chamber); and *Xenides-Arestis v Turkey*, Chamber judgment of 22 December 2005, application no. 46347/99.

[49] The Right Honourable Lord Woolf, *Review of the Working Methods of the European Court of Human Rights*, December 2005, 39–40 (4.2). Report available at: http://www.echr.coe.int/ECHR/Resources/Home/LORDWOOLFREVIEWONWORKINGMETHODS.pdf.

implicit functions now made explicit—and made explicit not as complementary tasks, but rather as the basis of competing institutional visions. While, as noted above, a balance will ultimately have to be struck between these necessarily inter-twined roles, it remains that such openly 'existential' controversy is something of a novelty for the Court, reflecting the need for conscious self-definition as it embraces its enlarged, pan-European mandate.

It is further against this background that one must conceive of a recent 'systemic turn' in the Court's jurisprudence as regards the handling of repetitive or 'clone' cases. This systemic turn, in part, corresponds to a 'constitutionalist' vision of the Court's role. As the Court moves towards dealing with systemic violations of human rights in general terms, using individual cases to highlight underlying problems, a clear emphasis is being placed on its standard-setting function. The Court's innovative use of Article 13 in *Kudla*, or the development of a pilot judgment procedure as evidenced in *Broniowski*, are manifest attempts to move away from a situation in which large numbers of individual applicants concerned with the same underlying problem will seek relief in Strasbourg. The Court has sought, instead, to 'set the standard' in general terms, but to return the question of individual relief back to national authorities under the supervision of the Committee of Ministers. A new balance is thus sought, in which the Court acts in a 'constitutional' role, but with the right of individual remedy still ensured within the Convention system as a whole. Such a rebalancing, it should further be noted, entails no formal restriction on the right of individual access to Strasbourg, though if successful it will obviate the practical necessity of recourse to the European level in many cases.

This is not, of course, to argue that the Court has found a 'magic formula' for resolving its problems. Complex questions of both principle and practice arise in relation to such a broad attempt to rebalance the distribution of roles within the Convention system. Is there, for example, a risk of leaving applicants to the Court in a form of lengthy legal limbo, when proceedings regarding their application are suspended awaiting a pilot judgment?[50] Similarly, where the Court has required the provision of an appropriate domestic remedy for an identified structural problem under a reinvigorated Article 13, what forms of recourse are to be open to potential claimants, insofar as such a remedy is either not forthcoming or found to be wanting (as already exemplified in the *Scordino* case)? Questions of this type may be further multiplied, but the general point is already clear. The Court's move in a more 'systemic' direction is not so much in itself a solution to its current dilemma, as an appropriately recalibrated and apparently promising framework within which to deal with the dramatic environmental challenges which confront it. Such a framework, moreover, places particular emphasis on the successful (re-) articulation of the Court's wider patter of institutional relationships with both the

---

[50] See Philip Leach, 'Beyond the Bug River—A New Dawn for Redress before the European Court of Human Rights?' (2005) 10 European Human Rights Law Review 148, 162.

Committee of Ministers and national authorities. This, in turn, further engages with wider questions of institutional reform.

The question of the Court's relationship with the Committee of Ministers is interestingly dealt with in Protocol 14, which introduces two new mechanisms whereby the Committee may bring matters before the Court. On the one hand, the Protocol institutes a form of infringement proceedings,[51] modelled on that which exists in European Union law. This provision permits the Committee, by a two-thirds majority vote, to make a reference to the Court seeking a determination as to whether a State party has fulfilled its obligations regarding the execution of a judgment. On the other hand, the Protocol also introduces a form of clarificatory ruling. Under this provision, the Committee of Ministers, again by a two-thirds majority vote, may request 'a ruling on a question of interpretation' where it has found that its supervision of the execution of a Court judgment has been hindered by the existence of problems surrounding the interpretation of that judgment.[52] In both cases, new possibilities for dialogue between the Court and the Committee are thus created, strengthening the sense of the Convention as an interlocking set of institutions in which both the judicial and the political elements have distinctive and necessary roles. The clarificatory ruling procedure would seem particularly promising in this respect, insofar as it allows for a considerable flexibility of response on the part of the Court. Using the procedure, the Court would have the possibility of engaging in quite subtle forms of 'remedial dialogue', setting out the parameters of required national action in light of both its previous ruling and subsequent developments, without having to deliver a further, formal judgment.[53]

Beyond its relationship with the Committee of Ministers, the 'decentralization' of Strasbourg jurisprudence also, of course, raises anew the question of the institutional relationship between the Court and its national judicial counterparts. It is perhaps unsurprising, in this light, that there has been a renewed academic interest in the possible introduction of a preliminary ruling procedure within the Strasbourg system, on the model of that which exists in EU law.[54] Such proposals

---

[51] Protocol 14, Art. 16(4), amending Art. 46 ECHR.

[52] Protocol 14, Art. 16(3), amending Art. 46 ECHR.

[53] By way of contrast, the Court itself, during the drafting of Protocol 14, expressed significant doubts as to the desirability of introducing a form of infringement proceedings into the Convention system. It repeatedly expressed its view that the introduction of such proceedings risked a potentially invidious confusion of the political and judicial roles within the Convention system. See the Position Paper of the European Court of Human Rights, 12 September 2003 (n 28 above) 11 and the Response of the European Court of Human Rights, 2 February 2004 (n 31 above) paras. 27–31. There would seem to be much to justify the Court's doubts in this regard. The Court would, in infringement proceedings, effectively be called upon to provide a judicial confirmation of a decision which had already been reached by the Committee of Ministers as to the continued existence of a breach. The interpretive procedure, by way of contrast, allows considerably more scope to the Court, as it would not have to render a direct verdict on State (non-)compliance.

[54] More recent statements of support for the adoption of a preliminary ruling procedure notably include: Benoît-Rohmer, 'Il faut sauver le recours individuel...' (n 16 above); Dominique Ritleng, 'Le renvoi préjudiciel communautaire, modèle pour une réforme du système de protection de la

have a long pedigree,[55] and raise a now well-known set of concerns principally related to the structural differences between the Community and the Convention legal orders.[56] Yet, weighed against such concerns, stand the very considerable, potential benefits of placing the relationship between the Court and its national interlocutors on a more positive and structured footing. At present, the Court's relationship with national courts is largely defined by situations in which the European Court is finding fault, ie in which it finds a violation of the Convention where, by definition, all domestic remedies have been exhausted. The existence of some form of preliminary ruling procedure would fundamentally alter this dynamic—allowing national courts to refer questions to the Court, and subsequently make their own rulings on the basis of such referrals, in the exercise of a more positive role as 'Convention courts'. Undeniably, the opening of a new channel of access to Strasbourg raises workload considerations, at least over the short-to-medium term.[57] Nevertheless, it is difficult to escape the conclusion that the introduction of such a direct link between the Court and its national interlocutors forms a necessary institutional complement, over the longer term, to the wider rebalancing of institutional roles suggested by the recent turn in the European Court's jurisprudence.

It is, indeed, perhaps finally in light of such broader systemic considerations that the Court's position as a 'constitutional court' should be understood. The Court, if it is successfully to face the challenges which now confront it, must consciously continue to elaborate its role within the context of a wider constitutional order, assuming its responsibilities for both the development of Convention rights and the overall maintenance of the Convention system. Differences will no doubt continue to surface as to where the balance between these two roles should be struck in any individual circumstance. That the Court should engage in such broad institutional politics appears, nonetheless, to be an ineluctable part of its role as the judicial guarantor of a 'constitutional instrument of the European public order'.[58]

CEDH?' (2002) 7/3 L'Europe des Libertés 3 and 'La réforme de la CJCE, modèle pour une réforme de la Cour européenne des droits de l'homme' (2002) 14 Revue universelle des droits de l'homme 288; and Piet van Dijk, 'Een efficiënt en effectief stelsel van toezicht op de naleving van het EVRM' (2003) 28 NJCM-Bulletin 394, 397–98.

[55] The first proposals for the adoption of a form of the (then) EEC preliminary ruling procedure in the Convention system date from 1960. For the longer-term historical background of the ideas see; Andrew Drzemczewski, *European Human Rights Convention in Domestic Law: A Comparative Study* (1983), 330–41 and Lammy Betten and Joost Korte, 'A Procedure for Preliminary Rulings in the Context of the Merger' (1997) 8 Human Rights Law Journal 75.

[56] See notably, Ronald St. John McDonald, 'The Luxembourg Preliminary Ruling Procedure and its Possible Application in Strasbourg', in Georges Flécheux (ed.), *Mélanges en Hommage à Louis-Edmond Pettiti* (1998) 593–603.

[57] This difficulty was particularly stressed in the Report of the Evaluation Group to the Committee of Ministers on the European Court of Human Rights, EG Court (2001) 1, EG Court (2001) 1, 27 September 2001, 35 (para. 84). This influential report argued that, while proposals concerning a preliminary ruling procedure might warrant further study, 'the Court simply does not have the capacity at present to take on the extra duties which those suggestions would involve'. The full document is available as at n 30 above.   [58] See n 18 above.

4

The Scope of the Right to a Fair Trial Guarantee in Non-Criminal Cases in the European Convention on Human Rights

*David Harris**

Introduction

Some of the more perplexing problems in the interpretation of the European Convention on Human Rights concern the application of the guarantee of the right to a fair trial in Article 6(1) to non-criminal cases. Does it apply to all cases in which a person's legal rights are being decided, or is it more limited than that? In the latter case, how far does it extend? These are the questions that will be explored in this essay. As will be seen, the Court's interpretation of the wording of Article 6 has evolved over time, to the point where its fair trial guarantee has a much greater reach than was first apparent and, in particular, provides a basis for controlling executive action by governments far more than might have been expected. At the same time, the theoretical basis for the Court's interpretation of 'civil rights and obligations' remains far from clear.

Private Law Meaning of 'Civil Rights and Obligations'

According to Article 6(1), it applies 'in the determination' of a person's 'civil rights and obligations'. In their early jurisprudence, the Strasbourg authorities established that the phrase 'civil rights and obligations' incorporated, by the use of the word 'civil', the distinction between private and public law, with 'civil' rights and obligations being rights and obligations in private law.[1] This distinction has long

---

* This essay is a revised version of a part of Ch 6 of David Harris, Michael O'Boyle, and Colin Warbrick, *The Law of the European Convention on Human Rights* (OUP, 2nd edn, 2006) (in preparation).
  [1] *Ringeisen v Austria* A 13 (1971) 1 EHRR 455, para 94 and *König v FRG* A 27 (1978) 2 EHRR 170, para 95.

been significant in civil law systems for jurisdictional and other purposes[2] and has more recently become important in United Kingdom administrative law.[3] On the basis of it, rights and obligations in the relations of private persons *inter se* clearly fall within Article 6, but some rights and obligations at issue in the relations between the individual and the State (eg the right to nationality and the obligation to pay taxes) do not, the problem in the latter case being to know where to draw the line. Criminal law is in a special position. Decisions taken in the 'determination of . . . any criminal charge' are included by a separate part of the wording of Article 6(1).[4] Ancillary decisions relating to criminal proceedings are not subject to Article 6 on the criminal side and not otherwise subject to Article 6 as decisions determinative of 'civil rights and obligations'. They are excluded both because of the distinction between private and public law and also, as the Court has preferred to emphasize, because, if certain decisions in criminal proceedings are specifically covered by Article 6(1), others, by inference, are not.[5]

It follows from the above that the Convention does not guarantee a fair trial in the determination of all of the rights and obligations that a person may arguably have in national law. However, as will be seen, the gaps in the coverage of Article 6 have been significantly, if somewhat confusingly, reduced by interpretation. Indeed, whereas the Court sometimes still relies upon the public law–private law divide when excluding rights or obligations as not being 'civil',[6] more recent jurisprudence, by which more and more rights and obligations have been brought within Article 6, is not always easy to explain in terms of any distinction between private and public law that is found in European national law.

Before examining further the Court's, and earlier the Commission's, use of the idea of private law rights and obligations, it should be noted that in two early cases the Court left open the question whether there is an exact equation between 'civil' rights and obligations and rights and obligations in private law. In *König v FRG*[7] and later in *Le Compte v Belgium*[8] it stated that it did not have to decide 'whether the concept of "civil rights and obligations" . . . extends beyond those rights which have a private nature'. It is not clear what the Court had in mind by this. One possibility is that human rights protected by the Convention might be 'civil' rights in the sense of Article 6.[9] However, although

    [2] See Rudolph Schlesinger, Hans Baade, Peter Herzog, and Edward Wise, *Comparative Law* (6th edn, 1998) 498ff.

    [3] See William Wade and Christopher Forsyth, *Administrative Law* (9th edn, 2004) 649.

    [4] A particular factual situation may concern both a criminal charge and civil rights and obligations, although the case will normally be dealt with under one head only: see *Albert and Le Compte v Belgium* A 58 (1983) 5 EHRR 533, para 30. Criminal proceedings may be determinative of 'civil rights' in some jurisdictions, eg in criminal defamation cases, or if a victim is joined as a civil party.

    [5] *Neumeister v Austria* A 8 (1968) 1 EHRR 91 (right to bail not a 'civil right' for this reason).

    [6] eg *Ferrazzini v Italy* 2001-VII 327; 34 EHRR 1068, para 27 GC.

    [7] A No 27 (1978) 2 EHRR 170, para 95.

    [8] *Le Compte, Van Leuven and De Meyere v Belgium* A 43 (1981) 4 EHRR 1, para 48.

    [9] See the *Alam and Khan v UK Nos 2991/66 and 2992/66*, 10 YB 478 (1967) line of cases, concerning the right to family life, discussed in David Harris, 'The Application of Article 6(1) of the

the Court has not expressly retracted the statements made in the *König* case, it has not repeated them since the *Le Compte* case in 1981.

An Autonomous Convention Meaning

The adoption of a private law meaning of 'civil' rights and obligations raised from the outset the question of the boundary between private and public law for the purposes of Article 6. One approach would have been to have applied a doctrine of *renvoi* by which the Court simply accepted the classification of a particular right or obligation in the defendant State's legal system. This would have led to the application of Article 6 differentially between the contracting parties, given that different States classify borderline cases differently. In fact, the Court has, from the beginning, as with the parallel Article 6 concept of a 'criminal charge', held that 'civil' has an autonomous Convention meaning, so that the defendant State's classification is not decisive.[10] In a particular case, therefore, a right that is regarded as a matter of public law in the legal system of the defendant State may be treated as falling within Article 6 and vice versa. With the Court applying an autonomous Convention meaning of 'civil' rights and obligations and expanding its scope over time, the position has been reached in which most substantive rights that an individual may arguably claim under national law fall within Article 6 unless they quintessentially concern the exercise of the public power of the State.

Although adopting an autonomous Convention meaning of 'civil' rights and obligations, the Court has refrained from formulating any abstract definition of the term, beyond distinguishing between private and public law.[11] It has instead preferred an inductive approach, ruling on the particular facts, or categories, of cases as they have arisen. Even so, there are certain general guidelines that emerge from the cases. First, 'only the character of the right at issue is relevant'.[12] The 'character of legislation which governs how the matter is to be determined (civil, commercial, administrative law, etc.) and that of the authority which is invested with jurisdiction in the matter (ordinary court, administrative body, etc.) are

European Convention on Human Rights to Administrative Law' (1974) 47 BYIL 157, 167 (1974–75), in which the Commission seemed for a while to adopt such an approach. This approach concentrates on the 'rights', as opposed to the 'obligations', part of civil rights and obligations.

[10] *König v FRG* A 27 (1978) 2 EHRR 170, para 88. In *Porter v UK* No 15812/02 hudoc (2003) DA, the Court accepted a national court classification for the purposes of argument.

[11] In *Benthem v Netherlands* A 97 (1985) 8 EHRR 1, para 34, the Court declined the Commission's invitation, ibid., Com Rep, para 91, to give guidance on the matter.

[12] *König v FRG* A 27 (1978) 2 EHRR 170, para 90. The wording quoted is phrased only in terms of 'rights', omitting 'obligations'. This tends to happen because most of the cases under Art. 6 are brought by claimants, not defendants. For 'obligations' cases, see eg *Muyldermans v Belgium* A 214-B (1991) 15 EHRR 204 Com Rep (F Sett before Court) and *Schouten and Meldrum v Netherlands* A 304 (1994) 19 EHRR 432.

therefore of little consequence'.[13] This guideline has minimal significance for cases involving disputes between private persons, which will invariably be governed by national private law and usually be within the jurisdiction of the 'ordinary courts'. It is, however, of critical importance in cases that involve the relations between a private person and the State. In national law systems that traditionally have made use of the distinction between private and public law, the classification of such cases generally turns upon whether the State is acting in a sovereign or non-sovereign capacity in its dealings with the private person concerned.[14] For the purpose of Article 6, however, whether the State has 'acted as a private person or in its sovereign capacity is... not conclusive';[15] instead, the focus is entirely upon the 'character of the right'.

Secondly, when determining the 'character of the right', the existence of any 'uniform European notion' that can be found in the law of the contracting parties is influential. This inference can be drawn from the *Feldbrugge* and *Deumeland* cases.[16] There the Court found that there was no 'uniform European notion' (which by implication would have been followed) as to the private or public law character of the social security rights before it and was forced to make a choice in respect of rights it considered to have a mixed private and public law character.[17]

Thirdly, although the classification of a right or obligation in the law of the defendant State is not decisive, that law is nonetheless relevant in that it necessarily determines the content of the right or obligation to which the Convention concept of 'civil' rights and obligations is applied. For example, in *König*,[18] when deciding whether the right to practise medicine was a matter of private or public law, the Court scrutinized West German law to see whether, in the law of the defendant State in the case, the services offered by the medical profession were a part of a public service or were, although subject to State regulation, essentially a matter of private law contract between doctor and patient. For this reason, despite the autonomous nature of 'civil' rights and obligations, it would be possible for the same right or obligation to be subject to Article 6 as it exists in one legal system but not as it is found in another.

Finally, the Court adopts a 'restrictive interpretation, in accordance with the object and purpose of the Convention, of the exceptions to the safeguards

[13] *Ringeisen v Austria* A 13 (1971) 1 EHRR 455, para 94, quoted in the *König* case A 27 (1978) 2 EHRR 170, para 90.

[14] eg, the State will be acting in a sovereign capacity when it exercises a power of deportation or expropriation. It will be acting in a non-sovereign capacity when it does something that a private person might do, such as buying chairs for an office. An act such as the purchase of guns for the army raises more difficult problems.   [15] *König v FRG* A 27 (1978) 2 EHRR 170, para 90.

[16] *Feldbrugge v Netherlands* A 99 (1986) 8 EHRR 425, para 29 and *Deumeland v FRG* A 120 (1986) 8 EHRR 448, para 63. Cf *König v FRG* A 27 (1978) 2 EHRR 170, para 89. See also *Pellegrin v France* 1999-VIII 207; 31 EHRR 651 GC.

[17] Cf *Muyldermans v Belgium* A 214-B (1991) 15 EHRR 204 Com Rep (F Sett before Court), para 56.   [18] A 27 (1978) 2 EHRR 170, para 89. See also *Perez v France* hudoc (2004).

afforded by Article 6(1)'.[19] This consideration was relevant in *Pellegrin v France*[20] when the Court ruled that some disputes concerning employment in the public service fall within Article 6.

Rights and Obligations in the Relations Between Private Persons

Applying its inductive approach, the Court, and earlier the Commission, has developed an extensive jurisprudence classifying rights and obligations as being civil or not for the purposes of Article 6. This jurisprudence is considered in the following pages. The first point to be made is that it establishes, in accordance with the position uniformly found in European national law, that the rights and obligations of private persons in their relations *inter se* are 'civil' rights and obligations. Thus, cases concerning such relations in the law of contract,[21] commercial law,[22] insurance law,[23] the law of tort,[24] the law of succession,[25] family law,[26] employment law[27] and the law of personal[28] and real[29] property have been regarded as falling within Article 6.

State Action Determining Private Law Rights and Obligations

The position is more complicated in cases involving the relations of private persons with the State. In accordance with its approach in the *König* case, in such cases the Court looks solely to the character of the right or obligation that is the subject of the case when deciding whether Article 6 applies. If that right or obligation falls within private law, then any State action that is directly decisive for it must either be taken by a tribunal that complies with Article 6 or, if it is administrative action, challengeable before such a tribunal. What is remarkable, and a tribute to the Court's creativity, is the identity and nature of the right and obligations of private persons that the Court has recognized as private law rights and obligations in this context. Most significantly, it has recognized certain rights of a very general character, such as rights that have a pecuniary nature or consequences and the right to family life, as being 'civil' rights. When, as is common, State action is determinative of such rights, it is controlled by Article 6.

---

[19] *Pellegrin v France* 1999-VIII 207; 31 EHRR 651 GC, para 64.   [20] ibid.
[21] *Ringeisen v Austria* A 13 (1971) (contract for the sale of land).
[22] *Barthold v FRG* A 90 (1985) 7 EHRR 383 (unfair competition).
[23] Implied in *Feldbrugge v Netherlands* A 99 (1986) 8 EHRR 425 and *Deumeland v FRG* A 120 (1986) 8 EHRR 448.   [24] *Golder v UK* A 18 (1975) 1 EHRR 524 (defamation).
[25] *C. D. v France* hudoc (2003).   [26] *Airey v Ireland* A 32 (1979).
[27] *Buchholz v FRG* A 42 (1981) 3 EHRR 597 (unfair dismissal).
[28] *Bramelid and Malmström v Sweden* Nos 8588/79 and 8589/79, 38 DR 18 (1983) Com Rep; CM Res DH (84) 4 (share valuation).
[29] *Pretto v Italy* A 71 (1983) 6 EHRR 182 (sale of land).

Pecuniary Rights

The key determinant in cases involving State action is often whether the right or obligation in question is pecuniary in nature or, if not, whether the State action that is decisive for the right nonetheless has pecuniary consequences for the applicant.[30] If so, the case will generally fall within Article 6, unless the State is acting within one of the areas that 'still form part of the hard core of public authority prerogatives',[31] such as taxation or the control of aliens. Although the Court commonly states that 'merely showing that a dispute is "pecuniary" in nature is not in itself sufficient to attract the applicability of Article 6',[32] this is mainly intended to allow for the 'public authority prerogative' exception: in cases to which that exception does not extend, Article 6 will generally apply if a pecuniary dimension, for which the Court usually looks, is present.[33] The following paragraphs concern rights and obligations that are sometimes classified as 'civil' under other headings by the Court but that all have a pecuniary dimension.

The Right to Property

The right to property is clearly a right with a pecuniary character. As a result, State action that is directly decisive for real or personal property rights is determinative of 'civil' rights and hence governed by Article 6. Thus, decisions by the State concerning the expropriation[34] or the regulation of the use of private land[35] have been held to be subject to the right to a fair hearing. With regard to personal property, decisions by the State as to a person's capacity to administer property,[36] or that are otherwise decisive for personal property rights[37] are controlled by Article 6.

---

[30] See eg *Editions Periscope v France* A 234-B (1992) 14 EHRR 597 and *Stran Greek Refineries and Stratis Andreadis v Greece* A 301-B (1994) 19 EHRR 293.

[31] *Ferrazzini v Italy* 2001-VII 327; 34 EHRR 1068 GC, para 29.   [32] ibid, para 25.

[33] eg the obligation of a French public accountant to repay public monies lost by his negligence is within Art. 6, despite its public law dimensions, because of its pecuniary impact on the accountant: *Martinie v France* No 58675/00 hudoc (2004) DA. On surcharges on UK local authority officers, see *Porter v UK* No 15812/02 hudoc (2003) DA.

[34] *Sporrong and Lönnroth v Sweden* A 52 (1982) 5 EHRR 35 and *Zanatta v France* hudoc (2000). See also *Raimondo v Italy* A 281-A (1994) 18 EHRR 237, para 43 (confiscation) and *Poiss v Austria* A 117 (1987) 10 EHRR 231 (land consolidation).

[35] For planning or building permission cases, see *McGonnell v UK* 2000-II 107; 30 EHRR 289; *Chapman v UK* 2001-I 41; 33 EHRR 399 GC; *Haider v Austria* (2004) hudoc DA. See also *Gillow v UK* A 109 (1986) 11 EHRR 335. For other land use cases, see *Zander v Sweden* A 279-B (1993) 18 EHRR 175 (water extraction); *Papadopoulos v Greece* hudoc (2003) (mineral exploitation); *Ludescher v Austria* hudoc (2001) (farming); *Posti and Rahko v Finland* hudoc (2002) (fishing); and *Oerlemans v Netherlands* A 219 (1991) 15 EHRR 561 (nature conservation).

[36] *Winterwerp v Netherlands* A 33 (1979) 2 EHRR 387 (mentally disordered person).

[37] *Vasilescu v Romania* 1998-III 1064; 28 EHRR 241 (seizure of property); *Lithgow v UK* A 102 (1986) 8 EHRR 329 (compensation for nationalization); *Ruiz-Mateos v Spain* A 262 (1993) 16 EHRR 505 (restitution); *Tinnelly and McElduff v UK* 1998-IV 1633; 27 EHRR 249 (public contracts); *Pafitis v Greece* 1998-I 436 27 EHRR 566 (shareholders' voting rights); *Sablon v Belgium* hudoc (2001) (bankruptcy); *Credit and Industrial Bank v Czech Rep* hudoc (2003) (compulsory

Where the State decision concerning real or personal property is taken by an administrative authority (as opposed to a tribunal), there must be the possibility of challenging it before a tribunal that complies with Article 6.

The Right to Engage in a Commerical Activity or to Practise a Profession

The right to engage in a commercial activity, which similarly has a pecuniary character, is also a civil right.[38] Hence State action by way of the withdrawal of a commercial licence or other authorization to engage in a commercial activity is controlled by Article 6.[39] The same is true of the right to practise a liberal profession.[40]

Article 6 applies to the *grant* of a licence or other authorization to undertake a commercial activity or practise a profession as well as a decision to withdraw it. In the *König* case,[41] the Court had emphasized that the case was one of the *continued* exercise of a right to operate a medical clinic and to practise medicine, distinguishing between a decision to grant a licence in the first place and the legitimate expectation that a licence-holder has in its continuance. In *Benthem* and the later cases,[42] however, Article 6 has been applied to applications for new licences, provided that the grant of the licence is not a discretionary decision by the State.

The Right to Compensation for Illegal State Action

The Court's jurisprudence also recognizes as 'civil' the right to compensation from the State for injury resulting from illegal State acts, again on the basis of its pecuniary nature. Thus, in *X v France*,[43] the Court held that a claim for damages

---

administration); *British American Tobacco Co Ltd v Netherlands* A 331A (1995) 21 EHRR 409 (patent applications and rights); *Procola v Luxembourg* A 327-A (1995) 22 EHRR 193 (milk levy).

[38] There may be an overlap between this right and the right to property. In *Benthem v Netherlands* A 97 (1985) 8 EHRR 1, para 36, the Court noted that the licence had a proprietary character (being assignable) and that its grant was 'closely associated with the right to use one's possessions'.

[39] See eg *Tre Traktörer Aktiebolag v Sweden* A 159 (1989) 13 EHRR 309 (sale of alcohol); *Kingsley v UK* 2002-IV 57; 35 EHRR 177 GC (gaming); *Pudas v Sweden* A 125-A (1987) 10 EHRR 380 (transport); *König v FRG* A 27 (1978) 2 EHRR 170 (medical clinic); *Benthem v Netherlands* A 97 (1985) 8 EHRR 1 (liquid petroleum gas); *Hornsby v Greece* 1997-II 495; 24 EHRR 250 (private school). Where disqualification from a commercial activity results from a criminal conviction, Art. 6 may be complied with by the criminal proceedings: *X v Belgium* No 8901/80 (1981) 23 DR 237.

[40] See eg *König v FRG* A 27 (1978) 2 EHRR 170 (medicine); *GS v Austria* hudoc (1999) (pharmacy); *H v Belgium* A 127 (1987) 10 EHRR 339 (law); *Thlimmenos v Greece* 2000-IV; 31 EHRR 411 GC (accountancy); *Guchez v Belgium* No 10027/82 (1984) 40 DR 100 (architecture); *Wilson v UK* No 36791/97, (1998) 26 EHRR CD 195; and *X v UK* No 28530/95 (1998) 25 EHRR CD 88 (company director).   [41] A 27 (1978) 2 EHRR 170.

[42] A 97 (1985) 8 EHRR 1. Cf *Allan Jacobsson v Sweden* A 163 (1989) 12 EHRR 56; *Nowicki v Austria* hudoc (2005); *Kraska v Switzerland* A 254-B (1993) 18 EHRR 188; and *De Moor v Belgium* A 292-A (1994) 18 EHRR 372.

[43] A 234-C (1992) 14 EHRR 483. Cf *H v France* A 162-A (1989) 12 EHRR 74. See also *Z v UK* 2001-V 1; 34 EHRR 97 GC.

in an administrative court for contracting AIDS from a blood transfusion because of government negligence fell within Article 6. Although the case concerned the exercise of a general regulatory power by a Minister, and hence was clearly a matter of public law in France, its outcome was 'decisive for private rights and obligations', namely those concerning pecuniary compensation for physical injury. The same approach was adopted in *Editions Périscope v France*,[44] where the applicant company had ceased trading because of pecuniary losses caused by an illegal decision by a public authority refusing it a tax concession. The Court held that the decision of an administrative court on the applicant's claim for compensation for damage sustained through the fault of the public authority determined the applicant's 'civil' rights. In a brief statement of reasons, the Court noted that 'the subject matter of the applicant's action was "pecuniary" in nature and that the action was founded on an alleged infringement of rights which were likewise pecuniary rights', so that the right in question was a 'civil' one. The Court's approach in these two cases involved finding a pecuniary interest in a very general sense and supposing that such an interest has a private law character.

X v France and *Editions Periscope* have been followed by other cases in which claims for compensation for illegal State acts have been held to concern 'civil' rights. These include claims for compensation for ill-treatment by the police,[45] unlawful detention,[46] unreasonable delay in judicial proceedings,[47] breach of contract,[48] the seizure of property,[49] and a miscellany of other claims.[50]

Statutory rights to compensation against the State for 'wrongful conviction and unjustified detention' in connection with criminal proceedings also fall within Article 6.[51] The cases have involved compensation for detention where the proceedings are discontinued,[52] the accused is acquitted,[53] or the conviction is quashed on appeal.[54] Such cases concern a right to compensation provided by the

---

[44] A 234-B (1992) 14 EHRR 597, para 40.

[45] *Assenov v Bulgaria* 1998-VIII 3264; 28 EHRR 652 and *Balogh v Hungary* hudoc (2004) (assault); *Baraona v Portugal* A 122 (1987) 13 EHRR 329 (illegal arrest); *Veeber v Estonia* hudoc (2002) (illegal search and seizure); *Ait-Mouhoub v France* (1998) 30 EHRR 382 (police theft, forgery, etc); *Kaukonen v Finland* No 24738/94 (1997) 91-A DR 14 (malicious prosecution).

[46] *Aerts v Belgium* 1998-V 1939; 29 EHRR 50.

[47] *Pelli v Italy* No 19537/02 hudoc (2003) DA (Pinto law).

[48] *Stran Greek Refineries and Stratis Andreadis v Greece* A 301-B (1994) 19 EHRR 293.

[49] *Air Canada v UK* A 316-A (1995) 20 EHRR 150.

[50] See eg *Beaumartin v France* A 296-B (1994) 19 EHRR 485 (claim for compensation under a treaty); *Neves e Silva v Portugal* A 153-A (1989) 13 EHRR 535 (official malpractice); and *S.A. Sotiris and Nicos Atee v Greece* No 39442/98 hudoc (1999) DA (refusal of State subsidy).

[51] *Humen v Poland* hudoc (1999) para 57 GC. The payment of compensation must be as of right, not discretionary: *Masson and Van Zon v Netherlands* A 327 (1995) 22 EHRR 491.

[52] *Goc v Turkey* 2002-V 193; 35 EHRR 134 GC *and Werner v Austria* 1997-VII 2496; 26 EHRR 310.　　　　　　　　　　　　　　　　　　[53] *Lamanna v Austria* hudoc (2001).

[54] *Georgiadis v Greece* hudoc (2000) 24 EHRR 606 and *Humen v Poland* hudoc (1999) GC. See also *Halka v Poland* hudoc (2001).

State under national law where the detention is not necessarily in breach of Article 5 of the Convention, but the detainee is not finally convicted.[55]

Although not involving an illegal act, a claim under a State's criminal injuries compensation scheme may, because of its pecuniary character, fall within Article 6 if the scheme provides for a legal right to compensation, and not an ex gratia payment.[56]

The Right to Social Security and Social Assistance

One of the most remarkable developments in the Court's jurisprudence has concerned the classification of rights to social security and social assistance which the Court has held fall within Article 6. Initially, in the companion cases of *Feldbrugge v Netherlands*[57] and *Deumeland v Germany*,[58] the Court adopted a balancing approach, and in both cases found that the private law aspects of the social security rights concerned outweighed their public law aspects, so that Article 6 applied. However, the Court has since gone further and established that 'the development in the law that was initiated by those judgments and the principle of equality of treatment warrant taking the view that today the general rule is that Article 6(1) does apply in the field of social insurance, including even welfare assistance'.[59] In addition, the Court has stressed that such rights are of a pecuniary, or economic nature.[60] Since the Court adopted this position, disputes concerning social security and social assistance rights have routinely been accepted as falling within Article 6, commonly without argument to the contrary by the defendant State.[61] The right need not be linked to a contract of employment[62] or

[55] Article 5 provides its own *lex specialis* fair trial guarantees for challenges to the legality of detention (Art. 5(3)(4)) or for claims for compensation for detention in breach of Art. 5 (Art. 5(5)). Article 6 does not apply.

[56] *Gustafson v Sweden* 1997-IV 1149; 25 EHRR 623 (a legal right) and *August v UK* hudoc (2003) 36 EHRR CD 115 (ex gratia payment). Article 6 does not apply to discretionary State compensation for a natural disaster: *Nordh v Sweden* No 14225/88 (1990) 69 DR 223.

[57] A 99 (1986) 8 EHRR 325 (employment sickness benefit).

[58] A 120 (1986) 8 EHRR 448 (industrial injuries benefit).

[59] *Schuler-Zgraggen v Switzerland* A 263 (1993) 16 EHRR 405, para 46 (invalidity pension). See also *McGinley and Egan v UK* 1998-III 1334; 27 EHRR 1 (disability pension); *Pauger v Austria* 1997 III 38; 25 EHRR 105 (widower's pension); *Grof v Austria* No 25046/94, (1998) 25 EHRR CD 39 (maternity benefit). For a case of welfare assistance, see *Salesi v Italy* A 257-E (1993) 26 EHRR 187 (disability allowance for destitute persons); and *Wos v Poland* No 22860/02 hudoc (2005) DA (forced labour compensation). The distinction between social security and welfare (or social) assistance is not wholly clear; generally persons receive differing amounts of welfare assistance to cover individual basic needs, rather than the same amount of benefit for all qualifying persons, as is the case with social security.

[60] *Schuler-Zgraggen v Switzerland* A 263 (1993) 16 EHRR 405, para 46 (the applicant 'suffered an interference with her means of subsistence' and was claiming an 'individual economic right').

[61] See eg *Duclos v France* 1996-VI 2163; 32 EHRR 86. If the issue is raised, the Court typically notes the right's pecuniary nature when finding that it is a 'civil' right: see *Sussmann v Germany* 1996-IV 1158; 25 EHRR 64, para 42.

[62] See eg *Lombardo v Italy* A 249-B (1992) 21 EHRR 188 (public service pension). The rights in the *Feldbrugge* and *Deumeland* cases were so linked.

depend upon contributory payments.[63] There must, however, be entitlement as a matter of legal right for those who qualify—disputes about benefits or assistance given by the State in its discretion are not included.[64] This is not to do with the civil or non-civil character of the benefit or assistance, but because Article 6 extends only to disputes about 'rights'.

Non-Pecuniary Civil Rights and Obligations

Although an important touchstone, the pecuniary dimensions of a right or obligation is not the only test for a 'civil' right or obligation. Other rights or obligations of private persons may qualify, again by reference to the general perception of them in national law as private law rights or obligations, with which the State may not interfere without due process. One right of a non-pecuniary character to which Article 6 applies is the right to respect for family life. Thus, State action that is directly decisive for this right, such as decisions placing children in care[65] and restricting the contact of prisoners with their families,[66] have been held to be regulated by Article 6.

Other non-pecuniary rights that have been recognized as 'civil rights' are the rights to life,[67] physical integrity,[68] liberty,[69] private life,[70] access to administrative documents,[71] a reputation (and to a remedy to protect it),[72] freedom of expression and assembly (unless used for political purposes)[73] and freedom of association.[74] Most of the rights listed in this paragraph are human rights protected by the Convention, although no reference to this link is made in Court judgments.[75] Generally, the Court merely states, without giving reasons, that a non-pecuniary right is a 'civil' right, or even just acts on the basis that it is such a right without addressing the matter.[76] At most, the Court usually refers only to the equation

---

[63] *Salesi v Italy* A 257-E (1993) 26 EHRR 187. See also *Stec v UK* No 65731/01 hudoc (2005) DA.

[64] *Salesi v Italy* A 257-E (1993) 26 EHRR 187 and *Mennitto v Italy* 2000-X; 34 EHRR 1122. See also *Gaygusuz v Austria* 1996-IV 1129; 23 EHRR 364.

[65] *Olsson v Sweden (No 1)* A 130 (1988) 11 EHRR 259. See also *Keegan v Ireland* A 290 (194) 18 EHRR 342 (adoption) and *Eriksson v Sweden* A 156 (1989) 12 EHRR 183 (fostering).

[66] *Ganci v Italy* 2003-XI.   [67] *Athanassoglou v Switzerland* hudoc (2000) GC.

[68] ibid, and *Taskin v Turkey* hudoc (2004).

[69] *Laidin v France (No 2)* hudoc (2003). See also *Aerts v Belgium* 1998-V 83; 29 EHRR 50 (a pecuniary right case: compensation for illegal detention) and *Reinprecht v Austria* No 67175/01 hudoc (2004) DA.   [70] *Mustafa v France* hudoc (2003) (choice of surname).

[71] *Loiseau v France* No 46809/99 hudoc (2003) DA.

[72] *Tolstoy Miloslavsky v UK* A 323 (1995) 20 EHRR 442 and *Werner v Poland* hudoc (2001) 36 EHRR 491.   [73] *Reisz v Germany* No 3201/96, 91-A DR 53.

[74] *A.B. Kurt Kellermann v Sweden* hudoc (2003) 37 EHHR CD 161 DA and *Apeh Uldozotteinek Szovetsege v Hungary* 2000-X; 34 EHRR 849.

[75] Such a link was made in the case of the *pecuniary* right to property in Art. 1, First Protocol to the Convention in *Procula v Netherlands* A 326 (1995) 22 EHRR 193. The Art. 13 requirement of an effective remedy suggests that there may well be an 'arguable right' in national law where there is a breach of most Convention rights, but Art. 13 does not necessarily require a right enforceable in the courts and some Convention rights (e.g. the right to free elections: Art. 3, First Protocol) are public law rights.   [76] See eg the family life cases cited above.

between 'civil rights and obligations' and 'private (law) rights and obligations'[77] established in its early jurisprudence. Exceptionally, in *O'Reilly v Ireland*,[78] it examined in some detail the public and private law elements of a local authority's statutory duty to repair a road and the applicants' standing as residents on the road to seek an order of mandamus to require its repair, finding on balance that the private law elements predominated.

Public Law Rights and Obligations

Following from the private law reading of the word 'civil', claims concerning a number of rights and obligations are not subject to Article 6 because of their public law character. However, their number is limited and in decline. The Court's parsimonious approach to the exclusion of rights and obligations on public law grounds is governed by two general considerations. First, in accordance with the object and purpose of the Convention, a 'restrictive interpretation' must be adopted when deciding whether a right or obligation is excluded from the safeguards of Article 6.[79] Secondly, the Convention is a living instrument that must be interpreted dynamically.[80] The significance of this second consideration was explained by the Court in *Ferrazzini v Italy*[81] as follows.

Relations between the individual and the State have clearly developed in many spheres during the 50 years which have elapsed since the Convention was adopted, with State regulation increasingly intervening in private law relations. This has led the Court to find that procedures classified under national law as being part of 'public law' could come within the purview of Article 6 under its 'civil' head if the outcome was decisive for private rights and obligations, in regard to such matters as, to give some examples; the sale of land, the running of a private clinic, property interests, the granting of administrative authorizations relating to the conditions of professional practise or of a licence to serve alcoholic beverages. Moreover, the State's increasing intervention in the individual's day-to-day life, in terms of welfare protection for example, has required the Court to evaluate features of public law and private law before concluding that the asserted right could be classified as civil.

However, the Court continued, 'rights and obligations existing for an individual are not necessarily civil in nature'.[82] Giving political rights and obligations, some kinds of public employment, the expulsion of aliens and the obligation to pay taxes as examples, the Court stated that rights and obligations that relate to matters that 'still form part of the hard core of public authority prerogatives'[83] remain

---

[77] *Apeh Uldozotteinek Szovetsege v Hungary* 2000-X; 34 EHHR 849, para 34.
[78] Hudoc (2003) DA. Semble the Court was analysing the applicants' 'right' to have the road repaired. [79] *Pellegrin v France* 1999-VII 207; 31 EHRR 651 GC, para 64.
[80] *Ferrazzini v Italy* 2001-VII 327; 34 EHRR 1068 GC, para 26.
[81] ibid, para 27. Footnotes omitted. But in some contexts the tendency has more recently been for the withdrawal of the State, involving deregulation and privatisation. [82] ibid, para 28.
[83] ibid, para 29.

excluded. In the case of such rights or obligations, the fact that there may in some cases be a pecuniary dimension to the right or to the consequences of its infringement is outweighed or overridden by its fundamentally public law character.

The Obligation to Pay Tax

On its facts, *Ferrazzini* concerned the obligation to pay taxes to the State. The Court held that disputes arising out of this obligation are not determinative of a person's 'civil' obligations because of its public law nature. Although the obligation has pecuniary elements, 'the public nature of the relationship between the taxpayer and the tax authority remains predominant'.[84] In contrast, in *Schouten and Meldrum v Netherlands*[85] it was held that Article 6 does apply to the applicant's obligation to pay social security contributions. Following the approach it had used in the *Feldebrugge* case in respect of social security benefits, the Court decided that the private law features of the obligation outweighed its public law features.

Polticial Rights and Obligations

As to political rights and obligations, in *Pierre-Bloch v France*[86] it was held that the right to stand for election to a national parliament does not fall within Article 6, because 'such a right is a political and not a "civil" one'. In *Pierre-Bloch*, the applicant, who had been elected to the French National Assembly, was found to have exceeded the election expenses limit and as a penalty was disqualified from standing for election for a year, made to forfeit his seat, and required to pay a sum equal to the expenses excess. Despite the pecuniary consequences of the decision, Article 6 was held not to apply: 'proceedings do not become "civil" merely because they raise an economic issue'.[87] Generally, the right to engage in political activities is not a 'civil' right, so that, for example, disputes concerning the right to vote[88] or the dissolution of a political party [89] also do not fall within Article 6. Disputes

---

[84] *Ferrazini v Italy* 2001-VII 327; 34 EHRR 1068 GC. See Sylvie Lopardi 'The applicability of Article 6 of the Convention to tax related proceedings' (2001) 26 European Law Review, Human Rights Supp 58. See also *Emesa Sugar N.V. v Netherlands* No 62023/00 hudoc (2005) DA (customs duties); and *Smith v UK* (1995) 21 EHRR CD 74 (UK poll tax). Surcharges imposed for non-payment of tax may involve a 'criminal charge' within Art. 6: *Vastberga Taxi Aktiebolag v Sweden* hudoc (2002).

[85] A 304 (1994) 19 EHRR 432. Followed in *Meulendijks v Netherlands* hudoc (2002).

[86] 1997-VI 2206; 26 EHRR 202. See also *Tapie v France* No 32258/96 (1997) 88-A DR 176; *Asensio Serqueda v Spain* No 23151/94, (1994) 77-A DR 122; and *Guliyev v Azerbaidjan* No 35584/02 hudoc (2004) DA. All kinds of election disputes fall outside Art. 6: see eg *Priorello v Italy* No 11068/84 (1985) 43 DR 195 (challenge to local election).

[87] 1997-VI 2206; 26 EHRR 202, para 51.

[88] *Hirst v UK* No 74025/01 hudoc (2003) 37 EHRR CD 176 DA (prisoner's right to vote).

[89] *Yazar, Karatas, Aksoy and the HEP v Turkey* hudoc (2002) 36 EHRR 59. See also *Reisz v Germany* No 32013/96 hudoc (1997) DA.

concerning the election of an officer of a non-governmental organization[90] or of an employees' council representative[91] are excluded on a similar basis.

Entry, Conditions of Stay, and Removal of Aliens

Disputes concerning the entry, conditions of stay, and removal of aliens also fall on the public law side of the line. In *Maaouia v France*,[92] the Court held that proceedings concerning the rescinding of an exclusion order against an alien physically present in France did not concern his 'civil' rights. More generally, the Court stated that 'decisions regarding the entry, stay and deportation of aliens do not concern the determination of an applicant's civil rights or obligations', and that this is so even though, in the case of an exclusion order, the decision 'incidentally' has 'major repercussions on the applicant's private and family life or on his prospects of employment'.[93] The approach in the *Maaouia* case was applied to the extradition of aliens in *Mamatkulov and Askarov v Turkey*.[94]

In the *Maaouia* case, the Court reached its conclusion that Article 6 did not apply to the 'expulsion of aliens' on the basis that the Seventh Protocol to the ECHR[95] provides procedural safeguards for aliens who are to be expelled, which would not have been necessary if the right to a fair hearing in Article 6 already applied. Although the Court did refer to the Commission's jurisprudence to the same effect that was based instead on the public law character of expulsion decisions, the Court relied solely on the Seventh Protocol for its decision.[96] This reasoning cannot apply to the entry or conditions of stay of an alien, to which the Seventh Protocol does not apply. It is likely that the Court would here rely upon the fact that these matters are a 'part of the hard core of public authority prerogatives'.[97]

Employment in the Public Service

To some extent, rights and obligations concerning employment in the public service are excluded from Article 6. Before its decision in *Pellegrin v France*,[98] the Court followed an approach by which Article 6(1) did not apply to disputes that

---

[90] *Fedotov v Russia* hudoc (2004) DA.   [91] *Novotny v Czech Rep* hudoc (1998) DA.
[92] 2000-X ; 33 EHRR 1037 GC.
[93] ibid, paras 40 and 38. Article 6 does not apply to asylum cases: *P v UK* No 13162/87 (1987) 54 DR 211 and *Taheri Kandomabadi v Netherlands* hudoc (2004) DA. The right to freedom of movement in EU law is a public law right and hence not within Art. 6: *Adams* and *Benn* Nos 28979/95 and 30343/96, (1997) 88 DR-A 137.
[94] 2005-GC. The extradition of nationals is also presumably excluded.
[95] See Art. 7(1) of the ECHR.
[96] Concurring, Judge Bratza would have preferred the Court to have followed the Commission's reasoning in exclusion decisions, which was based on the 'substantial discretionary and public order element'.   [97] *Ferrazini v Italy* 2001-VII 327; 34 EHRR 1068 GC.
[98] 1999-VIII 207; 31 EHRR 651 GC.

related to 'the recruitment, careers and termination of employment of civil servants'[99] generally, unless the claim involved a 'purely' or 'essentially' economic right, such as the payment of the employee's salary.[100] Finding this approach increasingly difficult to apply, the Court replaced it in the *Pellegrin* case by a functional test based upon the nature of the employee's work. It held that in the case of public service employment that involves the exercise of a public function traditionally associated with the State, Article 6 does not apply; in other kinds of public service employment, it does.[101] The exclusion from the scope of Article 6 of employment falling on the 'public function' side of the line was justified by the Court on the basis that in such cases the holders of such posts wield 'a portion of the state's sovereign power' and 'the state therefore has a legitimate interest in requiring of these servants a special bond of trust and loyalty'.[102]

In the *Pellegrin* case, the Court gave employment in the armed forces and the police as examples of the kinds of public service employment that are excluded from Article 6(1).[103] Also excluded is the employment of judges[104] and diplomats.[105] In the *Pellegrin* case itself, the applicant was employed overseas by a French government ministry as a high level technical adviser to a foreign government. It was held that Article 6 did not apply to his dispute with the State as to whether he was medically fit for work, as his job gave him 'considerable responsibilities in the field of the State's finances, which is, *par excellence*, a sphere in which States exercise sovereign power'.[106] On the other side of the line, in *Frydlender v France*,[107] the applicant was also employed by a French government ministry abroad, but this time his relatively low level role at a French embassy was to promote French export sales, with limited financial responsibility, with the result that Article 6 applied. In other cases, the employment of teachers in State schools[108] and universities[109] and of junior civil servants[110] has been held to fall within Article 6, as has employment in other public institutions which do not perform the traditional public functions of the State.[111] When applying its functional test,

---

[99] *Massa v Italy* A 265-B (1993) 18 EHRR 266, para 26.

[100] See the cases cited in *Pellegrin v France* 1999-VIII 207; 31 EHRR 651 GC, para 59. The exception also required that the case did not involve the exercise of discretionary power by the State: ibid.

[101] Public service employment has an autonomous Convention meaning: ibid, para 63. It is immaterial whether or not the person concerned is classified as a civil servant under national law.

[102] ibid, para 65.

[103] ibid, para 66. See *Stanczuk v Poland* hudoc (2001) DA (secret police) and *Kiratoglu v Turkey* hudoc (2002) DA (armed forces).

[104] *Yilmazoglu v Turkey* No 36593/97 hudoc (2003) 37 EHRR CD 234 DA. See also *Werner v Poland* hudoc (2001) 36 EHRR 491 (Court appointed lawyer).

[105] *Martinez-Caro de la Concha Castaneda et al v Spain* No 42646/98 hudoc (2000) DA.

[106] 1999-VIII 207; 31 EHRR 651, para 70.

[107] 2000-VII 151; 31 EHRR 1152 GC. See also *Fogarty v UK* 2001-XI 157; 34 EHRR 302 GC.

[108] *Volkmer v Germany* No 39799/98 hudoc (2001) DA.

[109] *Petersen v Germany* No 29793/98 hudoc (2001) DA.

[110] *Devlin v UK* hudoc (2001) 34 EHRR 1029 (administrative assistant).

[111] See eg *Grass v France* hudoc (2000) (works department); *Pramov v Bulgaria* hudoc (2000) (transport); *Satonnet v France* hudoc (2000) (medical centre); *Castanheira Barros v Portugal* hudoc (2000) (criminology institute).

the Court has regard to whether or not the category of activity or post in question is considered to involve 'employment in the public service' in EC law.[112] Since they concern the post-employment period, decisions about a public service employee's pension always falls within Article 6, whether the employment involves the exercise of 'a public function' or not.[113]

Although the *Pellegrin* test is an improvement upon the confused situation that preceded it, there will always remain borderline cases in which the result of its application will be difficult to predict and it is noticeable that, whereas it causes Article 6 to apply to some cases which would previously have been excluded,[114] there are also cases in which the reverse is true.[115] An approach by which employment in the public service was subject to Article 6 without exception would avoid these uncertainties or inconsistencies and be more consistent with a human rights approach. Such an approach is proposed in the joint dissenting opinion of Judges Tulkens, Fischbach, Casadevall, and Thomassen in the *Pellegrin* case, who state that whereas civil servants have traditionally had a special status in the public law of many European States, 'that justification has now largely lost its significance' as 'most member states have "judicialised" civil service disputes, if not entirely then at least in part'.[116]

Other Public Law Rights and Obligations

An obligation which is a part of 'normal civic duties in a democratic society' also falls outside Article 6.[117] Thus an obligation to pay a fine[118] or to give evidence in court proceedings[119] is not a 'civil' obligation to which Article 6 applies. Other kinds of public law cases that have been regarded as falling outside Article 6 include cases concerning the rights to nationality,[120] liability for military service,[121]

---

[112] See EC Commission Communication, *Freedom of movement of workers and access to employment in the public service of the Member States*, OJEC No C 72, 18 March 1988. The guidance in this communication, *inter alia*, classifies judges, tax officials, and diplomats as public servants, but excludes employment in public health care services, non-military research establishments, public transport, electricity and gas supply, post and telecommunications, and radio and television.

[113] *Pellegrin v France* 1999-VIII 207; 31 EHRR 651 GC, para 67. See eg *Trickovic v Slovenia* hudoc (2001) (military pension); *Truhli v Croatia* (2001) hudoc; *Silveri v Italy* hudoc (2000) (police pension); *Vasilopoulou v Greece* hudoc (2002) (judicial pension). But see *R v Belgium* hudoc (2001).

[114] See eg *Huber v France* 1998-I 105; 26 EHRR 457 (school teacher's suspension: Art. 6 held not applicable, pre-*Pellegrin*).

[115] See eg *Mosticchio v Italy* hudoc (2000) (army salary) and *Couez v France* 1998-V 2256 (police salary), both within Art. 6, pre-*Pellegrin*.

[116] See also the concurring opinion of Judge Jambrek and the dissenting opinion of 11 Commissioners in *Maillard v France* 1998-III 1292; 27 EHRR 232.

[117] *Schouten and Meldrum v Netherlands* A 304 (1994) 19 EHRR 432, para 50.   [118] ibid.

[119] *BBC v UK* No 25798/94 hudoc (1996) DA.

[120] *S v Switzerland* No 13325/87 (1988) 59 DR 256. See also *Peltonen v Finland* No 19583/92 (1995) 80-A DR 38 (passport); and *X v UK* No 8208/78 (1978) 16 DR 162 (peerage).

[121] *Nicolussi v Austria* No 11734/85 (1987) 52 DR 266 and *Zelisse v Netherlands* No 12915/87 (1989) 61 DR 230.

certain matters relating to the administration of justice,[122] education,[123] medical treatment[124] and public housing.[125]

Concluding Comments

As will be apparent, although the Court has maintained its private law meaning of 'civil' rights and obligations, its evolving jurisprudence has led to a position in which, in addition to disputes between private persons, Article 6 regulates more kinds of disputes between the individual and the State than that meaning might suggest. Thus, cases concerning the public control of land, the regulation of commercial or professional activities or practice, compensation claims against the State, social security and welfare assistance rights, and some cases of public employment now fall within the bounds of the right to a fair trial. This results partly from the extensive interpretation given by the Court to the word 'determination' in Article 6(1), but also from the Court's dynamic understanding of what amounts to a private law right or obligation for the purposes of Article 6. The ingenious use of such all-embracing concepts as the rights to property or to engage in commercial activities and especially the emphasis upon the pecuniary dimension of a right or obligation has engineered considerable inroads into the realms of public law and administrative justice—sometimes to the point where the Court's attempt to explain its decisions in terms of private and public law as these concepts are understood in national law appears to be artificial and unconvincing.

It is arguable that the Court might do better to reformulate its approach in terms of an abstract definition of 'civil' rights and obligations that starts from a different premise. The Court's attempt to rationalize its approach in the *Ferrazzini* case has some merit, but is not ultimately convincing or of comprehensive application. Given that European States now commonly provide, or can be expected to provide, judicial remedies in areas such as taxation, the control of aliens and electoral matters, the dynamic approach to the interpretation of Article 6 that the Court properly adopts should lead it to a different conclusion from one which still seeks to exclude disputes in the area of 'public authority prerogatives'. Instead, 'civil' rights and obligations might be interpreted as referring to all legal rights and

---

[122] *Schreiber and Boetsch v France* No 58751 hudoc (2003) DA (challenge to a judge); *X v FRG* No 3925/69 (1970) 32 CD 56 (legal aid), but see *Gutfreund v France* hudoc (2003), paras 39–44; *B v UK* No 10615/83 (1984) 38 DR 213 (lawyers' costs); and *Atkinson Crook and The Independent v UK* No 13366/87 (1990) 67 DR 244 and *Loersch et al v Switzerland* Nos 23868–9/94 (1995) 80-A DR 162 (court reporting). On the disciplining of prisoners (which may involve a 'criminal charge'), see *McFeeley v UK* No 8317/78 (1980) 20 DR 44, now subject to *Ganci v Italy* 2003-XI.

[123] *Simpson v UK* No 14688/89 (1989) 64 DR 188 (elementary education) and *X v FRG* No 10193/82 (1984) 7 EHRR 135 (university).

[124] *L v Sweden* No 10801/84 (1988) 61 DR 62 Com Rep, para 87; CM Res DH (89) 16.

[125] *Woonbron Volkshuisvestingsgroep v Netherlands* No 47122/99 hudoc (2002) 35 EHRR CD 161. And see *X v Sweden* No 9260/81 (1983) 6 EHRR 323 (tenants' associations).

obligations that an individual arguably has under national law, regardless of the area of law concerned and the nature of any involvement by the State.[126] This would be in line both with human rights expectations and evolving national practice in administrative law in European States. The difficulty with such an approach, the Court has stated, is that the principle of dynamic interpretation 'does not give the Court the power to interpret Article 6(1) as though the adjective "civil" . . . were not present in the text'.[127] However, in view of its juxtaposition with 'criminal' in the wording of Article 6(1), the term 'civil' could—without doing violence to the text—be read as meaning any right or obligation in law that is not a criminal one. Short of that, some extension of the Court's present approach would be to emphasize the pecuniary character of the obligation to pay tax[128] and of some other public law rights and obligations, or of the pecuniary consequences of their breach. A further pragmatic extension of the Court's understanding of the scope of Article 6(1) would be to consider that insofar as States actually have courts or tribunals (including, for example, immigration or tax tribunals) with jurisdiction to determine cases concerning rights and obligations of whatever kind in national law, these should comply with Article 6.[129]

The satisfactory end result of such developments would be that a person would be guaranteed a 'right to a court' in the sense of Article 6 both to assert or question any arguable legal 'right or obligation' that the person has under national law and to challenge by means of judicial review any administrative decision taken by the State that directly affects such rights or obligations. While it may not have been intended when the Convention was drafted that the right to a fair trial in Article 6 should have such a wide application, an extensive reading along these lines would be fully in line with the perception of the right to a fair trial as a human right.

---

[126] Cf the dissenting opinion of Judge Loucaides in *Maaouia v France* hudoc (2000) 33 EHRR 1037 GC. For another proposal, see the dissenting opinion of Messrs Melchior and Frowein in *Benthem v Netherlands* (1983) Com Rep B 80, para 10.

[127] *Ferrazzini v Italy* 2001-VII 207; 34 EHRR 1068 GC, para 30.

[128] See the dissenting opinion of Judge Lorenzen, joined by Judges Rozakis, Bonello, Straznicka, Firsan, and Fischbach, in the *Ferrazzini* case.

[129] Cf the approach by which Art. 6 applies to whatever appeal courts states have, and see the dissenting opinion of Mr Alkema in *Maillard v France* 1998-III 1292; 27 EHRR 232.

5

Deference Owed Under the Separation of Powers

*Tom Zwart**

Introduction

The question of how much deference is due to the decision-maker was discussed at length for the first time in *R. v Secretary of State for the Environment, ex p. Nottinghamshire CC*.[1] Both this case and the subsequent case of *R. v Secretary of State for the Environment, ex p. Hammersmith and Fulham LBC*[2] concerned fiscal issues, which were considered political rather than legal in nature. According to Lord Scarman, in such a context, there would be room for curial intervention only if the challenged act was so absurd that the decision-maker 'must have taken leave of his senses'.[3] Consequently, a less intrusive test than the *Wednesday* standard, which had been developed and applied in *Associated Provincial Picture Houses Ltd. v Wednesbury Corp*,[4] was proposed. This modification of the *Wednesday* test is usually referred to as 'super-*Wednesbury*'. At approximately the same time in *R. v Home Secretary, ex p. Bugdaycay*,[5] and *R. v Home Secretary, ex p. Brind*,[6] a more rigorous standard of review than *Wednesbury*—known as 'sub-*Wednesbury*'— emerged in cases involving human rights.

As Lord Hope rightly predicted in *R. v Director of Public Prosecutions, ex p. Kebilene*, it is clear that the entry into force of the Human Rights Act (HRA) has given the issue of deference new impetus.[7] When deciding cases under the HRA, courts are frequently called upon to determine the degree of deference due to the political arms of government.[8] Interestingly, these HRA cases often appear to pull

---

* The author is indebted to Angus Johnston and Gordon Anthony for their valuable comments on an earlier draft of this article.

[1] [1986] 1 AC 240, 247, 250 *per* Lord Scarman.   [2] [1990] 1 AC 521.

[3] *R. v Secretary of State for the Environment, ex p. Nottinghamshire CC* [1986] 1 AC 240, 247.

[4] [1948] 1 KB 223.   [5] [1987] AC 514.   [6] [1991] AC 696.

[7] [2000] 2 AC 326, 380–81.

[8] See generally P.P. Craig, *Administrative Law*, (5th edn, 2003) 585–88; H.W.R. Wade & C.F. Forsyth, *Administrative Law*, (9th edn, 2004) 369–71.

in opposite directions. For example, when an issue is raised in the area of national security or counter-terrorism, the case law indicates that the court is to accord latitude to the decision-maker. However, when the decision taken affects the Convention rights of the claimant, the court is expected to subject it to a more rigorous examination.

This essay discusses the way in which the courts have dealt with this dilemma and how they ought to resolve it. To this end the circumstances that trigger deference will be described. The fact that the leniency prescribed by deference and the 'anxious scrutiny' called for by the HRA do not always mix will be discussed. After the potential rationale for deference as identified by the courts has been set out, the case will be made that the separation of powers is the true theoretical justification for according deference to the administrative decision-maker. To underpin this argument, some comparative observations will be made.

For the purpose of this essay, 'deference' will be regarded as the latitude to be accorded by the courts to the discretionary judgment of the original decision-maker. Although Lord Hoffmann was undoubtedly right when he observed that the word 'deference' is less than fortunate because of its overtones of servility,[9] it will nevertheless be used throughout the essay. For better or for worse, the word has become current in the debate on the relationship between the courts and the executive, both in England and in other jurisdictions. It has become particularly popular in US administrative law, from which it probably originated, but even there it is not without its critics. Thus, Justice Scalia has described the term as 'mealy-mouthed'.[10] This contribution will focus mainly on the deference due to the administrative decision-maker rather than that owed to parliament.

Although both concepts spring from the same well, deference has to be distinguished from non-justiciability. A court will not deal with a case that it deems non-justiciable, that is, which raises issues that would be inappropriate for a judge to decide and which should instead be resolved by political means. Justiciability, therefore, is a threshold issue. If the court decides that the case is justiciable, it may nevertheless come to the conclusion that, rather than forming its own judgment on the issues raised, it should give considerable weight to the assessment by the original decision-maker. The question of whether to accord deference, therefore, will only arise after the court has determined that it should decide the case.

Mapping Out the Grounds for Deference

The different factors, circumstances, and approaches identified by the courts as calling for deference will be set out below. While in the majority of cases the subject-matter of the litigation was considered to be decisive, in other cases the

---

[9] *R. (Prolife Alliance) v BBC* [2004] 1 AC 185, 240.
[10] Antonin Scalia, 'Judicial Deference to Administrative Interpretations of Law' (1989) 39 Duke L.J. 511, 514.

type of action involved was deemed more important. In HRA cases, due weight was also given to the nature of the Convention right invoked by the claimant.

The Subject-Matter of the Litigation

In *R. (Mahmood) v Home Secretary*, Laws L.J. held that the intensity of review in a public law case will depend upon the subject-matter in hand.[11] This approach received a seal of approval in the judgment of the House of Lords in *R. (Daly) v Home Secretary*.[12] Two clusters of 'high policy' topics have emerged in the case law as being worthy of deference. The first cluster consists of issues related to public finances and national economic policy, the second covers topics related to security and foreign relations.

The need for the courts to defer to the primary decision-maker when issues of public expenditure and tax distribution are involved was recognized in the *Nottinghamshire* case.[13] More leeway is also due where the issues involve questions of macro-economic policy.[14] The allocation of resources has also been seen as a trigger for deference in several cases.[15]

National security has traditionally been recognized as an area where great weight should be given to the judgment of the political branches.[16] Issues relating to counter-terrorism receive the same treatment.[17] A considerable degree of deference will also be accorded to acts related to the security of the State's borders and the defence of the realm.[18] The political branches enjoy considerable leeway also in the area of immigration.[19] In *Home Secretary v Rehman*, Lord Hoffmann noted that foreign policy is the responsibility of the government and not of the courts.[20]

Courts have, on the other hand, also identified issues on which they are allowed to form their own judgment, for example, criminal justice,[21] the requirement of a

---

[11] [2001] 1 WLR 840, 847.   [12] [2001] 2 AC 532, 548 *per* Lord Steyn.

[13] *R. v Secretary of State for the Environment, ex p. Nottinghamshire CC* [1986] 1 AC 240, 250 *per* Lord Scarman.

[14] *R. v Secretary of State for the Environment, ex p. Hammersmith and Fulham LBC* [1990] 1 AC 521, 597 *per* Lord Bridge; *R. v Director of Public Prosecutions, ex p. Kebilene* [2000] 2 AC 32, 381 *per* Lord Hope; *R. v Ministry of Defence, ex p. Smith* [1996] QB 517, 540 *per* Simon Brown L.J; *A v Home Secretary* [2005] 2 AC 68, 108 *per* Lord Bingham, 135 *per* Lord Hope, 160–61 *per* Lord Walker; *Carson and Reynolds v Secretary of State for Work and Pensions* [2003] EWCA Civ 797, para 73 *per* Laws L.J.

[15] *R. v Cambridge Health Authority, ex p. B* [1991] 1 FLR 1055, 1073 *per* Sir Tomas Bingham M.R. (as he then was); *R. (Prolife Alliance) v BBC* [2004] 1 AC 185, 240 *per* Lord Hoffman; *International Transport Roth GmbH v Home Secretary* [2003] QB 728, 767 *per* Laws L.J; *A v Home Secretary* [2005] 2 AC 68, 160–61 *per* Lord Walker; *Carson and Reynolds v Secretary of State for Work and Pensions* [2003] EWCA Civ 797, para 73 *per* Laws L.J.

[16] *A v Home Secretary* [2005] 2 AC 68, 128 *per* Lord Nicholls, 134 *per* Lord Hope, 160–61 *per* Lord Walker; *Huang v Home Secretary* [2005] EWCA Civ 105, para 52 *per* Laws L.J.

[17] *R. v Director of Public Prosecutions, ex p. Kebilene* [2000] 2 AC 326, 381 *per* Lord Hope; *A v Home Secretary* [2005] 2 AC 68, 108 *per* Lord Bingham.

[18] *International Transport Roth GmbH v Home Secretary* [2003] QB 728, 766 *per* Laws L.J.

[19] *R. (Farrakhan) v Home Secretary* [2002] QB 1391, at 1418 *per* Lord Phillips M.R.

[20] [2003] 1 AC 153, 192–93.

[21] *International Transport Roth GmbH v Home Secretary* [2003] QB 728, 766 *per* Laws L.J.

fair trial,[22] and the protection of rights,[23] especially the rights of minorities.[24] Very prominent among these, of course, is the courts' responsibility to give effect to the rights and freedoms contained in the European Convention on Human Rights.[25]

Law Versus Policy

While determining the proper scope of review, the courts have sometimes distinguished between questions of law and questions of policy. They have held that questions of law are for the courts to decide. This view was expressed by Lord Bingham in *A v Home Secretary*,[26] the case concerning the suspected terrorists detained without trial in Belmarsh prison (the *Belmarsh* case). According to his Lordship, the greater the legal content of any issue, the greater the potential role of the court because under the British Constitution it is the function of the courts and not of political bodies to resolve legal questions. The formulation of policy, however, depends upon political judgement and should therefore be left to the political branches. Thus, in *Huang v Home Secretary*, Laws L.J. held that respect for democracy requires a margin of discretion to be accorded to the democratic decision-maker and that this principle primarily applies where the subject of the decision is the formation of policy.[27] This law-policy dichotomy closely resembles the policy-operational distinction applied by courts in the area of negligence.[28] There courts, for reasons of constitutional propriety, will decline to examine negligence claims against public authorities involving sensitive policy issues.

The Character of the Right Involved

Since the entry into force of the HRA, English courts have often taken the character of the right involved into account when determining the degree of deference to be accorded in any given case. Thus, in *Kebilene* Lord Hope made clear that it is easier for the courts to recognize an area of judgment where the Convention itself requires a balance to be struck, and much less so where the right is stated in terms

[22] *A v Home Secretary* [2005] 2 AC 68, 108 *per* Lord Bingham.
[23] *R. v Director of Public Prosecutions, ex p. Kebilene* [2000] 2 AC 326, 381 *per* Lord Hope; *A v Home Secretary* [2005] 2 AC 68, 108 *per* Lord Bingham, 134–35 *per* Lord Hope, 160–61 *per* Lord Walker.　　　　[24] *A v Home Secretary* [2005] 2 AC 68, 135 *per* Lord Hope.
[25] *Huang v Home Secretary* [2005] EWCA Civ 105, paras 30 and 55 *per* Laws L.J; *Home Secretary v Limbuela* [2004] EWCA Civ 540, para 129 *per* Carnwath L.J; *International Transport Roth GmbH v Home Secretary* [2003] QB 728, 754 *per* Simon Brown L.J; *R. (Bloggs 61) v Home Secretary* [2003] 1 WLR 2724, 2750 *per* Keene L.J.　　　　[26] [2005] 2 AC 68, 102.
[27] [2005] EWCA Civ 105, para 52; see also *R. v Ministry of Defence, ex p. Smith* [1996] QB 517, 556 *per* Sir Thomas Bingham M.R. (as he then was); *R. (Prolife Alliance) v BBC* [2004] 1 AC 185, 240 *per* Lord Hoffmann.
[28] See Duncan Fairgrieve, *State Liability in Tort, A Comparative Law Study* (2003), 59–63; Simon Deakin, Angus Johnston, and Basil Markesinis, *Markesinis and Deakin's Tort Law* (5th edn, 2003) 157–60 and 376–81.

which are unqualified.[29] There can be no doubt that this statement is an authoritative description of the law.[30]

Intriguingly, however, in *Kebilene* Lord Hope also made clear that even where a right is stated in terms which are unqualified, it may still be appropriate for the court to accord some deference to the decision-maker in view of the particular competence that decision-maker may have. Auld L.J. adopted a similar position in *R. (Bloggs 61) v Home Secretary*,[31] where he explained that the intensity of the courts' review is greatest in Article 2 ECHR cases, because of the fundamental and unqualified nature of the right to life. In spite of this, however, the court may still owe the agency some deference because of its special responsibility with regard to the subject-matter of the litigation.[32]

Contextual Approach

Although Lord Steyn noted in *Daly* that 'in law context is everything',[33] it has to date played only a modest part in the discussion on deference. In *R. (Prolife Alliance) v BBC*,[34] a political party opposed to abortion was entitled to air a party election broadcast. It submitted a video for this purpose, which contained footage of an actual abortion, including images of aborted foetuses. The BBC refused to transmit this material because the images were deemed to be too graphic to be broadcast.

In his judgment, Laws L.J. made it clear that he considered the context in which the broadcast would take place to be highly relevant.[35] According to his Lordship, if the material had been intended to be included in an episode of a TV soap, the courts would have undoubtedly deferred to the broadcaster's refusal to show it. If the context were to have been entertainment, the courts would also pay a very high degree of respect to the broadcaster's judgement. Within the context of day-to-day news reporting, the broadcaster's margin of discretion might be somewhat more constrained, but would still remain very considerable. However, since the material was to be included in a party election broadcast, only modest weight should be given to the broadcaster's views because under those circumstances the court has an overriding constitutional responsibility to protect political speech.

The Court of Appeal found that the BBC's decision not to show this party election broadcast was incompatible with Article 10 ECHR. The House of Lords came to a different conclusion, despite the fact that the contextual approach

---

[29] [2000] 2 AC 326, 381.

[30] *International Transport Roth GmbH v Home Secretary* [2003] QB 728, 766 *per* Laws L.J; *A v Home Secretary* [2005] 2 AC 68, 108 *per* Lord Bingham.   [31] [2003] 1 WLR 2724, 2746.

[32] Similarly, see Keene L.J. in the same case at 2750.   [33] [2001] 2 AC 532, 548.

[34] [2004] 1 AC 185; see Ivan Hare, 'Debating Abortion—The Right to Offend Gratuitously' (2003) 62 CLJ 525 and 'Method and Objectivity in Free Speech Adjudication: Lessons from America' (2005) 54 ICLQ 49.   [35] [2004] 1 AC 185, 206.

seemed to resonate with some of their Lordships. Their Lordships relied mainly on a construction of the statutory framework and the applicable broadcasting guidelines.[36]

The Limited Impact of Deference in HRA Cases

The dilemma facing judges in HRA cases where deference may be due has already been mentioned. This dilemma was eloquently described in Lord Walker's speech in the *Belmarsh* case.[37] His Lordship pointed out that, since the case involved both national security and individual liberty, it called for the simultaneous application of two tests that contradict each other. First, the court was expected to show a high degree of respect for the Secretary of State's assessment of the security risks based on his access to secret intelligence sources. On the other hand, the court was obliged to scrutinize closely the practical effect which the measures could have on individual human rights.

The crucial question, of course, is how to reconcile these two approaches in a satisfactory way. As has been discussed above, on the basis of *Kebilene* the courts should accord some degree of deference to the decision-maker, even if a fundamental or unqualified right is involved. That is not, however, how the courts usually operate.[38] In the majority of cases where the challenged act belongs to the area of discretionary judgement of the decision-maker, but at the same time affects a Convention right, the courts will subject it to the rigorous examination associated with the HRA. Or, in the words of Simon Brown L.J. in *International Transport Roth GmbH v Home Secretary*:

'It is suggested that this is a case of high constitutional importance. Perhaps it is. Certainly it raises questions as to the degree of deference owed by the courts to the legislature and executive in the means used to achieve social goals. But judges nowadays have no alternative but to apply the Human Rights Act 1998. Constitutional dangers exist no less in too little judicial activism as in too much. There are limits to the legitimacy of executive or legislative decision-making, just as there are to decision-making by the courts.'[39]

The judgment in the *Belmarsh* case exemplifies this approach.[40] In this case, Lord Bingham conceded that the decision taken by the Home Secretary ought to command respect. Nevertheless, he felt that a proportionality test should be applied because human rights were involved.[41] Lord Hope noted that the executive and the legislature are to be accorded a wide margin of discretion in matters relating to

---

[36] ibid, 225 *per* Lord Nicholls, 244 *per* Lord Scott, 251 *per* Lord Walker.

[37] [2005] 2 AC 68, 162.

[38] *R. (Bloggs 61) v Home Secretary* [2003] 1 WLR 2724 and *R. (Farrakhan) v Home Secretary* [2002] QB 1391, being the exceptions; see also Sadat Sayeed, 'Beyond the Language of "Deference"' (2005) JR 111, 119–20.   [39] [2003] QB 728, 754.

[40] In its judgment the Court of Appeal did accord deference to the decision-maker, see [2004] QB 335.   [41] [2005] 2 AC 68, 110.

national security, especially where the Convention rights of others, such as the right to life, may be put in jeopardy.[42] However, his Lordship went on to subject the decision to a proportionality test because of the absolute nature of the right to liberty.[43] Lord Walker acknowledged that the political branches of government enjoy a wide margin of discretion as far as safeguarding national security is concerned.[44] He nevertheless emphasized that the courts have a special duty to look very closely at any questionable deprivation of individual liberty.

In the *Belmarsh* case, therefore, their Lordships sacrificed a more lenient attitude, which was due because the case concerned a national security issue, in order to apply a strict test prescribed by the presence of the right to liberty. This 'either/or' approach, whereby the need to scrutinize strictly decisions affecting Convention rights trumps the need to accord deference to the decision-maker, is reminiscent of the line taken in *R. v Ministry of Defence, ex p. Smith*,[45] although that case produced the opposite result. There, Sir Thomas Bingham M.R. (as he then was) conceded that although the human rights issue involved called for more anxious scrutiny, the court should in the end adhere to the *Wednesbury* standard of review because the case concerned a policy regarding the defence of the realm. The 'all or nothing approach' currently displayed by the courts is all the more striking if one considers the declarations made by several judges that the scope of review should be regarded as a spectrum or a sliding scale.[46]

Although the courts usually opt for the more stringent of the two relevant tests, a more balanced approach was adopted in two recent cases. In *Bloggs 61*, after having subjected the decision to the most anxious scrutiny standard, Auld L.J. came to the conclusion that it was well within the bounds of what was reasonable.[47] More importantly, in *R. (Farrakhan) v Home Secretary*,[48] Lord Phillips M.R. made the crucial observation that when a court applies a test of proportionality, the margin of appreciation or discretion it accords to the decision-maker is all-important for it is only by acknowledging the margin of discretion that the court avoids substituting its own decision for that of the decision-maker. His Honour found that the decision of the Secretary of State was proportionate because he *provided a sufficient explanation for it*.[49] This suggests that his Lordship reviewed whether the decision of the Secretary of State was within a reasonable range of options, rather than assessing himself whether the right balance had been struck.

This approach matches the test Lord Phillips proposed in *Mahmood*.[50] There his Lordship asserted that, when anxiously scrutinizing an executive decision that

---

[42] ibid, 134.   [43] ibid, 135.   [44] ibid, 160–61.   [45] [1996] QB 517.

[46] ibid 556 *per* Sir Thomas Bingham M.R. (as he then was); *International Transport Roth GmbH v Home Secretary* [2003] QB 728, 761 *per* Laws L.J; *Carson and Reynolds v Secretary of State for Work and Pensions* [2003] EWCA Civ 797, para 73 *per* Laws L.J; *A v Home Secretary* [2005] 2 AC 68, 102 *per* Lord Bingham.   [47] [2003] 1 WLR 2724, 2748; see also Keene L.J. in the same case at 2750.

[48] [2002] QB 1391, 1417.   [49] ibid, 1419, emphasis added.

[50] [2001] 1 WLR 840, 857.

interferes with human rights, the court should ask the question, applying an objective test, whether the decision-maker could reasonably have concluded that the interference was necessary to achieve one or more of the legitimate aims recognized by the Convention. This deferential test has not been greeted with universal approval. Thus, Edwards has argued that this is a watered-down version of the proportionality test that does not meet the level of scrutiny required by the HRA.[51] In his view, the standard proposed by Lord Phillips amounts to 'judicial avoidance' and may even result in 'judicial abdication' of the courts' role under the HRA.

The Rationale for Deference

The answer to the question as to which of the two approaches described above is to be preferred depends upon what should be considered the true rationale of deference. In the case law several justifications have been offered for according deference to the decision-maker. It has been explained in functional terms, been portrayed as part of the discretion of the courts, and been founded upon the separation of powers. All three options will be explored in this paragraph.

Functional Explanations

In several cases the courts have expressed the view that the expertise which the decision-maker enjoys in a certain area—and correspondingly the courts' lack thereof—calls for deference.[52] Similarly, due weight should be given to the judgment of the decision-maker if he has more experience with regard to the subject-matter of the litigation,[53] or is otherwise better placed functionally than the courts to deal with it.[54]

Deference at the Courts' Discretion

Two commentators, Jeffrey Jowell and Murray Hunt, seem to accept that the courts enjoy discretion when deciding whether to accord deference.[55]

---

[51] R.A. Edwards, 'Judicial Deference under the Human Rights Act' (2002) 65 MLR 859, 868, 872.

[52] *R. v Ministry of Defence, ex p. Smith* [1996] QB 517, 556 *per* Sir Thomas Bingham M.R. (as he then was); *A v Home Secretary* [2005] 2 AC 68, 137 *per* Lord Hope; *International Transport Roth GmbH v Home Secretary* [2003] QB 728, 767 *per* Laws L.J.; *Home Secretary v Rehman* [2003] 1 AC 153, 195 *per* Lord Hoffman; *R. (Bloggs 61) v Home Secretary* [2003] 1 WLR 2724, 2746 *per* Auld L.J. and at 2750 *per* Keene L.J.

[53] *R. v Ministry of Defence, ex p. Smith* [1996] QB 517, 556 *per* Sir Thomas Bingham M.R. (as he then was); *Huang v Home Secretary* [2005] EWCA Civ 105, para 53 *per* Laws L.J; *R. (Bloggs 61) v Home Secretary* [2003] 1 WLR 2724, 2746 *per* Auld L.J. and at 2750 *per* Keene L.J.

[54] *R. (Farrakhan) v Home Secretary* [2002] QB 1391, 1418 *per* Lord Phillips M.R.

[55] Jeffrey Jowell, 'Judicial Deference: Servility, Civility or Institutional Capacity?' (2003) PL 592; Jeffrey Jowell, 'Judicial Deference and Human Rights: A Question of Competence' in Paul Craig and

Jowell has drawn an interesting distinction between institutional and constitutional competence.[56] Institutional competence refers to the capacity of a body
to make the relevant decision. The question that is asked is which body is best
equipped to decide the issue in hand—the court or the authority which is being
reviewed. Factors to be taken into account in answering this question include
the respective expertise of the two institutions, the investigative techniques at
their disposal and their access to information. Constitutional competence, on the
other hand, refers to the authority of a body to decide the relevant question. The
question asked is which body is authorized to take the relevant decision under
the constitutive rules which allocate decision-making power to bodies exercising
public functions in a democracy.

Jowell points out that, based upon the appropriate division of powers in a
democracy, the legislature and the executive enjoy superior constitutional status to
decide matters of public interest and policy because they are responsible to the
public through the democratic process. The executive is accountable to Parliament,
the members of which are elected by the people. When reviewing a decision taken
by a public official or parliament, courts are therefore to presume that the
reviewed body is constitutionally best suited to decide the matter. Under these
circumstances, the courts ought to accord deference as a matter of constitutional
competence.

Jowell argues, however, that the constitutional position has changed as a result
of the entry into force of the HRA. In respect of qualified rights, it is now up to the
courts to decide whether a breach of a right is justified in a democratic society
because such action promotes certain necessary public interests. It is for the public
official or parliament to justify that breach. As a result, the primacy of representative status and political accountability has been erased. The ultimate judgement
of whether the correct balance has been struck between the right in question,
the public interest in overriding that right, and the essential requirements of a
democratic society, is for the courts. Since the courts enjoy constitutional authority in this area there is no need for them to accord deference to the decision-
making body.

However, the fact that the courts have constitutional competence in the area
covered by the HRA does not mean that they will never accord deference to the
reviewed bodies. The courts should be sensitive to the fact that their ability to
determine the public interest is subject to limitations and shortcomings.[57] For
example, it is not easy for the courts to second-guess the executive's assertion as to

Richard Rawlings (eds), *Law and Administration in Europe, Essays in Honour of Carol Harlow* (2003)
67; Murray Hunt, 'Sovereignty's Blight: Why Contemporary Public Law Needs the Concept of
"Due Deference"' in Nicholas Bamforth and Peter Leyland (eds), *Public Law in a Multi-Layered
Constitution* (2003) 337.

[56] Jowell, 'Judicial Deference and Human Rights: A Question of Competence', n 55 above, 72–75
and 80–81.
[57] Jowell 'Judicial Deference: Servility, Civility or Institutional Capacity?', n 55 above, 595.

whether national security is likely to be endangered because the executive does indeed have special information and expertise on this matter. Jowell argues, therefore, that it is quite appropriate for courts to acknowledge modestly that there will be occasions where other bodies will be better equipped to decide certain questions.[58]

At first sight, this theory could be characterized as functional. When a court decides to defer to the reviewed body, it is simply conceding that the decision-maker is better placed functionally to deal with the issue. This approach may find support in *Huang*, where Laws L.J. acknowledged that courts may defer to government when for practical reasons they are in no position to arrive at an autonomous decision.[59] However, the essence of Jowell's approach is that it is largely up to the courts themselves to decide whether or not to recognize the primacy of the other branch in a particular area. When a court concedes competence to another branch of government, such a concession is not a matter of law, nor based upon any legal principle.[60] In Jowell's view, therefore, deference is not a constitutional imperative but a concession made by a court that acknowledges that it is less well equipped to deal with a particular issue. It is submitted that the outcome of Jowell's theory is that the margin of discretion left to the other branches may be extended or reduced at will by the courts, or even abolished altogether.

This discretionary character of deference is amplified by Jowell's view that the courts should not be too eager to defer to the other branches. First, if a court feels that deference is warranted in a particular case, it should never sign a blank cheque whereby the entire decision is effectively delegated to the other branch of government.[61] Secondly, courts should also not defer too lightly. They should guard against a presumption that matters of public interest are outside their competence. Thus, Jowell warns that a realistic sense of their own limitations should not lead the courts to disparage their own legitimacy, nor to deny their own authority, on account alone of their lack of accountability to the electorate.[62] There is no need to defer to Parliament or its agents on the basis of their legitimacy as bodies which command 'majority approval'. Quite the contrary, under the HRA the courts are expected to guard democratic rights against the unnecessary intrusion by the representatives of the popular will.[63] As a result, courts are now the ultimate arbiters of the necessary qualities of a democracy in which the popular will is no longer always expected to prevail.[64]

Hunt is critical of the way that deference has been conceptualized in the debate so far.[65] He rejects the use of 'spatial metaphors' that presuppose the existence of an area within which primary decision-makers are simply beyond the reach of

---

[58] ibid, 598.   [59] *Huang v Home Secretary* [2005] EWCA Civ 105, para 52.
[60] Jowell 'Judicial Deference: Servility, Civility or Institutional Capacity?' n 55 above, 599.
[61] ibid, 598.   [62] ibid, 601.   [63] ibid, 601.   [64] ibid, 599.
[65] This criticism is shared by Edwards, 'Judicial Deference under the Human Rights Act', n 51 above, 863–66, who considers deference to be a flawed and unprincipled doctrine.

judicial interference.[66] Hunt disagrees with this approach because it treats certain areas of decision-making as being beyond the reach of legality, and within the realm of pure discretion.[67] In this way, the progress that has been made in the area of public law through the opening up of what were formerly considered zones of immunity from judicial review is threatened.[68]

Hunt suggests that deference theory should instead be founded upon the 'culture of justification' introduced by Mureinik[69] and Dyzenhaus.[70] In this approach 'deference as submission' should be distinguished from 'deference as respect'. Deference as submission occurs when the court treats a decision or an aspect of it as non-justiciable and refuses to embark upon a review of it because it considers it beyond its competence. Deference as respect, on the other hand, presupposes that the court, while reviewing whether the decision is justifiable, gives some weight to it because of the reasons which are offered for it by the primary decision-maker.[71] An important element of this approach is the concept of 'due deference', that is, the idea that in certain circumstances there may be good reasons why it is appropriate for courts not to interfere with decisions of the legislature or the executive. Interestingly, according to Hunt, the primary decision-maker must earn such deference from the courts by openly demonstrating the reasons why its decision is worthy of curial respect.[72] This, too, suggests that deference is subject to the ebb and flow of judicial discretion.

Separation of Powers

Academics used to deny that the concept of separation of powers underlies the British Constitution.[73] Their case was considerably strengthened by the fact that there are significant overlaps between the three branches of government. There is growing evidence, however, that the concept of separation of powers plays an important part in British law.[74] Thus, in *Duport Steels v Sirs*, Lord Diplock emphasized that the British Constitution, though largely unwritten, is firmly based upon the separation of powers.[75] In *Prolife*, Lord Hoffmann asserted that under the separation of powers, the question of which branch of government in

---

[66] Hunt, 'Sovereignty's Blight: Why Contemporary Public Law Needs the Concept of "Due Deference"', n 55 above, 338.   [67] ibid, 338–39.

[68] ibid, 347.

[69] Etienne Mureinik, 'A Bridge to Where? Introducing the Interim Bill of Rights' (1994) 10 SAJHR 31, in particular 40–43.

[70] David Dyzenhaus, 'Law as Justification: Etienne Mureinik's Conception of Legal Culture' (1998) 14 SAJHR 11.

[71] Hunt, 'Sovereignty's Blight: Why Contemporary Public Law Needs the Concept of "Due Deference"', n 55 above, 346–47 and 351–52.   [72] ibid, 340.

[73] See eg J.A.G. Griffith and Harry Street, *Principles of Administrative Law* (3rd edn, 1963) 16; Stanley de Smith and Rodney Brazier, *Constitutional and Administrative Law* (8th edn, 1998) 17–21.

[74] Colin Munro, *Studies in Constitutional Law* (2nd edn, 1999) 328–32.

[75] [1980] 1 WLR 142, 157; see also Lord Scarman in the same case at 169.

any particular circumstance has the decision-making power and what the legal limits of that power are, is a question of law.[76] He therefore went one significant step further than Sir John Donaldson M.R. who, in *R v HM Treasury, ex p. Smedley*, still described the separation of powers as a constitutional convention.[77]

Although one cannot deny that close ties exist in the UK between the executive and the legislature, this does not mean that there is no place for the concept of the separation of powers. Frequent interaction between both branches of government is fairly common in most liberal democracies, even in those such as the US, which has a strong commitment to the concept. But as long as it is accepted that there are boundaries between both branches which ought not to be transgressed, the separation of powers remains a viable doctrine. The case of *R. v Home Secretary, ex p. Fire Brigades Union*, which concerned the separation of powers in all but name,[78] proved that in Britain the concept is still very much a live issue in the area of executive–legislative relations.

It is obvious that the separation of powers has a profound impact on the relations between courts and administrative authorities. Thus, in *M v Home Office*, Nolan L.J. (as he then was) made the crucial observation that the proper constitutional relationship of the executive with the courts is that courts will respect all acts of the executive within its lawful province, and that the executive will respect all decisions of the court as to what its lawful province is.[79] Not surprisingly, therefore, in a number of cases the English courts have suggested that deference is related to the separation of powers, either indirectly or directly.

The link with the concept of separation of powers was more indirect in cases where the courts asserted that the other branches were worthy of deference because of their democratic legitimacy.[80] Thus, Lord Hoffmann expressed the view in *Rehman* that national security assessments have to be entrusted to persons responsible to the community through the democratic process: 'If the people are to accept the consequences of such decisions, they must be made by persons whom the people have elected and whom they can remove.'[81]

Such an approach was criticized, however, by Lord Bingham in the *Belmarsh* case.[82] His Lordship did not accept the argument that because judges are not elected and are not answerable to Parliament they should yield to the other branches. Judges are charged with interpreting and applying the law 'which is universally recognised as a cardinal feature of the modern democratic state, a

[76] [2004] 1 AC 185, 240.   [77] [1985] QB 657 at 666.
[78] [1995] 2 AC 513; the concept was referred to by one of the dissenters, Lord Mustill, at 567, but within a different context.   [79] [1992] QB 270 314–15.
[80] *R. v Director of Public Prosecutions, ex p. Kebiline* [2000] 2 AC 326, 381 *per* Lord Hope; *Home Secretary v Rehman* [2003] 1 AC 153, 195 *per* Lord Hoffmann; *International Transport Roth GmbH v Home Secretary* [2003] QB 728, 762–65 *per* Laws L.J. and at 780 *per* Jonathan Parker L.J; *Huang v Home Secretary* [2005] EWCA Civ 105, paras 51 and 55 *per* Laws L.J; *A v Home Secretary* [2005] 2 AC 68, 135 *per* Lord Hope; *R. (Farrakhan) v Home Secretary* [2002] QB 1391, 1418 *per* Lord Phillips M.R.   [81] *Home Secretary v Rehman* [2003] 1 AC 153, 195.
[82] *A v Home Secretary* [2005] 2 AC 68, 110.

cornerstone of the rule of law itself'. He therefore rejected the argument put forward by the Attorney-General that the courts, being 'non-democratic' institutions owe deference to the 'democratic' branches. This view is shared by Clayton, who has argued that, because civil servants and local officials do not have a direct connection with the voters who make choices through the ballot box, they do not have democratic legitimacy.[83] According to Clayton, it is difficult to understand why in Convention cases judges have less legitimacy than civil servants.

In other cases, a more direct reference has been made to the need to adhere to the separation of powers. In his speech in the *Nottinghamshire* case, the first English case in which the scope of review was discussed, Lord Scarman clearly connected deference to the role that is constitutionally appropriate for the courts under the separation of powers.[84] According to his Lordship, the separation of powers places constitutional limits upon the exercise of the power of judicial review.[85]

In *Rehman*, Lord Hoffmann also assumed a close link between deference and the separation of powers. In his Lordship's view there are certain inherent limitations in the powers of the judicial branch of government arising from the principle of separation of powers. However broad the jurisdiction of a court or tribunal, the exercise of the judicial function must recognize the constitutional boundaries between judicial, executive, and legislative power.[86] His Lordship explained that having jurisdiction to decide a particular matter does not oblige a court to exercise strict scrutiny.[87] In *Prolife*, his Lordship built upon the speech that he had delivered in *Rehman*. He again asserted that the answers to the question of which branch of government has the decision-making power in any particular instance, and what the legal limits of that power are, depend upon the separation of powers.[88]

Clayton[89] and Sayeed[90] have also acknowledged that deference is tied to the separation of powers concept. Clayton has emphasized, however, that the role of this concept in English public law is far less important than in the US system. Hunt, on the other hand, considers the separation of powers to be a formalistic concept that cannot be relied upon to clarify the rationale of 'due deference'.[91]

---

[83] Richard Clayton, 'Judicial Deference and "Democratic Dialogue": the Legitimacy of Judicial Intervention under the Human Rights Act 1998' (2004) PL 33, 40.

[84] *R. v Secretary of State for the Environment, ex p. Nottinghamshire CC* [1986] 1 AC 240, 247, 248, 249 and 250.

[85] ibid, 250–51; similarly, see *R. v Secretary of State for the Environment, ex p. Hammersmith and Fulham LBC* [1990] 1 AC 521, 597 *per* Lord Bridge.   [86] [2003] 1 AC 153, 191.

[87] ibid, 192.   [88] [2004] 1 AC 185, 240.

[89] Clayton, 'Judicial Deference and "Democratic Dialogue": the Legitimacy of Judicial Intervention under the Human Rights Act 1998', n 83 above at 40.

[90] Sayeed, 'Beyond the Language of "Deference" ', n 38 above, at 111.

[91] Hunt, 'Sovereignty's Blight: Why Contemporary Public Law Needs the Concept of "Due Deference" ', n 55 above, at 340 and 347.

The Case for the Separation of Powers as the
Rationale of Deference

There is some important comparative evidence to support the view that sometimes an arm of Government, which is competent to deal with a particular issue, is
nevertheless under a constitutional duty to yield to another branch.

The decision of the US Supreme Court in *Chevron U.S.A., Inc. v Natural
Resources Defense Council, Inc.*, is a case in point.[92] It concerned rules issued by the
Environmental Protection Agency (EPA) under the Clean Air Act. The Carter
EPA had promulgated very strict regulations which were environmentally
friendly, but unwelcomed by many in the business community. When the Reagan
Administration came into office, the EPA replaced the existing rules with regulations which gave companies more leeway. Not surprisingly, these rules were
challenged by the National Resources Defense Council, an ecological organization. Since these different sets of rules were rooted in an interpretation of the same
statutory language, the question before the Supreme Court was how courts should
treat agency interpretations of Acts of Congress. Should judges rely upon their
own construction of the statute or should they respect the agency's interpretation?

At first sight, it appeared likely that the Supreme Court would allow courts to
impose their own construction upon ambiguous statutes. In *Marbury v Madison*,
Chief Justice Marshall had asserted that 'it is emphatically the province and duty
of the judicial department to say what the law is'.[93] It is difficult to reconcile such
an approach with that of accepting the judgement of an agency on a question of
law. However, in *Chevron* the Supreme Court held that the doctrine of the separation of powers did not allow courts to exercise fully their competence to say what
the law is and that courts should ordinarily yield to an agency's interpretation of
the statutes they administer unless their construction was unreasonable.[94] Courts
must defer to the agencies out of respect to Congress's wish to entrust regulatory
responsibility to agencies and to ensure that policy choices, which are a necessary
element of interpreting statutes, are being made by persons answerable to the
political branches rather than unelected judges. According to the Supreme
Court in *Chevron*, it is the constitutional duty of the court to defer to agency

---

[92] 467 U.S. 837 (1984).
[93] 5 U.S. (1 Cranch) 137 (1803); Lord Bingham relied upon a similar maxim in *A v Home
Secretary* [2005] 2 AC 68, 102.
[94] *Chevron U.S.A., Inc. v Natural Resources Defense Council, Inc.* 467 U.S. 837 (1984), 843–44
and 865–66; Cynthia Farina, 'Statutory Interpretation and the Balance of Power in the
Administrative State' (1989) 89 Columbia Law Review 452, 456; Maureen Callahan, 'Must Federal
Courts Defer to Agency Interpretations of Statutes?: A New Doctrinal Basis for Chevron U.S.A. v.
Natural Resources Defense Council' (1991) Wis. L. Rev. 1275, 1286–87; Daniel Lovejoy, 'The
Ambiguous Basis for Chevron Deference: Multiple-Agency Statutes', (2002) 88 Va. L. Rev. 879, 887;
contra Scalia, n 10 at 515.

interpretation of law, despite the fact that under that same Constitution it is the responsibility of the judicial branch to interpret the law.

It is not only the judiciary that may be reined in by these constitutional requirements. For example, the separation of powers sets limits on the extent to which legislative powers may be delegated to executive branch officials. Under the American 'non-delegation' doctrine—which is something of a misnomer—delegation of legislative powers by Congress to administrative agencies is therefore acceptable only as long as 'an intelligible principle' is attached.[95] It may also be noted that under Article 7, Chapter 11 of the Swedish Instrument of Government, the legislature is not allowed to interfere with decisions taken by administrative authorities in individual cases.[96]

It is clear that the judiciary has also sometimes benefited from the limits set to the roles of the other branches. Thus, in *Dodo v The State*, the South African Constitutional Court held that Parliament is allowed to enact legislation laying down mandatory sentences as long as it preserves the courts' power to apply and adapt a general principle to the individual case.[97] According to Justice Ackermann, under the separation of powers it should be left to the courts to determine each case individually. In Australia, an act of the New South Wales legislature, which paved the way for the detention of a person specified therein, was deemed contrary to the separation of powers by the Australian High Court.[98] Similarly, Article I, Section 9, paragraph 3 of the US Constitution bans the passing of bills of attainder, that is, acts of the legislature pronouncing individual persons guilty of crimes. In *U.S. v Brown*, the Supreme Court clearly linked this ban to the separation of powers:[99]

'The Bill of Attainder Clause was intended not as a narrow, technical (and therefore soon to be outmoded) prohibition, but rather as an implementation of the separation of powers, a general safeguard against legislative exercise of the judicial function or more simply—trial by legislature.'

The separation of powers is founded upon the idea that separate responsibilities have been entrusted to each of the branches of government by the constitution in order to preserve individual liberty and to prevent abuse of power.[100] The three branches are allowed to use the instruments at their disposal within, but not outside, their assigned territory. Of course, these territories are not hermetically sealed off from one another—in border areas the branches will sometimes exercise co-authority. When courts defer to the decision-maker, they give effect to the

---

[95] *J.W. Hampton, Jr. & Co. v U.S.* 276 U.S. 394 (1928).
[96] Sweden's Supreme Administrative Court has struck down legislation on the basis of this provision in the *Barsebäck* judgment.   [97] CCT 1/01 CC (2001).
[98] *Kable v Director of Public Prosecutions (NSW)* (1996) 189 CLR 51.
[99] 381 U.S. 437 at 440 (1965).
[100] See M.J.C. Vile, *Constitutionalism and the Separation of Powers* (2nd edn, 1998), in particular at 1–22.

limits of their constitutional mandate. If the courts were not to pay respect to the responsibility of the other branches in this way, they would simply fail in their constitutional duty. Giving latitude to the other branches, therefore, is a constitutional imperative prescribed by the separation of powers. As Lord Hoffmann has explained convincingly in the *Prolife* case, the courts are expected to delineate the respective responsibilities of the arms of Government.[101] They have the final say in this area, not because they can act on their own free will, but because the separation of powers is a legal concept and it is their duty to say what the law is.

Commentators like Jowell and Hunt also believe that it is for the courts to decide whether deference is due.[102] However, unlike Lord Hoffmann, they do not perceive this responsibility as part of the courts' duty to interpret and apply the law but as a matter of discretion. Hunt has expressed the view that the other branches ought to earn the respect of the courts by providing convincing reasons for their decisions. Jowell has argued that some deference might be accorded by the courts to the other branches as a result of certain perceived institutional shortcomings of the judiciary. He has called upon the courts to exercise restraint in yielding ground to the primary decision-maker. This approach places deference in a vulnerable position. When judges can decide, without any normative limitation, how much latitude is owed to the other branches and at the same time are encouraged to downplay their own institutional shortcomings, the discretionary area of judgement left to the primary decision-maker runs the risk of being reduced to zero.

This risk can be illustrated by referring to developments that have taken place in Germany. In the *Multiple-Choice Exam*[103] case, a medical student, who had failed a multiple-choice exam, challenged some of the questions before the administrative courts. These courts pointed out that, on the basis of existing case law, they were supposed to accord great deference to the experts that had composed the exam. The courts would only intervene if a question was manifestly wrong or had no foundation in science. Since neither could be said of the contested questions, review was denied.

The student subsequently filed a constitutional complaint with the Federal Constitutional Court challenging the limited review exercised by the administrative courts. She claimed that her right to recourse to the court, as guaranteed by Article 19, section 4 of the German Constitution, had been violated. The Court felt that the applicant's complaint was well-founded. Since the administrative courts had been unwilling to look into her objections to the contested exam, they had denied her the right to an effective remedy. The Court pointed out that the citizen is entitled to an effective review by the courts. They should undertake,

---

[101] [2004] 1 AC 185, 240.
[102] See Jowell, 'Judicial Deference: Servility, Civility or Institutional Capacity?'; Jowell, 'Judicial Deference and Human Rights: A Question of Competence'; Murray Hunt, 'Sovereignty's Blight: Why Contemporary Public Law Needs the Concept of "Due Deference"', n 55 above.
[103] BVerfGE 84, 59.

therefore, a thorough examination both of the law and the facts concerning the challenged decisions. They may not simply rely upon the determinations made by the administrative authorities.

Consequently, the margin of discretion with regard to exams should be very limited since otherwise it would be impossible to guarantee an effective review by the courts. The courts are expected to review whether the exam authorities have adhered to the prescribed standards. As far as medical exams were concerned, the courts should ascertain whether the questions were understandable, clear, and not open to debate. A question which does not meet these standards is unlawful. It is the task of administrative courts to exercise this kind of review, if need be with the help of experts. The German administrative courts are not altogether happy with this approach, feeling caught between a rock and a hard place.[104] While the Constitutional Court pushes for exacting review, administrative authorities complain of government by the judiciary.

If one accepts that when displaying deference the courts can act at their own discretion, one denies the normative force of the separation of powers. As a consequence, the danger exists that it would be very difficult to impose this concept upon the other two branches. One cannot have one's cake and eat it. If the courts can act at will, then so too can the other branches. This would mean that some of the safeguards to protect the role of the courts, that have been inferred form the separation of powers, would become irrelevant. No longer would there be any objection to Parliament charging individuals with crimes and punishing those charged for committing them. The legislature would be allowed in individual cases to abolish the duty to act fairly or to overrule the judgment reached by the court. It is obvious that such an unattractive state of affairs is likely to result in the arbitrariness and abuse of power that the separation of powers is designed to prevent.

Conclusion

It is submitted that the separation of powers is an essential element of the constitutional fabric that ought to set limits upon the respective responsibilities of the various arms of Government. This concept underlies the idea that acts of the decision-maker should sometimes command respect. In other words, rather than a discretionary act on the part of the courts, according deference to the other branches is a constitutional imperative. In order to take the concept of separation of powers seriously, courts should use a less exacting test when deference is due. In HRA cases, this means that they will have to combine the rigour associated with Convention rights and the leniency resulting from the margin of discretion into

---

[104] Norbert Niehues, 'Die Bindungswirkung und Umsetzung Verfassungsgerichtlicher Entscheidungen' (1997) Neue Juristische Wochenschrift, 557.

an intermediate test. This is what the Canadian Supreme Court consistently does when confronted with a case where different factors call for *prima facie* conflicting levels of scrutiny.[105] The test set out by Lord Phillips in *Mahmood*[106] and applied by him in *Farrakhan*[107] is perfectly suited to this type of situation.

This raises the question of whether the European Court of Human Rights would be willing to accept that such an intermediate test could be applied in Convention cases, considering its opposition to the sub-*Wednesbury* standard of review in cases such as *Smith and Grady v United Kingdom*[108] and *Hatton and others v United Kingdom*.[109] If one accepts that deference is a constitutional imperative prescribed by the separation of powers, it should be covered by the margin of appreciation left by the Strasbourg Court to the national authorities. Or, in the words of Laws L.J. in *Roth*:[110]

'Being a domestic tribunal, our judgment as to the deference owed to the democratic powers will reflect the culture and conditions of the British state. Such a judgment will itself enjoy (in any future debate at Strasbourg) a margin of appreciation, according to the Strasbourg court's own case law.'

If the European Court of Human Rights were not, however, to recognize that the constitutional justification for applying such a test is covered by the margin of appreciation, then there is something wrong with Strasbourg, rather than English, law.

---

[105] See *Canada (Director of Investigation and Research) v Southam Inc.* [1997] 1 SCR 748, and generally David J. Mullan, *Administrative Law* (2001) 61–83.   [106] [2001] 1 WLR 840, 856.
   [107] [2002] QB 1391, 1417–19.   [108] (1999) 29 EHRR 493.
   [109] (2002) 34 EHRR 1.   [110] [2003] QB 728, 765.

6

Judicial Policy in a Transforming Constitution

Hugh Corder

Introduction

The word 'transformation' is not to be found in the Constitution of the Republic of South Africa (1996),[1] nor was it used in the 'interim' Constitution of 1993.[2] Indeed, the use of the adjective 'transitional' for the latter (which I prefer), emphasizes the passage between two fixed points which was the avowed aim of the first step in South Africa's two-stage move from apartheid to a constitutional democracy.[3] The final Constitution, on the other hand, provides not only for a process of 'changing the form, character and nature of'[4] the systems of law and governance of the South African State, but also the very substance of socio-economic relationships. This apparent silence has, however, led some political opponents to argue that the South African government's pursuit of the goals of social and economic transformation through law and policy is neither necessitated by nor sanctioned in the Constitution.

The folly of such a point of view becomes apparent as one traverses, even at a very high level, the language of the opening and closing passages of the 1993 Constitution, and countless provisions of the 'final' Constitution. The Preamble of the transitional Constitution states:

'We, the people of South Africa declare that—

Whereas there is a need to create a new order in which all South Africans will be entitled to a common . . . citizenship in a sovereign and democratic constitutional state in which there is equality between men and women and people of all races so that all citizens shall be able to enjoy and exercise their fundamental rights and freedoms . . . '

---

[1] Act 108 of 1996.   [2] Act 200 of 1993.

[3] For a detailed contemporary account of the first phase of constitutional change, see Hugh Corder, 'Towards a South African Constitution' (1994) 57 MLR 491; for a review of constitution-making over a longer period, see Hassen Ebrahim, *The Soul of a Nation* (1998).

[4] These I take to be the essential elements of a 'transition'.

Of greater significance is the language of what became known as the 'Postamble'[5] to the same Constitution:

'National Unity and Reconciliation

This Constitution provides a historic bridge between the past of a deeply divided society characterised by strife, conflict, untold suffering and injustice, and a future founded on the recognition of human rights, democracy and peaceful co-existence and development opportunities for all South Africans, irrespective of colour, race, class, belief or sex.

The adoption of this Constitution lays the secure foundation for the people of South Africa to transcend the divisions and strife of the past, which generated gross violation of human rights, the transgression of humanitarian principles in violent conflicts and a legacy of hatred, fear, guilt and revenge. These can now be addressed on the basis that there is a need for understanding but not for vengeance, a need for reparation but not for retaliation, a need for ubuntu but not for victimisation . . .

With this Constitution and these commitments we, the people of South Africa, open a new chapter in the history of our country . . . '

What is important to appreciate is that this 'preambular' type of ringing declaration enjoyed greater significance in law than is the case according to the usual rules of statutory interpretation. Section 232(4)[6] provided that, in interpreting the Constitution, the fact that any provision appeared on the fringes, so to speak (and the National Unity and Reconciliation statement was expressly mentioned), did not mean that it was of any lesser status than a 'mainstream' provision, and should 'for all purposes be deemed to form part of the substance of this Constitution'. Indeed, the Postamble in particular was of critical importance in the outcome of a number of cases, chief among them *Azanian Peoples Organisation (AZAPO) v President of the Republic of South Africa*.[7]

The Preamble to the 1996 Constitution continues the theme thus:

'We, the people of South Africa, . . . adopt this Constitution . . . so as to—

Heal the divisions of the past and establish a society based on democratic values, social justice and fundamental human rights;

Lay the foundations for a democratic and open society in which government is based on the will of the people and every citizen is equally protected by law;

Improve the quality of life of all citizens and free the potential of each person; and

Build a united and democratic South Africa able to take its rightful place as a sovereign state in the family of nations.'

The statement of 'founding values'[8] further emphasizes such visionary sentiments, adding references to human dignity, supremacy of the constitution and the rule of law, and a system of 'democratic government, to ensure accountability, responsiveness and openness'.

---

[5] As the concluding part of Act 200 of 1993 came to be known. This part bore no section number and appeared after the final section of the Constitution, s 251. It is widely acknowledged to have been drafted and agreed to by the main parties in the final, nocturnal hours of the negotiation process which gave rise to the transitional Constitution—hence the 'postamble'.

[6] Of Act 200 of 1993.   [7] 1996 (4) SA 671 (CC).   [8] Act 108 of 1996, s 1.

In the light of these repeated exhortations to ideals which encapsulate much of the best to which organized humanity can strive through the law, contrasted with the forms of government and legal rules which characterized the apartheid regime in the half-century before the new constitutional dispensation, who could argue honestly that the Constitution is not all about 'transformation' of social relations through the law? In the absence of a disjuncture between the above statements of purpose and the rest of the constitutional provisions, a proposition that has not been heard, no one can be in any doubt that the design and detail of the 1996 Constitution seeks to 'transform' South Africa.

The words on paper must, naturally, be given life by Parliament and the executive, and there has been no shortage of policy- and law-making activity by successive national governments since 1994, much of it aimed at various aspects of social and economic transformation. (Provincial and local government have been far less effective and productive.) Similarly, in cases of doubt about the scope and meaning to be given to constitutional or statutory language, judgments of the superior courts assume great practical significance. To what extent has the judiciary been willing to engage with the complexity of the transformative agenda in the Constitution, national legislation, and policy? What can be learned about the capacity of 'the law' to facilitate transformation?

These questions demand extensive answers, beyond the ambit of the current piece.[9] They must be seen against the history of the role of the judiciary in colonial and apartheid South Africa, with its record of overwhelming support for successive racist and unjust governments, constrained externally by the doctrine of parliamentary sovereignty as received in its Diceyan splendour, with none of the restraints on legislative power inherent in the idea of the rule of law. Within its ranks, many studies[10] have shown that the judiciary was limited by the nature of its membership, by the confines of its educational and professional foundations, by its lack of critical engagement with more than the form of the disputes brought to it for resolution and, on significant occasions, by a lack of courage when faced with an uncomfortable choice.[11]

This track-record is not a promising one as the basis for imaginative participation in as revolutionary a project as is represented by the Constitution, especially when it is appreciated that all judges serving at the time of the adoption of the new dispensation in 1994 were entitled to continue in office—and all of them did so. There has, naturally, been a substantial degree of change in the composition of the

---

[9] Much naturally depends on one's view of the authority of the law and its relationship to the economy. Influenced by the work of EP Thompson and others, I subscribe to the notion of the 'relative autonomy' of the law and I proceed from such a vantage point.

[10] Among them, Albie Sachs, *Justice in South Africa* (1973); John Dugard, *Human Rights and the South African Legal Order* (1978); and David Dyzenhaus, *Hard Cases in Wicked Legal Systems* (1991).

[11] Such as in *Minister of the Interior v Lockhat* 1961 (2) SA 587 (A); *Rossouw v Sachs* 1964 (2) SA 551 (A); *South African Defence and Aid Fund v Minister of Justice* 1967 (1) SA 263 (A); *Omar v Minister of Law and Order* 1987 (3) SA 859 (A); and *Staatspresident v UDF* 1988 (4) 830 (A).

judiciary since then,[12] and it may be argued that a positivistic approach to the judicial office could be helpful, as a fundamental change of the legislative framework will not trouble the judges too much, for they will continue to apply a different sort of statutory regime with the same uncritical vigour with which they enforced the laws of apartheid. Perhaps of greater significance, however, is the widely acknowledged adherence to principles of legality and justice on a few important occasions by the judges under apartheid and earlier,[13] and even more frequently by courageous lawyers in practice and the academy.[14] These incidents, which occurred throughout the twentieth century, as well as the basis of the South African legal system in the Europe of the enlightenment[15] and the formal independence of the practising profession and the courts,[16] contributed substantially to the political commitment of the negotiating parties to the social democratic basis of the Constitution, and to the belief that the law could provide the means to achieve transformation in wider society.

This belief was translated into statute law and administrative action in the short term in pursuit of 'national unity and reconciliation', as a vital element in the process of 'transition', itself a part of more thorough-going 'transformation'. I am thus drawing a temporal distinction between the two concepts, linked as they are: I see the process of 'transition' embracing the work of the Truth and Reconciliation Commission[17] and any number of steps taken immediately to abolish the more obvious statutory and administrative pillars of injustice. Challenges to the constitutional validity of many such laws found their way rapidly to the Constitutional Court, which had no difficulty in upholding

---

[12] By late 2003, about one-third of the 214 superior court judges were black (compared with one out of 164 judges 10 years earlier); recent estimates are that about 60% of all such judges have been appointed since the end of apartheid in 1994. See Penuell Maduna, 'Address at the Banquet of the Judicial Officers' Symposium'; and MT Moerane, 'The Meaning of Transformation of the Judiciary in the new South African Context' (2003) 120 SA Law Journal 663 and 708 respectively, at 665 and 713.

[13] Such as *Harris v Minister of the Interior* 1952 (2) SA 428 (A); *R v Ngwevela* 1954 (1) SA 123 (A); and *Minister of Law and Order v Hurley* 1986 (3) SA 568 (A).

[14] See the published work of Anthony Mathews, *Law, Order and Liberty in South Africa* (1971); Geoff Budlender, 'Law and Lawlessness in South Africa' (1988) 4 SA Journal on Human Rights 139; B van D. van Niekerk, '... Hanged by the Neck until you are dead' (1969) SA Law Journal 457 and (1970) 87 SA Law Journal 60; and Arthur Chaskalson, 'The past ten years: a balance sheet and some indicators for the future' (1989) 5 SA Journal on Human Rights 293.

[15] See the contributions to D.P. Visser (ed.), *Essays on the History of Law* (1989) for a discussion of the origins of many aspects of South African law.

[16] Security of judicial tenure has been formally present in the South African Constitution since 1909, while the practising profession is structured in form and traditions on those of England. For a brief summary, see Hugh Corder, 'Judicial authority in a changing South Africa' (2004) 24 Legal Studies 253, 254–55.

[17] For a reflection on the interface between the Commission and the legal profession (including the judiciary), see David Dyzenhaus, *Truth, Reconciliation and the Apartheid Legal Order* (1988). For a more general review of its work, see Charles Villa Vicencio and Wilhelm Verwoerd (eds), *Looking back, Reaching Forward* (2000).

them.[18] In a sense, the focus on 'transition' (to be seen most prominently in legal form in the 'transitional' Constitution of 1993) provides the impetus, the platform for a much more extensive, fundamental, and longer-lasting process of the 'transformation' of social and economic relations. This latter process is, as we have seen, not only sanctioned expressly in many parts of the Constitution, but is also an indispensable part of any attempt to entrench the constitutional democratic form of government in South Africa.

In other words, the substantial continuation of the patterns of empowerment and impoverishment established and entrenched by colonialism and apartheid is inimical to the entire logic of the Constitution. In addition, should such patterns not be urgently addressed, there will be no social and political legitimacy for the constitutional project, which is then likely to suffer the fate of similar ambitious schemes in the post-colonial world. While the legislature and the executive have primary responsibility for initiating and implementing policies and programmes which are aimed at redressing the race-based imbalances of power and wealth, the response of the courts is a critical element in any such process. Judges must be sensitive to the constitutional imperatives and to the social climate, while exercising vigilance in upholding the values of the Constitution, particularly the rule of law and good governance.

While issues of transformation have surfaced on a number of occasions in the courts since 1994, this article seeks in a highly selective way to assess the temperature of judicial policy in response to the transformative agenda, by focusing on just two recent cases in the Constitutional Court. Both cases raise highly significant questions about the role of the law (and the courts) in shifting the socio-economic balance, yet from very distinct perspectives. I hope by a detailed consideration of the judgments to provide a sense of judicial responses to such issues, and to speculate on the road ahead. From my earlier work[19] on the role of the appellate judiciary in the period after Union in South Africa (1910 to 1950), I have good reason to believe that a comparative analysis of the respective jurisprudence of the two periods will be revealing, but this altogether more ambitious project lies in the future. There may well be useful lessons for other jurisdictions facing similar problems.

In focusing on judicial policy in this way, I make three (hopefully uncontroversial) assumptions: that judges are important cogs in the administration of justice, the more so when they have the power ultimately to give meaning to the words of as authoritative a document as a supreme constitution; that, in exercising this authority, judges face choices *to an extent*, through the variability of facts and the imprecision of language; and that, in choosing meaning, judges are

---

[18] See eg *S v Makwanyane* 1995 (3) SA 391 (CC); *S v Zuma* 1995 (2) SA 642 (CC); *S v Mhlungu* 1995 (3) SA 867 (CC); and *S v Williams* 1995 (3) SA 632 (CC).

[19] Hugh Corder, *Judges at Work* (1984).

Judges

influenced by policy, articulated (for example in basic constitutional or social values) or inarticulate.

The Cases

I will deal with the cases in the order in which the Constitutional Court heard them.

Bato Star Fishing (Pty) Ltd v Minister of Environmental Affairs and Tourism and Others[20]

This dispute arose from the allocation of fishing quotas in the Western Cape, where the ownership of the fishing industry was dominated by white people. One of the objectives of the Marine Living Resources Act, according to which a Total Allowable Catch (TAC) and quotas were to be determined, was '...the need to restructure the fishing industry to address historical imbalances and to achieve equity within all branches of the fishing industry'. [21] The respondent Ministry initially indicated that 'up to 25%' or 'a notable proportion' of the TAC would be allocated to consortia representing the historically disadvantaged, but in the end only 2 per cent was so allocated. Bato Star was such a company, and they pursued the alleged 'invalidity' of the allocations by way of judicial review of administrative action in the Cape High Court, where they succeeded in having the decision set aside as being 'unreasonable'. The Minister duly appealed to the Supreme Court of Appeal, which swiftly and peremptorily upheld the appeal.[22] The Court invoked due 'deference' as the basis for its view that it would be entirely inappropriate for it to question the reasonableness of the allocation of quotas, given the complexities of the fishing industry. Thus, the matter came before the Constitutional Court in late 2003. In unprecedented fashion, the Court duly delivered itself of two unanimous judgments in March 2004, dismissing the appeal. In order of appearance in the reports,[23] the first judgment written by Justice O'Regan addresses the administrative review issues, and constitutes the most authoritative and complete treatment of the current state of South African administrative law by any court since 1994. In several incisive passages[24] the Court dealt with review for reasonableness as envisaged by the Bill of Rights[25] and the related statute, the Promotion of Administrative Justice Act[26] (PAJA). It concluded that '...the review functions of the court now have a substantive as well as a procedural ingredient', although '...the distinction between appeals and reviews continues to be significant' and the court '...should take care not to

---

[20] 2004 (4) SA 490 (CC).   [21] Act 18 of 1998, s 2 (j).
[22] Reported as *Minister of Environmental Affairs and Tourism v Phambili Fisheries and Another* 2003 (6) SA 407 (SCA).   [23] See n 20 above for the citation, hereafter referred to as *Bato Star*.
[24] ibid, paras 43 to 48.   [25] Constitution, Act 108 of 1996, s 33.   [26] Act 4 of 2000.

usurp the functions of administrative agencies. Its task is to ensure that the decisions taken by administrative agencies fall within the bounds of reasonableness as
required by the Constitution.'[27]

In reaching these conclusions, the Court was influenced by recent pronounce-
ments of the House of Lords[28] which assisted in persuading it to abandon the
apparent adoption of the 'Wednesbury unreasonableness' approach by the South
African Parliament in the PAJA.[29] The Court also was careful not to set too much
store by the notion of 'judicial deference', emphasizing that it did not imply 'judicial timidity or an unreadiness to perform the judicial function'.[30] This judgment
thus marks an important milestone in the development of the law of judicial
review of administrative action in South Africa.[31]

For present purposes, however, the other unanimous judgment, penned by
Justice Ngcobo, is of greater significance. While its opening and closing paragraphs indicate that it concurs with the judgment of O'Regan J,[32] Ngcobo J stated
that he wrote separately 'to emphasise the importance of transformation in the
context of the Marine Living Resources Act'.[33] In his view (shared by all the other
members of the Court), the answer to the issues raised in the appeal 'depends, in
the first place, on the place of transformation in our constitutional democracy,
and, in the second place, on how the phrases "have regard to" or "have particular
regard to" are to be understood in the context of the Constitution and the Act.
The exercise is essentially one of statutory interpretation.'[34] The judgment thus
provides the fullest direct treatment so far of the judicial view of the notion of
'transformation' as enshrined in the Constitution, as well as a fair sense of how far
the highest court in the country is prepared to go in holding the executive to
account for the achievement of this notion in a 'polycentric' context.

The essence and flavour of the judgment can best be gained by a consideration
of the following selection of quotations from it:

'South Africa is a country in transition . . . from a society based on inequality to one based
on equality.

Our constitutional order is committed to the transformation of our society . . . [It]
recognises that decades of systematic racial discrimination entrenched by the apartheid
legal order cannot be eliminated without positive action being taken . . . We are required to

---

[27] *Bato Star*, para 45.
[28] In particular, the speech of Lord Cooke in *R v Chief Constable of Sussex, ex p. International
Trader's Ferry Ltd* [1997] (1) All ER 129 (HL) at 157, and Lord Hoffman in *R (on the application of
Prof-Life Alliance) v British Broadcasting Corporation* [2003] 2 All ER 977 (HL), paras 75 to 76; relied
on in para 44 of *Bato Star*.   [29] Act 4 of 2000, s 6(2)(h).
[30] See *Bato Star*, para 46.
[31] The series of judgments delivered in the Constitutional Court on 30 September 2005 in
*Minister of Health v New Clicks South Africa (Pty) Ltd and Others (Treatment Action Campaign and
Innovative Medicines South Africa as Amici Curiae)*, case CCT 59/04, thus far unreported, may in
time come to assume greater significance.   [32] See *Bato Star*, paras 69 and 110 to 115.
[33] ibid, para 69.   [34] ibid, para 71.

do more than that. The effects of discrimination may continue indefinitely unless there is a commitment to end it.

But transformation is a process. There are profound difficulties that will be confronted... We must not underestimate them. The measure that brings about transformation will inevitably affect some members of the society adversely, particularly those coming from the previously advantaged communities. It may well be that other considerations may have to yield in favour of achieving the goal we fashioned for ourselves in the Constitution. What is required, though is that the process of transformation must be carried out in accordance with the Constitution.'[35]

Ngcobo J then applied the same process of analysis to the Marine Living Resources Act[36] and section 2 (j) in particular in order to ascertain the appropriate meaning *in this context* of the words 'have regard to'.[37] He acknowledged being troubled by an interpretive approach which gave undue weight to the ordinary meaning of the phrase; rather, he said: '[t]he process of interpreting the Act must recognise that its policy is founded on the need both to preserve marine living resources and to transform the fishing industry, and the Constitution's goal of creating a society based on equality in which all people have equal access to economic opportunities'.[38] Applying the latter approach to the interpretation of the phrase allowed the Court to privilege the entry to the fishing industry of those 'from historically disadvantaged sectors of society'.[39] In sum:

'All these considerations point inexorably to the conclusion that the words "have regard"... in the constitutional and statutory context, require a decision-maker to give more than lip service to section 2(j). The decision must address the need for transformation in a meaningful way when decisions are made, and be able to demonstrate that this has been done. A failure to do so is unlawful, and the ensuing decision is open to attack.'[40]

At this point, and ignoring the opening paragraph, the legal representatives of Bato Star could have been forgiven for thinking that the language indicated at least a minority judgment in their favour.[41] Not so, however, for Ngcobo J continues:

'The duty of the courts... does not extend to telling the functionaries how to implement transformation.... The transformation can take place in various ways.... Exactly how this is to be done is complex and difficult and ultimately a matter of policy.'[42]

In assessing Bato Star's complaint, the Court held that the appellant had not made a case that the allocation (of 2 per cent of the TAC) to encourage transformation was 'in the context... so insignificant as to amount to failure to give effect to

---

[35] See *Bato Star*, paras 73, 74, and 76, respectively.   [36] ibid, paras 78 to 82.
[37] ibid, para 83ff.   [38] ibid, para 92.
[39] Act 18 of 1998, s 18 (5), as set out in *Bato Star*, para 96.
[40] *Bato Star*, para 99.   [41] ibid, paras 100 to 103.   [42] ibid, para 104.

transformation'.[43] This conclusion is reached despite a further judicial broadside in the immediately preceding paragraphs of the judgment that:

'No one would dispute the need to maintain stability in the industry.... But transformation is required by both the Constitution and the Act. And that change sometimes comes at a cost...[T]here are profound challenges facing our nation in meeting our constitutional commitment to transformation. The transformation process will inevitably have an adverse impact on some individuals, particularly those that have always been advantaged and, at times, on the industry. These are some of the challenges we will have to confront as a nation in transition. But transformation cannot be sacrificed at the altar of stability. It must be carried out responsibly and its adverse impact must be minimized.... It would be ironical indeed if the effects of past unfair discrimination...were now to be used to exclude [those discriminated against] from the very industry under the new legal order.'[44]

The significance of this unanimous judgment of the Constitutional Court for any discussion of the judicial view of its role in transformation is apparent. I will reflect further on these extracts below, but for the present would note the following:

(i)   the frequent use of the personal pronouns 'we' and 'our';

(ii)   the juxtaposition (interchangeability?) of the words 'transition' and 'transformation';

(iii) the clear and repeated warnings that those advantaged by past unfair discrimination should anticipate feeling the adverse effects of transformation; and

(iv)   the apparent pulling-back-from-the-brink of declaring the Ministerial action to be unlawful by Ngcobo J, perhaps to secure the support of all the fellow members of the Court for his views on transformation, which he would not have enjoyed had he upheld the appeal.

Against this background, let us consider the approach of the Constitutional Court in a different but equally urgent aspect of transformation, that of the provision of basic shelter to thousands of homeless urban dwellers.

President of the Republic of South Africa and Another v Modderklip Boerdery (Pty) Ltd (Agri SA and Others, Amici Curiae)[45]

Access to land, both rural and urban, lies close to the heart of most South Africans. Dispossession of land was the main objective of imperial and settler conquest in the nineteenth century, and was the principal means of ensuring white-minority hegemony and largely rural segregation in the first half of the twentieth century. From 1948, one of the keystones of apartheid was the ruthless pursuit of urban

---

43 ibid, para 110.   44 ibid, paras 106 and 107.
45 2005 (5) SA 3 (CC), hereafter *Modderklip*.

segregation of racial groups as defined, including the destruction of many areas of mixed residence, particularly in the older cities and towns.[46] It goes without saying that a programme of land redistribution must be a critical element in the success of any attempt at transformation of the socio-economic sphere in South Africa.[47]

Access to housing for low-income and unemployed South Africans is an acute problem, particularly in the larger urban areas, and is exaggerated by the removal over the past two decades of the artificial legislative and regulatory barriers which apartheid erected on racist grounds. It was to be expected, therefore, that the 'right to property' question would have loomed large in the constitutional negotiations of the early 1990s, and would have been strongly contested. So it was, both in the interim[48] and final Constitutions, leading to a right to property currently in place[49] which is unusually (for the South African Bill of Rights) negatively phrased: 'No one may be deprived of property except in terms of law of general application, and no law may permit arbitrary deprivation of property.' The section goes on to deal extensively with the conditions under which property may be expropriated, and provides for an obligation on the State to foster access to land and an entitlement for those dispossessed of property after 1913 to 'restitution of that property or to equitable redress'.[50]

In addition, the section in the Bill of Rights which follows immediately is that which deals with 'the right to have access to adequate housing'.[51] Furthermore, this section places a qualified obligation on the State to achieve this right, and provides safeguards against eviction from a home or the demolition of a home. Parliament has in turn adopted a raft of legislation in regard to land and housing.[52] This is the legislative and social context in which the *Modderklip* case was fought through the courts.

The immediate factual background[53] which gave rise to the dispute was the establishment on private land of an informal settlement (of about 4,000 shacks housing about 18,000 people) over a five-month period in 2000. These people were attempting to escape the overcrowding in the formal township of a city east of Johannesburg, but the owner of the land (used for agriculture) objected to this unlawful occupation of its land, and was granted an eviction order by the Transvaal High Court against the occupiers. The residents ignored this order of

---

[46] For a detailed examination of the development of the law of property in South Africa, see the contributions to 1985 *Acta Juridica*, (on the theme 'Land Ownership: A Changing Concept'). In particular, see TRH Davenport, 'Some Reflections on the history of land tenure in South Africa, seen in the light of attempts by the state to impose political and economic control', 53 to 76.
[47] For a recent review and analysis of this question, see Jill Zimmerman 'Property on the Line: Is an expropriation-centred land reform constitutionally permissible?' (2005) 122 SA Law Journal 378 and the authorities cited there.   [48] Act 200 of 1993, s 28.
[49] Act 108 of 1996, s 25 (1).   [50] ibid, ss 25 (5) and 25 (7).   [51] ibid, s 26.
[52] See eg the Restitution of Land Rights Act, Act 22 of 1994; the Development Facilitation Act, Act 67 of 1995; and the Prevention of Illegal Eviction from and Unlawful Occupation of Land Act, Act 19 of 1998.   [53] See *Modderklip*, paras 2 to 16.

Court; the Sheriff refused to carry it out without a substantial monetary deposit to cover her costs; the laying of criminal charges against the residents proved ineffective (the local prison could not accommodate those sentenced); and informal appeals by the land-owner to various governmental authorities proved fruitless. The number of unlawful residents grew to 40,000 within a few months.

Modderklip thus returned to court to enforce its rights against several government agencies. The State was in an awkward position: it was reluctant to give the impression that 'land invaders' would be preferred in the provision of formal housing over those who were patiently waiting their turn on various housing lists, and the land on which the settlement had been established was unsuitable for housing, so that costly alternative provision would have to be made. The Transvaal High Court[54] once more found for the farm-owner, granting it an order which confirmed its rights to property, and reminding the State of its constitutional obligations[55] to assist both the 'squatters' to find housing and the courts to ensure their independence and effectiveness.

The occupiers and government duly appealed to the Supreme Court of Appeal (SCA) against both the initial eviction order and the orders set out immediately above. The SCA unanimously rejected the appeal,[56] invoking the right to equality in favour of Modderklip, in the sense that it had no duty as an 'individual' to bear the burden of accommodating 40,000 people on its land. However, as the return of the land was not a feasible option, it ordered 'constitutional damages' by way of relief to Modderklip, as some form of financial compensation for the temporary loss of the use of the land. Thus, the occupiers would be permitted to remain on the land, until the orderly process of the provision of formal housing would allow them to be re-settled. The State then appealed against this decision to the Constitutional Court, which handed down a unanimous dismissal of the appeal in May 2005, with costs against the State.

This judgment is the one particularly under review for present purposes: significantly, perhaps, it was written by Acting Chief Justice Langa (now the Chief Justice). After reviewing the proceedings in and orders of the courts below, the Constitutional Court found for Modderklip, but preferred to do so not so much on the basis of the rights to property and to housing of the respective parties, but rather on the maintenance of the rule of law[57] and the right of Modderklip to have access to court.[58] The Court found that the rule of law created an obligation on the State 'to provide the necessary mechanisms for citizens to resolve disputes that arise between them', an obligation enhanced by the rights to have

---

[54] See *Modderklip Boerdery (Edms) Bpk v President van die Republiek van Suid Afrika en andere* (2003) 1 ALL SA 465 (T).   [55] Act 108 of 1996, s 165(4).
[56] See *Modderfontein Squatters, Greater Benoni City Council and President of the Republic of South Africa and others v Modderklip Boerdery (Pty) Ltd (Agr SA and Legal Resources Centre, Amici Curiae)* 2004 (6) SA 40 (SCA).
[57] One of the founding values of the Constitution, see Act 108 of 1996, s 1(c).
[58] ibid, s 34.

access to court.[59] While the basis of its decision was thus different from that adopted by the SCA, the Court agreed[60] that the form of relief ordered should be endorsed.

In reaching these conclusions, the Constitutional Court made the following remarks relevant to the present investigation:

'The problem of homelessness is particularly acute in our society. It is a direct consequence of apartheid urban planning which sought to exclude African people from urban areas, and enforced this vision through policies regulating access to land and housing which meant that far too little land and too few houses were supplied to African people. The painful consequences of these policies are still with us 11 years into our new democracy, despite government's attempts to remedy them. The frustration and helplessness suffered by many who still struggle against heavy odds to meet the challenge merely to survive and to have shelter can never be underestimated. The fact that poverty and homelessness still plague many South Africans is a painful reminder of the chasm that still needs to be bridged before the constitutional ideal to establish a society based on social justice and improved quality of life for all citizens is fully achieved.

[The State] is also obliged to take reasonable steps, where possible, to ensure that large scale disruptions in the social fabric do not occur in the wake of the execution of court orders, thus undermining the rule of law.

Land invasions of this scale are a matter that threatens far more than the private rights of a single property owner. Because of their capacity to be socially inflammatory, they have the potential to have serious implications for stability and public peace. Failure by the State to act . . . would be a recipe for anarchy.

I am mindful of the fact that those charged with the provision of housing face immense problems. . . . [T]he situation of local government can never be easy. The progressive real-isation of access to adequate housing . . . requires careful planning and fair procedures made known in advance to those most affected. Orderly and predictable processes are vital. Land invasions should always be discouraged. . . .

If social reality fails to conform to the best laid plans, reasonable and appropriate responses may be necessary.'[61]

In the light of such remarks, it is perhaps not surprising that Langa ACJ chose to seek refuge in the relatively safe harbour of a 'procedural' remedy such as effective access to court process and the evocation of the lofty ideals of the rule of law, rather than taking a stance (as the SCA had done) on whether the property rights of Modderklip and the housing rights of occupiers had been breached.[62] Yet the tenor of this judgment is markedly less direct and engaged with the process of social transformation, and is in line with the more typical discourse of the Court when confronted by issues of social justice. Indeed, the *Bato Star* judgment of Ngcobo J is really the exception in its relative bluntness and passion.

On the basis of these two judgments, let us consider what lessons can be drawn about judicial policy when faced with challenges at the interface of wealth and

---

[59] See *Modderklip*, paras 39 to 51.   [60] See paras 53 to 61.
[61] ibid, paras 36, 43, 45, and 49, respectively.   [62] ibid, para 26.

poverty, which is where the transformative agenda of the Constitution most urgently needs to be observed.

Judging a Transformative Constitution

Karl Klare wrote a remarkably prescient piece on this issue almost 10 years ago.[63] Describing the Constitution ambiguously as having a 'postliberal' agenda, and having dealt in detail with 'models of what can and should happen in adjudication', and with the 'autonomous role of legal culture in shaping and steering adjudication', he analysed the early responses to transformative constitutionalism in three cases before the Constitutional Court. He then concluded:

'To be transformative and transparent, rights discourse and legal reasoning need to be more candid and self-conscious about the politics of adjudication, indeed, they need to make a *virtue* of what has traditionally been thought of as a dilemma...An opening to transformation requires South African lawyers to harmonize judicial method and legal interpretation with the Constitution's substantively progressive aspirations. The burden of my argument is that law and legal practices *can* be a foundation of democratic and responsive social transformation, but that this requires us to evolve an updated, politicized account of the rule of law.'[64]

It seems to me that the Constitutional Court in *Bato Star* and *Modderklip* shows distinct signs of developing such a revised account of the rule/role of law.

Others have joined the debate about transitional and transformative jurisprudence, leading to a relatively substantial body of writing[65] which traverses both the constitutional project generally[66] as well as specific aspects of it.[67] There is widespread agreement among these commentators on the transitional and transformative objectives of the South African brand of constitutionalism adopted in 1994 and 1996, although views differ on exactly what type of transformation is envisaged. It is clear, however, that judicial interpretation of the founding constitutional values[68] will play a critical role in realizing such objectives. 'Transformational adjudication', as it is styled, marks a departure from the 'rule based interpretation' of the past, and is informed by '... the attainment of the collective good, through redistributive fairness in an open and accountable

---

[63] 'Legal Culture and Transformative Constitutionalism' (1998) 14 SA Journal on Human Rights 146. [64] ibid, 187–88.

[65] See Marius Pieterse, 'What do we mean when we talk about transformative constitutionalism?' (2005) 20 SA Public Law 155, and the literature to which he refers.

[66] See for example Dennis Davis, *Democracy and Deliberation* (1999) and Heinz Klug, *Constituting Democracy* (2000), especially in the 'Introduction'.

[67] See in particular Cathi Albertyn and Beth Goldblatt, 'Facing the Challenge of Transformation: Difficulties in the Development of An Indigenous Jurisprudence of Equality' (1998) 14 SA Journal on Human Rights 248.

[68] Such as equality—see the detailed treatment in Albertyn and Goldblatt, ibid.

society'.[69] It invites the judges '...into a new plane of jurisprudential creativity and self reflection about legal method, analysis and reasoning...'.[70]

In the context of this debate and on the basis of the judgments discussed above, I would argue that judicial policy can be a distinct force in pursuit of social justice, and that the judges of the Constitutional Court are deeply conscious of that force and their responsibility to express it. Critical in determining the limits of such responsibility is an acute and sensitive understanding of the judicial interface with the legislative and executive departments, and it is appropriate that discussion of 'deference' has assumed prominence of late.[71]

To this point, the Court has attempted a cautious and conscious building of trust with the other arms of government, as well as fostering public confidence in its own role. Bills of rights and written constitutions have a distinct transformative potential, but need to be approached with great care, and not idealized.

---

[69] See Justice Dikgang Moseneke, 'The Fourth Bram Fischer Memorial Lecture: Transformative Adjudication' (2002) 18 SA Journal on Human Rights 309, 314–15. The writer is now South Africa's Deputy Chief Justice.   [70] ibid, 316.
[71] Initiated by the article by Cora Hoexter, 'The future of judicial review in South African Administrative Law' (2000) 117 SA Law Journal 484.

7

Litigating the Agreement: Towards a New Judicial Constitutionalism for the UK from Northern Ireland?

John Morison and Marie Lynch[*]

'...anyway, it's all just politics in a legal vocabulary'
A lawyer from one of the negotiating teams

Introduction

It has been said that the words 'Northern Ireland' are the two most boring in the English language. For generations of news consumers, even within Northern Ireland, this may have been the case with cold, bitter violence seeming to over-whelm the quiet decency of most people there, and political intransigence snub-bing out all attempts at building something better. In the unaccustomedly heady days of the spring of 1998, however, Northern Ireland seemed to have its moment. Here was a historical peace agreement, brokered by two Governments, overseen by a superpower and witnessed by the world who presumed that with the hand-shakes (which no-one can quite remember witnessing) that the 'troubles' were over, finally. As international attention moved on Northern Ireland could be filed under 'lessons learned', and left as an academic curio for those interested in post-conflict societies. Of course, the reality confounded this view. With only two years of operational government out of the eight-year life of the peace process to date, Northern Ireland now appears as a tiresome anomaly within peace processes gen-erally and within a constitutionally reformed UK where a narrative of devolution could wait no longer for the story of government in Northern Ireland to fit the pattern.

* The authors would like to acknowledge with gratitude all those interviewees who gave gener-ously of their time and views. We would also like to thank Dr Alison Mawhinney for her excellent research assistance and Sir Ronnie Weatherup and Dr Gordon Anthony for assistance in uncovering additional cases where the Agreement was cited. All errors are of course the responsibility of the authors, who are writing in a purely personal capacity.

But the architecture provided by the Belfast Agreement and the Northern Ireland Act 1998 (hereafter the NIA 1998) should have continuing interest. Not only does it remain in essence the only show in town as regards the future governance of Northern Ireland, but beyond this it has particular resonance for constitutionalism more generally and that version of constitutionalism that the UK more generally is struggling towards in a post-devolution, post-human rights dispensation. The negotiations around the Belfast Agreement and the NIA 1998 had something of the quality of a 'hot moment' of constitutional development—a period of accelerated collective mobilization as Unger describes it.[1] Although the subject-matter was peripheral, and in some ways secondary to the main constitutional action of the Blair devolution reforms, it is in fact strikingly more significant than most of these efforts at updating Britain's seventeenth-century constitution to something that is perhaps more appropriate for the twentieth century.[2] Part of this significance comes from the degree of constitutional ingenuity that this chronic problem required from those more accustomed to the more straightforward context of Westminsterism. This ensured that some of the traditional, sovereignty-based absolutes could be at least challenged by thinking from elsewhere. This was linked to the necessity to recognize and find an accommodation for the legitimate interests and traditions of other identities and states, particularly those relating to the Republic of Ireland. This in turn increased the imperative of ensuring that the accommodation was rooted within an international context, which not only raised the stakes and widened the range of input, but also located the settlement firmly within international standards and protections. This is linked to the way in which this ancient, almost primal, quarrel about conflict and difference actually foreshadows fundamental rifts in wider society. Within the British constitutional mainstream there are newly urgent issues of race, religious fundamentalism, and social exclusion as well as increased interest in how the agenda of rights and equality might be used to provide the fundamental material to build answers to questions about how to live together. Northern Ireland is struggling towards what Loughlin describes as the third order of the political,[3] where institutional form is being given to the political conflicts that it contains. As it does so this struggle seems to contain many of the features that now preoccupy mainstream British constitutionalists within their new order of post-devolution, post-Human Rights Act constitutionalism. Northern Ireland appears almost as a lightening rod that earths many of the elemental forces within constitutionalism more widely.

To understand what has happened with the Belfast Agreement and the NIA 1998, and how this then impacts upon the new and emerging version of

---

[1] See Roberto Unger, *Politics: The Central Texts* (1997).

[2] See John Morison, 'The Case against Constitutional Reform' (1998) 25 Journal of Law and Society 510 and Dawn Oliver, *Constitutional Reform in the UK* (2003).

[3] See Martin Loughlin, 'Constitutional Law: the Third Order of the Political', in Nicholas Bamforth and Peter Leyland (eds), *Public Law in a Multi-Layered Constitution* (2003).

post-Westminster style constitutionalism, we must first ask how what has happened in the Northern Ireland context corresponds with developments elsewhere. In the first section of this essay, the peace process in Northern Ireland is examined briefly in terms of how it fits with a range of constitutional innovations elsewhere. These include developments within the wider scheme of devolution and ideas of constitutional legislation within the UK, notions of transitional justice as pioneered in a number of international contexts, as well as a range of ideas about a foundational 'constitutional moment'.

The conclusion of this initial review is that while the Belfast Agreement and the NIA 1998 share some elements of many of these other constitutional innovations, the process in Northern Ireland is not adequately described by reference to any of these alone. Indeed, we must consider the Northern Ireland constitutional project as something *sui generis*. It is a thing apart for a place that remains apart from the UK mainstream. However, interestingly, it can be seen as a harbinger of what might come to the mainstream. This means that mainstream interest should be focused on developments in Northern Ireland not only for what they might reveal more generally about narrow issues, such as how a multi-party executive might operate in a vaguely Westminster system, or how clashes between legislatures should be resolved—although this might be quite interesting—but because of what it says about a future, new look, British-style constitutionalism.

Because the experience of the Agreement is regarded as so important more generally, this essay then focuses on the details of the experience. It draws upon an ESRC-funded research project which the authors, along with Stephen Livingstone, carried out into the role of law and litigation in articulating Northern Ireland's emerging constitutional framework.[4] This project involved extensive interviews with politicians, civil servants and lawyers from Belfast, London, and Dublin. These interviews were undertaken with the objective of exploring: (1) the background to the drafting of the Agreement and its subsequent translation into the NIA 1998; (2) some further details about the operation of new forms of executive government since 1998 and the relationships between different parts of the State; and, (3) the approach of the parties and lawyers in a series of legal cases that arose from the Act and its wider impact. Exploring these themes across some 50 interviews with leading figures from the political, governmental, and legal world who were closely involved in the creation and outworking of the Agreement, the project findings provide various insights. These include not only what the parties thought they were creating through the Agreement, but also how this new constitutional dispensation actually operated, and some of the important

---

[4] This project, L21925114, was commissioned with the ESRC's Devolution and Constitutional Change programme. See further http://www.devolution.ac.uk/. An earlier, very much shorter version of this essay, reporting on the project, is published as John Morison, 'Towards a New Constitutional Doctrine for Northern Ireland? The Agreement, the Litigation and the Constitutional Future', in Paul Carmichael, Colin Knox, and Robert Osbourne (eds), *Devolution and Constitutional Change in Northern Ireland* (2007).

consequences that it has for the operation of government generally, and the role of law and courts in particular, in this new sort of post-Westminster constitutionalism. The remainder of this essay address these themes in turn before coming back to what this means for constitutionalism more generally.

The Agreement in a Wider Constitutional Context

There are a variety of people who are prepared to describe the settlement provided by the Belfast Agreement and the NIA 1998 as something new and different. Prime Minister Tony Blair famously felt the 'hand of history' on his shoulder and those involved in producing the Agreement declared, 'we, the participants in the multi-party negotiations, believe that the agreement we have negotiated offers a truly historic opportunity for a new beginning...a fresh start'. The long title of the NIA 1998 describes it ambitiously as 'An Act to make new provision for the government of Northern Ireland' and indeed this theme is picked up in much of the academic commentary with, for example, books and articles carrying references in their titles to ideas of 'a new beginning',[5] a 'constitutional moment',[6] and 'a new politics'.[7] References to 'democratic renewal'[8] and 'political transformation'[9] also appear, as do calls for 'rethinking'.[10] There is also much reference to the Northern Ireland arrangements in comparative terms with settlements in South Africa[11] and elsewhere.[12] Campbell, Ní Aoláin, and Harvey[13] refer to the settlement as being at the 'frontiers of legal analysis' and McCrudden too sees the

---

[5] For eg, Colin Harvey, 'The New Beginning: Reconstructing Constitutional Law and Democracy in Northern Ireland', in Colin Harvey (ed.), *Human Rights, Equality and Democratic Renewal in Northern Ireland* (2001) 9–52.

[6] Kieran McEvoy and John Morison, 'Beyond the 'Constitutional Moment': Law, Transition, and Peacemaking in Northern Ireland' (2003) 26 (4) Fordham International Law Review 961.

[7] Jennifer Todd, 'A new territorial politics in the British Isles?' in John Coakley, Brigid Laffan, and Jennifer Todd (eds), *Renovation or Revolution? New territorial Politics in Ireland and the United Kingdom* (2005) and Jonathan Tong, *The New Northern Ireland Politics?* (2005), although the presence of question marks in these more recently published works may be seen as significant.

[8] Colin Harvey (ed.), *Human Rights, Equality and Democratic Renewal in Northern Ireland* (2001).

[9] Kieran McEvoy, 'Law, Struggle and Political Transformation in Northern Ireland' (2000) 27 Journal of Law and Society 542.

[10] For eg, Paul Dixon 'Rethinking the international and Northern Ireland: a critique' and Michael Cox, 'Rethinking the International and Northern Ireland: a defence', in Michael Cox, Adrian Guelke, and Fiona Stephen (eds), *A Farewell to Arms? Beyond the Good Friday Agreement* (2006) 409–26 and 427–42.

[11] For eg, see John McGarry, 'Political Settlements in Northern Ireland and South Africa' (1998) 46 (5) Political Studies 853.

[12] See eg, Christine Bell, *Peace Agreements and Human Rights* (2000); John McGarry (ed.), *Northern Ireland and the Divided Worlds: Post-Agreement Northern Ireland in Comparative Perspective* (2001); John McGarry and Brendan O'Leary, *The Northern Ireland Conflict: Consociational Engagements* (2004).

[13] Colm Campbell, Fionnuala Ní Aoláin, and Colin Harvey, 'The Frontiers of Legal Analysis: Reframing the Transition in Northern Ireland' (2003) 68 Modern Law Review 317.

experience in Northern Ireland 'raising issues at the heart of the British constitutional tradition, as it was and as it might become'.[14]

Notwithstanding the current uncertainties about devolution, this continuing willingness to see the Agreement as in some way constitutive, as standing above ordinary politics or regular law in a way that successfully moves on from the past to redefine the future through a single 'constitutional moment', stands in contrast to constitutional traditions within the UK more generally. There, notwithstanding a recent acceleration of reforms, constitutionalism tends to mean a gradual process of accretional change to traditional forms. What is in place in Northern Ireland, even if it is not currently in full working order, does seem to be something different. In particular, the reaction to the Northern Ireland settlement raises the question of whether it might be better to see the Agreement as representing not simply the high-water mark of the traditional Westminster style constitutionalism—as it is operated in the slightly alien context of Northern Ireland[15]—but as amounting to something new. How is the Northern Ireland constitutional experience to be seen?

It might seem possible to fit the Northern Ireland constitutional experience into the wider project of reform, devolution, and modernization in the UK that has occurred since 1998. Indeed, while acknowledging its very different history and the specialized nature of its outworkings, it might perhaps be possible to regard Northern Ireland as, at bottom, an example of devolution in its new and modern format.[16] As discussed elsewhere,[17] textbook writers have adopted differing strategies to accommodate Northern Ireland. Some seek to accord devolution there the same treatment as in Scotland and Wales, others simply refer to it as something different (which most often they do not discuss much further), and a significant minority choose to omit Northern Ireland completely from their accounts of the UK constitution. Beyond the textbooks, some commentators on the UK constitution do maintain a watching brief on Northern Ireland as something that will, at some stage, take up its place within the overall scheme of devolution. While the size of Northern Ireland will inevitably render it of marginal interest to those within the larger structures, the fact of its existence as a part of the wider UK system should assure it a moment of more general interest. After all, the Northern Ireland structures contribute towards the asymmetry of the overall settlement and its history of a previous devolved system for 50 years from 1920 provides particular instances of evolutionary directions not taken this time as with, for example, the history of the separate Northern Ireland Civil Service.

---

[14] Christopher McCrudden, 'Northern Ireland, The Belfast Agreement, and the British Constitution', in Jeffrey Jowell and Dawn Oliver (eds), *The Changing Constitution* (2004) 196.

[15] See further John Morison and Stephen Livingstone, *Reshaping Public Power: Northern Ireland and the British Constitutional Crisis* (1995).   [16] See eg, Noreen Burrows, *Devolution* (2000).

[17] See Kieran McEvoy and John Morison, 'Beyond the "Constitutional Moment": Law, Transition, and Peacemaking in Northern Ireland' (2003) 26 (4) Fordham International Law Review 961–95 and 988–89.

Thus, there are various monitoring exercises that include Northern Ireland on the same terms as elsewhere, although of course the findings reported generally serve to demonstrate its difference.[18] Books on particular themes within devolution also struggle to accommodate Northern Ireland comfortably within the modernization and devolution theme and generally the Northern Ireland chapter is one about exception and difference.[19] Within wider research projects on devolution the position is similar. In initiatives such as the ESRC *Devolution and Constitutional Change* programme,[20] Northern Ireland was reasonably well represented among the 35 projects given funding, but the origins of the constitutional settlement within a major conflict and the difficult issues of identity that remain outstanding combine with the circumstances of suspension to give the projects something of an outsider feeling. This is perhaps best summed up in the Programme's final Report, which describes devolution in Northern Ireland as being both 'rare' and 'special'—rare because of the increasing frequent suspensions and special because it is bound up inextricably with the wider peace process.[21] The situation is perhaps more extreme with the Leverhulme *Nations and Regions: Constitutional Change and Identity* programme. Here Northern Ireland gets a very limited coverage indeed within accounts (mainly) of relationships between Scotland and England.[22] Even from the think-tank perspective there seems limited awareness of Northern Ireland as anything more than anomalous. For example, the Institute of Public Policy Research (IPPR) project on *The Future of the Constitution*,[23] although focused on the 'movement from a political to a legal constitution' does not seem to identify Northern Ireland as an instance where this trend is well developed.

Indeed, many commentators are happier to put Northern Ireland within a consociationalism box[24] where it is thus something different from the rest of the UK and, as McCrudden points out in his contribution to this volume, closer to the experience of countries such as Belgium, South Africa, Zimbabwe, India, the Netherlands, Austria, Switzerland, Cyprus, Lebanon, Macedonia, Bosnia Herzegovina, etc., which have adopted such arrangements. Indeed the fact that the Northern Ireland constitutional experience can be stowed away here has the additional advantage that it might seem to belong more to the political scientist than to the lawyer. But of course this is wrong. The Northern Ireland constitutional experience may be different but it is different in a way that is central to the

---

[18] See eg, the Constitution Unit's Devolution Monitoring project and its State of the Nations Devolution Yearbook series at http://www.ucl.ac.uk/constitution-unit/research/devolution/devo-monitoring-programme.html.

[19] See eg, Robert Hazell and Richard Rawlings (eds), *Devolution, Law Making and the Constitution* (2005).   [20] http://www.devolution.ac.uk/index.htm.

[21] http://www.devolution.ac.uk/final_report.htm.

[22] See further http://www.institute-of-governance.org/forum/Leverhulme/TOC.html.

[23] See further http://www.ippr.org.uk/research/teams/project.asp?id=1805&pid=1805.

[24] See further Brendan O'Leary, 'The Nature of the Agreement', in John McGarry and Brendan O'Leary (eds), *The Northern Ireland Conflict: Consociational Engagements* (2004) 261.

UK experience. Furthermore, it is different in ways that may be hugely instructive to the more general experience there. So how does what has come about in Northern Ireland measure up to experience elsewhere, and how does it fit into various theoretical conceptions?

It may be thought that ideas within what might be termed the 'due deference debate' can be stretched to accommodate this new constitutional dispensation. This is interesting particularly in relation to any new role for the judges under the Agreement. This debate, focusing on the 'proper' constitutional role for judges, is perhaps the closest that orthodox constitutionalism comes to addressing the foundations of the constitutional framework in the UK.[25] While some of the detail of this debate has become rather sterile, the idea has emerged that there is now perhaps something new in the constitution and that this ushers in a new role, in particular for the judges. Jowell, for example, argues that 'the conception of democracy which the ECHR advances differs fundamentally from that which has prevailed hitherto in the United Kingdom' and that the 'courts are now charged by Parliament with delineating the boundaries of a rights-based democracy'.[26] Lord Steyn endorses Jowell's view and rejects the idea that there is anything undemocratic about the creative law-making role of the courts in a modern democracy.[27] Elliott argues that while the key features of this modern version of British constitutionalism—human rights, membership of the EU, and devolution—might currently seem to be vulnerable to an exercise of sovereign power, there is a new view of the constitutional order available to challenge the traditional model.[28] This comes from the judicial approach taken in *Thoburn v Sunderland City Council*.[29] Here Sir John Laws develops ideas about 'constitutional statutes' which have a different status to ordinary law and introduces what Elliott describes as a new approach where the doctrine of parliamentary sovereignty no longer insulates ordinary legislation from judicial evaluation. Instead the 'constitutional statutes' along with other evidence of the prevailing fundamental values in the political and constitutional order are to be used by the judges to interpret the nature and extent of legislative authority in relation to the context and values of the contemporary constitution. In a similar vein, Clayton suggests that we might consider following the Canadian example to devise a constitutional theory of

---

[25] For some recent examples of this long-running debate see Mark Elliott, *The Constitutional Foundations of Judicial Review* (2001); T.R.S. Allan, 'The Constitutional Foundations of Judicial Review: Conceptual Conundrum or Interpretive Inquiry?' (2002) 61 Cambridge Law Journal 87; Paul Craig, 'Constitutional Foundations: the Rule of Law and Judicial Review' (2003) Public Law 92; Christopher Forsyth and Mark Elliott, 'The Legitimacy of Judicial Review' (2003) Public Law 286.

[26] Jeffrey Jowell, 'Judicial deference: servility, civility or institutional capacity?' (2003) Public Law 592 and Jeffrey Jowell, 'Judicial Deference and Human Rights: A Question of Competence', in Paul Craig and Richard Rawlings *Law and Administration in Europe* (2003) 67–81.

[27] See 'Deference: A Tangled Story' (2005) Public Law 346.

[28] Mark Elliot, 'Embracing 'Constitutional' Legislation: Towards Fundamental Law?' (2003) 54 Northern Ireland Legal Quarterly 25.

[29] [2002] 3 WLR 247. Cf. Lord Bingham in *Watkins v Home Office and others* [2006] UKHL 17.

adjudication in terms of a 'democratic dialogue'.[30] Dyzenhaus writes of Dworkin's great contribution to legal theory being the idea that the rule of law has justificatory character where 'law is not only about setting clear goals but also about argument as to what those goals should be'.[31] Murray Hunt goes further and suggests that now we have to abandon the language of sovereignty in favour of the language of justification.[32] Following Dyzenhaus's efforts to build upon the work of Etienne Murenik, where the idea of legality appears as a 'culture of justification', Hunt argues that we should replace the Diceyean view of constitutionalism with a 'more coherent vision of constitutionalism which combines a non-positivist role for courts in articulating and furthering the fundamental values to which society is committed, at the same time as giving a meaningful role to the democratic branches and the administration in the definition and furtherance of those values'.[33]

These sorts of ideas are strengthened by approaches from jurisdictions where judges either traditionally or because of some constitutional innovation take a more active approach within an understanding of the constitutional framework which encourages this. Some of these may seem to have particular application to the Northern Ireland constitutional juncture. Alan Hutchinson, with the Canadian experience in mind, writes of the need for a positive view of the role of the courts in sustaining democracy. He proposes an approach where '*laws* and *persons* interact in mutually sustaining ways in the democratic practice of just governance: judges are neither so overwhelmed by laws such that their room for personal judgement disappears or so untouched by the pull of laws such that their room for personal judgement is unconstrained'.[34] The rule of law here is a sort of institutional morality that conditions the exercise of authority and discretion. Hutchinson makes the point that, like the general mix between the rule of law and its other constitutional components, 'the democratic demands of the rule of law will be context specific: sometimes, it will play a minor role and sometimes it will play a much larger one'.[35] In particular, he argues, in transitional societies the rule of law rather than grounding the legal order, serves, in the words of Teitel, 'to mediate the normative shift in justice that characterises these extraordinary periods'.[36] It may be that in such circumstances judges are best placed to effect

---

[30] Richard Clayton, 'Judicial Deference and 'Democratic Dialogue': The Legitimacy of Judicial Intervention under the Human Rights Act 1998' (2004) Public Law 33.

[31] David Dyzenhaus, 'Recrafting the Rule of Law', in David Dyzenhaus (ed.), *Recrafting the Rule of Law: The Limits of Legal Order* (1999) 1–12.

[32] See Murray Hunt, 'Sovereignty's Blight: Why Contemporary Public Law Needs the Concept of "Due Deference"', in Nicholas Bamforth and Peter Leyland (eds), *Public Law in a Multi-Layered Constitution* (2003) and Hunt's contribution to this volume.   [33] ibid, 340.

[34] Alan Hutchinson, 'Rule of Law Revisited: Democracy and Courts', in David Dyzenhaus (ed.), *Recrafting the Rule of Law: The Limits of Legal Order* (1999) 196–224 at 197 (emphasis in original).

[35] ibid, 215.

[36] ibid, 216, Hutchinson quoting Ruti Teitel, 'Transitional Jurisprudence: The Role of Law in Political Transformation' (1997) 106 Yale Law Review 2009.

such changes and that this suggests an enhanced role for them. Indeed within wider ideas of 'transitional constitutionalism' there are a number of features which might seem to accommodate aspects of the constitutional circumstances of Northern Ireland. Whereas traditionally constitutionalism is viewed as foundational and forward looking, transitional constitutionalism looks back to undoing problems of the past as well as laying foundations for the future.[37] It is also provisional, subject to revision, and contested, where the boundary between 'ordinary' and 'constitutional' politics becomes blurred. Such a description may seem to resonate in Northern Ireland and require both a new constitutional practice and theory. In particular it may require judges to use their power creatively 'not to "block" democracy but to make it more deliberative', as Sunstein describes it.[38] It may involve what Karl Klare describes in the South African context as a 'transformative constitutionalism'. This invites 'a new imagination and self-reflection about legal methods, analysis and reasoning consistent with its transformative goals . . . where judicial mindset and methodology are . . . examined and revised so as to promote equality, a culture of democracy and transparent governance'.[39] A closely related idea is that described by Dorf and Sabel as 'democratic experimentalism'.[40]

This study is not the first to comment on the way in which the Agreement and the NIA 1998 have been undervalued in constitutional theory terms. Campbell, Ní Aoláin, and Harvey point out that it cannot simply be accommodated into traditional accounts of UK constitutionalism as an act of the Westminster Parliament making provision for devolved government of one part of the Kingdom.[41] The basis for governing Northern Ireland has shifted from simply being what the Westminster Parliament decrees to relying on an Agreement backed by an international treaty and underpinned by the dual referendums.[42] Indeed what we have in Northern Ireland is not just a constitutional settlement about how to solve issues over how to govern, but also a peace agreement. This brings into the constitutional arena all sorts of immediate issues about disarmament, prisoners, and victims. Some of these might be seen as particular to Northern Ireland rather than

---

[37] See further Ruti Teitel, *Transitional Justice* (2000) and 'Transitional Justice Genealogy' (2003) 16 Harvard Human Rights Journal 69.

[38] Cass Sunstein, *Designing Democracy: What Constitutions Do* (2001).

[39] Karl Klare, 'Legal Culture and Transformative Constitutionalism' (1998) 14 *South African Journal on Human Rights* 146, 156.

[40] Michael Dorf and Charles Sable, 'A Constitution of Democratic Experimentalism' (1998) 98 Colombia Law Review 267. Here, again in the particular circumstances of South Africa's transition, the approach of the Constitutional Court in *Government of South Africa v Grootboom* [2000] (11) BCLR 1169 (S.Afr.) on housing rights within the constitution is analysed as an instance of a court developing a particular approach, whereby it begins with a constitutional principle stated at a fairly high level of abstraction and works with legislators and executive officials to implement plans to fulfill the incompletely specified constitutional requirement, which are then fleshed out further in subsequent cases and in a dialogue with other constitutional actors.

[41] Campbell, Ní Aoláin, and Harvey, 'The Frontiers of Legal Analysis: Reframing the Transition in Northern Ireland', n 13 above.

[42] See Kieran McEvoy and John Morison, 'Beyond the 'Constitutional Moment': Law, Transition, and Peacemaking in Northern Ireland' (2003) 26 (4) Fordham International Law Review 961.

general to the UK, and as transitional rather than more fundamental. However, the Northern Ireland settlement is concerned also with longer-term elements to do with providing a constitution in terms of answering basic ethical questions about how to live together.[43] The fact that it seeks the answer to this in terms of ideas of human rights, equality, and good relations should be of very considerable interest beyond the immediate experience of Northern Ireland. A constitution that can move towards accommodating (at least) two groups with very different views on their constitutional past and future should be of interest well beyond its local context. When this is combined with a willingness to move beyond the Diceyan orthodoxy of Westminster sovereignty and into a constitutional form that is conditioned by a range of international interests and rooted in international law then this is very exciting indeed.

What has happened in Northern Ireland then seems to amount to something new and different. There are various general ideas from the North American context that might be adopted to help explain what this is. There are notions of a constitutional revolution occurring through the agency of a particular coalition of forces taking control[44] or gradual processes of change and consolidation across dominant sets of institutions or ideology.[45] However, these do not seem fully to fit the circumstances. Most interestingly perhaps there is Bruce Ackerman's idea of a general process of constitutional history involving a series of 'constitutional moments' occurring within a narrative of continuing 'normal politics'.[46] Ackerman's idea of a 'constitutional moment' is as a rare juncture when the political and the constitutional interact in an occasion of constitutional transformation. This has been experienced in the US only three times—in the Founding, the Reconstruction, and the New Deal. It provides a new and different foundation for the constitution. Ackerman suggests that such a constitutional moment only comes about after a sophisticated engagement between the different branches of government and the people giving their explicit, unequivocal, and sustained approval in a process where the interaction between separation of powers and national elections serves as the vehicle for constitutional transformation. While there are elements of this that might have application to Northern Ireland— particularly around the electoral approval that came from the referenda—this too must be rejected as it does not seem to capture all that is potentially important about the post-Agreement constitution. Indeed, one of the major features of the constitutional settlement in Northern Ireland is its anti-foundational foundation.

[43] See further John Morison, 'Democracy, Governance and Governmentality: Civic Public Space and Constitutional Renewal in Northern Ireland' (2001) 21 Oxford Journal of Legal Studies 287.
[44] Jack Balkin and Stanford Levinson, 'Understanding the Constitutional Revolution' (2001) 87 Virginia Law Review 1045.	[45] Mark Tushnet, *The New Constitutional Order* (2004).
[46] Bruce Ackerman, *We the People: Foundations v.1* (1991); *We the People: Transformations* (1998). See Rivka Weill, 'We the British People' (2004) Public Law 380, for an attempt to apply this approach in the UK context.

Perhaps the constitutional dispensation in Northern Ireland is almost unique in this regard. It is certainly striking that the Northern Ireland settlement not only offers the potential of a departure from Diceyan notions of sovereignty of Westminster but that it does so without reference to ideas of popular sovereignty which elsewhere appear inevitably as the alternative foundation of constitutionalism. In other words, and in contrast to Ackerman's account, there is no single foundational event or moment where the new order is created and thus fixed in a constitutive moment as a concrete expression of a contract or political accommodation for a new polity.

This is certainly different and it makes the Agreement special. Balibar has written of the 'obsessive, spectral return of popular sovereignty in regimes of democratic citizenship', complaining that there seems no other way to think about how to develop democracy, legitimacy, or political decision-making—the big constitutional problems—without bringing in an idea of a community of citizens sharing some essential qualities and allegiances which can transcend their differences and form the foundation of their political/constitutional community.[47] Thinking particularly about transnational citizenship in the context of the European Union, he argues that the strong preferences that are observable generally for notions of democratic principles, democratic guarantees of individual and collective rights and democratic citizenship—although standing as an alternative to the idea of simple popular sovereignty—nevertheless require some sort of reference to 'the people'. The people (or *demos, peuple, Volk*) here are present as both those who are to be protected *and* as those who are limiting themselves by imposing upon themselves this democratic framework which necessarily blurs (at least formally) the differences and conflicts in society. What the Agreement offers, arguably, is something very different. There is no 'We, the People...' moment where society is reconstituted in the classic republican mode with individuals seeing themselves as somehow possessing some commonality among themselves that transcends other allegiances so that the universal rights expressed here can form a basis for a common citizenship. Instead, conflict and exclusion remain manifest. Indeed the Agreement structures seek simply to provide a place where these conflicts can be contained and worked upon over time with the instruments of rights, equality, and partnership that are provided. Within the Belfast Agreement model there is no need to experience what Balibar describes as the 'relativisation of social differences and competing belongings in favour of a strong manifestation of democratic reciprocity'.[48] Instead, as we shall return to later, conflict is acknowledged, difference is accommodated, and institutional power is separated and divided among competing factions.

Let us now turn to how this new dispensation came about and how it has been received.

---

[47] Etienne Balibar, *We the People of Europe? Reflections on Transnational Citizenship* (2004) 183–90.   [48] ibid, 186.

Making the Agreement—Law and Consitutionalism

The basic story of how the Agreement came about has been told extensively in other places. This project focused particularly on the extent to which considerations about law and litigation played a role in its formulation. Among those key figures we interviewed the overall impression was that law was secondary with the view being, as one informant put it, that the Agreement 'was first and foremost always a political endeavour... [law] played a role but it wouldn't have been significant'.[49] Politicians and officials on all sides stressed that the emphasis was very much on getting *political* agreement and that in the highly pressurized context of the negotiations there was insufficient time to go into what they perceived as the 'fine detail of law'. Some participants did not feel that the absence of full-time legal support was a disadvantage and were 'happier with having negotiating skills rather than having legal skills'.[50] Indeed there was some scepticism about the role of lawyers. As a senior Sinn Féin negotiator told us, '... one thing that we have found in our contact with legal people is [they] would give us as many different opinions as there are lawyers out there! And so at the end of the day the final judgment has to be made by ourselves.'

There were differing reports about the extent to which individual parties sought or used legal advice. One observer from the senior ranks of the Irish Government told us, 'My clear impression [was] that the British Government and Sinn Féin and the Ulster Unionists used lawyers a lot, other parties less.' Indeed there was a general view that Sinn Féin had made the most extensive use of legal advice and they indicated that additionally they had received a large amount of unsolicited legal advice.[51] Most of this focused on issues around policing, human rights, equality of opportunity, and perhaps proved more significant at the stage of converting the Agreement to an Act than at the stage of negotiating the Agreement itself. The Ulster Unionist Party, in common with the SDLP and

---

[49] This did not stop some negotiators, particularly those with a legal background, acting in a way that suggested a strong legal element. As a member of one party's talks team recalled, 'I still have memories of Bob McCartney [a QC and founder member of the small UK Unionist Party] bowing to [Senator] Mitchell as he entered, as you would in the High Court.'

[50] As one of the leaders of the Women's Coalition told us, 'we did a lot of preparation... we would call meetings in my house and... prepare the next day's meeting. We would circulate papers and we would have people write papers, analytical papers and preparatory papers and Senator Mitchell would say at the table often, we were the only people giving him papers!'

[51] Interviewees from Sinn Féin told us, 'obviously the negotiations for all parties were fronted by the elected representatives... [but] we had a legal team there, two solicitors and a barrister, not working full time, but as we got closer to Good Friday they were there permanently... We would have regular consultation with them and with other solicitors. We took legal opinion as well from people based in the South, people with international experience.' A representative from one of the smaller parties told us, 'I remember... going into a room that we would have used for bilaterals and discovering a set of [Sinn Féin] lawyers working on lap tops... I think that was mainly on human rights, equality of opportunity and safeguards sections.'

Alliance, had a number of lawyers, both academic and practising among their negotiating teams, and appeared to turn to them to examine draft proposals but not in any particularly systematic or legalistic way. On more than one occasion it was suggested the UUP leader's background in law had inhibited negotiations as matters of detail were pursued to the detriment of broader principles.[52] A member of one of the smaller unionist/loyalist parties had indicated that they would have liked to have retained legal advice but were unable to do so as they did not have the resources. Indeed there was a view that such issues would be looked after by the larger, Ulster Unionist Party.[53]

The position of the two governments on legal advice was especially interesting. The UK, which appeared to be in receipt of considerable legal advice from both Home Office and Foreign Office lawyers (the latter in respect of Strands Two and Three) adopted much the same approach as the parties, with the emphasis very much on getting the political deal sorted out with the idea that it could all be translated into law once agreed. The possibility of subsequent legal challenges was foreseen but officials appeared to be confident that the courts would not wish to become too embroiled in political controversy and, even if they did, matters could always be sorted out by subsequent legislation. It was also interesting that as the negotiations spanned across the remit of several UK Departments, the legal advice was drawn from different sources and used from a variety of perspectives. As one senior official in Northern Ireland put it, 'we found ourselves at different stages talking to the Foreign Office, the NIO, the Attorney General's Office, even the Lord Chancellor's Office . . . there was almost, I won't say a pass the parcel, but nobody was ever in a position really to give you an authoritative view on anything without consulting with four or five other bodies and that tended to make the procedures very cumbersome and slow'.

This differed from the Irish Government approach, which was markedly more holistic, perhaps as a consequence of the tradition of a written constitution.[54] The Irish Government, though again stressing the need to deal with things at the political level and not to become too preoccupied with legal technicalities, appeared rather more concerned with the legal form, at least as respects Strand Two. Several

[52] As one UUP interviewee put it, 'any legal issues were deferred to Trimble basically'. The UUP leader's background also exerted an influence beyond the party. The leader of the small Progressive Unionist Party told us, 'we were under the impression that Trimble, having, we imagined, earned his living as a teacher of constitutional law [sic] was well placed and [also] they had people like Austin Morgan and other barristers . . . . They certainly made play of having other people . . . in other negotiations in London . . . and it was indicated to us that they were on top of these things.'

[53] As we were told, 'maybe it is a rather naïve approach but when the Ulster Unionists look relatively comfortable with something then we made the presumption "well, it mustn't be too bad" because they were generally nervous about everything. We presumed . . . that they had enough legal minds concentrating on such issues.'

[54] As a senior Irish civil servant told us, 'the lawyers were very much a part of all of it where there were major legal constitutional issues involved . . . in fact our Attorney General's Office was deeply involved . . . particularly on our side because we were changing a written constitution unlike the British system.'

of those who worked on the Irish Government side during the negotiations indicated to us an awareness of the development of constitutional review by the Irish courts in general and of challenges to the Anglo-Irish Agreement and the Nice Treaty in particular.[55] The advice of the Attorney-General was sought on these matters and Irish officials undoubtedly spent considerable time identifying a formulation for the repeal of Articles 2 and 3 of the Irish Constitution which would satisfy the Irish courts as well as the political parties to the negotiations. Officials also seemed well aware of the broader implications of these constitutional changes, especially for the issue of Irish citizenship and immigration law, which subsequently became apparent in litigation.[56] On the other hand, Irish officials seemed much less interested in the likely impact of these changes in UK constitutional law and were often bemused by how British constitutional culture operated.[57] Sometimes, however, the different cultures produced unexpected coincidences in approach. For example, we were told that, for very different reasons, both the Irish Government and the Unionist parties were anxious to nest aspects of the agreement in international law. As one Irish official put it, 'we were certainly concerned, in order to ensure a legal certainty to the thing, to emphasise the international aspect of it... [and] you would find echoes of that for quite different reasons on the Unionist side. You know, for them if it was between two sovereign states as far as they were concerned then that wasn't a problem.'

Of course the dynamics of being in a negotiation process had a strong impact. On the one hand there were settled positions taken at the start. As an official from the Irish Government told us, 'as you can imagine, we would have had exhaustive preparations for this over three or four years in the run in before the Good Friday Agreement was even ever started like. Myself and... other people would have been around all their departments for a year and a half settling what our negotiation position was, what particular bodies we were prepared to put into North–South stuff and examining the whole thing minutely.' On the other hand, there was also the timetable of negotiations, the need to meet the Easter deadline and perhaps a general sense of 'now or never' that meant paradoxically that some very important elements were glossed over. As one of the negotiators commented on the feeling towards the end of the process, 'people probably then would have signed up to anything... there was weariness and... the feeling that the Agreement

---

[55] A senior Irish civil servant said, 'I was always conscious too that anybody who was politically against aspects of the Agreement, there would be an obvious incentive there for them to bring a judicial review application to expose the weaknesses in it if you didn't attend to these sort of problems. If you look at something like the *Boland* case down here you can see how the courts can be used to exploit any political weakness of that sort.'

[56] Commenting on the approach of the Irish team, a senior British source expressed the view that, 'I think they felt that organisationally it was easier for them and also culturally because of the written constitution... [they] were always aware that they had this constitution to protect.'

[57] 'I would say too and I don't mean this in any sense critically but one of the difficulties you have in dealing with legal issues with the UK in any negotiations, is that their system is such that responsibility for legal issues is very unclear and very divided.'

was the broad principles, we couldn't go into any further detail'.[58] In some ways while this timetable produced agreement it certainly did reduce the element of involvement from all but the very major players in negotiations which may have planted seeds of resentment. As one middle-ranking member of the Ulster Unionist Party's negotiating team told us, 'I think the handling of the final six hours of the entire thing made people think "well hang on a second here" ... people hadn't slept for two days, people were getting abusive telephone calls from the White House, it was just a bizarre way to tie up a complicated set of negotiations and the truth was of course the complicated negotiations had been done by other people, it was just a matter of "here's the dotted line, you sign".'

The approach to law that was evident during the negotiations continued with the translation of the Agreement into the NIA 1998. There was some limited comment made to us regarding the unusual nature of the Agreement as the basis for legislation and how this departed from the type of briefing papers those drafting legislation would normally rely upon. Generally, however, very few of those we spoke to seemed in any way aware of the constitutional significance of drafting a statute to delineate the basis for the government of part of the UK on the basis of a broad-ranging agreement endorsed by Northern Ireland's political parties, the Irish Government and referendums in Northern Ireland and the Republic of Ireland, and couched in international law. While the basis for legislation may well be seen now as significantly different from usual it was still looked upon as essentially a normal set of policy instructions for the drafting of a statute. Previous constitutional legislation, such as the Government of Ireland Act 1920 and the Northern Ireland Constitution Act 1973, was drawn on to shape the legislation, as was some of the devolution legislation for Scotland and Wales.[59]

Although appreciation of the constitutional originality of the legislation may have been limited, the political nature of the more general process, however, did assert itself to give a slightly different character to the legislation. We were told 'it was not like a normal exercise in Government legislation where ministers determine the policy and decide whether their clauses reflect that or not'. The political importance of the Agreement and its broad-brush nature meant that much of the detail remained to be filled in. This produced a slightly different dynamic. As one Member of Parliament expressed it to us, 'it was important that we had gone through the scrutiny within Parliament but in this case the scrutiny within

[58] One of the political party's team told us how, 'I can remember John Alderdice saying at that stage, "we are not rewriting this document, we are picking the six or eight things that matter most that we might get changed". If we had another eighteen months we would have fallen apart anyway.' Conversely one of our interviewees, Martin Mansergh, has written of how in the last hours of negotiation he witnessed the Taoiseach Bertie Ahern and Mo Mowlam being required to answer some 77 unsatisfied demands from Sinn Féin and their backroom team (See *The Irish Times*, 27 August 2005).

[59] There were slightly conflicting views among our respondents. For example, we were told that 'the NIO civil servants just saw it as replicating large chunks of the Scotland Act with the various tweaks that were required' but a senior civil servant from the NIO claimed 'it is fair to say we drew more on the sort of historical record of devolution in NI than what was going on in Scotland and Wales'.

Parliament wasn't actually in some ways the critical consideration. The critical consideration was [whether] the parties by and large think it was a fair recognition, a fair implementation of the Good Friday Agreement.'

Formal input into the parliamentary process was of course confined to those parties who actively participated in the Westminster Parliament, and therefore excluded the Irish Government and abstentionist Sinn Féin. However, it was clear that both, and especially the latter, made their views well known to the UK Government and contributed to the shaping of the legislation. Irish Government officials told us, 'our primary focus was to argue that the Agreement wasn't being implemented as it had been agreed... people went regularly to London too in the course of those various pieces of legislation going through Parliament and we lobbied and talked to people and then some amendments were actually proposed'. Sinn Féin too acknowledged the importance of supervising the translation from political agreement to law and maintained their input was effective.[60] The Northern Ireland parties who did participate in parliament of course had the most detailed scrutiny role and some used this opportunity to continue negotiations. As one senior official complained, 'indeed David Trimble felt at perfect liberty for example to move amendments to the critical principle of consent clauses that they had all signed up to in the Good Friday Agreement saying... you know, "I'm in Parliament so I can subject it to normal parliamentary scrutiny"'. The SDLP was less engaged generally but did take a particular interest in the North/South bodies and how they related to the Executive, and in accountability to the Assembly. The DUP was less concerned with detail and more with finding general opportunities to play out their opposition to the process and make the argument that it was all flawed from the beginning. It is striking how uneven was the recognition even at the political level that this was a constitutional statute of some significance. In a sense the political rather than the legal/constitutional remained the dominant dynamic.[61] Discussions about law, both from inside and outside Parliament, focused on matters of technical detail even if several of these, such as the scope of the powers of the Human Rights Commission and the Equality Commission, were of considerable wider significance. However, the template for drafting was drawn very extensively from the Agreement and the job focused on the essentially political task of giving effect to

---

[60] Sinn Féin negotiators insisted that 'the detail of the Agreement... what effectively comes out then from the British Government in terms of legislation, all needs to be very carefully watched... and obviously we did keep a very close eye on all of that... we had direct access to the highest levels of the British Government and to the highest levels of the Irish Government, so they weren't under any illusions whatsoever about our particular stance on a particular aspect of legislation'.

[61] This contrasted to the approach in the Republic of Ireland where the constitutional was, we were told, very much to the forefront as an organizing principle. As a senior government official there told us, 'it was interesting that, in a sense having the Constitution in a way gives you more flexibility than the British side where they have to work out what the rules are first and then run round all the different departments'.

the Agreement in UK law, as is reflected in the preamble to the NIA 1998. While there was some recognition in some quarters of the potential of the courts as another constitutional actor, this remained limited.[62]

Overall the impression obtained during the research of the role of law within the negotiations leading to the Agreement and the NIA 1998 was that it played a fairly minor part. This was due in large measure to the very traditional perceptions of law held by most of the participants. Law was envisaged as simply whatever set of rules the parties to Agreement could be made to agree upon. At most law and litigation was seen as a potential irritant—something one official suggested legally minded Ministers had to be discouraged from relying on. The focus was very firmly on getting a political deal and then reducing it to some sort of legal form. It was clearly hoped that if this was done competently then the opportunities for one of the parties to challenge the workings of the deal would be few. Even if someone was minded to do so, it was hoped that they could be persuaded from this by political means but if that proved unsuccessful most felt the courts would be unwilling to become involved. Even if the courts did become involved, it was felt that fresh legislation could always be passed to set things right again. There was little sense that anyone saw the law in a more positive sense, as a repository of values and norms that could be drawn upon to help construct and sustain whatever agreement was reached. This is of course one of the functions constitutional law plays in many countries, where the constitution is not simply a set of rules but also a set of values and principles on which the society is founded and around which the institutions of the society are structured around. Contrary to the position in the UK, where traditionally constitutional law has been seen as no different from any other law—with the Act of Union having the same status as the Dentists Act—in many countries the constitution is seen as having a 'higher' status, and as a text whose content is reflective of broader ideas about the relationship of citizens to each other and to the State.

At first sight it may not seem surprising that those involved in negotiations about Northern Ireland's constitution operated on the basis of traditional notions of constitutional law. However there are perhaps three reasons why this might have been otherwise and more far-reaching views of constitutional law might have been articulated.

First, even at the time of the Agreement, and perhaps more so subsequently, there were signs of a change within UK constitutional discourse itself. The recognition of the supremacy of EU law, the incorporation of the ECHR, devolution legislation and the widening scope of judicial review have led judges and other commentators to begin to re-evaluate the nature of UK law and the constitutional

---

[62] As one UK civil servant told us 'certainly I had the impression that one was always fighting for attention to explain to people that actually this could be very tricky and that it would be unfortunate if you got everyone politically agreed and the whole thing got derailed because somebody brought a judicial review'.

relationship of the courts to other branches of government.[63] Most graphically, as noted already, in *Thoburn v Sunderland City Council*,[64] the courts were developing the idea of 'constitutional statutes' which have a different status than ordinary statutes. In time this may lead to the courts developing a more extensive articulation of the structure and norms of the constitution, one which develops more clearly the scope of their role in a way which goes beyond the mere checking of whether conduct conforms to clear rules. It is certainly clear that a new understanding of the position and role of judges more generally has been contemplated as a necessary element of an unfolding constitutional story in the UK generally. As Lord Steyn expressed the position:

'We do not in the United Kingdom have an uncontrolled constitution . . . In the European context the second Factortame decision made that clear . . . The settlement contained in the Scotland Act 1998 also points to a divided sovereignty. Moreover, the European Convention on Human Rights as incorporated into our law by the Human Rights Act 1998, created a new legal order . . . The classic account given by Dicey of the doctrine of the supremacy of Parliament, pure and absolute as it was, can now be seen to be out of place in the modern United Kingdom. Nevertheless, the supremacy of Parliament is still the general principle of our constitution. It is a construct of the common law. The judges created this principle. If that is so, it is not unthinkable that circumstances could arise where the courts may have to qualify a principle established on a different hypothesis of constitutionalism.'[65]

Secondly, a number of commentators have suggested that traditional British notions of constitutional law, where the law is simply the reflection of the wishes of those who have gained political power, may be particularly inappropriate to the context of a divided society such as Northern Ireland. In such a society law too easily can become a tool for instability and oppression. Those who find themselves in a political minority may well have the fear that political defeat could lead to a diminishing of their citizenship. At the level of institutional detail the Agreement, with its provisions for weighted voting and entrenched human rights guarantees, as well as the way in which it overlays the 'constitutional' with international normative frameworks, marks a move away from this type of majoritarian, winner-takes-all constitutionalism. However, it may be argued, the shift needs to go further to reflect ideas about the purpose of the constitution itself. Arguably the constitutional process itself in Northern Ireland was a demonstration of the phenomenon of a constitution that moves beyond the

---

[63] See Tom Hickman, 'Constitutional Dialogue, Constitutional Theories and the Human Rights Act 1998' (2005) Public Law 306. Writing within the context of the more modest constitutional revolution in Scotland, Aidan O'Neil identifies the tensions around the judicial role that are introduced to the constitutional traditions of the UK after seven years of devolution. See further 'Stands Scotland where it did?' Devolution, Human Rights and Scottish Constitution Seven Years On' (2006) 57 Northern Ireland Legal Quarterly 102.   [64] [2002] 3 WLR 247.

[65] *Jackson v Attorney General* [2005] 3 WLR 733, para 102.

boundaries of a national constitutionalism with its intra-State constitutional sphere within which relationships between different identities are to be reconciled and accommodated. It may be that the Northern Ireland constitutional process is an instance of what Neil Walker identifies as a new legal genus that is emerging in the post-Westphalian territory of constitutionalism.[66] Within this, according to Walker, there are appearing a whole range of future understandings of constitutionalism that fundamentally challenge the existing normative or representational basis of constitutionalism by envisaging new constitutional settlements within the existing territorial frames, where 'traditional "international" relations between states develop in new "constitutional" ways, either interfering directly in the institutional structures and normative frameworks of domestic law or carving out a relatively autonomous space of political organisation in which the writ of the state runs increasingly faintly and unevenly'.[67] At the internal level of political contestation, constitutional politics will be based (and here Walker follows James Tully) on mutual recognition—'a recognition within the authoritative (and so officially "recognised") constitutional vision, of the legitimacy of other constitutional visions, and an "agonistic" process of negotiation between these alternative visions on the basis of consent and mutual respect'.[68] It may be thought that such an arrangement is counter-intuitive as it is unrealistic to expect an evenly weighted negotiation between different and conflicting frameworks of constitutional thought within an authoritative structure developed from within one of the frameworks in question. Nevertheless, according to Tully and Walker, it is the best way to foster an 'inter-cultural dialogue' where citizens with diverse and opposing identities can come together to determine how to negotiate agreements about how to live together over time 'in accordance with the three conventions of mutual recognition, consent and cultural continuity'.[69] While it could not necessarily be expected that this sort of understanding of the evolution of legal and constitutional norms would be consciously or explicitly stated by those developing the Northern Ireland settlement, it is eminently clear that something new was being created here to overcome the limitations of the old Westminster models.

A third reason why more exciting approaches to law might have been more apparent in the creation of the Agreement comes from the fact that traditional, historical views of the British Constitution and of constitutional relationships present there, were never likely to be true of the new situation in Northern Ireland. These characteristics include strong parliamentary government (where

---

[66] See Neil Walker, 'The Idea of Constitutional Pluralism' (2002) 65 Modern Law Review 317. See also 'After the Constitutional Moment' in Ingolf Pernice and Miguel Poiares Maduro (eds), *A Constitution for the European Union: First Comments on the 2003 Draft of the European Convention* (2004).   [67] ibid, 355.

[68] ibid, 354, Walker citing James Tully, *Strange Multiplicity: Constitutionalism in an Age of Diversity* (1996).

[69] Tully, *Strange Multiplicity: Constitutionalism in an Age of Diversity*, n 68 above, 30.

the winning political party will always be able to claim a high level of democratic support for its actions), collective responsibility of ministers to the cabinet and strong traditions of ministerial accountability to Parliament. Where these characteristics are present, as Guarnieri and Pederzoli observe,[70] courts will largely be deferential to the executive and will be reluctant to enter the political fray. However, in Northern Ireland the arrangements provided by the Agreement and NIA 1998 meant there was always likely to be a weak Executive, with high potential for conflict among its members and a limit on the extent to which members of the Executive were likely to be accountable to the Assembly. In addition, power was fragmented away from both the Assembly and Executive by the possibility of legislation being subjected to judicial review on a range of competence grounds, notably those relating to human rights and equality—and by the creation of various quangos and independent commissions. Such conditions, as in federal setups, create the opportunity for more extensive conflict between, rather than within, power centres, and a greater opportunity for courts to intervene, especially as the democratic legitimacy of other branches of government is not quite as overwhelming as in a strong parliamentary system. It says something for the limited constitutional thinking which took place at the time of the Agreement that the parties appeared to believe they could make significant changes in the nature of the legislature and executive from that which prevailed in the traditional Westminster model but largely leave the judicial branch untouched. What thinking there was, which fed into the commitment to the Criminal Justice Review, focused largely on the issue of whether the judiciary were in some way 'representative' of the community where they operate. While this is an important issue in itself it might be thought likely that this had the potential only to deteriorate into an unsatisfactory squabble about politicizing the judiciary and undermining judicial independence if broader questions about the role and structure of the courts in the type of democracy that the Agreement envisages are not addressed.

The particular understanding of constitutional law which those who negotiated the Agreement proceeded on may seem an esoteric point of somewhat limited interest. However, it is important because as the study found, important litigation resulting from the Agreement and the Act has depended on what approach to the constitution the courts hold. This is especially clear in *Robinson*,[71] where ironically, the court's willingness to depart from traditional understandings of constitutional law proved highly beneficial for the government's case. This is explored in more detail below, where it is argued that a more explicit articulation of such a different constitutional approach might be most beneficial for the development of a more satisfactory constitutional regime for Northern Ireland and instructive for the rest of the UK. Before moving to this, however, it is important

---

[70] Carlo Guarnieri and Patrizia Pederzoli, *The Power of Judges* (2003).
[71] [2002] UKHL 32.

to highlight some of the findings about the specific experience of cabinet government in Northern Ireland's devolved administration and the constitutional problems which this posed.

Operating the Agreement—Cabinet Government and the Reality of Relationships Between Different Parts of the State

As we develop further the constitutional context of the Agreement it is important to sketch out in a little more detail the singular elements relating to the formation and operation of executive government under the Agreement. This is not only to demonstrate one of the more constitutionally innovative elements but also to illustrate the background to some of the important litigation where the constitutional understandings of many of the actors were tested.

There is no doubt that the blueprint for government in Northern Ireland is different from that in the rest of the UK. Not only is legislation to be made under a different dispensation,[72] but particularly, the executive power is organized and operated in a different way.[73] This is a consequence not only of the high level agreement over elements such as consent and minority protection but also of both the founding documents and the way in which they allowed freedom to the parties to fill in the details.

The NIA 1998 said relatively little about such issues, beyond specifying the formal circumstances in which Ministers could be appointed and dismissed. More extensive detail was provided in the Agreement itself and in a subsequent ministerial code agreed between the parties and later approved by the Assembly in 2000. The Agreement clearly envisaged that each Minister was to be given a high degree of autonomy. Paragraph 24 indicates that 'Ministers will have full executive authority in their respective areas of responsibility, within any broad programme agreed by the Executive Committee and endorsed by the Assembly as a whole.' The Executive Committee is stated, in paragraph 19, to be 'a forum for the discussion of, and agreement on, issues which cut across the responsibilities of two or more Ministers, for prioritizing executive and legislative proposals and for recommending a common position where necessary (e.g. in dealing with external relationships)'. The one collective responsibility of Ministers is to 'agree each year, and review as necessary, a programme incorporating an agreed budget linked to

---

[72] See Gordon Anthony and John Morison, 'Here, There, and (Maybe) Here Again: The Story of Law Making for Post-1998 Northern Ireland', in Robert Hazell and Richard Rawlings (eds), *Devolution, Law Making and the Constitution* (2005) 155–92.

[73] For discussion of the architecture of the Agreement see eg, Brendan O'Leary, 'The Nature of the Agreement' (1999) 22 Fordham Law Journal 1628 or Richard Wilford (ed.), *Aspects of the Belfast Agreement* (2001). For an account of the operation of executive power, see the Northern Ireland section of the Constitution Unit's Devolution Monitoring project at http://www.ucl.ac.uk/constitution-unit/publications/devolution-monitoring-reports/index.html.

policies and programmes, subject to approval by the Assembly, after scrutiny in Assembly Committees, on a cross-community basis'.

In the absence of detailed structures in the legislation the parties to the talks, and those inhabiting the structures, had a significant role. This was to alter the basic position in important ways and perhaps introduce several elements which were to test the Agreement and its legal basis. It certainly meant introducing political elements directly into the institutional design of the Agreement. As one civil servant told us, 'the whole of the infrastructure in devolution was decided by the politicians themselves without a lot of advice from civil servants about how things actually work, and work in practice...'. This was not always regarded as ideal and the dynamics of the political process often crossed imperatives for good organization in government. For example, another civil servant complained to us 'they had a view that it was actually a good idea to split some functions up between departments because it would force the politicians in charge of the two departments to work together. Now I think that was a very naive view.... It wasn't being done in the interests of good governance, it was being done to achieve a political deal.'

Surprisingly, however, some of the more controversial issues were not as difficult as might be expected. We were told by one of the negotiating teams that 'the cross-border stuff was done very quickly but there was a lot of discussions on the Northern Ireland Assembly and what shape it should take and whether it should be a parliament and whether it should be an Assembly.... Its methods of voting were done very quickly, though there was a lot of talk about safeguards that we were going to put in, in terms of the cross-community voting.' Some of this was made less in the spirit of constitutional innovation than for political reasons.[74] For example, we were told by one of the Ulster Unionist Party's negotiating team that the original Ulster Unionist proposals were essentially to have Welsh-style devolution with the entire Executive function being exercised by the Assembly. Although it was admitted that this would be cumbersome it was initially preferred because 'it got over the political embarrassment of us sitting round the Cabinet table with de Brún and McGuinness [from Sinn Féin]'. Another Unionist source said that the experience of local government, and in particular the role of committees there, had overly influenced unionist negotiators: 'I think the fatal error was giving almost complete executive control over the departments to the executive minister.' This view was shared, perhaps for different reasons, by some of the civil servants, with one London-based member of the NIO remarking to us, 'I do find it very sad that political parties simply own departments of Government.'[75]

---

[74] Perhaps as a consequence of the political input the results of this constitutional engineering were not always as intended. A senior member of the DUP told us, 'Strangely the structure that they set up, which I have no doubt was set up to aid the minority actually ended up aiding us. Even the voting systems were an aid to us and caused Trimble most of his major problems.'

[75] At the ground level, civil servants in Belfast were unenthusiastic about this approach, perhaps anticipating some of the problems. As one complained to us, 'we were told this was what was going to happen, and to make it work, which we tried to do because it was a political decision and it was being done for political reasons'.

Of course, all this differs very markedly from the situation in the rest of the UK. In UK constitutional law the rules governing the formation and operation of the Executive have largely been a matter of constitutional convention. Appointment is made by the Prime Minister and the convention of collective responsibility requires the cabinet to speak with one voice. The power of the Prime Minister to dismiss a cabinet minister for speaking or acting in a way which is out of line with an agreed collective decision provides an effective means of ensuring such decisions are respected. As ministers have, with few exceptions, been drawn from the same political party as the Prime Minister, difficulties with regard to inter-executive disputes are rare. This form of cabinet government also facilitates a free flow of information between officials as, whatever their department, all are ultimately working for the same government.[76] Such a system of Executive formation is of course closely tied to the simple majority voting system and the corollary of this system is that usually one political party will have a majority in the House of Commons. The adoption of PR systems in Scotland and Wales raised the possibility that this would not always be the case in the devolved Assemblies, and coalition rather than single party governments have indeed become the norm. In Northern Ireland the combination of PR and the use of the D'Hondt system for the appointment of the Executive made it not merely likely, but indeed inevitable, that the Executive would be made up of parties which had opposed each other in the election. In such circumstances the possibility of establishing collective responsibility on the traditional Westminster model were slim, and disappeared when election results produced the outcome that two of the Ministers would be drawn from the DUP, which refused to sit in the Executive in protest at the inclusion of Sinn Féin. The consequences of operating such as system far from the Westminster norm were eloquently expressed to us by a DUP Minister:

'I mean a lot of people still think of an Executive in British terms, you know, the Cabinet where there's collective responsibility, the Prime Minister hires and fires and everybody is expected to go along to Cabinet meetings. This was an altogether different creation. There was no collective responsibility ... the power was vested in ministers rather than in the Assembly which meant that the Assembly could say and do what it wanted: the committees could say and do what they wanted .... I was taking the decision and what was true of me was true of every other minister. It meant that we could operate in a silo; we didn't require any Executive approval for anything .... We didn't need to go to Executive meetings. As soon as a Programme for Government, which was a very vague concept anyway, was passed we worked within it. If there was money in our Department we spent it, nobody could say or do anything ... and I don't think that I ever felt that I had been disadvantaged by not being at a Cabinet meeting.'

The generally political charged element in the structures of government, and the autonomy of Ministers in particular, was not helpful to the development of

---

[76] See Terence Daintith and Alan Page, *The Executive in the Constitution: Structure, Autonomy and Internal Control* (1999).

consensus politics. The story of the decline of the first rounds of devolution in the post-Agreement era bears this out. However, for our purposes it was significant because it contributed towards establishing a constitutional condition where some of the basic legal and constitutional understandings within the Agreement were to be tested further. It connects particularly to the litigation about nominations to the North–South Ministerial Council,[77] and litigation about refusing the release of ministerial papers to non-participating ministers.[78] It also raises what are new and important issues about how civil servants operate in such circumstances and give advice, as well as constitutional issues about the funding of such cases between different government departments from departmental budgets. It is to some of these that we now turn.

Litigating the Agreement

The Agreement has thrown up a number of cases. Most but not all of these touch on the interpretation of the NIA 1998, others raise aspects of the Agreement, such as the policing provisions, which were given effect in other legislation. One might also argue that the many human rights cases which have come before the courts in Northern Ireland in recent years are related to the emphasis placed in the Agreement on human rights.[79] Most of the cases followed up in detail by the project were cases brought by politicians, indeed sometimes by members of the government against each other—something unusual in UK constitutional law but not in many other parts of the world. Although the number of cases is relatively small, they do raise a number of interesting points. The research focused on nine particular cases, where extensive interviews were carried out with the parties involved.

1. *Re Williamson's Application for Judicial Review* CA [2000] NI 281.

2. *In re an Application by Seamus Treacy and Barry MacDonald for Judicial Review* 6 January 2000; *Re Treacy's and another's Application for Judicial Review* QB [2000] NI 330.

3. *In the matter of an application by Bairbre de Brún and Martin McGuinness for judicial review* 2001 NIQB 3; *In the matter of applications by Bairbre de Brún and Martin McGuinness for judicial review* 2001 NICA 43.

4. *In the matter of an application by Conor Murphy for judicial review* 2001 NIQB 34.

---

[77] *In the matter of applications by Bairbre de Brun and Martin McGuinness for Judicial Review* 2001 NICA 43.

[78] *In the matter of an application by Maurice Morrow and Gregory Campbell for Judicial Review* 2002 NIQB 4.

[79] See further Gordon Anthony, 'Public Law Litigation and the Belfast Agreement' (2001) 8 European Public Law 401; Brice Dickson, 'The House of Lords and the Northern Ireland Conflict—A Sequel' (2006) 69 (3) Modern Law Review 383.

5. *In the matter of an application by Maurice Morrow and Gregory Campbell for leave to apply for judicial review* 2001 NIQB 13; *In the matter of an application by Maurice Morrow and Gregory Campbell for judicial review* 2002 NIQB 4.

6. *Re Northern Ireland Human Rights Commission's Application for Judicial Review* CA [2001] NI 271; *In Re Northern Ireland Human Rights Commission (Northern Ireland)* [2002] UKHL 25.

7. *In the matter of an application by Peter Robinson for leave to apply for judicial review* 2001 NIQB 39; *In the matter of an application by Peter Robinson for leave to apply for judicial review* 2001 NIQB 42; *In the matter of an application by Peter Robinson for judicial review* 2001 NIQB 49; *In the matter of an application by Peter Robinson for judicial review* 2002 NICA 18A; *Robinson v Secretary of State for Northern Ireland and Others (Northern Ireland)* [2002] UKHL 32 [2002] NI 390.

8. *In the matter of an application by Mark Parsons for judicial review* 2002 NIQB 46; *In the matter of an application by Mark William John Parsons for judicial review* 2003 NICA 20.

9. *In the matter of an application by Damien McComb for judicial review* 2003 NIQB 47.

Additionally, there were two subsequent cases of particular interest:

In the matter of an application by Stephen James McClean for Judicial Review and In the matter of a decision of the Sentence Review Commissioners 2003 NIQB 32; *In the matter of an application by Stephen James McClean for Judicial Review and In the matter of a decision of the Secretary of State for Northern Ireland* 2003 NIQB 31; *In the matter of an application by Stephen McClean for Judicial Review and in the matter of a decision of the Sentence Review Commissioners* 2004 NICA 14; *In re McClean (Original Respondent and Cross-appellant) (On Appeal from the Court of Appeal Northern Ireland) (Northern Ireland)* [2005] UKHL 46.

In the matter of an application by Peter Neill for judicial review 2005 NIQB 66; *In the matter of an application by Peter Neill for Judicial Review* 2006 NICA 5.

There are a number of general issues arising from this litigation. First, the volume of cases is fairly low. Some civil servants to whom we spoke suggested that they had expected more.[80] There was a view that the very nature of the Agreement structures might engender conflict. As one civil servant said, 'there was this very novel relationship between the members of the Executive. They weren't there by agreement, they were there in a sense because the electorate put them there.' Indeed among the issues that those interviewed expected to come to court, and did not, were the provisions regarding designation of political parties and in particular its effect on the potency of Alliance Party votes; the redesignation of the Alliance Party; the 'resignation' of the Deputy First Minister (described by a DUP Minister as 'the one case I think we should have taken and didn't'); the extent of

---

[80] For example, a NIO civil servant told us that, 'everybody had a big fear that we would be involved in hours of continuous litigation'.

Ministerial powers, particularly in relation to the Programme for Government; and, in the Republic of Ireland, the status of the North–South bodies and the Ministerial Council in relation to the Constitution.[81]

Notwithstanding expectations, litigation remained limited. Several factors appear to be responsible for this. First, there was widespread, if not universal, satisfaction with the negotiating process and the ensuing Agreement and Act. As one of the political negotiators put it, 'we had achieved a lot through the actual Agreement itself and through the Northern Ireland Act which we felt reasonably faithfully reflected the Agreement... there is no need for us to be litigious'. Secondly, the influence of individuals should not be underestimated. Clearly some parties had politicians or advisers who were more legally minded than others, and who were therefore, more likely to be analysing developments with a view to potential litigation.[82] A third factor relates to resources. Certain politicians, for example, claimed that they could not justify the use of party funds to explore speculative legal points and looked enviously at the ability of those in government to use public money to pursue disputes between the parties.[83] Also there was a general view that the courts would not be willing to become involved in difficult matters of political controversy.[84] This view was reinforced by decisions such as that in the *Williamson* case where the invocation of 'soft edged review' by Kerr J and then on appeal by the Lord Chief Justice Carswell suggested a judicial reluctance to become involved in high-profile political disputes. The judgment in this case expressed the view that 'the court should in such circumstances be somewhat more ready than in some other cases to assume a higher degree of knowledge and expertise on the part of the decider'.[85] The signals given in this decision were

---

[81] Interestingly, however, North–South issues were seen in the UK context as being relatively non-contentious. It was explained to us that having been a historically difficult issue the comparatively long and sometimes difficult time spent negotiating this section ensured they got 'the architecture right' in producing a system which worked, thereby avoiding the necessity of resort to the courts. Indeed, one Irish civil servant remembers David Trimble dismissing this as a 'non-issue'.

[82] As one barrister close to the Ulster Unionist party told us, 'the line always was "but our leader is a great lawyer and... if our lawyer leader says it is okay then it is okay". The implication being that if it didn't turn out okay then the great white knight of litigation would come on and save the day.'

[83] We were told by one political advisor simply that the party was open to using litigation 'as long as the party is not paying for it' and there is a Minister able to use government money. One barrister told us of a strategy that was used whereby 'very often political parties would trawl their membership to find somebody who can attract legal aid and then be the person who would then take an action'.

[84] For eg, we were told by one barrister, commenting on the politically controversial decision of the moderate Alliance party to redesignate itself temporarily as Unionist in order to facilitate the formation of an Executive, that although this was a very arguable legal issue 'it was never put and I think it is telling that their lawyers didn't put it because again the minds of lawyers as much as the judiciary were focused on the statutory rather than the constitutional'.

[85] *In the matter of an application by Michelle Williamson for Judicial Review* (CA) [2000] NI 281. Lord Carswell went on to say, 'The area with which the [the Sentences (NI) Act 1998] is concerned is delicate and sensitive, and it is hardly surprising that strong views should be held on it or that decisions within this area should give rise to serious differences of opinion. It is part of the democratic process that such decisions should be taken by a minister responsible to Parliament, and so long as the

referred to as one reason why some of the most controversial issues—such as the extent to which decommissioning had taken place and whether this constituted a breach of the Agreement[86]—have not been taken before the courts.

The most prominent reason overall, however, appeared to be that most politicians instinctively disliked turning to the courts to resolve what they saw as essentially political issues. It was only as a last resort or a lack of alternative option that such an undertaking was chosen.[87] The views across the parties were remarkably similar on this with, to take just two examples, members of diametrically opposed political parties telling us that going to court was 'an opting out of the political process . . . a vote of no confidence'; and that 'we would have much preferred to have had the problems and the difficulties resolved politically by, if you like, a coming together of political leaderships to resolve these matters'.[88] Even the legal personnel involved in the cases shared this view to some extent. One of the barristers connected to a case remarked on how he advised potential litigants that the political process was 'a politically preferable i.e. a much surer way to solve disputes'. Moreover, unlike in many political systems where points of constitutional impasse can be resolved only by the courts, there was for some parties another outlet via a reference to the British or Irish Government to put pressure on one side or the other.[89] Indeed, it is perhaps no accident that two of the most high-profile cases were brought by the anti-agreement DUP, which did not previously have a reputation for using the courts, but which lacked the possibility of resort to either government to enforce their view of the Agreement.

In carrying out the research we were struck by the degree to which both politicians and lawyers involved in those cases that were pursued generally sought only short-term tactical gains and espoused fairly traditional approaches to legal interpretation. Rather than seeing the courts as a medium through which to clarify the law, we were told, 'everybody is looking for a short fix out of a problem rather than

manner in which they are taken is in accordance with the proper principles the courts should not and will not step outside their proper function of review.'

[86] Cf. *In the matter of an application by Sinn Féin for Judicial Review* [2005] NI 412, Sinn Féin unsuccessfully sought judicial review of the finding of the International Monitoring Commission and of a direction by the Secretary of State that he was not satisfied, for the purposes of financial support for political activity, that Sinn Féin were committed to non-violence and exclusively peaceful and democratic means.

[87] As a senior representative from one party (who did in fact litigate) put it, 'there is risk that you could lose authority and standing . . . it's the credibility that you start losing if you take politics into the court all the time [that means that] you have to do it somewhat sparingly'. More cynically perhaps it was a barrister who told us, 'I think politicians are loath to use the courts . . . [because] the voting public can't see what is going on.'

[88] Cf the view expressed to us by a senior civil servant in the Republic of Ireland who told us, 'we were regularly getting advice from Sinn Féin to take this thing to the International Court . . . We would have grave reluctance to do it, if we did that would be a signal of a breakdown in trust, a severe breakdown in trust.'

[89] Indeed one well-known political journalist who we interviewed painted a vivid picture of the 'continual political crises [where] one lot rushes down to see Brian Cowan [the Irish foreign Minister] to ask him to back them up and the other lot rushes over to find whoever they can find at Westminster because most of them don't trust the Secretary of State . . . '.

a real comprehensive response to the problem'.[90] Those cases which did come
before the courts, therefore, tended to be pursued for fairly narrow tactical reasons. This did not inevitably mean that a straightforward legal victory was being
sought.[91] Indeed, a legal ruling on its own was not seen as particularly important
goal.[92] Generally some sort of wider political point was being pursued and the
courts were only one avenue for pursuing this. Even those who professed little
faith in the legal/judicial system viewed going to court as potentially productive in
this cause.[93] Overall, however, the emphasis remained very much on particular,
individual gains rather than more strategically on winning particular interpretations of the Agreement and NIA 1998. For example, there was the *De Brún and
McGuinness* application for judicial review where David Trimble refused to nominate two Sinn Féin Ministers to the North–South Ministerial Council (N/SMC)
as section 52 of the NIA 1998 required him on the avowedly political grounds
that he wished to pressurize Sinn Féin to use its influence to secure IRA decommissioning. In the judicial review application, the applicants obtained a declaration that the First Minister's decision to refuse to nominate the applicants to
meetings of the N/SMC had been taken to pursue a purpose collateral to section 52,
and as a direct result of this judgment the two ministers were able to resume their
roles on the N/SMC.[94] Similarly, in the *Morrow and Campbell*[95] case the High
Court granted a declaration that the decision not to pass on certain confidential
papers was in breach of a substantive legitimate expectation and thus ensured that
DUP ministers were accorded the rights of their office.[96]

[90] Only one politician interviewed (interestingly perhaps from Sinn Féin) recognized the value of
having a judicial ruling that 'would guide future decisions in this respect and . . . would give an indication of an interpretation of the Northern Ireland Act . . . that would give a steer when certain difficulties might arise in the future'.

[91] A legal representative close to one of the main Unionist parties told us how a 'good' case might
sometimes mean one where 'even if you lose you will have been making a political point'. On the
other hand Sinn Féin told us, 'even if you subscribe to the view that it is an absolute waste of time
with regard to possible judgment, it is another platform on which to articulate [your views] . . . .
We've fairly successfully used the courts in that respect. . . . With the Martin McGuinness and
Bairbre [de Brún] challenge to the Trimble refusal to make the nominations [to the North–South
Ministerial Council] . . . we won it publicly in the public domain . . . in terms of the media presentation of the issue.'

[92] As a DUP Minister put it, 'Nobody sat down and said "let's go to the House of Lords".'

[93] A Sinn Féin Minister told us, 'just because the courts rule against [us] we wouldn't necessarily
always consider that as a loss as such. It would be better if they ruled in favour but if we have highlighted the issue I would still be happy enough to go down that road.' A DUP insider, commenting
on the party's loss in the House of Lords in *Robinson*, was able to boast that at least 'We got good
PR—the fact that the LCJ and the former LCJ for NI agreed with us.'

[94] As Bairbre de Brún, told us, 'it was very clear by then that there was simply no possibility of
taking this forward through the political structures and that therefore in order to be able to carry out
my ministerial responsibilities I had to take legal action . . . [or] be seen as acquiescing in the non-
carrying out of certain of my functions'.

[95] See *In the matter of an application by Maurice Morrow and Gregory Campbell for Judicial Review*
2002 NIQB 4, where two DUP ministers found that they were continually being denied important
documents which had immediate relevance to the Departments for which they were responsible, on
the basis that with their opposition to the Agreement they might break confidentiality.

[96] Coughlin J held that, 'the DUP ministers were entitled to expect that the respondents
would . . . act in accordance with a fair, rational and clearly articulated policy when implementing any

As the body of litigation is considered as a whole it is interesting to note how by and large the settled understandings of politicians and officials have been reflected in the cases which have come before the courts. It is also noteworthy how the legal arguments employed have not been particularly adventurous with, in particular, a marked judicial reluctance to move beyond deciding cases on anything but the most narrow grounds. The status accorded to the Agreement (rather than the NIA 1998) within the litigation is particularly revealing here, as it is perhaps indicative of the sort of wider understanding of the constitutional as opposed to legal status of the new dispensation. In general, politicians saw the Agreement rather than the NIA 1998 as the key document. This may be due to the understanding of most politicians as having been involved in a political process of negotiation rather than a legal process of drafting.[97] It may also be related to levels of legal understanding and role that politicians generally play.[98] On the other hand, lawyers generally took the Act as their main reference point, with one barrister telling us, 'the Agreement is all very fine but the Northern Ireland Act is really what we relied on'.[99] This did not mean that the Agreement was not used by lawyers, although of course, the degree to which it could be deployed depended on the argument that was being made.[100] This use of the Agreement can be seen as being linked to some sense of the litigation being different from the ordinary. Although it was certainly uneven and by no means a view universally held, there was undoubtedly at least a feeling reported to us by some lawyers that there are some issues in the litigation that were constitutional matters that may require constitutional arguments. As one barrister expressed it, 'The Agreement is much more fundamental than a consultation paper or a white paper to which regard could be had in interpreting legislation.'

This 'constitutional' approach was not reflected generally, however, within the courts in Northern Ireland where the Agreement, and the constitutional arguments which developed from it, were not universally well received. As one barrister expressed it, 'As far as I can see the courts just treat the Northern Ireland Act as they do any order in council. I haven't seen any judge get misty eyed about fundamental rights or constitutional founding documents. I think the judiciary here see

---

decision. To inform the applicants that they would be provided with confidential documents in practice and subsequently introduce an entirely new factor i.e. the failure of the applicants to participate in meetings of the Executive does not fulfil an expectation.'

[97] ibid.

[98] As a civil servant told us, 'The parties would look at the Agreement if only because the Agreement is more accessible. I mean all the politicians have read it, whereas the Act is a bit of a bitch. Sorry—the Act is very difficult and complex to understand! They all know it, so the Agreement tends to be for politicians the first reference point and not the Act. The Act is more the reference point for the civil servants.'

[99] As another barrister expressed it, 'It is a piece of legislation and like all other legislation we work it.'

[100] For eg, as one counsel told us, 'In *de Brún* the Agreement was looked at in great detail. Strand 2 was very detailed, very useful... [In *Murphy*] the Agreement wasn't used as much... it was in the skeleton [argument] but not to the forefront... yes, it is a long way from a constitutional document but the closest we are going to get is *de Brún*... Carswell does refer to the Agreement in *de Brún*'.

it as a piece of legislation and they work with it.' This view did not always go down well with some politicians or sometimes even their counsel. One barrister close to the SDLP expressed to us the view that 'the Agreement should be considered much more than it has been by the courts. I mean we have seen it being treated by the courts as an aid to statutory interpretation and we don't feel that that is the proper level of attention to be given to the Agreement. Nor has any recognition been given to the fact that it is an international treaty.'

Some of the early cases that arose illustrated the attitude that would be taken in the Northern Ireland courts to constitutional arguments in general, and constitutional arguments that departed from the Diceyean orthodoxy in particular.

In the judicial review taken by the Sinn Féin MLA Conor Murphy, it was contended that regulations introduced by the then Secretary of State, Peter Mandelson, during a period of suspension of the devolved institutions, to permit the flying of the Union flag over Government buildings, were inconsistent and contrary to the undertakings given in the Good Friday Agreement in that they failed to pay regard to 'partnership, equality and mutual respect' between opposing political parties. Rejecting this argument, Kerr J also refuted the contention that Peter Mandelson agreed to introduce the legislation concerning the flying of flags for reasons of political expediency.[101] In a response reminiscent of 'soft-edged review' as developed in *Williamson*, Kerr J suggested that even if the Secretary of State had made his decision based on this reason, the judge was of the opinion that the decision could not be quashed on that account alone, because such a decision being 'the stuff of politics ... is not subject to judicial review'.[102] We found that this case incurred a high level of criticism from several of those that we interviewed, who felt that the court here departed from the intention and spirit of the Agreement and particularly from its parity of esteem provisions. As might be expected there was disappointment amongst some politicians, and indeed some civil servants, about the situation regarding flags in general, if not the reasoning in the case.[103] But more significantly there was perhaps a sense among some in the legal community that an opportunity to do things differently had been missed. One of the more politically engaged lawyers expressed the view that 'the wording in the Agreement is vague and obviously it is the legislation that has legal force, but as an interpretative aid it is unique, and much stronger. And we haven't

[101] It was argued that the real purpose of the Secretary of State's decision was to accommodate the Ulster Unionist party, specifically to enable Mr Trimble to encourage his party to return to government after the suspension period.

[102] Indeed, Kerr J made the point that the legal mechanisms that allowed the flying of the flag were regulations introduced on the basis of order in council and that since they were within the Assembly's competence they could therefore be changed by the Assembly.

[103] One civil service source expressed a view that we heard several times when he said, 'the whole spirit of the Agreement is, I would have thought, that when you come to the issue of the national flags you have to say "wow, we've got a big issue here in the light of this Agreement we've negotiated" ... and you sit down ... But just to say the solution to the flags issue was instead of having 21 Union Jack days there was 16 or something ... big deal!'

seen that translated across yet by the courts. Nor a proper engagement of what the Agreement means…and that to us came across very clearly in the *Conor Murphy* case.'

The *Treacy and McDonald* case, where two barristers successfully disputed the wording of the declaration required for admittance to the senior bar, raised some similar issues in terms of how the courts handle concepts of parity of esteem in a post-Agreement world. The fact that the case came about at all was seen by some to be significant. While the major influence towards taking this case might be seen as Bar Council support, and the main reason for winning it was an unexpected development around a letter written by the then Lord Chief Justice, it was accepted by one of those involved that 'the courts now aren't immune to what is going on outside this building. The face of the judges is unquestionably changing'—although this was attributed as much to the Human Rights Act as to the NIA 1998. Of course this change is not sufficient for some. Another barrister (not involved directly but commenting on the case) suggested that 'you felt that philosophically the judiciary had not understood the significance of the Agreement and…in fact the House of Lords is much better at understanding it than the courts here'.

Indeed the different approaches taken by the House of Lords and the courts in Northern Ireland emerged as a particularly interesting feature in our research. In the *Human Rights Commission*[104] case, the House of Lords was willing to read into the relevant provisions of the NIA 1998, despite an explicit absence, a power of intervention which would allow the Commission to make submissions on human rights law to courts, tribunals, and inquests. In coming to his decision, Lord Slynn acknowledged that as the NIA 1998 was 'for the purpose of implementing' the Belfast Agreement therefore it was relevant in making his decision to note the emphasis in the Agreement on the 'protection and vindication of the human rights of all'. It was this emphasis that permitted him to conclude that despite the absence of overt permission, a general reading of the relevant subsections of the Act conferred on the Commission 'general powers to promote the understanding of human rights law and practice and to review its adequacy and effectiveness'. The majority of 4:1 in the House of Lords overturned both the Northern Ireland Court of Appeal's decision,[105] and that of the then Lord Chief Justice of Northern Ireland, Sir Robert Carswell, who in the first instance had, even with a 'broad and sympathetic construction', felt unable to read even an implied power into the relevant statutory provision. For some legal observers in Northern Ireland this suggested a more progressive approach towards interpreting the new constitutional situation in Northern Ireland.[106] This view was not always shared by those who

---

[104] [2001] NI 271 (NI); [2002] UKHL 25 (House of Lords).   [105] With Kerr J dissenting.
[106] One barrister expressed the view to us that 'in the *Human Rights Commission* case, there was a much stronger engagement there than you would have seen in the Northern Ireland courts…Comparisons were also made to the early jurisprudence of the nascent Republic of Ireland's courts, [and] some thought given to the constitutional structures of the state and what they meant.'

had a closer acquaintance with the House of Lords. One London-based barrister we interviewed told us that 'I would say that, the Law Lords don't want any Northern Ireland cases because of the "otherness" of Northern Ireland . . . they just don't want to get involved in the politics of Northern Ireland. It is not that they are frightened of constitutionalism . . . but [they] are frightened of a constitutional decision which is seen to encroach on the territory of the Executive or a Parliament. That's what they're frightened of. They will move mountains to help an ordinary man and woman who's a victim . . . but they won't get dragged into a squabble between Northern Ireland ministers, that's just not their role.'

Nevertheless, the House of Lords was drawn again into constitutional litigation from Northern Ireland with the landmark case of *Robinson v Secretary of State for Northern Ireland and Others (Northern Ireland)*,[107] where the Lords were willing to consider the NIA 1998 as a constitutional document with Lord Hoffman stating that the Act is 'a constitution for Northern Ireland, framed to create a continuing form of government against the background of the history of the territory and the principles agreed in Belfast'.[108] Categorizing the 1998 Act as a constitution in this way has consequences as it permits the courts to interpret its provisions 'generously and purposively, bearing in mind the values which the constitutional provisions are intended to embody'. In the *Robinson* judgment, this interpretative methodology meant that the Northern Ireland Assembly had the power to elect Mr David Trimble and Mr Mark Durkan as First Minister and Deputy First Minister outside the statutory six-week period that had been established by the Northern Ireland Act 1998 for such an election. This flexible interpretation of the Lords, of course, was at variance with the Lord Chief Justice, Sir Robert Carswell's dissenting judgment in the Northern Ireland Court of Appeal, which favoured a strict literalist approach to the NIA 1998.[109]

It is interesting too how various parties saw and interpreted the political nature of the cases in the different courts. One political party interviewee who was involved in litigation told us how he was 'struck by how political the whole thing

---

[107] [2002] UKHL 32.

[108] See para 25 and also the judgments of Lords Bingham and Millet. In this way their Lordships acknowledged the import of the Act and the preceding Agreement and seemed to elevate the statute to sit alongside other constitutional landmarks as the Bill of Rights 1689, the European Communities Act 1972 and the Human Rights Act 1998. See further the discussion of *Thoburn v. Sunderland City Council*, [2002] 3 WLR 247, above, and Laws LJ recommendation that we should acknowledge that there are a hierarchy of Acts of Parliament: 'there exists rights which should properly be classified as constitutional or fundamental . . . '.

[109] 'It is a difficult and invidious task for judges sitting in a court of law to adjudicate upon matters which have a highly charged political content, where the exercise of political judgment is at the centre of decision-making. That is the task imposed upon us by law and we have to discharge our function in the manner required of a judicial tribunal, looking only to those matters which are properly within our purview. Those matters are concerned solely with the interpretation of the governing statute, and I have sought to construe its terms in such a way as to ascertain and give effect to the intention of Parliament and eschewing all other considerations.' See further Marie Lynch, 'Robinson v. Secretary of State for Northern Ireland: Interpreting Constitutional Legislation' (2003) Public Law 640.

was at first instance' but also how he 'didn't expect it in the Lords' and was surprised by how they 'set a lot of store in keeping the Agreement alive'. Other more legally informed informants told us how in the Northern Ireland courts 'you were left with a clear impression that if there had been a different balance on the Bench you might have had a different outcome' and we were given detailed and personalized accounts of how they saw the 'draw' in terms of the judges allocated at different levels.

Of course it was inevitable that the courts both locally and in the House of Lords would operate within the political context. Indeed all parties to the cases saw them clearly as political matters.[110] For example, a number of interviewees referring to the *Robinson* case noted not only the involvement of a 'big hitter' in the person of the Attorney-General for the respondents, but also how his submission used such dramatic terminology as the 'nuclear option' when asking the Lords to consider the consequences of their accepting the DUP's arguments. This political character to the cases was of course inevitable. As one barrister speaking in relation to one of the major cases informed us:

'Undoubtedly there are political overtones in the judgments, I don't suggest otherwise because we invited them to politicise themselves, that was part of argument . . . . We invited them to view . . . first of all that to give effect to a political accord they should interpret [a relevant section] in a particular way . . . . So they had to look at the political accord and immerse themselves in that. We invited them to consider the bloody history of Northern Ireland which you couldn't dissociate from the political accord. And we invited them to the view that the political accord had brought about stability in Northern Ireland and that to reject our argument would create serious instability with all the negative consequences.'

As the litigation reviewed above is surveyed, it is possible to draw some limited conclusions about its overall effect in practical terms. Although there is little evidence that the litigation had major impact on the lives of those living within Northern Ireland or indeed on the day-to-day conduct of politics, there have been some noteworthy features. First, the ability to go to court facilitated the continuance of the democratically elected institutions where otherwise they would have terminated. Secondly, the courts were at least able to provide an alternative means of finding a remedy for some difficult political problems. However, despite these advantages, it should be remembered that resort to the courts by politicians invariably indicates a failure of the political process and a breakdown of trust.[111]

---

[110] It was, however, curious to note how some of the political actors were surprised that the courts were so politically aware. As one complained to us, 'Is it the job of the Law Lords to determine what the outcome or the fallout might be from a decision that they would take? Do they take their decision based on what the repercussions are going to be or do they take it on the basis of the evidence that is before them.' Conversely, another said more cynically that, 'it was very clear that there was a presumption in favour of the Government position and I'm not sure if that's a legal requirement or not'.

[111] As one Sinn Féin politician lamented to us, 'Sinn Féin scored a legal political victory in the courts and asserted their right to go to a N/SMC but did it in any way assist in the process of bringing

It is also noteworthy that there has been a marked judicial reluctance to move beyond deciding cases on anything but the most narrow grounds. In some early cases, such as *Murphy* or *De Brun and McGuinness*, the court indicated a general view that the actions of the Secretary of State were not inconsistent with the Agreement but without spending a significant amount of time on the interpretation of its status or content. The House of Lords decision in *Robinson* suggested that the Agreement was relevant at least to the interpretation of the NIA 1998 and that its relevance flowed more from the sense of overall purpose it gave to that Act, rather than specific commitments contained or not contained within it.[112] Since then the High Court in Northern Ireland has suggested in the subsequent case of *In the matter of an Application by Damien McComb for Judicial Review* a wider application where the Agreement may be relevant to the interpretation and application not just of the NIA 1998 but also of other legislation passed under its 'aegis'. In this case, Kerr J (as he then was) disagreed with the Recorder's assertion that the Belfast Agreement was aspirational only. Citing a section of Lord Hoffman's judgment in *Robinson*, he stated that though it referred to the effect that the Agreement had on the nature of the NIA 1998, it supported the conclusion that the terms of the Agreement could affect one's approach to 'the interpretation and application of statutory provisions made under its aegis'.[113] In that case it was the sentence review legislation. This approach has also been applied to policing where in *Re Parson's Application* the NI High Court dismissed an application for judicial review of a 'quota' whereby recruitment to the Police Service of Northern Ireland was to take place on a 50:50 basis as between Protestants and Catholics. Kerr J expressed the view that 'it cannot seriously be disputed that a police force should be representative of the community it serves. That has been recognised and endorsed by all the parties who supported the Belfast Agreement. The Agreement had in turn been endorsed by 71% of the voting population ... These circumstances provide formidable support for (the) method of recruitment.'[114] It could be imagined that similar reasoning could apply to (at least) criminal justice and victims legislation as these also flow from explicit provisions in the Agreement.[115] Whether one might eventually argue that all legislation

the Ulster Unionists and Sinn Féin closer together in terms of political understanding and in political co-operation?'

[112] See further Marie Lynch, 'Robinson v. Secretary of State for Northern Ireland: Interpreting Constitutional Legislation', n 109 above.

[113] Consequently, Kerr J concluded that the fact of the applicant's release under the Northern Ireland (Sentences) Act 1998 should have been considered by the department when making the decision as to whether he should be granted a taxi driver's licence, his application for judicial review was granted, and an order quashing the decision of the Recorder was made. See also *In re McClean* [2003] NIQB 31; [2004] NICA 14; [2005] UKHL 46, where, on appeal from the Court of Appeal Northern Ireland, Lords Bingham and Scott talked in terms of interpreting prisoner legislation in the spirit of the Agreement (paras 27 and 49).   [114] Para 34.

[115] *In The Matter of an Application by Peter Neil for Judicial Review* [2005] NIQB 66; [2006] NICA 5, which related to whether or not an anti-social behaviour order (ASBO) was lawful in light of equality scheme obligations under s 75 NIA 1998. Girvan J also referred to the judgments of Lords

passed in Northern Ireland post-1998 is really under the 'aegis' of the Agreement is a moot point. If this were to be the case, then the Agreement would clearly have attained the 'constitutional status' Lord Hoffman suggests in *Robinson*, and could act as a signal to constitutional development elsewhere in the UK.

Conclusion: the Courts and New Constitutional Understandings

This chapter offers two sets of conclusions. The first set relates to the new circumstances in Northern Ireland, while the second considers how the constitutional innovation there impacts more widely.

The Belfast Agreement introduced a new constitutional landscape. The Agreement is unusual because of its basis in rights, equality, and partnership, and perhaps unique in the way in which it is conditioned by various external stakeholders and then rooted in international law. It provides less of a 'once and for all' solution and more of a constitutional space in which the people of Northern Ireland can park the big constitutional issues of self-determination and engage with the important, everyday constitutional issues about how to live together. The NIA 1998 is less revolutionary. It is closer to the usual Westminster model (and therefore vulnerable to another exercise of sovereign power such as the Northern Ireland Act 2000, which can simply sweep it away). Notwithstanding the Agreement's abiding constitutional significance (as opposed to its mere political importance) not all those who negotiated the Agreement were necessarily aware that they were doing anything other than securing a political deal. Indeed, despite some important expressions to the contrary the courts most often simply used the law to regulate some of the unstable relationships within the governmental structures. This does not mean that the courts' role in articulating a new constitutional framework is not of enduring importance. It does not mean either that if people had resorted to the courts more often, or if the courts had done a different job, this would have saved the Agreement structures from their periods of failure and that Northern Ireland's constitutional politics would now be flourishing. As Hamilton famously observed, the courts are the 'weakest branch' of the constitution and struggle always to impose their will on the legislature or executive. Indeed, while courts may interpret or develop a constitution they cannot make it by themselves.[116]

Bingham and Hoffman in *Robinson*. He went on to say that the equality provisions 'are part of a statute intended to be a new constitution for Northern Ireland framed against the background of the history of Northern Ireland and the principles agreed in the so-called Good Friday Agreement. The Agreement was the product of multi-party negotiations and was intended to be a balanced and carefully nuanced constitutional arrangement.' See also *In the Matter of an application by Sinn Féin for Judicial Review* [2005] NI 412, and *In the Matter of an application by Brenda Downes for Judicial Review* [2006] MQB 77.

[116] Here the phrase 'Courts' should be interpreted not only to mean the judiciary but the wider legal culture, which too must take responsibility for the way in which understandings about the Agreement

An analogy could be developed whereby we see the representatives of the two Governments and their international supporters along with the locally based negotiators as the *architects* of the settlement. The local politicians in the Assembly and other structures are then the *builders* of the constitutional edifice within which the people of Northern Ireland are the *inhabitants* who live and work. Within this analogy the judges are perhaps designers who can shape parts of the structure and adjust elements that are not functioning as they should. But the courts are not responsible for making the Agreement work. If Northern Ireland's political parties do not wish to reach agreement and operate together the courts cannot force them to do so. Moreover, even if the courts do perform their traditional role of explicating who is right in disputes about the meaning of an agreement the parties have reached, the parties will always have the statutory outlet to get the law changed.[117] The ability of the courts to impose their will on contending parties in Northern Ireland is further undermined by the capacity of parties to appeal to other bodies, including the British and Irish Governments. A court decision would undoubtedly have a political impact but is unlikely to be a decisive one.

Nevertheless, the research does suggest that the use of the courts in inter-executive disputes such as *De Brún and McGuinness* or *Morrow and Campbell* indicates they can play a useful role and one that can be built on. Trust was not significantly undermined by the resort to the courts and all parties appeared to accept the result. We would suggest that this is something which could be built on if devolved government is restored to Northern Ireland and which might diminish the instability inherent in attempting to construct a government in a deeply divided society. However, for this to occur a number of things may have to take place.

One is that the courts would need to accept, and then play a more active role in explicating, Northern Ireland's constitutional norms. These are constitutional principles which, while remaining within the UK system, differ somewhat from those which prevail at Westminster. As with courts in many other constitutional democracies their role may shift from being there simply to decide disputes on the meaning of a particular statutory provision or common law rule to more broadly articulating the underlying constitutional principles and how this particular dispute relates to them. Such an approach could help structure and guide both institution building and political decision-making in Northern Ireland. However,

---

are developed. See further Stephen Livingstone, 'And Justice for All? The Judiciary and the Legal Profession in Transition', in Colin Harvey (ed.), *Human Rights, Equality and Democratic Renewal, in Northern Ireland* (2001) 131–62; and Stephen Livingstone, Kieran McEvoy, Rachel Rebouche, and Paul Mageean, *Lawyers, Judges and Human Rights in the Northern Ireland Transition* (2006).

[117] For eg, it is quite clear that if the Secretary of State had lost the *Robinson* case there would not have been an election; instead retrospective legislation would have been passed to validate the appointment of the First and Deputy First Minister, even if this might have carried significant political costs.

this will only be possible if all parties, including the UK Government, show a greater willingness to abide by decisions of the courts as a means of resolving political disputes.[118] Secondly, there needs to be a recognition that judges may be doing a different role than the essentially technical task of deciding disputes. If one suggests that in a complex constitutional democracy they may have to articulate constitutional values and resolve the balance of power between different power centres in the constitution, then it may be we are looking for different sorts of people than have been judges in the past. This is not to criticize the current judiciary, who have been acting according to one vision of the judicial role, nor is it to suggest that the judiciary should be effectively politicized. Rather it is to note that in such a complex democracy, especially if a Bill of Rights is added in, judges will inevitably be drawn into political disputes and that those best suited to the role may be those who can carefully negotiate tensions between law and politics, not those who think they should be avoiding the latter altogether. This vision may suggest a different concept of 'merit' from that which prevails if the judicial task is essentially technical. These are issues with which the Northern Ireland Judicial Appointments Commission will engage.[119] It suggests further that there may be a need to revisit the structure of the judiciary. It is far from clear that all courts will need to deal with such complex constitutional issues. The vast majority of cases will still turn on factual disputes and routine legal interpretation. In many continental European States provision is made for a Constitutional Court to which complex constitutional issues can be referred, leaving other courts free of the need to deal with such issues. The idea of a Constitutional Court surfaced only briefly in the negotiations and then was advanced largely on the South African analogy, that there was a need for a 'new' court to develop public confidence in the new constitution. This analogy found little favour with some and the issue was not pursued to any great extent. Moreover, there are significant constitutional problems in fitting a Northern Irish Constitutional Court into the UK judicial hierarchy. However, if the case for a Constitutional Court is based more on the need for the courts to play a different role it may receive a more sympathetic hearing.[120]

These conclusions about how the Agreement impacts on the constitutional politics of Northern Ireland do not exhaust the importance of the Northern Ireland constitution for the wider UK constitutional context. As has been argued consistently, there is much in the new constitutional dispensation there that instructs us more widely about directions that can be taken in the new post-devolution, post-Human Rights Act British constitution. Indeed, we believe that the anti-foundationalist foundations of the Northern Ireland constitution

[118] The example of President Mandela's acceptance of the decision of the Constitutional Court in the *Western Cape* case [1995] (4) SA 877 (CC), federalism decision is particularly valuable in demonstrating that judicial power is in large part dependent on political willingness to acknowledge its authority. [119] See http://www.nijac.org/Live/NIJAC_Site.htm.
[120] See further Brice Dickson, 'A Constitutional Court for Northern Ireland?', in Andrew Le Sueur (ed.), *Building the UK's New Supreme Court* (2004).

can perhaps indicate how a new, post-Diceyean constitution might develop beyond the sovereignty mode.

The lesson of the Northern Ireland constitution for the UK more widely is not just that it shows how that most troubled part of the polity might begin to find answers to how to live together through rights-based mechanisms which emphasize recognition of difference, equality, and partnership. It is rather to indicate a whole new approach to constitutionalism generally. We should consider the Northern Ireland settlement as less about the British standing above the quarrelling natives and producing a constitutionally ingenious fix to an historic problem and more about a challenge to the whole British style of constitutionalism. Here we have an approach that suggests that the State itself is a constitutional actor and should submit to a constitution of rights, equality, and process. The Belfast Agreement (and to a lesser extent the NIA 1998) pick up and run further and faster with trends nascent in the Human Rights Act 1998 that speak towards encompassing the State within the law rather than the State being simply the source of law as to how it runs its affairs best. Although the peace process is often portrayed simplistically as either the more or less complicit British having a final meddle in a post-colonial spasm, or in a narrative where the British and others are standing above the various factions of uneasy Irish who need to have peace brokered between them, it is much more than either of these crude stereotypes. There is an element about the people of Ireland—both within the north and across the border—trying to find ways to accommodate each other and decide fundamental questions about how to live together. But it is also about all actors, including the State submitting to, and then contributing to, a constitution which provides a framework of law and rights to challenge fundamentally the existing normative or representational basis of sovereignty-based constitutionalism. This is different from the other constitutional settlements in Britain, which are mainly about rearranging institutions and modernizing the operation of government. It picks up on nascent trends in the Human Rights Act 1998, and by rooting these in international standards and a politics of recognition, it changes the sphere of operation of the constitution as nothing else in the Blair project has done.

The implications of this for all constitutional actors are huge and will need to be worked out. However, as the focus here is largely on judges we would like to say that as UK judges generally begin to think about how they can begin to fashion a full Bill of Rights from the Human Rights Act 1998 and the meagre and largely atheoretical jurisprudence from Strasbourg, they might like to consider more closely the challenges already introduced by the Northern Ireland constitution. This will involve an acknowledgement of the political nature of the judicial role in a constitution of rights and devolution, European standards, and post-Dicyean justification. Martin Shapiro and Alec Stone Sweet have written about how acknowledging that the American courts are significant actors in American politics produces 'a considerable liberation of intellectual energies', thereby allowing us to think about the dynamics of the constitution unhampered by 'endlessly sophisticated reassertion(s) of judicial independence, neutrality, and apoliticism'.[121] Such an acknowledgment in the UK context would produce a similar liberation. This is so particularly as we seek to understand the foundations of the new constitution in ways that move beyond traditional references to simple ideas of parliamentary sovereignty. This task of developing these understandings is something that Stephen Livingstone would have relished and it is a significant loss to all of us that he is not here to do so further.

---

[121] See Martin Shapiro and Alec Stone Sweet, *On Law, Politics and Judicialization* (2002) 4. Commenting on the impossibility of squeezing politics out of a system of entrenched human rights law, Conor Gearty recently talked in terms of how it is a 'perpetuation of a Lockean delusion to believe that these pre-political truths exist' and how 'persevering with such folly merely causes the guardians of these impossible truths—the judiciary—to be infected with the very political virus from which they are supposed to be protecting the rest of their society'. See Conor Gearty, *Can Human Rights Survive?* The Hamlyn Lectures 2005 (2006) 86.

PART II
TRANSITION

8

The Battle for Transitional Justice: Hegemony, Iraq, and International Law

*Christine Bell, Colm Campbell, and Fionnuala Ní Aoláin**

Introduction

This essay explores the interplay of two seemingly contradictory international law trends impacting on transitional justice discourses. In the first, transitional justice appears as an attempt to extend the reach of international law, in particular its human rights and humanitarian standards, both in negotiated transitions from violent conflict, and in shifts from authoritarian rule to more liberal political arrangements.[1]

The second (contradictory) trend is that of an apparent move away from international law as a restraining force, and the (re)presentation of it as uniquely susceptible or subject to the interpretations and retrenchment of the hegemonic power—the United States.[2] There are many illustrations of this dominance, but it can most evidently be seen in the apparent assault on the United Nations Charter limitations on the use of force (evidenced in Iraq, and to a lesser extend in Kosovo and Afghanistan), and what appears to be the attempted interpretative re-shaping of the agreed treaty definitions of torture.[3]

* We are grateful to Professor David Kretzmer of the Hebrew University Jerusalem and to Professor Ruti Teitel of New York Law School for their comments on a draft of this essay, and to Ita Connolly (Transitional Justice Institute) and Catherine O'Rourke (Transitional Justice Institute) for assistance with research in its production. Responsibility for the views expressed lies solely with the authors.

[1] See generally Christine Bell, Colm Campbell, and Fionnuala Ní Aoláin, 'Justice Discourses in Transition' (2004) 13 Social and Legal Studies 305 (for overview of a broad notion of transitional justice discourse and its relationship to international law).

[2] This trend is identified by many as the 'Bush Doctrine'. See National Security Strategy of the United States of America, March 2006, at http://www.whitehouse.gov/nsc/nss/2006/index.html; Thomas Franck, 'Preemption, Prevention and Anticipatory Self-Defense: New Law Regulating Recourse to Force?' (2004) 27 Hastings International and Comparative Law Review 425; Philippe Sands, *Lawless World America and the Making and Breaking of Global Rules* (2005).

[3] Karen J. Greenberg and Joshua L. Dratel (eds), *The Torture Papers: The Road to Abu Ghraib* (2005). Notable, and discussed later, is the traction of domestic and international law in response, see eg The McCain Amendment to the 2006 Department of Defence Appropriations Bill, at http://mccain.senate.gov/index.cfm?fuseaction=NewsCenter.ViewPressRelease&Content_id=1611.

Both trends can offer a nuanced view of international law's relationship to politics. However, ultimately they appear to reinforce two quite different views of this nexus, providing opposite answers to the question of whether law has a normative compliance-pull or is merely politics in disguised form.[4]

The first trend assumes a significant degree of autonomy in international law norms. Crucially, law is seen as having a mediating capacity.[5] In short States are understood to be required to accommodate their behaviour to the norms of international law, even if assessments of compatibility are likely to involve a range of contextual factors (including the 'pull' of powerful States on the law).[6]

The second trend appears to bolster more 'realist' dismissals of international law as almost completely defined by the interplay of international power politics, and therefore having little independent autonomous normative basis and little mediating capacity in the case of powerful States.[7] On this view a clash between legal norms and the exercise of hegemonic power is likely to lead either to norm-shift (facilitating the hegemon), or to a dismissal of international law by the hegemon (thereby weakening law's compliance-pull for all States).

Clearly these contradictory trends preceded both the 'war on terror' and the war in Iraq, but both these conflicts have given a new vitality to time-worn controversies. The debate is driven in large part by the fact that the central foreign actor in the Iraq legal *imbroglio*, the US, enjoys an unprecedented military, political, and (to a lesser extent), economic superiority.[8] It is clear that since the end

---

[4] The resonance to the realist school of international law is clear. See generally Kenneth N. Waltz, *Theory of International Politics* (1979); Inis L. Claude, *Power and International Relations* (1962); Ernest Haas, 'The Balance of Power: Prescription, Concept, or Propaganda' (1953) 5 World Politics 442; Kenneth N. Waltz, 'Realist Thought and Neorealist Theory' (1990) 44 Journal of International Affairs 21; A.F.K. Organski, *World Politics* (2nd rev. ed., 1968).

[5] In Antonio Cassese's formulation, international law is not simply a prescriptive framework, but also a 'mediating paradigm', Antonio Cassese, *International Law in a Divided World* (1986).

[6] Cf Higgins's view of international law as a 'process' in which '. . . context is always important', Rosalyn Higgins, *Problems and Process: International Law and How We Use It* (1994) 8. See generally Louis Henkin, *How Nations Behave* (2nd ed., 1979) and Harold Hongju Koh, 'Why Do Nations Obey International Law?' (1997) 106 Yale Law Journal 2599.

[7] For other realist accounts of international law, see Hans J. Morgenthau, *Politics Among Nations: The Struggles for Power and Peace* (6th ed., 1985); Edward Hallet Carr, *Twenty Years' Crisis, 1919–1939*: An Introduction to the Study of International Relations (2nd ed., 1951); George Frost Kennan, *Realities of American Foreign Policy* (1954); Dean G. Acheson, 'Foreign Policy of the United States' (1964) 18 Arkansas Law Review 225; Arnold Wolfers, *Discord and Collaboration: Essays on International Politics* (1962).

[8] Michael Byers and Georg Nolte (eds), *United States Hegemony and the Foundations of International Law* (2003); Michael J. Glennon 'American Hegemony in an Unplanned World Order' (2000) 5 Journal of Conflict and Security Law 3; Rosemary Foot, S. Neil McFarlane and Michael Mastanduno (eds), *US Hegemony and International Organizations: The United States and Multilateral Institutions* (2003). For a view on the positive obligations this creates for the US, see Lea Brilmayer, *American Hegemony: Political Morality in a One Superpower World* (1994). For a discussion of the UK position vis-a-viz US hegemony, see Colm Campbell, ' "Wars on Terror" and Vicarious Hegemons: The UK, International Law, and the Northern Ireland Conflict', (2005) 54 International and Comparative Law Quarterly 321. For analyses of Gramsci's views on hegemony (focusing on hegemonic processes rather than hegemonic states) see n 24 below.

of the Cold War, the position occupied by the US has been less that of a 'super power', than, in the words of the former French foreign minister, Herbert Vredine, a 'hyperpower'.[9] The strength of this dominance inevitably brings to the fore debates about the future of international law, and specifically whether international law has any normative restraining force in respect of the exercise of hegemonic power.[10]

Discussion of the applicability of 'transitional justice' analyses to the Iraqi situation further sharpens these issues. The US and its coalition partners have chosen to adopt and justify their actions in Iraq by using amongst others, the label of transitional justice to characterize them.[11] Thus, 'transition' in Iraq has become a site for engagement with broader debates about the direction of both international law and transitional justice. Justifications for the invasion have been variable and mutable (notoriously so), but with the failure to find weapons of mass destruction, the human rights abuses and the undemocratic nature of the former Ba'athist regime have assumed ever greater importance as providing a retrospective justification to validate the political legitimacy of the invasion.[12] Within this frame the intervention was aimed, at least partly, at effecting a 'transition to democracy'. Having intervened, the occupying power was left with little choice but to police the past that confronted it using classic transitional justice mechanisms. Specifically it resorted to the processes of lustration and criminal trial as the means to deal with the 'past' of the previous regime.

---

[9] Hubert Védrine and Dominique Moisi, *France in an Age of Globalisation* (2001). However, holding this position is not without negative implications for the State. See Eyal Benvenisti, 'The US and the Use of Force: Double Edged Hegemony and the Management of Global Emergencies' (2004) 15 European Journal of International Law 677, 677–700 (discussing global and US approaches to the management of global security risks).

[10] American Journal of International Law Symposium, 'Future Implications of the Iraq Conflict' (2004) 98 American Journal of International Law 1.

[11] US official discourse frequently uses the term 'transition' with reference to Iraq, eg in President Bush's speech of 1 May 2003 referring to '[T]he transition from dictatorship to democracy', at http://www.whitehouse.gov/news/releases/2003/05/print/20030501-15.html. Likewise, the rhetoric of 'justice' has been invoked in relation to the establishment of the Iraqi Special Tribunal to try Saddam Hussein and senior Ba'ath party officials. In language couched in familiar transitional justice terms, the US-installed administrator stated in 2004 that '[T]his Special Tribunal serves a purpose beyond bringing criminals to justice. The Tribunal becomes a national remembrance for the hundreds of thousands murdered by Saddam's regime.' The speech also emphasized Bremer's establishment of a 'National Commission for Remembrance' to considered proposals on 'how best to memorialize the suffering of Iraq's many communities under Saddam' (therefore excluding abuses associated with the invasion), 'Turning the Page', the televised speech by L. Paul Bremer III, Administrator, Coalition Provision Authority, 23 April 2004, at http://www.iraqcoalition.org/transcripts/20040423_page_turn.html. See generally Eric Stover, Hanny Megally, and Hania Mufi, 'Bremner's "Gordian Knot": Transitional Justice and the US Occupation of Iraq' (2005) 27 Human Rights Quarterly 830. For a 'transitional justice' analysis from within the US military see 'Rule of Law in Iraq: Transitional Justice under Occupation', a monograph by Major Leonard J. Law, United States Army, School of Advanced Military Studies, US Army Command and General Staff College, Fort Levenworth, Kansas, at http://www.smallwarsjournal.com/documents/law.pdf.

[12] See speech by George W. Bush to the United States Chamber of Commerce on the 20th Anniversary of the National Endowment for Democracy, 6 November 2003, at http://www.whitehouse.gov/news/releases/2003/11/print/20031106-2.html.

Implementation of this approach included the direct role played by the US-installed administrator in the 'de-Ba'athicization' programme affecting the military, police, civil service, and other government structures. It is also evidenced by the trial of Saddam Hussein and some senior Ba'athist officials (albeit with the US ostensibly at arm's length, though providing much practical and jurisprudential infrastructure).[13]

In these processes the US has played the role of the primary instigating subject. Paradoxically, however, US actions in Iraq and more generally in the 'war on terror' may have also cast it in a different and much less comfortable role—that of the possible object of transitional justice. Allegations of abuses in Abu Ghraib and the Guantanamo Bay regime provide the most cogent examples.

Examination of transitional justice discourse in Iraq has a contemporary analytic currency in several spheres. First, it throws light on the nature of the hegemonic project and its relationship to law. Secondly, it provides a new perspective on the fluidity of contemporary transitional justice discourses. Most importantly, it shows the importance of transitional justice discourse to the hegemonic project, revealing a point of resistance for those asserting the normative force of international law in general, and the importance of its human rights norms in particular. Part I of this essay maps the current fluidity of both the transitional justice and the hegemonic projects, exploring a range of possible meanings for both terms. Part II illustrates how transitional justice and hegemony interact in two specific areas: 'dealing with the past' and 'governance in transition'. These examples are used to claim that transitional justice discourse is a key battleground in the move towards hegemony.[14] Rather than taking solely an abstract critical approach, the analysis in this essay is also presented in instrumental terms—the aim is to provide an understanding of the ideological battleground that can inform those who wish to resist the dismantling of international human rights law, or indeed international law itself. The goal here is to continue Stephen Livingstone's legacy of combining academic rigour and insight to real-world struggles for justice. The essay points to the resilience of international law's normative force, rooted not just in principle, but in its ability to offer practical tools for emerging from conflict and political change. It argues that while the fact of US dominance has to be recognized, this dominance will not necessarily be successful in co-opting transitional justice and human rights discourse in the exercise of hegemonic power.

---

[13] For somewhat differing assessments of resort to the Iraqi Special Tribunal for the trial of Saddam Hussein, see Ruti Teitel, 'The Law and Politics of Contemporary Transitional Justice' (2005) 38 Cornell International Law Journal 3; Farhad Malekian, 'Emasculating the Philosophy of International Criminal Justice in the Iraqi Tribunal' (2005) 38 Cornell International Law Journal 38, and Tom Parker, 'Prosecuting Saddam: The Coalition Provisional Authority and the Evolution of the Iraqi Special Tribunal' (2005) 38 Cornell International Law Journal 3.

[14] Some have argued that this goes further and constitutes an attempt to establish 'empire', see Michael Hardt and Antonio Negri, *Multitude: War and Democracy in the Age of Empire* (2005).

Transitional Justice and Hegemony

Transitional Justice

While transitional justice has traditionally been conceived of as a discourse centrally concerned with 'dealing with the past', Teitel has usefully set out an historiographic genealogy which identifies three phases in a more nuanced use of the term.[15] Phase I grew from the immediate experience post-Second World War, and was characterized by reliance on a past-focused international law-mandated model of criminal accountability exemplified in the Nuremberg trials. While the on-going relevance of this phase was limited given its historical contingency, a key legacy was its move from collective to individual accountability. Phase II, which began with the decline of Soviet power that ultimately led to the end of the Cold War, was marked by a reliance on domestic national devices—typically the 'truth commission' (also past-focused). These were often employed in clearly instrumentalist 'nation-building' projects with a contingent relationship to domestic political constraints. The key legacy of this phase lies in the mediation of international law's normative demands in the light of the dilemmas posed by the need to sustain 'peace' (conceived as the absence of violent conflict). Creative approaches to the competing demands of accountability and amnesty through novel institutional mechanisms, such as truth commissions, were justified as necessary to effecting transition.[16] In Phase III, the contemporary phase, Teitel argues that the importance of the 'past-focus' of transitional justice has given way to a 'steady-state transitional justice' which has moved 'from the periphery to the center'.[17] The most obvious 'steady state' mechanism is the newly created International Criminal Court (ICC). While this would seem to mark a return to the Phase I universalization of the rule of law, Teitel demonstrates a much more ambivalent view of transitional justice as a concept which operates to universalize the exception (rule of law as secondary to the needs of transition). The concept may therefore be open to appropriation in an attempt to re-work mainstream understandings of international legal norms.

What was viewed as a legal phenomenon associated with extraordinary post-conflict conditions now increasingly appears to be a reflection of ordinary times. There is a process of normalization with ambivalent consequences, particularly when this conception of transitional justice is yoked to the instrumental goals of the war on terror.[18]

---

[15]　Ruti Teitel, 'Transitional Justice Genealogy' (2003) 16 Harvard Human Rights Journal 69.

[16]　See the South African Truth and Reconciliation Commission model and the justifications for it, in particular: South African Truth and Reconciliation Commission Report Vol.1, Ch 5, para 100 (1999); *Azanian Peoples Organization (AZAPO) and Others v President of the Republic of South Africa and Others*, CCT17/96, 15 July 1995, 25 (South African Constitutional Court dismissal of challenge to amnesty law as a violation of international law).

[17]　Teitel, *Transitional Justice Genealogy*, n 15 above, 89.　　[18]　ibid, 90.

To give an example, this 'steady-state' transitional justice tends to conflate humanitarian and human rights law (though the degree of this overlap remains contested). The conflation is most evident in the statutes and jurisprudence of the International Criminal Tribunal for the Former Yugoslavia and the International Criminal Tribunal for Rwanda, which draw heavily from both legal streams.[19] Conflation has been useful during violent conflict in bringing the restraining application of law to bear on both State and non-State actors.[20] However, as Teitel points out, conflated application in the transitional justice situation also enables the on-going application of humanitarian law post-conflict, that is, in times of 'peace'. In a subtle way this underwrites and legitimates the 'war' against terrorism by suggesting that these standards have a broader relevance, particularly in the context of this permanent war, which requires exceptionality all the time.[21] While transitional justice discourse may operate to extend the reach of international human rights and humanitarian law, it may also work less positively by enabling agendas of the US and others, to exercise dominance, in particular regional or conflict-specific contexts. The discourse can facilitate dubious legal categorizations which provide ongoing arguments for exceptionality, with dominant states uniquely empowered to claim whether and how international law applies.

Hegemony

The term 'hegemony' has a range of possible meanings in the fields of international relations, international law, and in analyses of social domination, thus demanding clarification of terminology.[22] Rather than emphasizing hegemony as straightforward 'predominance' with its connotations of unilateral or hierarchical exercises of power (the classic 'realist' understanding in international relations), this essay suggests that the term may more usefully be employed as referring to a project for dominance by powerful States through ideological redefinition. This view is compatible with Nolte's interpretation of Triepel's view of hegemony as being less the power of a State to force another State to behave in a certain way, than as a characteristic relationship between the attitude of the leading State and the attitude of those which it leads. This involves softer exercises of power located

---

[19] Statute of the International Criminal Tribunal for the former Yugoslavia, U.N. Doc. S/RES/827 (1993), Art. 1–5; Statute of the International Criminal Tribunal for Rwanda, U.N. Doc. S/RES/955 (1994), Art. 1–4.

[20] For somewhat differing views from the International Court of Justice on parallel application, see *Legality of the Threat or Use of Nuclear Weapons*, Advisory Opinion (1996); *International Court of Justice Reports* 226 (1997); 35 *International Legal Materials* 809 (1996) (*Nuclear Weapons*); *Legal Consequences of the Construction of a Wall in the Occupied Palestinian Territory*, Advisory Opinion, 9 July 2004, at http://www.icj-cij.org/icjwww/idocket/imwp/imwpframe.htm (*The Wall*).

[21] This is the argument also made by Kretzmer when he notes a recent tendency of States to activate the applicability of international humanitarian law so as to allow maximum action against so-called combatants. David Kretzmer, 'Targeted Killing of Suspected Terrorists: Extra-Judicial Executions or Legitimate Means of Defence?' (2005) 16 European Journal of International Law 171.

[22] See n 8 above.

somewhere between subordination and mere influence,[23] an understanding that can be buttressed by transposition to the international arena of Gramsci's view of hegemony as the process by which a powerful group produces 'consent' to its domination.[24] In domination by force, ideology need play little role; in consensual dominance, ideology is likely to be central.

Hegemony as 'predominance' tends to lead to the stark legal choices favoured by realists; international law either moulds itself to the requirements of the hegemon or the hegemon ignores it with impunity. However, the more nuanced, softer conception of hegemony lays the groundwork for a more finely tuned conceptualization of the hegemon's engagement with international law.

The possible relationship of hegemony to international law set out by Michael Byers suggests a spectrum between soft and hard options.[25] When the hegemon's preferred course of conduct runs up against international legal norms a number of possibilities present themselves.[26] The first is to violate the law. This leads to anarchy in international affairs, which is likely to prove inefficient for the hegemon's exercise of power, requiring constant threats of the use of force. The second option is to create an exceptional regime for the hegemon.[27] International law may permit such a regime, but in practice there is likely to be significant resistance to its creation (particularly if the special regime sanctions the use of force). Even where such agreement is possible, there are costs to the hegemon in placing itself outside the frame of the well-established doctrine of sovereign equality. The third option is to change the generally applicable rules so as to further the hegemon's own interests. This is in many respects the most attractive choice for the hegemon, particularly if the general rules can be changed in a manner that while claiming to be

---

[23] See Georg Nolte, 'Conclusion: A Historical Question and Contemporary Responses', in Michael Byers and Georg Nolte (eds) *United States Hegemony and the Foundations of International Law*, n 8 above, 492–93, drawing on Heinrich Triepel *Die Hegemonie—Ein Buch von Fuhrenden Staaten* (1938). Also note, *inter alia*, Benvenisti's account of the relationship between hegemony and common security, n 9 above.

[24] For an analysis of Gramsci's view of hegemony (which were based on power-relations within the capitalist states of Gramsci's time) see Joseph V. Femia, *Gramsci's Political Thought: Hegemony, Consciousness and the Revolutionary Process* (1981). For transposition of Gramsci's analyses to the international law arena see Balakrishnan Rajagopal, *International Law from Below: Development, Social Movements and Third World Resistance* (2003) 17–21. For differing interpretations of the applicability of Gramscian analyses to the field of international relations, see William I. Robinson, 'Gramsci and Globalisation: From Nation-State to Transnational Hegemony' (2005) 8 Critical Review of International Social and Political Philosophy 559, and Robert W. Cox, 'Gramsci, Hegemony and International Relations: An Essay in Method' (1983) 12 Millenium: Journal of International Studies 162. The focus in this paper remains on international law and the hegemonic State (rather than on hegemony by transnational social groups).

[25] Michael Byers, 'Preemptive Self-defense: Hegemony, Equality and Strategies of Legal Change' (2003) 11 The Journal of Political Philosophy 171; cf Detlev F. Vagts, 'Hegemonic International Law' (2001) 95 American Journal of International Law 848.

[26] Byers, *'Preemptive Self-defense: Hegemony, Equality and Strategies of Legal Change'*, n 25 above, *passim*.

[27] On exceptional regimes generally, see Oren Gross, 'Chaos and Rules: Should Responses to Violent Crises Always Be Constitutional?' (2003) 112 Yale Law Journal 1011.

of general application, in effect privileges its position. The fourth option is one of co-operation and compromise—which is self-explanatory and also compatible with the exercise of 'soft' hegemony.

Byers argues convincingly that the US's current approach is closest to the third option (change generally applicable rules to further its own interest), with some shades of the fourth. Reliance on this third option reveals the importance of the ideological dimension to the hegemonic project. Change produced by straightforward military and political domination represents a hard notion of hegemony, while change produced by an ideological shift to which States become bought-in (and to that extent 'consent'), represents 'soft' hegemony, which paradoxically stands to be more profound.

It was suggested above that the ambivalences identified in the third phase of transitional justice discourse have created a key battleground in which to assert such an ideological shift, based on redefining central meanings of international law. This is because transitional justice discourses revolve around arguments over the need for an exceptional application of law during transition. Transitional justice's orientation around debates about exceptionality point to a 'twilight zone' for law that is uniquely susceptible to manipulation.[28] While transitional justice discourses have generally attempted to use this malleable quality of law to deliver liberal and transformative outcomes, its darker side is revealed by its contemporary appropriation. This can be illustrated by an exploration of two sites of intense attrition on the contemporary global transitional justice and human rights landscape: 'dealing with the past', and 'governance in transition'.[29]

Illustrating the Battlefield

Dealing with the Past

As noted above, the term 'transitional justice' has been most associated with attempts of successor regimes to hold past human rights abusers to account.[30] Transitional justice discourses with respect to the past seemed to provide evidence of the extending reach of human rights law, and in particular an attempt by international law to 'plug a gap' with respect to past violations of human rights. This

---

[28] Cf Oscar Schachter, 'The Twilight Existence of Nonbinding International Agreements' (1977) 71 American Journal of International Law 296.

[29] For an overview of what we conceive of as the broad transitional justice terrain, see Bell, Campbell, and Ní Aoláin, 'Justice Discourses in Transition', n 1 above, 305. See also Ruti Teitel, *Transitional Justice* (2000); *The Rule of Law and Transitional Justice in Conflict and Post-conflict Societies, Report of the Secretary-General*, UN Doc. S/2004/616.

[30] See Diane F. Orentlicher, 'Settling Accounts: The Duty to Prosecute Human Rights Violations of a Prior Regime' (1991) 100 Yale Law Journal 2537; Neil J.Kritz (ed.), *Transitional Justice: How Emerging Democracies Reckon with Former Regimes* (1995); Martha Minow, *Between Vengeance and Forgiveness: Facing History after Genocide and Mass Violence* (1998).

approach was viewed as exerting a normative constraint on peace agreements, with a particular salience in relation to the thorny issue of amnesty. As Arroht-Arriaza and Gibson noted in 1998, over time 'the trend has been from broader to more tailored, from sweeping to qualified, from laws with no reference to international law to those which explicitly try to stay within its strictures'.[31] These shifts were underwritten by a number of developments in international law—the creep of universal jurisdiction for serious international crimes;[32] the notion that the repression of breaches under Protocol II (1977) to the 1945 Geneva Conventions might involve a mandatory rather than a permissive jurisdiction;[33] and the establishment both of *ad hoc* Tribunals for the former Yugoslavia and Rwanda, and of the International Criminal Court.[34] The increasing use of both humanitarian and human rights law as a means to address conflict-related violations appeared to offer broader opportunities for addressing all levels of violent conflict, and all its actors.[35] The UN has, since its famous 'dissent' from the broad amnesty of Sierra Leone's Lomé Agreement, nailed its colours to the mast as a 'normative negotiator', unwilling to sign peace agreements with blanket amnesties or mechanisms which rely on the death penalty.[36] These developments cannot be dismissed as anything other than a clear move in the direction of increased accountability, and an extension of human rights and humanitarian law's constraints.

Other developments, however, point to a more ambiguous relationship between transitional justice and international law. As Teitel points out, Nuremberg's

---

[31] Naomi Roht-Arriaza and Lauren Gibson, 'The Developing Jurisprudence on Amnesty' (1998) 20 Human Rights Quarterly 843, 884.

[32] Theodore Meron, *Human Rights and Humanitarian Norm as Customary Law* (1998), 235–44. See also Michael Bothe, 'War Crimes in Non-International Armed Conflicts' in Yoram Dinstein and Mala Tabory (eds), *War Crimes in International Law* (1996).

[33] Meron, *Human Rights and Humanitarian Norm as Customary Law*, ibid, 252, argues that national States should be regarded as having an obligation to prosecute, as 'a failure to prosecute violators of clauses other than grave breaches would call into question a state's good faith compliance with its treaty obligations'. It can be argued, however, that if a discretion to prosecute exists, then it is the exercise of this discretion which must be done in good faith.

[34] On these developments, see generally Christine Bell, *Peace Agreements and Human Rights* (2000); see also Christine Bell, *The Role of Human Rights in Peace Agreements* (2006), Ch 5. Cf *Report of the Independent Expert to Update the Set of Principles to Combat Impunity, Diane Orentlicher, Addendum: Updated Set of Principles for the Protection and Promotion of Human Rights through Action to Combat Impunity*, UN Commission on Human Rights, 61st Sess., Item 17, UN Doc. E/CN.4/2005/102/Add.1 (8 February, 2005). Statute of the International Criminal Tribunal for the former Yugoslavia, U.N. Doc. S/RES/827 (1993); Statute of the International Criminal Tribunal for Rwanda, U.N. Doc. S/RES/955 (1994). Rome Statute of the International Criminal Court, 17 July 1998, U.N. Doc. A/CONF.183/9.

[35] See Colm Campbell, 'Peace and the Laws of War: The Role of International Humanitarian Law in the Post-Conflict Environment' (2000) 82 International Review of the Red Cross 627.

[36] See Peace Agreement between the Republic of Sierra Leone and the Revolutionary United Front of Sierra Leone (RUF/SL), 7 July 1999, Art. IX (amnesty provision); See *Seventh Report of the Secretary-General on the United Nations Observer Mission in Sierra Leone*, UN SCOR, UN Doc. S/1999/836 (1999) (reporting the UN disclaimer); cf Teitel, *The Rule of Law and Transitional Justice in Conflict and Post-conflict Societies*, n 29 above (provides for a series of recommendations for negotiations, peace agreements, and Security Council mandates).

model of accountability had begun to move the focus of responsibility from State action to that of individuals (Phase I). This shift in focus became more marked in Phase II, as domestic or hybrid mechanisms 'privatized' transitional justice. Its imprint can also be seen in the international community's failure to define 'crime of aggression' in the Rome Statute of the ICC;[37] in continual pressure for opt-outs for the human rights violations of international peacekeepers; and indeed in the accountability gaps for international actors more generally during transition (Phase III).[38]

A second ambivalence can be seen in the use of international transitional justice mechanisms as in-effect *ex post facto* face-savers for the international community in situations where a failure to act decisively meant that it stood accused of enabling dramatic human rights abuses (Bosnia), and even genocide (Rwanda). The imposition of an international mechanism to deal with human rights abuses in the wake of these conflicts operated so as to subtly assist the development of a (still contested) doctrine of humanitarian intervention, as evidenced most clearly by the situation of Kosovo.[39]

These ambivalences have operated at the centre of the search for ideological shift in the situation of Iraq and the 'war on terror' (the two being linked in this context). In Iraq, the US has used past-focused transitional justice discourse to justify and underwrite 'de-Ba'athicization' processes, which had a clear link to notions of victory in the preceding conflict.[40] Aside from serious questions over the competence of the process, US labeling of it as 'transitional justice' attempts at a subtle level to justify its own role as 'democratizer' rather than 'occupier'—casting it in a 'quasi-UN' position.

This also facilitated the US in defining 'the' conflict (or the undemocratic era for which accountability is required)—as being the one that preceded and was 'ended' by its own use of force.[41] The difficulty of using current transitional justice discourse to address the rights and wrongs of recourse to inter-State conflict has

[37] Although technically, drafting continues and so this may be resolved. See Rome Statute of the International Criminal Court, 17 July, 1998, U.N. Doc. A/CONF.183/9, Art. 5.2.

[38] Guglielmo Verdirame, 'UN accountability for human rights violations in post-conflict situations', in Nigel White and Dirk Klassen (eds), *The UN, Human Rights and Post-Conflict Situations* (2005); John Cerone, 'Reasonable measures in unreasonable circumstances: a legal responsibility framework for human rights violations in post-conflict territories under UN administration', in White and Klassen, *The UN, Human Rights and Post-Conflict Situations*, op cit. 42, 80; Frederic Megret and Florian Hoffmann, 'The UN as a Human Rights Violator? Some Reflections on the United Nations Changing Human Rights Responsibilities' (2003) 25 Human Rights Quarterly 314.

[39] Cf Teitel, 'Transitional Justice Genealogy', n 15 above, 91.

[40] See, 'Coalition Provisional Authority Memorandum Number 1: Implementation of De-Baathification Order No. 1' (CPA/ORD/16 May 2003/01); 'Coalition Provisional Authority Memorandum Number 5: Establishment of the Iraqi De-Baathification Council Order' (CPA/ORD/25 May 2003/05; 'Coalition Provisional Authority Memorandum Number 7: Delegation of Authority Under De-Baathification' Order No. 1 (CPA/ORD/16 May 2003/01. 'Turning the Page', the televised speech by L. Paul Bremer III, Administrator, Coalition Provision Authority, 23 April 2004, at http://www.iraqcoalition.org/transcripts/20040423_page_turn.html.

[41] See further n 11 above.

enabled the US to invoke the term while resisting its application to its own acts. The more the US can use the discourses of transitional justice, human rights, and democratization to characterize and justify its actions, the more it can validate its own democratic and peace-building credentials in Iraq. This potentially enables the US to distinguish its own actions from those of the previous regime. The use of transitional justice discourses to bring accountability mechanisms to bear on Saddam regime violations, and the rejection of the discourse with relation to US/coalition forces, are not straightforward acts of hypocrisy or inconsistency. Rather, they evidence an ideological battle, potentially serving to redefine both human rights 'values' and 'transitional justice'.[42]

The debates concerning torture are particularly revealing in relation to the question of confining transitional justice discourses to the pre-war situation in Iraq. If the reach of the norm can be limited, there may be no 'past' for which US/coalition forces to be called to account for.[43] Two prongs to the assault on the torture norm can be identified—the first substantive, the second procedural. Central to the substantive assault is the definition of the term 'torture', and more particularly, the issue of hegemonic control over its definition. The Bush Administration has given somewhat inconsistent responses to the question of what constitutes torture[44] and whether or not US forces and/or agents were engaged in practices that might be defined as torture.[45] There is a suggestion that the definition of torture should be dependent on context, privileging the behaviour of democratic over non-democratic States, in a way that echoes the language of the infamous doctrine of (former) US Secretary of State Jean Kirkpatrick drawing a distinction between authoritarian and totalitarian regimes.[46]

The second prong of the attack on the torture norm operates quite differently. It focuses on reducing liability or accountability for the torture of others. The torture of unjust regimes can in practice be permitted, and even enabled, by decisions that it does not taint the use of evidence by western liberal democracies

---

[42] *In Larger Freedom: Towards Development, Security and Human Rights for All, Report of the Secretary-General*, UN Doc. A/59/2005 (2005), para 128 (referring to 'the universal values [sic] of the rule of law, human rights and democracy').

[43] This paradox is not without substantial legal significance. If we remember the *Nicaragua v US*, ICJ, 27 June, 1986, decision in which it was noted that reference to the norm itself, even as its content and effect were being disputed, constituted evidence of the customary law status of the questioned norm.

[44] See Karen J.Greenberg (ed.), *The Torture Debate in America* (2005).

[45] Some of these inconsistencies can be found in the response of many democratic States to times of crisis, see eg *Ireland v UK* (1978) 2 EHRR 25; David Kretzmer, *The Occupation of Justice: The Supreme Court of Israel and the Occupied Territories* (2002); Ruth Gavison 'The Role of Courts in Rifted Democracies' (1999) 33 Israel Law Review 216. See also Eyal Benvenisti, 'Role of National Courts in Preventing Torture of Suspected Terrorists', The Symposium: The Changing Structure of International Law Revisited (Part 2)' (1997) 8 European Journal of International Law 596.

[46] Jeane J. Kirkpatrick, 'Dictatorships and Double Standards', (1977) *Commentary*, November, 34–45.

whose reputation depends on not carrying out torture.[47] Thus, the blanket nature of the prohibition is undermined by placing the burden of proof on those being tortured, reversing decades of treaty-making and jurisprudential trends that have pushed the norm towards requiring States to take positive steps to ensure that torture does not occur.[48]

This two-pronged (substantive and procedural) attack would seem to bear out Byers' multi-faceted account of the relationship of the US hegemon to international law. The US position on torture is a complex one, with the situation still in flux. However, it provides some evidence of an attempt at norm-redefinition so as to meet its own preferences while maintaining a formal commitment to the prohibition on torture in international law.

Governance in Transition

The relationship between transitional justice discourse and the battle for hegemony can similarly be illustrated by the quite different example of 'governance and rule of law in transition'. The deployment of inter-State force, from Bosnia, to Kosovo, to East Timor, and to Afghanistan, has given rise to a need to reconstruct domestic constitutional processes, post-victory (or post-settlement), while providing for governance in the transitional period during which they are being reconstructed. These situations evidence an emerging pattern in how this process is managed.[49] First, UN Security Council (UNSC) resolutions establish a mandate for establishment of an International Territorial Administration (ITA).[50] Secondly, the ITA appoints a Transitional Government—multi-ethnic where relevant—which is gradually given increasing powers.[51] Thirdly, there is a progression (though sequencing can vary) in the Transitional Government's role, from consultation towards limited direct exercise of power, in an attempt to prepare the way for elections[52] and the drafting of a new constitution to replace the interim

---

[47] See *A and others v Secretary of State for the Home Department* (No 2) [2005] 3 WLR 1249; [2005] UKHL 71 HL; The Center for Human Rights and Global Justice, 'Torture by Proxy: International Law Applicable to "Extraordinary Renditions"' (2005).

[48] Convention Against Torture and Other Cruel, Inhuman or Degrading Treatment or Punishment, UN Doc. A/39/51 (1985), Art. 2.

[49] This next section is drawn from Christine Bell, 'Peace Agreements: Their Nature and Legal Status' (2006) 100 American Journal of International Law 1–40.

[50] Kosovo: SC Res. 1244 (19 June 1999). East Timor: SC Res. 1272 (25 October 1999). Afghanistan: SC Res. 1378 (14 November 2001).

[51] Kosovo: UN Doc. UNMIK/REG/2000/1 (2000) (established Joint Interim Administrative Structure, thereby implementing the agreement signed on 15 December 1999 by the Kosovo Albanian political party leaders present at the talks leading to the Rambouillet Accords). East Timor: UN Doc. UNTAET/REG/1999/2 (1999), 2000/23 (2000), 2000/24 (2000). Afghanistan: SC Res. 1383 (6 December 2001) (endorsing Agreement on Provisional Arrangements in Afghanistan Pending the Re-establishment of Permanent Government Institutions, 5 December 2001, UN Doc. S/2001/1154 (2001) [hereinafter Bonn Agreement]) I(4)).

[52] East Timor: UN Doc. UNTAET/REG/2001/2 (2001). Kosovo: UN Doc. UNMIK/REG/2001/9 (2001) (Constitutional Framework for Provisional Self-Government). Afghanistan: Bonn Agreement, n 51 above, I(4).

structures of governance.[53] Interestingly, despite the lack of UN resolution underwriting the conflict,[54] and the primacy of the US rather than the UN in transition, Iraq follows the pattern, and so reveals the ideological battle ground.[55]

The need for constitutional rupture, and renewal, reconstruction, and relegitimation of political and legal institutions is prefigured in all peace processes. In the processes of the early 1990s in El Salvador and Guatemala for example, radical reform of political and legal institutions represented a triumph of human rights and democracy over repression.[56] Those assessing the transition in retrospect, note that the international community played a critical norm-promotion role, which assisted in moving those waging the conflict to more liberal positions, which then needed to be sustained and internalized through domestic institutions, and reflected in domestic politics.[57] It can be argued that this account underestimates the role of domestic and transnational civil society in shaping and even creating international commitments to norm-promotion.[58] In the processes of many Central American States the involvement of civil society had some

[53] East Timor: UN Doc. UNTAET/REG/2001/2 (2001). Kosovo: UN Doc. UNMIK/REG/2001/9 (2001). Afghanistan: Bonn Agreement, n 51 above, I(6).

[54] Although there are arguments that UN SC Res. 1441 (8 November 2002) provided authority for use of force, in our view the better view is that it did not, see Sands, *Lawless World America and the Making and Breaking of Global Rules*, n 2 above, 174–203; an open letter published in the British *Guardian* newspaper, signed by 16 French and British academic specialists in international law (based at Oxford, Cambridge, the London School of Economics, and the University of Paris), stated that 'there is no justification under international law for the use of military force against Iraq'. 'War Would Be Illegal' *Guardian* (UK), 7 March 2003, 29.

[55] (1) Mandate: SC Res. 1483 (22 May 2003) recognizes the UK and the US as occupying forces under unified command ('the Authority'). (2) Transitional government: CPA/REG/13 July 2003/06 (established the Governing Council of Iraq as the principal body of the Iraqi interim administration with a consultative role); Law of Administration for the State of Iraq for the Transitional Period, 8 March 2004, at http://www.cpa-iraq.org/government/TAL.html (providing for vesting an Iraqi interim government consisting of a president, prime minister, and cabinet of ministers with full sovereignty; CPA/REG/9 June 2004/9 (dissolving the Coalition Provisional Authority). (3) Elections: Law of Administration for the State of Iraq for the Transitional Period, op cit (elections held on 30 January 2005). (4) New Constitution: Law of Administration for the State of Iraq for the Transitional Period, op cit (National Assembly responsible for drafting constitution).

[56] Guatemala: Agreement on a Firm and Lasting Peace, 29 December 1996. See further Stephen Baranyi, *The Challenge in Guatemala: Verifying Human Rights, Strengthening National Institutions and Enhancing an Integrated UN Approach to Peace* (1995). El Salvador: Joint Declaration Signed on 4 October 1994 by the Representatives of the Government of El Salvador and of the Frente Farabundo Martí para la Liberació Nacional (FMLN), 1994, *at* http://www.usip.org/library/pa.html. See further Americas Watch, *Accountability and Human Rights: The Report of the United Nations Commission on the Truth for El Salvador*, (1993) Vol. V, Issue Nr. 7, 2 ('While many aspects of implementation of the peace accord remain in question, the accord itself is a stunning document, addressing many of the root causes of the conflict and establishing concrete mechanisms for change.').

[57] Mark Peceny and William Stanley 'Liberal Social Reconstruction and the Resolution of Civil Wars in Central America' (2001) 155 International Organization 149; Kathryn Sikkink and Ellen.L. Lutz, 'International Human Rights Law and Practice in Latin America' (2000) 54 International Organization 633.

[58] Kathryn Sikkink, 'Human rights, principled issue-networks, and sovereignty in Latin America' (1993) 47 International Organization 411.

importance to legitimating the outcome of negotiations, given the limited legitimacy and local accountability of political elites.[59] Thus, the involvement of both civil society and international actors in what was, in essence, the fashioning of constitutional shifts of power, were seen as progressive, positive, and legitimating, giving rise to talk of new models of 'participatory' or 'deliberative democracy'.

In the 'use of force' situations set out above however, the International Territorial Administrations involved international actors taking on the role of government almost completely.[60] Unrepresentative appointees drawn frequently from civil society (often justified, interestingly, by the presence of women), provided the only connection to local accountability within transitional political institutions which were given little real power.

This UN' use of ITAs has been criticized as raising difficult questions of the accountability and legitimacy of international actors themselves.[61] The difficulties of accountability, like those of dealing with the past, reflect the peculiarities of the transitional situation and the difficulty of applying international law to its novel governance arrangements. Accountability here occupies the twilight zone created by the transitional situation's exceptional nature. The legal basis of even UN ITA accountability under UN-promulgated international norms is unclear, given the transitional and constantly transiting locus of power, and the difficulties of precisely locating sovereignty during transition. ITAs, however, still have political and moral justifications based on arguments that they are necessary to providing government during transitional periods, when domestic governance lacks legitimacy, capacity, or both.[62] However, these justifications logically lose their force as time passes.[63] Over time, a failure to return governance to democratically accountable domestic actors begins to create a situation where the legitimacy and capacity of international governance itself can increasingly fall foul of the same criticisms levelled against the former domestic (undemocratic) regime.[64]

The normative ambiguities of ITAs are accentuated as regards Iraq and the role of the US and its allies. Here it can again be argued that these ambiguities have enabled the hegemon to attempt a fundamental re-definition of law's normative application. In Iraq, the post-use of force status of the US and other forces was that of occupier.[65] This made the situation entirely different from earlier examples

---

[59] ibid.

[60] See generally Ralph Wilde, 'From Danzig to East Timor and Beyond: The Role of International Territorial Administration' (2001) 95 American Journal of International Law 583.

[61] Ralph Wilde, 'Representing International Territorial Administration: A Critique of Some Approaches' (2004) 15 European Journal of International Law 71; Outi Korhonen 'International Governance in Post-Conflict Situations' (2001) 14 Leiden Journal of International Law 495.

[62] Wilde, 'From Danzig to East Timor and Beyond: The Role of International Territorial Administration', n 60 above.

[63] Bell, 'Peace Agreements: Their Nature and Legal Status', n 49 above.   [64] ibid.

[65] See SC Res. 1483 (22 May 2003) (recognizing the UK and US as occupying forces under united command). The US accepted the application of the Geneva Conventions, however note *New York Times* article, stating that lawyers seemed to be arguing inapplicability, 'U.S. Disputed Protected Status of Iraq Inmates', New York Times, 23 May 2004, 29.

of UN ITAs, as it meant that a normative framework was clearly applicable: the Hague Regulations and Geneva IV standards define and limit the power of occupiers, and regulate their relationship with the indigenous population.[66] For the US the easiest way around their status as occupiers was to co-opt the pattern of other ITA's so as to present elections as the 'end-point' of occupation, and their own on-going presence as rooted in the consent of a domestic sovereign. The US fashioned an incremental transition similar to that of previous ITA patterns, establishing first a Governing Council of Iraq with a consultative role, giving it increasing powers, holding elections, and providing for a new constitution to be drafted. At each point, UN SC Resolution endorsement was obtained.[67] UN SC Resolutions also were used to 'clarify' the occupation powers of the US and its allies, using the argument that Geneva IV did not provide for the needs of the gradual transition, such as the need for occupiers to engage in domestic constitutional reform, or management of oil resources.[68]

These UN SC Resolutions endorsed a presentation of the situation as one where a transition of power from occupier to Iraqi government was in progression, enabling the US to move towards the position where the negative badge of 'occupier' could be set aside altogether. The resolutions also affirmed the US argument that there was a need to legalize an extraordinary occupation power to meet the extraordinary needs of the transitional situation.[69]

This approach culminated in UN SC Resolution 1546 (2004), which is startling in its revelation of the power of transitional arguments in the pursuit of hegemony through (re)definition of law. UN SC Resolution 1546 (2004) endorsed the formation of the sovereign Interim Government of Iraq, and welcomed the fact that on the date for transfer of power to the Interim Government 'the occupation will end and the Coalition Provisional Authority will cease to exist, and that Iraq will reassert its full sovereignty'.[70] It endorsed the proposed framework for transition, and also declared 'that the multinational force shall have the authority to take all necessary measures to contribute to the maintenance of security and stability in Iraq in accordance with the letters annexed to this resolution...'.[71] It arguably therefore brought an end in law to the 'occupation'.[72] The International

---

[66] Geneva Convention (IV) for the Protection of Civilian Persons in Time of War, 12 August 1949, 6 U.S.T. 3516, 75 U.N.T.S. 287, Arts 47–78; Hague Convention No. IV Respecting the Laws and Customs of War on Land, 18 October 18, 1907, 36 Stat. 2277, Arts 43–56.

[67] SC Res. 1500 (14 August 2003) (welcoming establishment of Governing Council of Iraq); SC Res. 1511 (16 October 2003) (welcoming establishment of preparatory constitutional committee); SC Res. 1546 (8 June 2004) (endorsing proposed framework for transition). See further Bell, 'Peace Agreements: Their Nature and Legal Status', n 49 above.

[68] Remarks of John B. Bellinger, III, Legal Adviser, US Department of State, *United Nations Security Council Resolutions and the Application of International Humanitarian Law, Human Rights and Refugee Law*, International Conference, San Remo, Italy, 9 September 2005.

[69] See eg SC Res 1483 (22 May 2003), 1511 (16 October 2003) and 1546 (8 June 2004). See also Bellinger, ibid.   [70] SC Res 1546 (8 June 2004), paras 1 and 2.

[71] ibid, para 10.

[72] See Adam Roberts, 'The End of Occupation: Iraq 2004' (2005) 54 International and Comparative Law Quarterly 27.

Committee of the Red Cross position is that a situation of occupation has ended—while aspects of the Geneva Conventions relating to internal conflict may still apply, the US has ceased to be an 'occupier'.[73] However, UN SC Resolution 1546 simultaneously enabled occupation-like powers, notably the power to detain security internees, to be extended to the new 'non-occupation' stage of transition. These arguments derive not from the text of the Resolution itself, but from the letter attached by Colin Powell that is referred to in the resolution. This letter describes the powers that the 'multinational force' will need to do its work, sometimes borrowing the language of Geneva IV.[74] It is currently being argued that UN SC Resolution 1546, read with this letter, in effect creates a new mini-law of (non)occupation peculiar to the Iraq transition, which not only replaces the law of occupation, but also overrides the human rights treaty commitments of the US and its allies.[75] Both the US State department and the British Government have asserted that UN SC Resolution 1546 trumps their own human rights treaty commitments, including (in the case of the UK) those under Article 5 of the European Convention on Human Rights which could preclude British forces from administrative detention.[76] The label of transition has therefore been used to attempt to remove the formal constraints of international humanitarian law, and to give extraordinary powers to the erstwhile occupation forces.[77] This has all been achieved, not through a rejection of law, but through use of UN SC Resolutions. As Alvarez notes, this arguably poses a greater threat to international law because:

'[T]he hegemon can do only so much to alter the fundamental sources on international obligation on its own. But when acting with the Council, the hegemon can do almost anything, while still appearing to be acting consistently with the Charter's vague Principles and Purposes.'[78]

In general therefore, the use of ITA's by the UN illustrates a lack of clarity around the question of the legitimate functions of third party States/international actors in transitional situations, thereby illustrating the difficulties with applying the traditional normative frameworks to ITA actors. However, in Iraq

---

[73] Speech delivered by Professor Daniel Thürer, Member, International Committee of the Red Cross, *Current Challenges to the Law of Occupation*, 6th Bruges Colloquium, 20–21 October, 2005 (his main reason for asserting this is that the Iraq Government has the authority to ask multinational forces to leave). But note Roberts, ibid.

[74] Colin Powell's letter appended to SC Res. 1546 provides for 'internment where this is necessary for imperative reasons of security', SC Res. 1546 (8 June 2004) app. The Fourth Geneva Convention provides that the Occupying Power may subject protected persons to internment 'for imperative reasons of security', Geneva IV, n 66 above, Art. 78.

[75] Bellinger, n 68 above; *The Queen (On the Application of Hilal Abdul-Razzaq Ali Al-Jedda) v Secretary of State for Defence* [2006] EWCA Civ 327.   [76] ibid.

[77] Cf Giorgio Agamben, *State of Exception* (2005); Giorgio Agamben, *Homo Sacer: Sovereign Power and Bare Life* (1995).

[78] Jose E.Alvarez, 'Editorial Comment: Hegemonic International Law Revisited' (2003) 97 American Journal of International Law 873, 887.

the US has, with some success, exploited the peculiarities of transition to attempt to create a re-defined legal framework, ideologically shaped to buttress its hegemonic position.[79]

Conclusions

To return to the central question of the relationship of the exercise of hegemonic power to international law, the following conclusions suggest themselves. First, exploration of the operation of the hegemon in the situation in Iraq and in relation to the 'war on terror' tends to support Teitel's thesis that contemporary transitional justice discourse does not have a linear progressive normative direction, but is much more ambivalent. This is a key element in the context in which the rhetoric of transitional justice is being employed in the exercise of US hegemony.

At one level this can be considered as a somewhat cynical appropriation of the concept. However, it also evinces a perceived need to be seen to operate within analytical frameworks that have global currency, referenced to binding legal norms; there is a perceived need to manifest a commitment to the ideology of the rule of law as a device for the exercise of hegemonic power. This tends to reinforce Byers's overall conclusions concerning the relationship of the hegemon to international law. Rather than a rejection of international law, or an attempt to carve out exceptions for the US alone, there is a deeper attempt to redefine the law for everyone so as to enable US exceptionalism in practice. While at first blush the relationship of transitional justice discourse to international law evidences two competing trends, these trends can also be conceived of as paradoxically linked, in the sense that the rhetoric of the former (transitional justice as extending the reach of international law to exceptional situations) is used to justify the hegemon's pursuit of an ideological redefinition of what international law requires.

However, rather than leave this analysis as a somewhat depressing (though necessary) critical evaluation, a second conclusion, concerning the battle for human rights activism suggests itself. This battle is still being fought; it is not clear that the international legal norms on the use of force have shifted so as to provide an expansive doctrine of pre-emptive self-defence. Were such a change to have occurred, there would have been no need to seek to rely on pre-existing UN Security Council resolutions to justify the intervention in Iraq. Yet these resolutions provided the sole legal justification advanced by the US's prime ally (the UK) for invasion, and they also provided the prime US legal (rather than political) justification. Similarly, it is not clear that the legal norms in relation to torture

---

[79] Cf US Department of State, *Post-conflict Reconstruction Essentials Task Matrix* (1 April 2005), at http://www.state.gov/s/crs/rls/52959.htm (indicating a 'patterned' approach to post-conflict reconstruction which appears to suggest a US view of future transitional authority roles, although note caveats in the preface as regards the need to be appropriate for context).

have shifted. Despite the rhetoric in the immediate aftermath of 9/11, the US has more recently been at pains internationally to emphasize its rejection of torture.[80] Domestically, the McCain amendment has undercut the attempted redefinition of the concept, and the international community has shown little appetite for accepting US practice as indicative of a norm-shift.[81] In short, while the context of US hegemony has impacted upon the debate as to the requirements of international law in such spheres as the use of force and the prohibition of torture, the resilience of the norms in question suggests that they possess a significant degree of autonomy.

This resilience of international law's normative core lies beyond political will and the strength of existing institutional safeguards (such as domestic and international human rights machinery). It lies also at the ideological level. The difficulty in co-opting the discourse of transitional justice and human rights to dismantle them is that, instead of having your cake and eating it, there is a cognitive dissonance which has to be resolved. It is unclear that it will be resolved in favour of the hegemon. The ideological space which the US wishes to occupy is a difficult one to carve out in any coherent way. Any attempt to co-opt transitional justice and human rights language as justification for hegemonic unilateralism can backfire. The fact that the US has chosen to invoke legal norms and the rhetoric of transitional justice in the exercise of hegemony, has, of necessity, created particular sites of resistance.[82]

The increasing anchoring of peace processes in human rights standards in recent decades has come about not simply because of an abstract commitment to the standards; the anchoring has also been shown to have instrumental benefits in assisting transition.[83] This aspect of reliance upon human rights standards (as 'a good way of doing business') goes some way to explaining the hegemon's choice to re-define international law rather than to reject it outright. However it also makes clear the line of counter-hegemonic resistance to a project that seeks to weaken international human rights norms. This resistance must be based on ongoing human rights advocacy, which seeks to re-assert normative understandings of its core through traditional modes of lobbying, political debate and international

---

[80] US Secretary of State, Condoleeza Rice, stated on 5 December 2005 that '[T]he United States does not transport, and has not transported, detainees from one country to another for the purpose of interrogation using torture', at http://usinfo.state.gov/mena/Archive/2005/Dec/05–762606.html.

[81] 'Alleged Secret Detentions in Council of Europe Member States', Information Memorandum II (Strasburg: Council of Europe Committee on Legal Affairs and Human Rights, 22 January 2006) AS/JUR (2006) 03.

[82] As Krisch points out, in this context international law occupies an 'ambivalent position . . . as both a tool for the exercise of dominance and as an element of resistance to it'. Nico Krisch, 'International Law in Times of Hegemony: Unequal Power and the Shaping of the International Legal Order' (2005) 16 European Journal of International Law 369.

[83] See further Bell, *Peace Agreements and Human Rights*, n 34 above; see also Bell, *The Role of Human Rights in Peace Agreements*, n 34 above (dealing with pragmatic arguments for those in conflicts to use human rights standards).

and domestic litigation. This can be further built by developing the arguments for human rights standards and instruments as offering not just clear normative standards, but a pragmatic way of organizing the business of democracy, and giving substantive content and practical mechanisms to the word 'peace'.[84] In short, it points to the importance of asserting and developing notions of the pragmatic imperative for an international rule of law.

---

[84] ibid.

9

Human Rights and Conflict Resolution

Tom Hadden

Introduction

Almost everyone agrees that human rights are most at risk and most abused during ethnic and communal conflicts, especially when they develop into armed conflicts, and that they are best protected by bringing the conflict to an end as soon as possible, or better still by preventing it.

Most activists in the human rights community also argue, as a corollary, that the effective protection of human rights—past, present, and future—is an indispensable element in any lasting settlement.

This second proposition is not so enthusiastically endorsed by many of those in the conflict resolution community.[1] Their primary focus is more on the need for negotiation and compromise and some argue that strict adherence to human rights principles may sometimes stand in the way of an agreed settlement. One example is the need in some circumstances for the negotiation of a general amnesty for participants in the conflict rather than an insistence on the prosecution and punishment of those responsible for all serious human rights violations. Another is the difficulty in dealing with the human rights principle of self-determination for all peoples within the context of negotiations between States and separatist groups. A third is the choice between accepting ethnic separation and insisting on the return of displaced populations and the restitution of their property.

Some conflict resolution experts might add that there is no compelling empirical evidence for the validity of the second proposition. They can point to the more or less satisfactory resolution of some long-standing conflicts in which there has not always been strict adherence to human rights principles, as for example in Chile, Sierra Leone, and perhaps also in Northern Ireland. It may be added that

---

[1] For a general account of these issues see Michelle Parlevliet, 'Bridging the Divide: Exploring the Relationship between Human Rights and Conflict Management' (2002) 11/1 *Track Two* Centre for Conflict Resolution, Cape Town.

international intervention in an attempt to enforce human rights principles has in some recent cases made the situation worse rather than better. This points to the need for an assessment of the balance of advantage in utilitarian terms rather than the more demanding principles of human rights protection. An approach of that kind, as will be seen, is more readily accepted within the law of armed conflict through the concept of acceptable collateral damage in the pursuit of agreed objectives.

How can these conflicting positions be reconciled? Are we to say that some human rights principles can be abandoned in the interests of conflict resolution? Or can they be reformulated in such a way as to preserve the essentials of both approaches?

One way to achieve a reconciliation between the two approaches may be to focus on different needs and priorities at different stages in conflict prevention and resolution.

This will involve a careful consideration of four main issues: (i) the priority to be accorded to individual rights as opposed to a more utilitarian assessment of how to achieve the best outcome for the greatest number of people; (ii) the choice between judicial adjudication on rights and the negotiation of compromises; (iii) the question of timing or at what stage particular human rights issues can best be addressed; and (iv) the respective roles of national and international actors and agencies.

Recent Developments in the United Nations Approach to Conflict Resolution

Within the United Nations there has been a gradual development along these lines from the somewhat simplistic provisions in Chapters VI and VII of the United Nations Charter for mediation followed only by sanctions and military intervention. The initial step, despite the absence of any express Charter authorization, was the regular deployment of peacekeeping forces along ceasefire lines between opposing armed forces, aptly described as action under Chapter VI 1/2. More recently, the categorization of United Nations operations has been further extended in Boutros Ghali's *Agenda for Peace*[2] report to cover some or all of the following distinct types of activity:

Conflict prevention: preventive diplomacy designed to prevent disputes from arising, to prevent existing disputes from escalating into conflicts, and to limit any conflict from spreading.

---

[2] *An Agenda for Peace: Preventive Diplomacy, Peacemaking and Peace-keeping* (1992), available at http://www.un.org/Docs/SG/agpeace.html; the explanations in the text are not direct quotations but are drawn from the wording in various sections of the report.

Peacekeeping: deployment of a United Nations presence in the field, normally
with the consent of all the parties concerned.

Peace making: action designed to bring hostile parties to agreement, essentially
through the peaceful means provided for under Chapter VI of the UN Charter.

Peace enforcement: the use of sanctions and military force to maintain or restore
international peace and security under Chapter VII of the UN Charter.

Peace building: post-conflict efforts to identify and support structures which will
tend to consolidate peace and the restoration of order, including disarming
warring parties, repatriating refugees, reforming government institutions, and
advancing efforts to protect human rights.

The practical implementation of these has been further clarified in the detailed
review of current United Nations practice in the Brahimi Report[3] and more
recently in the Report of the Secretary-General's High Level Panel.[4] In addition,
the United Nations has been drawn into full-scale transitional administration by
international personnel in Bosnia, Kosovo, and East Timor, again despite the
absence of any formal provision in the Charter.[5] It has also embarked on a more
general policy of preparing individual country assessments in which the risks and
immediate prospects of ethnic or economic conflict are analysed and made available to all those involved in conflict prevention or resolution.[6]

The more general implications of this rapidly developing approach to international intervention have been spelled out in an independent international report,
The Responsibility to Protect.[7] The authors concluded that in certain circumstances
the United Nations Security Council has an obligation to organize or authorize
intervention to prevent large-scale human rights abuses, and that if it fails to do so
the pressure on other States to act may be irresistible; they added, however, that
any military action in cases of this kind must be proportionate and that there must
be a reasonable prospect of success. Pragmatic considerations of that kind have
clearly been uppermost in the mind of members of the United Nations Security
Council in respect of the situations in Chechnya and Darfur, despite compelling
evidence of large-scale human rights violations. In Chechnya any kind of international military intervention in the 'internal affairs' of Russia as a major world
power was clearly regarded as out of the question. In Darfur the prospect of any
form of uninvited military intervention by Western powers in a major Islamic
power seemed equally unrealistic in political terms, given the continuing controversy and problems over Western intervention in Iraq.

---

[3] Report of the Panel on United Nations Peace Operations, UN Doc. A/55/305-S/2000/809.
[4] Report of the High Level Panel, *A More Secure World: Our Shared responsibility*, UN Doc.
A/59/565 (2005).
[5] For a general account of the legal basis of the transitional administrations in Kosovo and East
Timor, see Matthias Ruffert, 'The Administration of Kosovo and East Timor by the International
Community' (2001) International and Comparative Law Quarterly 613.
[6] See eg United Nations System Staff College, *Early Warning and Preventive Measures* (2002).
[7] International Commission on Intervention and State Sovereignty, *The Responsibility to Protect*
(2001).

An Account of Human Rights Activity at Various Stages in Conflict Resolution

This list of different forms of conflict prevention and resolution can be further expanded to highlight the different roles of the human rights and conflict resolution communities at each stage in the process, focusing not on the detailed analysis of particular cases as described in the extensive literature but on the general nature of the processes involved.

Country reporting

Reports on human rights violations, especially those involving different ethnic or religious minorities or communities, by national and international Non-governmental Organizations (NGOs) and by United Nations Special Rapporteurs and other international agencies can help to alert the international community to a potentially violent conflict. This form of human rights activity, however, is generally focused on individual incidents or practices and does not often extend to a more detailed analysis of the underlying causes or their possible longer term resolution. The objective and the result in most cases is limited to alerting the international community to the scale of human rights abuses rather than suggesting ways in which the underlying problems which give rise to the abuses might be addressed. In so far as the process has been formalized, for example in respect of the consideration of communications of human rights violations under the Resolution 1503 procedure within the Human Rights Commission, it is likely to lead to more of the same rather than the development of proposals for international action.[8]

Conflict prevention

More intensive involvement by international human rights agencies, such as the Office of the United Nations High Commissioner for Human Rights or the OSCE High Commissioner for National Minorities, can help to identify the underlying tensions and engage with the various parties in an attempt to develop programmes and policies which may assist in diminishing the risk of more serious conflict, as in the recent international intervention in Macedonia. As already indicated, the Office of the United Nations High Commissioner for Human Rights has embarked on a policy of preparing country assessments in which the level of risk of conflict and possible preventive measures are outlined. Similar structures have been established within the OSCE, particularly in respect of minority issues. The High Commissioner for National Minorities has developed a practice of pro-active intervention with a view to promoting direct dialogue between government and

---

[8] For a general account of the development and limited impact of the procedure see Joan Fitzpatrick, *Human Rights in Crisis* (1994) 116–51.

minority representatives.[9] These interventions are in principle based on established human rights standards in respect of minorities. But in practice they leave a good deal of flexibility for negotiation of the most appropriate measures in the particular circumstance of each country,[10] and there is typically no resort to any kind of formal adjudication let alone attempts at enforcement. Interventions of this kind have aptly been referred to as human rights diplomacy.

Human rights monitoring and human rights protection

The deployment of international human rights monitors at early stages in a violent or armed conflict may help to diminish the risk of more serious violations and the resulting escalation of the conflict, as in the deployment of human rights monitors in El Salvador before the negotiation of a final settlement and in Kosovo before the escalation of the fighting. The very different outcome in these two cases, however, indicates that action of this kind may be more effective as an integral part of peace building than as a preventive measure. The inability of the monitors in Kosovo to take effective action in the absence of political progress soon led to their withdrawal. Proponents of conflict resolution might argue that direct engagement with both sides in an emerging conflict, as in respect of the NATO and European Union intervention in Macedonia, would often be a better strategy.

These concerns have led to a renewed debate on the respective merits of employing human rights monitors merely to observe and report on violations as opposed to expecting them to take action to protect those most at risk. But it is reasonably clear that these are different functions which will require different forms of training and different procedures in the field of operation.[11] Monitoring and reporting on human rights violations typically involves adopting an objective and detached approach aimed at establishing precisely what has happened and whether it breaches international human rights standards. Getting involved in action to protect the rights of those at risk and those who have already suffered violations is likely to involve direct engagement and negotiation with actual or potential perpetrators and perhaps also legal or practical action to secure redress for victims.

Peacekeeping

The deployment of international peacekeeping forces between opposing armed forces in the context of a negotiated ceasefire may help to stabilize the situation

---

[9] John Packer, 'The OSCE High Commissioner on National Minorities', in Nazila Ghanea and Alexandra Xanthaki (eds), *Minorities, Peoples and Self-Determination* (2005) ch. 14.

[10] See generally, Tom Hadden, 'Integration and Separation: Legal and Political Choices in Implementing Minority Rights', in Ghanea and Xanthaki, *Minorities, Peoples and Self-Determination*, n 9 above, ch. 10.

[11] These issues are currently under consideration by a team at the University of Norttingham; see Daniel Moeckli, *An Emerging Profession: Towards a Doctrine of Human Rights Field Work*, Sixth Annual Conference of the Association of European Human Rights Institutions, NUI Galway, 2005.

and to protect refugees or internally displaced civilians. Experience in Kashmir, Cyprus, South Lebanon, and elsewhere, however, has shown that action of this kind may result in perpetuating a stand-off in an unresolved conflict rather than assisting in its resolution.[12] This traditional form of peacekeeping has been regarded as essentially a military operation in which there has been little scope for the involvement of human rights personnel. Military commanders in the field would typically seek to establish relationships with the opposing forces and to intervene to prevent the escalation of shelling or incursions on either side. But they have not usually been expected or encouraged to look for longer term resolutions of the underlying conflict.

More recently, peacekeeping operations, such as those in Somalia, Sierra Leone, and the Democratic Republic of Congo, have sought to adopt a more active role, both in defeating or disarming those involved in civil wars or insurgencies and also in attempting to sponsor or facilitate negotiations on longer term peace agreements. There is some dispute over the extent to which these separate roles can be successfully combined.[13] Some argue that the most useful and potentially lasting contribution of peacekeeping forces is to 'win the war' by imposing their authority throughout the territory; others that it is better to aim at achieving a temporary cessation of hostilities so that other contributors to conflict resolution missions can have a better chance of achieving a negotiated settlement. On either view it is clear that the traditional concept of creating a buffer zone between the opposing sides has been superseded by one in which the search for a longer term resolution of the conflict is an essential element in the overall mandate.

Humanitarian aid

This more active form of peacekeeping is often linked to the creation of conditions in which intervention by international aid agencies, such as the UNHCR and the ICRC and their non-governmental counterparts, may help to protect the lives and rights of all those affected by an ongoing conflict, from refugees and internally displaced civilians to prisoners of war and other detainees. One of the major problems in humanitarian intervention in this limited sense is the issue of consent for access to the area of conflict. In principle, States are required to grant access to humanitarian agencies,[14] but this has sometimes been denied on the ground that humanitarian assistance is in effect helping to prolong an insurgency. There is also a potential difference between the strict principle of impartiality and non-involvement to which humanitarian agencies are committed, and the

---

[12] Recent and past experience is discussed in Ramesh Thakur and Albrecht Schnabel (eds), *United Nations Peacekeeping Operations: Ad Hoc Missions, Permanent Engagement* (2001).

[13] For an account of the ongoing debate on these issues, see Tim Woodhouse and Oliver Ramsbottom (eds.), *Peacekeeping and Conflict Resolution* (2000).

[14] There are formal provisions to facilitate access in both international armed conflicts (Geneva Convention IV, Arts 142–43) and non-international armed conflicts (common Article 3 and Protocol II, Art. 18) and also in the Abo Declaration of Minimum Humanitarian Standards (1991) Art. 15.

commitment of members of the human rights community not to stand by and do nothing in the face of serious human rights violations. There is often a difficult choice to be made between condemnation and withdrawal as opposed to staying on to provide as much assistance to victims as possible.

This raises further difficult issues in respect of the protection of aid workers. Most humanitarian agencies prefer to work without military protection, not least to maintain the principle of strict impartiality. But their primary objective of the delivery of essential food and medical aid to civilians may not always be practicable without security protection, and if that cannot be provided on an impartial basis the fundamental human rights of refugees and internally displaced civilians may have to be sacrificed to the safety of humanitarian personnel. In this and in the related issue of relative priorities in the allocation of food and medical aid to aid workers, able-bodied civilians and those who may be too weak or ill to survive, there are unavoidable decisions to be made as to whose human rights are to be sacrificed for the benefit of others. In practice the decision will often be based on an assessment of the risk to aid workers rather than the protection of the rights of those affected by the conflict. Risk assessments of this kind, in which the protection of the security and lives of the international aid workers are given much higher priority than those of the civilian population at risk, do not fit easily with the underlying principles of human rights law in which all are to be treated equally and any form of discrimination is to be avoided.

Human rights enforcement

Intervention by international forces with a view to the prevention of genocide and other systematic human rights violations must be clearly distinguished from purely humanitarian intervention. It will often involve the overthrow and eventual replacement of abusive regimes, as was the objective in Kosovo, Afghanistan, and Iraq, and poses even more difficult issues. The deployment of military forces without the consent of the State government, with or without the authorization of the Security Council, inevitably involves decisions on the balance of advantage in the protection of human rights.[15] Any large-scale military intervention will almost inevitably result in the death of innocent civilians and the widespread destruction of property and essential infrastructures. The question is whether the costs in terms of loss of human life and more general disruption can be justified in terms of the benefits to be obtained by military intervention.

Assessments of this kind are built into the laws of armed conflict in which the infliction of what is known as 'collateral damage' is accepted provided that it is proportional to the military objective which is being pursued.[16] Utilitarian

---

[15] The legal and moral issues are analysed in detail in Nicolas Wheeler, *Saving Strangers: Humanitarian Intervention in International Society* (2000).

[16] The most general formulation of this principle is in Art. 54 of Additional Protocol I to the Geneva Conventions which prohibits 'indiscriminate attacks ... which may be expected to cause

calculations involving an assessment of the numbers of deaths and injuries which may be justified in pursuit of a longer-term objective are less easy to reconcile with the underlying commitment in human rights law to the protection of the funda- mental rights of every individual. Hence the rather different approach by military lawyers and human rights lawyers to the killing of civilians caught up in one way or another with an armed conflict. The military approach is to accept that mis- takes in the heat of battle are inevitable while the human rights approach is more demanding and seems to require that those responsible for mistakes should be brought to account.[17] There is clearly a need in any proposed military inter- vention of this kind for a realistic and hard-headed assessment of the relative costs and benefits, not least for the population of the territory. In more general terms it can be argued that in times of conflict and in respect of military action of any kind, the criterion of the greatest happiness of the greatest number in the longer term may have to be preferred to the protection of the human rights of each individual person.

Peace building

In the aftermath of serious armed conflict or in 'failed states' in which the struc- tures of central government have broken down a longer term involvement by international agencies and personnel may help in restoring stability and good gov- ernance. This will typically involve a wide range of activities, from the imposition of a transitional international administration to the deployment of international administrative and security personnel to advise and assist national officials. Here too a different approach may be adopted by human rights activists and those trained in conflict resolution in some of the distinctive aspects of what is now referred to as the process of post-conflict peace building.

(a) Retraining or re-establishing national military or police forces

The restructuring of the military, the police, and other security forces is almost always a contested issue, not least since those involved in the conflict on either side are likely to have been responsible for serious human rights violations. Many of those working in the international human rights community typically campaign for the removal or 'lustration' of all those who have been responsible for or asso- ciated with human rights abuses during the conflict.[18] But there are dangers in

---

incidental loss of civilian life, injury to civilians, damage to civilian objects ... which would be exces- sive in relation to the concrete and direct military advantage anticipated'.

[17] These issues have been at the centre of some recent cases on the extent to which the obligations to protect life under the European Convention on Human Rights apply to situations of armed con- flict, notably *Bankovic v Belgium and Others* (2001) 11 Butterworths Human Rights Cases 435, and *Regina (Al Skeini) v Secretary of State for Defence* (2005) 2 WLR 1401.

[18] See generally Symposium on the Problems of Lustration, in *Law and Social Inquiry* (1995), especially Martin Los, 'Lustration and Truth Claims: Unfinished Revolutions in Central Europe' 117–61 and Arthur Stinchcombe, 'Lustration as a Problem of the Social Basis of Constitutionalism', 245–73.

pursuing policies of this kind in too comprehensive a manner or in too short a time scale. If the established police and security forces are removed and replaced by an international force with little local knowledge, there may be a period of lawlessness, as for example in Kosovo and Iraq. It may be better to concentrate initially on promoting or installing a more acceptable set of commanders while retaining and seeking to retrain the bulk of existing local forces, as for example in Northern Ireland. This may involve postponing any attempt to deal with alleged violators until the situation has been stabilized. It may also be desirable to focus attention on the recruitment of members of previously excluded minorities or communities and in some, though not all, cases to incorporate members of opposition forces. The underlying objective should be to limit the role of international police and security personnel to what is essential and to maintain and assist in the reformation of as much as possible of the established structures for law and order.

(b) Negotiation of new political and constitutional arrangements

The negotiation of new political and constitutional arrangements is likely to raise a wider set of issues. Except in cases where one or other faction has effectively won the conflict and expelled their opponents, as in East Timor, the active involvement of leaders of all the major communities or factions, whether or not they have been involved in abuses during the conflict, is likely to produce the most acceptable and stable settlement. As in the case of policing and security, this may involve avoiding or postponing any attempt to deal immediately with allegations of human rights violations during the conflict. It is also likely to require the negotiation of significant compromises on some major human rights claims, notably those of self-determination or autonomy for minority communities,[19] and a good deal of constitutional creativity, for example in respect of the extent and duration of provisions for power-sharing or con-sociation in government.[20] There is continuing dispute on the extent to which this may necessitate a degree of 'constructive ambiguity' in the formulation of agreements at different stages in development of peace processes to permit the leaders of different factions to assert different interpretations of contested issues.[21] There is also considerable uncertainty on the extent to which these agreements can or should be subject to strict legal interpretation or enforcement.[22] In this process the skills of mediation and political flexibility

---

[19] The difficulty in dealing with these issues within a human rights or internal law framework is discussed in Geoff Gilbert, 'Individuals, Collectivities and Rights', in Ghaneaand Xanthaki, *Minorities, Peoples and Self-Determination*, n 9 above, ch. 8.

[20] For a detailed account of some of the difficulties in achieving lasting settlements in communally divided States, see Ian O'Flynn and David Russell (eds), *Power Sharing: New Challenges for Divided Societies* (2005).

[21] This issue is extensively discussed in respect of the peace process in Northern Ireland in Christine Bell and Kathleen Cavanaugh, 'Constructive Ambiguity or Internal Self-Determination? Self-Determination, Group Accommodation and the Belfast Agreement' (1999) 22 Fordham International Law Journal 1345.

[22] See Christine Bell, 'Peace Agreements: Their Nature and Legal Status' (2006) 100 American Journal of International Law 374–412.

are likely to be more useful than those of experts in human rights or formal legal adjudication.

(c) Organizing and monitoring democratic elections

The process of establishing new electoral structures and the organization and monitoring of elections is a more or less discrete and technical operation on which there are only very general human rights standards. The main human rights conventions refer only to the principles of democracy and the need for regular free and fair elections without prescribing any very clear guidelines on what is an acceptable electoral system.[23] But since the choice of electoral systems and constituency boundaries is likely to pre-determine the eventual result, those involved must have a fairly clear idea of the political structure, they wish to produce. The essential requirements are an understanding of the theory and practice of integrative, con-sociational and federal structures and an ability to negotiate and implement a set of electoral procedures that will help in achieving the desired result and are acceptable to the parties to the conflict.[24] These are not typically skills that are well developed within the human rights community. Human rights workers are more likely to be useful in the more limited role of electoral monitoring, for which specific training is relatively well developed and which does not require much more general experience either of human rights or of conflict resolution.

(d) Dealing with the past

Dealing with past human rights violations may involve contested choices between establishing national, international, or hybrid human rights courts, negotiating appropriate amnesties or prisoner releases, organizing truth and reconciliation commissions and assisting in providing reparations for victims of human rights violations. As already indicated, this is an area in which there is continuing controversy between most human rights activists who support the principle of 'no impunity' of any kind and others who claim that amnesties of varying kinds are necessary in the interests of peace and reconciliation.[25] In the absence of any compelling evidence that either of these absolutist positions is always effective, a more pragmatic approach may be more productive. Depending on the particular circumstances of the conflict the indefinite postponement of prosecutions and punishment, as for example in Argentina and Chile, or concentrating only on those most responsible, as in Sierra Leone, or using amnesties as a means of getting at

---

[23] See *Human Rights and Elections*, United Nations Centre for Human Rights, Professional Training Series No 2 (1994).

[24] Some of the possible objectives and procedures are discussed in detail in Donald L. Horowitz, *Ethnic Groups in Conflict* (1985) ch. 8.

[25] The prevailing human rights standards, calling for the right to a remedy, the right to truth and the duty to investigate, the duty to prosecute and punish, and the right to reparations for victims, were finally agreed in 2005 after lengthy negotiation in the *Basic Principles and Guidelines on the Right to a Remedy and Reparation for Victims of Gross Violations of International Human Rights Law and Serious Violations of International Humanitarian Law*, UN Doc. E/CN.4/2005/L.10/Add.1.

the truth, as in South Africa, or developing communal restorative justice alternatives, as in Rwanda, may be the best strategy for securing longer term peace and stability.[26] If this is accepted, a detailed analysis of what appears to make the best contribution to the resolution of the conflict in various types of case may be a better preparation for effective involvement by international agencies than a prior commitment to any particular set of human rights principles.

(e) Righting past wrongs

Another equally difficult issue is the extent to which the practical effects of the conflict, notably in respect of ethnic cleansing and the return of refugees and internally displaced persons should be insisted on. There is a difficult choice to be made in many cases between attempting to restore the pre-conflict population distribution, as for example under the Dayton Accords in Bosnia, and accepting and stabilizing the redistribution that has taken place.[27] There are strong arguments in terms of the rights of individual refugees and displaced persons for insisting on the right to return to homes or property which they were forced to leave during the conflict. But it is almost always difficult to reverse the 'facts on the ground' that have been created, not least because of the threats and dangers faced by individuals returning to a radically different communal environment. Pragmatic considerations may point towards alternative policies of managed population exchange with compensation for those adversely affected in the interests of avoiding or minimizing further communal conflict. Where the communal separation is less serious, procedures to remedy past communal discrimination and inequality by the adoption of positive measures to achieve a better balance in public and private sector employment may also be called for in pursuit of human rights standards and are likely to be easier to implement. Experience in most cases, however, suggests that progress towards communal integration and effective equality will take a long time and that an attempt to move too quickly may increase rather than diminish the risk of further communal conflict.

(f) Arranging for future human rights protection

It is usual for internationally sponsored peace agreements to include provision for the creation of national human rights institutions or ombudsmen and other forms of internal monitoring. Newly established human rights commissions, however, must themselves make difficult strategic decisions on whether they are to focus on independent adjudication on alleged violations, direct involvement in mediation between opposing factions or more general promotional and educational

---

[26] The balance between human rights and political considerations in such cases is discussed in Tom Hadden, 'Punishment, Amnesty and Truth: Legal and Political Approaches', in Adrian Guelke (ed.), *Democracy and Ethnic Conflict: Advancing Peace in Deeply Divided Societies* (2004) ch. 11.

[27] These issues are discussed in detail in Christine Bell, *Human Rights and Peace Agreements* (2000) ch. 8.

activities.[28] In some situations, as in respect of contested marches and the Holy Cross School affair in Northern Ireland, mediation may be a more productive approach than an attempt to adjudicate on conflicting rights or to demonstrate solidarity with one or other side. In others, as in respect of the serious disorders in Gujarat, embarking on a detailed independent investigation and report may be the best strategy. There is a particular problem in attempting to persuade or shame non-State paramilitary forces into accepting and implementing general human rights principles.[29]

Some General Features

This account of the range of activities by members of the human rights and con-flict resolution communities at various stages in the processes of conflict preven-tion and resolution draws attention to a number of significant features.

To begin with it may help to recognize that there is typically a shift from a focus on the rights of individual human beings at earlier and later stages in dealing with conflicts and their resolution towards a more utilitarian approach when the con-flict is at its height. At that level there is a tendency to accept that the rights of individuals may be subordinated to what is regarded, rightly or wrongly, as the protection of the wider national population. This may occur during military enforcement activity of any kind, notably under the doctrine of acceptable collat-eral damage in pursuit of a legitimate military objective. It may also be inevitable in refugee and relief camps during prolonged conflicts and famines and after natural disasters in situations in which limited resources must be applied to the best advantage of the greatest number of potential survivors.

It may also help to recognize that there is typically rather less emphasis in the process of conflict resolution on judicial adjudication on human rights issues and rather more on the skills of negotiation and compromise. This is because the serious human rights violations that regularly accompany sustained ethnic or communal conflicts are best regarded as symptoms of the conflict rather than as an essential element of its underlying causes. Understanding the nature of those underlying issues is likely to require the skills of social and political science rather than human rights law. Furthermore, finding a way to achieve the compromises that are almost certainly required for any workable settlement is likely to require expertise in mediation and negotiation rather than in formal adjudication on conflicting claims.

[28] These issues are discussed in detail in Stephen Livingstone and Rachel Murray, *Evaluating the Effectiveness of National Human Rights Institutions: The Northern Ireland Human Rights Commission* (2005).
[29] International Council on Human Rights Policy, *Ends and Means: Human Rights Approaches to Armed Groups* (2000).

There is also likely to be a need for the prioritization and implementation of rather different human rights principles and standards at different stages in the process. In particular there is likely to be more ready acceptance of the postponement or fudging of difficult or contested issues—sometimes referred to as constructive ambiguity—in the initial stages of conflict resolution even if there is a fairly clear answer in human rights terms, to permit the development of mutual confidence between the conflicting parties. Timing is as much of the essence in the delivery of human rights as in most other spheres.

Finally, there is a need to ensure the appropriate development of internal national capacity in all these areas and to avoid giving too dominant a role to international personnel, whether in policing and security or in the development of the elements of a peace process. This is likely in its turn to require a less dogmatic approach to human rights principles and a greater readiness to encourage and accept the contribution to policies and practices by those most directly involved in or affected by a particular conflict, even if they have been responsible for past violations.

All this points to the need to accept some limitations on the role of human rights lawyers as they have traditionally been perceived and to develop different and more extensive forms of training and specialization for members of the human rights community involved in each of the various forms of activity involved in conflict resolution. In simpler terms it may be better to start with an understanding of the processes of conflict resolution and of the contribution that human rights may make at each stage rather than with a list of rights that are to be implemented or adjudicated on in all circumstances.

10

Habits of Mind and 'Truth Telling': Article 2 ECHR in Post-Conflict Northern Ireland

Gordon Anthony and Paul Mageean

Introduction

One of the developments that transitional justice literature identifies as key to the emergence of agreed democratic structures in a contested polity is accountability for past human rights abuses.[1] Where the process of transition results in previous State structures being superseded in their entirety, accountability will often take the form of prosecutions that may, for instance, be heard by international war crimes tribunals.[2] However, where the State is not superseded but rather part reinvented in the light of a new accord between constituent groupings, the issue of accountability can become significantly different.[3] While prosecutions may still follow, a greater emphasis may be placed upon 'truth telling' mechanisms like inquiries and commissions that seek both to explain past violations by State and non-State actors and to foster reconciliation.[4] The justification for such mechanisms is typically that they offer a form of accountability more suited to a compromise political settlement, although that accountability may in turn be negatively affected by a number of considerations. Prominent among these is the prior and continuing legal culture of the original State, albeit as modified to the emerging context (the bind between legal culture and non-State actors is more problematic given the normative link between State and law[5]). Legal culture has been linked to

---

[1] See eg Neil J Kritz (ed.), *Transitional Justice: How Emerging Democracies Reckon with Former Regimes* (1995–6, Vols 1–3).

[2] Richard J Goldstone, *For Humanity: Reflections of a War Crimes Investigator* (2000).

[3] On different State models and transition, see Fionnula Ní Aoláin and Colm Campbell, 'The Paradox of Transition in Conflicted Democracies' (2005) 27 Human Rights Quarterly 172.

[4] Michelle Parlevliet, 'Considering Truth: Dealing with a Legacy of Gross Human Rights Violations' (1998) 16 Netherlands Quarterly of Human Rights 141.

[5] But for consideration of humanitarian law as offering terms of reference for non-State actors, see Kieran McEvoy, 'Human Rights, Humanitarian Interventions and Paramilitary Activities in

'habits of mind' that may be more open or closed to, among other things, new legal arguments, revised institutional structures, and/or wider debates about law and society.[6] As habits tend, by definition, to be set and difficult to disengage, processes of truth telling may have to vie with precepts, doctrines, and procedures that may not always or easily complement wider notions of accountability and control. Under those circumstances, it is likely that a process of transition will remain partially—maybe even largely—incomplete.

The purpose of this essay is to assess the impact that habits of mind in UK constitutional law have had—and continue to have—on processes of truth telling in Northern Ireland. Northern Ireland's truth telling processes have their origins both in the Belfast/Good Friday Agreement of 1998 (the paradigm example of political compromise: hereinafter the 'Agreement'[7]) and in the Article 2 ECHR requirement that States conduct full and effective investigations into the circumstances of controversial deaths that are caused directly or indirectly by State actors.[8] The corresponding argument in this essay is that prevailing legal habits that take form around core constitutional doctrines and judicial reasoning have, in some significant respects, prevented the fuller bedding down of truth telling processes. This has been most pronounced in respect of meeting the requirements of Article 2 ECHR, as developed by the European Court of Human Rights (ECtHR) in relation to unresolved deaths in Northern Ireland.[9] The ECtHR has, in short, held that a range of procedures and practices need to be modified individually and/or collectively to ensure that the UK is able to discharge its minimum international obligations. However, while the UK Parliament and government have since made a number of important changes (some of which were introduced in direct response to Article 2 ECHR judgments and some of which were domestic initiatives), there remain areas of difficulty associated both with judicial interpretation of the Human Rights Act 1998 that gives effect to the ECHR and with government approaches to, among other things, the suppression of evidence. Although these difficulties reflect UK-wide debates about the constitutional significance of the Human Rights Act 1998 and related constitutional initiatives,[10] they have a particular resonance in Northern Ireland, where political problems with the working through of the

---

Northern Ireland' in Colin Harvey (ed.), *Human Rights, Equality and Democratic Renewal in Northern Ireland* (2001) 215.

[6] See generally Karl Klare, 'Legal Culture and Transformative Constitutionalism' (1998) 14 South African Journal of Human Rights 146.

[7] See Brendan O'Leary, 'The Nature of the Agreement' (1999) 22 Fordham International Law Journal 1628.

[8] Fionnuala Ni Aolain, 'The Evolving Jurisprudence of the European Convention Concerning the Right to Life' (2001) 19 Netherlands Quarterly of Human Rights 21.

[9] See, most notably, *Jordan v UK* (2003) 37 EHRR 2; *Kelly v UK*; *McKerr v UK* (2002) 34 EHRR 20 *& Shanaghan v UK* (Appls No. 30054/96 & 37715/97, May 4, 2001); *McShane v UK* (2002) 35 EHRR 23; and *Finucane v UK* (2003) 37 EHRR 29.

[10] On the significance of the Act see, eg Murray Hunt, 'The Human Rights Act and Legal Culture: The Judiciary and the Legal Profession' (1999) 26 Journal of Law and Society 86.

Agreement have resulted in the ongoing suspension of the local institutions.[11] Those institutions were premised upon a unique form of participatory democracy that was to define the process of transition from conflict (with competence in policing and criminal justice to follow[12]), but suspension has resulted in the 'new' politics of the Agreement being replaced for the moment by the 'old' politics of direct rule.[13] This essay will thus link the constitutional model that underpins suspension to the habits of mind that have informed judicial interpretation of the Human Rights Act 1998 and suggest that they have coalesced to complicate both the practical and contextual workings of transition and truth telling. The essay will, in that way, also complement the long-standing thesis that constitutional doctrines that are problematic in UK law more generally can be particularly so in the context of Northern Ireland.[14]

The essay begins with a section that describes both the Article 2 ECHR critique of UK legal culture and the constitutional context of post-conflict Northern Ireland. It next surveys how the government and the courts have reacted to the Article 2 ECHR critique in terms of institutional adaptation and in terms of the recasting (or otherwise) of legal precepts. Focusing first on the significance of a number of institutional reforms—notably to the Coroners Courts, mechanisms for police accountability, and to the Department of the Director of Public Prosecutions (DPP[15])—the essay next examines case law in which the courts have exhibited a reluctance to embrace to the full the dynamics of Article 2 ECHR. This reluctance was manifest most clearly in the House of Lords judgment in *In Re McKerr*,[16] which held that the Human Rights Act 1998 does not have retrospective effect and cannot apply to controversial deaths that pre-date the Act's coming into force in October 2000.[17] The essay describes the uncertainty that this ruling has generated in terms of the investigation of unresolved deaths in Northern Ireland; and it then considers the significance of the Inquiries Act 2005 which may now govern inquiries into some of the conflict's most controversial killings.

---

[11] Northern Ireland Act 2000 and Northern Ireland Act 2006; SI 2002/2574, SI 2003/1155, SI 2003/2592, SI 2004/1105, SI 2004/2505, SI 2005/868, SI 2005/2046, SI 2006/1012, and SI 2006/2132.

[12] Policing and criminal justice are reserved matters under paras 9–11 of Sch. 3 to the Northern Ireland Act 1998 but may be transferred to the Assembly in accordance with s. 4 of the Act. And see Northern Ireland Miscellaneous Provisions Bill, clauses 16–20 (available at http://www.nio.gov.uk/st-andrews-agreement.pdf).

[13] On which see Gordon Anthony and John Morison, 'Here, There, and (Maybe) Here Again: The Story of Law making for Post-1998 Northern Ireland' in Robert Hazell and Richard Rawlings (eds), *Devolution, Law making, and the Constitution* (2005) 155.

[14] See eg John Morison and Stephen Livingstone, *Reshaping Public Power: Northern Ireland and the British Constitutional Crisis* (1995) and Christopher McCrudden, 'Northern Ireland, the Belfast Agreement, and the British Constitution' in Jeffrey Jowell and Dawn Oliver (eds), *The Changing Constitution* (2004) 195.

[15] Now the Public Prosecution Service of Northern Ireland (PPS): see the Justice (Northern Ireland) Act 2002, s 29.   [16] [2004] 1 WLR 807.

[17] SI 2000/1851.

The conclusion offers some more general and evaluative comments, particularly in the light of ongoing attempts to restore the local institutions.[18]

Article 2 ECHR, The Human Rights Act 1998, and the Agreement

The ECtHR Critique of UK Practice

The aspect of Article 2 ECHR that has proven most problematic in Northern Ireland is that concerned with the procedural, or adjectival, element to the right to life.[19] While the interpretation of the Article originally focused almost exclusively on whether the use of force by State agents under particular circumstances was proportionate,[20] the Article now imposes additional obligations on the State in respect of, first, its preparation for the use of force[21] and, secondly, for the subsequent investigation of that use of force[22] (the Article also imposes positive obligations on the State *vis-à-vis* relations between private parties[23]). The Article does not as such require that prosecutions be brought in respect of each and every use of force, as it is couched in terms that accept that force may be absolutely necessary—and thereby legitimate—in a number of defined circumstances.[24] But where force is resorted to, Article 2 ECHR imposes an obligation to conduct a full, effective, and open investigation into the circumstances surrounding the use of force and any resulting loss of life[25] (the House of Lords accepts that the obligation continues in international law until the requisite investigation is held[26]). The Article in turn also requires that the law provide for the criminal prosecution of those State actors who are considered to have acted unlawfully, whether through their direct or indirect involvement in a death.

---

[18] The most recent proposals are those contained in 'The St Andrews Agreement' (2006) available at http://www.nio.gov.uk/st_andrews_agreement.pdf.

[19] The Article reads: '(1) Everyone's right to life shall be protected by law . . . (2) Deprivation of life shall not be regarded as inflicted in contravention of this Article when it results from the use of force which is no more than absolutely necessary: (a) in defence of any person from unlawful violence; (b) in order to effect a lawful arrest or to prevent the escape of a person lawfully detained; (c) in action lawfully taken for the purpose of quelling a riot or insurrection.'

[20] eg *Stewart v UK* D&R (1984) 162.

[21] See, most famously, *McCann, Farrell and Savage v UK* (1996) 21 EHRR 97.

[22] eg *Kaya v Turkey* (1998) 28 EHRR 1.

[23] eg *Osman v UK* (2000) 29 EHRR 245. And see in Northern Ireland, eg *Re E's Application* [2004] NIQB 35 and [2006] NICA 37.

[24] See n 19 above. For wider and comparative analysis of the issue of responsibility for use of force as a human rights abuse, see Tom Hadden, 'Punishment, Amnesty and Truth: Legal and Political Approaches' in Adrian Guelke (ed.), *Democracy and Ethnic Conflict: Advancing Peace in Deeply Divided Societies* (2004) 196.

[25] *R (Amin) v Secretary of State for the Home Department* [2004] 1 AC 653.

[26] See *In Re McKerr* [2004] 1 WLR 807.

The ECtHR's corresponding critique of principle and practice in Northern Ireland (there have been cases arising from England and Wales too[27]) has focused primarily on the lack of transparency and effectiveness in the post-use of force investigative process. The principal authorities remain *Jordan*, *Kelly*, *McKerr*, and *Shanaghan v UK*,[28] which were centrally concerned with the lack of investigation and accountability when State actors had been involved directly and indirectly in the use of force (in *Jordan*, the applicant's son was killed when a member of the (then) Royal Ulster Constabulary (RUC) who was pursuing his car opened fire as Jordan tried to escape [Jordan was an IRA member, but unarmed at the time]; in *Kelly*, the applicant's son, together with seven other armed IRA members and a civilian, was killed by SAS soldiers dug into position around a police station which the IRA was attacking; in *McKerr*, the applicant's father, together with two other companions, was shot dead by undercover RUC officers [they were members of the IRA, but unarmed]; and in *Shanaghan*, the deceased, who was not a member of the IRA, was shot dead by a masked gunman shortly after the police informed him that his personal details had fallen into the hands of loyalist paramilitaries [the circumstances suggested official involvement in the murder]). While the cases each raised fact-specific and separate issues, they pointed collectively to a number of systemic failings in the investigative and prosecutorial processes.[29] For example, Coroners Courts were criticized as offering too limited an inquiry into the circumstances surrounding controversial deaths. The Coroners legislation, which requires inquests to ascertain 'how' the deceased came about their death,[30] had previously been interpreted to mean that the function of an inquest was to consider 'by what means' death had occurred rather than 'by what means and in what broad circumstances'.[31] This more narrow formulation, which was intended to ensure that inquests did not pre-judge matters of criminal and/or civil liability, was criticized by the ECtHR for closing off the type of investigation that would be all the more necessary for the families of the deceased in the event that criminal proceedings or some other fact-finding exercise did not take place.[32] The ECtHR in similar vein criticized: the rule of procedure whereby Coroners could not compel individuals who had been involved in the use of force to give evidence at an inquest;[33] the delay

---

[27] eg *Edwards v UK* (2002) 35 EHRR 487.

[28] See *Jordan v UK* (2003) 37 EHRR 2; *Kelly v UK* (Appl. No. 30054/96, May 4, 2001); *McKerr v UK* (2002) 34 EHRR 20; and *Shanaghan v UK* (Appl. No. 37715/97, May 4, 2001). See also, *McShane v UK* (2002) 35 EHRR 23 and *Finucane v UK* (2003) 37 EHRR 29.

[29] For fuller analysis of the cases, see Fionnuala Ni Aolain, 'Truth Telling, Accountability and the Right to Life in Northern Ireland' (2002) 5 European Human Rights Law Review 572.

[30] Coroners Act (Northern Ireland) 1958, s. 31(1) and, in England and Wales, s 11(5)(b)(ii) of the Coroners Act 1988, and the Coroners Rules 1984, SI 1984/552, rr 36, 42, and 43.

[31] *Re Ministry of Defence* [1994] NI 279, considering *R v HM Coroner for North Humberside and Scunthorpe, ex p Jamieson* [1995] QB 1.

[32] *Jordan*, paras 128–30; *Kelly*, paras 123–24, *McKerr*, para 145, *Shanghan*, paras 109–13.

[33] *Jordan*, para 127; *Kelly*, para 121, *McKerr*, para 144. Rule 9(2) of the Coroners (Practice and Procedure) Rules (NI) 1963 at that time read: 'Where a person is suspected of causing the death, or

in holding inquiries in the various cases;[34] the absence of legal aid for some of the families of the deceased;[35] the use of public interest immunity certificates to suppress evidence on key issues;[36] and the non-disclosure of witness statements to families prior to the inquiry.[37]

Criticisms were also made of the role of the police in investigating the use of force and of the DPP in deciding whether to bring criminal proceedings against the State actors involved. In respect of the police it was considered that there was a lack of independence as between the investigating and implicated officers and soldiers, which resulted in the overall investigation being affected by concerns about impartiality;[38] and the corresponding criticism of the DPP was of the need for transparency and accountability in respect of prosecution decisions.[39] While criminal proceedings had been initiated in the *McKerr* case, decisions were taken in the other cases not to prosecute and no reasons were given publicly to explain these decisions. Although this was consistent with DPP policy, it was criticized by the ECtHR as contrary to the requirements of openness and legality that inhere in Article 2 ECHR, particularly as judicial review was in general not available in Northern Ireland for the purposes of challenging the DPP's failure to give reasons.[40] Thus, in the *Jordan* case, the ECtHR, having noted that the domestic courts had already said that the circumstances of the death 'crie(d) out for an explanation', concluded: 'There was no reasoned decision available to reassure a concerned public that the rule of law had been respected. This cannot be regarded as compatible with the requirements of Article 2, unless that information was forthcoming in some other way. This however is not the case.'[41]

The Human Rights Act 1998 and the Agreement

The judgments in *Jordan, Kelly, McKerr*, and *Shanaghan* were delivered on 4 May 2001, which was just over three years after the conclusion of the Agreement and seven months after the coming into force of the Human Rights Act 1998. Viewed in the abstract, this should, of course, have meant that the judgments would have had maximum impact at the level of the UK more generally and in Northern Ireland in particular. Not only does the Human Rights Act 1998 require domestic

---

has been charged or is likely to be charged with an offence relating to the death, he shall not be compelled to give evidence at the inquest.'

[34] *Jordan*, paras 136–40, *Kelly*, paras 130–34, *McKerr*, paras 152–55, *Shanaghan*, paras 119–20.

[35] *Jordan*, para 132.   [36] *McKerr*, paras 149–51.

[37] *Jordan*, para 134; *Kelly*, paras 126–28; *McKerr*, paras 147–48; *Shanaghan*, paras 116–17. On the position in NI law before the judgments see eg *R v HM Coroner at Hammersmith ex parte Peach* [1980] 2 All ER 7; *In Re Mailey* [1980] NI 102; *In Re Devine and Breslin's Application* [1988] 14 NIJB 10.

[38] *Jordan*, paras 118–21; *Kelly*, para 114 (re: RUC officers investigating the actions of SAS soldiers who had liaised with the RUC prior to the actions); *McKerr*, paras 128–29, 138–41, *Shanaghan*, paras 104–5.

[39] *Jordan*, paras 122–24, *Kelly*, paras 116–18, *Shanaghan*, paras 106–8.

[40] See eg *Re Adams' Application* [2001] NI 1.   [41] (2003) 37 EHRR 2, para 124.

authorities in the UK to have regard to the judgments,[42] the Agreement, as outlined above and as originally conceived, also envisaged a new constitutional context in the Northern Ireland polity that had first given rise to the cases. While the apex of that context was, and is, the reconciliation of the constitutional demands of Irish Nationalism and Ulster Unionism,[43] the Agreement's related emphasis on human rights, equality, victims' rights, reform of policing, reform of the criminal justice system, decommissioning of paramilitary weapons, and democratic process were also key.[44] These priorities essentially went to the heart of the practical process of transition in post-conflict Northern Ireland that was thought would characterize the bedding-down of the Agreement. Some of the priorities thereby clearly dovetailed with the ECtHR judgments insofar as they appeared to provide prior recognition at the local level of the legitimacy of several of the criticisms made by the Strasbourg Court.

The Agreement's promise of a new constitutionalism has, however, yet to be fully realized and it is here that arguments about prevailing legal habits begin.[45] Although the principal reason for the truncated working of the Agreement is political distrust among Northern Ireland's political parties, that distrust plays out in a wider UK constitutional order that continues to be defined by the (much criticized) legal habit of reliance on the doctrine of Parliamentary sovereignty.[46] This doctrine has meant that the Westminster Parliament has been able to place the Northern Ireland Act 1998 that gives effect to many of the institutional aspects of the Agreement in temporary abeyance,[47] and the doctrine has on that basis seemingly also denied much of the argument about the constitutional integrity of the Agreement and of its signing as a definitive 'constitutional moment'.[48] Just as

---

[42] ss 2, 3 and 6.

[43] Through the consent principle (as now manifest in the Northern Ireland Act 1998, s 1 and Art. 3 of the Irish Constitution 1937) and the creation of a Northern Ireland Assembly, a North/South Ministerial Council (and related implementation bodies) and a British–Irish Council. See further Brendan O'Leary, 'The Nature of the Agreement', n 7 above; and John Morison and Gordon Anthony, 'An Agreed Peace? The Institutions of Democratic Governance in the Belfast Agreement 1998 and the Northern Ireland Act 1998' (1999) 11 European Review of Public Law 1313.

[44] See further Harvey, *Human Rights, Equality and Democratic Renewal in Northern Ireland*, n 5 above. And on the significance of Human Rights in particular, see Paul Mageean and Martin O'Brien, 'From the Margins to the Mainstream: Human Rights and the Good Friday Agreement' (1999) 22 Fordham International Law Journal 1499.

[45] It is now generally accepted that some change to aspects of the Agreement is inevitable: 'the St Andrew Agreement' (2006), available at http://www.nio.gov.uk/st_andrews_agreement.pdf.

[46] The leading critique remains Murray Hunt, *Using Human Rights Law in English Courts* (1997) chs 1–3. Although note that there are increasing judicial soundings to the effect that the doctrine— itself a judge-made construct—is of lessening contemporary value: see eg *Thoburn v Sunderland City Council* [2003] QB 151 (Laws LJ) and *Jackson v Attorney-General* [2005] 3 WLR 733, 767–68, para. [102] (Lord Steyn).

[47] Northern Ireland Act 2000; SI 2002/2574, SI 2003/1155, SI 2003/2592, SI 2004/1105, SI 2004/2505, SI 2005/868, SI 2005/2046, SI 2006/1012, and SI 2006/2132.

[48] The Northern Ireland Act 1998, as read with Agreement, has been described as a constitution for Northern Ireland: see *Robinson v Secretary of State for Northern Ireland* [2002] NI 390. For commentary on the constitutional significance of the Agreement, see Kieran McEvoy and John Morison,

significantly, the interplay of political distrust and Parliamentary sovereignty has prevented the emergence of the fuller type of deliberative democracy that the Agreement was premised upon and which was deemed necessary for the Agreement and each of its component parts fully to take form.[49] The Agreement envisaged interdependence rather than mutual exclusion among Northern Ireland's political communities, but the 'staccato' nature of institution-building has stunted the development of the Agreement's consociational elements.[50] 'Constitutional law' may therefore be 'the third order of the political' and a mature working through of difference and conflict,[51] but the undercurrent of Parliamentary sovereignty would for the meantime appear to have at least part prevented the fuller maturation of Agreement politics.

Similar points can also be made about the positioning of the Human Rights Act 1998 within the wider UK constitutional order. The Act was central to a broader programme of constitutional reform throughout the UK that sought to modernize constitutionalism and its related processes.[52] However, while the Act has recast institutional relations in a manner that, for instance, provides for 'constitutional dialogue' between the courts and the Westminster legislature,[53] its more general grounding in the doctrine of the (final) sovereignty of Parliament remains problematic.[54] The criticism here is not that the Act prefers a constitutional model centred on legislative supremacy—there are well-founded concerns about permitting courts to invalidate primary legislation[55]—but rather that that model can in turn

---

'Beyond the "Constitutional Moment": Law, Transition, and Peacemaking in Northern Ireland' (2003) 26 Fordham International Law Journal 961.

[49] See Colin Harvey, 'Contested Constitutionalism: Human Rights and Deliberative Democracy in Northern Ireland' in Tom Campbell, Keith Ewing, and Adam Tomkins (eds), *Sceptical Essays in Human Rights* (2001) 163. On the relationships between constitutionalism, democracy, and human rights, see further David Feldman, ch. 20.

[50] The term 'staccato' was used by Lord Bingham when describing the stop-start nature of the institutions under the Northern Ireland Act 1998: see *Robinson v Secretary of State for Northern Ireland* [2002] NI 390, 395. On the consociational nature of the Agreement, see O'Leary, 'The Nature of the Agreement', n 7 above; and for a critique of the Northern Ireland Act 2000, see John Morison, 'Democracy, Governance and Governmentality: Civic Public Space and Constitutional Renewal in Northern Ireland' (2001) 21 Oxford Journal of Legal Studies 287.

[51] The terms are Martin Loughlin's: see 'Constitutional Law: The Third Order of the Political' in Nicholas Bamforth and Peter Leyland (eds), *Public Law in a Multi-Layered Constitution* (2003) 27.

[52] For an early account, see Rodney Brazier, 'The Constitution of the United Kingdom' (1999) 58 Cambridge Law Journal 96. But see also John Morison, 'The Case Against Constitutional Reform?' (1998) 25 Journal of Law and Society 510.

[53] See Tom Hickman, 'Constitutional Dialogue, Constitutional Theories and the Human Rights Act 1998' (2005) Public Law 306.

[54] On the design of the Act, see David Feldman, 'The Human Rights Act 1998 and Constitutional Principles' (1999) 19 Legal Studies 165. For criticism of case law under the Act see Keith Ewing, 'The Futility of the Human Rights Act' (2004) Public Law 829. But see also Anthony Lester, 'The utility of the Human Rights Act: a reply to Keith Ewing' (2005) Public Law 249.

[55] For a strong reassertion of the value of political, as opposed to legal/common law, constitutionalism, see Adam Tomkins, *Our Republican Constitution* (2005).

yield to a model of constitutional dualism that regards national law as ultimately distinct from, and superior to, international law.[56] Thus, even though there have been cases in which the courts have adopted a pragmatic approach to the relationship between national law and international law under the terms of the Human Rights Act 1998,[57] there have been others in which the courts have forcefully restated the enduring relevance of constitutional dualism and of national law and the ECHR as essentially separate entities. The seminal example remains the *In Re McKerr* judgment of the House of Lords that was noted above and which is returned to below.

Prospective Changes: The UK Government Response to Article 2 ECHR

Whatever the particular constitutional dynamics of the national system into which *Jordan, Kelly, McKerr,* and *Shanaghan* were to be received, the UK government remained obliged, as a matter of international law, to introduce measures that would implement the judgments of the ECtHR.[58] The government's corresponding response—contained in a 'package of measures' presented to the Committee of Ministers of the Council of Europe[59]—focused on three principal areas identified as problematic; namely the workings of Coroners Courts, mechanisms of police accountability, and the DPP policy on the giving of reasons (although the beginnings of some of the measures were, as noted above, already in place before the judgments).

Coroners Courts

Changes to the Coroners Courts have centred on the ECtHR's concerns about the transparency and effectiveness of inquests. While the changes have not yet been fully endorsed—the Council of Europe Committee of Ministers has reserved its opinion on how far the measures comply with Article 2[60]—they have clearly gone

---

[56] See, in the context of EU membership, Ian Ward, 'Dualism and the Limits of European Integration' (1995) Liverpool Law Review 29.

[57] The leading examples are those concerning the 'Belmarsh detainees': see *A & Ors v Home Secretary* [2005] 2 WLR 87 and *A & Ors v Home Secretary (No 2)* [2006] 1 All ER 575.

[58] ECHR Art. 46.

[59] See Council of Europe Interim Resolution Res DH (2005) 20, *Action of the Security Forces in Northern Ireland (Case of McKerr against the United Kingdom and five similar cases)*, adopted by the Committee of Ministers on 23 February 2005 at the 941st meeting of the Ministers' Deputies. Measures taken or envisaged to ensure compliance with the judgments of the European Court of Human Rights in the cases against the United Kingdom listed in Appendix III. Available at: http://www.coe.int/T/E/Com/press/News/2005/20050224_rec_cm.asp.   [60] ibid.

some distance towards ECHR compliance for the future. Changes have therefore been made to the rule that previously prevented inquests from compelling police officers or others involved in the use of force from appearing as witnesses,[61] and there is now also pre-inquest disclosure to the next-of-kin of individuals who die in police custody or a result of police action.[62] Legal aid is likewise (potentially) available for legal representation at inquests;[63] and a general restructuring of the Coronial system in the light of the Luce Review has been carried out for purposes of, among others, avoiding delay.[64]

The problem of the range of verdicts that are available to Coroners and their juries has in turn been remedied in case law. In *Sacker* and *Middleton*,[65] the House of Lords held that the word 'how' in Coroners legislation in England and Wales— which is in substantially the same terms as the Northern Ireland legislation— should no longer be given the restrictive reading of 'by what means'.[66] Focusing on the interpretive obligation under section 3 of the Human Rights Act 1998, the House of Lords held that 'how' should instead be read to mean 'by what means and in what broad circumstances'. While the judgments will be seen, below, to have generated some confusion on the question of retrospectivity (both cases concerned deaths in prison which pre-dated the coming into force of the Act but which were being investigated after October 2000), their more general significance lies in the fact that they allow Coroners Courts to make fuller findings on the circumstances surrounding deaths in respect of which the Coroners Court is to be the principal forum for investigation. As the House said: 'To meet the procedural requirement of Article 2 an inquest ought ordinarily to culminate in an expression, however brief, of the jury's conclusion on the disputed factual issues at the heart of the case.'[67]

---

[61] Coroners (Practice and Procedure) (Amendment) Rules (Northern Ireland) 2002, SR 2002/37, amending Rule 9(2) of the Coroners (Practice and Procedure) Rules (NI) 1963.

[62] This position changed not as a result of Art. 2 ECHR *per se*, but of the 1999 MacPherson report into the murder of Stephen Lawrence. A Home Office Circular issued after the report—see http://www.statguidance.ipcc.gov.uk/docs/Home%20Office%20Circular%2031.doc—provided that pre-inquest disclosure should be given and this position has since been adopted and implemented by the Chief Constable of the PSNI. Note, however, that it is unclear whether the Prison Service of Northern Ireland similarly considers itself bound in respect of deaths in prison: see Prison Service Order PSO 1301 Investigating a Death in Custody http://pso.hmprisonservice.gov.uk/PSO_1301_deaths_in_prison_custody.doc.

[63] The Lord Chancellor has issued a direction under Art. 12(8) of the Access to Justice (Northern Ireland) Order 2003 which provides for funding for next-of-kin at inquests: see http://www.nilsc.org.uk/uploads/publications/documents/consolidated%20%20LC%20Direction%2023404.pdf: and *Re Collette Hemsworth's Application for Judicial Review (No 2)* [2004] NIQB 26.

[64] See *Death Certification and Investigation in England, Wales and Northern Ireland: The Report of a Fundamental Review 2003*, Cm 5831.

[65] *R (Sacker) v West Yorkshire Coroner* [2004] 1 WLR 796 and *R (Middleton) v West Somerset Coroner* [2004] 2 WLR 800.

[66] Coroners Act 1988 s 11(5)(b)(ii), and the Coroners Rules 1984, SI 1984/552, rr 36, 42, 43. The corresponding NI legislation is Coroners Act (Northern Ireland) 1958, s 31(1).

[67] *R (Middleton) v West Somerset Coroner* [2004] 2 WLR 800, 810, para 20.

Policing and the DPP

Reforms to policing have focused on the ECtHR's concerns about a lack of institutional independence in the investigation of deaths by the police, although the reforms here pre-date the Article 2 judgments.[68] Each of the killings in the four cases were investigated by officers of the (then) RUC, and the ECtHR considered that such officers could not be regarded as independent from officers of the same force or, indeed, from soldiers who worked in co-operation with the police. The corresponding reforms have thus seen the creation of the office of the Police Ombudsman for Northern Ireland.[69] The office, which is staffed independently of the police, is now responsible for all investigations where the police—though not the army—have been involved in the use of live rounds. Use of force by the army would however appear to remain to be investigated by the police, a position which is, on the finding in *Kelly*, inconsistent with Article 2 ECHR.

The approach to the giving of reasons by the DPP has meanwhile been altered in the Code for Prosecutors in Northern Ireland. While the more general policy of not giving reasons for decisions remains unaffected, the Code recognizes that 'there may be cases arising in the future, which (the DPP) would expect to be exceptional in nature, where an expectation will arise that a reasonable explanation will be given for not prosecuting where death is, or may have been, occasioned by the conduct of agents of the State'.[70] The Code continues by noting that there may still be compelling grounds for not giving reasons in such cases, for example where there are duties under the Human Rights Act 1998. But the Code now also recognizes that, where a death is caused by the State, 'it will be in the public interest to reassure a concerned public, including the families of victims, that the rule of law has been respected by the provision of a reasonable explanation. The (DPP) will reach a decision as to the provision of reasons, and their extent, having weighed the applicability of public interest considerations material to the particular facts and circumstances of each individual case.'[71]

Retrospective Difficulties: *In Re McKerr* and the Inquiries Act 2005

The remaining problems that the wider process of truth telling in Northern Ireland has faced have followed from the fact that the above changes are essentially prospective in effect and do not demand reinvestigation of the cases that gave rise

---

[68] Linda Moore and Mary O'Rawe, 'A New Beginning for Policing in Northern Ireland?' in Harvey, *Human Rights, Equality and Democratic Renewal in Northern Ireland*, n 5 above.

[69] Police (Northern Ireland) Act 1998.

[70] Available on the PPSNI website http://www.ppsni.gov.uk/site/default.asp   [71] ibid.

to them (awards of just satisfaction were made) or, moreover, govern other unresolved deaths in the Northern Ireland conflict. Here, and in the absence of the
government voluntarily undertaking fresh investigations, reliance has been placed
upon the Human Rights Act 1998 in a number of attempts to compel Article 2
ECHR compliant investigations. Such attempts have, however, failed because the
courts have read the Human Rights Act 1998 from the above noted dualist constitutional perspective that precludes retrospective effect (the *In Re McKerr* judgment[72]), and the issue of accountability has therefore become one for 'political'
rather than 'constitutional' resolution. While this perhaps begs the question of
where 'politics end' and 'constitutions begin',[73] the failure to constitutionalize the
issue of accountability in the sense of placing it under the Human Rights Act 1998
has resulted in a number of other particularly high-profile deaths—including
some which the ECtHR has also found to have violated Article 2 ECHR[74]—
assuming a central place in debates about the accountability gap. As this debate
has (largely) taken place against the backdrop of the suspension of the Northern
Ireland institutions, this factor too has complicated the intended links between
truth telling and the emergence of a new constitutionalism. Indeed, while the
Northern Ireland institutions would not in themselves have been competent to
legislate to order Article 2 ECHR compliant investigations,[75] their functioning
would nevertheless have added to the context of transition that the Agreement
envisaged and in which unresolved deaths—and a range of other issues—should
have been addressed. In their absence, the matter has instead been left to *ad hoc*
inquiries and related legislation.

In Re McKerr

In Re McKerr was an application for judicial review brought on foot of *McKerr v
UK* in which the son of the deceased sought mandamus to compel the Secretary of
State to order an Article 2 ECHR compliant investigation into his father's death in
1982 (the applicant also sought damages, as well as a declaration that he had a
continuing right to an investigation and that the Secretary of State was in breach
of Article 2 ECHR and section 6 of the Human Rights Act for so long as he failed
to order a full investigation). The application was first dismissed by the High
Court in Northern Ireland, which considered that the earlier award of damages by
the ECtHR had compensated the applicant for the violation of Article 2 ECHR
and that the violation had at that stage ceased.[76] However, the Northern Ireland
Court of Appeal disagreed, and made a declaration that the applicant had a

[72] [2004] 1 WLR 807. The position was less clear before the judgment of the House of Lords: see
Re Jordan's Application [2003] NIQB 1; *Re David Wright's Application* [2003] NIQB 17; *Re Jordan's
Application* [2003] NICA 54; *Re McCaughey and Grew's Application* [2004] NIQB 2.
[73] See further Loughlin, 'Constitutional Law: The Third Order of the Political', n 51 above.
[74] *Finucane v UK* (2003) 37 EHRR 29.   [75] See n 12 above and text.
[76] Unreported, 27 July 2002.

continuing right to an investigation.[77] While the Court declined to order an investigation—the government had at that time recently made submissions to the Committee of Ministers on how it might comply with the ECtHR's earlier judgment and the Court considered that a mandatory order would be inappropriate—it nevertheless considered that the absence of a full investigation remained actionable: 'the appellant's claim is well founded . . . there is a continuing breach of Article 2(1) which requires to be addressed by the respondent Government . . . we propose to allow the appeal and make a declaration that the respondent Government has failed to carry out an investigation which complies with the requirements of Article 2 of the Convention'.[78]

The Secretary of State appealed to the House of Lords, where the central question became whether the Human Rights Act 1998 could have retrospective effect such as would allow it to apply to a death that predated the Act's coming into force by, in this instance, 18 years. As the House of Lords had already held on several occasions that the relevant provisions of the Act preclude retrospective effect,[79] the applicant argued that the nature of the Article 2 ECHR obligation in this case in effect transcended the provisions of the domestic legislation (the point being that the obligation was continuing and that, while it had its origins in 1982, it still existed post-2000 and thereby came under the Act). The House of Lords however disagreed and allowed the appeal. The decisive factor for their Lordships was the dualist distinction between domestic law and international law, such as impacted upon the domestic relevance of a continuing obligation in international law. Although there was some discussion in the case of the problematic nature of constitutional dualism that founded the distinction,[80] their Lordships ultimately held that the continuing obligation in the case was confined to the international law sphere. The position in domestic law was different and had to be determined with reference to the Human Rights Act 1998, which it was clear could not apply to events that pre-dated October 2000.[81] Given this, Lord Nicholls emphasized that there could be no investigative obligation in domestic law, as any obligation first required that the events giving rise to it came within the temporal reach of the Act. The continuing obligation in international law—which had its origins in 1982—was therefore irrelevant:

'Having had the advantage of much fuller arguments I respectfully consider that (some other UK courts) fell into error by failing to keep clearly in mind the distinction between (1) rights arising under the Convention and (2) rights created by the 1998 Act by reference

---

[77] *Re McKerr's Application* [2003] NI 117.

[78] *Re McKerr's Application* [2003] NI 117, 122, para 13 (Carswell LCJ).

[79] Ss 7 and 22, and eg *R v Lambert* [2002] 2 AC 545 (as read in the light of *R v Kansal* [2002] 1 All ER 257); *Wainwright v Home Office* [2003] 4 All ER 969; *R v Lyons* [2003] 1 AC 976; and *Wilson v First County Trust (No 2)* [2004] 1 AC 816.

[80] See in particular the judgment of Lord Steyn: [2004] 1 WLR 807, 817 ff.

[81] Comparable arguments about continuing obligations had also failed in other cases in Northern Ireland: see eg *Re Adams' Application* [2001] NI 1 and *Re Jordan's Application* [2003] NICA 54.

to the Convention. These two rights now exist side by side. But there are significant differences between them. The former existed before the enactment of the 1998 Act and they continue to exist. They are not as such part of this country's law because the Convention does not form part of this country's law. That is still the position. These rights, arising under the Convention, are to be contrasted with rights created by the 1998 Act. The latter came into existence for the first time on 2 October 2000. They are part of this country's law. The extent of these rights, created as they were by the 1998 Act, depends on the proper interpretation of that Act. It by no means follows that the continuing existence of a right arising under the Convention in respect of an act occurring before the 1998 Act came into force will be mirrored by a corresponding right created by the 1998 Act. Whether it finds reflection in this way in the 1998 Act depends upon the proper interpretation of the 1998 Act.'[82]

Other members of the House of Lords sought further to justify the retrospective effect conclusion with reference to the pragmatic consideration that, in the absence of a cut-off point, every pre-2000 death—or violation of a Convention right—could then potentially found an action.[83] Whatever the merit in the argument—one counterpoint is that the right to life is qualitatively different from other rights in the ECHR and thereby demanding of greater judicial invention—its legitimacy was part affected by the House of Lords judgments, on the same day, in the *Sacker* and *Middleton* cases that were considered above.[84] These cases, again, concerned pre-October 2000 deaths in prison which were the subject of Coroners inquiries after the date of the coming into force of the Human Rights Act 1998. In holding that the relevant legislation should be construed in the light of the section 3 obligation in the Human Rights Act 1998, the House afforded the Act a retrospective effect that was apparently inconsistent with the finding in *In Re McKerr*. That inconsistency was not however addressed as problematic, and the House sought to explain the disjuncture simply by stating: 'In (these appeals) no question was raised on the retrospective application of the Human Rights Act and the Convention. They were assumed to be applicable. Nothing in this opinion should be understood to throw doubt on the conclusion of the House in *In Re McKerr*.'[85]

The inconsistency between *McKerr* and *Sacker/Middleton* generated an inevitable uncertainty in the Northern Ireland courts, where it was initially thought that there were the two options of either distinguishing *McKerr* or following it.[86] For instance, in *Re Jordan's Application*, the Northern Ireland Court of Appeal chose to

---

[82] [2004] 1 WLR 807, 815.

[83] The point was put at it's highest by Lord Hoffman: 'Otherwise there can in principle be no limit to the time one could have to go back in history and carry out investigations . . . It would in principle be necessary to investigate the deaths by state action of the Princes in the Tower.' See [2004] 1 WLR 807, 827, para 67.

[84] *R (Sacker) v West Yorkshire Coroner* [2004] 1 WLR 796 and *R (Middleton) v West Somerset Coroner* [2004] 2 WLR 800.   [85] [2004] 2 WLR 800, 819.

[86] And see also in England and Wales, *R (Challender) v Legal Services Commission* [2004] EWHC 925 and *Commissioner of Police for the Metropolis v Hurst* [2005] EWCA 890. Note that the inconsistency is, at the time of writing, on appeal before the House of Lords in the *Hurst* case and in *Re McCaughey and Grew's Application* [2005] NI 344, considered below.

distinguish *McKerr* when holding that an incomplete inquest into the death of Pearse Jordan (a case which had already gone to Strasbourg[87]) should be conducted in the light of *Sacker* and *Middleton*.[88] Girvan J reached this conclusion on the ground that while *McKerr* has established definitively 'that the obligation to carry out an Article 2 compliant investigation (does) not apply where the death' predates the Act, the case does not deal with the situation which 'applies in the present case where there (is) an ongoing and incomplete inquest in respect of the deceased which falls to be completed subsequent to the commencement of the Human Rights Act'.[89] Holding in particular that the interpretive obligation in section 3 of the Human Rights Act is of general application and that it applies to legislation that predates the Act, the Court noted that this may, as in *Sacker* and *Middleton*, allow facts that predate the Act to give rise to a question of interpretation in a post-October 2000 context. While the Court in turn accepted that there should be no revised interpretive approach where this would affect vested or pre-existing contractual rights,[90] it cited authority to the effect that interpretive changes are permissible so long as they only have an impact upon procedure and do not create injustices for the parties.[91] Having thus concluded that the application of 'section 3 to the conduct of inquests . . . would not interfere with any vested rights and would merely affect the procedure of an inquest which has only really started', the Court considered that the guiding principles for the instant case were to be found in *Sacker* and *Middleton*, rather than *McKerr*: 'In *McKerr* there was no question of an ongoing incomplete inquest . . . The coroner must conduct that inquest in accordance with domestic law but the domestic law duties of the coroner and the jury fall to be interpreted in a manner which is consistent with the Convention. This conclusion is in accordance with the decisions in *Middleton* and *Sacker*.'[92]

The Northern Ireland Court of Appeal was however to adopt the opposite approach in *Re McCaughey and Grew's Application*,[93] where Girvan J's comments in *Jordan* were read as *obiter*. This was an appeal against a decision of the High Court that held that the Chief Constable of the Police Service of Northern Ireland (PSNI) was under a continuing duty by virtue of section 8 of the Coroner's Act (Northern Ireland) 1959 and Article 2 ECHR to provide the Coroner with certain police documents relevant to an inquest into the deaths of the applicants' sons (deaths which had, again, occurred pre-2000).[94] In allowing the appeal, the Court of Appeal considered at length the Court's earlier decision in *Jordan* before concluding that it had been wrong to distinguish *McKerr*. Kerr LCJ, who delivered

---

[87] See nn 28–41 above, and text.   [88] [2004] NICA 29 and [2004] NICA 30.
[89] [2004] NICA 29, para 13 (Girvan J).
[90] ibid paras 20–23, considering *Wilson v First County Trust (No 2)* [2004] 1 AC 816. See also Nicholson LJ's judgment at [2004] NICA 30, para 39.
[91] [2004] NICA 29, para 22, citing *Republic of Costa Rica v Erlanger* [1876] 3 Chan 62, 69.
[92] ibid, para 23.   [93] [2005] NI 344.
[94] *Re McCaughey and Grew's Application* [2004] NIQB 2.

the judgment of the Court, stated that the flaw in the Court's earlier approach lay in the fact that section 3 of the Human Rights Act can only apply where the ECHR is of application. Finding that neither the appellant in *Jordan* nor the respondents in the instant appeal had access to the ECHR because of the non-retrospectivity of the Human Rights Act, he stated that section 3 could not be in issue here—or in *Jordan*—because the deaths involved had occurred before the Human Rights Act came into force: 'Lord Hoffman (in *McKerr*) put it bluntly, "Either the Act applies to deaths before 2 October 2000, or it does not". He held that it did not.'[95]

The Cory Process and the Inquiries Act 2005

McCaughey and Grew is but one example of the large number of other conflict-related incidents that give rise to Article 2 ECHR issues but which now fall out-with the Human Rights Act 1998. During the conflict, there were approximately 360 deaths caused by members of the police and/or army while on duty in Northern Ireland,[96] some of which have been investigated and some of which, as with *Jordan* and *McCaughey and Grew*, remain subject to ongoing inquiry. More controversial still is the number of deaths which can be attributed to some extent to collusion between the police and/or army on the one hand, and (generally) loyalist paramilitaries on the other. A small group of such cases has since become synonymous with ongoing problems with truth recovery while at the same time assuming the key political significance that was mentioned above (their resolution being viewed by some as central to the reinvigoration of the overall political process in Northern Ireland). The most high-profile cases involve serious and credible allegations of official collusion in the murders of two prominent human rights lawyers, Patrick Finucane and Rosemary Nelson, Catholic man Robert Hamill, and the leader of the loyalist paramilitary group, the Loyalist Volunteer Force, Billy Wright (one of the few cases concerning alleged collusion between State agents and republican paramilitaries). In terms of the institutional changes made in the light of the Agreement and/or Article 2 ECHR, the cases raise further concerns about the functioning of the police, the army, and other intelligence agencies, the DPP, police complaints mechanisms, the courts, and indeed officials and ministers at the heart of government.[97] The cases have therefore long been understood (potentially) to demand further changes to the institutions already affected by the process of transition in Northern Ireland. Aspects of the corresponding government response to them have, however, served only to raise further questions about old and emerging obstacles to truth.

[95] [2005] NI 344, 358, para 44.
[96] See generally Fionnuala Ní Aoláin, *The Politics of Force: Conflict Management and State Violence in Northern Ireland* (2000).
[97] The *Finucane* case itself has already given rise to a finding of a violation of Art. 2: see *Finucane v UK* (2003) 37 EHRR 29.

The principal difficulty is concerned with the form that investigations into the deaths should now take. For instance, it had long been argued that the deaths could only be fully and properly investigated by independent public inquiries, and the Article 2 ECHR jurisprudence of the ECtHR added to such arguments to the extent that it tended to undermine the integrity of the investigations already carried out (each of the killings had been subject to separate police and, in two of the cases, coronial investigation). The UK government refused to establish such inquiries for a sustained period of time, but it finally agreed, together with its Irish counterpart, to invite a retired Canadian Supreme Court judge, Peter Cory, to examine the four cases along with two in the Irish Republic (both governments agreed to comply with the judge's findings and to establish inquiries in their respective jurisdictions should they be recommended[98]). The judge subsequently recommended public inquiries in each of the four cases (along with one case of alleged collusion in the Republic of Ireland that had resulted in the deaths of two senior RUC officers),[99] and the UK government responded to the recommendations in the Nelson, Hamill and Wright cases by establishing statutory inquiries under the relevant legislation (the Police (Northern Ireland) Act 1998 in the cases of Hamill and Nelson; and the Prisons Act (Northern Ireland) 1953 in Wright). Its response to the recommendation in respect of the Finucane case was, however, very different. In that case, which arguably raised the most potentially damaging allegations of official misconduct, the government failed to establish an inquiry under what would have been the most suitable domestic legislation (the Tribunals of Inquiry (Evidence) Act 1921), but indicated instead that new legislation would have to be enacted. Thus, even though the Tribunals of Inquiry (Evidence) Act 1921 had been the basis of the Saville Inquiry into the events of Bloody Sunday in Northern Ireland, the government felt that the older legislation was inappropriate for addressing the circumstances surrounding the murder of Mr Finucane. The government in consequence introduced (what became) the Inquires Act 2005.

The 2005 Act has been the subject of significant criticism, most notably from within the judiciary. Not only does the Act remove from Parliament, and give to Ministers, the power to establish inquiries into matters of public importance,[100] it also provides a framework that governs: the appointment of inquiry chairmen and members; the setting of terms of reference; and the conduct of inquiry proceedings.[101] The Act moreover confers powers on the Minister in relation to the conclusion or suspension of an inquiry;[102] the restriction on public access to inquiry proceedings;[103] the disclosure of evidence to the inquiry;[104] and the publication of the reports of inquiries.[105] Such powers of restriction have been said by some to

---

[98] See http://www.justice.ie/80256E01003A02CF/vWeb/pcJUSQ5XKJ5C-en.

[99] The reports as relate to Northern Ireland are available at http://www.nio.gov.uk/index/media-centre/media-detail.htm?newsID=9220; and for those in respect of the Republic of Ireland, see http://www.justice.ie/80256E010039C5AF/vWeb/pcJUSQ5XEL6Q-en.

[100] Inquiries Act 2005, s 1. [101] ibid, ss 3–14 & 17–23. [102] ibid, ss 13–14.
[103] ibid, s 19. [104] ibid, ss 19–20. [105] ibid, s 25.

have brought about a fundamental shift in the manner in which the actions of government and public bodies can be subjected to scrutiny in the UK,[106] and the Joint Committee of Human Rights in Parliament has also noted that the scope for interference in the workings of inquiries raises concerns about the legislation's compatibility with Article 2 ECHR.[107] Even more telling have been the criticisms by Lord Saville, the chair of the Bloody Sunday Inquiry, who has highlighted the legislation's (potential) impact on the needed independence of inquiries. In a letter to Baroness Ashton at the Department of Constitutional Affairs, he voiced particular concern about restriction notices and orders, and said: 'I take the view that this provision makes a very serious inroad into the independence of any inquiry and is likely to damage or destroy public confidence in the inquiry and its findings, especially in cases where the conduct of the authorities may be in question.' He added that such ministerial interference with a judge's ability to act impartially and independently of government would be unjustifiable and that neither he nor his fellow judges on the Bloody Sunday Inquiry would be prepared to be appointed as a member of an inquiry that was subject to a provision of that kind.[108]

Of course, it remains to be seen quite how the legislation will work in practice. Nevertheless, the fact that it was introduced to give effect to a recommendation in a report that sought finally to bring to an end concerns about a number of controversial deaths suggests once again that legal habits of mind—in this instance the government's emphasis on national security[109]—can impact negatively on processes of truth telling and accountability. The prevailing influence of such habits can, for instance, also be seen in the government's recent decision to convert the inquiries established into the murders of Billy Wright and Robert Hamill under the Prisons Act (Northern Ireland) 1953 and the Police (Northern Ireland) Act 1998, respectively into inquiries under the Inquiries Act 2005.[110] Proceedings to challenge the lawfulness of the decisions have since been initiated, and some of the central arguments have again focused on Article 2 ECHR. The final judgment of the court(s) should doubtless reveal much about how far—if at all—Article 2 ECHR exists as an overarching constitutional norm in Northern Ireland's present constitutional context.

Conclusion

This essay began by stating that transparency and accountability are central to any meaningful process of transition, but that the fuller attainment of those values in

106 BIRW critique on Inquiries Act www.birw.org.
107 http://www.parliament.uk/parliamentary_committees/joint_committee_on_human_rights.cfm
108 Available at http://www.birw.org/Saville%20letters.html
109 Laurence Lustgarten, *In From the Cold: National Security and Parliamentary Democracy* (1994).
110 Statements of Secretary of State Peter Hain, 23 November 2005 and 29 March 2006, www.nio.gov.uk (the transfer of inquiries is provided for by s 15 of the Inquiries Act 2005).

Northern Ireland has, for the moment, been frustrated by the truncated working of the Agreement and by the response of the UK government and courts to Article 2 ECHR. In developing the point with reference to the imagery of habits of mind, the essay has highlighted in particular the problematic nature of the doctrine of Parliamentary sovereignty, both in the manner in which it has negated some of the constitutionalizing potential of the Agreement as well as in the way in which it places domestic human rights law at one remove from international norms. While the difficulties in respect of Article 2 ECHR have played out in the wider UK constitutional order, they have had an obvious and politically added importance in Northern Ireland, where suspension of the Assembly has increased the accountability void. Even without the complicating consideration of the Inquiries Act 2005 and related government decisions, the wider story of Article 2 ECHR has thus illustrated again how core precepts of the UK constitution can be of questionable value in the Northern Ireland polity.[111]

Whether—or how far—this means that habits of mind in UK constitutional law will continue to retard the process of transition is perhaps less apparent. Certainly, and in terms of Parliamentary sovereignty and the Agreement, it is arguable that the structures for devolution in Northern Ireland may, in any event, only result in further complexities. Attempts to restore the institutions have, for instance, recently been linked to the devolution of policing and criminal justice to a Ministry that may be given to one party in the Assembly or, as *per* the consociational design of the Agreement, shared between two.[112] This, at one level, is potentially very significant as a restored Assembly would then have competence not just in respect of unresolved deaths caused by State actors but also those caused by paramilitary organizations (whose actions are, for the moment, among those being examined by a specially constituted Historical Enquiries Team[113]). However, while the Assembly may wish to legislate for a more comprehensive truth-telling mechanism—the model that is most frequently cited is a truth and reconciliation commission of the kind famously established in South Africa[114]—the fact that 'national security' remains an excepted matter under the Northern Ireland Act 1998[115] may result in any legislative initiative giving rise to a 'devolution issue'.[116] National security is defined in the Northern Ireland Act 1998 to include 'special powers and other provisions for dealing with terrorism or subversion', and it may be that the outworking of a fuller truth-telling process would infringe upon such matters. On the

---

[111] See Morison and Livingstone, *Reshaping Public Power: Northern Ireland and the British Constitutional Crisis*, n 14 above; and McCrudden, 'Northern Ireland, the Belfast Agreement, and the British Constitution', n 14 above.

[112] Northern Ireland Miscellaneous Provisions Bill, clauses 16–20 (available at http://www.publications.parliament.uk/pa/ld200506/ldbills/110/2006110.htm).

[113] See http://www.psni.police.uk/index/departments/historical_enquiries_team.htm

[114] On which see Richard A Wilson, *The Politics of Truth and Reconciliation in South Africa: Legitimizing the Post-Apartheid State* (2001). [115] Sch 2, para 17.

[116] Sch 10. On which see further Graham Gee, 'Devolution and the Courts' in Robert Hazell and Richard Rawlings (eds), *Devolution, Law making, and the Constitution*, n 13 above, 252.

assumption that an Assembly Bill could be both introduced and be enacted as law,[117] any subsequent hearing of the 'devolution issue' would thus require the courts to consider closely the nature of the lines that demarcate power in the UK and to assess whether a literal reading of the Northern Ireland Act 1998 should be allowed to frustrate the purpose of related legislation on policing and criminal justice.

However, even without such intergovernmental tensions, it is clear that the process of truth telling remains ill-defined and incomplete. Although the UK government and courts may themselves choose to redraw the domestic boundaries within which Article 2 ECHR must develop—the question of the retrospective effect of Article 2 is again pending before the House of Lords[118]—*In Re McKerr* and the Inquiries Act 2005 appear more as set positions than moveable markers. Given this, it may be that the impetus for further change will once more have to come from within the Council of Europe. When considering the content of the package of measures introduced in the light of *Jordan, Kelly, McKerr,* and *Shanaghan,* the Committee of Ministers of the Council of Europe noted that 'certain general measures remain to be taken and that further information and clarifications are outstanding with regard to a number of other measures, including, where appropriate, information on the impact of these measures in practice'.[119] While the Committee thus welcomed the measures that had been adopted in respect of Coroners and police investigations (among other things), it indicated that further changes may be needed if the UK government is to discharge fully its minimum international obligations. Should that change not be forthcoming, further censure of the UK could only serve to highlight a retrospective and defining problem that goes far beyond the limited number of cases heard by the ECtHR.

---

[117] Northern Ireland Act 1998, ss 10–11 and 14.   [118] See n 86 above.
[119] See Council of Europe Interim Resolution Res DH (2005) 20, *Action of the Security Forces in Northern Ireland (Case of McKerr against the United Kingdom and five similar cases),* n 59 above.

11

The Impact of the Human Rights Act in Northern Ireland

Brice Dickson

Introduction

Amidst all the controversy surrounding the extent to which human rights are protected in Northern Ireland it is surprising that so little attention has been paid to the impact of the Human Rights Act 1998. Passed at Westminster in the same month as the Northern Ireland Act 1998[1]—which implemented significant parts of the Belfast (Good Friday) Agreement of 10 April 1998[2]—the Human Rights Act incorporated into the laws of all parts of the UK most of the rights contained in the European Convention on Human Rights of 1950.[3]

The Act was intended to ensure that all public authorities in the UK—including 'any person certain of whose functions are functions of a public nature'[4]—act compatibly with Convention rights. If they do not do so they can be sued by any victim of the act in question.[5] For such breaches courts and tribunals can give whatever remedies they think appropriate within their existing powers.[6] The Act also obliges courts to give effect to legislation, 'so far as it is possible to do so', in a way which is compatible with Convention rights,[7] but in situations where legislation is too clearly in contravention of Convention rights to be interpreted in this way courts are empowered to invalidate it if it is subordinate legislation or to

---

[1] The Human Rights Act received the Royal Assent on 9 November 1998 and the Northern Ireland Act on 19 November 1998. But the earlier Act did not come fully into force until 2 October 2000.

[2] Cm 3883.

[3] More precisely it said that Arts 2 to 12 and 14 of the Convention, Arts 1 to 3 of Protocol 1, and Arts 1 and 2 of Protocol 6 (all as read with Arts 16 to 18 of the Convention) are to have effect for the purposes of the Human Rights Act 1998. These are called, by s 1(1), 'the Convention rights'.

[4] s 6(3)(b).

[5] s 7. By s 7(5) the victim must bring his or her claim within one year of the act occurring or within such longer period as the court considers equitable. Section 7(7) makes it clear that 'victim' means what it means in Art. 34 of the European Convention on Human Rights, which specifies who can bring applications to the European Court.

[6] s 8.

[7] s 3.

declare it incompatible if it is primary.[8] Issuing a declaration of incompatibility sends a clear message to Parliament and to law-enforcers that the legislation in question should be considered a dead letter. If it needs to be replaced by new legislation one method of doing so is for a government Minister to fast-track an amendment by processing a 'remedial order' through Parliament.[9]

Amongst campaigners for human rights in Great Britain there was much rejoicing at the passing of the Act.[10] It was seen as a huge leap forward, and one that was long overdue. Its enactment was a vindication of the calls made in preceding years by a number of senior judges and respected lawyers for incorporation of the Convention. There was particular admiration for the way in which the Act was drafted, and especially for the way it struck a workable balance between empowering judges and at the same time safeguarding the doctrine of Parliamentary sovereignty. There were hopes that the Act would presage a change to the human rights culture of British society and reduce the number of applications brought against Britain in the European Court of Human Rights.[11] But there were, of course, many sceptics. Left-wing commentators feared that the Act would give too much power to judges and not address the most serious human rights abuses in the country—poverty, ill-health, and marginalization.[12] Right-wing commentators feared that it would lead to excessive political correctness and a waste of public money. The media and some church organizations complained that the Act could *lessen* their existing freedoms. Some judges hinted that it was superfluous[13] or that it would politicize their role.[14] A few philosophers thought that the whole rights discourse was an unproductive way of forging a responsible and trustworthy society.[15]

---

[8] s 4. Any court or tribunal can invalidate subordinate legislation but only the High Court or above can issue a declaration of incompatibility. 'Primary legislation' and 'subordinate legislation' are defined in s 21.

[9] s 10. So far only one such order has been issued consequent on a declaration of incompatibility—the Mental Health Act 1983 (Remedial) Order 2001, SI 2001/3712. Curiously, no such order has been made for Northern Ireland, even though the defect it remedied (in ss 72(1) and 73(1) of the Mental Health Act 1983) also exists in arts 77(1) and 78(1) of the Mental Health (NI) Order 1986.

[10] See generally Francesca Klug, *Values for a Godless Age: The Story of the United Kingdom's New Bill of Rights* (2000) ch. 1. She claims, at p 19, that over £1 million was spent promoting the new Act.

[11] Murray Hunt, 'The Human Rights Act and Legal Culture: The Judiciary and the Legal Profession' (1999) 26 Journal of Law and Society 86.

[12] Prominent amongst the academic critics has been Keith Ewing. See his 'The Futility of the Human Rights Act' (2004) PL 829, and also Anthony Lester, 'The Utility of the Human Rights Act: A Response to Keith Ewing' (2005) PL 249.

[13] Lord McCloskey, a retired Scottish judge, allegedly said that the Act would be 'a field day for crackpots, a pain in the neck for judges and legislators, and a goldmine for lawyers'. This remark was endorsed by Michael Howard, leader of Her Majesty's Opposition, in an article he wrote for the *Daily Telegraph* on 10 August 2005.

[14] See eg Sir Robert Carswell, the then Lord Chief Justice of Northern Ireland, in an address to the Conference of the World Police Medical Officers in Vancouver in 1999 (1999) 6 Journal of Clinical Forensic Medicine 249.

[15] See eg Baroness O'Neill in her Reith Lectures, *A Question of Trust* (2002).

In Northern Ireland, curiously, there was very little public debate about the potential consequences of the Act. As so often, local politicians and commentators were fixated with more parochial concerns, in particular the rolling out of the Belfast Agreement. Even the references within that Agreement to the incorporation of the European Convention on Human Rights into the law of Northern Ireland went almost unnoticed.[16] The Committee on the Administration of Justice (CAJ), the leading non-governmental human rights organization in Northern Ireland, said virtually nothing about the Act,[17] and political parties, too, were strangely reticent. Democratic Unionist and Ulster Unionist MPs were not particularly supportive of the Act when it was passing through Parliament: Peter Robinson and David Trimble voted for a proposed amendment which would have suspended the effect of a declaration of incompatibility until the European Court had pronounced on the matter.[18]

Given this silence, it is reasonable to examine whether the Act has actually made much of an impact in Northern Ireland. How to measure that impact is problematic, but attempts to do so are nevertheless worthwhile. If progress on the human rights front is not carefully recorded, efforts to enhance protection of rights still further may be easier to thwart. After setting the commencement of the Act in context, this essay looks at the attention paid to it by Northern Ireland's legislators, government, public authorities, and legal professionals. It concludes that the influence of the Act has indeed been significant, even if the rights in question have not always been protected as fully as they might have been.

The Context of the Act's Commencement

Following the enactment of the Human Rights Act the British government decided to delay its commencement by nearly two years so that all public authorities could have the opportunity to prepare for its coming into force. Judges, in particular, were to be given specialist training and £4.5 million was set aside to allow the Judicial Studies Board to run appropriate courses.[19] Judges from Northern Ireland were included in that training, several of them becoming trained as trainers themselves. The Judicial Studies Board of Northern Ireland also sent some judges and magistrates to be trained in Strasbourg in 1999 and since 1998 has itself organized some 15 training sessions specifically devoted to human rights for local judges at all levels.[20] These sessions have been addressed by academic and practitioner

[16] It is given less than a page in Austen Morgan's 600-page book *The Belfast Agreement: A Practical Legal Analysis* (2000) 376–77.

[17] On the other hand, the Law Centre (NI), through its director Les Allamby, produced a very useful guide to the Act, *Rights in Progress*, in 2002. A second edition appeared in 2004.

[18] HC Debs, 1997–98, Vol 317, col 1294–1311.

[19] Klug, *Values for a Godless Age: The Story of the United Kingdom's New Bill of Rights*, n 10 above, 33.

[20] Letter from the secretary to the Judicial Studies Board, 15 February 2006.

experts from Northern Ireland and elsewhere and are still organized on an *ad hoc* basis as the need arises.

In January 2000 the Home Office established a Task Force to help the government and other public authorities prepare for the commencement of the Human Rights Act and to promote awareness of it. A representative from the Northern Ireland Human Rights Commission (NIHRC)[21] was invited to attend the monthly meetings of this Task Force, as was someone from the CAJ. Over the following 18 months each national government department, including the Northern Ireland Office (NIO), made a presentation to the Task Force on how it was getting ready for the Act. The Task Force also worked with the Home Office in publishing guidance on the Act for all departments.[22] In due course the Office of the First Minister and Deputy First Minister (OFMDFM) produced similar guidance for government departments in Northern Ireland this has been updated and circulated to all civil servants in Northern Ireland in 2006.[23] The OFMDFM has a Human Rights Unit, the job of which is to ensure that all areas of legislation, policy, and administrative practice in Northern Ireland's government departments comply with the Human Rights Act.[24]

In September 2000 the NIHRC, for its part, co-published with the Citizenship Foundation a booklet explaining in plain terms what the Human Rights Act should mean in practice for people living in Northern Ireland. It also accepted invitations to give training on the Act to various public bodies,[25] although it made clear its view that the primary obligation for bringing civil servants up to speed with the Act rested on the government itself, not on an underfunded quango which had been established with much more wide-ranging duties.[26] The Commission has since run many events at which the consequences of the Human Rights Act for the law of Northern Ireland have been addressed and Commission representatives have spoken about the Act at numerous conferences, seminars, roundtables, workshops, and annual meetings. Most recently the Commission has begun to publish what may eventually become a series of practical guides to rights

[21] This is a statutory body set up by s 68 of the Northern Ireland Act 1998 as a result of the Belfast Agreement. The current author was Chief Commissioner of the Commission from 1999 to 2005. He attended several meetings of the Task Force.

[22] Responsibility for human rights legislation has since been transferred from the Home Office to the Department for Constitutional Affairs (the former Lord Chancellor's Department), where a Human Rights Unit maintains web pages detailing new developments in the field: www.humanrights.gov.uk. The Home Office's initial guidance on the Act has been replaced by the DCA's 'Study Guide'. The Department of Health also has a site with guidance on the Act for health bodies: www.doh.gov.uk/humanrights.   [23] The new document is called *Get In On The Act*.

[24] www.ofmdfmni.gov.uk/index/equality/human-rights/human-rights-about-us.htm.

[25] Including the Probation Board of Northern Ireland, the Housing Executive of Northern Ireland and the OFMDFM. The Commission also posted on its website some materials on the Act for use in training on human rights more generally: see www.nihrc.org/documents/pubs/et/material_HR2001.doc.

[26] See eg Recommendation 9 in the Commission's 'Report to the Secretary of State Required by Section 69(2) of the Northern Ireland Act 1998' (2001), available at www.nihrc.org/documents/pubs/ hrc/effectiveness.doc.

protected by the Act.[27] It has been aware since its inception of the significance of the Act and agrees with the view of the Parliamentary Joint Committee on Human Rights that human rights commissions can play an important role in ensuring its effective implementation.[28] It has nevertheless been taken to task for not fully auditing what Northern Irish public authorities did to prepare for the implementation of the Act and for not using work on the Act as 'a valuable pilot exercise and potential template' for later training on any Bill of Rights that may be enacted for Northern Ireland.[29] In its Strategic Plan for 2006–09 the Commission has listed as one of its top objectives the introduction to the public sector of a human rights impact assessment framework to measure compliance with the Act.[30] The Plan also commits the Commission to promoting the Human Rights Act, to monitoring the case law resulting from it and to securing changes in public policy to reflect the Act.[31] If vigorously pursued, this strategy will represent a step-change in the NIHRC's approach to the Act.

Besides committing the British government to incorporate the European Convention into the law of Northern Ireland,[32] the Belfast Agreement said that the new NIHRC would be tasked with advising the British government on the scope for enacting at Westminster a Bill of Rights for Northern Ireland that would comprise not just the rights in the European Convention but also rights reflecting the particular circumstances of Northern Ireland, the principle of mutual respect for the identity and ethos of both communities, and the principle of parity of esteem.[33] Starting more than six months before the Human Rights Act came into force, the NIHRC has pursued its work on a Bill of Rights with considerable dedication ever since. It has consulted very widely and published two drafts of a Bill to date, in September 2001 and April 2004. Unfortunately its proposals have not met with anything like unanimous support amongst political parties, the NGO community, or academics.[34] As regards the relationship between the proposed Bill and the Human Rights Act the Commission's second draft states that '[t]he Convention rights as set out in the Human Rights Act 1998 shall be considered a part of the Bill of Rights for Northern Ireland' and adds '[t]he other rights protected by the European Convention . . . shall also be considered a part of the Bill

---

[27] Mark Kelly, *The Right to Life* and *The Right Not to be Ill-Treated* (2005).

[28] *Work of the Northern Ireland Human Rights Commission*, 14th Report, 2002–03, para 5.

[29] Stephen Livingstone and Rachel Murray, *Evaluating the Effectiveness of National Human Rights Institutions: The Northern Ireland Human Rights Commission* (2005) 94. The Bill of Rights is discussed below.

[30] At p. 10. This is the third objective within the Commission's first aim, which is to build a human rights culture in Northern Ireland.   [31] ibid, 15–16.

[32] Para 2 of the 'Rights, Safeguards and Equality of Opportunity' section: 'The British Government will complete incorporation into Northern Ireland law of the European Convention on Human Rights (ECHR), with direct access to the courts, and remedies for breach of the Convention, including powers for the courts to overrule Assembly legislation on grounds of inconsistency.'

[33] ibid, para 4.

[34] See eg the articles included in (2001) 52 NILQ 229–406 and the essay in this book by Christopher McCrudden, ch. 15.

of Rights for Northern Ireland'.[35] Some responses to this proposal have suggested that the Bill should not simply embrace the Human Rights Act and add rights to it but that the Human Rights Act should be repealed and the whole standard-setting process for Northern Ireland started afresh.[36] This position is apparently based on the view that the current enforcement system in the Human Rights Act is flawed, since it does not allow incompatible primary legislation to be declared invalid, it can be activated only by 'victims', and it is not operated by a new court with new judges.[37] To those who do not share this view it might seem that in this context the perfect can easily become the enemy of the good.

The Act and Legislators

While the Home Office Task Force was sitting in London, a call went out to all government departments to review the legislation they were responsible for in case it appeared to breach Convention rights. The outcome of the NIO's review has not been published but we do know that it threw up queries concerning the law on the release of life-sentenced prisoners (see below). Neither the NIO nor the Northern Ireland Assembly felt the need to introduce legislation along the lines of the Scottish Parliament's Convention Rights (Compliance) (Scotland) Act 2001, which dealt not only with the release of lifers but also with an array of other issues such as the composition of the Parole Board for Scotland, the rules on legal aid, and the prohibition of homosexuality.

As part of the devolution arrangements for Scotland, Wales, and Northern Ireland, Westminster decreed that each of the devolved legislatures was barred from making any law which breached the Human Rights Act. For Northern Ireland this prohibition took effect on 2 December 1999, when the Northern Ireland Assembly at last became operational.[38] A provision of an Act passed by that Assembly is, accordingly, 'not law' if it is incompatible with any of the Convention rights.[39] Moreover, whenever a Bill is introduced into the Assembly, or before then, the Minister responsible for it must publish a statement saying that in his or her view the Bill is within the legislative competence of the Assembly and therefore not in breach of Convention rights.[40] All Bills introduced into the

[35] Draft s 20(2) and (3).

[36] This is the view of the CAJ and of the Council for the Homeless.

[37] The establishment of a new court is supported by, amongst others, the SDLP, NICVA, the CAJ, the Children's Law Centre, and the Women's Coalition.

[38] See the Northern Ireland Act 1998 (Appointed Day) Order 1999 (SI 1999/3208) and the Northern Ireland Act 1998 (Commencement No 5) Order 1999 (SI 1999/3209). In Wales and Scotland the equivalent provisions took effect on 1 April 1999 and 6 May 1999, respectively.

[39] Northern Ireland Act 1998, s 6(1) and (2)(b). Assembly Acts are 'subordinate legislation' for the purposes of the Human Rights Act (see s 21) and so can be invalidated by any court or tribunal if found to be incompatible with Convention rights (see n 8 above).

[40] ibid, s 9. This kind of statement is comparable to that required at Westminster under s 19 of the Human Rights Act.

Assembly so far (36 Acts were passed during the 31 months in which the Assembly managed to function between December 1999 and October 2002[41]) have had such statements attached to them and none of these was challenged in the Assembly.[42] Nor have any of the resulting Acts been challenged on human rights grounds in the courts.[43]

The Assembly, when it is not suspended, also has the power to consider draft Orders in Council which the UK government proposes to make for Northern Ireland on reserved matters, such as criminal justice.[44] Proposals for these Orders must be presented to Westminster at least 60 days before an actual draft is laid and it is during this period that the Assembly may report its views to the Secretary of State (or *must* do so if he or she so requests).[45] The Assembly has so far set up *ad hoc* committees to consider four such proposed Orders and in each case the committee has had regard to the compatibility of the proposals with the Human Rights Act after taking evidence from, amongst others, the NIHRC. The reports of the committees have all been endorsed by the full Assembly and transmitted to the Secretary of State.

In relation to the first of these Orders, the Financial Investigations (NI) Order 2001, a majority of the *ad hoc* committee strongly backed the goal of preventing criminals profiting from their criminal activities, but individual committee members had concerns regarding the Order's impact on what are, in effect, Article 8 Convention rights regarding solicitor/client confidentiality and legal professional privilege.[46] A majority of the committee looking at the Life Sentences (NI) Order 2001 welcomed the attempt to bring the law into line with the requirements of the European Convention (and in advance of any such changes in England and Wales[47]) but warned that some requirements of the Human Rights Act were still

---

[41] This number of Acts compares favourably with the 44 Acts which the Scottish Parliament enacted in the three years 2000–2002 (during which there were no periods of suspension.)

[42] Contrary to a recommendation of the NIHRC made in June 2001, the Assembly decided not to establish its own human rights committee but instead to 'mainstream' human rights proofing throughout all the other committees (see 1st Report of the Committee on Procedures, *Review of the Legislative Process in the Northern Ireland Assembly*, 2002, paras 3.4.1–3.4.6). The NIHRC had concerns about aspects of the Assembly's Adoption (Intercountry Aspects) Bill 2001, Family Law Bill 2001, and Social Security Fraud Bill 2001, but the Assembly did not share these.

[43] But there have been challenges to Orders in Council which started life as Assembly Bills: see n 60 below and the accompanying text. For a more general account of law-making in Northern Ireland post-1998, see Gordon Anthony and John Morison, 'Here, There, and (Maybe) Here Again', in Robert Hazell and Richard Rawlings (eds), *Devolution, Law Making and the Constitution* (2005), ch. 5.

[44] Such an Order must be referred by the Secretary of State to the Northern Ireland Assembly before it is laid at Westminster. See Anthony and Morison, 'Here, There, and (Maybe) Here Again', n 43 above, 179–84.   [45] Northern Ireland Act 1998, s 85(4) and (5).

[46] www.niassembly.gov.uk/record/reports/010206.htm#4. For the NIHRC's views see www.nihrc. org/documents/landp/50.doc.

[47] A point which did not go unnoticed when the House of Lords eventually declared part of the relevant English legislation to be incompatible with Convention rights: see *R (Anderson) v Secretary of State for the Home Department* [2003] 1 AC 837, paras 29 (Lord Bingham), 42 (Lord Steyn) and 77 (Lord Hutton).

not being met.[48] The committee examining the Criminal Injuries Compensation (NI) Order 2002 went so far as to recommend that the legislation should not be laid as a draft Order at Westminster in its current form.[49] The removal of a right of appeal to the courts against the size of a compensation award was condemned as liable to be challenged under the Human Rights Act 1998.[50] As with other committee reports, however, this one cut no ice when the draft Order was eventually laid at Westminster.[51] In the case of the Access to Justice (NI) Order 2003, which radically altered the system for delivering legal aid in Northern Ireland, the UK government again rushed ahead regardless of *ad hoc* committee reservations.[52] One can sum up the history of this scrutiny of draft Orders in Council by saying that, while the Northern Ireland Assembly, despite its internal differences based on community allegiances, undertook its role with admirable regard for the requirements of the Human Rights Act, Parliamentarians at Westminster were easily persuaded to discount these human rights concerns and to rubber-stamp the government's proposals. Only one of the laws in question has as yet been challenged in court—successfully as it happens[53]—so it may be that most of the Assembly's concerns were not justifiable after all, but it is regrettable that compatibility with Convention rights was not discussed at greater length on the floor of the two Houses at Westminster.

A few other Orders in Council, made at times when the Assembly was suspended, might have provoked further concerns about human rights if they had been discussed by an *ad hoc* committee. In the event, they too received rather cursory treatment at Westminster.[54] The NIHRC, and some NGOs, made representations to the NIO *à propos* the Protection of Children and Vulnerable Adults (NI)

---

[48] www.niassembly.gov.uk/record/reports/010312.htm#5. For the NIHRC's views see www.nihrc. org/documents/landp/52.doc. Both the *ad hoc* committee and the Commission saw potential breaches of Art. 6 of the Convention in, for example, the discretion given to the Secretary of State to decide whether the early release provisions should apply to certain prisoners. But when finally enacted the provisions in question—Arts 5(4), 10(1), 10(2), 11(1) and 11(2)—remained unaltered. See also n 53 below.

[49] www.niassembly.gov.uk/record/reports/011126.htm#7.

[50] The committee also felt that the government's assumption that a tariff system would be in the best interests of victims of crime was erroneous and that the proposed new system was actually a cost-saving exercise based on the removal of paid legal assistance for claimants.

[51] It was approved by the House of Commons on 11 July 2001 (without any debate) and by the House of Lords on 12 July 2001. At the request of the chairperson of the Select Committee on Northern Ireland Affairs the proposed Order had also been debated by the Northern Ireland Grand Committee on 22 March 2001, 10 days after the Assembly's approval of the *ad hoc* committee's report.

[52] The Assembly approved the *ad hoc* committee report on 2 July 2002. The proposed Order was debated by the Northern Ireland Grand Committee on 24 October 2002, laid before Parliament on 19 December 2002, approved by the House of Commons on 25 January 2003 and approved by the Lords on 6 February 2003.

[53] In *Re King's Application* [2003] NI 43 words were read into Art. 11 of the Life Sentences (NI) Order 2001 by the Court of Appeal (using s 3 of the Human Rights Act 1998) to ensure that the Order's release scheme would apply to prisoners already serving life sentences when the Order came into force. This partly vindicated points made by the NIHRC and an *ad hoc* committee of the Assembly (see n 48 above).

[54] Draft Orders, being secondary legislation, cannot be amended while being debated—they have to be accepted or rejected *in toto*.

Order 2003,[55] the Commissioner for Children and Young People (NI) Order 2003,[56] the Criminal Justice (NI) Order 2004,[57] the Anti-social Behaviour (NI) Order 2004[58] and the Special Educational Needs and Disability (NI) Order 2005.[59] But all of these were eventually enacted in virtually identical terms to those originally proposed by the government. The legitimacy of the Anti-social Behaviour (NI) Order has since been challenged, twice, in the Northern Ireland High Court, on the ground that its enactment was not preceded by an equality impact assessment as required by section 75 of, and Schedule 9 to, the Northern Ireland Act 1998. Both challenges, however, failed,[60] and Convention rights did not feature in the judgments except to the extent that in the second case the judge drew upon the European Court's decision in *Moreno-Gomez v Spain*[61] to stress that Article 8 of the European Convention obliges States to consider legislation mitigating the real social problems of anti-social behaviour.

The Flags (NI) Order 2000 was made at Westminster at a time when the Assembly was suspended, but it was commenced at a time when the Assembly had been restored. Conor Murphy, a Sinn Féin Member of the Assembly, sought judicial review of the Secretary of State's decision to enact the Order as well as the consequential Flags Regulations (NI) 2000. He argued that the decision was contrary to the Good Friday Agreement in that such contentious legislation (specifying, for example, when the Union flag should be flown from public buildings in Northern Ireland) should have been approved by a cross-community vote in the Assembly. Kerr J, as he then was, had little difficulty in rejecting this argument and Mr Murphy was not able to rely on any alternative argument based on the Human Rights Act because the European Convention has nothing to say about how legislation should be enacted for a divided society, nor about concepts such as 'parity of esteem' and 'mutual respect for the identity and ethos of both communities'.[62]

Although there are various mechanisms in place allowing draft Assembly legislation to be challenged on the basis of the Human Rights Act,[63] the judiciary in

---

[55] This legislation started life as an Assembly Bill. For the NIHRC's views see www.nihrc.org/documents/landp/72.doc.

[56] For the NIHRC's views see www.nihrc.org/documents/landp/54.doc and 87.doc.

[57] For the NIHRC's views see www.nihrc.org/documents/landp/136.doc.

[58] For the NIHRC's views see www.nihrc.org/documents/landp/120.doc.

[59] For the NIHRC's views see www.nihrc.org/documents/landp/116.doc.

[60] *Re an Application by the Northern Ireland Commissioner for Children and Young People* [2004] NIQB 40; *Re Peter Neill's Application* [2005] NIQB 66 and [2006] NICA 5. But see also *Re NIHE's Application* [2005] NIQB 71, where Girvan J ruled, contrary to a previous ruling of the Court of Appeal of England and Wales, that a magistrates' court does not have the power to grant an interim anti-social behaviour order on an *ex parte* application, and *Re Landlord Association of Northern Ireland's Application* [2005] NIQB 22, where the same judge invalidated part of a scheme drawn up by the Northern Ireland Housing Executive (making landlords of houses in multiple occupation responsible for the anti-social behaviour of their tenants and guests) because it breached Art. 1 of Protocol 1 to the European Convention (the right to enjoyment of one's possessions).

[61] (2005) 41 EHRR 40.   [62] *Re Murphy's Application* [2001] NI 425.

[63] I identified eight such mechanisms in Anthony Lester and David Pannick (eds), *Human Rights Law and Practice* (2nd ed., 2004), paras 6.43–6.56.

Northern Ireland have made it clear that pre-enactment review by the courts will rarely be allowed (certainly if the legislation emanates from Westminster):

'When the Executive seeks to put before Parliament legislation on which there are human rights issues, the courts must be slow to intervene to stop such legislation being considered by Parliament itself, bearing in mind the various checks and balances that exist under the legislation and bearing in mind the individual citizen's rights to be protected under the Human Rights Act after the legislation is enacted in the way fixed by that Act.'[64]

As regards post-enactment review, the Northern Ireland Court Service has calcu- lated that, of the 585 occasions on which the Human Rights Act has been raised in Northern Ireland's courts between 2000 and 2005, in only 20 cases (3.4 per cent) has the validity of domestic legislation been challenged.[65] In only one case since 2000 has a court in Northern Ireland declared a piece of legislation to be incom- patible with Convention rights: in criminalizing consensual anal intercourse between a man and a woman, section 62 of the Offences against the Person Act 1861 was held to be in breach of the right to a private life, taken in conjunction with the right not to be discriminated against, because anal intercourse between two people of the same gender is not a crime.[66]

Sinn Féin sought a declaration that section 12 of the Political Parties, Elections and Referendums Act 2000—a Westminster Act—was incompatible with Con- vention Article 10 (the right to freedom of expression), Article 14 (the right not to be discriminated against) and Article 3 of Protocol 1 (the right to free elections). Section 12 had the effect of disqualifying a party from receiving a policy develop- ment grant unless it had at least two MPs who had sworn allegiance to the Crown under the Parliamentary Oaths Act 1866. The case was lost in the High Court and the Court of Appeal,[67] mainly on the basis that the grants in question were designed to assist parties which, unlike Sinn Féin, were busy with activities involved in Parliamentary attendance. After a hearing in London, Sinn Féin was given leave to appeal to the House of Lords, but a few months later it mysteriously withdrew its petition, for reasons that remain unclear.

The Act and Government Departments

Since 2 December 1999 no Minister in the Northern Ireland government, and no Northern Ireland government department, has had power to do any act which is incompatible with any of the Convention rights.[68] To date no case has been taken

---

[64] *Re an Application by the Northern Ireland Commissioner for Children and Young People* [2004] NIQB 40, para 15 (Girvan J).

[65] Table 4 of the Court Service's latest statistics on the Human Rights Act 1998. See the text at n 123 below.

[66] *Re McR's Application* [2003] NI 1. This remains the only case in the UK where a High Court declaration of incompatibility has not been appealed by the Crown.

[67] *Re Sinn Féin's Application* [2004] NICA 4.   [68] Northern Ireland Act 1998, s 24(1)(b).

to court alleging that any such act is incompatible.[69] The Human Rights Act was not relied upon, for example, when the Democratic Unionist Party successfully sought judicial review of the decision by the First Minister and Deputy First Minister to withhold Executive Committee papers from DUP ministers.[70] Nor did it feature when Sinn Féin successfully sought judicial review of the First Minister's decision to refuse to nominate Sinn Féin ministers for meetings of the North–South Ministerial Council.[71]

There is, no doubt, acute awareness of the Human Rights Act within the NIO, the department of the British Government which retains total responsibility for Northern Ireland during periods of direct rule and more limited responsibility—for 'excepted' and 'reserved' matters—during periods when the Northern Ireland Assembly is not suspended.[72] But the NIO has not produced and circulated its own Human Rights Act guidance, preferring instead to rely upon materials produced centrally by the Department for Constitutional Affairs, and the department has certainly not escaped challenges to its actions on human rights grounds.[73]

Early in 2000, for example, fearing a difficult 'marching season' in Northern Ireland, the NIO proposed commencing the Human Rights Act earlier than planned—in April rather than October 2000—for the specific purpose of allowing challenges to be lodged against determinations of the Parades Commission made under the Public Processions (NI) Act 1998. When asked for its views on this proposal, the NIHRC advised against it and the government followed that advice. The NIHRC was not opposed to the early commencement of the Human Rights Act in principle, but it felt that early commencement would be inappropriate if it was confined to one particular sphere of activity (marching, but not protesting) and to one particular aspect of that activity (determinations made by the Parades Commission, but not decisions made by the police or the Secretary of State).

Sinn Féin challenged a direction given by the Secretary of State under section 51B(2) of the Northern Ireland Act 1998[74] whereby he ordered that money payable to Sinn Féin under the Financial Assistance for Political Parties Act (NI) 2000[75] should not be paid for the year 2004–05. This was a 'punishment' for ongoing republican violence identified by a report of the Independent Monitoring Commission.[76] The party relied on Convention Article 6 (the right to a fair trial)

[69] The Department of Economic Development was held to have acted contrary to Art. 6 *before* the Human Rights Act came into force: *Cowan v Department of Economic Development* [2000] NI 122.
[70] *Re Morrow's and Campbell's Applications* [2001] NI 261.
[71] *Re de Brún's and McGuinness' Applications* [2001] NI 442 (Court of Appeal).
[72] For details of excepted and reserved matters see Schs 2 and 3, respectively, to the Northern Ireland Act 1998.
[73] The Human Rights Act played no part in the litigation over whether the Secretary of State had acted lawfully in refusing to declare that the IRA ceasefire had ended: *Re Williamson's Application* [2000] NI 281 (decided by the Northern Ireland Court of Appeal six months before the commencement of the Act).
[74] Inserted by the Northern Ireland (Monitoring Commission etc) Act 2003, s 8.
[75] An Act of the Northern Ireland Assembly.   [76] In its first report, 2003–04, HC 516.

and Article 1 of Protocol 1 (the right to enjoyment of one's possessions). Weatherup J, relying on the European Court of Human Rights' decision in *Pierre Bloch v France*,[77] held that Article 6 was not engaged because the right in question (to financial assistance) was a not a 'civil right' within the terms of Article 6.[78] Nor was Article 1 of Protocol 1 of any help because, even if the money at issue was deemed to be 'possessions' for the purposes of that article, the State was entitled to control its use 'in accordance with the general interest'. Here, the general interest in question was securing compliance with the commitment to non-violence and exclusively peaceful and democratic means—that was a perfectly legitimate aim and the means used to achieve it were not disproportionate or discriminatory.

The NIO's system for granting protection to persons under threat has also come under scrutiny in recent years. The NIHRC engaged with the department at a very high level on this issue, urging it to change its schemes so as to make them more obviously compliant with Convention Article 2 (the right to life).[79] In the end the Commission decided not to seek judicial review of the schemes in its own name but it did support applicants in two further cases where the NIO's decision not to grant protection was so challenged. In both cases the judge held that the NIO had applied the wrong test when deciding not to grant protection.[80] As a result the NIO's 'Key Persons Protection Scheme' has had to be amended to take account of the Human Rights Act. In a separate case, however, Kerr J held that Article 2 of the Convention had not been breached when the NIO refused to remove a Sinn Féin councillor's ineligibility for a personal protection weapon because not enough time had elapsed since his last criminal conviction.[81]

The Act and Public Authorities

Judging by the frequency of the requests received by the NIHRC to provide input into training sessions for staff working in public authorities—and for members of the boards of such authorities—the impact of the Human Rights Act is far from negligible in those circles too. In September 2000 the Commission published a document entitled *Advice for Public Authorities Preparing for the Human Rights Act*.[82] This recommended adoption of action plans within each public authority and close liaison with relevant government departments. It also suggested that each authority should not only establish a unit to provide assistance to employees who wish to know more about the implications of the Act but

---

[77] (1998) 26 EHRR 202.   [78] *Re Sinn Féin's Application* [2005] NIQB 10.

[79] See www.nihrc.org/documents/pubs/hra/keyperson.doc.

[80] *Re Frazer's Application* [2004] NIQB 68 and *Re Brolly's Application* [2004] NIQB 69. See also *Re W's Application* [2004] NIQB 67 and *Re Murray's Application*, unreported 2004.

[81] *Re Meehan's Application (No.2)* [2002] NIJB 317. The claim to a personal protection weapon also failed in *Re Frazer's Application*, n 80 above.

[82] www.nihrc.org/documents/pubs/hra/hr_advice.doc.

also create a loose-leaf manual to allow staff to keep abreast of developments in the human rights field. The NIHRC itself, in the same month, produced a straightforward guide to how the Human Rights Act affects Northern Ireland.[83] Unfortunately the Commission has not been able to conduct research into what kind of impact the Human Rights Act has had amongst public authorities generally. Nor does any such research appear to have been conducted by others. In Northern Ireland there has been nothing comparable to the study conducted by the Audit Commission on how the Human Rights Act has affected public services in England and Wales.[84]

Probably the most important of the non-governmental public authorities affected by the Act are the police. Summing up how the police have reacted to the Act in Northern Ireland is difficult, but by and large the picture is a rosy one. The RUC and, since 2001, the Police Service of Northern Ireland (PSNI), opened themselves up to extensive evaluation of their human rights training by the NIHRC, which has published four reports on the subject to date.[85] The first of these was rather critical of the police's 'Workbook on the Human Rights Act' but the police have responded positively to these and other criticisms. They have also (though belatedly) established their own 'Human Rights Programme of Action', in line with the first recommendation in the Patten Report of 1999, and they have devised a Code of Ethics[86] which is modelled not just on the requirements of the Human Rights Act but on those of other international human rights documents as well. The Human Rights and Professional Standards Committee of the Northern Ireland Policing Board reviews the PSNI's compliance with human rights standards[87] and in 2005 it published its first *Annual Report on Human Rights*, compiled by the Board's Human Rights Advisors Keir Starmer and Jane Gordon.[88] Amongst the 61 recommendations in this report are proposals that, as matters of priority or urgency, student officers should be better trained on positional asphyxia, training materials on the use of force should be revised, the policy on integrity testing should be developed, and arrangements for effective communication with the Parades Commission should be reviewed. The Police Oversight Commissioner regularly reports on how faithfully the police are implementing

---

[83] www.nihrc.org/documents/pubs/hra/hr_impact.doc. This was sourced from the Commission's booklet 'Human Rights ImpAct', co-published with the Citizenship Foundation.

[84] *Human Rights: Improving Public Service Delivery* (2003).

[85] *The RUC's Training on the Human Rights* Act (2000); *An Evaluation of Human Rights Training for Student Police Officers* (2002); *Probationer Constables and Student Officers* (2004): *Course for All* (2004).

[86] Available on the PSNI's website: www.psni.police.uk.

[87] In accordance with a Monitoring Framework published by the Board in 2003.

[88] The same advisors also produced *A Report on the Policing of the Ardoyne Parade 12 July 2004*. They concluded that that policing operation complied with the Human Rights Act 1998 but they expressed three serious concerns (summarized at paras 26–28): (a) that a judge's ruling on 9 July 2004 that those participating in a public procession excluded those who follow, proceed with or accompany lodges and bands along an entire parade route 'will have a profound and detrimental effect on the ability of the PSNI to police parades in the future'; (b) that there are insufficiently clear and agreed lines of communication between the Parades Commission and the PSNI; and (c) that the arrangements in place for joint operations between the PSNI and the military are ineffective.

the recommendations of the Patten Commission, including those on human rights,[89] and the Police Ombudsman's Office also applies the Human Rights Act when considering whether complaints against the police can be substantiated.[90] The PSNI, in short, can be held to account for its alleged human rights breaches in several ways, and rightly so. The learning curve vis-à-vis the Human Rights Act has been a steep one for the organization, and the record is not entirely unblemished,[91] but there is good reason to believe that the PSNI is ahead of most if not all other police services in these islands as regards its willingness to subject its policies and operations to human rights proofing and review.[92] So far it has survived challenges brought against it in the courts on human rights grounds.[93]

Neither the NIHRC nor any other human rights organization has evaluated the extent to which the Prison Service of Northern Ireland has complied with the Human Rights Act, but the NIHRC has paid a lot of attention to complaints raised by individual prisoners and has researched the conditions experienced by women prisoners[94] as well as the systems in place for investigating the worryingly high number of deaths occurring in prisons.[95] While it is arguable that the letter of the Human Rights Act is being complied with, the spirit of the Act may not be. The Prison Service has not always been convincing about the extent of training it provides to its staff on the Human Rights Act and reports by HM Inspectorate of Prisons bear out some concerns.[96] In *Re TP (a minor)'s Application*,[97] the Youth Justice Agency was upbraided for detaining a remanded juvenile in the Intensive Support Unit of a juvenile justice centre for nearly five months without regularly assessing the impact of this isolation on his Article 8 rights. Even more remarkably, in *Martin v Northern Ireland Prison Service*,[98] Girvan J held that the slopping out arrangements for prisoners at Magilligan Prison in County Derry also amounted to a breach of Article 8 (although not of Article 3). In *Re McConway's*

---

[89] See in particular his 14th report (September 2005), which was dedicated to human rights and accountability. In his 15th Report (December 2005), devoted to training, the Commissioner concluded that with respect to human rights training the PSNI had demonstrated its commitment to achieving a human rights-focused culture of policing as intended by the Patten Commission (p 17).
[90] A judicial review application against the Police Ombudsman based on Art. 2 of the Convention failed in *Re the CAJ's Application* [2005] NIQB 25.
[91] Mary O'Rawe, 'Human Rights and Police Training in Transitional Societies: Exporting the Lessons of Northern Ireland' (2005) 27 HRQ 943, 963–96. The Chief Constable also apologized for heavy-handed policing when Sinn Féin's offices were raided at Stormont in 2002.
[92] The Policing Board's *Annual Report on Human Rights* found that the PSNI had done more than any police service anywhere else in the UK to achieve human rights compliance (Introduction).
[93] eg *Re E's Application* [2006] NICA 37, where the Court of Appeal held that the PSNI had not breached the Human Rights Act through the manner in which it policed the Loyalist 'protest' at the Holy Cross Girls' Primary School in 2001.   [94] *The Hurt Inside* (rev ed., 2005).
[95] There have been at least nine in Northern Ireland since June 2002.
[96] See eg the reports on HMP Magilligan (2001) and Hydebank Wood (2005).
[97] [2005] NIQB 64 (Weatherup J), applying *Re Connor's Application* [2004] NICA 45 (see the text accompanying n 113 below).
[98] [2006] NIQB 1. On Art. 8 the judge distinguished *Re Karen Carson* [2005] NIQB 80, and on Art. 3 he distinguished the Scottish decision of *Napier v Scottish Ministers* [2002] UKHRR 308.

Application,[99] however, the Court of Appeal rejected a challenge to a Prison Service decision to refuse security clearance to someone wanting to work in a prison and innumerable other judicial review applications brought by prisoners relying on the Human Rights Act have for the most part failed.[100] In the same field, challenges to decisions of the Sentence Review Commissioners based on the Human Rights Act have also not succeeded, including one taken as far as the House of Lords.[101]

The Parades Commission has also had occasion to pay close attention to the Human Rights Act. At an early meeting with the NIHRC in 1999 it seemed disappointed that the Act would not provide a 'quick fix' for the problems associated with marching and that the applicable law was at times uncertain.[102] When preparing its evidence for the Quigley Review of the Parades Commission and of the Public Processions (NI) Act 1998,[103] the NIHRC had internal differences of opinion over the extent to which the Public Processions (NI) Act 1998 needed to be amended to take account of Convention rights. On one view the Act did not need to be amended at all because the Parades Commission, being a public authority, was already bound to act compatibly with Convention rights. On another view, the Act did require amendment because its requirement that the Parades Commission, when deciding whether to impose conditions on any public procession, must have regard (for example) to 'any impact which the procession may have on relationships within the community',[104] raised the possibility that a Convention right could be infringed on a ground not permitted by the Convention. Some Commissioners wanted the Act to refer in particular to the right to freedom of assembly, as enshrined in Article 11 of the Convention. Others thought that it would be wrong to mention that article without also mentioning other articles, such as Article 8 (the right to respect for one's private and family life, home, and correspondence) and Article 10 (the right to freedom of expression). The advice submitted to Sir George Quigley mentioned all of these options. In his report, Sir George recommended that the Public Processions Act should be amended to make specific reference to Article 11 of the Convention and that new guidelines should be prepared, making it clear that the Parades

---

[99] [2004] NICA 44.

[100] A typical example is *Re Swift's Application* [2005] NIQB 1, where the judge rejected a prisoner's challenge of a decision refusing him home leave to attend his daughter's First Holy Communion.

[101] *Re McClean* [2005] UKHL 46. See also *Re Sheridan's Application* [2004] NIQB 4, where the independence of the Commissioners was unsuccessfully challenged.

[102] The NIHRC published a report entitled *Parades, Protests and Policing: A Human Rights Framework* in March 2001. The Parades Commission's approach to Convention rights was vindicated by the Court of Appeal in *Re Pelan's Application*, unreported, 2001, where Nicholson LJ said that the Commission was in a very much better position than the court to reach a balanced decision on competing human rights, and that the court should be slow to intervene in the resolution by the Commission of those human rights.

[103] The Report of the review was published by the NIO in 2003: see www.nio.gov.uk/quigley_review_ of_the_parades_commission.pdf.   [104] Public Processions (NI) Act 1998, s 8(6)(c).

Commission should take into account the extent to which a planned parade would affect the rights and freedoms of others under any article of the Convention.[105] This recommendation, however, was rejected by the government. All it agreed to do was to extend the remit of the Parades Commission to include the control of meetings organized as protests against parades.[106] The issue of whether the decision-making procedures of the Parades Commission are in conformity with Article 6 of the Convention (because they provide for evidence to be given in confidence) is still unsettled. In 2006, the House of Lords ruled that the Commission should make greater disclosure of the documents it relies upon when rechecking its determinations.[107]

The education sector in Northern Ireland has probably done more than any other to take on board the consequences of the Human Rights Act. In doing so it has been aided significantly by the NIHRC and an NGO, the Children's Law Centre (CLC). In 2003 the Commission and the Department of Education co-published guides to the Act for schools and for school managers and, along with the five education and library boards, they produced in 2004 a study pack for secondary school children on what human rights really mean and how they can best be protected in Northern Ireland.[108] The CLC, for its part, obtained funding from the Department for materials on human rights awareness for school managers.[109] A recent court decision, unfortunately, suggests that current awareness is not as high as it should be.[110] The selection criteria applied by a grammar school in South Belfast, which were in line with 'model' criteria issued by the local education board, were held to be discriminatory on grounds of disability and so in breach of Article 2 of Protocol 1 to the Convention (the right to education) when read in conjunction with Article 14 (the right not to be discriminated against).

Within the past two years, the housing, health, and social services sectors in Northern Ireland have also demonstrated that they are not as *au fait* with the Human Rights Act as they should be. The courts have stressed in particular that the public authorities in question have not properly taken into account the implications of Article 8 (the right to a private and family life, etc).[111] Thus, in *Re Shay Donnelly*,[112] the Court of Appeal granted judicial review to a tenant who

---

[105] See n 103 above, paras 15.13–15.17.
[106] Public Processions (Amendment) (NI) Order 2005.
[107] *Tweed v Parades Commission for Northern Ireland* [2006] UKHL 53. This decision has a more general significance for the rules relating to disclosure in judicial review applications in England and Wales.   [108] *Bill of Rights in Schools: A Resource for Post-Primary Schools* (2004).
[109] www.childrenslawcentre.org/Childrens%20Law_output.pdf.
[110] *McGuigan v Belfast Education and Library Board* [2005] NIQB 60 (Morgan J).
[111] See *Re Misbehavin' Ltd's Application* [2005] NICA 35, where Belfast City Council had refused to grant the applicant a sex establishment licence. The Court of Appeal held that the applicant's rights under Art. 10 and Art. 1 of Protocol 1 had not been properly considered. An appeal is pending in the House of Lords.
[112] [2003] NICA 55. See also *Re Landlord Association of Northern Ireland's Application*, n 56 above.

complained that the Housing Executive had refused to commence possession proceedings against a neighbour whose family had persistently harassed the applicant. In *Re Connor's Application*,[113] where a health and social services trust had refused to permit the appellant, a person subject to a guardianship order because of her mental state, to live permanently with her husband, the Court of Appeal held that, as the trust had not made an appraisal of the appellant's Article 8 rights, the interference with those rights had to be assumed to be unjustified unless a contrary view would have been inevitable if the appraisal had in fact been made. In *Re Family Planning Association of Northern Ireland's Application*[114] the Court of Appeal held, again on the basis of Article 8, that the current law on abortion in Northern Ireland is uncertain and in need of clarification by the Department of Health, Social Services and Public Safety. Just as remarkably, in *AR v Homefirst Community Trust*,[115] the same court held that a health trust had failed to take account of the Article 8 rights of an alcoholic mother whose baby had been placed in care one day after he was born. This was again the finding in *Re W and M*,[116] a case on the freeing of two sibling children for adoption, where Gillen J made quite plain his unease at the (unidentified) trust's conduct:

'I reiterate that I find the breach of the rights in this case to be flagrant and the courts must make clear that such breaches of Article 8 of the European Convention on Human Rights will not be tolerated. Although I am assured that steps have been taken now to ensure that this Trust will afford compliance to Convention rights in the future, it is clear to me that employees at all levels in this Trust require training in the fundamental impact that the Convention has on the type of decision that was to be made in this instance. The public interest requires that all Trusts throughout Northern Ireland grasp this concept.'[117]

In *Re P (A Child)*,[118] on the other hand, where what was in question was the compatibility with Article 8 of the statutory prohibition on an unmarried couple adopting a child,[119] Gillen J held that the difference in treatment between the applicants and a married adoptive couple was objectively justifiable in the sense that it had a legitimate aim, namely the best interests of children, and that the difference bore a reasonable relationship of proportionality to that aim. As the judge put it:

'In this case the interests of these two individual applicants must be balanced against the interests of the community as a whole. It is for this society through Parliament to

113 [2004] NICA 45. See also *Conway v Kelly* [2005] NIQB 29, a civil action for assault, where Deeny J prohibited disclosure to the defendant of a psychiatric report on the plaintiff because otherwise the latter's Art. 8 rights would have been breached; disclosure was restricted to the defendant's legal and medical advisers.   114 [2004] NICA 37, reversing Kerr J at first instance.
115 [2005] NICA 8. This case, and the next to be cited, were the focus of a presentation entitled 'Where is the ECHR leading us?' given by the Northern Ireland High Court judge specializing in family law matters, Gillen J, at a conference in Belfast on 6 March 2006 (copy with the present author).
116 [2005] NIFam 2. A later challenge to the subsequent decision to free the children for adoption, based on the alleged bias of the decision-maker, was rejected: [2006] NIFam 6.
117 ibid, para. 23.   118 [2006] NIFam 5.
119 The prohibition is to be found in the Adoption (NI) Order 1987, Art. 14(1).

determine the setting in which the advantages of adoption can best be achieved. I do not consider it is the court's task to substitute its own view for that of the legislature in this instance.'[120]

In 2004 researchers at the University of Ulster's UNESCO Centre conducted research on behalf of the NIHRC to review the current extent of, and scope for, human rights education and training in Northern Ireland.[121] Their survey was based on responses from 46 public authorities (as well as four professional associations, 11 NGOs and 22 education institutions). It revealed that most of the respondents already provided training around Convention rights but it recommended that further support should be provided to organizations, especially public bodies, to provide more such training, better materials, awards and prizes, accredited courses, and training for trainers. The research conducted for the present essay lends weight to the need for such steps.

The Act and Legal Professionals

The Northern Ireland Court Service keeps statistics on the number of times the Human Rights Act is raised in cases heard in Northern Ireland's courts. Tables 1 and 2, below, are based on the latest available figures.[122] They demonstrate clearly that by far the most common Convention right referred to (by some margin) is Article 6—the right to a fair trial—and that the only other Convention rights which are fairly regularly referred to are Articles 2 (the right to life), 3 (the prohibition on torture, etc), 5 (the right to liberty) and 8 (the right to a private life, etc). The context in which these references are made is overwhelmingly that of judicial review, with the next most common context, surprisingly, being cases heard by the Social Security and Child Support Commissioners. For some reason there was a dramatic fall in the number of references in judicial review cases during 2004 and 2005. Perhaps barristers have become more aware of how far the judges will allow them to push human rights arguments in such cases?

The Court Service estimates the success rate for arguments based on the Human Rights Act in Northern Ireland at 17.6 per cent (103 of the 585 occasions on which Convention rights have been relied on[123]), but it has not made it clear what is meant by 'success' in this context—does it imply that the judge decided the case in favour of the party relying on the Act or simply that the judge upheld that

---

[120] [2006] NIFam 5, para 23.
[121] *Review of Human Rights Education and Training* (2005).   [122] *Human Rights Act* (2006).
[123] ibid, Tables 3 and 6. The statistics also reveal (Table 7) that the Act was raised in a total of 393 cases, but they urge caution here because the figure is an estimate. Furthermore, the statistics do not include cases heard before industrial tribunals (because these do not fall within the Court Service's bailiwick).

Table 1. Convention rights relied on in the courts, 2000–2005

	Art 2	Art 3	Art 5	Art 6	Art 8	Other arts	Totals
Court of Appeal	1	2	1	11	2	7	24
Queen's Bench	3	—	2	3	5	2	15
Judicial reviews	29	13	16	69	74	55	256
Chancery	—	—	—	—	4	—	4
Family proceedings	—	—	4	1	2	2	9
Crown Court	1	2	2	26	1	2	34
Bail office	—	—	5	1	—	—	6
Magistrates' court (criminal)	—	—	1	19	1	1	22
Youth courts	—	—	—	2	—	—	2
Social Security/Child Support Commissioners	1	1	—	150	6	53	211
Pensions Appeal Tribunal	—	—	—	2	—	—	2
Totals	35	18	31	284	95	122	585

Table 2. Frequency of reliance on the Human Rights Act in the courts, 2000–2005

	2000	2001	2002	2003	2004	2005	Totals
Court of Appeal	—	8	3	3	1	6	21
Queen's Bench	6	5	2	1	1	—	15
Judicial reviews	28	84	50	83	11	—	256
Chancery	3	1	—	—	—	—	4
Family proceedings	9	—	—	—	—	—	9
Crown Court	10	12	7	3	—	1	33
Bail office	6	—	—	—	—	—	6
Magistrates' court (criminal)	15	3	1	3	—	—	22
Youth courts	2	—	—	—	—	—	2
Social Security/Child Support Commissioners	5	13	40	68	44	38	208
Pensions Appeal Tribunal	—	1	—	—	1	—	2
Totals	84	127	103	161	58	45	578

party's particular argument on the Act regardless of the ultimate outcome of the case? The published statistics even reveal how much time judges have spent on Human Rights Act points: in the last six years almost 525 hours have been devoted to them,[124] which means that each point has required less than one hour of judicial time.

[124] ibid, Table 5.

To date the judges in Northern Ireland appear to have faithfully applied the Human Rights Act in ways which tally with the approach of the English judiciary.[125] The senior judges have certainly been prepared to hear arguments based on European Court jurisprudence and countless judgments are peppered with analyses of that jurisprudence. In the vast majority of cases, though, the courts have held that the Convention rights have not been breached.[126] There are few examples of the Northern Ireland Court of Appeal reversing a High Court decision on a European Convention point, and fewer still of the House of Lords reversing the Northern Ireland Court of Appeal. In the one case where that did occur, *Re McKerr*,[127] it was the Court of Appeal which took a much more pro-Convention stand.[128] It made a declaration that the obligation to hold an investigation which complied with the requirements of Convention Article 2 was a continuing one, even though the death in question had occurred in 1982.[129] The House overturned this ruling, holding that there was no such continuing obligation and that the right to enforce Convention rights in British courts arose only when the 1998 Act came into force on 2 October 2000, not while the Convention was still unincorporated into UK law.

Section 3 of the Human Rights Act requires judges and others to read and give effect to legislation, so far as it is possible to do so, in a way which is compatible with Convention rights. In England this duty has been complied with even when it has meant reading new words into legislation, rearranging existing words alongside new words, or deleting words. The clearest example of section 3 being applied to date in Northern Ireland is *Re King's Application*,[130] where 12 words were read into article 11 of the Life Sentences (NI) Order 1991 in order to make it compatible with Article 6 of the Convention.

Both the Bar Council and the Law Society, and groups within those professions, have organized training courses and conferences at which the implications of the Human Rights Act have featured prominently. SLS Legal Publications (NI) Ltd, based in the School of Law at Queen's University, has likewise run numerous relevant events. Senior judges have addressed and/or chaired such events. In 2003 Matrix Chambers, in conjunction with the NIHRC, held an event on the Act in Belfast at which Cherie Booth QC spoke. Lawyers have also banded together as

[125] For a survey of Northern Ireland case law up to the end of 2003 see Brice Dickson, 'Northern Ireland', in Anthony Lester and David Pannick (eds), *Human Rights Law and Practice*, n 63 above, paras 6.59–6.128.
[126] One of the most high-profile cases was *Re Parsons' Application* [2004] NI 38, where the Court of Appeal held that the positive discrimination provision requiring 50% of new recruits to the PSNI to be Catholics (see s 46(1) of the Police (NI) Act 2000) was not a breach of Arts 9 or 14 of the Convention.
[127] [2004] 1 WLR 807. See also the essay by Gordon Anthony and Paul Mageean in this book ch. 10.
[128] [2003] NI 117.
[129] [2003] NICA 1. See generally, Fiona Doherty and Paul Mageean, *Investigating Lethal Force Deaths in Northern Ireland: The Application of Article 2 of the ECHR* (2006). [130] [2003] NI 43.

the Human Rights Practitioners Group, which meets regularly at the offices of the NIHRC and is serviced by the Commission's Case Worker. She periodically compiles a summary of the notable cases which have raised Human Rights Act issues in Northern Ireland and circulates these to all members of the group.

Conclusion

Measuring the impact of any piece of legislation is notoriously difficult. The Northern Ireland Court Service can provide information on the number of times the Human Rights Act has been argued in court and court judgments can be trawled through to see what role the Act has played in the outcome of cases. On that basis one can make an estimate of how many, and what kind of, cases have been decided in the way that they have precisely because the Human Rights Act is in force. But one cannot easily assess what influence the Act has had, outside the courtroom, on the behaviour of law- and policy-making organizations, law enforcement bodies, and all the other public authorities operating in Northern Ireland. More empirical work would be required before a definitive evaluation on that front would be possible. Meanwhile, it is abundantly clear from the piecemeal evidence currently available that the influence of the Act has already been profound.

The relative ease with which the Act has infused the legal system is a cause for hope that, if and when a Bill of Rights is eventually enacted for Northern Ireland, as the Belfast Agreement envisages (but does not guarantee), it too will gain quick and ready acceptance. As there will be no parallel rolling out of such a Bill of Rights in other parts of the UK (nor, probably in Ireland) the road to acceptance will be rockier, but if the Bill's commencement is preceded by a year or so of preparatory training courses and information booklets there is no reason to suppose that it will be unduly problematic. This will be all the more likely if the Bill of Rights is modelled on the Human Rights Act as regards the interpretation and invalidation of other legislation, a position which is embodied in the NIHRC's second draft of the Bill of Rights.[131] It may be less likely if the Bill of Rights gives power to judges to allocate economic and social rights, for at present this is mostly the preserve of elected politicians rather than the courts. But the Human Rights Act does protect some such rights already—the right to property, the right to form a trade union, and the right to education, for example—and the sky has not fallen in on either the judges themselves or the society they serve.

Sceptics may counter that the Human Rights Act has proved to be largely irrelevant to several outstanding human rights 'issues' in Northern Ireland—such as

---

[131] *Progressing a Bill of Rights for Northern Ireland* (2004), 87–91.

how to ensure that people are properly held to account for behaviour they indulged in prior to the Belfast Agreement, how to reduce poverty and improve health care, and how to guarantee fair and effective power-sharing arrangements across the communities. They might contend that a much more radical human rights initiative is required if those larger issues are to be dealt with. The reality is, however, that the issues just mentioned are all highly political in nature and human rights activists will themselves disagree as to how best to deal with them. The Convention was not designed to provide answers to those problems and in relation to them it would be inappropriate to blame the Act which incorporates Convention rights into Northern Ireland's law for not doing more than the Convention itself can do.

12

Dangerous Constitutional Moments: the 'Tactic of Legality' in Nazi Germany and the Irish Free State Compared

Gerard Quinn

Law Considered merely as order contains ... its own implicit morality. This morality or order must be respected if we are to create anything that can be called law, even bad law.[1]

Introduction

Dangerous constitutional moments can occur during any process of transition. This essay focuses on two such moments. The first involved the deconstruction of the Weimar Constitution in the early 1930s to pave the way for the Nazi terror. The sheer ease with which that Constitution could be deconstructed from within was striking and continues to reverberate through the decades. The second involved the deconstruction of the Irish Free State Constitution (1922) at around the same time, which eventually paved the way for the highly successful 1937 Constitution of Ireland.

Obviously, these processes had vastly different motivations and led to dramatically different outcomes. In the former case it led to a totalitarian State. In the latter case it led to a more sustainable democratic constitutional order. Yet both processes involved the adroit use of law to undo itself. Legal formalities were consciously manipulated to transform the existing legal order. This so-called 'tactic of legality' presents object lessons to us today and especially during moments of heightened sensitivity as one regime transitions into another.

Many twentieth-century constitutions contained amending provisions that allowed for some susbstantive re-moulding of the constitutional order by the executive without recourse to Parliament or to the People through referenda. Indeed,

[1] Lon Fuller, 'Positivism and Fidelity to Law—a Reply to Professor Hart' (1958) 71 Harv. L. Rev 630, at 645.

these provisions were generally inserted into Dominion constitutions in order to allow for some free play in the joints of new and relatively autonomous legal systems; and the Weimar Constitution of 1919 allowed for (too many) possibilities for rule by Executive decree. These powers were not generally intended to be used to overturn the fundamentals of the legal order and usually had very short time limits (four years or so). They were, however, cast broadly and the lack of explicit limitations could (and did) give rise to the impression that the amending power could be used not merely to 'improve' the technical functioning of the sinews of constitutional power but to actually transfigure the constitutional order itself.

Indeed such was the case with Article 48 of the Weimar Constitution, which enabled the Federal President to decree the suspension of constitutional rights and the infamous Enabling Act 1933, whereby the Reichstag effectively created a parallel source of legislation and vested it in the Executive. The Executive's legislative power even extended to amending the Weimar Constitution itself without even a vestige of parliamentary or legal control.

At least as a matter for formal law, such was also the case under the 1922 Irish Free State Constitution, Article 50 of which allowed for a limited period of grace within which the 1922 Constitution could be amended. Some democratic controls were in place—but were adroitly removed. Article 50 was invoked by the Irish Free State Oireachtas (Parliament) at the behest of the Executive to amend itself in order to extend its own life by a further eight years and to remove the possibility of any reference to the People by way of referendum. In this way, the Irish Free State Constitution was purged of various 'marks of subordination' insisted upon by the British negotiators of the Anglo-Irish Treaty of 1921, and thus paved the way for a wholly new (and extremely successful) Constitution in 1937.[2]

With the benefit of hindsight, the end result in the shape of the 1937 Constitution may have been worth it. But the 'tactic of legality' could have gone badly wrong. Indeed, when endorsing this 'tactic of legality' in 1935 in the famous case of *State (Ryan and Others) v Lennon and Others*, at least one judge in the Irish Supreme Court even went so far as to exclaim that the Legislature had thereby handed over its power to the Executive.[3] The majority in the Supreme Court placed no limits on the use of the amending power and its conception of the 'law' did not offer up any normative resistance to a potential slide toward totalitarian rule. The decision represents the apogee of legal positivism in Ireland. Consciousness of its defects—if not outright embarrassment—motivated de Valera to draft a tighter Constitution in 1937 (even though he had been one of the main beneficiaries of the elasticity of the 1922 Constitution) and emboldened future Irish Supreme Courts to adopt a much more robust approach to policing the Constitution.

---

[2] See generally, Vincent Grogan, 'Irish Constitutional Developments' (1951) Studies 386.
[3] LXIX, The Irish Law Times (1935) 125; Chief Justice Kennedy.

It is important to recall that rule by executive decree is not new. It was resorted to in many legal orders in continental Europe during successive periods of political crisis or instability in the hope that the ship of state would right itself and the need for the use of these powers would dissipate. Indeed, it is important to recall that such powers had a venerable precedent. Dictatorship was an entirely legal institution in the Roman Republic provided it was limited to six months and freely voted into existence.[4]

It goes without saying that a certain attitude—especially in the judiciary—is necessary toward these powers and the conditions under which they may be exercised in order to maintain the overall integrity of the legal and political order. Otherwise, such power can be legally used to hollow out the legal order and replace it with something quite different and qualitatively distinct. Unless checked, the 'tactic of legality' can too easily be used to undermine the very essence of the legal order whilst maintaining the outward appearance of legality.

Using Law to Undo Itself—The 'Tactic of Legality' in Nazi Germany

The Weimar Constitution is widely acknowledged as having been amongst the most democratic of its day. The previous Constitution placed the Kaiser at the apex of the political and legal order. He alone appointed the Chancellor and the Government (which was not formally accountable to the Reichstag) and directly controlled the army. The elected Reichstag (lower house) could block legislation but could not itself legislate.

This concentration of power could not stand after the calamitous defeat of the Great War. In October 1918 (one month before defeat and the Kaiser's abdication), the Government voluntarily declared itself accountable to the Reichstag (perhaps in anticipation of defeat). The abdication of the Kaiser in November 1919 was followed by an interim Government accountable to the Reichstag. A national election was held in January 1919 which led to a new German National Assembly, and a new and thoroughly democratic constitution was adopted by that Assembly in August 1919 in the town of Weimar. It envisaged a Federation of 17 States (Lander) with a clear separation of powers at Federal level and constrained by a set of strong fundamental rights enforced by an independent judiciary.

The text of the Weimar Constitution was admirably clear. Indeed, it could be taken as the very epitome of a liberal-democratic constitution. Part I of the Weimar Constitution dealt with the 'Structure and Tasks of the Federation'. It provided a roadmap for the dispersal of competencies as between the Federal government and the States. Exclusive Federal competencies in fields such as foreign relations,

---

[4] See generally, Andrew Lintott, *The Constitution of the Roman Republic* (2003).

national defence, etc, were set out in Article 6. Legislative competencies (presumably concurrent unless pre-empted) in areas such as civil law, penal law welfare, etc, were set out under Article 7.

Importantly, and marking a sharp break with the preceding constitutional order, Article 1 announced that the German Federation was a republic and that '[S]upreme power emanates from the people'. Federal law was declared supreme (Article 13) and the states were obliged to execute Federal law. This was important since the Federal apparatus relied almost exclusively on the state apparatuses to enforce Federal law. The potential for conflict was therefore in-built given the possibility that states could be controlled by political factions antithetical to the Federal government. State governments were constitutionally bound to remedy defects in the execution of Federal law (Article 15). Article 17 bound each state to have and retain a republican constitution.[5] Indeed, and in keeping with this republican vein, Article 109 provided that titles of nobility could no longer be conferred.

The Lower House (Reichstag) was elected by an equal and secret ballot and on the basis of proportional representation (list system). Unfortunately this system may have contributed to the failure of the centre ground to hold and the proliferation of extreme splinter parties. Interestingly, Article 21 was to the effect that members of the Reichstag were to 'represent the entire nation. They have to follow nothing but their conscience and are not bound by instructions.' The framers were obviously alive to the danger of extreme factionalism, especially in the context of a polarized political environment. Members enjoyed the usual privileges and immunities (eg from arrest) one would expect of parliamentarians (Article 37)—immunities that were ruthlessly ignored later in a Nazi-dominated chamber. Its term of office was four years. If dissolved by the President (at his absolute discretion) fresh elections had to be held within 60 days. Legislation could only be initiated in the Reichstag (Article 68) or by the Federal Government before the Reichstag. The Reichstag also had the power to demand the presence of the Chancellor and individual members (Article 33). Interestingly, the Reichstag could move to try the Chancellor or a Reich minister before the courts for consciously violating the constitution (Article 59). It is interesting to speculate that if the Enabling Act had not been passed, whether Article 59 would have afforded a means of removing Hitler from power. In any event, this power was never used. Clearly the fulcrum of political power lay in the Reichstag under the Weimar Constitution.

The Upper House (Reichstrat) was an appointed assembly and represented the constituent states (Articles 60 and 61). It could not propose legislation and it could not amend legislation. There was a limit on the members that could be appointed

---

[5] For a parallel, see Art. IV, s 4 of the US Constitution to the effect that 'The United States shall guarantee to every State in this Union a Republican form of Government.'

from each state to prevent the Reichstrat being dominated by larger states such as Prussia. Article 61 contained an interesting clause already envisaging the eventual addition of Austria as part of the Federation (but presumably on the basis of free consent).

The hereditary office of Kaiser (which term derived, like the office of Tzar, from Caesar) was discontinued. Functionally, the new office of Federal President fulfilled part of the duties of the Kaiser. He could dissolve the Lower House before its full four-year term came to an end—precipitating fresh elections and possible political turmoil. Unlike members of the Reichstag who were elected locally, he was elected nationally and for a longer seven-year term. The Office was therefore cloaked in elevated legitimacy. He could be removed through a plebiscite initiated in the Reichstag but only if two-thirds of the members agreed to put the matter to the people (Article 43). He appointed and dismissed the Federal Chancellor (Article 53—subject to a vote in the Reichstag under Article 54). He therefore had to make difficult decisions regarding the constellation of political opinion and support in the Reichstag for particular candidates for that office. He became the ultimate arbiter of political conflict, which was an onerous responsibility given the polarization of German society in the 1920s and 1930s. Article 47 conferred on him 'supreme command over the whole of the armed force of the federation'—creating an important pole of loyalty for the professional army, which always formed the bulwark of the republic. Hitler always knew he had to keep the army loyal and was even prepared to sacrifice his own most loyal supporters to that end.

It was the Reich President—and not the Chancellor—who formally represented the German State for the purposes of international law. He 'concludes alliances and other treaties with foreign powers in the name of the Reich' (Article 45). This should not be overstated since the Chancellor and his Ministers conducted all relevant negotiations. A declaration of war could only be signed under Reich law, which effectively created a veto for the President. In case of temporary absence or unavailability or where the presidency ends prematurely (eg death) his functions were transferred to the Chancellor (Article 51(9)). Long-term incapacity required a Reich law.

The President was required to authenticate all laws constitutionally enacted. He could refuse to sign a given piece of legislation for whatever reason and submit it to a popular plebiscite (Article 73). Similar powers were conferred in the event of disagreements between the Reichstag and the Reichsrat or if a substantial number of Reichstag members agreed. Indeed, a plebiscite had to be held if one-tenth of the enfranchised voters demanded a new draft law be presented. These were important democratic checks.

Furthermore, the President held certain exceptional powers under Article 48 which were triggered when he judged that one of the component states had failed to perform its duties to obey the constitution and/or to enforce Federal law.

The infamous Article 48 read (in part):

'If a state fails to perform the duties imposed upon it by the federal constitution or by federal law, the President ... may enforce performance with the aid of the armed forces.

If public order and security are seriously disturbed or endangered within the Federation, the President ... may take all necessary steps for their restoration, intervening, if need be, with the aid of the armed forces.

For the said purpose he may suspend for the time being, either wholly or in part, the fundamental rights described in Articles 114, 115, 117, 118, 123, 124, and 153. The President has to inform the Reichstag without delay of any steps taken in virtue of the first and second paragraph of this article. The measures to be taken are to be withdrawn upon the demand of the Reichstag.'

The rights covered by Article 48 were quite fundamental and were set out in Part II of the Weimar Constitution: Article 114 covered the right to liberty and due process; Article 115 dealt with the privacy of one's residence; Article 117 dealt with privacy more generally in terms of correspondence and other forms of communications; Article 118 dealt with freedom of expression; Article 123 dealt with the right of peaceful assembly; Article 124 dealt with freedom of association; and Article 153 dealt with the right of private property. All of these rights, in their own way, preserved the possibility of autonomous individual action—a zone of autonomy that is vital in any vibrant democratic order and which was quickly closed down under the Nazis.

There was no requirement of proportionality in the measures adopted following a Presidential decree to suspend any of the above rights under Article 48. Further, there was no sunset provision that would require any such decree to lapse unless expressly renewed. And the exercise of the power was not subject to parliamentary sanction—much less judicial review. This lack of side-constraints was to prove fatal since there was nothing to stop a temporary suspension of rights to meet a passing emergency becoming permanent to suit the unlimited political ambitions of the Nazis.

With respect to the judicial branch, Article 102 established that 'judges are independent and subject to the law only'. They were given lifetime tenure (Article 104). Importantly, Article 105 went on to provide that 'extraordinary courts are inadmissible. No one may be withdrawn from his lawful judge ...'. The latter phrase was undoubtedly meant to protect courts against executive or legislative moves to strip them of jurisdiction over pending cases. On paper at least, the judicial branch has the formal independence to display judicial statesmanship and bring normative resistance to bear against the Nazis.

The Weimar Constitution provided that it could be amended by legislation but only if two-thirds of those present in the Reichstag voted in favour (Article 76). Even then, the people (or one-tenth of the enfranchised voters) could demand a plebiscite for the change to come into effect.

The march toward the totalitarian nightmare in Germany began in the immediate aftermath of the Great War. Many regarded those who agreed to the 1918
armistice as 'November Criminals'. The improvidence of the Versailles settlement further served to humiliate ordinary Germans and the political ineptitude
of President Wilson to ensure a steadying American presence in the League of
Nations did not augur well. Parenthetically, Franklin Delano Roosevelt witnessed
the debacle at Versailles at first hand in his capacity as under-Secretary of the Navy
and resolved not to repeat Wilson's errors when re-creating global institutions
in the 1940s.[6]

It is plain that the Weimar Constitution contained many normative opportunities for those who were bent on its destruction. Hitler turned to the 'tactic of
legality' after learning from his earlier mistakes. His biggest mistake was to confront the military power of the State with his own rag-tag army. The failure of his
Beer Hall Putsch of 1923 led him to the view that military means alone would
not do. By all means he had to maintain an armed wing of the Nazi political party
(one that, in time would also have to be disciplined in order to keep the professional army loyal), but after the Putsch he resolved to enter the system 'legally'
and to begin to dismantle it 'legally' from within using its own powers. This was
an entirely cynical and highly deliberate tactic. While his tactic was a 'tactic of
legality', his goal was the very perversion of legality.[7] As Hitler explained:

'In this Constitutional way [i.e., using the tactic of legality] we shall try to gain decisive
majorities in the legislative bodies so that the moment we succeed we can give the State the
form that corresponds to our ideas.'[8]

When Hitler was named Chancellor by President Von Hindenburg in January
1933 (despite not having a majority in the Reichstag) he immediately (ie within
24 hours of assuming the office) prevailed upon the President to dissolve the
Reichstag and call fresh elections to take place in March of that year in the hope
of increasing his party's representation. This seemed feasible as he could now use
the full propaganda and other resources of the State to drown out the voices of
the other parties and so help get his party returned in larger numbers. Six days
before the election the Reichstag fire broke out. The Nazi's seized on the possibility that the fire might have been a signal for a wider communist uprising.[9]
In these circumstances Hitler leaned on President Von Hindenburg to invoke

---

[6] A good account of the lessons not lost on Roosevelt is contained in Conrad Black, *Franklin
Delano Roosevelt: Champion of Freedom* (2005).

[7] See eg H.W. Koch, '1933: The Legality of Hitler's Assumption of Power', in H.W. Koch (ed.),
Aspects of the Third Reich (1985) and, by the same author, *In the Name of the Volk: Political Justice in
Hitler's Germany* (1989).

[8] Peter Caldwell, '*National Socialism and Constitutional Law: Carl Schmitt, Otto Koellreutter, and
the Debate over the Nature of Nazi States, 1033–1937*' (1994–1995) 16 Cardozo L.Rev 404.

[9] A Presidential decree was adopted on 29 March 1933 enabling the death penalty to be applied
retroactively to Van de Lubbe, the suspected arsonist.

Article 48 to suspend many constitutional protections. Von Hindenburg relented. The decree stated:

'Order of the Reich President for the Protection of People and State
On the basis of Article 48, paragraph 2 of the Constitution of the German Reich, the following is ordered in defense against Communist state-endangering acts of violence:

§1.   Articles 114, 115, 117, 118, 123 and 153 of the Constitution of the German Empire are suspended until further notice. It is therefore permissible to restrict the right of personal freedom [habeas corpus], freedom of opinion, including freedom of the press, the freedom to organise and assemble, the privacy of postal, telegraphic and telephonic communications, and warrants for house searches, orders for confiscations as well as restrictions on property, are also permissible beyond the legal limits otherwise prescribed.'

This gave the green light to the authorities in the various states that Federal civil rights law would be no obstacle to harsh treatment. No guidance was given as to how the decree was to be implemented. Those states already under Nazi control (eg Prussia) were ruthless in giving free rein for mass summary arrests. Hermann Goering was in fact the interior minister in Prussia. There was nothing—in law or in fact—to hold ground on the slippery slope toward undifferentiated terror against all and not just the communists. This had the (wholly intended) effect of politically neutering the communists in the run-up to the election.

When Hitler returned as Chancellor after the March 1933 election he was still dependent on coalitions. His party's vote did increase (by some 5.5 million to 17.3 million) but it was still not enough to propel him into a majority position. He knew that opposition in civil society could be effectively quelled through repressive measures made possible by the Presidential decree. However, he still lacked an absolute majority in the Reichstag and was forced to come to terms with coalition partners who still laboured under the illusion that they could control him and his party. He could deal with the remaining impediments to absolute power either by abolishing the Reichstag or by getting it to voluntarily amend the constitution to create a parallel legislative authority lodged in the Government (ultimately in him personally). The former option would destroy his image as someone who valued democracy and who clung scrupulously to legal forms. In keeping with his 'tactic of legality' he chose to preserve the veneer of a parliamentary process whilst at the same time utterly disregarding its actions. He chose the latter option.

Some weeks after the general election of March 1933 Von Hindenburg opened the new parliamentary session at the site of the tomb of Frederick the Great in the Potsdam Garrison Church. After the ceremonies the new parliament opened in the Kroll Opera House in Berlin (demolished after the War), and there was only one item on the agenda—the so-called *Enabling Act (Law to Remedy the Distress of the People and the Reich)*. The preface to the Act stated that 'the Reichstag has enacted the following law, which has the agreement of the Reichsrat and meets the requirements for a constitutional amendment'. The effect was to amend the Weimar Constitution. Article 1 stated that 'In addition to the procedure prescribed by the constitution, laws of the Reich may also be enacted by the government of the Reich . . . '. Thus, simply, a parallel legislative stream was opened. It was to have devastating consequences.

Article 2 of the Enabling Act went on to provide that 'Laws enacted by the government of the Reich may deviate from the constitution as long as they do not affect the institutions of the Reichstag and Reichsrat. The rights of the President remain undisturbed.' In effect, the parallel legislative power thus created could be exercised without regard to any remaining constitutional constraints provided only that the *institutions* of parliament were not altered. Hitler had no intention of abolishing these institutions as their outward show of democracy served his propaganda purposes well (he simply never allowed them to function properly). The core question was not so much whether the edifice of parliament would be allowed to remain standing but what would happen if a difference arose as between the parliamentary legislative stream and the governmental legislative stream. This was answered emphatically under Article 2 by insuring that other constitutional constraints did not apply. Such a clash would become highly theoretical in any event as other political parties were progressively deemed illegal. Interestingly, there had been other Enabling Acts in the history of the Weimar Constitution but none contained a clause such as Article 2.

Article 3 of the Enabling Act stated that laws enacted by the Reich government shall be issued by the Chancellor and announced in the Reich Gazette. This seems to have been scrupulously adhered to. Article 3 also stipulated that Articles 68–77 would not apply to laws decided upon by the Government. Article 77 dealt with the process whereby the Constitution itself could be amended (requiring a two-thirds quorum and a vote of two-thirds of those present). Henceforth, the Government (in effect Hitler) could amend the Constitution at will.

Article 4 explicitly freed up the hand of the government (which meant the Chancellor) with respect to treaties. Even where such treaties affected Reich legislation (ie had some domestic impact) they were not subject to approval by 'bodies concerned with legislation'. Hitler thus won carte blanche with respect to foreign relations. There was one genuflection to liberal sensibilities. Article 5 enacted a sunset clause. It was to the effect that the Enabling Act would cease to be in force on 1 April 1937. This was a cruel April Fool's joke since the rump Reichstag (composed henceforth exclusively of Nazis) was prevailed upon to periodically extend the life of the Enabling Act.

The Centre party voted with the Nazis in favour of the Enabling Act. All communists who had been returned in the general election were removed (their mandate was considered 'dormant'). Twenty-six SPD delegates were arrested before arriving at the session (and were thus unable to vote). The final vote was 441 to 94 (all 94 were SPD members). Apparently the SPD considered abstaining from attending to deprive the Reichstag of a quorum but the President of the Reichstag (Hermann Goering) changed the rules of procedure to enable him to declare any member 'absent without cause' to be considered as present.

Hitler (through cabinet) could now rule by decree. This unbounded power sat uneasily alongside the formal niceties of the 'normal' parliamentary process in the Reichstag. Formal cabinet meetings were rare and non-existent during World War II. In effect, Hitler now wielded absolute power. The *Fuhrerprinzip*—meaning total personal rule by the Fuhrer—was now a reality. The use made of this power was startling.[10]

First, all power was centralized and all remaining poles of political power sub-ordinated. A law was decreed in 1934 subordinating the States (*Law for the Reconstruction of the Reich*),[11] Article 1 of which abolished popular assemblies of the Lander. Article 2 transferred the sovereign powers of the Lander to the Reich. Indeed, Article 4 of that law stated that 'The Reich Government may issue new constitutional laws.' The 1933 *Law against the Establishment of Political Parties* stated simply that 'The National Socialist German Workers Party constitutes the only political party in Germany' (Article 1) and went on to criminalize the forma-tion of other parties. A 1933 *Law for the Restoration of the Civil Service* eroded the independence of the professional civil service and allowed for the dismissal of 'non-Aryan' civil servants.

Indeed, judges were converted into civil servants. There was to be no expect-ation that the judges would administer the law independently; rather the task of the judge was to apply the law in keeping with the spirit of the Nazi regime (*volksgeist*).[12] The most striking illustration of the new judicial atmosphere is to be found in the Rohm purge. In his zeal, Ernst Rohm, who led the SA (Stormabteilung or brown shirts), which was in many respects a parallel Nazi army alongside the regular army, went too far ahead of what mainstream political opinion (and especially the professional army) could bear. His revolutionary antics and disdain for democratic politics threatened Hitler's more cautious attempt to manoeuvre the centre ground and capture power. Hitler's answer was simply to exterminate him and his senior colleagues in the infamous 'night of the long knives' on 30 June 1934. This was simply murder. All liberal-democratic constitutions contain prohibitions against retrospective penal sanctions. Some time later Hitler justified the murders in the Reichstag by effectively asserting that the *Fuhrerprinzip* enabled him to retroactively render legal what was in fact illegal at the time. He said:

'If anyone reproaches me and asks why I did not turn to the regular courts for conviction of the offenders, then all I can say to him is this: in this hour I was responsible for the fate of the German people, and thereby I became the supreme judge of the German people...

I gave the order to shoot ringleaders in this treason, and I further gave the order to cauterise down the raw flesh of the ulcers of this poisoning of the wells of our domestic

---

[10] See generally, Michael Stolleis, *The Law under the Swastika: Studies on Legal History in Nazi Germany* (1998); and Christian Joerges and Navraj Singh Ghaleigh (eds), *Darker Legacies of Law in Europe: the Shadow of National Socialism and Fascism over Europe and its Legal Traditions* (2003).

[11] 1934 Reichgesetzblatt, Pt 1, 75.

[12] See generally, Ingo Muller, *Hitler's Justice: The Courts of the Third Reich* (1991).

life . . . Let the nation know that its existence—which depends on its internal order and security—cannot be threatened with impunity by anyone! And let it be known for all time to come that if anyone raises his hand to strike the State, then certain death is his fate.'[13]

On a separate occasion Hitler said:

'History will never forgive us if in this historic hour we allow ourselves to be infected by the weakness and cowardice of our bourgeois world and use the kid glove instead of the iron fist.'[14]

Thus, Hitler effectively rendered legal what was clearly illegal in retrospect! This *Fuhrerprinzip* also led to a decree enabling the Government to direct sentencing in criminal cases and indeed to set up a special criminal court, or People's Court, to try treason—the notorious *Volksgerictshof* (VGH). Only the presiding judge and one assisting judge had to have a legal qualification. No appeal lay against its convictions or sentences. This made an utter mockery of Article 105 of the Constitution.

Criminal law in liberal-democratic regimes does not normally impose sanctions unless there is some degree of moral culpability on the part of the offender. Our criminal law punishes people not for who they are but for what they do (crimes of behaviour) and only then if it is done with criminal intent. The Nazis stood this tradition on its head and began enacting 'crimes of condition'—ie criminalizing people for their condition. Indeed, the notion of the 'political criminal'— one whose criminality was evidenced by a certain *attitude* toward the Nazi State— entered currency. This created much room for the discretionary enforcement of the criminal law.

This shift toward criminalizing people for who they are and not for what they do began early in the *Law for the Protection of Hereditary Health: The Attempt to Improve the German Ayran Breed* (14 July 1933). This law authorized widespread sterilization of anyone suffering from an 'inheritable disease', which was interpreted broadly to include blindness, deafness, schizophrenia, and even alcoholism. It was but a short step to the exceptionally cruel medical experiments conducted on the authority of the Nazi high commend throughout the 1930s and 1940s.

The Reich Citizenship Law of September 1935 (enacted in the Reichstag) was to the effect that citizenship was confined to those who are of 'German or kindred blood' (Article 2). Additionally, citizenship was confined to those who 'through his behaviour, shows that he is both desirous and personally fit to serve loyally the German people and the Reich'. This was followed up by a decree in November 1935 which baldly pronounced that 'a Jew cannot be a citizen of the Reich' (Article 4) and which forcibly retired all Jews then in the civil service. A *Law for the Protection of German Blood and German Honour* was enacted in September 1935 which forbade inter-marriage between German nations and Jews and also forbade 'relations outside marriage' between the same.

---

[13] See Alan Bullock, *Hitler and Stalin: Parallel Lives* (1993) 383.   [14] ibid, 348.

Hitler's stance on the criminal law was lauded by a leading German lawyer, Carl Schmitt.[15] Professor Caldwell sums up the philosophy of Carl Schmitt as follows:

'[he first denies] the authority of the *Rechtsstaat* [rule of law] within a "truly" German system, and then linking it with bourgeois liberalism and Jewish lawyers of the nineteenth century... He argued that the *Rechtsstaat* had historically been part of the invasion of Germany by liberal ideas in 1789. The *Rechtsstaat* carried with it a humanism, a tendency to treat all people equally. It thus stood in direct opposition to Christianity, and allowed the "usurer" to swindle the hardworking population.... The *Rechtsstaat* implied a separation of powers, not their concentration. It promoted individual freedom and pacifism, not the strong state.'[16]

Having eliminated or absorbed all political institutions that could muster opposition Hitler then began to homogenize civil society. Reich trustees of labour were set up to suppress independent trade unions and substitute for them a party trade union that infiltrated every workplace.[17] Universities were purged of dissenting voices. The intent was plain: to block all possibilities for even imagining any alternative to the Nazi programme. Many tenured faculty were purged. Many others were enthusiastic. An accommodation was reached with religious denominations, which effectively neutered them as a potential pole of opposition.

The Enabling Act was also used to extend the Government's powers to amend the Constitution at will. This was used to abolish the Reichstrat and indeed to abolish the office of the Presidency upon Von Hindenburg's death in August 1934. The Office of the Presidency was simply merged with that of the Chancellor! Interestingly, Hitler obliged the professional army to take an oath of loyalty not to the office of the Presidency as such (which was now transferred into his office) but to himself personally as Fuhrer. All of this amounted to what Professor Caldwell calls 'Nazi anticonstitutionalism'.[18]

Perspectives on Nazi 'Legality'

Was any of this legal? There are at least four approaches one might take in denying the epithet 'lawful' to the Nazi regime.

One might grin and bear Nazi legality. This was the view of H.L.A. Hart, who must surely rank as one of the more sophisticated legal positivists of the twentieth century. No matter how much one detests Nazi 'law'—as Hart surely did—it was

---

[15] Carl Schmitt, 'The Fuhrer Protects the Law' (1934) German Law Gazette.

[16] Caldwell, '*National Socialism and Constitutional Law: Carl Schmitt, Otto Koellreutter, and the Debate over the Nature of Nazi States, 1033–1937*', n 8 above, at 420.

[17] For analysis see Franz Neumann, 'Labor Mobilization in the National Socialist New Order' (1942) 9 Law & Contemp. Probs 544.

[18] Caldwell, '*National Socialism and Constitutional Law: Carl Schmitt, Otto Koellreutter, and the Debate over the Nature of Nazi States, 1033–1937*', n 8 above, at 399.

still nevertheless 'law'. In his famous exchange with Professor Lon Fuller on the subject, Hart draws a distinction between the recognition of law as, law on the one hand and political obligation to obey that law on the other.[19] This is not wholly convincing since political obligation is intimately tied to the rule of law.[20] But it is a measure of his extreme discomfiture at having to defend Nazi law as law.

Another approach is to insist—as the Gustav Radbruch insisted in his post-positivist phase—that certain core human values transcend time and place. As Radbruch stated:

'In manifold ways, the rulers of the twelve year dictatorship gave unlawfulness, even crime, the form of a statute. Even institutionalized murder is said to have been founded on a statute, admittedly in the monstrous form of an unpublished secret law. The inherited conception of law, namely positivism and its theory that "a statute is a statute", which was the indisputably dominant theory for decades among German jurists, was defenceless and powerless against such an unlawfulness in the form of a statute. The adherents of this theory were compelled to recognise every unjust statute as law.'[21]

The legal order, in order to be cognisable as a legal order, must pivot on—and be bounded by—these values, otherwise it ceases to be a legal order. This is a respectable position and strongly buttressed by natural law-thinking. However, and maybe because of its connectedness to natural law-thinking, it does not exhaust all the counter-arguments that could be made against Nazi 'law'. For one thing, it comes perilously close to sanctioning retroactive penal law—something against which the 'rule of law' is stoutly opposed.

A third approach would be to stand back from these transcendent values and to peer deeply into the 'rule of law' tradition itself. From this perspective, the 'rule of law' tradition suggests many *desiderata* in the law (like clarity, predictability, treating like cases alike, etc) which, if not met, deny the 'legal order' any claim to legality. This is certainly the view strongly advocated by Franz Neuman.[22] It is interesting to note that Neumann did not want to rest the case against Nazi law entirely on natural law arguments since, as a labour lawyer, he saw how such arguments could be abused by courts against the rights of workers. Instead, he saw certain *desiderata* (serving particular values such as freedom of conscience and liberty) as immanent within the 'rule of law' tradition. In a sense, the 'rule of law' carried its own set of values that could be detached from natural law-thinking. This too, is the general approach taken by Professor Lon Fuller in his answer to H.L.A. Hart.[23] Fuller develops his arguments further in his magisterial 1964

---

[19] H.L.A. Hart, 'Positivism and the Separation of Law and Morals' (1958) 71 Harv. L.Rev. 593.

[20] See eg Carole Pateman, *The Problem of Political Obligation: a Critical Analysis of Liberal Theory* (1979).

[21] Gustav Radbruch, 'Die Erneurung des Rechts' (1947), repr. in Werner Maihofer (ed.), *Naturrecht oder Rechtpositivismus* (1966); quoted in Caldwell, '*National Socialism and Constitutional Law: Carl Schmitt, Otto Koellreutter, and the Debate over the Nature of Nazi States, 1033–1937*', n 8 above.

[22] Franz Neumann, *The Rule of Law* (translation, 1985).

[23] Lon Fuller, 'Positivism and Fidelity to Law: a Reply to Professor Hart', n 1 above.

opus *The Morality of Law* by identifying what he calls the 'inner morality' of law and legality.[24]

The approach of Neumann and Fuller is an interesting attempt to bring normative resistance to bear against Nazi 'law' without relying on supposed universal values. Yet one suspects that since the 'rule of law' tradition (at least in modernity) is itself coterminous with the great revolution of English liberal constitutional-thinking from the 1680s onwards that it too is ultimately anchored on these transcendent values.

Yet another approach is to move away from supposed universal values—whether in their own right or as embodied in the 'rule of law' tradition—and to focus instead on what it means (both practically and normatively) to belong to a democratic society. At one level, an open-ended democratic system that pivots on the sovereignty of the people should be able to carve out its own destiny and select its own fundamental values (or indeed, no values) without any artificial boundaries. And yet a curious paradox arises. If we truly value an open-ended democratic process then we should be concerned with obstacles and dangers that cause that process to implode. It follows that some practical or prudential limits against popular sovereignty are required if only to save the democratic process from itself. Quite what these limits are is open to debate. Yet no matter where the line falls, it is clear that the Nazis exceeded it by destroying the very essence of a democratic order.

A variation of the above argument (the argument from democracy) is to straightforwardly assert that democracy harbours within it its own set of values.[25] After all, why treat each vote equally unless we are committed to the ideal that there is something of inestimable worth in each human being regardless of intellect, or social class or other attribute?

It is certainly striking that the framers of the European Convention on Human Rights were particularly alive to the need to preserve an open democratic political system. For example, during the relevant debates in the Consultative Assembly of the Council of Europe, Sir Ungoed-Thomas, former Solicitor General for England and Wales, stated:

'What we are concerned with is not every case of injustice which happens in a particular country but with the question whether a country is ceasing to be democratic.'[26]

These sentiments were typical of those who contributed to the relevant debate in the Consultative Assembly on the Convention. They demonstrate not merely a deontological concern for the inherent rights of man but also an instrumental concern for the preservation of the best process known to protect and advance those rights—the institutions of democracy.

[24] Lon Fuller, *The Morality of Law* (1964).
[25] For an exquisite account of this approach to democratic theory and law in the jurisprudence of Justice William Brennan, see Frank Michelman, *Brennan and Democracy* (2005).
[26] Vol II, *Collected Version of the Traveaux Preparatories*, 166.

It is now universally accepted that Nazi law was not law. But the basis for such judgement varies. Probably, on balance, some combination of the Lon Fuller argument—looking deeply into the 'rule of law' tradition and finding within it its own limitations—with the argument from democracy (both practical and normative) suffices to ground the judgment.

Using Law to Undo Itself—The 'Tactic of Legality' in the Irish Free State

The 'tactic of legality' was resorted to by Hitler in order to infiltrate the legal order and hollow it out—leaving a shell that cast a thin veneer of respectability over naked power. He saw the Weimar Constitution as a stepping stone to absolute power and had no problem retaining it as an empty fossil and ornament for outside consumption. The 'tactic of legality' was resorted to in the Irish Free State for vastly different reasons.

The Irish Free State Constitution was always going to be a stepping stone. Few people—or at least few people South of the border—were enthused by it. All would seek to change it one way or another. Its fate was doomed from the beginning; yet it is the way it was undone that gives some cause for concern.

The Proclamation of a Republic in 1916—ever since considered the root of title to the legal legitimacy of the Irish State by most Irish constitutional scholars—contained many lofty goals for a sovereign Irish people. It famously committed the new entity to 'cherish all the children of the nation equally', and it genuflected before an ideal of a pluralistic democracy that respected difference and rejected attempts to manipulate difference for political ends. Yet the dream of an independent sovereign all-Ireland Republic was to remain just that. The General Election of 1918 witnessed the meltdown of the Irish Parliamentary Party and the rise of Sinn Féin, especially in the South. Instead of taking their seats in Westminster the new Sinn Féin MPs convened their own Parliament (First Dáil) in Dublin. In British constitutional eyes this was an illegal assembly. From the perspective of republican legal thought, this assembly owed its authority to the Proclamation in 1916. The First Dáil issued a Declaration of Independence reaffirming the 1916 Proclamation. It adopted a highly egalitarian Democratic Programme and proceeded to create a parallel State apparatus alongside the existing British apparatus. Eventually a parallel court system was set up (the so-called Dáil Courts) with local (ie non-legal) members.[27] The First Dáil reaffirmed the Proclamation and indeed re-issued it in French. Efforts to gain entry into the peace conference at Versailles were made but rebuffed.

The Government of Ireland Act 1920 sought to deliver on the more moderate and longstanding demand of home rule and led to the creation of two

---

[27] See generally Mary Kotsonouris, *Retreat from Revolution: the Dáil Courts, 1920–1924* (1994).

Parliaments—one in Belfast and another in Dublin. Another (British) general election was held in May 1921 and the Sinn Féin MPs returned again opted to convene a Second Dáil rather than sit in the House of Parliament for Southern Ireland as envisaged under the Government of Ireland Act. The War of Independence raged between January 1919 until 11 July 1921 when a truce between the parties was put into effect. This eventually led to an agreement on 6 December 1921 which was always referred to as the 'Treaty' by the Irish side on the assumption that the Irish State had existed since 1916 and therefore had the requisite legal capacity to conclude treaties under international law. On the British side it was styled *Articles of Agreement for a Treaty* on the assumption that only one sovereign power was engaged unless and until it acquiesced in the creation of another sovereign power. As appended to the Irish Free State Constitution it appears as *Articles of Agreement for a Treaty*.

The Treaty (or Articles of Agreement) did not deliver on the Republic as sought. Instead it conferred 'mere' dominion status on a new Irish Free State (Article 1). The new dominion was subject to Imperial law, which at that time was quite restrictive but was later liberalized by the Statute of Westminster in 1931 to afford more autonomy to the Dominions. An oath of allegiance to the Crown was required of members of the new Parliament in the South. The territorial integrity of the new entity would not be complete. Naval facilities in particular would remain with the Royal Navy. Article 16 did provide interesting protections for religious minorities left on either side of the emerging border.

The Treaty was narrowly 'ratified' by the Second Dáil (meeting in UCD) on 14 January 1922 (by a vote of 64:57). It was this ratification that was considered vital on the Irish side. Article 18 of the Treaty required that it be formally ratified on the Irish side by the Parliament for Southern Ireland set up under the Government of Ireland Act 1920. It was agreed to do so as a formality. This time, however, the Sinn Féin representatives were ominously absent and the vote was 64:0. This latter meeting set up the Provisional Government with Michael Collins as its Chairman. On 16 January 1922, the Provisional Government began assuming all the powers of the outgoing British administration. On 31 March 1922, the UK Parliament conferred the force of law on the Treaty through the Irish Free State (Agreement) Act.

The stage was thus set for a bloody and divisive Civil War and for the preparation of a new Constitution for the Irish Free State.[28] A new general election was called by the Provisional Government in 1922 and resulted in the Third Dáil or Constituent Assembly (sitting as a single chamber with no oath of loyalty required) whose main purpose was to draft and enact a new Constitution. A Dáil Committee was set up to draft the Constitution. As Colm Gavin-Duffy

---

[28] See generally, Leo Kohn, *The Constitution of the Irish Free State* (1932). On the drafting of the 1922 Constitution, see Brian Farrell, 'From First Dáil through Irish Free State', ch. 2 in Brian Farrell (ed.), *De Valera's Constitution and Ours* (1988) ch. 2.

noted 'three drafts were prepared and submitted for approval to the British Government'.[29]

The Constituent Act which was passed on 25 October 1922 contained some prefatory language and just three brief sections. It was mirrored in a Westminster Statute: Act to Provide for the Constitution of the Irish Free State. The preface (later to become significant) to the Constituent Act stated that Dáil Éireann was sitting as a Constituent Assembly and that 'all lawful authority comes through God to the people'. Section 1 was to the effect that the Constitution contained in the First Schedule shall be the Constitution of the Irish Free State. Section 2 subordinated the new Constitution to the Articles of Agreement for a Treaty contained in the Second Schedule. In effect, and in case of inconsistency between the two documents, the Treaty would prevail. The third section dealt with citation.

The Irish Free State Constitution (set out as the First Schedule to the Constituent Act) reflected many of the perceived 'marks of subordination' imposed under the Treaty. The Dominion status of the new entity was emphasized in Article 1—counterbalanced by Article 2 that predicated the legitimacy of all governmental authority on the sovereignty of the People. The Crown was denominated a constituent element of the new Parliament (Oireachtas) under Article 12. Article 17 spelt out the oath of allegiance required of members of the Oireachtas. The King's personal representative could reserve legislation to the Privy Council (Article 51), who would have the last say over appeals from the new Supreme Court, which was not to be supreme after all (Article 66). Interestingly, the Constitution would only come into force by parallel enactments in the Constituent Assembly and the British Parliament and announced by Proclamation of the King (Article 83).

Despite these 'marks of subordination' the 1922 Constitution did innovate in other respects. It genuflected toward the national aspiration of the State by recognizing Irish as an official language (Article 4) and showed republican sympathies by prohibiting the grant of new titles of nobility (Article 5). The judicial branch was given effective independence (Article 64). Importantly, the new High Court was explicitly given the new original jurisdiction to invalidate laws for inconsistency with the constitution (Article 65), with the possibility of an appeal to the Supreme Court. The Constitution did contain some fundamental rights (nowhere called such and not bundled under a clear chapeau of rights) such as the right to liberty and habeas corpus (Article 6), the right to the inviolability of the dwelling (Article 7), freedom of expression, the right of assembly (Article 9), the right to fair trial in the regular courts and by a jury of one's peers (Article 72), and a right against retroactive penal sanction (Article 43).

It was clear that both Cumann nGaedheal (pro-Treaty party that later became Fine Gael) and the new Fianna Fáil party established in 1927 (anti-Treaty but

---

[29] Colm Gavan-Duffy, 'Lecture on the Origin of the Two Irish Constitutions', delivered at University College Cork, 15 February 1988. Text on file with the author.

resolved to work within the system) would agitate to leverage change. The groundwork for this was laid by Irish diplomats (in association with diplomats from other Dominions) who successfully agitated for a change of Imperial law at successive Imperial conferences in the 1920s. This led to the Statute of Westminster 1931, which would be exploited to great effect by Eamonn de Valera when in power. But it is equally clear that both major parties deployed a 'tactic of legality' to deconstruct the 1922 Constitution from within.

A series of counter-terrorism emergency laws were adopted in the late 1920s to counteract rump republican violence against the fledgling Free State. One stumbling block to effective legislation was the very human rights that set the 1922 Constitution apart. The Government could neutralize the human rights provisions by successively amending the Constitution. But there were formidable obstacles. Article 50 of the Constitution contained the main provision dealing with amendments. It reads:

'Amendments of the Constitution within the terms of the Scheduled Treaty may be made by the Oireachtas but no such amendment, passed by both Houses of the Oireachtas, after a period of eight years from the date of the coming into operation of this Constitution, shall become law, unless the same shall, after it has been passed or deemed to have been passed by the said two Houses of the Oireachtas, have been submitted to a Referendum of the people, and unless a majority of the voters on the register, or two thirds of the votes recorded, shall have been cast in favour of such amendment. Any such amendment may be made within the said period of eight years by way or ordinary legislation and as such shall be subject to the provisions of Article 47 hereof.'

It is plain from Article 50 that an eight-year period of grace was to be given to the Government and the Oireachtas to amend the Constitution. This was apparently added very late in the drafting process.[30] Following this period of grace, any such amendment had to be put to the people by way of referendum. An added insurance was built in against abuse in the sense that any amendment proposed within the eight-year period of grace would always be subject to Article 47, which created a democratic check not unlike those contained in the Weimar Constitution. If two-fifths of the members of the Dáil (Lower House) or a majority of members of the Seanad (Upper House) made a written demand that the amendment be suspended and put to the people in a referendum then it had to go to a popular vote. The eight-year period of grace was set to expire in 1930.

A series of amendments were in fact introduced by the Government and enacted by the Oireachtas relying on Article 50. Amendment 10 was enacted in 1928 which deleted the reference to Article 47 in Article 50.[31] So the Article 47 safeguard was now gone. Since the eight-year period of grace was useful and coming to an end, Amendment 16 was enacted in 1929 to extend the operation of

---

[30] Gerard Hogan, 'A Desert Island Case set in the Silver Sea: The State (Ryan) v Lennon', in Eoin O'Dell (ed.), *Leading Cases of the Twentieth Century* (2000) 82.
[31] Constitution (Amendment No 10) Act 1928 (No 8 of 1928).

Article 50 for another eight years. Thus, Article 50 was used to amend itself, bringing the period of grace up to 1937.

Within this extended period (and by definition beyond the first eight years) a new substantive amendment was enacted (Constitution (Amendment No 17) Act, 1931).[32] It was styled an *An Act to Amend the Constitution by Inserting Therein an Article Making Better Provision for Safeguarding the Rights of the People and Containing Provisions for Meeting a Prevalence of Disorder*. The Act itself contained only two sections. Section 1 was to the effect that a new Article 2A would be inserted into the Constitution following Article 2. The new Article 2A was contained in a Schedule to the Act. The second section simply dealt with citation. The Schedule itself was nearly as long as the original Constitution! It is a remarkable document containing Five Parts, 34 sections, and an annex of seven sections. There was no possibility of putting such a fundamental alteration of the Constitution to the People by way of referendum since the reference to Article 47 had already been removed from Article 50 by Amendment 10.

Effectively, Amendment 17 enabled the Executive Council (the cabinet under the 1922 Constitution), whenever it is 'of opinion that circumstances exist which render it expedient' to initiate Parts II, III, and IV of Article 2A which sets up a parallel legal system to try terrorist-related offences (Section 1(2)). Section 2 was to the effect that 'Article 3 and every subsequent Article of this Constitution shall be read and construed subject to the provisions of this Article.' This subordinated the rest of the Constitution to Article 2A. It is unclear why Articles 1 and 2 of the Constitution were left unaffected. Part II of Article 2A made provision for a Constitution (Special Powers) Tribunal. All five members of the Tribunal were to be members of the Defence Forces and there was no requirement for legal training or qualification. Indeed they were removable at will (Section 4(2)). It had full control of its own proceedings and could bar the public from attending (Section 5(3)). Section 6 conferred on the Tribunal the competence to try any office listed in the Annex to the Schedule. The Annex listed the usual range of terrorist-related crimes. In addition, Section 7 of the Annex was to the effect that the Tribunal could try:

'any offence whatsoever (whether committed before or after this Article was inserted into the Constitution . . .) in respect of which the Executive Minister certifies in writing that under his hand that to the best of his belief the act constituting such offence was done with the object of impairing or impeding the machinery of government or the administration of justice.'

There could be no appeal from decisions of the Tribunal—nor was it subject to *certiorari* (Section 6(5)). Furthermore, the Tribunal should substitute a greater sentence than the one normally specified for the relevant offence up to and including the death penalty (Section 7(1)). No coroner's inquest could follow

---

[32] No 37 of 1931.

the imposition of the death penalty (as was usually the case following judicial execution (Section 7(5)). Extensive immunities were conferred on members of the Tribunal in the exercise of their functions. Extensive powers of arrest and examination of suspects were conferred on the police under Part III. Part IV prohibited unlawful organizations who were defined extremely broadly. Amongst other matters, Part V restricted freedom of assembly.

The constitutionality of Article 2A was bound to be ventilated. If found unconstitutional it would give rise to the strange paradox of an unconstitutional constitution! The substance of Article 2A was objectionable in itself as it erected a parallel legal process within the Constitution. It neutered other countervailing provisions of the Constitution dealing with the right to liberty, due process, and fair trial and it conferred powers on the Executive and on the Tribunal, going far beyond what the Constitution could ordinarily bear and was affront to the conscience of those who held the 'rule of law' dear. Furthermore, it could only have been validly enacted in 1931 by the Oireachtas (without recourse to a popular referendum) if Amendment 16 of 1929 (extending the period of grace for a further eight years) had itself been validly enacted. It therefore put directly into question the validity of the 'tactic of legality' used to sideline important protections in the Constitution. Could the Constitution be used to undo itself?

The issue—or complex set of issues—arose squarely in 1934 in an application for habeas corpus and Prohibition: *State (Ryan and others) v Lennon and others*.[33] The respondent Lennon was the governor of Arbour Hill Detention Barracks where Ryan and others were awaiting trial before the Tribunal. The case came before a Divisional High Court (Sullivan P, Meridith and O'Byrne JJ), where the application was unanimously rejected by the High Court panel and its decision upheld by a three-judge Supreme Court (Fitzgibbon and Murnaghan JJ and Kennedy CJ).

The President of the High Court, Sullivan P, framed the issue narrowly as one of statutory interpretation. The issue thus framed was one of measuring legislation against the Constitution—a novel task for a common law judge. While he laid stress on the familiar canon of statutory construction (that the words should be given their ordinary and natural meaning), he nevertheless followed the views of the Privy Council which were to the effect that statutes containing constitutions should be liberally interpreted.[34] He rejected the argument that the word 'amend' in Article 50 had to be confined to 'improvements' or the 'removal of faults'. Amendment 16 was therefore validly enacted and Amendment 17—which was dependent on Amendment 16—stood.

The opening sentence in the judgment of Meridith J gave a strong hint of what was to follow. He explicitly denied that he could have recourse to any principles lying outside the text of the Constitution and declined the invitation from

---

[33] Vol. LXIX, The Irish Law Times (1935) 125.
[34] *Edwards v Attorney General for Canada* (1930) AC 124.

counsel to 'rove at large' in search of (external) legal principles. For example, he rejected the principle of *delegates non potest delegare* (since the people conferred a limited period of grace on the Executive it could unilaterally extend this period). This was one such 'external' principle that was not importable into the analysis. Article 50 itself could have been explicitly exempted from its own operation— but it was not. Meredith J next focused on the argument that even if Amendment 16 was valid, that it did not necessarily or automatically follow that Amendment 17 (Article 2A) was valid, since it was 'so radical as to amount to a repeal of the Constitution'. The essence of the argument was that some Articles were so 'fundamental' that they could not be eroded. Meredith J countered that all Articles were fundamental in a Constitution (and there could thus be no distinction between minor and fundamental provisions). He pointed out that if it was intended to except certain Articles from the remit of Article 50 then it should have been clearly stated. This point was not lost on the drafters of the 1937 Constitution, who took care to highlight fundamental rights in a separate and prominent part of the Constitution. It was put to the High Court that if no Article was exempt from Article 50 then there was no principle in the Constitution, however sacred, (eg proportional representation) that could not be swept away. Meredith J did not demur:

'Well, the truth must be faced, however unpalatable: there is nothing in Article 50 to prevent the abolition of proportional representation. Such is the devastating effect of Article 50.'[35]

The third High Court judge, O'Byrne J, dealt with the argument put by counsel that since the new Constitution rested on popular and not parliamentary sovereignty (cf the prefatory language in the Constituent Act as mirrored in Article 2 of the Constitution which was unaffected by Article 2A), more space was created for the judiciary to acknowledge some 'fundamentals'. He characterized—and rejected—the argument as being among 'various other questions of philosophical interest'.

The High Court decision was immediately appealed to the Supreme Court. Counsel for the State included Gavin-Duffy SC, who was on the official Irish delegation at the Treaty negotiations and who later distinguished himself as a liberal President of the High Court. The Chief Justice was Hugh Kennedy, who was the first, and highly successful, Attorney-General in the new Irish Free State. Three judges in all composed the Supreme Court panel: Kennedy CJ, Fitzgibbon J, and Murnahan J. Both Fitzgibbon and Murnahan JJ voted to uphold the High Court decision. Kennedy CJ issued what is perhaps the most famous dissenting judgment in Irish constitutional history.

Fitzgibbon J denied that the term 'amendment' as used in Article 50 was confined to 'improvement'. He cited 'amendments' to the US Constitution that were

---

[35] See n 33 above, 130.

in fact repeals. He also felt that the judiciary could have no function in judging what was, or was not, an 'improvement' since such judgments lie within the exclusive province of the political branches of Government. To hold otherwise would be to stray impermissibly beyond the judicial remit. While section 2 of the Constituent Act anchored the Constitution in the Treaty (and so erected some fundamental barriers), and while this was reflected in the opening lines of Article 50, no other barriers were to be found on the face of Article 50.

Fitzgibbon J in the Supreme Court stressed that the open-ended power to amend the Constitution in Article 50 did not extend to amendments of the Constituent Act, nor to the phrase 'within the terms of the Scheduled Treaty' as it appears in Article 50 itself. Even if this phrase had not appeared in Article 50 it was nevertheless operative through section 2 of the Constituent Act. Yet this was a pyrrhic concession since the Treaty did not anchor any fair trial rights (although it anchored education rights for minorities). No Articles in the 1922 Constitution were denominated on their face as 'fundamental' (unlike other Constitutions). Fitzgibbon J also gave short shrift to the more abstract argument that 'there are certain rights, inherent in every individual, which are so sacred that no Legislature has authority to deprive them'. He surveyed the rights tradition in the Anglo-American legal tradition (within which he situated Ireland) to the effect that certain universal rights pre-exist and hover above the State. Fitzgibbon J conceded its strength but doubted its universality given the diversity of other rights traditions including the General Will theory in France. He repudiated the notion that a judge can have resource to some vague 'spirit' of the text. To the argument that minorities had been induced to give loyalty to the new State because of the presence of fundamental protections in the text he retorted that everyone signed up to Article 50 and were therefore stuck with the consequences. In what is perhaps the most caustic line in any Irish Supreme Court judgment he concluded that Amendment 17 set out the:

'[c]onditions under which liberty is enjoyed "in this other Eden, demi-Paradise, this previous stone set in the silver sea, this blessed plot, this earth, this realm this" Saor Stat.'[36]

Murnaghan J framed the issue as one of constitutionality in the strict sense and would not decide the matter on the wisdom or otherwise of the legislation. He did, however, vent his extreme displeasure of Article 2A in the following revealing terms:

'The extreme rigour of the Act in question [inserting Article 2A] in such that its provisions pass far beyond anything having the semblance of legal procedure and the judicial mind is staggered at the very complete departure from legal methods in use in these Courts.'

This was precisely the stance taken by Professor Lon Fuller, who went on to characterize the Nazi legal order as no legal order at all. Murnaghan J did not carry his

---

[36] See n 33 above, 151.

own insight to its logical conclusion and noted, like Fitzgibbon J, that no Articles were highlighted as 'fundamental' or otherwise segregated from the rest and all were therefore equally amenable to amendment. Murnaghan J, similar to Professor Fuller, took the view that the Treaty was 'fundamental' (ie the Article 50 amending power could not reach it) since this was the effect of section 2 of the Constituent Act.

The judgment of Kennedy CJ is lengthy and rightly celebrated. He elaborated at length the content of Article 2A to reveal just how far it departed from accepted practice. Like Murnaghan J, he stated:

'In general it may be said that some of the provisions to which I have been referring are the antithesis of the rule of law and are, within their scope, the rule of anarchy.'[37]

Here one can catch an echo of the analysis made famous by Professor Lon Fuller. One would have wished that he would have developed this argument by using it as a separate ground of unconstitutionality.

In sharp contrast to his brethren in the majority, he took the view that 'the new Article 2A is no mere amendment in, but effects a radical alteration of, the basic scheme and principles of the Constitution'.[38] Echoing (unconsciously) the effects of the Nazi Enabling Act, Kennedy CJ said:

'[T]he net effect, then, is that the Oireactas has taken judicial Power from the Judiciary and handed it to the Executive, and has surrendered its own trust as a Legislature to the Executive Council.'[39]

His general approach in testing the constitutionality of Article 2A could not have been more different to that of the majority. While he would bow to 'lawful' amendments, he would adopt the posture of a watchdog to 'protect against unlawful encroachments and to maintain intact, in so far as in us lies, the principles and provisions in the Constitution for the protections of the liberties of the citizens'.[40] He focused first on the prefatory words contained in the Constituent Act which acknowledged that 'all lawful authority comes from God to the people . . .'.

In doing so he did two things. First, he opened up a window onto universal principles reflected in the Constitution but anchored externally. In effect, he used the text as an invitation to stray beyond the text (a style that Robert Bork later called 'false textualism' in a different context).[41] He asserts that every act, whether legislative or executive or judicial, in order to be lawful must be capable of being justified under the authority declared to be derived from God. This was already going very far and is reminiscent of the use made by the US Supreme Court of natural law reasoning in the 1930s—which prompted President Roosevelt (with the active collaboration of the colourful Irish-American lawyer, Tommy 'the Cork'

---

[37] ibid, 133.   [38] ibid, 134.   [39] ibid, 135.   [40] ibid, 136.
[41] Robert Bork, *The Tempting of America: the Political Seduction of the Law* (1997).

Corcoran) to attempt to pack the court.[42] In particular, Kennedy CJ, found the power to substitute the death penalty for any penalty under law impossible to reconcile with natural law. As Gerard Hogan correctly points out, this was not the religiously inspired natural law-thinking that dominated Irish jurisprudence in the 1960s and 1970s.[43] If anything, it resonates with classic liberal legal and political thinking about the 'rule of law'.

Secondly, Kennedy CJ focused on the doctrine of 'popular sovereignty' contained in the preface to the Constituent Act (which was not amenable to Article 50). If the People in the Constituent Assembly set up a particular method of amendment (with safeguards in the form of referenda) then these safeguards were inviolable.

Parenthetically, he never comes to terms with the potential clash between natural law-thinking and popular sovereignty (a tension that would convulse Irish constitutional jurisprudence later in the 1980s and 1990s as the 'liberal agenda' sunk roots). Gerard Hogan rightly states that the 'key question' is whether he would have relented with his natural law approach if Article 2A had in fact been democratically endorsed through a referendum.[44] Hogan speculates that he would not and points to a series of later decisions according to which the Supreme Court took sides with 'people power' in a face-off with natural law. For example, the core issue in *Re Article 26 and the Information (Termination of Pregnancies) Bill* in 1995 was whether 'natural law' fundamentals placed an insuperable roadblock in the way of amendments to the Constitution which were otherwise democratically decided upon by the people. Hamilton CJ, writing for the Supreme Court, came down emphatically on the side of 'people power' over 'natural law' and stated:

'The People were entitled to amend the Constitution in accordance with the provisions of Article 46 of the Constitution and the Constitution as so amended by the Fourteenth Amendment is the fundamental and supreme law of the State representing as it does the will of the People.'[45]

This decision decisively marginalized (if not eliminated) natural law from Irish constitutional jurisprudence, and thus created space for the democratic will of the people to be respected. It implicitly follows the advice of Oliver Wendell Holmes: judges should not get in the way of the people. Yet its complete genuflection before 'popular sovereignty' is disconcerting.

Kennedy CJ found another restriction of the power to amend the Constitution in section 2 of the Constituent Act (linking—and rendering subordinate—the Constitution to the Treaty). His analysis was long and ponderous and touched on the fascinating issue of the State of the Treaty under domestic law. It is relevant to subsequent debates about the 'constitutionality' of the crafting of the 1937

[42] For an entertaining account of the role of Corcoran in the Court Packing Plan, see David McKean, *Peddling Influence: Thomas 'Tommy the Cork' Corcoran and the Birth of Modern Lobbying* (2005).
[43] Gerard Hogan, n 30 above, 95.   [44] ibid, at 96.
[45] *Re Article 26 and the Information (Termination of Pregnancies) Bill* [1995] 1 IR 43.

Constitution and the legality of the abrogation of the Treaty (which it required). Unlike the majority, he took the view that the way the various rights were expressed in the Constitution was intended to signal that they were in some way 'fundamental'. Like Meredith J he noted (but, unlike Meredith J, with disapproval) that if the extension of the eight-year period of grace was lawful:

'It can be continued indefinitely in time and scope of amendment, ultimately even to the exclusion of the people from all voice in legislation and administration and in open mockery of Article 2 of the Constitution.'[46]

He declared that Amendment 16 was beyond the scope of Article 50. If this fell, then so too did Amendment 17 (Article 2A).

What was the result? Amendment 16 was upheld by the majority in the Supreme Court. The result was that the 1922 Constitution could now be amended by the legislature without the need to hold a referendum. Amendments of the Irish Free State Constitution now lay with the legislative at the behest of the Executive. The stage was set for a radical dismantling of the 'marks of subordination' of the Treaty and the 1922 Constitution. Legislation amending the Constitution was subsequently introduced to get rid of the oath of loyalty,[47] to deny the possibility of taking appeals to the Privy Council from the Supreme Court,[48] to abolish the office of Governor General,[49] and the removal of the King as the Head of State. The constitutionality of the removal of the right of appeal to the Privy Council was fought all the way up to the Privy Council since that right was in fact entrenched in the Treaty. The latter body sanctioned the abolition of the right of appeal (thus making itself redundant with respect to Irish appeals) on a theory that the Statute of Westminster of 1921 had given the Irish the power to abrogate the Treaty.[50]

The groundwork was now laid for the introduction of the 1937 Constitution. Gerard Hogan points out that these amendments might otherwise have been difficult to obtain through referenda given the polarized character of Irish political opinion at the time.[51] A Constitution Revision Committee met throughout 1934. The Oireachtas enacted the Executive Authority (External Relations) Act 1936, which marginalized the King to external affairs (receiving credentials). The Irish Free State remained part of the Commonwealth and did not in fact leave it until 1948 (curiously not under de Valera). Its decision to leave was political—there was nothing in the 1937 Constitution forcing it to do so. Contrariwise, there would appear to be no constitutional obstacle to the Republic of Ireland rejoining the Commonwealth!

---

[46] See n 33 above, 140.   [47] Constitution (Removal of Oath) Act 1933 (No 6 of 1933).
[48] Constitution (Amendment No 22) Act 1933 (No 45 of 1933).
[49] Constitution (Amendment No 27) Act 1936 (Act No 57 of 1936).
[50] *Moore v Attorney General for the Irish Free State* [1935] AC 484.
[51] Hogan, n 30 above, 88.

The lesson of the foregoing was that there were no anchors in the 1922 Constitution that could have saved it from the fate of the Weimar Constitution. To his immense credit, de Valera opted to strengthen the emerging 1937 Constitution by explicitly denominating human rights as 'fundamental' and sending a strong signal to the courts that they should robustly defend them. This was done in Articles 40–44 of the 1937 Constitution. But if de Valera, or any other President of the Executive Council of the Irish Free State, could muster enough votes in the Dáil, they could have begun dismantling our democratic system without any let or hindrance from the courts.

Conclusions

The neutering of fundamental human rights protections by Presidential decree under Article 48 of the Weimar Constitution served to quell civil society in its opposition to the Nazis. The disastrous Enabling Act enabled the Nazis to systematically deconstruct the separation of powers, to concentrate power in one Office (and ultimately in one person) and to eliminate all political activity hostile to the Nazi party by banning all parties except the Nazi party. The 'tactic of legality' worked. Germany was a society in shock and in flux. It was clearly in transition—but to what no one knew. There was certainly no justice in this transition. The use made of this power shocked the conscience of mankind and led to a web of human rights protections that served, in the words of Sir Ungoed-Thomas, not merely to advance justice for individuals, but also to preserve the democratic system which is itself one of the best guarantors of freedom.

The Irish Free State was also in transition almost from the moment of its birth. The judgment of Kennedy CJ must surely rank as one of the leading and early judgments of the twentieth century against the use of the 'tactic of legality'. The ambiguity in his judgment adverted to by Gerard Hogan continues to trouble. If Article 2A had been democratically decided would Kennedy CJ lay down his principled objections and bow to the will of the people no matter how misguided he may have thought them to be? Indeed, was the Supreme Court right in the 1995 abortion information referral to elevate 'popular sovereignty' as almost the supreme principle of the Constitution? I venture to think not.

Clearly the natural law tradition has run its course and the Supreme Court was right to demote it beneath 'popular sovereignty'. Yet it is precisely because one values 'popular sovereignty' that space should be created for courts to prudentially intervene to save systems from self-destructing and to place limits on the 'tactic of legality' toward that end. At least such intervention would not ostensibly be motivated by an illegitimate wish to substitute one substantive view point (that of the judge) for that of the people. Rather, it would be motivated to preserve the democratic system according to which the people can democratically decide.

Kennedy CJ did at least intimate in his dissenting judgment that he found the content of Article 2A to violate the 'rule of law'. In addition, Lon Fuller does provide a very full theory on how and why this theory should help inform our understanding of the proper limits of the law.

The Irish Free State was never going to go the way of the Weimar Republic. Yet it is submitted that a close study of the 'tactic of legality' as used in both systems helps one gain a better insight into why it is important to ensure that courts are adequately equipped to save democratic institutions from self-destruction.

13

Ireland, The European Convention on Human Rights, and the Personal Contribution of Seán MacBride

*William Schabas**

Introduction

Ireland missed out on the seminal event in international human rights law, the drafting of the Universal Declaration of Human Rights by the Commission on Human Rights and the General Assembly of the United Nations in 1947 and 1948.[1] Denied membership in the organization until 1955, the Republic of Ireland did not participate in the initial standard-setting debates within the international community in the area of human rights. With adoption of the Universal Declaration of Human Rights by the General Assembly, on 10 December 1948,[2] the focus of attention shifted in some ways to the more daunting task of codifying what had been described as a 'common standard of achievement' into binding treaty norms. Two parallel efforts were soon underway. Within the United Nations, work proceeded on the international covenant, a process only completed in 1966.[3] At the same time, the newly minted Council of Europe proceeded with adoption of the Convention for the Protection of Human Rights and Fundamental Freedoms (Convention).[4] The European effort went much more rapidly, and the

* Aisling O'Sullivan provided the research assistance for this essay. The author wishes to acknowledge the financial support of the Irish Research Council for the Humanities and Social Sciences.

[1] See Johannes Morsink, *The Universal Declaration of Human Rights, Origins, Drafting & Intent* (1998); Mary Ann Glendon, *A World Made New, Eleanor Roosevelt and the Universal Declaration of Human Rights* (2001).   [2] GA Res. 217 A (III), UN Doc. A/810.

[3] GA Res. 2200 A (XXI). By that time, the original draft covenant had been split in two, and distinct treaties were adopted distinguishing between civil and political rights, on the one hand, and economic, social, and cultural rights, on the other. The Universal Declaration of Human Rights made no such separation between the two categories. See generally Manfred Nowak, *UN Covenant on Civil and Political Rights, CCPR Commentary* (2nd rev. ed., 2005).

[4] It was the first general human rights treaty. Though never intended to be anything but regional in scope—many of the European governments who participated were also actively working on the

Convention text was formally approved in November 1950. The relative ease of adoption, compared with the parallel process in the United Nations, reflects the homogeneity of the Western European members of the Council of Europe at the time. There was also, no doubt, a greater sense of urgency borne from the continent's recent experience with devastating armed conflict and of atrocities perpetrated by totalitarian regimes.

Though absent from the United Nations drafting efforts in these early years, Ireland played a major role in the drafting and adoption of the European Convention on Human Rights. It was not the first State to ratify the Convention, but was among those whose participation was necessary for it to enter into force on 3 September 1953. Ireland was the first State to make a declaration under Article 46 of the Convention, by which it recognized the jurisdiction of the European Court of Human Rights. Officials in the Department of Justice had assured the government that there was virtually no chance Ireland could actually be brought before the Court, given their perception that Irish legislation was consistent with the provisions of the Convention. But they insisted on the symbolic importance of such a gesture. Ironically, given what we can now see as the naïve equanimity of government bureaucrats, Ireland was respondent in the first case to be litigated before the European Court of Human Rights.

At the centre of Ireland's engagement with the European Convention on Human Rights was an extraordinary personality, Seán MacBride. As Minister of External Affairs in the Inter-party government that ruled from 1948 to 1951, MacBride piloted Ireland's participation in the negotiations that led to adoption of the Convention on 4 November 1950. He was also largely responsible for the momentum that drove Ireland's ratification of the Convention and its acceptance of the European Court's compulsory jurisdiction, although this took place under the subsequent government. Soon after his government was defeated, MacBride reinvented himself as one of the world's pre-eminent human rights lawyers. As counsel for Gerard Richard Lawless, he initiated the petition that led to Ireland's first case at the European Court of Human Rights.

The Early Career of Seán MacBride

MacBride's life is intimately bound up with many of the legends of recent Irish history. He was born in France in January 1904, where he spent his early years. His father, Major John MacBride, made a name fighting with the Boers against the British in South Africa. Passionately engaged in the struggle for Ireland's independence, John MacBride was executed following the Easter Rebellion. Seán's mother, Maud Gonne, was the unrequited love of Nobel laureate William Butler

---

draft human rights covenant within the United Nations system—the ethnocentric drafters omitted the adjective 'European' in the title of the Convention. Colloquially, however, it has always been known as the 'European Convention on Human Rights'.

Yeats. As a teenager, MacBride moved from Paris to London with his mother who, according to his recently published memoirs, 'used to haunt the British Embassy in Paris to try to get a passport'. When she finally succeeded, it was on the condition she would go to London and no farther.[5]

But come to Ireland she did, with her son Seán, who soon joined Na Fianna, a paramilitary republican organization that had been founded by Countess Markievicz, who was herself a frequent visitor to the MacBride household. MacBride was soon transferred from Na Fianna to the Irish Republican Army (B Company of the 3rd Battalion), to which MacBride became attached, operated out of a Catholic Boys Club on Great Brunswick Street (now Pearse Street). B Company launched frequent ambushes on British troops and Black and Tans, who travelled through the area from their barracks to the inner city.[6] Michael Farrell has described MacBride as 'an able guerrilla fighter and a good organiser'.[7] Those were different times, of course. Today, MacBride would be stigmatized as a 'child soldier', in breach of Article 38 of the Convention on the Rights of the Child[8] and the Optional Protocol to the Convention on the Rights of the Child on the Involvement of Children in Armed Conflicts,[9] both of which have been ratified by Ireland. His recruiters would be guilty of war crimes under customary international law,[10] and be subject to prosecution before the International Criminal Court in the event that Ireland itself failed to do so.[11]

At the beginning of 1921, MacBride became commander of the Active Service Unit of B Company. In his memoirs, MacBride referred to his early practical taste of legal work, during this period. He assisted solicitor Michael Noyk and junior counsel Charles Wyse-Power, both of whom defended republican prisoners, by collecting evidence and gathering and preparing affidavits from witnesses.[12] Throughout the 1920s, MacBride continued his close affiliation with the IRA. He was even arrested as a suspect in the assassination of Kevin O'Higgins in 1927. MacBride had been travelling to Belgium or Holland to obtain fruit pulp and equipment for Maud Gonne's jam factory at their home in Roebuck House, which provided employment for ex-prisoners.

---

[5] Caitriona Lawlor (ed.), *Seán MacBride: That Day's Struggle: A Memoir 1904–1951* (2005) 9.

[6] ibid, 20–21.

[7] Michael Farrell, 'The Extraordinary Life and Times of Seán MacBride: Part 1', *Magill*, Christmas 1982, 18.

[8] UN Doc. GA Res. 44/25, Annex (1989), Art. 38(3). Also: *Protocol Additional II to the 1949 Geneva Conventions and Relating to The Protection of Victims of Non-International Armed Conflicts*, (1979) 1125 UNTS 609, Art. 4(3)(c).　　　　　　　　　　　　　　　　　　　　[9] UN Doc. A/RES/54/263.

[10] *Prosecutor v Norman* (Case No. SCSL-04-14-AR72(E)), Decision on Preliminary Motion Based on Lack of Jurisdiction (Child Recruitment), 31 May 2004.

[11] Pursuant to Art. 8(e)(vii) of the Rome Statute of the International Criminal Court, UN Doc. A/CONF.183/9. Because Ireland has so far failed to enact implementing legislation concerning the International Criminal Court, prosecution for recruitment of child soldiers would seem problematic before the country's criminal courts, and ought to trigger more or less automatically the exercise of jurisdiction by the Court, in accordance with Art. 17.

[12] Lawlor, *Seán MacBride: That Day's Struggle: A Memoir 1904–1951*, n 5 above, 31.

'Some days after I got home, suddenly, in the middle of the night, the police erupted into the house, came into my bedroom and arrested me. They handcuffed me and took me off to Bridewell. I was treated quite roughly and I was charged there with the assassination of O'Higgins. I told them that this was nonsense; I wasn't even in the country at the time. But they paid no attention to this … I was put on an identification parade at which a number of other prisoners … I think it was the gardener of the O'Higgins house, together with another witness, who identified me as having been the person who had assassinated Kevin O'Higgins. I mention this because it shows how unreliable identification can be.'[13]

The poet William Butler Yeats, who had known Seán since he was a child, remained suspicious of his involvement in the murder, however. He wrote to Olivia Shakespear: 'He was & probably is a friendly simple lad but has been subject to a stream of terrible suggestion & may not have been able to resist. Any one ordinary would think him devoted to making peace but there are others who have a different story & it is impossible to sift out the truth.'[14]

MacBride left the IRA in 1937. He told Michael Farrell that this was the result of the enactment of the Constitution, Bunreacht na hÉireann.[15] MacBride contended that the removal of the British monarchy as head of the Irish State and the continued commitment to Irish unity, indicated by Articles 2 and 3, enabled republicans to achieve their remaining objectives through political process. In his own words, he considered that 'once the 1937 constitution was adopted, the whole position of the country was radically altered'.[16]

MacBride qualified as a barrister in 1937, taking silk as senior counsel in less than six years.[17] He was soon litigating important human rights issues before the Irish courts. MacBride challenged provisions of the Offences against the State Act 1939,[18] by way of habeas corpus in the High Court.[19] He argued that the 1939 Act in its entirety, and more specifically, the provision for the deprivation of liberty without trial, was repugnant to the Constitution. High Court Justice Gavan Duffy acknowledged the 'very careful and elaborate argument' of MacBride, saying that the protection of the personal rights of the citizen was 'too important to pass over in silence'. He held that legislation providing for internment without trial, 'outside the great protection of our criminal jurisprudence and outside even our special courts', did not respect the right to liberty of the person, in breach of Article 40(4), and unjustly attacked the personal rights of the citizen, contrary to Article 40(3)(1) of the Constitution. The Court ruled in favour of the applicant and ordered his release.[20]

---

[13] Lawlor, *Seán MacBride: That Day's Struggle: A Memoir 1904–1951*, n 5 above, 107.
[14] Letter to Olivia Shakespear of 7 September 1927, cited in Roy Foster, *W.B. Yeats, A Life, II. The Arch Poet*, (2003) 726, fn 3.
[15] Farrell, n 7 above, 'The Extraordinary Life and Times of Seán MacBride: Part 1', 25.
[16] Lawlor, *Seán MacBride: That Day's Struggle: A Memoir 1904–1951*, n 5 above, 123.
[17] Farrell, 'The Extraordinary Life and Times of Seán MacBride: Part 1', n 7 above, 25.
[18] Offences Against the State Act 1939 (No 13 of 1939).
[19] *State (Burke) v Lennon* [1940] IR 136.
[20] The High Court decision was appealed by the State to the Supreme Court which, like the House of Lords in *Cox v Hakes*, held that there was no appeal from a successful habeas corpus application in the High Court. See *State (Burke) v Lennon* [1940] IR 136, 157–79.

The declaration of unconstitutionality resulted in the enactment of new legislation, the Offences against the State (Amendment) Bill 1940.[21] Administrative powers of internment were then readily and extensively applied. In an attempt to gain political status, many of the internees went on hunger strike, to tragic ends. MacBride acted on behalf of the families of numerous hunger strikers at the inquests into their deaths in confinement.[22] One of those whose interests he represented, Seán MacCaughey, had been an ex-Chief of Staff of the IRA. MacCaughey had refused to wear prison clothes and was kept in solitary confinement for four years wearing only a blanket. After his death, following a hunger strike, MacBride and solicitor Con Lehane represented the family at the inquest.[23] At the conclusion of a celebrated cross-examination of the prison doctor, MacBride asked: 'Have you got a dog, Dr Duane?' 'Yes', he answered. MacBride: 'Would you allow your dog or dogs to be treated in the way in which this man has been treated?' Dr Duane questioned whether he was required to answer the question, but the coroner gave no reply. MacBride told Dr Duane that he must answer the question. 'Again there was a long silence. Then the doctor said, "No, I would not allow my dog to be treated in this way".'[24]

Clann na Poblachta was established on 4 July 1946 in Barry's Hotel, Dublin, with many of its founding members sharing, with MacBride, a legal background as well as a strongly republican tinge.[25] MacBride's party obtained 13.2 per cent of the popular vote and 10 seats in the 1948 election, enough for it to participate in the Inter-party Government composed of Fine Gael, Labour, National Labour, Clann na Poblachta, and Clann na Talmhan. Seán MacBride was named Minister of External Affairs.

The Council of Europe and Drafting of the European Convention on Human Rights

The Council of Europe was established in London on 5 May 1949.[26] Seán MacBride was authorized by Cabinet to represent Ireland at its founding conference, and 'subject to certain conditions specified in its decision, to sign, subject to ratification the draft Statute of the COE prepared for submission to the Conference'.[27] *The Irish Times* editorialized: 'We are more than glad that Ireland has been one of the founder-States of the Council of Europe. Mr MacBride has

---

[21] Offences against the State (Amendment) Act 1940.
[22] MacBride represented the families of Tony D'Arcy and Jack McNeela, who died in April 1940. Farrell, 'The Extraordinary Life and Times of Seán MacBride: Part 1', n 7 above, 29.
[23] Lawlor, *Seán MacBride: That Day's Struggle: A Memoir 1904–1951*, n 5 above, 134.
[24] ibid, 135.   [25] Eithne Mac Dermott, *Clann na Poblachta* (1998) 17.
[26] 'Letter sent from the High Commissioner for London, John W. Dulanty, to the Department of External Affairs, 25 April 1949, enclosing invitation addressed to the High Commissioner'. NAI DFA 417/39/1 Pt II.
[27] Memorandum for Government on the Establishment of the Council of Europe, 2 June 1949, NAI DFA 417/39/1 Pt II.

already played an active part in its organization, feeling, quite properly, that this little country has something to contribute to the common pool of European endeavour.'[28]

The Council of Europe was governed by two bodies, a Committee of Ministers made up of representatives from the governments of Member States, and a Consultative Assembly, composed of elected parliamentarians from Member States. MacBride represented Ireland at the first session of the Committee of Ministers in August 1949. The four Irish delegates to the Consultative Assembly included Eamonn De Valera. From the outset, there was considerable tension between the two bodies. MacBride, though a representative of government sitting on the Committee of Ministers, tended to sympathize with the Assembly. The Irish media reported heated debates in the Ministers' meeting 'and it seems now that many of the delegates to the Council have been protesting against the undue authority that has been assumed by the Ministers. The power of the Committee of Minister to control the agenda is viewed by the smaller States as an "over-riding veto" contrary to "the spirit of the whole project".'[29]

Ireland argued, unsuccessfully, that the statute of the Council of Europe should contain a reference to 'Christian civilisation'. Ireland also tried to obtain a pre-ambular reference to 'the national right of self-determination'.[30] It soon became clear that in the aftermath of the Second World War, Western European States were anxious to emphasize unity rather than diversity.[31] MacBride tried yet another angle, calling for the Council to develop mechanisms for the peaceful settlement of disputes and for the resolution of boundary problems, but again without success. MacBride saw the whole effort as one 'which would give the Irish delegates an opportunity more or less to put the British in the dock'.[32] This was sometimes described as the policy of the 'sore thumb', and MacBride was its foremost practitioner. He considered that Ireland's important role was effectively nullified by the injustice suffered by the artificial division of the country 'against the wishes of the overwhelming majority of its people'. MacBride believed that partition precluded Ireland 'from taking our rightful place in the affairs of Europe'.[33]

The 'sore thumb' policy was almost surely misunderstood by Ireland's treaty partners in the Council of Europe, who clearly did not share MacBride's obsession in establishing priorities for the first new European organization. *The Irish Times* observed that accusations of a police state in Northern Ireland left other delegates cold: 'They have seen, and some of them have been inmates of concentration camps ... and having lived through the anti-Jewish campaign, are not inclined to listen very carefully to tales of religious persecution in Northern Ireland.'[34] To

[28] 'Europe's Council', *The Irish Times*, 11 August 1949.   [29] ibid.
[30] The Charter of the United Nations, Art. 1(2), describes one of the purposes of the United Nations as being 'the principle of equal rights and self-determination of peoples'.
[31] Memorandum for the Government (classified 'Top Secret'), 10 February 1949, NAI DFA 417/39/1 Pt II.   [32] 'Europe's Council', The *Irish Times*, 11 August 1949.
[33] 112 *Dáil Debates* Col. 905 (20 July 1948).
[34] 'Out of Turn', *The Irish Times*, 13 August 1949.

what extent this was a serious attempt to promote Irish policy on an international plane and how much this was simply pandering to domestic sentiment is difficult to assess. *The Irish Times* suspected that rather than lack of international experience accounting for MacBride's 'tactless error', the real explanation was political competition between the Inter-party Government and the opposition, Fianna Fáil. *The Irish Times* expressed 'some sympathy with MacBride ... In order to satisfy the members of his own party, and with De Valera at Strasbourg keeping a close eye on his actions, he was bound to make a gesture against partition.' Dáil Debates seem to confirm this. MacBride was being constantly questioned about his success in promoting the issue of partition in Europe and the US. But *The Irish Times* warned that it 'would be a great pity if the first appearance of the Republic's representatives at an international gathering should degenerate into a contest between Opposition and Government in an effort to catch domestic votes. Strasbourg assuredly is not the place for such trial of strength.'[35]

Drafting of the European Convention on Human Rights began with a motion adopted during the first session of the Council of Europe's Consultative Assembly on 19 August 1949.[36] Earlier, in its submissions to the Preparatory Commission of the Council, Ireland had made three proposals for inclusion on the agenda, one of them 'defence of the basic political, civil and religious rights of man'. The Consultative Assembly resolution said that the Council of Europe should 'accept the principle of collective responsibility for the maintenance of human rights and fundamental freedoms ... ' and that, to this end, it 'should immediately conclude a convention'.[37] MacBride was fully supportive of this Consultative Assembly initiative, noting that it 'had also raised great interest' in Ireland.[38]

Despite the State's absence from the United Nations, Irish policy-makers were clearly well aware of the parallel standard-setting process underway in New York. A Department of External Affairs memorandum noted that not all of the rights listed in the Universal Declaration of Human Rights had been included in the Consultative Assembly resolution.[39] Another memorandum said that the outline of the draft convention contained rights 'considered as essential to guarantee personal independence and human dignity' ('so-called "professional" freedoms and "social" rights were excluded by the Assembly, the view of the Assembly's Legal Committee being that it was necessary in the first place to guarantee political democracy in the European sphere and then co-ordinate the various economies as a preliminary to the generalisation of social democracy').[40]

Detailed debates on the Convention took place within the Council's Committee of Legal Experts, where Ireland was represented by its Attorney-General,

---

[35] ibid.
[36] *Collected Edition of the "Travaux préparatoires" of the European Convention on Human Rights,* Vol. I, Dordrecht: Martinus Nijhoff, 1985, 36–155; MacEntee Papers, UCD Archives Department, P67/763, 4.   [37] ibid.
[38] ibid, 12.
[39] Notes taken at meeting, 5 November 1949, NAI DFA 417/39/24. The notes are unsigned, but were presumably written by Frederick Boland.   [40] NAI DT S.14921A, para 2.

Cecil Lavery. According to MacBride's memoirs, he had first met Lavery at the Mount St. Benedict School, when he resumed his schooling after his arrival in Ireland in 1917 from Paris. Later, as was one of the prosecutors in the District Court, Lavery had laid charges against MacBride, who was eventually acquitted by a jury. MacBride admired Lavery, saying he was 'a man for whom I had great respect, a close friend of mine'.[41]

An important discussion took shape about the general approach of the proposed convention on human rights. This was the debate between 'enumeration' and 'definition'. Britain argued for the definition of rights and their limitations 'in a detailed manner as possible', arguing that it would be impossible for States to undertake to respect rights whose formulation was not sufficiently precise.[42] The more continental approach, to which Ireland subscribed, urged a general formulation of human rights, and was driven by a commitment to principles of natural law. According to Fredrick Boland, Permanent Secretary in the Department of Foreign Affairs, who served as Vice-Chairman of the Conference of Senior Officials of the Council of Europe, any formulation of fundamental natural rights necessitated 'statements of principle rather than cautious and crushing legal definitions'.[43] The debate sharpened in Boland's exchanges with Samuel Hoare, of the British Foreign Office. Boland recounted Hoare's presentation: 'A long silence followed the British statement and it looked for a moment as if the discussion would collapse.'[44] Ireland made a statement arguing that '[t]he more declaratory, and the less contractual, the Council of Europe Convention was, the better'.[45]

Britain's approach was highly positivistic, and may have been driven by its own lack of experience with a written constitution. Similar arguments were being made by the British in the United Nations Commission on Human Rights, where they had prevailed in the draft text of the international covenant adopted in 1949.[46] Boland criticized the United Nations draft covenant, noting that the 'caution and mutual suspicion of Lake Success had no place in the Council of Europe'. He said that 'history showed that the best texts were those drawn up in general terms'.[47] The British attempted to provide a comprehensive enumeration of exceptions to the right to life (such as proportionate use of force in defence of a person from unlawful violence, effecting a lawful arrest, and lawful action to quell a riot), a list of detailed exceptions concerning penal servitude to the general prohibition of slavery, and so on. Most of these appear in the final version of the

---

[41] Lawlor, *Seán MacBride: That Day's Struggle: A Memoir 1904–1951*, n 5 above, 17, 117 and 159.

[42] *Collected Edition of the "Travaux préparatoires" of the European Convention on Human Rights*, Vol. I, Dordrecht: Martinus Nijhoff, 1985, Vol. IV, 8.

[43] Report on Conference, NAI DFA 417/39/96/19 Pt 1A.   [44] ibid, para 4.   [45] ibid.

[46] U.N. Doc. E/1371. See James Simsarian, 'Draft International Covenant on Human Rights Revised at Fifth Session of United Nations Commission on Human Rights' (1949) 43 American Journal of International Law 779.

[47] *Collected Edition of the "Travaux préparatoires" of the European Convention on Human Rights*, Vol. I, Vol. IV, 108.

European Convention on Human Rights, attesting to the ultimate triumph of the British position.

One of the main stumbling blocks in the negotiations was the right of individual petition to the European Commission of Human Rights. On this point, Ireland was particularly vocal in its support. It ran up directly against the British, who were not at all keen on the idea. MacBride said that a 'convention on human rights which did not grant any right of redress to individuals was not worth the paper it was written on'.[48] A compromise text was eventually agreed to, by which States could ratify the Convention yet not accept the right of individual petition. In order to establish jurisdiction of the European Commission on Human Rights to receive individual petitions, a special declaration was required, in accordance with Article 25. Eventually, all delegations but one—Ireland—voted in favour of the text. Ireland said it was prepared to have its vote registered as an abstention in order to achieve unanimity.[49]

A headline in The *Irish Times* encapsulated Ireland's approach to the substance of the draft convention: 'Irish Defend Human Rights Charter Against Socialists'.[50] The reference to 'socialists' was code for the British and Scandinavian governments, where the welfare state approach that would subsequently prevail throughout most of Europe, including Ireland, had already taken root. In particular, Ireland was insistent about inclusion of the right to property in the draft text. The right to property has had its place in the catalogue of human rights since the time of the Enlightenment. But it was only included in the Universal Declaration of Human Rights in the form of a compromise provision reflecting ideological tensions: 'Everyone has the right to own property alone as well as in association with others. No one shall be arbitrarily deprived of his property.'[51] There were arguments that property had no place in the draft European Convention because it was an economic right.[52] The Irish contended that this was no reason to object, because other economic rights had been included in the Consultative Assembly draft. In reply to a British motion aimed at deletion of the provision, the Irish delegates attempted to clarify the misunderstanding that the clause was directed against measures of nationalization.[53] A senior official in the Department of External Affairs, Michael Rynne, said that '[t]he British text ... would, I imagine,

---

[48] *Collected Edition of the "Travaux préparatoires" of the European Convention on Human Rights*, Vol. I, Dordrecht: Martinus Nijhoff, 1985, Vol. V, 112.   [49] ibid, 114.

[50] The *Irish Times*, 9 September 1949.

[51] *Universal Declaration of Human Rights*, GA Res. 217 A (III), UN Doc. A/810, Art. 17.

[52] There were similar debates in the United Nations Commission on Human Rights about where, in the two international covenants, the right to property belonged. No agreement was reached, and the draft article was simply omitted from the two instruments. See William A. Schabas, 'The Omission of the Right to Property in the International Covenants' (1991) 4 Hague Yearbook of International Law 135.

[53] Notes prepared by the Secretariat on the reasons for the amendments to the Convention for the protection of Human rights and fundamental freedoms adopted by the Consultative Assembly, 25 August 1950, C of E Doc. CM (50) 96.

be condemned by any Churchman as much too "utilitarian"'.[54] A compromise text was eventually adopted: 'Every national or legal person is entitled to the peaceful enjoyment of his possessions. Such possessions cannot be subjected to arbitrary confiscation. The present measures shall not however be considered as infringing, in any way, the right of a State to pass necessary legislation to ensure that the said possessions are utilized in accordance with the general interest.'[55] But even this formulation was too controversial, and in the final throes of negotiations the British and their allies managed to exclude the right to property from the draft convention.

A text on political freedom prepared by the Drafting Sub-Committee was accepted unanimously in the Consultative Assembly's Committee on Legal and Administrative Questions, in which Seán MacEntee participated.[56] It read: 'The High Contracting parties undertake to respect the political liberty of their nationals and, in particular, with regard to their home territories, to hold free elections at reasonable intervals by secret ballot under conditions which will ensure that the government and legislature shall represent the opinion of the people.'[57] Once again, the British were fervently opposed, and the provision was later dropped in order for negotiations to progress. Michael Rynne wrote: 'This is an article of real importance to us, if we want to exploit it to hit at the Six-County gerrymandering system.'[58] He noted that the reference to 'home territories' was 'certainly cynical and suggestive of drastic reservations affecting colonial peoples'.[59] For obvious reasons, Ireland did not share the tender sensibilities of other Western European States about democracy in their colonies. Ireland also advocated inclusion of a provision prohibiting restriction on the rights of national minorities to give expression to their aspirations by democratic means, but to no avail.[60]

A third right of great concern to Ireland was that of parents to secure the religious education of their children. Article 26(3) of the Universal Declaration of Human Rights affirms that '[p]arents have a prior right to choose the kind of education that shall be given to their children'. Here too, the British were opposed to including the right within the European Convention. A text proposed by Seán MacEntee was adopted by the Consultative Assembly: 'Every person has the right to education. The function assumed by the State in respect of education and

---

[54] Letter from Michael Rynne to V. Iremonger, 19 February 1950, NAI DFA 417/39/19/1a.

[55] C of E Doc. CM/WP I (51) 40. Compare with the version finally included in the first Protocol: 'Every natural or legal person is entitled to the peaceful enjoyment of his possessions. No one shall be deprived of his possessions except in the public interest and subject to the conditions provided for by law and by the general principles of international law. The preceding provisions shall not, however, in any way impair the right of a State to enforce such laws as it deems necessary to control the use of property in accordance with the general interest or to secure the payment of taxes or other contributions or penalties.'   [56] NAI DFA 417/39/19/2.

[57] ibid, 10.

[58] Letter from Michael Rynne to V. Iremonger, 19 February 1950, NAI DFA 417/39/19/1a.

[59] ibid, 5.

[60] 'Amendments by the Irish delegation'. *Collected Edition of the "Travaux préparatoires" of the European Convention on Human Rights*, Vol. I, Vol. V, p. 60. See also: C of E Doc. CM 1 (50) 2 A 1863.

teaching may not encroach upon the right of parents to ensure the religious and moral education of their children in conformity with their own religion and philosophical convictions.'[61] The strong association between the State and the Catholic Church no doubt influenced the Irish position. Michael Rynne wrote that 'there seems to be, for us, an ever-present conflict between Catholic teachings, non-Catholic liberalism and the relentless necessities of our own day-to-day internal administration'. He warned, in words reminiscent of more recent critics of the European Convention and of legislation to incorporate it into Irish national legislation, that Ireland '[m]ust be careful not to be run into over-generous undertakings which would not fit our existing "way of life"'.[62]

MacBride 'reserved his opinion' on the draft Convention during the August 1950 session of the Committee of Ministers. He spoke of the fact that the draft Convention 'now had a long history', beginning with the Committee of Ministers requesting the Consultative Assembly for an opinion. After referrals to the Experts and the Senior Officials, the resulting text represented 'a compromise which was less effective than his Government would have wished, as it omitted a number of points which they felt should be included'. He described the Convention as weaker in its provisions than the draft Convention produced by the United Nations, referring specifically to the omission of the protection of political rights. Irrespective of this inadequacy, MacBride told the Committee of Ministers that the Irish Government had accepted the text 'in order to get agreement, thinking that it represented the limit of compromise'.[63]

Signing the Convention

The penultimate draft of the Convention was considered by the Irish government, in preparation for the final meeting of the Committee of Ministers, scheduled to take place in Rome in early November 1950, at which it was planned to adopt a definitive text of the Convention. The Consultative Assembly continued to push for changes, and MacBride was supportive of the process; but he subsequently came to the view 'from contacts and discussions with his colleagues in the Committee of Ministers that there may be opposition to the acceptance of the amendments proposed by the Assembly and that it is unlikely that any substantial changes will be made in the draft submitted to the Assembly'. He was concerned that 'any reluctance on the part of Ireland to sign this Convention would be capable of being misinterpreted ... and might be construed as a lack of interest in a problem which is very real to those peoples of Western Europe who have suffered under totalitarian regime'. MacBride himself 'share[d] the view of the

---

[61] NAI DFA 417/39/19/2. See also C of E Doc. CM (50) 96, 6.
[62] Letter from M. Rynne to T. O'Driscoll, 3 February 1951, NAI DFA 417/39/19/1a, 3.
[63] *Collected Edition of the "Travaux préparatoires" of the European Convention on Human Rights*, Vol. I, Vol. V, 112.

Irish representatives to the Consultative Assembly that the draft Convention ... has many imperfections which are only partially cured by the amendments proposed by the Assembly'.[64]

A memorandum circulated within the Department of External Affairs, where William Butler observed that the Consultative Assembly recommendations were consistent with Irish policy. Butler said that '[t]hey still fall short of the ideal but we might perhaps accept them in the spirit that the Convention, with these additions, is just beginning of progress towards more complete protection of all human rights ...'. The Department recommended that the draft Convention be signed, subject to ratification, and that a full power be issued to MacBride for this purpose.[65]

The Department of External Affairs was of the opinion that detailed examination of the draft Convention by other government departments was necessary 'before ratification takes place with a view to seeing whether any legislation will be necessary for the purpose of implementing any of the provisions of the Convention or whether any reservations under Article 64 would necessary'.[66] But apparently the Department did not consider such detailed study to be necessary prior to signature. Under customary international law applicable at the time, signature subject to ratification was a preliminary act of largely symbolic significance indicating an intent to be bound by the treaty. Signature had, and still has, limited legal consequences. By signing the treaty, Ireland would be obliged not to defeat the object and purpose of the treaty prior to its entry into force for Ireland,[67] but nothing more. Perhaps for this reason, MacBride and the officials at the Department of External Affairs did not attach much importance to consultation within the government prior to signature. But perhaps MacBride was also nervous that cautious officials in other departments might delay even signing of the draft convention, and deny MacBride the glory of fully participating in the planned November ceremony. Perhaps MacBride had already anticipated potential compatibility problems of Irish legislation, notably the Offences Against the State Act, with which he had had so much personal experience prior to his political career.

On 21 October 1950, the Department of External Affairs transmitted a memorandum on the subject to the Department of the Taoiseach. Two days later, the Department of the Taoiseach answered that 'no observations appear to be called for, so far as this Dept is concerned'. But it added that '[n]o doubt the Dept of Justice has considered whether the provisions of paragraphs (1)(c) and (3) of Article 5 of the Convention would necessitate the making of a reservation under Article 64 thereof, in light of the provisions of the Offences Against the State

---

[64] Memo circulated to all members of the government in advance of meeting on 24 October 1950, NAI DT S.14291 A, para 14.

[65] Memorandum from W. Butler and V. Iremonger to T. O'Driscoll, 7 October 1950, NAI DFA 417/39/19/2. [66] ibid.

[67] The customary legal obligation was later codified in Art. 18 of the *Vienna Convention on the Law of Treaties*, (1979) 1155 UNTS 331.

(Amendment) Act, 1940'.[68] The provisions to which the Department of the Taoiseach was referring concern arbitrary detention and the right to contest pre-trial detention before a court.

This was a courteous way of reminding the Department of External Affairs that colleagues in the Department of Justice had to be consulted. In fact, nothing of the sort had taken place. The urgent and unusual nature of the subsequent exchanges can be judged by the fact that the first significant contact between the Department of Justice and the Department of External Affairs on the subject took the form of a Saturday night telephone conversation, only hours before MacBride was scheduled to leave for Rome in order to sign the Convention.[69] The Department of Justice later stated: '[T]his Dept was not given an opportunity of expressing its views on the Convention before it was submitted to government, and ... we have fears that the Convention may restrict the powers of the Government to intern without trial under the Offences against the State Act 1940'.[70] Thomas Costigan of the Department of Justice complained to the Department of the Taoiseach: '[A]lthough [External Affairs] were aware of the fact that this Convention was being prepared, and although the draft, adopted by the Committee of Ministers, has been available to them since August last, we first heard of the existence of this Convention on 23rd instant [23 October 1950] when we received a Minute from [External Affairs] telling us that their Minister would ask the government at their meeting on Tuesday 24th instant for authority to sign ...'. Moreover, 'from inquires which we have made, we understand that the draft Convention would not have been referred to us even at that stage, only for the fact that the Dept of the Taoiseach suggested to [External Affairs] that they should refer the Convention to us'.[71]

Costigan protested that Justice had 'not had the time to make a careful examination, but from the examination which we have been able to make ...' there were three concerns. The first issue arose with respect to Article 5 of the draft Convention, on arrest and detention, something the Department of the Taoiseach had already signalled in its memorandum of 23 October. According to Costigan, '[i]t may be that there is nothing inconsistent between Article 5 of the Convention and the Offences against the State (Amendment) Act 1940, but I have some doubts'. In his Saturday night telephone conversation with T. O'Driscoll of the Department of External Affairs, Costigan had said he had 'made it clear that I assumed that even if the 1940 Act were "ultra vires" the Convention we would not be guilty of any violation of the Convention by merely allowing the 1940 Act to remain unrepealed, so long as we did not take any action under the Act'. He said

[68] Response of Taoiseach's Department to request for observations, 27 October 1950, para 1, NAI DT S.14291 A.
[69] Minute recounting telephone conservation of Department of the Taoiseach with T. O'Driscoll, 27 October 1950, NAI DT S.14291 A.
[70] Letter from Thomas Coyne to D. Costigan, 30 October 1950, NAI DT S.14291 A.
[71] Minute accompanying letter to Department of the Taoiseach, 30 October 1950, NAI DT S.14291 A, para 2.

he was 'very doubtful whether the Minister for Justice would be prepared at the present time to introduce any legislation to amend the Offences against the State Act'. Accordingly, 'propaganda could be used against us for keeping it on the Statute Book, even if we never operated it'.[72]

The Department of Justice was also concerned about the provisions of Article 6, which protects the right to a fair trial, and more specifically the requirement that anyone charged with a criminal offence be entitled to free legal assistance when the interests of justice so require. Costigan explained that under Irish law, 'as you are aware we have no scheme for the provision of free legal assistance, except in capital cases'. Finally, Costigan expressed concern about the provisions establishing a right of petition to the European Commission of Human Rights, which had been so cherished by MacBride himself during the drafting of the Convention. According to Costigan, a right of individual petition 'would provide publicity for malicious and groundless charges against governments, and might injure the reputation of States'.[73]

The dispute between the Departments of Justice and External Affairs simmered for several days, but did not prevent MacBride from signing the Convention in Rome on 4 November 1950. He made a final effort at the meeting of the Committee of Ministers to strengthen the draft, asking whether it could 'not accept at least one or two of the amendments proposed by the Consultative Assembly'. But the British were adamant. Ernest Davies of the Foreign Office said that his government 'would find it very difficult at that stage to accept the amendments of the Assembly and he knew that certain of his colleagues shared this view'. David Maxwell-Fyfe concurred, suggesting that 'the Assembly would be most disappointed if the Convention were not signed in Rome, even without the amendments which had been proposed'.[74] The controversial provisions on property rights, education, and elections were not included in the final version. But there was agreement to proceed immediately with negotiations for a protocol to the Convention in which these rights could be recognized. This was principally the result of initiatives from MacBride.

Ratification of the European Convention by Ireland

Initially, there was a widespread belief that ratification of the Convention should be authorized by a resolution of the Dáil. MacBride ordered that 400 copies of the Convention be printed and circulated in the Dáil 'with a resolution for its acceptance at the earliest possible moment'. He insisted this was 'a matter of first priority for this reason (importance of Convention) and because of the important

[72] Minute accompanying letter to Department of the Taoiseach, 30 October 1950, NAI DT S.14291 A, para 2. [73] ibid, para 3(b).
[74] *Collected Edition of the "Travaux préparatoires" of the European Convention on Human Rights*, Vol. I, Vol. VII, 26.

effect this Convention may have on the question of partition of this country'.[75] The proposed resolution insisted upon the contribution made by Irish representatives to the Consultative Assembly during the drafting stages.[76] MacBride's Department may have annoyed some civil servants because of lack of consultation, especially with regard to signature of the Convention. But it had always been deferential, again largely due to MacBride's personal views, towards the Consultative Assembly in which Irish parliamentarians, including members of the opposition, were represented.

The relevant government departments took the position that no new legislation was required in order for Ireland to ratify the European Convention.[77] With respect to declarations accepting the jurisdiction of the European Commission and the European Court of Human Rights, the government was divided. MacBride felt strongly that Ireland should accept the jurisdiction of the Commission, relying upon the argument that 'both in the Committee of Ministers and in the Consultative Assembly, the Irish representatives have been prominent in their urging that the present Convention does not go far enough in protecting human rights'.[78] The Department of Justice was in disagreement on this point. As for the Court, its creation was envisaged by the Convention but would not be automatic. In fact, the European Court of Human Rights only came into existence several years after the beginning of operations of the Commission. But while acknowledging the lack of urgency in this respect, MacBride also considered that Ireland should make an unconditional declaration in respect of the Court.[79] The memorandum prepared by the Department of External Affairs for Government highlighted the importance of a declaration accepting the jurisdiction of the European Commission and the European Court of Human Rights: 'If such a declaration is not made, Ireland will appear in the position that, while urging the extending Amendments referred to . . . , she is unwilling fully to implement even the existing Convention.'[80] The Attorney-General was astonishingly sanguine about the prospect that the petition mechanisms would be used against Ireland. He said that '[i]n practice, however, the likelihood of this country being brought before the Commission or the Court is very remote, as all the "rights" set out in the Convention are already conceded here'.[81]

---

[75] Letter from the Department of External Affairs to the Procurements Office, 17 November 1950, NAI DFA 417/39/19/2.

[76] Memorandum for the Government: Approval by the Dáil and subsequent ratification of the Convention, March 1951, NAI DFA 417/39/19/2. See also, letter from W. Butler to T. O'Driscoll, 24 November 1950, NAI DFA 417/39/19/2.

[77] Letter from Department of the Taoiseach to the Department of External Affairs, 29 November 1950, DFA 417/39/19/2, para 3. [78] ibid, para 6.

[79] ibid, para 7.

[80] Minute of Department of External Affairs to Department of Taoiseach, 15 March 1951, NAI S14921A; Letter from Secretary to the Government to Department of External Affairs, 7 April 1951, NAI S14921A. See also, Minute of Department of Taoiseach , 15 March 1951, NAI S14921A, para 5.

[81] Memorandum for the Government: Approval by the Dáil and subsequent ratification of the Convention, March 1951, NAI DFA 417/39/19/2.

Meanwhile, negotiations progressed on the protocol to the Convention. At a series of meetings held during 1951, a draft text was hammered out. Reacting to one attempt to postpone or abort the process, Michael Rynne:

' ... protested very vigorously and at some length. I said that the Irish Government had, since the very commencement of the preparation of the Rome Convention, felt that the three rights we were now debating were among the most important of all. Ireland's signature of the Convention had been made subject to a clear understanding that the three extra rights were going to be treated in a special Protocol which would become an integral part of the Convention itself. We objected to any tendency to lower an 'Iron Curtain' (presumption play on words intended) between dozen or so rights protected by the Convention and the three quite similar and particularly sacrosanct human rights now being provided for.'[82]

Ireland argued, for example, that the adjective 'religious' should be removed from the provision on parental control over education, so as to permit broader protection. Ireland also pleaded for the use of 'right' instead of 'liberty' of parents, a point on which it was initially unsuccessful but that eventually prevailed. On the subject of political rights, the Irish negotiators kept 'the Six-county position firmly in mind'.[83] Michael Rynne wrote: 'Irish interventions in favour of a draft more likely to satisfy European public opinion (and Irish ideals) were patiently listened to and occasionally endorsed in perfunctory tones of some of the other representatives (often by British!), but they seldom resulted in any material change in the original Secretariat or British texts.'[84] This did not trouble the Irish negotiators too much. T. O'Driscoll observed that '[e]ven if the wording or substance are not all we desire, provided they are not objectionable, I feel the Minister would prefer to see agreement on that basis than further postponement'.[85] Ireland's representatives concluded that the provisions of the draft protocol were the result of protracted discussions and represented the 'maximum possibilities of agreement'.[86]

The Department of External Affairs did not repeat the mistake it had made six months earlier with respect to signature of the Convention. This time, it sought observations not only from the Department of the Taoiseach, but from the Department of Justice, the Department of Education, the Attorney-General, and the Department of Finance.[87] There were no objections, and the only comment came from the Attorney-General, who felt 'that while something more positive might have been welcomed, no objection could be made to this compromise and

---

[82] Committee of Experts on Human Rights: Conference of Legal Experts, 18–19 April 1951, para 3, NAI DFA 417/39/19/1a.   [83] Minute from Michael Rynne. NAI DFA 417/39/19/1a.

[84] Committee of Experts on Human Rights: Droit à l'education: Proposition française, 19 April 1951, NAI DFA 417/39/19/1a.

[85] Letter from T. O'Driscoll to Junior Officials, NAI DFA 417/39/19/1a.

[86] Report of the Committee of Experts on Human Rights, 6 June 1951, NAI DFA 417/39/19/1a. See also C of E Doc. CM/WP VI (51) 20.

[87] Letter from T. O' Driscoll to various Departments, 24 April 1951, NAI DFA 417/39/19/1a.

that no legislation would be required'.[88] MacBride was duly authorized to sign the draft protocol, subject to modifications that might be adopted by the Committee of Ministers.[89]

However, the draft protocol floundered, and was not adopted at the next session of the Committee of Ministers. A Department of External Affairs memorandum described 'prolonged and difficult negotiations with the Committee of Ministers and between the Committee of Ministers and the Consultative Assembly', adding that Britain, Sweden, and Turkey intended to formulate reservations concerning the right to education because the terms of draft Article 2 conflict with certain provisions in their national law.[90]

By this time, the Inter-party government had fallen, and MacBride was no longer a government minister. The new government examined a revised draft of the protocol in 1952.[91] Once again, the relevant Departments of Justice, Finance, and the Taoiseach were consulted and had no particular comments, but the Department of Education did not approve of Article 2 and said it could not recommend acceptance of a text 'which would not specifically endorse the right of parents to send their children to schools other than those established by the State'. Signature of the draft protocol was authorized but with the proviso that it is 'made clear by the Minister at the time of signature that the Government do not regard Article 2 of the Protocol as representing their views as to the right of parents to send their children to schools other than those established by the State'.[92] The matter was reconsidered, and the following text was agreed upon: 'Article 2 of the Protocol is not sufficiently explicit in ensuring to parents the right to provide education for their children in their homes or in schools of the parents' own choice, whether or not such schools are private schools or are schools recognised or established by the State'.[93] The declaration was duly recorded when Ireland signed the Protocol, on 20 March 1952, on the same day that it was opened for signature. It was also included in Ireland's instrument of ratification, filed on 25 February 1953.[94]

Ireland had decided to await adoption of the protocol before ratifying the Convention itself. In October 1951, the Department of External Affairs proposed that Ireland proceed with ratification rather than await the approval of Dáil Éireann. It had changed its mind about the wisdom of seeking Dáil approval, and noted that was not required by the Constitution.[95] Later, the

[88] Minute of the Government Secretary to the Department of External Affairs, 3 May 1951, NAI DT S.14921A.   [89] ibid.
[90] Minute by T. O'Driscoll to the Department of the Taoiseach, 23 June 1951, NAI DT S.14921 A.
[91] Minute of Department of External Affairs (John J. Ronan, Secretary of the Department) to the Department of the Taoiseach, 5 March 1952, NAI DT S.14921B.   [92] ibid.
[93] ibid. The Department of Taoiseach said that the Department of External Affairs and Education should be informed of the change in writing.
[94] Protocol to the Convention for the Protection of Human Rights and Fundamental Freedoms, CETS No.: 9. 'Protocol No. 1', as it is now known, entered into force on 18 May 1954, following the tenth ratification.
[95] Minute of Department of External Affairs (William Butler) to Department of the Taoiseach, 17 October 1951, NAI S.14921B.

government would be criticized in the press for its failure to consult the Dáil.[96] A new memorandum was submitted to the government by the Department of External Affairs on the subject of ratification.[97] The Department of Justice had agreed that no legislation was required, but was concerned about the issue of legal aid, and mooted a reservation to Article 6(3)(c) of the Convention. The Department of External Affairs took the view that no reservation to Article 6 was necessary.[98] The Minister for Justice was also not as comfortable as External Affairs with unqualified recognition of the jurisdiction of the European Commission.[99] The Department of External Affairs was insistent upon the importance of prompt ratification, explaining that Ireland had argued that the Convention did not go far enough, and that therefore it should accept the instrument in as unqualified a manner as possible. But Cabinet agreed that there a reservation should be formulated.[100] When Ireland finally ratified the Convention, on 25 February 1953, a reservation to Article 6 was attached:

'The Government of Ireland do hereby confirm and ratify the aforesaid Convention and undertake faithfully to perform and carry out all the stipulations therein contained, subject to the reservation that they do not interpret Article 6.3.c of the Convention as requiring the provision of free legal assistance to any wider extent than is now provided in Ireland.'

Decades later, Ireland invoked the reservation before the European Court of Human Rights in a case challenging a lack of availability of legal aid in family law proceedings. The debate was access to a court, and the applicant relied upon Article 6(1), rather than legal aid in criminal matters, which is set out explicitly in Article 6(3)(c). It is a good example of exceedingly strict construction of reservations by human rights tribunals. It seems obvious enough that the original intent of the Irish reservation had been to exclude legal aid altogether, and not only legal aid in criminal justice. But the Court adopted a literal reading of the reservation, which only referred to Article 6(3)(c) ('[e]veryone charged with a criminal offence ... '). The European Court quite summarily dismissed Ireland's argument: 'As regards the Irish reservation to Article 6 para. 3 (c) (art. 6-3-c), it cannot be interpreted as affecting the obligations under Article 6 para. 1 (art. 6-1); accordingly, it is not relevant in the present context.'[101] The Court found that Ireland had a duty to provide legal aid in family law matters, even if by virtue of its reservation it had escaped liability for this in the field of criminal justice.

If MacBride had had his way, Ireland would probably have been the first State to ratify the European Convention on Human Rights. Ultimately, it was the sixth,

---

[96] 'A Grave Issue', Irish Independent, 28 February 1953.

[97] Department of External Affairs Memorandum for Government: Ratification of (I) Convention for the Protection of Human Rights and Fundamental Freedoms, Rome 4 November 1950 and of (II) the Protocol to that Convention, Paris 20 March, 1952, 20 January 1953, NAI S.14921B.

[98] ibid, para 8.   [99] ibid, para 7.

[100] Extract from Cabinet Minutes, 6 February 1953, G.C.6/150, NAI S.14921B. See also, Additional Memorandum for the Government on Proposed Ratification, 5 February 1953, NAI S.14921B.   [101] Airey v Ireland, Series A, No. 32, para 26.

after the United Kingdom (8 March 1951), Norway (15 January 1952), Sweden (4 February 1952), Germany (5 December 1952), and Saarland (14 January 1953).[102] Of the first six, only Sweden had accepted the jurisdiction of the European Commission on Human Rights to receive individual petitions, and no State had recognized the jurisdiction of the Court. Ireland was therefore the first State to make the declarations under Articles 25 and 46 accepting the right of individual petition and access to the Court, something that did not escape mention in the Irish press at the time.[103] Although he was no longer in government, MacBride's personal contribution to this process was immense, and it seems unlikely that in his absence Ireland would have taken such a lead. The fact is often lost sight of that Ireland was the first State *in the world* to accept a binding international petition mechanism before an international human rights court.

Ireland's ratification was sharply criticized by the *Irish Independent* in an editorial which, entitled 'A Grave Issue', said:

'It is scarcely necessary to call attention to the seriousness of these agreements to which the Irish nation is now committed. As far as we are aware neither the Legislature nor the Irish people have given any express authority to the Government to commit them to this agreement. Clearly it confers on an external judicial body the right to adjudicate on matters of purely Irish concern. Equally clearly it derogates from the exclusive juridical rights conferred by the Constitution on the Irish courts. It seems to us that this external court may even reverse or render nugatory a decision made by our Supreme Court.'[104]

At the time of ratification, Ireland sent the Council of Europe an Irish language translation of the Convention and the Protocol with the request that if it were to be published, it would be desirable to send a proof to Dublin for revision.[105]

MacBride uses the Convention Against Ireland and Britain

The election of 30 May 1951 had brought an end to the Inter-party Government, and returned De Valera and Fianna Fáil to power. MacBride's political career was not entirely over, but it was the last time he would sit in government or occupy a ministerial position. Clanna Poblachta returned very few seats in the 1951 election, although MacBride was one of those fortunate enough to be re-elected to the seat of Dublin South East. As an opposition TD, he managed to maintain his connection with the Council of Europe, and served as a delegate to the Consultative Assembly. In the mid-1950s, there was a flurry of activity around the prospect that MacBride might be elected president of the Consultative Assembly. MacBride

---

[102] Saarland became an integral part of Germany on 1 January 1957.
[103] 'Jurisdiction of Court accepted by Ireland', Irish Independent, 26 February 1953.
[104] 'A Grave Issue', *Irish Independent*, 28 February 1953.
[105] Letter from Seán G. Ronan to M. Paul Levy, Directorate of Information, 21 February 1953, NAI DFA 417/39/19/1B.

apparently campaigned for the job, and the response from the Irish government was favourable. Brendan O'Riordan, Ireland's Permanent Representative to the Council of Europe, wrote to MacBride: 'I think that you will see from these letters that your chances of the Presidency are quite good and, for my part, I hope that you will succeed. I think it would be an honour both for the Consultative Assembly and for Ireland if you were chosen.'[106] MacBride had a number of qualities that suited him for European leadership, including his political experience as Minister of Foreign Affairs and his fluent bilingualism in the two official languages of the Council, something that would have been (and still is) rather unusual for someone from an English-speaking country. Perhaps predictably, the British were opposed. They offered to support another Irish candidate, such as Senator James Crosbie, but not the former IRA man and son of a rebel executed in the aftermath of Easter 1916.[107]

MacBride was—not for the first time in his already illustrious career—reinventing himself yet again, as one of the world's first 'human rights lawyers'. He became involved in some of the initial litigation before both the European Commission and the European Court of Human Rights. Unlike Ireland, the UK did not initially accept the compulsory jurisdiction of the Commission with respect to individual petitions in accordance with Article 25 of the Convention. However, jurisdiction over inter-State petitions to the Commission was an automatic consequence of ratification. As a result, Greece filed a complaint against the UK concerning violations of the Convention in Cyprus, then still a British colony embroiled in a struggle for self-determination.[108] The petition was never adjudicated, but Greece had succeeded in opening another battlefront in the campaign for the independence of Cyprus. It subsequently discontinued the petition as political negotiations progressed. MacBride served as an advisor to the Greek government in the case. In 1959, when he attended ceremonies in Strasbourg as one of the individuals who had signed both the Statute of the Council of Europe and the European Convention on Human Rights, he received a message of appreciation from Cypriot leader Archbishop Makarios, who expressed 'sincere thanks and appreciation for all you have done in the cause of Cypriot freedom'.[109]

MacBride was not only in Strasbourg for ceremonial reasons. He was also there for hearings of the European Commission on Human Rights in the *Lawless* case, in which he acted on behalf of the petitioner. Gerard Lawless was an active republican with an impressive history of brushes with the law. In 1956, he had been involved in an armed raid in Keshcarrigan, County Leitrim, where guns and revolvers were stolen. In 1957, Lawless was convicted by Dublin District Court

[106] Letter from W.P. Fay to S. MacBride, 22 February 1956, NAI DFA P286.

[107] Letter from William Fay, Irish Ambassador to France, to Seán Murphy, Department of External Affairs, 20 March 1956, NAI DFA P286. Also, letter from Brendan O'Riordan to Ambassador William Fay, 14 March 1956, NAI DFA P286.

[108] On the Greek application, see A.W. Brian Simpson, *Human Rights and the End of Empire, Britain and the Genesis of the European Convention* (2001), 924 ff.

[109] 'Cypriot Archbishop thanks Mr. MacBride', Irish Independent, 20 April 1959.

after being caught in possession of a sketch map for an attack on certain frontier posts between the Irish Republic and Northern Ireland. Lawless was again arrested on 11 July 1957 at Dun Laoghaire, and charged with being a member of an unlawful organization. Lawless was told he would be released provided that he signed an undertaking in regard to his future conduct; but he refused. On 17 July 1957 Lawless was transferred from Military Prison to the Curragh Internment Camp, where he was held without charge or trial until 11 December 1957. On 16 August 1957, Lawless was informed that he would be released if he gave an under-taking in writing 'to respect the Constitution of Ireland and the laws' and not to 'be a member of, or assist, any organisation which is an unlawful organisation under the Offences against the State act 1939'.

Lawless presented an application for a writ of habeas corpus in the High Court. MacBride appealed denial of the application to the Supreme Court, where he sub-mitted arguments based upon the European Convention on Human Rights. On 8 November 1957, an application was submitted to the European Commission of Human Rights. MacBride argued that Lawless's detention had breached Articles 5 and 6 of the European Convention on Human Rights. The Commission decided that the arrest and detention of Lawless under section 4 of the Offences against the State (Amendment) Act 1940 was 'not a measure which is authorised by Article 5(1) of the Convention'. The Commission found, by a majority of 9:5, that there was a public emergency which threatened the life of the nation within the meaning of Article 15(1) of the Convention. Then, by 8 votes to 6, it held that the measures of arrest and detention taken by Ireland 'do [...] not exceed what is justifiable under Article 15 of the Convention'. Finally, the Commission declared that the case raised legal issues of fundamental importance in the application of the Convention, and upon which, therefore, it was desirable that the European Court of Human Rights pronounce itself. In accordance with the Convention as it then stood,[110] the Commission then referred the case to the Court.

Lawless was the first case to be heard by the European Court of Human Rights. Richard McConigal, the initial Irish judge on the Court, was designated to sit in the *Lawless* case, in accordance with the rule by which the judge nominated from a country sits in matters in which that country is respondent.[111] Six other judges were chosen by lot. René Cassin, the great French jurist who was later to win the Nobel Peace Prize for his work in drafting the Universal Declaration of Human Rights, was the presiding judge.[112] A sign of the infancy of human rights litigation

---

[110] The Commission was subsequently amended, by Protocol No. 9, CETS No. 140, allowing individual litigants to seize the Court directly after a hearing before the Commission. Ireland signed Protocol No. 9 (signature without reservation as to ratification) on 24 June 1994. Pursuant to Protocol No. 11, CETS No. 155, the Commission was abolished. Since it entered into force, on 1 November 1998, applicants have had direct access to the European Court of Human Rights after exhausting their domestic remedies. Ireland ratified Protocol No. 11 on 16 December 1996.

[111] In accordance with Art. 43 of the *Convention* (subsequently amended, see Art. 27(2) of the current version).

[112] Marc Agi, *René Cassin, Prix Nobel de la Paix (1887–1976), Père de la Déclaration universelle des droits de l'homme*, (Paris: Perrin, 1998).

was the denial of a right of audience to counsel for the victim. Lawless was 'represented' by Humphrey Waldock, the British member of the Commission who acted on its behalf in proceedings before the Court. In effect, there was no voice before the Court representing Lawless himself. Ireland had contested the Commission's initiative of sending a copy of its report to Lawless, saying it was confidential, and that its disclosure was prohibited by the Convention. The Court did not concur, although it denied the Commission's request that Lawless's personal submissions be filed with the Court.[113] The Court subsequently dismissed the petition on the merits, holding that Ireland was entitled to hold Lawless without trial by virtue of its right to derogation, in accordance with Article 15 of the Convention.

Eventually, MacBride even put his services to work at the European Court of Human Rights on behalf of the Irish government. During the height of the 'troubles', Ireland filed an inter-State application against the UK concerning abuse of prisoners within Northern Ireland's detention centres.[114] MacBride advised the Irish government on the application, which was successful before both the Commission and the Court. But that is another story.[115]

For specialists in international human rights law, the life of Seán MacBride really only becomes a subject of interest with his appointment as Minister of External Affairs and his involvement in the drafting of the European Convention on Human Rights. His participation then seemed to refocus what was already a most astonishing career, one whose overarching theme was a commitment to militant republicanism, followed by a transformation to legal forms of struggle upon enactment of the 1937 Constitution. By the 1950s, MacBride took his place as one of the world's pre-eminent human rights lawyers. He served as chairman of the international executive of Amnesty International and, in 1974, was awarded the Nobel Peace Prize. Had the position of High Commissioner for Human Rights existed at the time, his name would surely have appeared on the short list of distinguished candidates. One of the enigmas of his complex persona is the relationship between his early commitment to the armed movement and his subsequent dedication to peaceful forms of political activity, including a devotion to human rights and fundamental freedoms. Was this the epiphany of a gunman turned barrister (for some, perhaps, merely a betrayal), or rather a consistent and logical development in a life underpinned by a common thread of social justice? The shift from the Armalite to the courtroom is, in many ways, a recurring theme in Irish republicanism, and one with contemporary echoes.[116] But even today,

---

[113] *Lawless v Ireland*, Series A, No. 2 (*locus standi*); *Lawless v Ireland*, Series A, No. 3, paras 5–6. See also the discussion in *Lawless v Ireland*, Series A, No. 1 (preliminary exceptions).

[114] *Ireland v United Kingdom*, Series A, No. 25.

[115] This essay is part of a larger ongoing study into Ireland's participation in international human rights institutions.

[116] See eg Kieran McEvoy, 'Law, Struggle and Political Transformation in Northern Ireland' (2000) 27 Journal of Law and Society 542.

when MacBride's name is mentioned, there is often a slight tone of discomfort or embarrassment, rooted in the complexities of a modern-day iconic figure of the human rights movement with a past as a terrorist.

MacBride's life might well be taken as a metaphor for a broader theme in Irish political life. In that sense, the country's singular commitment to the European Convention on Human Rights would be taken as the consequence of its long and bitter history. The post-Second World War movement for human rights provided a vehicle for the promotion and enforcement of principles whose outlet had taken other forms in earlier decades. The standard explanation of the initial success of the European Convention on Human Rights as the first comprehensive binding international human rights instrument focuses upon the revulsion felt by the major Western European States about the terrible conflict they had barely survived. Without disputing the validity of such an analysis, the Irish contribution provides a somewhat different perspective, because neutral Ireland had largely avoided the brutality of the war. Its newfound attachment to international human rights norms, manifested by its seminal role in the negotiation of the Convention, can best be explained within the historical context of a State forged in the crucible of human suffering. MacBride's personal role in the process had its own peculiar aspects, yet in its broad lines it fits comfortably within a coherent theory of Irish legal and political development. A unique individual, MacBride was nevertheless a man of his times. His commitment to the adoption of the European Convention on Human Rights spoke for an emerging strand in the Irish world view. MacBride's genius lay in grasping the importance of international human rights law at such an early stage of its development.

14

Mobilizing the Professions: Lawyers, Politics, and the Collective Legal Conscience*

Kieran McEvoy and Rachel Rebouche

'In the ideal world, a Law Society or a Bar Council should function as the collective conscience of the legal profession. They should be the most vocal in not just defending the financial or institutional interests of their members but in deploying their skills and resources in defence of human rights and of the rule of law itself, despite whatever pressures the state and other powerful forces may deploy. Unfortunately however history teaches us that a range of factors often contribute to the opposite. If lawyers do the right thing it is often despite such groups rather than because of them.'[1]

Introduction

This essay considers the ways in which lawyers either do or do not make their voices heard in processes of political, social, and legal transformation. By examining a number of key moments of legal and political history in three distinct jurisdictions, it looks in particular at the interaction between those lawyers who do 'take a stand' and the professional bodies to which they belong. The purpose of that examination is to explore ways in which the potential for particular groups of lawyers to serve as the 'collective conscience' of the legal professional may be developed and enhanced.[2] Of course, as is well discussed in the literature reviewed

 * Kieran McEvoy would like to thank the staff of the Institute of Legal Research, School of Law, University of Berkeley, where his contribution to this essay was completed, in particular to Frank Zimring, Harry Scheiber, Karen Chin, and Toni Melucci for their assistance and support.
 [1] Interview Northern Ireland barrister, 25 August 2005.
 [2] As noted above the notion of collective conscience emerged from one practitioner in our field-work and we considered that it well captured some of the issues with which we were grappling. Obviously the concept resonates with Durkheim's concept of 'the totality of beliefs and sentiments common to the average citizens of the same society [which] forms a determinant system which has its own life: One may call it the collective or common conscience'. However we are not deploying the term here as synonymous with some sort of 'averaged out' or lowest common denominator form of consensus to which the Durkheimian concept is sometimes (mistakenly) applied. Rather, we are utlizing the notion of collective conscience to describe a more ambitious, far-reaching, and ultimately more

below, Law Societies, Bar Associations, Bar Councils, and the like tend to adopt conservative positions which favour the political and institutional positions of the State in which they practice and which is, in the final analysis, the guarantor over their continued de facto monopoly on the delivery of legal services. As will be seen below, often such positions are expressed in terms of maintaining the 'neutrality' or 'independence' of the profession and a denial of the political nature of such stances. However, we will argue that even in circumstances wherein the dominant forces in the legal community appear largely pliant to the interests of the State or other powerful institutional forces, progressive lawyers find ways to ignore, circumnavigate, or otherwise negotiate such institutional blockages and have their voices heard. In each of the examples discussed, it is ultimately the legal collectives which have shifted their stance. Often such movement has been made begrudgingly. However, we would argue that the process of *internationalization*, *popular mobilization*, and *acknowledgement of the past*, in the three jurisdictions discussed, have nudged along the established organizations of the profession towards a more honourable expression of what we have termed the 'collective legal conscience'.

The key moments or 'critical junctures' which we examine are drawn from a major comparative research project on the ways in which lawyers utilize and adapt to human rights discourses in times of profound political and legal transformation.[3] The rationale for conducting such comparative legal research are well rehearsed.[4] One of the features of human rights discourse in particular and of the broader process of increased globalization is that legal scholars and practitioners are increasingly required to be internationalist and comparativist in nature.[5] More generally, as Nelken has argued, comparative scholarship allows us to 'raise

courageous expression of what Halliday has described as 'moral authority', wherein technical legal knowledge and skills are deployed in a self-consciously *moral* and quite often *political* fashion because it is deemed by the professional organization involved to be 'the right thing to do'. The practical difficulties of determining such a path for legal associations is discussed at length below. Emile Durkheim *The Division of Labour* (1893\1933) 79; Roger Cotterrell *Emile Durkheim: Law in a Moral Domain* (1999); Terence Halliday 'Knowledge Mandates: Collective Influence By Scientific, Normative and Syncretic Professions.' (1985) British Journal of Sociology, 421, 429.

[3] This essay is drawn from research completed between 2002 and 2006 by the authors and Professor Stephen Livingstone. That project involved fieldwork in the United States, Canada, Northern Ireland, South Africa, Britain, and the Republic of Ireland. Over 130 interviews were conducted with judges and lawyers including five chief justices. All of those interviewees who wish to be anonymized are identified by the branch of the profession to which they belong and the date of the interview. For a more detailed discussion on the findings, see Stephen Livingstone, Kieran McEvoy, Rachel Rebouche, and Paul Mageean (2007) *Judges, Lawyers and Human Rights in the Northern Ireland Transition*.

[4] See eg David Nelken (ed.), *Comparing Legal Cultures* (1997); David Nelken (ed.), *Contrasting Criminal Justice: Getting From Here to There* (2000); Konrad Zweigert and Hein Koetz, *An Introduction to Comparative Law* (3rd ed.), (1998); Paul Roberts 'On Method: The Ascent of Comparative Criminal Justice' (2002) 22 Oxford Journal of Legal Studies 539.

[5] Christopher McCrudden, 'A Common Law of Human Rights? Transnational Judicial Conversations on Human Rights' (2000) 20 Oxford Journal of Legal Studies 499; William Twining *Globalisation and Legal Theory* (2002).

or sharpen awkward questions' about our own jurisdictions.[6] It can facilitate a process of reflection which allows actors to 'step back' from the immediacy of their own context, particularly when dealing with politically sensitive or difficult issues.[7] Providing an approach is adopted which avoids simplistic or mechanistic transpositions from one jurisdiction to another, but rather draws upon other experiences to thematize and frame that which is relevant, comparative research is an extremely useful analytical tool for moving debates beyond their localized context.[8]

In part one of the essay we first outline what is meant by the notion of a critical juncture and how a close examination of such a defining 'moment' can speak to broader political and sociological themes of more general applicability. Part two then considers key themes which emerge from the literature on the sociology of the legal professions more generally, and in particular with regard to the role of professional associations in contributing to the mores, values, and working practices which make up the legal culture of a given jurisdiction. Part three then considers the particularities of the responses of three different legal communities to such critical junctures. Although a range of overlapping strategies were deployed in each jurisdiction aimed at galvanizing lawyers, each is used heuristically to illustrate particular features of broader applicability. In Northern Ireland, we examine how *internationalization* became a key feature in breaking down long-held traditions of quietism within a legal community that was finally galvanized by the decision of the Law Society of Northern Ireland to call for public inquiries into the murders of two of its prominent members in circumstances which strongly suggested collusion by the security forces. In Canada, we explore the strategy of *popular mobilization* employed by feminist lawyers concerning their efforts to mainstream gender equality in the discussions preceding the introduction of the Canadian Charter of Rights and Freedoms. In South Africa, we examine a key moment in the Apartheid era when the Bar excluded one of its own members for his stance in opposition to the regime and the manner in which the profession engaged in a process of *acknowledgement* of that history through the Truth and Reconciliation Commission. In the final part of the essay we seek to draw together the lessons from these and other jurisdictions and attempt to frame those experiences within the 'cause lawyering' literature. In particular, we suggest that a more sophisticated notion of professionalism amongst lawyers and legal organizations may afford them the confidence and space to engage in contentious public conversations of which they could and should be a part.

---

[6] David Nelken, 'Whom Can You Trust: The Future of Comparative Criminology.' in D. Nelken (ed.), *The Futures of Criminology* (1994).

[7] Kieran McEvoy and Graham Ellison, 'Criminological Discourses In Northern Ireland: Conflict and Conflict Resolution, In Kieran McEvoy and Tim Newburn (eds.), *Criminology, Conflict Resolution and Restorative Justice* (2003).

[8] David Nelken, 'Beyond Compare? Criticizing "The American Way of Law" ' (2003) 28 Law and Social Inquiry 799.

Recognizing a Critical Juncture

Before exploring the ways in which lawyers are or are not mobilized, it might be useful to offer some guidance as to how one might recognize a key moment or critical juncture in the history of an organization, institution, or political system. The notion of a critical juncture applied in this context to the professional history of lawyers is derived from the literature on historical institutionalism. This is a rich comparative political science literature, the nuances of which are beyond the needs of the current essay. Summarizing for the sake of brevity, historical intuitionalism is the study of the ways in which particular institutions emerge over time and the ways in which such institutions influence the social and political world around them.[9] Originally heavily influenced by fairly rigid functionalist perspectives on the intersection of the social and political arenas as an overall system of inter-acting parts,[10] historical institutionalists have increasingly adopted an expanded perspective of determining *which* institutions matter (beyond obvious political institutions, such as parliaments) and the *ways* in which they matter.[11] They increasingly focus upon more subtle forms of 'cultural' relationships between individual actors and the institutions to which they belong.[12] They are sensitive to the operation of power, both within institutions themselves and in terms of broader sets of power relations between differing institutions.[13] Finally, historical institutionalist scholarship places considerable emphasis upon the significance of time. By tracking changes and continuities within particular institutions carefully (and avoiding simplistic linear narratives wherein, for example, institutions evolve in an inevitably liberal or progressive manner),[14] historical institutionalism provides us with the notion of 'critical junctures', key 'moments' or periods in the history of any institution which provide crucial insights into the ways in which organizations *see*, *act,* and *think* of themselves.

Some of the most persuasive writings on critical junctures are suffused with the notion of crisis, challenge, or significant change in the history of a given

[9] Kathleen Thelen, Sven Steinmo, and Frank Lonstreth (eds), *Structuring Politics: Historical Institutionalism in Comparative Analysis* (1992); Sven Steimo 'The New Institutionalism,' in Barry Clarke and Joe Foweraker (eds), *The Encyclopaedia of Democratic Thought* (2001).

[10] Ronald Chilcote, *Theories of Comparative Politics* (1981); David Knoke, 'Networks of Political Action: Towards Theory Construction' (1990) 68 Social Forces 1041.

[11] Peter Hall and Rosemary Taylor, 'The Potential of Historical Institutionalism' (1998) XLVI Political Studies 958.

[12] Kathleen Thelen, 'Historical Institutionalism In Comparative Politics' (1999) 2 Annual Review of Political Science 369. Ellen Immergut, 'The Theoretical Core of the New Institutionalism' (1998) 26 Politics and Society 5.

[13] Johannes Lindner and Berthold Rittberger, 'The Creation, Interpretation and Contestation of Institutions: Revisiting Historical Institutionalism' (2003) 41 Journal of Common Market Studies 445; Terry Moe, 'Power and Political Institutions' (2005) 3 Perspectives on Politics 215.

[14] Paul Pierson and Theda Skocpol, 'Historical Institutionalism In Contemporary Political Science' (2002) *Political Science the State of the Discipline*; Paul Pierson, *Politics in Time: History, Institutions and Social Analysis* (2004).

institution.[15] In particular, the ways in which particular institutions respond to such challenges is examined in the context of their 'legacy', and the ways in which such legacies are 'reproduced' both in terms of how the institutions function at a practical level but also in terms of the ways in which they are publicly perceived and remembered, and the ways in which an organizational self-image emerges.[16] Thus, for some scholars in this field, the specific configurations of a given institution may be crystallized as a result of a particular critical juncture.[17] At the very least, the ways in which an institution responds to critical junctures renders its workings more visible.[18]

By way of illustration, the murder of Stephen Lawrence and the subsequent MacPherson Inquiry would be widely accepted amongst policing scholars and practitioners alike to constitute a critical juncture in the history of British policing.[19] In the world of British prisons, the prison riots of the 1980s and the subsequent report of Lord Woolf is also seen by many as a defining period with a legacy which remains highly significant to this day.[20] In the legal world, despite a heated debate as to its actual transformative impact,[21] few would dispute that the introduction of the Human Rights Act 1998 was a key moment in the history of the British legal system. In each instance, as a result of incidents which occurred within their domain which were of considerable broader political significance, these institutions were hugely affected both internally and externally. For the actors within these institutions 'MacPherson', 'Woolf' or the 'Human Rights Act' became shorthand for a series of (often contested) meanings around which hotly disputed discourses such as 'institutional racism' in the police, 'moral crisis' within the prisons or the 'appropriate balance' between public safety and civil liberties coalesced. For actors within these institutions, such critical junctures provided important historical and cultural narratives in the development of an institutional

[15] Theda Skocpol, *States and Social Revolutions: A Comparative Analysis of France, Russia and China* (1979); Ruth Collier and David Collier, *Shaping The Political Arena: Critical Junctures, The Labor Movement, And Regime Dynamics In Latin America* (1991).
[16] Theda Skocpol, Ganz Marshall, and Ziad Munson, 'A Nation of Organizers: The Institutional Origins of Civic Voluntarism in the United States' (2000) 94 American Political Science Review 527.
[17] Thelen (1991) above n 12, 391 also makes the useful corrective point that the notion of particular institutional relations being crystallized (and thereby ensuring some degree of legacy which will last) should not be viewed as meaning that such relations stand still. Rather, as she points out, institutions which do achieve some form of historical continuity are often marked out by their capacity to adapt to changes in their environment.
[18] For a classic account, see Stuart Hall, Charles Critcher, Tony Jefferson, John Clarke, and Brian Robert, *Policing the Crisis: Mugging, the State and Law and Order* (1978).
[19] Michael Rowe, *Policing, Race and Racism* (2004); John Stevens, *Not for the Faint Hearted: My Life Fighting Crime* (2006).
[20] Michael Cavadino and James Dignan, *The Penal System: An Introduction* (2002); Alison Liebling, *Prisons and their Moral Performance* (2004).
[21] See eg the special issue of the Journal of Law and Society, especially Stephen Sedley, 'The Rocks or the Open Sea: Where is the Human Rights Act Heading?' (2005) 32 Journal of Law and Society 3; Luke Clements, 'Winner and Losers' (2005) 32 Journal of Law Society 34; Shami Chakrabati, 'Rights And Rhetoric: The Politics of Asylum and Human Rights Culture In The United Kingdom' (2005) 32 Journal of Law and Society 131.

memory and informed the mores and values which shaped the organizational culture. For those on the outside, they offered glimpses into comparatively closed worlds as well as useful historical 'moments' around which to frame broader social and political discussions concerning such institutions.[22]

Critical junctures therefore are defining moments in the history of organizations and institutions which offer us insights into how they work, the power relationship at work within and without, the ways in which they are perceived and remembered, and the ways in which they see themselves. The critical junctures we have chosen are in some senses eclectic. Certainly we are conscious that we could have chosen many others from the diverse histories of the legal communities in Northern Ireland, Canada, and South Africa. However, the junctures we decided to focus upon emerged organically from our fieldwork; they were all viewed as 'key moments' by the actors involved. In addition, we considered that they were illustrative of themes and strategies of broader applicability beyond the confines of each jurisdiction.

Legal Collectives and the Sociology of the Legal Profession

The origins of work on the sociology of the profession actually lie with the broader study of societies in transformation. Drawing upon the work of Weber and Durkheim, professions such as law or medicine were historically seen as amongst the most important and as stabilizing influences in a fast-changing world.[23] Up until the 1960s the sociology of the professions was heavily influenced by the emphasis which Durkheim in particular placed upon the professions and professional bodies as entities which represented *corps-intermediaires* (intermediate bodies) between the individual and the State.[24] His view was that in the context of increased division of labour and related social and political upheaval, such groups embodied the social forces which were required to prevent a breakdown in moral authority.[25] Later work on the professions began to look at how such groupings

[22] There is a similar notion contained with policing literature, referred to as 'signal events', which may be events or controversies which 'everyone knows about' regardless of whether the precise nature of such events has been established. See Martin Innes, 'Signal Crimes and Signal Disorders: Notes on Deviance as Communicative Action' (2004) 55 British Journal of Sociology 335. Such events may become watersheds, key markers in individuals' biographies and a focus around which experiences of and attitudes within and towards institutions such as the police may be structured, understood and articulated. See also Sharon Pickering, *Policing and Resistance in Northern Ireland* (2002) and Aogán Mulcahy, *Policing Northern Ireland: Conflict, Legitimacy and Reform* (2005).

[23] '...they inherit, preserve and pass on a tradition...they engender modes of life, habits of thought and standards of judgement which render them centres of resistance to crude forces which threaten steady and peaceful evolution...the great professions stand like rocks against which the waves raised by these forces beat in vain'. Alexander Carr-Saunders and Paul Wilson, *The Professions* (1933) (repr. 1964) 497.

[24] Terence Johnson, *Professions and Power* (1972); Keith MacDonald, *The Sociology of the Professions* (1995). [25] Emile Durkheim, *Professional Ethics and Civic Morals* (1957).

exercised 'license and mandate' over their work by virtue of the State and the support of political, social, or economic elites. Some such commentators were highly critical of the processes by which particular dominant professions are distinguished from other occupations, setting in place their own oversight and educational mechanisms and developing a particular sense of self-regard 'by virtue of professional myths imposed on a gullible public'.[26] The creation of a monopoly over access and services, the exercise of autonomous power over their own members, the particular relations of such groups with the political culture in which they operate, and the achievement of social status and reputation are amongst the most important features which sets apart such 'professions'.[27]

With regard to lawyers in particular, they too have been long identified as seeking to control admission to and training for the profession, to demarcate and protect jurisdiction within which they alone are entitled to practice, to impose their own rules of etiquette and practice upon one another and to defend and if possible to enhance their status.[28] As Western world societies questioned the irrational bases of social privilege, legal professions historically met this challenge by reforming the training, admission, and regulation of their members in ways which would limit numbers and organize forms of competition.[29] In effect, lawyers have sought to modernize the basis of their social advantage through monopolization.[30] The means through which that monopoly was maintained has historically been via organizations such as Bar Associations and Law Societies, which were charged with the task of the self-governance of the professions.

[26] ' . . . several dominant occupations (especially medicine and law) have come to occupy uniquely powerful positions in Western societies from which they monopolistically initiate, direct and regulate widespread social change. Several of the mechanisms which have facilitated these developments have been identified and discussed. Principal amongst them are the emergence of a mythology concerning professionalism.' John McKinlay 'On the Professional Regulation of Change, in Paul Halmos (ed.), *Professionalization and Social Change* (1973) 77. For a classic polemic on this process in the medical world, see Ivan Illich, *Limits to Medicine: Medical Nemesis, the Expropriation of Health* (1977). See also Andrew Abbot, *The System of Professions an Essay on the Division of Expert Labor* (1988), mirroring Nils Christie, 'Conflicts as Property' (1977) 17 British Journal of Criminology 1, on the ways in which lawyers have come to claim exclusive 'jurisdiction' over conflicts defined as 'legal disputes'. See also Lawrence Friedman, *Legal Culture and the Legal Profession* (1995).

[27] Magali Larson, *The Rise of Professionalism*: A Sociological Analysis (1977); Terence Johnson, 'The State and the Professions' in Anthony Giddens and Gavin Mackenzie (eds), *Social Class and the Division of Labour* (1982); Anne Witz, *Professions and Patriarchy* (1992); Keith MacDonald, *The Sociology of the Professions* (1995).

[28] Daniel Duman, 'The Creation and Diffusion of a Professional Ideology in Nineteenth Century England,' (1979) 27 Sociological Review 113; John Flood, *The Legal Profession in the United States* (3rd ed.) (1985). Michael Burrage, 'Revolution and the Collective Action of the French, American, and English Legal Professions' (1988) 13 Law and Social Inquiry 225; Hilary Sommerlad, 'Managerialism and the Legal Profession: A New Professional Paradigm' (1995) 2 International Journal of the Legal Profession 159; Terence Halliday, *Beyond Monopoly: Lawyers, State Crises and Professional Empowerment* (1987); Gerard Hanlon, 'Lawyers, the Market and Significant Others' (1997) 60 Modern Law Review 798; Fiona Kay, 'Professionalism And Exclusionary Practices: Shifting The Terrain Of Privilege And Professional Monopoly' (2004) 11 International Journal of the Legal Profession 11.

[29] See generally Richard Abel and Philip Lewis, *Lawyers in Society* (1988), esp. vol. 1.

[30] Mark Osiel, 'Lawyers as Monopolists, Aristocrats and Entrepreneurs' (2000) 103 Harvard Law Review 2009.

Much critical work on such entities has focused upon such organizations as the vehicles through which the pecuniary interests and professional monopolies of their members are maintained and promulgated.[31] Historically, such analysis has tended to concentrate on the weaknesses of the self-governance model in dealing with professional misconduct.[32] More sympathetic studies, particularly of American bar associations, suggest that once the dominance of the legal market was secured, the preoccupation with the maintenance of the monopoly gave way to an ethos of 'civic professionalism' wherein energies were directed towards the improvement of the legal systems in which their members operated.[33] Studies of other systems such as in England have been less charitable. For example, Abel in his seminal work in the English profession is scathing about the record of the Law Society and Bar Council on their lack of sustained engagement in matters of legal reform which did not impact directly on their own interests.[34] As he navigates the various attempts to erode the monopoly of legal service provision in the British context in the 1980s and 1990s, he summarizes:

'The greatest pitfall of self-governance [in England and Wales], however, is not tension among fractions or between professional and public interest, oligarchy and democracy, but apathy. Most lawyers just want to earn a living and leave politics to others... Like Rhett Butler, most lawyers frankly do not give a damn.'[35]

In very broad terms much of the literature on the sociology of the legal profession in general and of organizations within the professions in particular suggests a profession more interested in protecting itself and the status of its members. Viewed from such a reductionist perspective, the legal profession is individualist in nature and it secures its privileged status due in large part to its mechanisms for self-governance. Those mechanisms are, in the final analysis, guaranteed by the State in which lawyers operate.[36] In such a context, it is perhaps small wonder that

---

[31] See Richard Abel, 'The Rise of Professionalism' (1981) 6 British Journal of Law and Society 82; Terence Halliday, 'Professions, Class and Capitalism' (1983) 24 European Journal of Sociology 321, for a review. For a classic account with regard to medicine, see Jeffrey Berlant, *Profession and Monopoly: a Study of Medicine in the United States and Great Britain* (1975).

[32] David Wilkins, 'Who Should Regulate Lawyers?' (1992) 104 Harvard Law Review 799; Bruce Arnold and Fiona Kay, 'Social Capital, Violations of Trust and the Vulnerability of Isolates: The Social Organization of Law Practice and Professional Self-regulation' (1995) 4 International Journal of the Sociology of Law 321; Christine Parker, *Just Lawyers: Regulation and Access to Justice* (2000).

[33] See also John Halliday, above n 28; Michael Powell, *From Patrician to Professional Elite: The Transformation of the New York City Bar Association* (1988); Terence Halliday, Michael Powell, and Mark Granfors, 'After Minimalism: Transformations of State Bar Associations from Market Dependence to State Reliance, 1918 to 1950' (1993) 58 American Sociological Review 515.

[34] John Morison and Philip Leith, *The Barristers World and the Nature of Law* (1995); Andrew Levin and Jennifer Boon, *The Ethics and Conduct of Lawyers in England and Wales* (1999); Mary Seneviratne, *The Legal Profession: Regulation and the Consumer* (1999); Daniel Muzio, *The Professional Project and the Contemporary Re-Organisation of the Legal Profession in England And Wales* (2004).

[35] Richard Abel, *English Lawyers: Between Market and State* (2003) 470. For an interesting discussion on the break-up of lawyers monopoly on service provision in the United States see Herbert Kritzer, *The Professions Are Dead, Long Live the Professions: Legal Practice in a Postprofessional World* (1999) 33 Law and Society Review 713.   [36] Fiona Kay (2004), above n 28.

organized groups of lawyers do not do more to collectively 'rock the boat' and indeed may take a dim view of those lawyers who do.[37] Of course such a crude generalization fails to grasp much of the differences and nuances of the lived experiences of lawyers and legal organizations within and between different jurisdictions. It also fails to take account of a long tradition of progressive work (sometimes referred to as 'cause lawyering') carried out by individual lawyers, law firms, collective organizations and even, on occasion, established Bar Associations and Law Societies in a wide range of different contexts. This is a style of lawyering which we shall return to in the final section of this essay. For current purposes, however, this more cynical notion of lawyers and their capacity for mobilization provides a useful backdrop to the critical junctures explored below in Northern Ireland, Canada, and South Africa.

Critical Junctures in Context: Comparative Examples

The experiences discussed below in Northern Ireland, Canada, and South Africa at various critical junctures in their own legal history may help to elucidate some of the broader arguments concerning the mobilization of lawyers being explored here. Each of these societies have experienced considerable political and constitutional transformation. As is discussed elsewhere in this volume, the era since the paramilitary ceasefires in Northern Ireland has seen the introduction of the Belfast Agreement in 1998 and the Human Rights Act. Despite the stop-start nature of devolution, both of these pieces of legislation have had a important effect on the political and legal landscape in the jurisdiction.[38] In Canada, the Canadian Charter of Fundamental Rights and Freedoms has also had a profound impact on Canadian legal and political culture and the way in which Canadian political power is exercised.[39] In South Africa, the post-Apartheid 1996 South African Constitution was both a legal and symbolic marker in the dramatic transition from a racist legal system (based on the primacy of parliamentary sovereignty) to a system tied explicitly to the interpretation of entrenched rights.[40] As John Morison and Marie Lynch argue herein with regard to Northern Ireland, as Christopher Manfredi has underlined with regard to Canada,[41] and Rick Abel with regard to South Africa,[42] *some* lawyers were deeply imbued in the struggles

---

[37] As one colleague suggested at an earlier presentation of a version of this paper, 'what else would you expect from a bunch of lawyers?' Seminar, Institute of Governance, Queens University Belfast, 27 June 2006.

[38] Arthur Aughey, *The Politics of Northern Ireland: Beyond the Good Friday Agreement* (2005).

[39] See eg James Kelly, *Governing with the Charter: Legislative and Judicial Activism and the Framers' Intent* (2005).

[40] Hassen Ebrahim, *The Soul of a Nation: Constitution Making in South Africa* (1999).

[41] Richard Abel, *Politics by Other Means: Law in the Struggle Against Apartheid 1980–1994* (1994).

[42] Christopher Manfredi, *Feminist Activism in the Supreme Court; Legal Mobilization and the Women's Legal Education and Action Fund* (2004).

before and after these legal and constitutional initiatives and their outplaying on the political stage. In each instance, they were often blocked by powerful institutional forces both within and outside of their own profession. While the histories of these countries differ radically in other ways, we will argue that the search for peace in Northern Ireland, the creation of the Charter in Canada, and the struggle to end Apartheid in South Africa, created moments of change wherein an elevated collective legal conscience was possible.

Internationalization and the Collective Legal Conscience in Northern Ireland

We have argued elsewhere that a range of factors including the small size of the jurisdiction and legal community, the exigencies of the Northern Ireland conflict, the particularities of the relationship which many lawyers and judges have had with the State, all contributed to a legal culture which was (in very broad terms) conservative, positivistic, and shaped by a desire to avoid 'division' at all costs.[43] With a few exceptions, the self-image of lawyers in Northern Ireland during the conflict was of a profession striving to remain 'above' politics, a group of skilled professionals engaged in a collective process of upholding 'the rule of law'.[44] The numbers working 'at the coalface' of cases related to the violent conflict were small in comparative terms and, for the reasons discussed below, were loath to be seen as affiliated to the political causes of their clients.[45] A number of small collectives of critical lawyers did emerge for brief periods during the conflict and engaged in high-profile public commentary around civil rights, emergency laws and other conflict-related issues and performed a limited amount of pro-bono work. However, these organizations withered on the vine after a few years in existence.[46] In addition, in the early 1980s a local human rights NGO, the Committee on the Administration of Justice (CAJ), was established, which included practising lawyers amongst its early membership. CAJ became one of the most internationally respected local human rights NGOs in the world.[47] Those important exceptions

---

[43] Stephen Livingstone *et al* (2007) above n 3. See also Stephen Livingstone, *'And Justice for All?: The Judiciary and the Legal Profession in Transition'* in Colin Harvey (ed.), *Human Rights, Equality and Democratic Renewal in Northern Ireland* (2001).

[44] As one barrister interviewed jokingly described it to us, ' . . . the law is the law is the law, no politics, no context, just law'. Interview, 25 August 2005.

[45] See John Jackson and Sean Doran, *Judge Without Jury: Diplock Trials in the Adversary System* (1995); Steven Greer, *Supergrasses: A Study in Anti-Terrorist Law Enforcement in Northern Ireland*; Kieran McEvoy, *What the Lawyers Did During the War: Critical Junctures in the Legal Culture of Northern Ireland* (2006), paper presented to Institute of Governance Queens University Belfast, 26 June 2006.

[46] The two most prominent of these were the Northern Ireland Society of Labour Lawyers in the late 1960s and early 1970s and the Northern Ireland Association of Socialist Lawyers established in 1980–1981. The contribution of both are analysed at length in Livingstone *et al* (2006) above n 3; and Kieran McEvoy (2006), ibid.

[47] Eitan Felner, *Human Rights Leaders in Conflict Zones* (2003).

aside however, Northern Ireland has seen nothing like the public and collective legal activism which characterized aspects of feminist mobilization associated with the development of the Charter in Canada and the anti-apartheid struggle in South Africa. That culture of 'quietism' was perhaps best highlighted by the response of the legal profession to the murder of two of its own members, defence solicitors, Pat Finucane and Rosemary Nelson.

The murder of Pat Finucane by the Ulster Defence Association was one of the most controversial killings of the Northern Ireland conflict. Although a number of other lawyers and judges were also murdered by paramilitaries,[48] it was the persistent allegations of State collusion in the Finucane killing which arguably gave this killing such national and international prominence. In claiming responsibility for the murder the UDA claimed that Mr Finucane was a member of the IRA, a claim hotly disputed by his family and colleagues and refuted by the RUC and by retired Canadian Supreme Court Judge Peter Cory in his investigation into whether a public inquiry should be conducted into the circumstances of his death.[49] Mr Finucane's murder took place in a context wherein a number of prominent lawyers involved in defending Republican suspects had become increasingly concerned about threats made by police officers.[50] Certainly the level of personal animosity felt by some police officers towards Finucane and other defence lawyers was viewed as shocking by one experienced officer from Great Britain.[51] While Finucane had originally viewed these threats as a means to get his clients to talk during interrogation, he had become more worried in the year immediately preceding his death, both by the consistency of what his clients were relating to him and by the fact that such vicarious intimidating tactics were

[48] At least 18 paramilitary attacks were carried out against the judiciary, resulting in the murder of two magistrates, two county court judges, and in 1987 the deaths of senior judge Lord Justice Gibson and his wife in a bomb planted by the IRA. Republicans were also responsible for the murder of Unionist politician and law lecturer Edgar Graham and the killing of one member of the Director of Public Prosecutions office, as well as a number of attempted attacks on DPP staff. As well as the Finucane and Nelson murders, Loyalists were also involved in the killing of Queens University law student and Sinn Féin activist, Sheena Campbell. See Colette Blair, *Judicial Appointments: Research Report* 5 (Criminal Justice Review of Northern Ireland, 29); Tim Pat Coogan, *The Troubles* (1995) 204; David McKittrick, Seamus Kelters, Brian Feeney, and Chris Thornton, *Lost Lives: The Stories of the Men, Women and Children Who Died Through the Northern Ireland Troubles* (1999).

[49] '. . . there is nothing in the RUC files which indicates that Patrick Finucane was a member of PIRA, the IRA, or the INLA. It is apparent that two of his brothers were members of Republican organizations but a man cannot be held responsible for the criminal acts of his brothers. If this were not so, history would have held Abel as guilty as his murderous brother Cain . . . The presiding coroner confirmed that: 'The police refute the claim that Mr Finucane was a member of PIRA. He was just another law-abiding citizen going about his professional duties in a professional manner. He was well known both inside and outside the legal profession. He was regarded in police circles as very professional and he discharged his duties with vigour and professionalism.' Judge Peter Cory, *Cory Collusion Inquiry Report: Patrick Finucane* (2004) 11.

[50] In their comprehensive report on the intimidation of defence lawyers in Northern Ireland, the US-based Lawyers Committee for Human Rights concluded that '. . . credible evidence suggests that Patrick Finucane's murder was simply the most heinous instance of systematic harassment of defense lawyers for simply doing their job'. Lawyers Committee for Human Rights, *Human Rights and Legal Defense in Northern Ireland* (1993) 25.   [51] See eg John Stalker, *Stalker* (1998) 49.

accompanied by threatening telephone calls.[52] Most infamously perhaps, his murder was also preceded by comments in the House of Commons by Parliamentary Under-Secretary of State, Douglas Hogg MP, the previous month that '... there are in Northern Ireland a number of solicitors who are unduly sympathetic to the cause of the IRA'.[53]

In addition to compelling evidence of State collusion,[54] the complacency of the Northern Ireland legal community has been the subject of much outrage and scrutiny. The Bar Council, apparently taking the view that RUC threats were directed solely against solicitors, said nothing.[55] In what was described by the New York-based Lawyers Committee on Human Rights as a 'tepid' response, the Law Society issued a statement condemning the murder, but did not follow this up with calls for an inquiry or measures to protect the independence of lawyers.[56] A public meeting was held shortly after the murder but no decision on official Law Society action resulted other than raising the matter privately with

[52] Amnesty International, *United Kingdom: Human Rights Concerns* (1991) 56; British Irish Rights Watch, *Intimidation of Defence Lawyers in Northern Ireland*, (1992a); British Irish Rights Watch *Intimidation of Defence Lawyers in Northern Ireland Update* (1992b).

[53] *Hansard*, House of Commons, Standing Committee B, 17 January 1989, col. 508. When challenged by the SDLP's Seamus Mallon, Mr Hogg repeated the allegation claiming, 'I state it on the basis of advice I have received, guidance that I have been given by people who are dealing with these matters and I shall not expand on it further.' Mallon later prophetically remarked in the debate, 'I have no doubt that there are lawyers walking the streets or driving on the roads of Northern Ireland who have become targets for assassins' bullets as a result of the statement that has been made tonight...' (*Hansard*, col. 519). Hogg subsequently admitted to the Guardian newspaper that his briefings came from the RUC (Guardian, 13 June 2001). The third of a series of enquiries conducted by former Metropolitan Chief Constable Sir John Stevens into this case and related allegations of collusion ultimately concluded that the Minister's comments were based on information provided by the RUC, and that '... they were not justifiable and that the Minister was compromised'. Sir John Stevens, *Stevens Enquiry 3: Overview and Recommendations* (2003 11).

[54] The intelligence which led to Finucane's murder was co-ordinated by Brian Nelson, a UDA member and Army's Force Research Unit agent. The principal weapon was supplied by another RUC Special Branch agent, William Stobie. Both Nelson and Stobie claimed that they had informed their respective handlers of the plan to kill Finucane. Ken Barrett, one of the prime actors recently convicted of the murder, was also an RUC informer. When Brian Nelson was arrested in 1990 and faced 34 charges including two counts of murder, the Attorney-General told the court that after 'a scrupulous assessment of the possible evidential difficulties and a rigorous examination of the interests of justice', 15 charges were to be dropped, including the two murders. These facts have been the subject of three investigations by the former Chief of the Metropolitan Police, Sir John Stevens, and an independent report by Judge Cory, both of whom found evidence that collusion had taken place. Judge Cory recommended public inquiries into this and three other cases. The British government announced the need for a new Inquiries Act to deal with the Finucane killing and subsequent Inquiries and indicated that because of the sensitivities of national security in this case, much of the Inquiry will have to be held in private. See Committee for the Administration of Justice (CAJ) *Additional Submission to the Criminal Justice Review (in relation to Patrick Finucane case)* (1999); British & Irish Rights Watch *Justice Delayed: Alleged State Collusion In The Murder of Patrick Finucane and others* (2000); John Stevens (2003) ibid; Lawyers Committee for Human Rights *Beyond Collusion: The UK Security Forces and the Murder of Patrick Finucane* (2003); Peter Cory, (2004) above n 49; Justin O' Brien, *Killing Finucane: Murder in Defence of the Realm* (2005).

[55] Stephen Livingstone (2001), above n 43.

[56] Lawyers Committee for Human Rights, (1993) above n 50, 61. In 2004 the Lawyers Committee for Human Rights changed its name to Human Rights First.

the authorities.[57] Even the early attention paid by international human rights groups clearly created a level of discomfiture amongst some members of the Law Society. As Executive Director Mike Posner of the Lawyers Committee for Human Rights recounted with regard to his organization's 1992 meeting with the Law Society:

'We came to Belfast and we saw the Bar Council and the Law Society, and the Law Society meeting I would say was actively hostile. I mean they were so uncomfortable that we were there; we had a very hard time trying to find somebody to talk to us. When we finally met this sort of administrator of the place who was just icy cold and we got an earful about how our members don't care about this and there's a few "types" that take these political cases and they know what they're getting themselves into . . . The more we got into it the worse it got in a way, and they were clearly not interested. So we walked out really disgusted with them and I think eventually on that trip we wound up seeing one of the lay leaders, one of the officers. He was a little more polite but he wouldn't meet us in the Law Society's headquarters; he met us in some place where nobody would see him and he said, "I sort of agree with some of the things you're saying but I can't really say it out loud".'[58]

The continued failure of the Law Society to either call for a public inquiry into the killing of Pat Finucane or to offer more fulsome public support to other lawyers subject to threats and harassment became a source of much criticism. The Lawyers Committee concluded in their 1993 report that, ' . . . we are left with the impression that, for a large part of the legal profession in Northern Ireland, the obligation of lawyers to assert fundamental human rights against abuses by the state is a low priority: and if not the legal profession, who will do so?'.[59] The UN Special Rapporteur for the Independence of Judges and Lawyers was even stronger. As well as supporting the call for an independent judicial inquiry into the killing and the allegations of collusion, he argued that the failure of both the Law Society and Bar Council to stand up in defence of their colleagues meant that they had failed to meet their professional obligations under Principle 25 of the UN Basic Principles on the Role of Lawyers.[60]

Throughout the 1990s the vocal criticism of the Lawyers Committee and the UN Special Rapporteur for the Independence of Judges and Lawyers and the calls for an independent inquiry into collusion by State forces in the Finucane killing was augmented by a range of influential national and international legal groupings. By 2002 these included Claire Palley (UK nominee to the UN Sub-Commission on the Prevention of Discrimination and the Protection of

[57] Lawyers Committee for Human Rights, *At the Crossroads: Human Rights and the Northern Ireland Peace Process* (1996).   [58] Interview with Mike Posner, 14 June 2002.

[59] Lawyers Committee for Human Rights (1993) above n 50, 41.

[60] Principle 25 states that ' . . . professional associations of lawyers shall cooperate with governments to ensure that everyone has effective and equal access to legal services and that lawyers are able, without improper interference, to counsel and assist their clients in accordance with the law and recognised professional standards and ethics'. See Param Cumaraswamy *Report of the Special Rapporteur on the Independence of Judges and Lawyers, Param Cumaraswamy, on a Mission to Great Britain and Northern Ireland* E/CN.4/1998/39/Add.4 (1998).

Minorities), Peter Burns (UK Rapporteur for the UN Committee Against Torture), Amnesty International, the International Federation of Human Rights, the UN Special Representative on Human Rights Defenders, Helsinki Watch, the International Commission of Jurists, the International Bar Association, the American Bar Association, and the New York Bar Association.[61] These international bodies were also joined by influential national and local organizations including Liberty, the Haldane Society, the Northern Ireland Standing Advisory Commission on Human Rights (SACHR), the Committee on the Administration of Justice, and British Irish Rights Watch.[62] The Finucane family, together with the law firm Madden and Finucane, in which Mr Finucane was a founding partner, also engaged in a long-running campaign to keep the case high on the political agenda through lobbying in the US, Britain, and Ireland, a poster and letter-writing campaign, and a number of legal actions including a case lodged at the European Court of Human Rights.[63]

Despite the considerable build-up of international pressure, the Law Society of Northern Ireland maintained its position of remaining 'neutral' on the question of calling for a public inquiry into the Finucane killing for over 10 years. That position was eventually reversed in an Extraordinary General Meeting of the Law Society in May 1999, which overturned the position of the Law Society's ruling council. That meeting took place two months after a second murder of a nationalist solicitor by Loyalist paramilitaries, also amidst widespread allegations of State collusion in her death.

Rosemary Nelson was a private practitioner based in Lurgan whose practice involved a mixture of civil, matrimonial, and criminal work. Following her involvement as the solicitor acting in a number of high-profile cases, in a similar fashion to Finucane, she began to record threats, including death threats from RUC officers via her clients.[64] Ironically, Rosemary Nelson was one of the 33 lawyers who had called for an independent inquiry into the Pat Finucane murder the previous January.[65]

What distinguished Rosemary Nelson was that as a result of these threats, and in particular in the light of the murder of Pat Finucane, she became the subject of a high-profile international and national campaign designed to highlight her plight. For example, in his 1998 report, the UN Special Rapporteur on the Independence of Judges and Lawyers, paid special attention to these death threats and, in a televized interview, suggested that Mrs Nelson's life could be in danger.[66] In September 1998 she gave evidence to an American Congressional Committee

---

[61] See Lawyers Committee (1996), above n 57; Lawyers Committee for Human Rights (2003), above n 54; and Geraldine Finucane, *The Long Road to Truth: PJ McGrory Memorial Lecture* (2004) for an overview.   [62] Geraldine Finucane, ibid.

[63] Interview, Belfast solicitor involved in the Finucane campaign, 21 February 2003. See also *Finucane v UK* (2003) 37 EHRR 29.   [64] Peter Cory (2004), above n 49.

[65] Statement issued by 33 lawyers, 14 January 1998, 'Equal Protection Under the Law'. Available at http:/www.serve.com/pfc.

[66] Param Cumaraswamy, *Report on the Mission of the Special Rapporteur to the United Kingdom of Great Britain and Northern Ireland, 5 March 1998*, E/CN.4/1998/39/Add.4. (1998).

reiterating her concern for her personal safety. Several organizations including Amnesty International, Lawyers Committee for Human Rights, British-Irish Rights Watch, and the Committee on the Administration of Justice wrote to the Northern Ireland Office and RUC, and made known their concerns for her safety. Despite that campaign, in March 1999 Rosemary Nelson was murdered by a group calling itself the 'Red Hand Defenders'.[67] Despite a much more commendable reaction by the legal establishment to the Nelson murder, given that the Extraordinary General Meeting of the Law Society which was to discuss both murders took place not long after the Nelson killing, feelings understandably continued to run high.

In May 1999 a group of 20 petitioners proposed three resolutions to the EGM: (1) to call for an independent inquiry into the circumstances surrounding the murder of Pat Finucane; (2) to call for an independent inquiry and investigation into the murder of Rosemary Nelson; and (3) to pass a motion of no confidence in the Council of the Law Society and to call for their immediate resignation.[68] The first motion was overwhelmingly carried, the second was also carried, but by a narrow majority of only nine votes,[69] and the third motion was defeated. Speaking after the vote, Law Society President Catherine Dixon said: 'I have never seen so many solicitors in my entire life. A third of our membership turned out and they all came out because these were big important and sensitive issues for them. We have espoused neutrality for 30 years but the Society has called for this so we must move with it.'[70] While some prominent Unionist solicitors criticized the political 'take over' of the Law Society,[71] Catherine Dixon herself commented on the 'constructive, sober and positive manner of the debate'.[72]

The additional voice of the Law Society calling for such an inquiry did not immediately tilt the political axis. During the Weston Park political negotiations in 2001, the British and Irish governments agreed to appoint a judge of international standing to investigate allegations of State collusion with terrorists in the deaths of Pat Finucane, Rosemary Nelson, and four other cases and that 'in the event that a Public Inquiry is recommended in any case, the relevant Government will implement that recommendation'.[73] Former Canadian Supreme Court Judge

[67] Peter Cory (2004), above n 49.

[68] The petitioners also issued a press release stating, 'On March 11th the Council of the Law Society declined to support a call for an independent inquiry into the murder of Pat Finucane and the signatories of the petition feel that this view is unrepresentative of the feelings of the profession as a whole. The petitioners feel that it is astounding that the society, of which Pat Finucane was a member, is the only professional lawyers association in these islands that is refusing to endorse legitimate calls for an inquiry.' Irish News, 1 May 1999, 'Solicitors Insist Law Society Council Resigns'; 'Lawyers' Society Facing Turmoil: Resign Demand to Officers at Crunch Meeting', Belfast Telegraph, 11 May 1999.

[69] Many of those present argued that given the investigation into Rosemary Nelson's death was a mere two months old, it was perhaps premature to call for an independent inquiry at such an early stage. Interview with Solicitor, 14 February 2002.

[70] 'Law Society U-turn over Nelson Death', Irish News, 12 May 1999.

[71] Ms Arlene Foster MLA in Belfast Telegraph, 12 May 1999, 'Unionists Hit Out As Law Society Backs Probe'.

[72] 'NI Solicitors Overturn Council's Decision on Finucane Inquiry', *The Irish Times*, 12 May 1999.

[73] http://cain.ulst.ac.uk/events/peace/docs/bi010801.htm, para 19.

Peter Cory was appointed in May 2002 and delivered his findings in October 2003. In five of the six cases, including Finucane and Nelson, Cory found evidence of collusion and recommended public inquiries.[74] The establishment of the Finucane inquiry was originally delayed by ongoing police investigations. These obstacles were ultimately cleared with the conviction of UDA man and Special Branch informer, Ken Barrett, in September 2004 for his part in the murder.[75] The three other inquiries in Northern Ireland (including Nelson) were established with powers of subpoena equal to those of the Bloody Sunday Tribunal.[76] In April 2005, the British government introduced new legislation under which it said the Pat Finucane inquiry would be established. On 7 April 2005 less than a week after the publication of the Cory reports and on the final day of session before Parliament closed—the government pushed through the repeal of the Tribunals of Enquiry (Evidence) Act 1921 (under which public inquiries such as the Bloody Sunday Tribunal had previously been established and which gave such tribunals the same evidential power as the High Court) and passed the Inquiries Act 2005. As is discussed in this volume by Anthony and Mageaan (Chapter 10), that Act arguably marks a significant move towards executive control over many aspects of a public inquiry. The legislation has been opposed by many of the organizations and institutions who have been long involved in the Finucane case, by Judge Cory himself and by Lord Saville, the current chairman of the Bloody Sunday Inquiry.[77] The Finucane family have continued to insist that they will not take part in an inquiry established under the terms outlined in the Inquiries Act.[78] Their campaign continues.

While the Law Society EGM may not have had an immediate political effect, it was self-evidently an important 'moment' in the legal history of Northern Ireland. In interviews with those who were at the meeting that night, it was clear that something historical was taking place. While the evening was not without its heated moments and some clear sectarian overtones,[79] those who made the arguments concerning the need for independent inquiries continuously stressed the

---

[74] Judge Cory defined collusion as the State security services 'ignoring or turning a blind eye to the wrongful acts of their servants or agents or supplying information to assist them in their wrongful acts or encouraging them to commit wrongful acts' (above n 49, at p 21).

[75] 'Finucane's Killer Jailed Amid Clamour for Inquiry', The Guardian, 17 September 2004.

[76] The Billy Wright Inquiry was established under the Prison Act (Northern Ireland) Act 1953. The Robert Hamill and Rosemary Nelson Inquiries were established under the Police (Northern Ireland) Act 1998. However, the Wright Inquiry has since been redesignated to operate under the Inquiries Act.

[77] In a strongly worded letter to Baroness Ashton, Minister of the Department of Constitutional Affairs, Lord Saville, argued that the erosion of the powers of a Tribunal Chairman, previously established under the 1921 Act '... makes a very serious inroad into the independence of any inquiry; and is likely to damage or destroy public confidence in the inquiry and its findings, especially in any case where the conduct of the authorities may be in question.... As a judge, I must tell you that I would not be prepared to be appointed as a member of an inquiry that was subject to a provision of this kind.' 'Finucane Widow Urges Judges to Shun Inquiry', The Guardian, 14 April 2005.

[78] 'Family Reject Legislation', 26 November 2004, Press Release, available at http://www.serve.com/pfc/pf/inqubill/041126pf.html.

[79] 'Northern Solicitors Demand Inquiries', Sunday Tribune, 16 May 1999.

point that the matters at hand were human rights concerns. While one solicitor made the argument that the demographic changes to the solicitors' profession had a considerable impact on the vote,[80] most of those we interviewed agreed that voting on the three resolutions did not split along sectarian lines. As one solicitor stated, the real recognition of the legal profession was, 'that [calling for an inquiry into the murder of defence lawyers] was a human rights issue concerning a member of the Law Society and as such one which the Society could not fail to take a position on'.[81] Certainly the human rights framework facilitated lawyers in debating a difficult and sensitive topic in a reasonably mature and considered fashion. The traditional refrain that the call for inquiries into State collusion was too 'political',[82] or that the Law Society would split on sectarian grounds on the issue proved groundless.[83] Politically, however, internationalizing the campaign was absolutely crucial in shifting the position of the Law Society. Time and again lawyers interviewed for this research spoke of the sense of embarrassment, discomfort and pressure on the Law Society from such a cacophony of international legal voices. In such a context the Northern Ireland Law Society's silence on the death of two of its own members became deafening and ultimately untenable.

Of course the internationalization of the Finucane campaign for a public inquiry was but one part of a broader strategy which saw the Law Society shift its position. Criminal practitioners who had long felt isolated from the mainstream of the bulk of solicitors who ran the Law Society had begun to use their own committees and groupings within the Law Society structure as a platform for mobilization on this and other issues.[84] Two months before the EGM one prominent criminal practitioner, Barra McGrory, himself a target of death threats from the police and Loyalist paramilitaries similar to those that had preceded the Finucane and Nelson killings, took an unsuccessful judicial review action against the President of the Law Society.[85] The sobering reality should also be noted that,

---

[80] Interview with Solicitor, 25 November 2002.

[81] Interview with Solicitor, 21 February 2003.

[82] As the Law Society spokesperson interviewed for this research suggested, 'Well, at that time, it was felt that there was an overtly political dimension to all of this but some of our members took a different view...' Interview, 13 December 2002.

[83] For further analysis concerning the utility of the human rights framework in this regard, see Kieran McEvoy (2006) above n 45. The significance of the move by the Law Society was not lost on those who had been involved in the Finucane Campaign for several years. For example, Amnesty International described it as 'an historic step forward in the impartial defence of human rights in Northern Ireland'. 'Amnesty Shocked at Rights Failures', Irish News, 17 October 1999.

[84] Interview, Belfast Solicitor, 25 November 2002. One other criminal practitioner described the rationale for the creation of one such grouping (the Criminal Bar Association) thus, 'Everyone in that association is a member of the Law Society but really I think you can take it that if the criminal lawyers had felt that their interests would be fully ventilated and protected by the Law Society there would never have been any need for it.' Interview, Belfast Solicitor, 21 February 2003.

[85] McGrory was chairman of the Human Rights Committee of the Law Society and he challenged the refusal by the Law Society President and two senior office bearers to allow the committee, that he chaired, to consider a recently published report by a prominent NGO into the allegations of

in common with human rights defenders in many parts of the world,[86] the internationalization strategy which contributed to raising the domestic profile of Rosemary Nelson had its risks—it failed to protect Mrs Nelson from her assassins' bomb. With those caveats in mind however, it must be recognized that it con-tributed significantly to shifting the institutional position of a very conservative legal organization—an organization which some who had been heavily involved in the Finucane case for years had long viewed as hardly worth the effort.[87] It facilitated the Law Society of Northern Ireland in becoming, albeit belatedly, a voice of the collective conscience of a legal community speaking out against the killing of two of its own members in circumstances which suggested State collu-sion warranted an independent public inquiry. In ending that shameful organiza-tional silence, it also removed any final vestige of respectability to the suggestion that there was a view amongst Pat Finucane's fellow professionals that perhaps there was 'no smoke without fire' regarding his killers' allegations that he was a member of the IRA.

Drafting the Charter: Women's Mobilization and the Collective Legal Conscience in Canada

'The greatest achievement of the women's constitutional struggle may not have been the rewriting of the law, but the process of strengthening mass collective action whereby the anger of women crystallized into law.'[88]

Like South Africa, Canada's constitutional law underwent dramatic transform-ation with introduction of a new constitution that moved from a system of parliamentary sovereignty to a constitutionalism that emphasized entrenched rights—the Canadian Charter of Rights and Freedoms (the Charter) in 1982.[89]

---

collusion in the Finucane killing. The proceedings were abandoned when a full Council meeting of the Law Society was called which upheld the refusal to allow the Human Rights Committee to dis-cuss the relevant document. 'Law Body Blocking Report on Finucane', Irish News, 10 March 1999; 'NI Law Society Officers Trying to Stop Study of Murder Report', Irish Times, 10 March 1999; 'Lawyers Slam Finucane Hush-Up', Irish News, 12 March 1999; 'Law Society to Ignore Finucane Report', Irish News, 16 March 1999.

[86] UN Commission on Human Rights, *Promotion And Protection Of Human Rights Human Rights Defenders: Report Of The Special Representative Of The Secretary-General, Hina Jilani* (2004).

[87] 'Well you see my own view was that I didn't really expect the Law Society as a body to do any-thing, . . . so I wasn't really concentrating that much on the Law Society to be honest with you. Other people were more concerned about that, in fact other solicitors that I knew were more incensed about the fact that this wasn't happening than I was. I was sort of taking a view well look, we've got every other human rights and legal group in the world taking an interest in this and it didn't matter for me too much that the Law Society as a body wasn't supporting it. . . . I was sort of shrugging my shoulders, sort of saying "well look you know that is the type of body it is".' Interview, Belfast Solicitor, 21 February 2003.

[88] Judy Fudge, *The Effect of Entrenching a Bill of Rights Upon Political Discourse: Feminist Demands and Sexual Violence in Canada*, 17 International Journal of the Society of Law 445, 448 (1989).

[89] See generally Robert Sharpe and Kent Roach, *The Charter of Rights and Freedoms* (3rd ed., 2005); Donald Abelson, Patrick James, and Michael Lusztig, *The Myth of the Sacred: The Charter, the Courts,*

The language of the Charter was the subject of intense negotiations as legal scholars, practitioners, and activists sought to carve out a new role for themselves within a transformed constitutional order. For those invested in seeking equal status and equal benefits for all Canadians, the Charter was an opportunity to systematically revise how law afforded protection and access to resources to previously disadvantaged groups. Thus, feminist groups, childrens' advocates, first nations organizations, language lobbyists, gay rights groups, and a range of others were involved in a lively and spirited process to maximize rights protections for their and other constituencies.[90]

What is of particular interest for this essay is the ways in which feminist lawyers organized in seeking to influence the drafting of the equality provisions of the Charter. The first draft of the Charter included a vague right to equality and did not include a right to sex equality.[91] Yet when the process of drafting the Charter concluded in April 1982, the Charter was one of the most progressive constitutions in the world.[92] The women's movement, lawyers as well as activists, employed innovative, collective methods to lobby for equality rights.[93] In particular, we were struck in the Canadian context with the ways in which feminist lawyers circumnavigated the male-dominated realms of the legal elite professional organizations, such as the Law Society and Bar Association, and instead adopted a strategy of *mobilization* beyond the legal community.[94] In the Canadian context, the critical juncture for the Canadian legal feminist movement was its decision to work outside of the litigation system and focus its energies on creating popular support for women's rights. Of course, once successful, women activists would find it another struggle to sustain the hard-fought ground of the Charter within the litigation system they circumvented.[95]

Despite Canada's generally positive national and international image (which is inevitably juxtaposed to their neighbours to the south for good and ill),[96] pre-Charter Canadian legal culture was little different than most common law countries, where laws restricted women's participation in public life, prohibited the

and the Politics of the Constitution in Canada (2002); Philip Bryden and Stephen Davis (eds) *Protecting Rights and Freedoms: Essays on the Charter's Place in Canada's Political, Legal, and Intellectual Life* (1994).

[90] eg Rhadda Jhappan (ed.) *Womens' Legal Strategies in Canada* (2002); Katherine Covell and Brian Howe, *The Challenge of Children's Rights for Canada* (2001); Patrick Macklem, *Indigenous Difference and the Constitution of Canada* (2002); Jeremy Webber, *Reimagining Canada: Language, Culture, Community and the Canadian Constitution* (1994); Kathleen Lahey, *Are We Persons Yet: Law and Sexuality in Canada* (1999).

[91] Dale Gibson, *The Law of the Charter: Equality Rights* (2001); Ian Binnie 'Equality Rights in Canada: Judicial Usurpation or Missed Opportunity?' In Grant Huscroft and Paul Rishworth (eds), *Litigating Rights* (2002).   [92] See Sharpe and Roach, above n 89.

[93] Penny Kome, *The Taking of Twenty-Eight: Women Challenge the Constitution* (1983).

[94] Sheila McIntyre, 'Feminist Movement in Law: Beyond Privileged and Privileging Theory' in Jamman (ed.) (2002) above n 90.

[95] Gwen Brodsky and Shelagh Day, *Canadian Charter Equality Rights for Women: One Step Forward or Two Steps Back?* (1989).

[96] Seymour Lipset, *Continental Divide: The Values and Institutions of the United States and Canada* (1990).

ownership of private property and excluded women from professional life well
into the twentieth century.[97] For example, it was only in 1930 that the Privy
Council, sitting in London, held that the term 'person' which was a Canadian
requirement for standing for election, also included women.[98] After divorce,
fathers traditionally had legal authority over their children and custody was allocated accordingly.[99] The first significant overhaul of Canadian rape law in the
twentieth century did not occur until 1983 when a range of evidential requirements (eg the corroboration rule, the admissibility of evidence of 'general sexual
reputation' and the marital rape exception) were modified in order to make successful prosecutions more feasible.[100] As one feminist lawyer interviewed for this
research suggested to the authors, 'I know Canada has this reputation as a liberal
enclave where the rights of women and other traditionally discriminated against
groups are well protected. Let me tell you, Canada was no different. Any progress
that has been made on women's rights here has been hard won through blood,
sweat and tears.'[101]

Perhaps unsurprisingly, the legal profession historically reflected the subordinate position of women more generally in society. Change occurred early in the
twentieth century when individual women lobbied provincial legislatures to force
law societies to admit women.[102] As in South Africa, Canadian law societies are
self-regulating monopolies of legal practice. Lawyers were affiliated, but not
bound, by the policies of national organizations like the Canadian Bar Association
and province-based law societies. Legal professional organizations formed to protect their members' interests from government interference in a familiar exchange.
These self-regulating organizations could justify the power conferred upon them
by the State (a monopoly over the delivery of legal services) in exchange for regulating the competence and admission of legal practitioners.[103] Until the last 50
years, those members were exclusively men and it behoved an elite profession to
limit the admission to it. In this regard, a key historical role of Canadian law
societies, as elsewhere, was to exclude those believed to be of lesser character or less
suited to law (in this case, women).[104] When individual petitions to provincial
legislatures proved successful and a few women gained access to the profession,
law societies changed education requirements so that women would find it more
difficult to qualify for practice.[105]

---

[97] Diana Marjury, 'Women's (In)Equality Before and After the Charter' in Japphan (ed.) above,
n 90; Lyn Smith and Eleanor Wachtel, *A Feminist Guide to the Canadian Constitution* (1992) 45–46.
[98] *Edwards v AG of Canada* [1930] AC 124 ('The Persons Case').
[99] Marjury above, n 97, 105.
[100] See Maria Ros, 'The Struggle to Redefine Rape in the 1980s' in Julian Roberts and Renate Mohr
(eds), *Confronting Sexual Assault* (1984).   [101] Interview with Mary Ebert, 21 June 2002.
[102] Fiona Kay and Joan Brockman, 'Barriers to Gender Equality in the Canadian Legal Establishment,' Ulrike Schultz and Gisela Shaw, (eds), *Women and the World's Legal Professions* (2003) 52–53.
[103] Joan Brockman, *The Use of Self-Regulation to Curb Discrimination and Sexual Harassment in the
Legal Profession* (1997) 35 Osgood Hall Law Journal 209, 213.
[104] Joan Brockman (1997) ibid. 215.
[105] Kay and Brockman (2003) above, n 102, 53.

Despite the repeal of laws that banned women from the practice of law out-right, women continued to be excluded in practice from the legal profession well into the 1980s. For example, in 1971 only 5 per cent of lawyers were women. By 1981 this had risen to a mere 15 per cent.[106] With lesser numbers, and a powerful male-dominated organizational culture, women struggled to have issues of gender discrimination taken seriously by the legal profession. Before the Charter (and well into its life), law societies responded to sexism with unenforceable policy guidelines relating to how firms should change their conduct towards women.[107] This disadvantage suggests that women within the legal profession (and thus within legal professional organizations) already worked within a climate where their authority and competence was undermined. Under such continued conditions, women as potential agents of change faced an uphill battle in convincing trad-itional institutions like law societies to challenge the status quo.[108] Without such questioning from 'plausible' sources from within, the legal profession in the pre-Charter era largely continued to ignore women's multiple realities and failed to award credibility to such 'outsiders' stories.[109]

Finding limited gains from work within legal professional organizations or within the legal profession, groups of feminists including feminist lawyers focused considerable energy *outside* the legal profession such as in grassroots and charitable organizations.[110] In collecting and commemorating the stories of everyday women, a burgeoning women's movement began a process of making women's experiences 'mainstream' and women lawyers became prominent in that broader movement.[111] This modern, and more national, women's movement took shape in 1978 when the Canadian Parliament considered delegating the regulation of divorce to Canadian provinces. The Canadian Supreme Court had recently upheld a divorce decree of an Alberta provincial court that stripped a wife of ownership of a ranch she and her husband had worked jointly. In *Murdoch*, the Alberta court held that the wife had no legal rights to the ranch upon divorce because her name was not on the deed.[112] In response to Parliament's divorce proposals, women collected petitions and held public meetings against divorce reform.[113] The Parliament withdrew its proposals on divorce.

---

[106] ibid.

[107] Joan Brockman, *Gender in the Legal Profession: Fitting or Breaking the Mould* (2001).

[108] Regina Graycar, '*The Gender of Judgments: Some Reflections on "Bias,"* (1998) 32 University of British Columbia Law Review 1, 3. Graycar argues that the process of 'letting women in' the legal profession presupposes a position of marginalization. This is seen in the ways that 'gender' is defined—it is only used when we are talking about women: 'The word does not appear in an all male context, the gender of participants there being seemingly invisible.'   [109] Graycar, ibid, 19.

[110] Lynn Smith and Eleanor Wachtel, *A Feminist Guide to the Canadian Constitution* CACSW: ISBN 0662197852, August 1992, 45.

[111] Sherene Razack *Canadian Feminism and the Law: The Womens Legal Education and Action Fund and the Pursuit of Equality* (1991).   [112] *Murdoch v Murdoch* [1975] 1 SCR 423.

[113] Doris Anderson, popularly conceived as the leader of these efforts, was also the long-time editor of *Chatelaine*, a hugely popular women's magazine. Doris Anderson and the magazine would become essential in the first stages of women's organization with respect to the Charter. Starting in the late 1960s, Doris used the magazine to raise women's interest in gender equality.

Activism around the divorce issue achieved two important results. First, it created a small network of advocates who learned the skills necessary for lobbying the
federal government.[114] Because this network was successful in drawing public
attention to women's rights, the government created the Canadian Advisory
Council on the Status of Women (CACSW). Second, this network of women
believed that changing the existing and widely discredited Bill of Rights was the
first step to better protecting equality rights and thus better protecting women's
rights.[115] For example, in the *Bliss* case (1978), the Canadian Supreme Court held
that an employment policy denying pregnant women equal compensation was
not discriminatory because it treated all pregnant women the same and made no
distinction between male and females. As was happening in the US around the
Equal Rights Amendment, lawyers decided that amassing public support for
strong equality rights in the Charter would help them secure stronger women's
rights and women's rights consciousness, which could ultimately undo decisions
like *Bliss*.[116]

This move—reliance on popular pressure to change the law rather than litigating under the law—would characterize the movement's Charter campaign. As
Beth Symes, a prominent barrister in the movement, told the authors:

'It was literally going across Canada and speaking to whoever would hear us. We spoke to
farm women, we spoke in church basements, in trade unions—we spoke to an incredible
array of women and what was astonishing is how well it was received. People had the most
galvanizing stories about discrimination in their own lives.'[117]

While the focus of these feminist lawyers was primarily beyond the legal arena,
they nonetheless took advantage of the professional resources at their disposal. For
example, they made liberal use of the supplies and mail offices of their firms to
inundate Members of Parliament with letters and telephone calls. As another
lawyer recalled, 'The major law firms had no idea of their contribution to the
women's movement.'[118] These lawyers made similar use of whatever political
facilities they could get access to, including the congressional administrative
facilities of the few woman MPs. Beth Symes recalled:

'The few female members of Parliament opened their doors to us and every evening
women poured in to use parliamentary resources—we used the phones, mail, and copy

---

[114] Anne McLellan, 'Women and the Process of Constitution-Making' in *Conversations Among
Friends: Proceeding on an Interdisciplinary Conference on Women and Constitutional Reform* (ed.), Ed
David Schniederman (Centre of Constitutional Studies, Alberta Law Foundation: 1991) 10.
Women, and particularly women lawyers, organized along provincial lines to change bar admission
laws and other province-specific policies. The divorce campaign was an opportunity to organize on
the national level.
[115] As Sharpe and Roach, above n 89, 278, '... the courts performance under the Bill of Rights
was generally regarded as a disappointment'.
[116] Mary Eberts, 'Sex Based Discrimination and the Charter', *in* Anne Bayefsky and Mary Eberts
(eds), *Equality Rights and the Canadian Charter of Rights and Freedoms* (1985).
[117] Interview with Beth Symes, 21 June 2002.
[118] Interview with Mary Ebert, 21 June 2002.

machines. We spent so much time there that the guards mistook us for MP staffers. So when we arranged the conference on the draft Charter in 1981, we could hand out invitations personally to members in the halls—just walk up to them in the voting halls as if we worked for them!'

While their publicity campaign gained momentum, some remained sceptical that a Charter would actually produce enforceable equality rights in the context of a traditionally conservative bar and judiciary. Some feminists and others were fearful of creating a Charter that could not be repealed and the potential power of the judges under such a Charter. The disagreement caused a major split in Charter activists, causing some to abandon a constitutional project altogether. The pro-Charter movement quickly solidified, however, following the Government's unexpected cancellation of a national event on women and the constitutional drafting process. The pro-Charter wing of CACSW formed the Ad Hoc Conference of Canadian Women[119] which took on the mantle of planning the conference and using it as a platform to lobby Parliament for stronger equality rights.[120] Following the conference, Mary Eberts and Beverly Baines drafted a 'revised' Charter to present to Parliament. Conference delegates demanded that the Charter not only recognize 'equality under the law' but also 'equality before the law' and 'equal benefit of the law'. The Ad Hoc Conference called for the Charter to include a clear statement of equality between men and women. This separate right to sex equality would emphasize the importance of ending sexism in post-Charter Canada.[121] Parliament revised the equality provision to include rights to substantive equality. Section 15(1) of the Charter now reads:

'Every individual is equal before and under the law and has the right to the equal protection and equal benefit of the law without discrimination and, in particular, without discrimination based on race, national or ethnic origin, colour, religion, sex, age or mental or physical disability.'[122]

[119] Diana Majury, 'Women's (In)Equality before and after the Charter' in *Women's Legal Strategies in Canada*, (ed.) Radha Jhappan (2002).
[120] At the conference, a participant asked then Minister of Justice Jean Chrétien what type of equality rights he thought the Charter should include. Chretien famously answered 'Listen ladies, you will just have to trust me—we know what we're doing.' His response provoked predictable outrage. Mary Eberts Interview, 21 June 2002.
[121] Radha Jhappan, 'Appendix VII: Summary of the Resolutions Passed at the Ad Hoc Conference on Women and the Constitution, February 14 and 15, 1981' in Jhappan (ed.) (2002), above, n 119, 634–44. The Conference also recommended a right to reproductive freedom, a right to equality of economic opportunity and a non-discrimination statement that banned discrimination on the grounds of marital status, sexual orientation, and political belief that did not ultimately appear in the next draft of the Charter.
[122] As Sharpe and Roach, above, n 89, explain 279 'The insistence in the careful wording of section 15 that the guarantee includes equality before and under the law as well as equal protection and equal benefit of the law was meant to signal to the courts that section 15 was intended to be a much more powerful instrument of protection than its predecessor. In particular, the reference to equal protection echoed the Fourteenth Amendment to the US Constitution which had proved to be a powerful tool in the fight against racial discrimination . . . .the explicit protection in section 15 (2) of programs designed to ameliorate the conditions of disadvantaged individuals is intended to ensure that legislatures will not be discouraged from taking affirmative measures to enhance equality.'

As a result of women's lobbying efforts, Parliament also included a specific guarantee for equality between men and women. The draft subsequent to the final version allowed the legislature to suspend this right if necessary. After another round of lobbying, the exception was removed. Section 28 of the Charter reads:

'Notwithstanding anything in this Charter, the rights and freedoms referred to in it are guaranteed equally to male and female persons.'

For many, Section 28 signified an acknowledgement that 'the basis of all groups are men and women'.[123] Beverly Baines has argued, in thinking about the effect of the Charter, that the gender equality provision had an effect in terms of 'naming male privilege': 'Charter litigation provides a vehicle for women to name "objective" reality for what it is, a world organized consistently with male practices and beliefs.'[124] So whereas cases have not been litigated under Section 28, its language may have strengthened Section 15 rights indirectly by underscoring the importance of gender equality. The passage of Section 28 was heralded as a symbol of success for the women's movement because the constitutional recognition of gender equality meant success regarding one of the movement's primary goals, making gender concerns an issue of national concern.

The equality provisions did not come into effect for three years after Parliament ratified the Charter in April 1982. Parliament designed the delay to allow the government to amend existing laws as to be compatible with the new equality rights. In response, women's rights lawyers focused on three main activities: organizing a major conference on how the Charter would change existing law; writing a book about equality rights; and starting a new organization that would pursue Charter litigation and education—the Legal Education and Advocacy Fund (LEAF). When federal and provincial governments were slow to repeal discriminatory laws during the three-year period, LEAF filed lawsuits the first day that the equality provisions became active. In many ways, the creation of LEAF and its accompanying litigation strategy marked a new era for the women's rights movement in Canada. A movement which had relied on popular consent to meet its objectives now turned to a litigation strategy.[125]

While the mobilization and lobbying which led up to the Charter and the passage of the Charter itself with its strong equality Sections should rightly be regarded as a significant moment in Canadian political and legal history, it would be wrong to convey the impression that those involved in the struggle for equality in Canada were entirely victorious. While early litigation suggested promising results,[126] and LEAF's pursuance of section 15 litigation has been

---

[123] Anne McLellan, *Women and the Process of Constitutional Reform. A Discussion Paper Prepared for the Alberta Advisory Council on Women's Issues* (Edmonton: May 1991) 14; Jhappan, above, n 119, 634.
[124] Beverley Baines, '*Using the Canadian Charter of Rights and Freedoms*', in Beverly Baines and Ruth Rubio-Marin (eds) (2005) *The Gender of Constitutional Jurisprudence*, 54.
[125] Manfredi (2004), above n 42.
[126] *Andrews v The Law Society of Upper Canada* [1989] 1 SCR 143. This case concerned a male British lawyer who argued that restricting the practice of law to Canadian citizens violated his equality

widely discussed and applauded,[127] the consequences for women of Section 15 litigation is less than clear and hotly contested within the Canadian legal community.[128] Judy Fudge and Beverly Baines have suggested that while the inclusion of equality rights in Canada's Charter was heralded as a political victory, the actual results of Charter litigation have been mixed.[129] Litigation of Charter rights has yet to make meaningful gains in reducing the feminization of poverty.[130] Cases regarding income tax breaks and child care deductions—cases designed to put more money in women's pockets—have not been successful under equality provisions.[131] In addition, equality rights have been brought in many cases on behalf of men and not necessarily to further women's interests. Of 591 cases decided during first three years, less than 10 per cent were based on sex, 35 of which were brought by or on behalf of men.[132] Male defendants have sought to invoke equality and fair trial rights to strike down aspects of previous sexual assault legislation.[133] As a result, and perhaps inevitably, feminist organizations are spending time and resources in the courts defending legislation that it took many years to pass.

Similarly, within the ranks of the legal profession itself, the profession that feminist lawyers by and large chose to circumnavigate in pursuing their mobilization strategy, change comes slowly. Some feminist lawyers have made inroads into the upper echelons of these traditionally male-dominated domains.[134] Law societies, such as in Ontario, have established an equity office with quite a wide remit to tackle discrimination in the professions.[135] That said, women still

rights under the Charter on the basis of citizenship. LEAF intervened in the case and the Canadian Supreme Court ruled that the purpose of section 15 is to benefit those who have been historically disadvantaged. This decision meant that s 15 would be interpreted in the way that activists intended: not only should similarly situated people be treated alike, but also that the special needs of disadvantaged groups should be considered in the context of their unique position.

[127] See Christopher Manfredi above n 42.

[128] See Bruce Porter, *Twenty Years of Equality Rights: Reclaiming Expectations*, 23 Windsor Year book Access Justice 145 (2005); Rosanna Langer, *Five Years of Canadian Feminist Advocacy: Is It Still Possible To Make a Difference?*, 23 Windsor Year Book Access Justice 115 (2005); Majury, (2002), above n 119, 110.

[129] Fudge, above, 88, 445. [130] Baines, above, n 124, 72. [131] ibid.

[132] ibid, 52. [133] ibid, 451.

[134] Moore notes that '... while in 1987 women were about one fifth of practising lawyers, only 3 women were amongst the 40 "benchers" who made policy for the Law Society of Upper Canada. By 1995 first time candidate Mary Eberts topped the poll and women became a third of elected benchers, actually ahead of their proportion in the profession ... the core of this new caucus was female, but more than gender divided it from the old guard. "I was elected, I suspect, by lawyers who feel excluded from the Law Society and who serve clients who feel excluded from power" said one of them, family law practitioner Carole Curtis.' Christopher Moore *The Law Society of Upper Canada and Ontario's Lawyers: 1797–1997* (1997) 319–20.

[135] The mandates of these programs are variously conceived but are primarily concerned with issues such as: the diversity of the profession; employment equity initiatives within law firms; the development and implementation of workplace policies on discrimination and harassment; advice and support on the appropriate workplace accommodation for lawyers with special needs; offering training programs on equity and diversity; delivering public education; providing mentoring programs; and in some cases, community outreach and the like. See Rosemary Cairns Way, *Reconceptualizing Professional Responsibility: Incorporating Equality* (2002) 25 Dalhousie Law Journal 27.

face formidable obstacles. In 1993 Justice Bertha Wilson produced a report for the Canadian Bar Association that listed what she referred to as a 'somewhat numbing' list of barriers to women in the legal profession.[136] Similarly Joan Brockman's study of female lawyers in British Columbia found that women in the legal profession continue to face gender bias and gendered obstacles to the practice of law.[137] Women continue to be the primary caregivers of children, interrupting the pursuit of a partnership or disabling women from accruing seniority on the job because of time taken for childcare.[138] Of the women Brockman interviewed, 36 per cent reported being the targets of sexual harassment.[139] The more formal attempts of law societies to respond to gender concerns appear empty without resources or support of law firms. As Brockman concludes, '. . . despite ongoing attempts to educate firms about human rights and diversity, it continues to be as nightmarish an experience for students from equality-seeking communities as it was twenty years ago'.[140]

An awareness of the ongoing struggles to achieve real equality should not, however, detract from the achievements of those women who took the decision to go around their professional bodies, thus circumventing the male-dominated structures which were unresponsive to the ways in which law excluded them. Their activism on a popular level was incredibly important in changing institutional language regarding cultural receptiveness to sex equality. It made gender and other forms of equality in Canada become an intrinsic and impossible-to-ignore element of what Jeremy Webber has described as 'the Canadian Conversation'.[141] Inevitably that movement now seeks to gain ground in infusing a language of rights with the resources and substance that make it more applicable to women's lives. Following mobilization, they have become increasingly involved in the drawn-out business of legislation, litigation, and ultimately trying to transform their own professional bodies from within. It is at this juncture that the strategy of Canadian feminists meets the problems of legal reform that this essay has traced; namely, how the rule of law may actually become responsive to the experiences of marginalized groups; and perhaps more importantly, how a movement should deal with the vestiges of a legal system it worked so hard to change.

Acknowledging the Past and the Collective Legal Conscience in South Africa

The particular configurations of South African legal culture and the relationship between that culture and the development of the Apartheid regime has been well

---

[136] These included: sexual harassment; salary differentials; difficulties in obtaining articles; problems with work allocation; problems with promotion, including partnerships; segregation into certain areas of practice; and an unwillingness to accommodate female parents with family responsibilities. See Bertha Wilson *Touchstones for Change: Equality, Diversity and Accountability* (1993).

[137] Brockman (2001), above n 107.   [138] ibid, 213.   [139] ibid, 114–15.

[140] ibid, 41.   [141] Jeremy Webber (1994), above n 310.

documented.[142] As the South African Truth and Reconciliation Commission (TRC) verified in impressive detail, quite apart from the invidious and well-recorded outcomes of racial discrimination, detainees or suspected enemies of the State were regularly tortured or killed by the security forces, and State-sponsored assassinations and murders occurred throughout the Apartheid years (and particularly as the regime began to unravel).[143] The Commission did not only focus on those perpetrators and victims at the sharp end of the Apartheid regime. It also included an examination of the work of a range of institutions including business, labour, various government departments and, most interesting for current purposes, the judiciary and the legal profession.[144] Before we examine the background to a particular critical juncture (the disbarment of Bram Fischer) and the accounts given by the legal profession to the TRC in relation to it, it might be useful to offer some background to the particularities of South African legal culture.

The Apartheid system was not only unjust, it was also highly legalistic.[145] The chosen methods to achieve a societal hierarchy and the physical control of the living and working spaces of South African citizens based on racial categorization were primarily legal and bureaucratic.[146] As Joseph Lelyveld has argued, South Africa's white rulers were '…unusually conscientious about securing statutory authority for their abuses'.[147] Until the Apartheid regime began to disintegrate, its oppressive power was characteristically imposed '…not by the random terror of the death squad but by the routine and systematic processes of courts and bureaucrats'.[148] As Stephen Ellman demonstrates meticulously with regard to the emergency law regime in South Africa, the manifest injustice of Apartheid did not necessarily imply lawlessness.[149] Rather, the architects and supporters of white supremacist South Africa had a number of practical and ideological reasons for their apparent adherence to law.

---

[142] See eg Hugh Corder, *Judges at Work: The Role and Attitudes of the South African Appellate Judiciary 1910–1950* (1998) and (ed.) *Essays in Law and Social Practice* (1988); Christopher Forsyth, *In Danger for their Talents: A Study of the Appellate Division of the Supreme Court of South Africa from 1950–80* (1985); David Dyzenhaus, *Hard Cases in Wicked Legal Systems: South African Law in the Perspective of Legal Philosophy* (1991); Karl Klare, 'Legal Culture and Transformative Constitutionalism.' (1998) 4 South African Journal on Human Rights 146; Richard Abel *Politics by Other Means: Law in the Struggle Against Apartheid 1980–1994* (1994). For an excellent discussion on pre-Apartheid legal culture, see Martin Chanock, *The Making of South African Legal Culture 1902–1936: Fear Favour and Prejudice* (2001).

[143] Truth and Reconciliation Commission South Africa, Report Vols 1–5 (1998).

[144] See Alex Boraine, *A Country Unmasked: Inside South Africa's Truth and Reconciliation Commission* (2000). [145] Interview with Chief Justice Arthur Chastelson, 16 August 2002.

[146] William Dean, 'The Legal Regime Governing Urban Africans in South Africa: An Administrative Law Perspective' (1984) 105 Acta Juridica 106; Johannes Theodore Schoombe, 'Group Areas Legislation: The Political Control of Ownership and Occupation of Land' (1985) Acta Juridica 77. [147] Joseph Lelyveld, *Move Your Shadow: South Africa, Black and White* (1985) 81.

[148] Martin Chanock, 'Writing South African Legal History: A Prospectus' (1998) 30 Journal of African History 265.

[149] Stephen Ellman, *In a Time of Trouble: Law and Liberty in South Africa's State of Emergency* (1992).

First, law obviously had instrumental utility, both as a necessary systemic framework for the organization of capital and as a mechanism of repression. With regard to the latter, such broad discretion was conferred on those involved at the sharp end of enforcing the regime that it verged on 'the legalisation of illegality'.[150] Secondly, the legitimating capacity of law spoke to international audiences and to the self-image of many supporters of the regime that South Africa was a country distinguished from much of the rest of Africa by its much vaunted commitment to the rule of law. It set South Africa apart as somewhere more worthy of being seen as part of the 'Western Anglo-Saxon club'.[151] From the early part of the century, legalism was also, as Martin Chanock points out, utilized as a legitimating discourse *internally* amongst the white elites who ran the country to distinguish them from those that they ruled.[152] Thirdly, as Ellman contends, different variants of adherence to legality were part of the historical powers struggles between white South Africans (English speaking and Afrikaners) wherein chauvinistic reverence for their respective English common law and Dutch-Roman traditions meant that some *actual* adherence to law as a limitation on oppression was inevitable.[153]

The effect of the particular variant of legalism in the South African context was that the application of the State's considerable repressive powers was inevitably a honeycombed affair. As Abel argues, '...the courts oscillated between being compliant, even enthusiastic instruments of white domination and erecting obstacles, if only temporary, to the apartheid project'.[154] Similar to other contexts of social and political conflict, those opposed to the regime were highly conscious of both the material and the symbolic potential of the law and of the courtroom as an instrument and site of resistance.[155] Nelson Mandela, Oliver Tambo, Joe Slovo and many other leaders of the resistance movement were themselves lawyers who, while understandably cynical, nonetheless took law seriously.[156] Political prisoners, land rights activists, trade unionists, anti-censorship activists, and

[150] Stephen Ellman, *In a Time of Trouble: Law and Liberty in South Africa's State of Emergency* (1992) 175. See also Mike Brogden and Clifford Shearing, *Policing for a New South Africa* (1997).

[151] As one Nationalist MP opined in a parliamentary debate in 1985, '...the South African administration of justice and the judicature stand out as symbols of hope and confidence. Even South Africa's severest critics readily concede that the standard of the administration of justice in South Africa is of the highest order. Mr Andrew Young [former US Ambassador to the UN] spontaneously and readily concurred that the South African administration of justice complied with the highest standards'. Quoted in Abel (1995), Channock (2001) above, 41, 13.

[152] '...the judgements of the courts were a crucial part of the discourses which divided self and other; ruler and ruled; white and black'. above, n 142, 31.

[153] Stephen Ellman (1992), above n 149, 187.   [154] Richard Abel (1994), above n 41, 14.

[155] See eg Isaac Balbus, *The Dialectics of Legal Repression: Black Rebels Before The American Criminal Courts* (1973); Kieran McEvoy 'Law, Struggle and Political Transformation in Northern Ireland' (2000) 27 Journal of Law and Society 542.

[156] 'The court system, however, was perhaps the only place in South Africa where an African could possibly receive a fair hearing and where the rule of law might still apply. This was particularly true in courts presided over by enlightened judges who had been appointed by the United Party [the previous government to the Nationalist party, the architects of Apartheid]. Many of these men stood by

others involved in the broad liberation movement were all involved in sustained recourse to the courts in seeking to undermine the Apartheid legal apparatus.[157] Unlike for example in the Irish Republican tradition,[158] there were comparatively few of even the most militant activists who refused to either mount a defence at trial or to recognize the courts.[159] Of course in order for the resistant capacity of law to be properly exploited, there had to be lawyers willing to take on such cases.

Some of the most prominent jurists and lawyers in post-Apartheid South Africa made their reputations by their willingness to take on cases which challenged the status quo. Lawyers such as Arthur Chaskalson, Leonard Hoffman, Van Zyl Steyn, George Bizos have become iconic figures to a new generation of South Africans. Although the prestige and status of the Bar in particular could arguably have largely insulated them from criticism and promoted a greater daring amongst its members,[160] as David Dyzenhaus points out, during the 1960s and 1970s it was well known that there were very few human rights lawyers (then known as 'political lawyers') prepared to take on the defence of those whom most white South Africans regarded as subversive.[161] While that situation improved in the 1980s due to increased opportunities for funding and the development of a range of radical legal organizations, as is discussed below, the larger and more established collective voices of the legal profession are worthy of criticism for their stance during the struggle against Apartheid. Indeed to paraphrase Dyzenhaus, the visibility and vocality of those comparatively few outstanding lawyers who *did* take a stand (both inside and outside the court) has arguably allowed the silence of the many in the legal profession and their representative organizations (who said or did little) to escape without appropriate censure while continuing to pride themselves on their integrity and independence in maintaining the rule of law.[162]

As in the case of Northern Ireland, the South African context provides a rich array of critical junctures through which one might explore the role of such legal collectives. For illustrative purposes, however, we have chosen to focus on one in

the rule of law. As a student I had been taught that South Africa was a place where the rule of law was paramount and applied to all persons, regardless of their social status or official position. I sincerely believed this and planned my life based on that assumption. But my career as a lawyer and activist removed the scales from my eyes. I saw that there was a wide difference between what I had been taught in the lecture room and what I learned in the court... I never expected justice in the court, however much I fought for it, and though I sometimes received it.' Nelson Mandela, *The Long Walk to Freedom* (1995) 308–309.

[157] See generally David Friedrichs (ed.), *Law and the South African Legitimacy Crisis* (special issue) (1992) 16 Law and Social Inquiry; Abel (1995), above n 41; Fran Buntman, *Robben Island and Prisoner Resistance to Apartheid* (2003); Jurgen Schadeberg, *Voices from Robben Island* (1994).

[158] Kieran McEvoy (2000), above n 155.

[159] Stephen Ellman (1992), above, 159, 181. Ellman notes a prominent exception in the trial of *S v Masina and others*, where a group of *Umkhonto we Sizwe* activists (the military wing of the African National Congress) refused to recognize the right of 'civilian courts' to try them. They were ultimately represented by counsel in any case.   [160] Stephen Ellman (1992), ibid.

[161] David Dyzenhaus, *Judging the Judges: Judging Ourselves* (1998) 105.

[162] David Dyzenhaus, ibid 106–9.

particular—the decision by respected lawyer Bram Fischer to go underground rather than face trial and the response of the Johannesburg Bar to that decision.

Bram Fischer was a distinguished senior counsel of the Johannesburg Bar. Fischer was from an elite Afrikaner family, his father was Judge President of the Orange Free State and his grandfather had been a former prime minister of the Orange River Colony and a South African cabinet minister. In the 1950s and the 1960s Fischer, a lawyer specializing in mineral claims, became a prominent member of the South African Communist Party and a leading advocate against Apartheid.[163] In 1956 he served as counsel in the long-running treason trial in which Nelson Mandela and several other ANC leaders were ultimately acquitted. In 1964 he took on the position of lead counsel for the defence for Nelson Mandela and his co-accused in their Riviona trial in which they were sentenced to life imprisonment. Despite the urgings of his comrades on trial, he had initially been reluctant to take on the case because, as he and some of the accused were aware, some of the evidence uncovered at Riviona actually implicated him personally.[164] In 1964, he was arrested under the Suppression of Communism Act 1950. Such was his standing at the Bar (Fischer was a member of the Johannesburg Bar Council for much of his legal career), that after he was initially arrested he was permitted to leave South Africa on bail to argue a mining case in England before the Privy Council. However, when he returned to South Africa, after much agonizing, he went underground to work with the South African Communist Party, refused to stand trial, and the Johannesburg Bar, despite its reputation as being the most liberal Bar in South Africa,[165] struck Fisher from its rolls on the basis of 'dishonest conduct'.[166] The judge who presided over the trial to strike him from

[163] In the first Bram Fischer Memorial Lecture, President Nelson Mandela described him: 'Even his political opponents would agree with us his comrades that Bram Fischer could have become prime minister or the chief justice of South Africa if he had chosen to follow the narrow path of Afrikaner nationalism. He chose instead the long and hard road to freedom not only for himself but for all of us. He chose the road that had to pass through the jail.' He concluded that memorial lecture by saying, 'In any history written of our country two Afrikaner names will always be remembered. Happily, one is still with us, dear comrade Beyers Naude. The other is Bram Fischer. The people of South Africa will never forget him. He was among the first bright beacons that attracted millions of our young people to fervently believe in a non-racial democracy in our country.' Market Theatre Johannesburg, 9 June 1995. Fischer was also a model for the Dr Burger character in Nadine Gordimer's novel *Burger's Daughter* (1979). See http://www.anc.org.za/ancdocs/history/mandela/1995/sp0609.html
[164] Stephen Ellman, 'To Live Outside the Law You Must be Honest: Bram Fischer and the Meaning of Integrity' (2001) 26 North Carolina Journal of International Law and Commercial Regulation 798.
[165] Stephen Clingman, *Bram Fischer: Afrikaner Revolutionary* (1988). That liberalism has been attributed in part to the high numbers of lawyers of Jewish origin in the Johannesburg Bar, a fact that had been a source of some disquiet amongst the more conservative judiciary under Apartheid. Reinnhard Zimmermann, 'The Contribution of Jewish Lawyers to the Administration of Justice in South Africa' (1995) 29 Israel Law Review 250.
[166] *Society of Advocates v Fischer* 1966 (1) SA 133. The ratio of the decision of De Wet, JP with Hill and Boshoff JJ concurring was that Fischer had breached his solemn assurance that he would stand trial and that such a breach was dishonest conduct, sufficient to warrant his removal from the Roll of Advocates, see Stephen Clingman, ibid. In 1952 the Transvaal Branch of the Association of Law Societies had failed in a similar attempt to have Nelson Mandela struck from the Roll of Attorneys

the Bar roll was the same judge who had presided in the Riviona trial. Fischer penned a letter in which he explained his decision to refuse to stand trial:

'When an advocate does what I have done, his conduct is not determined by any disrespect for the law nor because he hopes to benefit personally by any offence he may commit. On the contrary, it requires an act of will to overcome his deeply rooted respect of legality, and he takes the step only when he feels that whatever the consequences to himself, his political conscience no longer permits him to do otherwise. He does it not because of a desire to be immoral, but because to act otherwise would, for him, be immoral.'[167]

Fischer was caught less than a year after absconding, tried and convicted for a range of charges including sabotage and sentenced to life imprisonment. At his trial he again articulated his rationale for his decision to abandon his commitment to the rule of law.

'My Lord when a man is on trial for his political beliefs and actions, two courses are open to him. He can either confess to his transgressions and plead for mercy, or he can justify his beliefs and explain why he has acted as he did. Were I to ask for forgiveness today, I would betray my cause. That course, my Lord, is not open to me. I believe that what I did was right, and I must therefore explain to your Lordship what my motives were; why I hold the beliefs that I do, and why I was compelled to act in accordance with them . . . I accept, my Lord, the general rule that for the protection of a society laws should be obeyed. But when the laws themselves become immoral, and require the citizen to take part in an organised system of oppression—if only by his silence and apathy—then I believe that a higher duty arises. This compels one to refuse to recognise such laws.'[168]

Fischer died nine years later in prison from cancer, a condition exacerbated by gross misjudgement by his prison doctor. As has been well analysed elsewhere,[169] his decision to take his struggle in opposition to the Apartheid regime outside the courtroom illustrates perfectly the legal and moral dilemmas of lawyers operating in unjust legal systems. What is of equal interest for our discussion is the way in which the collective conscience of the legal community was expressed, both at the time and subsequently.

Briefly by way of background, as in Northern Ireland, the structure of the South African legal profession did not necessarily lend itself to organized collective dissent against State abuses. As in the British system, the profession was and is divided, in this instance between advocates (the 'Bar') who alone are empowered to argue cases in the superior courts and attorneys who appear in the lower courts

because of his role in the Defiance Campaign, a non-violent protest in defiance of racist law. In that instance, Judge Ramsbotham rejected the application on the grounds that nothing Mandela had done reflected on his fitness to remain in the profession, *Incorporated Law Society, Trasnvaal v Mandela* 1954 (3) SA 102 (TPD).

[167] *Society of Advocates v Fischer* 1966 (1) SA 133, 135.
[168] Stephen Clingman, above n 165, 409–10.
[169] Stephen Ellman (2001), above n 164, Chief Justice Ismail Mahomed, *The Bram Fischer Memorial Lecture* (1998) 14 South African Journal of Human Rights 209.

but who generally do out-of-court work and instruct advocates.[170] Attorneys were organized into provincial law societies which formed the Association of Law Societies (ALS). Advocates were organized by city and belonged to the General Council of the Bar (GCB). The General Council of the Bar required consensus at the federal level for any public comment which inevitably meant a position of the lowest common denominator being adopted, with the Pretoria Bar in particular (the most conservative), continuously being able to block critical commentary.[171] The Bar generally adopted a position of only concerning itself with technical issues relating to the administration of justice, and that it 'should not engage itself in "political" issues or matters of policy'.[172] The Association of Law Societies also claimed in its submission to the Truth and Reconciliation Commission that 'politics was not the business of the organised profession'.[173]

As noted above, the relatively enlightened Johannesburg Bar began the process of striking Fischer from its roll a mere two days after Fischer failed to appear for trial, a move which Fischer found deeply personally hurtful.[174] Fischer's decision not to appear for his original trial was framed in legal terms. As he indicated by letter to the Court which disbarred him, he found himself unable to partake in a legal process wherein confessions would be extracted after a 90-day detention and this evidence would then form the basis by which a Minister could impose an indeterminate sentence. The General Council of the Bar argued in their submission to the TRC that the Johannesburg bar was faced with the invidious position that a senior practitioner had deceived the court by not appearing for his trial and therefore this justified his striking-off—something they now recognized as 'a grave injustice'.[175] As Dyzenhaus argues however, what actually happened is that in exercising 'indecent haste' the Bar took the initiative from the

[170] Francis du Bois, 'Introduction, History, System and Sources' in C.G. Van der Merwe and Jacques Du Plessis (eds), *Introduction to the Law of South Africa* (2004).
[171] The Pretoria Bar only began to admit non-whites to the Bar in 1980. In the general GCB submission to the Truth and Reconciliation Commission, the Pretoria Bar made a specific apology for their previous behaviour. 'The Pretoria bar as an institution failed in its duty to fulfil the legal profession's role of custodian of individual rights and the rule of law. Its refusal to join the other bars in protest also prevented the GCB from speaking on behalf of the entire profession with one voice. We apologise to our colleagues, the judiciary, the attorney's profession, the public at large and in particular the victims of unjust laws for these failures.' GCB Submission to the Truth and Reconciliation Commission, 1997 vol. 2, 210.
[172] South African Press Association, 'Bar Council Provides TRC with Three Volume Submission' 21 October 1997. As one prominent advocate told the authors, 'So one did what one could but we could have done more, but on the other hand the Bar is not a political organ or instrument, it is a pretty blunt instrument from that point of view and in fact could lose its independence or credibility if it becomes too involved in one or other side of the divide.' Advocate Milton Seglison (former chair of the General Bar Council), 5 August 2002.
[173] Association of Law Societies Submission to the Truth and Reconciliation Commission (1997), cited in Heide Rombouts, *The Legal Profession and the TRC: A Study of a Tense Relationship* (2002) 22, available at http://www.csvr.org.za/papers/papromb.htm.
[174] Clingman, above n 165.
[175] GCB, *Submission to the Truth and Reconciliation Commission* (1997), 193–197, cited in Dyzenhaus, above n 161, 98.

government in discrediting Fischer, thus assisting in obfuscating his intended message to his fellow white South Africans. The GCB continued to insist in their evidence to the TRC that there was no political motivation behind the striking-off, despite contemporaneous minutes of the period which showed direct communication between the Bar and the Minister suggesting how best to frame the affidavit to play down the politics of the application.[176] Of course, by acting as a proxy for the government (where they were in fact an applicant rather than implementing 'the law of the land'), narrowing the issue of Fischer's actions to one of personal integrity and abstracting his protest from the politics of South Africa, the actions of the Bar were *political* in the extreme.[177] Their continued denial of this some 30 years later is instructive. The TRC found that this continued failure of full acknowledgement to have been 'dishonest and to have besmirched the reputation of the bar even further'.[178]

As noted previously, Fischer's reputation has been restored posthumously by the new government in a number of ways including a very prominent series of lectures. In 2003 that restoration was formalized within the legal community when the Legal Resources Centre brought the first application of The Reinstatement of Certain Deceased Legal Practitioners Act on behalf of the daughters of Bram Fischer. This Act provides for the reinstatement on the roll of attorneys or advocates, of lawyers who were struck-off the roll because of their opposition to Apartheid. A full bench of the High Court, headed by the Judge President, granted the application.[179]

In many ways, Fischer was a precursor to broader mobilization of the legal profession and to groups of lawyers who were dismissive of the notion that the legal profession could possibly exist as a site of political neutrality in such a context.[180] Other lawyers drew direct inspiration from the stance that this white Afrikaner lawyer had adopted in the 1960s.[181] In the 1970s and 1980s new groups of progressive lawyers emerged such as the Black Lawyers Association (BLA) and the National Association of Democratic Lawyers (NADEL).[182] Both saw themselves as counteracting the GBC and ALS, which continued to refuse to take a stand on Apartheid.[183] Such groups emerged in part precisely because of the failings of the established legal collectives. As one prominent human rights lawyer told the

---

[176] GCB Minutes for 2 November 1965, GCB Submission to the Truth and Reconciliation Commission. [177] See Dyzenhaus, above n 161, 101.

[178] Cited in Rombouts, above n 173, 26.

[179] Legal Resource Centre, *Posthumous Readmission of Fischer to Roll of Advocates* (2003), available at http://www.lrc.org.za/Features/Bram_Post_Readmission.asp, accessed 26 July 2006.

[180] Antje Krog, *Country Called My Skull* (1998) 305.

[181] Interview with human rights lawyer, 3 March 2006.

[182] Blake (1997) see n 183 below, 1.

[183] The BLA was established in the 1970s to resist the prosecution of black lawyers who were practising in the Central Business Districts of 'white towns' in contravention of the Group Areas Act. See Black Lawyers Association website http://www.bla.org.za/. See also Michael Blake *'Rights Now'*, Newsletters of Nadel's Human Rights Research and Advocacy Project, September 1997 (Issue 1).

authors'... of course part of the campaign of the BLA was to isolate the apartheid tradition nationally, it was also to isolate the South African Law Society and the Bar councils because of what we regarded them as, essentially as apologists for the apartheid regime'.[184] Indeed in some ways they succeeded in that process, in particular in the wake of the transition.[185] However, many of the lawyers involved in these groups remain deeply cynical that the evidence given to the Truth and Reconciliation Commission by the General Bar Council and the Association of Law Societies was little other than:

'a naked attempt to rewrite history, to find the minutes of this meeting or that encounter with a minister to show that they were doing their bit, working away behind the scenes, making quiet representations. The reality is however, once the minister reassured them that there were genuine security reasons why this lawyer was being detained, or that defendants rights were being abused, they were all too happy to take such reassurances at face value to let the apartheid legal order continue unaffected with their feeble protests duly noted.'[186]

In reviewing the submissions of the GBC and the Association of Law Societies, as well as the secondary accounts of the oral evidence given, undoubtedly there is good reason for a degree of cynicism. Similar to many who appeared before the TRC,[187] both organizations attempted to put the best face possible on their organizational histories. However, the importance of the process of acknowledgement entailed in the South African TRC should not be underestimated.

First, the South African TRC was the first such body to attempt to include the conduct of the judiciary and the legal profession as significant institutional elements of the previous regime which should be called upon to account for their previous actions or inactions. Although as Dyzenahaus demonstrates, this largely failed with regard to the judiciary. The fact that the organizations of the legal profession gave evidence at all was significant.[188]

Secondly, as evidenced by the case of *Fischer* in particular, a formal process of acknowledgement of 'a grave injustice' perpetrated against a lawyer who took a stand against injustice was an important moment, not only for Fischer's family in terms of the broader process of his professional reinstatement but also for the South African legal profession as a whole. One of the lowest common denominators of organizations of lawyers such as bar councils or law societies is their capacity to act like trade unions or to represent the interests of their members—in effect to 'look after their own'. In South Africa, as noted above, often the GBC and

[184] Interview with Vincent Saldana, 6 August 2002.
[185] For example, membership in NADEL or BLA is now considered a qualification for the bench by the Judicial Service Commission who may ask nominees what they did during the Apartheid era concerning issues such as the detention or maltreatment of fellow lawyers. Interview with Judge Dennis Davis, 7 August 2002.
[186] Interview with South African human rights activist, former member of NADEL, 8 August 2002.
[187] Richard Wilson, *The Politics of Truth and Reconciliation in South Africa* (2001).

the ALS were timid in the extreme in standing up for lawyers who were detained, harassed or worse and in the *Fischer* case the GBC actually led the charge in going after a lawyer who had threatened the regime. An acknowledgement (no matter how begrudging or minimalist), of having failed even this most 'thin' notion of the professional responsibility of any professional organization of lawyers was nonetheless highly significant.

Thirdly and closely related is the fact that both the submissions of the GBS and ALS to the TRC contained an express acknowledgement that both had failed in their broader responsibility as organizations to, as the Pretoria Bar put it, fulfil the legal profession's role as 'custodians of individual rights and the rule of law'. True, the power of that submission was then somewhat undermined by the reiteration of the old adage that it was not the role of organizations to 'meddle in politics'. That said, the explicit acknowledgement of legal professionals as having such a broader responsibility is surely of wider significance in the longer term. Many of those we interviewed in South Africa argued that the mainstreaming of human rights discourses has been key to the attempts to transform the legal culture there. As Martha Minow have argued,[188] different variants of human rights discourses were also at the centre of the deliberations of the TRC. Based on the South African experience, there is a powerful argument to be made that the process of reconstructing fractured communal relations in post-conflict societies, which is based upon respecting the rights of the *other*, must also entail some formal process of coming to terms with the past.[189] If lawyers are to fulfil their potential as the custodians of such rights, then they too must be the subject of an honest appraisal of their past misdeeds.

Conclusion

As was noted at the outset of this essay, there is considerable cynicism amongst human rights and other progressive lawyers about the capacity of the legal profession to challenge the power of the State.[190] In Northern Ireland, Canada, and South Africa, lawyers deployed a range of strategies designed to challenge, ignore, circumnavigate, and ultimately shift the position of the professional organizations. They drew upon international resources and support to embarrass such bodies; they worked internal committee systems; they litigated; they mobilized in the communities; they established alternative organizations and, in the South African

---

[188] Martha Minow, *Between Forgiveness and Vengeance: Facing History* (2000).

[189] Priscilla Hayner, *Unspeakable Truths: Facing The Challenge Of Truth Commissions* (2001).

[190] For a useful discussion of the definitional complexities associated with the notion of progressive law and progressive lawyering, see generally David Kairys (ed.), *The Politics of Law: A Progressive Critique* (1998).

context, they lobbied for the professions to formally acknowledge their misdeeds of the past. In each jurisdiction, individual lawyers have stood out. Pat Finucane, Rosemary Nelson, Mary Ebert, Beth Symes, and Bram Fischer embody direct challenges to the profession's complacency and occasional complicity in injustice. Such efforts to shift professional organizations were not an end in themselves, rather they were part of larger political and social struggles. In Northern Ireland, the Finucane and Nelson cases speak directly to the issue of collusion and the culpability of the British State in murder. In Canada the struggle was to take advantage of a golden moment in legal and political history to maximize the chance for gender equality. In South Africa, the *Fischer* case and the acknowledgement of the wrong that occurred was symbolic of the broader evils of Apartheid. In each instance, the position of the organizations of the legal profession themselves was but one battleground in much larger conflicts.

Given the bigger issues at stake in each jurisdiction, one might well ask whether the positions adopted by the voices of the legal profession mattered so much in the grand scheme of things. The simple answer is that not only does law matter, but so do lawyers and so does what they say. They bring what Bordieu referred to as 'symbolic capital' to any debate—'authority, knowledge, prestige, and reputation'[191]—attributes which speak to the constitutive power of law (and lawyers) to shape difficult social and political debates. By way of example, as discussed elsewhere in this volume, the context of the War on Terror throws such matters into sharp relief. In the US, prominent lawyer and Harvard professor, Alan Dershowitz, has provoked considerable controversy by his suggestion that judges and lawyers should 'dirty their hands' by becoming involved in a system for the regulation of warrants for torturing terror suspects in certain specified instances.[192] On the other hand, the American Bar Association has won considerable plaudits from the human rights community for its firm stance in defence of human rights principles, including their support for the McCain Amendment prohibiting torture, domestic surveillance, the treatment and classification of enemy combatants, the conduct of military tribunals, and other issues.[193] Such organizations purport to speak 'on behalf of the profession'. As such, both in the current context of the War on Terror and in each of the jurisdictions we examined, the support, opposition, or sometimes acquiescence of the key voices of the legal profession is and was a highly prized asset for protagonists from all sides.

The tensions which manifest themselves between lawyers such as those discussed in this essay and their professional associations have been well developed elsewhere. In particular, the 'cause lawyering' literature is particularly insightful. This important field of scholarship, most famously mapped out by Sarat and

---

[191] Pierre Bordieu, *Outline of a Theory of Practice* (1977).

[192] See Alan Dershowitz, *Why Terrorism Works* (2002). For a range of responses to Dershowitz's suggestions, see Sanford Levinson (ed.), *Torture: A Collection* (2004).

[193] Speech of Michael Posner, Executive Director, 'Human Rights First to the American Bar Association Center for Human Rights', 14 February 2005, Salt Lake City, Utah.

Scheingold, has included analysis of the relationship between the work of lawyers on behalf of their clients and the broader political and ideological context in which they operate.[194] Although the definition of what constitutes cause lawyering is itself contested, at its core cause lawyering is often seen as a form of 'moral activism'.[195] It views the function of committed lawyers as elevating the moral self-image of legal professionals beyond the instrumentalist 'hired gun' approach which sees lawyers selling their services without regard to the ends. It seeks instead to reconnect law and morality and to make real the notion of lawyering as a 'public profession' whose function is more than the deployment of technical skills, but rather a vehicle through which to build a better society, thus in turn legitimating the legal profession as a whole.[196] For example, lawyers involved in traditional 'left of centre' work on anti-racism, poverty, death penalty, feminist issues and indeed more recently more traditionally conservative issues, including anti-abortion and religious lawyering have all been the focus on cause lawyering scholars. What unites the analysis of these very different spheres of lawyering is a more open acceptance that the intersection between law and politics is a reality in these areas of practice, which must be managed by those involved in it. To paraphrase Rick Abel, cause lawyering requires a much more open acknowledgement that the professional really is *political*.[197]

Where the literature on cause lawyering is of particular interest, for current purposes it is in its analysis of the processes required to achieve an organized voice in the legal profession and the powerful force that such a voice can become. Thus, for example, Sarat's fascinating account of the work of anti-death penalty lawyers in persuading the American Bar Association (ABA) to call for a moratorium on State executions is instructive. As with the debates in Northern Ireland concerning the Finucane and Nelson cases, those who lobbied successfully for the ABA to adopt the moratorium were successful because their arguments centred on *legal* issues (eg the quality of defence counsel and executive erosion of fair trial protections on capital cases) rather than generic political or moral arguments concerning the death penalty itself.[198] The ABA's call for a moratorium has in

[195] See generally Stuart Scheingold, *The Politics of Rights: Lawyers, Public Policy, and Political Change* (1974); Austin Sarat and Stuart Scheingold (eds.), *Cause Lawyering: Political Commitments and Professional Responsibilities* (1998); Austin Sarat and Stuart Scheingold (eds.) *Cause Lawyering and the State in a Global Era* (2001); Stuart Scheingold and Austin Sarat, *Something to Believe In: Politics, Professionalism and Cause Lawyering* (2004).

[195] David Luban, *Lawyers and Justice: An Ethical Study* (1988) vii.

[196] Sarat and Scheingold (1998), above n 195, 3. See also Robert Gordon, 'The Independence of Lawyers' (1988) 68 Boston University Law Review 1. As Alifieri argues with respect to lawyers involved in anti-death penalty litigation in the US '. . . progress in law and politics, however slow and inconsistent, turns on moral vision . . . Professing moral theory in practice is our professional responsibility'. See Anthony Alifieri, 'Mitigation, Mercy and Delay: The Moral Politics of Death Penalty Abolitions' (1996) 31 Harvard Civil Rights-Civil Liberties Law Review 352.

[197] Richard Abel, 'The Professional is Political' (2004) 11 International Journal for the Study of the Legal Profession 131.

[198] The then President of the ABA spoke against the motion on the moratorium precisely because he argued that the focus on the legal issues masked a broader political opposition to the death penalty.

turn been rightly credited with giving impetus and focus to the moratorium debate in the US, tailoring it to the issues outlined in their original report including racial and ethnic discrimination, competency, and compensation of counsel, lack of meaningful review in capital cases, and the execution of mentally disabled and juvenile offenders.[199] In short, and perhaps unsurprisingly, the lawyers who make up the membership of legal bodies *like* good legal argumentation and they *may*, in the final analysis, be persuaded by the value and power of a compelling legal case.[200]

In discussing such notable 'successes' in Northern Ireland, Canada, and South Africa (wherein established organizations within the profession have ultimately adopted a 'progressive' stance), a broader question arises as to whether such legal associations can fulfill the function of expressing the 'collective conscience' of the legal profession on a more sustained basis.

Some scholars have appeared to argue that lawyers' attainment of such an aspiration is indeed feasible. For example, Michael Perry has suggested an appealing vision of the legal profession as a 'moral community' wherein lawyers are the current bearers of a tradition and wherein a 'moral evolution' takes place, old norms are replaced and new ones emerge as each generation of the Bar tests, changes, and articulates that tradition as befits their era.[201] Similarly, Croft has suggested that the American legal profession should be understood as a 'deliberative moral community' underpinned by four broad principles: a respect for truth, fidelity to the law, a mediative role, and a commitment to public service.[202] While he acknowledges that such benchmarks are somewhat vague, he contends that such a reconceptualization would have a number of consequences, including transforming the organized Bar into a forum for promoting professional discourse and the vehicle through which '...a feeling of moral community' is developed.[203] Others appear more cynical. Citing Scheingold, Halliday asks 'what constitutes

---

'What you really have here is a vote up or down on the death penalty. Folks, bring it in the front door, don't try to get it in the back door... The Department of Justice thinks it's a bad idea. The White House thinks it's a bad idea. In my opinion our membership would think it's a bad idea... It is a wolf in sheep's clothing. The wolf is total opposition to the death penalty. The sheep's clothing is couched in constitutional rights.' Despite his opposition, ABA delegates voted by 270 to 119 in favour of the resolution calling for a moratorium. See Austin Sarat, 'State Transformation and the Struggle for Symbolic Capital: Cause Lawyers, the Organized Bar, and Capital Punishment in the United States' in Austin Sarat and Stuart Scheingold, above, 203.

[199] See ABA (2001) for a summary of the national and international response to the moratorium call.

[200] Stephen Ellman makes the same argument with regard to the ability of the Legal Resource Centre in South Africa to win the respect of the organized profession, in part because of the high quality of their legal work. Arthur Chaskelson, the LRC's founding director, later became the President of the Constitutional Court of South Africa. See Stephen Ellman, 'Cause Lawyering in the Third World' in Austin Sarat and Stuart Scheingold (1998), above n 195, 367.

[201] Michael Perry, *Morality, Politics and Law* (1990) 33–34.

[202] Colin Croft, 'Reconceptualising American Legal Professionalism: A Proposal for A Deliberative Moral Community' (1992) 67 New York University Law Review 1256.

[203] Colin Croft, ibid 1345.

and enables professional collective action? What constitutes the profession as a political actor? Does a profession act collectively when it does so in the name of most lawyers, some lawyers, lawyers in general, organised legal professions... how is it possible for professions to act at all, given divisions within professions?'[204] In a similar vein, Abel has suggested that '... certainly no contemporary national legal profession constitutes a community'.[205] Having completed this comparative project, on balance we would probably position ourselves on the side of the cynics, but only just.

In an increasingly diverse and fragmented legal profession, which is in turn faced with evermore complex political and ideological challenges, it is not feasible that the organized profession will always find space to *know* and to *speak* as lawyers' collective legal conscience. However, based upon the experiences highlighted above, we would suggest that such 'moments' or critical junctures are possible when all or some of these elements are present.

Firstly, the collective conscience of the legal profession is usually stirred into action by individual lawyers who demonstrate courage, integrity, and commitment in their work or their own public utterances. The example set by such individuals may provide leadership to other like-minded lawyers as well as shine a harsh light on the actions or inactions of their more sedentary colleagues.

Secondly, an expression of the collective conscience by the organized profession may well require a specific combination of circumstances to be successfully achieved. Within the scholarship on conflict resolution and political transformation more generally, there is a considerable emphasis on the notion of 'ripeness'.[206] Simply put, this is a view that *timing* is important. Conflicts may be ripe for resolution at a particular time because of a complex interaction of political, ideological, social, cultural, individual personalities, and other factors. As noted above, it is certainly no accident that the arguably more progressive moves within the legal communities of Northern Ireland, Canada, or South Africa all occurred at junctures wherein political transformation was arguably already well underway. In a sense, perhaps the organized legal profession is more likely to follow or at least move alongside rather than lead such processes of change.

Thirdly, the extent of the organized legal profession to take on the mantle of the profession's collective conscience will often be shaped by the skills, strategies, and tactics adopted by those pressing for such a role. Like most social or political organizations, bar associations and law societies respond to a combination of pressures from above, below and within. Thus, the tactics of internationalization, popular and political mobilization, the creation of alternative organizations, and

---

[204] Terence Halliday, 'Lawyers and Politics, The Politics of Lawyers: An Emerging Agenda' (1999) 24 Law and Social Inquiry 1005 1006.

[205] Richard Abel, 'Taking Professionalism Seriously' (1989) 41 Annual Review of American Law 59.

[206] Marieke Kleiboer, 'Ripeness of Conflict: A Fruitful Notion?' (1994) 31 Journal of Peace Research 109; Daniel Lieberfeld, 'Conflict "Ripeness" Revisited: The South African and Israel/Palestine Cases' (1999) 15 Negotiation Journal 63.

the utilization of internal committees and systems of governance may all be required. As noted above, they also respond best to styles of legal argumentation which resonate with their professional training, institutional culture, and organizational sense of self.

Finally, the expression of a collective conscience requires a much deeper and arguably more honest notion of professionalism than that which has heretofore dominated the professions.[207] The positivist myth of a politics-free legality amongst the legal professions in Northern Ireland, Canada, and South Africa was a flag of convenience for an avowedly political alignment with the least progressive political forces in each of those jurisdictions. An acknowledgement of that fact, such as through the admittedly imperfect contribution of the South African legal professions to the TRC, would be a useful first step in other countries (such as Northern Ireland) which are still struggling to come to terms with a violent past. More generally with regard to the future of professional associations, what is required is not an intellectually untenable and politically anaemic version of 'neutrality'. Rather, what is needed is a framework which provides both substance and meaning for lawyers' groupings and which gives them a steer through shark-infested political waters. Such a template may be an international human rights framework. International human rights standards, both those which relate directly to the conduct of the legal professional but also those of more general applicability who can give lawyers the confidence to become involved in public conversations which they should not avoid.[208] They provide the compass for an engagement in politics (which is inevitable) while avoiding the charge of political alignment (which is predictable). In the final analysis, it is ultimately through law that lawyers are enabled and emboldened to do the right thing.

[207] One interviewee for this project described this eloquently to one of the authors. 'I think it requires a rejection of the idea that professionalism is about erasing those parts of yourself that link you to real human communities. I think it's only through human communities of meanings that norms make sense and the Bar is one such community and its why actually I think the idea that we should get rid of bar associations would be a bad idea. We should try to make better use of Bar Associations but we shouldn't get rid of them. But we should also encourage lawyers to be grounded in communities of meaning that extend beyond the profession and beyond their workplace so that they can use those normative commitments in a way to check or ground those much more abstract professional commitments.' Interview with Professor David Wilkins, 5 March 2002.

[208] For further detailed discussion on the efficacy of the human rights framework in this context, see Livingstone *et al* (2007), above n 3.

15

Consociationalism, Equality, and Minorities in the Northern Ireland Bill of Rights Debate: The Role of the OSCE High Commissioner on National Minorities

*Christopher McCrudden**

Introduction

How far is the method of political accommodation of national, ethnic, and religious tensions termed 'consociationalism' or 'consociation' compatible or in tension with human rights obligations, particularly those concerning minority rights? Consociationalism is a term coined by Arend Lijphart to describe arrangements, utilized in several political systems with ethnic or other divisions, involving the sharing of power between segments of society joined together by a common citizenship but divided by ethnicity, language, religion, or other factors.[1] Under such a system, some entitlements and responsibilities are given to communities rather than to individuals. Generally, the four key elements of consociationalism are said to be: (1) the sharing of executive power among representatives of all significant groups; (2) communal autonomy, in which each group has a great deal of internal self-government, coupled with equality between the divided communities; (3) proportional representation and allocation of important resources and offices in society, such as positions in the civil service and judiciary; and (4) an explicit

* I am most grateful to the following who commented on an earlier draft: Brice Dickson, Maggie Beirne, Brendan O'Leary, Gordon Anthony, Colin Harvey, Martin O'Brien, Fionnuala Ní Aoláin, Christine Bell, Steven Ratner, John Morison, Tom Hadden, Bill Bowring, and Inez McCormack. Christine Chinkin helped enormously on several aspects of international law. Chief Commissioner Monica McWilliams responded on behalf of the Northern Ireland Human Rights Commission, which was given the opportunity to correct any factual errors, and did so. John Packer was offered the opportunity to comment on several drafts but did not do so. None bears any responsibility for the form or content of the essay, of course.
    [1] Arend Lijphart, *Democracy in Plural Societies* (1977).

minority veto on vital issues, resulting in practice in a mutual veto being able to be operated in practice by both the majority and minority community. Countries adopting these arrangements at various junctures in their histories include Belgium, South Africa, Zimbabwe, India, the Netherlands, Austria, Switzerland, Cyprus, Lebanon, Macedonia, Bosnia Herzegovina, and Northern Ireland (at least since the Belfast Agreement of 1998).[2]

There are both positives and negatives to such 'group' entitlements, using the term 'group' loosely for the moment. On the positive side, they can ensure that all groups are represented and have access to political and economic power. On the negative side, they treat individuals as members of groups and confer benefits not on the basis of only individual achievement but on group identity. Given that human rights ideology is often thought to see the individual as the only proper subject of human rights, we can see immediately that tensions may arise. We should be careful not to set up the tension between human rights ideology and consociational arrangements in too stark a way. There is an equally long tradition of viewing human rights as incorporating a strong communitarian or collective element, recognizing the importance of the relationship between the individual and the community. This is reflected in international human rights treaties such as those relating to the rights of indigenous peoples, and socio-economic and cultural rights. It is also reflected in the provisions regarding equality and non-discrimination, rights that are at the heart of protections of civil and political rights but also implicate important issues regarding the individual as associated with one or more groups. Considering the potential tensions, establishing the appropriate relationships between international human rights law and consociational arrangements is likely to be a complex interpretative task.

There has long been a heated debate between proponents and opponents of consociationalism. Prominent among the critics are some in the liberal, left, and feminist traditions.[3] There are two elements of criticisms from these quarters that form an important part of the debate in Northern Ireland over the acceptability of such arrangements there. The first objection is that consociation 'freezes and institutionally privileges (undesirable) collective identities at the expense of more "emancipated" or more "progressive" identities, such as those focused on class or gender'.[4] The 'opportunities for transforming identities are more extensive'[5] than supposed by the unduly pessimistic proponents of consociation. Second, consociational arrangements 'jeopardize important values, principles, and institutions'.[6] One prominent critic asserts that 'consociational democracy *inevitably* violates the

---

[2] I do not intend to argue further in support of the proposition that the Belfast Agreement has a strong consociational basis, see Brendan O'Leary, 'The Nature of the Agreement', in John McGarry and Brendan O'Leary, *The Northern Ireland Conflict: Consociational Engagements* (2004) 261–93.

[3] A prominent 'liberal' critique is that by Brian Barry, 'The Consociational Model and its Dangers' (1975) 3 European Journal of Political Research 393.

[4] Brendan O'Leary, 'Debating Consociational Politics, Normative and Explanatory Arguments', in Sid Noel (ed.), *From Power Sharing to Democracy* (2005) pp 3–43, at 5. O'Leary rejects these arguments.

[5] ibid, 5.   [6] ibid, 6.

rights of some groups and the rights of some individuals'.[7] During the course of this essay, I shall refer to these critiques of consociationalism as 'liberal', whilst recognizing that there are many variations of liberal, several of which may not share these criticisms of consociationalism, and recognizing that these criticisms are shared by those who would not necessarily regard themselves as liberals. Needless to say, these 'liberal' criticisms are met with equally robust defences by supporters of consociation.[8]

These political objections have sometimes been translated into objections based in interpretations of human rights law. A particular dispute in Northern Ireland, which developed between 2000 and 2005, illustrates some of the legal and political dimensions of the relationship between interpretations of international and regional human rights protection, on the one hand, and consociationalism of the type adopted in the Belfast Agreement, on the other. The issue arose in the context of continuing discussions from the time when the Belfast Agreement was concluded concerning whether Northern Ireland should adopt a 'Bill of Rights'.

The Agreement included a proposal to create a Northern Ireland Human Rights Commission (NIHRC), which would be:

'invited to consult and to advise on the scope for defining, in Westminster legislation, rights supplementary to those in the European Convention on Human Rights, to reflect the particular circumstances of Northern Ireland, drawing as appropriate on international instruments and experience. These additional rights to reflect the principles of mutual respect for the identity and ethos of both communities and parity of esteem, and—taken together with the ECHR—to constitute a Bill of Rights for Northern Ireland.'

The issue that I shall focus on is the debate that occurred over whether such a Bill of Rights should include protections for 'identity and community', and to the extent that it did, whether these protections would be in conflict with those aspects of consociationalism adopted in Northern Ireland that attempted to secure democratic and economic participation to both ethno-religious communities in Northern Ireland. Within the concept of consociationalism adopted and incorporated by the Belfast Agreement, I include both those provisions of the Agreement that established particular voting procedures in the legislature, and also those domestic anti-discrimination and equality policies that addressed the economic disparities between Catholics and Protestants in employment and attempted to ensure the fairer distribution of jobs, in both the public and private sectors. Although the latter predated the Agreement, it was underpinned by the Agreement. The important connection between the two is not only that, however, but also that both rely to some extent on using group identity as an important element in the way they are operationalized.

---

[7] Paul R. Brass, *Ethnic Conflict in Multiethnic Societies: The Consociational Solution and Its Critics* (1991) 334 (emphasis added), quoted in O'Leary (2005), 'Debating Consociational Politics, Normative and Explanatory Arguments', n 4 above, 6.

[8] O'Leary (2005), 'Debating Consociational Politics, Normative and Explanatory Arguments', n 4 above, provides such a defence.

The debate over such arrangements clearly has an important policy and political dimension to it, but the issue I want to address is the legal aspect of that debate as conducted in Northern Ireland. This involved the question of whether protections for 'identity and community' were required by international or regional human rights obligations to which the UK had subjected itself, and whether, legally, such obligations cast doubt on certain aspects of the Agreement itself and equality legislation because they adopted religio-political difference as part of the institutional arrangements for securing political power-sharing and a fairer distribution of employment. The legal issue was always likely to affect the policy and political debates, as legal obligations flowing from regional or international human rights obligations have often proven valuable as political trumps in the past in Northern Ireland.

When we speak of 'international and regional human rights obligations', however, it is clear that there is a multiplicity of agreements incorporating such protections and that the relationship and hierarchy between them may not be clear cut. In the Northern Ireland debate that is addressed here, the focus of attention was the extent to which rights protecting 'identity and community' should be included in the Bill of Rights, particularly because of the provisions of the Council of Europe Framework Convention on National Minorities, which both the UK and Ireland have ratified, and the implications of doing so.

A major problem that arises is how we are to tell what the Framework Convention prescribes. In common with most international and regional human rights conventions, there is no final judicial body established by the Convention with the authority to determine its meaning. In the absence of such a body, or an alternative single source of established interpretation, how should one go about determining the implications of the Convention, especially if the meaning of the Convention is deeply contested? Where there is no single authoritative body but several quasi-authoritative bodies it may give rise to the emergence of what has been termed 'forum shopping', in which individuals and organizations take advantage of the growing number of international and regional human rights institutions with quasi-authoritative status to choose that institution most likely to give the answer to a question of interpretation that most suits the questioner.

Forum shopping arises where individuals or organizations have a range of possible bodies with actual or purported jurisdiction to address their claims. Such forum shopping has been thought by some to have deleterious consequences: competition between decision-making bodies, legal uncertainty, and declining respect for law. Others consider it desirable in the human rights context where it 'encourages jurists to engage in a dialogue to elucidate and harmonize the [shared] legal norms'.[9] The availability of multiple interpreters has been analysed as but

---

[9] Laurence R. Helfer, 'Forum Shopping for Human Rights' (1999) 148 U. Pa. L. Rev. 285, 293. This article is generally useful for a discussion of the various arguments pro and con.

part of a larger phenomenon: the fragmentation of the international legal system, with (for some) a consequential loss of coherence and legal normativity, while for others such fragmentation demonstrates a welcome maturity and diversity in the international legal process.[10] In the Northern Ireland context this issue proved particularly controversial.

Two themes are explored here: first, the substantive issue of the appropriate relationship between the protection of 'identity and community' and consociation, which in part involved a debate as to how far the Bill of Rights should further underpin the Belfast Agreement[11] or contest its underpinnings, and, second, the issue of how to arrive at an authoritative interpretation of a human rights treaty, involving a choice of which international or regional institution to involve in addressing the issue, where there is multiplicity of such bodies, but no single authoritative body.

In the first section of the essay, I explain the Framework Convention and the formal mechanisms established to oversee its implementation, and how several other actors have become involved in applying the Convention, in particular the Organization for Security and Cooperation in Europe's (OSCE) High Commissioner on National Minorities (HCNM) and the Council of Europe's Venice Commission. The second section considers the equality and power-sharing arrangements in Northern Ireland, in particular those relating to voting arrangements in the Assembly and the provisions regarding employment equality, and how both involve the use of religio-political identity. The third section is the core of the essay, analysing the relationship between the HCNM and the NIHRC. The belated involvement of the Council of Europe, involving the establishment of an ad hoc group to address the issues, is discussed in the fourth section. Some tentative conclusions are then offered.

I was an active participant in the debates on these issues. Before these events, I had previously been a member (1984–1988) of the NIHRC's predecessor body, the Standing Advisory Commission on Human Rights (SACHR), which had been significantly involved in developing proposals that were included in reforming equality legislation. After finishing my term of office with SACHR, I was an advisor to the Shadow Secretary of State for Northern Ireland during the passage of the legislation that implemented these proposals. I was subsequently advisor to the Northern Ireland Committee of the House of Commons in its inquiry into fair employment legislation, in the late 1990s. During the events discussed below, I was frequently solicited for advice by several members of the NIHRC, the Committee on the Administration of Justice (a Northern Ireland-based, human rights, NGO), and others involved in the processes discussed. For example,

---

[10] See generally Kalypso Nicolaidis and Joyce L. Tang, 'Diversity or Cacophony?: New Sources of Norms in International Law' (2004) 25 Michigan J. International Law 1349.

[11] As was argued by Brendan O'Leary, 'The Protection of Human Rights under the Belfast Agreement', in Brendan O'Leary and John McGarry *The Northern Ireland Conflict: Consociational Engagements* (2004) 352.

throughout the period, I was a member of an advisory group, established by a Northern Ireland government department, considering the enactment of equality legislation.

Interpreting the Framework Convention on National Minorities

The Framework Convention Introduced

The Framework Convention on National Minorities grew out of lengthy discussions in the Council of Europe, stretching over 40 years. As early as 1949, the Parliamentary Assembly recognized the importance of wider protection of the rights of national minorities. In 1961, the Assembly recommended the inclusion of an article in a second additional protocol to the European Convention on Human Rights (ECHR) to guarantee to national minorities certain rights not thought to be covered by the Convention.[12] The committee of experts, which had been instructed to consider whether it was possible and advisable to draw up such a protocol, concluded that, from a legal point of view, there was no special need to make the rights of minorities the subject of a further protocol. However, the experts considered that there was no major legal obstacle to the adoption of such a protocol if it were considered advisable for other reasons. More recently, the Parliamentary Assembly recommended a number of political and legal measures to the Committee of Ministers, in particular the drawing up of a protocol or a convention on the rights of national minorities.

In October 1991, following the collapse of the Communist regimes of central and eastern Europe, and the growth of problems surrounding the position of minorities in these countries, the Steering Committee for Human Rights (CDDH) was given the task of considering, from both a legal and a political point of view, the conditions in which the Council of Europe could undertake an activity for the protection of national minorities, taking into account the work done by the Conference on Security and Co-operation in Europe (CSCE, the predecessor of the OSCE, to be discussed subsequently), the United Nations, and the Council of Europe. In May 1992, the Committee of Ministers instructed the CDDH to examine the possibility of formulating specific legal standards relating to the protection of national minorities. The CDDH established a committee of experts (DH-MIN), which was required to propose specific legal standards in this area,

---

[12] Since then, however, in parallel with the developments discussed in this section, the European Court of Human Rights has developed some degree of protection for minorities under the ECHR; see Christian Hillgruber and Matthias Jestaedt, *The European Convention on Human Rights and the Protection of National Minorities* (1994); Gaetano Pentassuglia, *Minorities in International Law* (2002) 119–127; Geoff Gilbert, 'The Burgeoning Minority Rights Jurisprudence of the European Court of Human Rights' (2002) 24(3) Human Rights Quarterly 36.

bearing in mind the principle of complementarity of work between the Council of Europe and the CSCE.

This culminated in a report to the Committee of Ministers of 8 September 1993, which included various legal standards that might be adopted and the legal instruments in which they could be incorporated. The CDDH noted that there was no consensus on the interpretation of the term 'national minorities'. When the Heads of State and Government of the Council of Europe's Member States met in Vienna at the summit of 8 and 9 October 1993, it was agreed that the rights of national minorities had to be protected and respected as a contribution to peace and stability. In particular, the Heads of State and Government decided to enter into legal commitments regarding the protection of national minorities. On 4 November 1993, the Committee of Ministers established an ad hoc Committee for the Protection of National Minorities (CAHMIN).

The committee, made up of experts from the Council of Europe's Member States, started work in late January 1994, with the participation of representatives of the CDDH, the Council for Cultural Co-operation, the Steering Committee on the Mass Media, and the European Commission for Democracy through Law (the Venice Commission, to be discussed subsequently). The High Commissioner on National Minorities of the CSCE and the Commission of the European Communities also took part, as observers. On 15 April 1994, CAHMIN submitted an interim report to the Committee of Ministers, which was then communicated to the Parliamentary Assembly.[13] In May 1994, the Committee of Ministers expressed satisfaction with the progress achieved. At its meeting in October 1994, CAHMIN decided to submit the draft framework Convention to the Committee of Ministers, which adopted the text on 10 November 1994. The Framework Convention was opened for signature by the Council of Europe's Member States on 1 February 1995, and entered into force on 1 February 1998.[14] The UK signed the Convention on the date it opened for signature and ratified it on 15 January 1998. Ireland also signed the Convention on 1 February 1995 and ratified the Convention as part of its commitments under the Belfast Agreement on 7 May 1999.

The Convention's Supervisory Mechanisms

The Convention provides that the Council of Europe's Committee of Ministers is entrusted with the monitoring of its implementation.[15] It is assisted by an

---

[13] Doc. 7109.

[14] For a detailed consideration of the Convention, see, in particular, Marc Weller, *The Rights of Minorities: A Commentary on the European Framework Convention for the Protection of National Minorities* (2005); Tove H. Malloy, *National Minority Rights in Europe* (2005).

[15] For a detailed description of the mechanisms, see Alan Phillips, 'The Framework Convention for the Protection of National Minorities' in Council of Europe, *Mechanisms for the Implementation of Minority Rights* (2005) ch. 5.

advisory committee, composed of members with recognized expertise in the protection of national minorities. A Resolution of the Committee of Ministers[16] determined the role of the advisory committee. The Advisory Committee is elected by the Committee of Ministers, but each member serves in his or her individual capacity. There is no equivalent to the European Court of Human Rights to receive individual complaints or inter-State complaints and interpret the Convention on an authoritative judicial basis. Instead supervision is based primarily on periodic State reports. The advisory committee adopts 'opinions' in respect of particular State party's implementation on the basis of these periodic reports. These 'opinions' are submitted to the Committee of Ministers, which may adopt resolutions containing 'conclusions' and 'recommendations'. In addition, it appears that the Advisory Committee (with the support of the Secretariat) provides technical advice and assistance to the authorities of the States parties, largely on the basis of requests received.[17]

In the view of Pentassuglia, writing just before the events to be discussed occurred, 'no binding decision can be adopted by the monitoring body. The non-judicial character of the procedure . . . reflects the [lack of] stringency of the treaty as a whole, and is clearly an off-shoot from the states' reluctance to secure supervision based on adjudication and redress'.[18] Instead, the Convention adopts a set of 'principles, the clarification and realization of which are to be fundamentally achieved at the domestic level. (. . .) [T]he convention contains programme-type provisions setting out objectives which the parties undertake to pursue (. . .) leaving the states concerned a measure of discretion in the implementation of the convention, in consideration of particular factual circumstances'.[19]

A similar, if rather more acerbic, view of the arrangements for monitoring and enforcement was taken by the European Court of Human Rights. In the *Chapman* case,[20] although the Court observed 'that there may be said to be an emerging international consensus amongst the Contracting States of the Council of Europe recognising the special needs of minorities and an obligation to protect their security, identity and lifestyle'[21] citing the Framework Convention amongst other authorities, the Court was 'not persuaded that the consensus is sufficiently concrete for it to derive any guidance as to the conduct or standards which Contracting States consider desirable in any particular situation. The framework convention, for example, sets out general principles and goals but the signatory States were unable to agree on means of implementation.'[22] This

---

[16] Resolution (97) 10, 17 September 1997.

[17] John Packer, 'Situating the Framework Convention in a wider context: achievements and challenges', in Council of Europe, *Filling the Frame: Five Years of Monitoring the Framework Convention for the Protection of National Minorities* (2004) 48.

[18] Pentassuglia, *Minorities in International Law*, n 12 above, 201.

[19] Pentassuglia, ibid, 132–33.

[20] *Chapman v United Kingdom* (Application no. 27238/95), European Court of Human Rights, 18 January 2001.   [21] ibid, para 93.

[22] ibid, para 94.

reinforced the Court's view of 'the complexity and sensitivity of the issues involved in policies balancing the interests of the general population (...) and the interests of a minority with possibly conflicting requirements'.[23]

Council of Europe's Venice Commission

A major theme of this essay is the extent to which bodies with no formal interpretative role in the Framework Convention have increasingly become involved in this task. The European Commission for Democracy through Law, better known as the Venice Commission, is one such body. It is a Council of Europe advisory body on constitutional matters. It was established in 1990 and has played a leading role in the adoption of national constitutions in Europe, particularly in those countries of central and eastern Europe making the transition to democracy. It also plays a role in crisis management and conflict prevention through constitution building and advice in particular situations. The Venice Commission is composed of 'independent experts who have achieved eminence through their experience in democratic institutions or by their contribution to the enhancement of law and political science'.[24] The members are senior academics, particularly in the fields of constitutional or international law, supreme or constitutional court judges, and members of national parliaments. Acting on the commission in their individual capacity, the members are appointed for four years by the participating countries but act in their individual capacity. In giving advice, the Venice Commission frequently refers to the Framework Convention on National Minorities as a benchmark against which to consider disputed issues regarding national minorities, and frequently offers legal interpretations of the Convention.[25]

OSCE and the High Commissioner on National Minorities

This picture of the monitoring and interpretation of the Framework Convention is further complicated by the existence of several other bodies that play a subsidiary, but nevertheless important role in the implementation of the Convention. For the purposes of this essay, particular attention must be given at this stage to the role of the OSCE's High Commissioner on National Minorities. The OSCE started life as the Conference on Security and Co-operation in Europe (CSCE) and was a product of the Cold War. It was established during the 1970s, originally as a mechanism for discussion on security issues between the communist

---

[23] ibid.   [24] Art 2 of the revised Statute.
[25] A good example is CDL-AD (2002) 1, Opinion on Possible Groups of Persons to which the Framework Convention for the Protection of National Minorities Could be Applied in Belgium, adopted by the Venice Commission at its 50th Plenary Meeting (Venice, 8–9 March 2002), on the basis of comments by: Mr Franz Matscher (Member, Austria), Mr Giorgio Malinverni (Member, Switzerland), Mr Pieter Van Dijk (Member, Netherlands), Mr Sergio Bartole (Substitute Member, Italy) (hereafter Venice Commission, Belgium Opinion), para 5.

countries of Eastern and Central Europe, and the democracies of Western Europe
and North America. Between then and the end of the Cold War which began in
the late 1980s, the CSCE provided a process by which the Soviet and Western
blocs could discuss measures which would lessen tension and begin to build a
degree of mutual confidence. Among these issues was the question of human
rights. Its primary rationale was the building of international security through
resolving conflict between States that may endanger that security. It was not a legal
mechanism for conflict resolution and agreements reached under its auspices were
not legally binding. It was a political mechanism that relied on political pressure
and reciprocation for its ability to achieve change.

When the Cold War eventually ended by the beginning of the 1990s, the
CSCE underwent a radical change. A 'Paris Charter for a New Europe' was signed
in November 1990. By 1992, the CSCE became an organization with more established, permanent institutions with more regular meetings between its members.
A Chairman and Secretary-General were appointed, and a Conflict Prevention
Centre and a Office for Free Elections were established. The CSCE was also
renamed the Organization for Security and Co-operation in Europe (OSCE),
indicating its more formal and permanent status. The OSCE remained, however,
a non-Treaty-based organization, operating politically and primarily oriented to
State security and avoidance of conflict. The Helsinki Summit in July 1992
approved a further institutional innovation: the creation of a High Commissioner
on National Minorities.[26] The CSCE had during its period of existence concluded
several agreements with minority rights protections, but the establishment of the
High Commissioner was a major institutional manifestation of the importance
the organization planned to give to minority rights in the future.

The mandate of the High Commissioner on National Minorities was originally
set out in the 1992 Helsinki Document. The role of the High Commissioner was
to 'provide "early warning" and, as appropriate, "early action" at the earliest possible stage in regard to tensions involving national minority issues that have the
potential to develop into a conflict within the OSCE area, affecting peace, stability, or relations between participating States'.[27] Within this mandate, the High
Commissioner will work in confidence and will act independently of all parties
directly involved in the tensions. The High Commissioner would base his or her
actions on OSCE principles and commitments. The High Commissioner will
not consider national minority issues in situations involving organized acts of
terrorism. Nor will the High Commissioner consider violations of CSCE commitments with regard to an individual person belonging to a national minority.
In considering a situation, the High Commissioner will take fully into account
the availability of democratic means and international instruments to respond to
it, and their utilization by the parties involved. A key element, from the perspective of the High Commissioner, is the 'condition of confidentiality—which

---

[26] CSCE, *Helsinki Summit Document: The Challenges of Change* (1992).   [27] ibid, para 23.

means that the HCNM acts through silent diplomacy'.[28] According to the High Commissioner this:

'...was meant to reconcile the need to establish such an office in the first place with the importance of avoiding any possible escalation that might be caused by his involvement. Often parties directly involved feel they can be more co-operative and forthcoming if they know that the discussions will not be revealed to the outside world. Conversely, parties may make much stronger statements in public than in confidential conversations, from the presumption that they should be seen to be maintaining a strong position or that they should try to exploit outside attention.'[29]

A full understanding of the role of the High Commissioner cannot be gained only by considering the formal mandate, since the working methods of the High Commissioner have developed subsequently in ways that add significantly to the bare bones of the mandate.[30] In particular, the two High Commissioners who have served have developed the role in a number of respects: first, in developing a mechanism of specific recommendations to particular governments, mostly in the form of a letter to that country's foreign minister, and these are sometimes also released to the general public and published on the High Commissioner's website. Second, High Commissioners have been instrumental in the development of several general recommendations in areas of particular concern to minorities. Third, High Commissioners have, on occasion, issued public statements on particular situations. Fourth, problem-solving workshops and projects have been initiated. Finally, the High Commissioner's office at The Hague has been expanded from two officials in 1993 to around 15 a decade later.

The relationship between the High Commissioner and the Framework Convention is somewhat complex. On the one hand, neither the OSCE nor the High Commissioner on National Minorities has any formal role under the Convention on National Minorities, which was a document drawn up by the Council of Europe, not the OSCE. On the other hand, the High Commissioner stresses that the Council of Europe drew extensively on the previous work of the CSCE on minorities issues in the drafting of the Framework Convention, and his legal adviser participated in the drafting of the Convention.[31] The High Commissioner both supports the implementation of the Convention in hosting conferences on the Convention, and draws on the Convention as a basis for his advice and recommendations to particular countries.

---

[28] http://www.osce.org/hcnm/13022.html.   [29] ibid.

[30] This paragraph draws significantly on Claus Neukirch, Karin Simhandl, and Wolfgang Zellner, 'Implementing Minority Rights in the Framework of the CSCE/OSCE', in Council of Europe, *Mechanisms for the implementation of minority rights* (2004) 159. For an illuminating discussion of the modus operandi of the HCNM, see Steven R. Ratner, 'Does International Law Matter in Preventing Ethnic Conflict' (2000) 32 NYU J Inter'l Law and Pol. 591. See also Walter A. Kemp (ed.), *Quiet Diplomacy in Action: The OSCE High Commissioner on National Minorities* (2001).

[31] Packer (2004), 'Situating the Framework Convention in a wider context: achievements and challenges', n 17 above, 46.

Speaking in October 2003, the then High Commissioner described how he referred:

'to the standards of the Framework Convention not only in regard to States Parties thereto, but also to other OSCE Participating States. Political commitments, as reflected in the legal language of the Framework Convention, allow me to strengthen my recommendations addressed to the States non-parties thereto. In this way the Framework Convention has become a common tool for the protection of national minorities.'[32]

Although he accepted that the High Commissioner has no explicit powers with regard to standard-setting or interpretation of OSCE commitments, he went on to stress that 'practical needs generate a need for clarifications of standards in the field of national minorities, particularly when I discuss with governments specific modalities and recommendations for their domestic regulations, policy-making and administrative decision-making'.[33]

The HCNM has stressed the need for consistency between his recommendations and the Opinions of the Advisory Committee and the Resolutions of the Committee of Ministers, and noted a 'developing synergy'[34] between the Framework Convention and the High Commissioner. In an interesting contribution, John Packer, formerly the Senior Legal Adviser to the High Commissioner and subsequently a Director in the Office of the High Commissioner, described in 2003 the 'particular close[ness]' of the co-operation between the Council of Europe and the High Commissioner, 'with contacts sometimes on a daily or even hourly basis'.[35] From the point of view of the Council of Europe, however, some of the operations of the OSCE may be less than desirable. In February 2005, the Secretary General of the Council of Europe proposed a merger between the Council of Europe and the OSCE, noting the tensions between the two organizations on occasion.[36] The experience of its involvement with Northern Ireland was also to cast a rather different light on this rather rosy picture painted by the High Commissioner and his staff.

---

[32] Rolf Ekéus, 'The role of the Framework Convention in promoting stability and democratic security in Europe', in Council of Europe, *Filling the Frame: Five years of monitoring the Framework Convention for the Protection of National Minorities* (2004) 26.   [33] ibid, 26.
[34] ibid, 27.
[35] Packer (2004), 'Situating the Framework Convention in a wider context: achievements and challenges', n 17 above, 47. He continued:
'Co-operation has taken place with various bodies or parts of the Council [of Europe], ranging from representatives of Member States (including the Committee of Ministers and Presidency), the Parliamentary Assembly and its relevant Committees and rapporteurs, the Advisory Committee under the Framework Convention, the Venice Commission, and not least of all the Secretary General and the Secretariat. Concretely, there have been numerous co-ordinated activities and actions, and several collaborations addressing, inter alia, the provision of advice on legislative reform, domestic policy development, etc. I wish to emphasise that this has been a very positive experience of constructive co-operation which is a hardly known story.'
[36] 'Too many of us in the human rights business, European leaders are told', Financial Times, 7 February 2005.

Consociationalism and Equality in the Northern Ireland Context

The Belfast Agreement attempted to reach an historic compromise between nationalists (predominantly Catholics) and unionists (predominantly Protestants) in Northern Ireland.[37] There are several aspects of these initiatives, which subsequently came to be considered controversial in the context of the NIHRC's consideration of the Bill of Rights.

The Cross-Community Agreement in the Assembly

The Northern Ireland Act 1998, which enacted the Agreement provided, first, that there would be special requirements concerning the need to ensure that certain key decisions in the Assembly would be taken on the basis of cross-community voting.[38] Members of the Assembly would register a designation of identity (nationalist, unionist, or other) for the purposes of measuring cross-community support in certain Assembly votes.[39] Two methods of showing cross-community support were provided for: *either* parallel consent was required, ie a majority of those members present and voting, including a majority of the unionist and nationalist designations present and voting, needed to vote in favour; *or* a weighted majority (60 per cent) of members present and voting, including at least 40 per cent of each of the nationalist and unionist designations present and voting, needed to vote in favour. The election of the First and Deputy First Ministers required the first method.[40] Other decisions requiring either method of cross-community support were designated in legislation, including election of the Chair of the Assembly, and the adoption of standing orders and budget allocations. In other cases a requirement to demonstrate cross-community support could be triggered by a petition of concern brought by a significant minority of Assembly members (30:108). The Chair and Deputy Chair of the Assembly were also to be elected on a cross-community basis.

There would be a committee for each of the main executive functions of the Northern Ireland administration. The chairs and deputy chairs of the Assembly committees would be allocated proportionally, using the d'Hondt system.[41] Membership of the committees would be in broad proportion to party strengths in the Assembly to ensure that the opportunity of committee places was available

---

[37]   The academic literature on the Belfast Agreement is extensive. For an overview, see Christopher McCrudden, 'Northern Ireland, the Belfast Agreement, and the British Constitution', in Jeffrey Jowell and Dawn Oliver (eds.), *The Changing Constitution* (6th ed., 2007).

[38]   Northern Ireland Act 1998, s 4(5).   [39]   ibid, s 4(5).   [40]   ibid, s 16(3).

[41]   For an explanation, see B. O'Leary, Bernard Grofman, and Jorgen Elklit, 'Divisor Methods for Segmented Portfolio Allocation in Multi-Party Executive Bodies: Evidence for Northern Ireland and Denmark' (2005) 49(1) American Journal of Political Science 198.

to all members. The appointment of those exercising executive authority was also subject to cross-community voting arrangements, and d'Hondt. Executive authority would be discharged on behalf of the Assembly by a First Minister and Deputy First Minister and up to 10 ministers with departmental responsibilities. Following the election of the First Minister and Deputy First Minister, the posts of ministers would be sequentially allocated to parties on the basis of the d'Hondt system in proportion to the number of seats each party has in the Assembly. Removal from office would also take place on a cross-community basis.[42]

That these provisions were controversial can be seen from the inclusion in the Belfast Agreement of a review of the Agreement's arrangements establishing institutions of government in Northern Ireland, 'including the details of electoral arrangements and of the Assembly's procedures, with a view to agreeing any adjustments necessary in the interests of efficiency and fairness'.[43]

Fair Employment Legislation

The Agreement also contained extensive reference to human rights and equality issues. Amongst other measures, it was agreed that existing equality legislation should be strengthened. Measures on employment equality included in a set of proposals[44] issued by the British Government during the talks process leading up to the Agreement would be adopted. These involved the extension and strengthening of anti-discrimination legislation, including the fair employment legislation that had been in operation since 1989, a review of the national security aspects of the fair employment legislation, a new, more focused initiative and a range of measures aimed at combating unemployment and progressively eliminating the differential in unemployment rates between the two communities by targeting objective need.

At first sight, it might seem strange to include such detailed measures on employment equality in a peace agreement that was so clearly addressing political change and the institutional adjustments necessary to ensure such change. The parties to the Agreement, however, accepted the argument that political change and social change were deeply interconnected and structural adjustments were needed on various fronts, hence the incorporation of such detailed references to issue of equality and discrimination. The Assembly arrangements are not only linked by the overall purpose of the Agreement but also by the methods chosen to accomplish this purpose. Both the Asssembly voting arrangements and the equality measures I am about to consider rely heavily on communal identity as the basis for their operation, hence the objections to them.

---

[42] The background to the 'cross community' voting arrangements in the Assembly is well set out by Lord Bingham in a decision of the House of Lords in *Robinson v Secretary of State for Northern Ireland and others* [2002] UKHL 32, 25 July 2002 (House of Lords).

[43] Agreement, Strand 1, para 36.   [44] White Paper, *Partnership for Equality* (1998).

The provisions on fair employment, as amended following the Agreement, are found in the Fair Employment and Treatment (Northern Ireland) Order 1998 (FETO 1998). This replaced and revised the scheme previously enacted in the Fair Employment Act 1976 (FEA 1976) and the Fair Employment Act 1989 (FEA 1989). The original 1976 legislation had been judged largely unsuccessful in achieving its goals, and replaced in 1989 by a considerably more extensive set of provisions.[45] The 1998 legislation extended the legislation beyond employment, and made some other less major amendments to the 1989 legislation. The basic scheme of the 1989 legislation was largely untouched, and it has been judged considerably more successful in its operation in comparison to the 1976 legislation. However, this basic scheme is now underpinned by the specific references in the Agreement to the legislation, further enhancing its legitimacy and status, at least politically, and (arguably) legally.

The FETO 1998 aims to provide remedies for religious and political discrimination. It also requires employers and others to undertake certain actions to ensure 'fair participation' and 'equality of opportunity' more generally between the two communities in Northern Ireland, ie Catholics and Protestants. Registered employers and public authorities must monitor the religious composition of their workforces. Such employers must also monitor the religious composition of applicants for employment. Public authorities and employers with more than 250 employees must also monitor the religious composition of those ceasing to be employed in the concern[46] and the religious composition of those promoted in the concern. A 'monitoring return' has to be completed yearly including this information and submitted in a prescribed form to the Equality Commission. If the Commission does not receive a return before the end of the specified time limit, the employer can be fined unless it can provide a reasonable excuse.

The original Bill presented to Parliament by the government in 1988 did not contain detailed provisions relating to the methods that must be adopted by employers in deciding how to work out the community affiliation of employees and job applicants, essentially leaving it to further legislation to specify what methods would be appropriate. Concern was expressed in Parliament that this approach was unsatisfactory, and that the main methods of monitoring should be specified on the face of the legislation and, most importantly, that they should be drawn up so at to ensure that the results of monitoring would be comprehensive, and accurate. Concern was expressed, in particular, by the official opposition: relying only on answers provided by individuals as to their community affiliation would be liable to result in inaccurate figures. There was a fear that there could well be systematic and organized resistance to providing information on community affiliation as part of a sustained campaign against the legislation, and that this would lead to the other provisions of the regulatory scheme that relied on accurate

---

[45] Christopher McCrudden, Robert Ford, and Anthony Heath, 'Legal Regulation of Affirmative Action in Northern Ireland: An Empirical Assessment' (2004) 24 Oxford Journal of Legal Studies 363.

[46] FETO 1998, Art. 52.

statistics becoming a dead letter.[47] As a result of these arguments, the Government agreed to introduce amendments, which were subsequently adopted, to ensure that several methods should be available to employers, not just the method of asking direct questions of the employee.[48]

As incorporated in the 1998 legislation, and subsequently set out in detail in subsidiary legislation,[49] the employer is required to apply the 'principal method' to all employees and applicants. It provides for the community to which a person is treated as belonging to be determined by reference to his or her written answer to a direct question regarding his or her community affiliation.[50] Where the 'principal method' does not result in an employee or job applicant being treated as a member of the Protestant or Roman Catholic communities then the employer has the option of applying the 'residuary method'.[51] The code of practice issued by the Equality Commission recommends that 'in every case where an individual cannot be treated as belonging to a community under the principal method, [the employer is] strongly recommended to use the residuary method in order to determine the community background of the individual'. Where the employer chooses not to, or where this method produces no determination, the employee or applicant is to be treated as if the community to which he or she belongs cannot be determined.

What the 'residuary method' for discovering community affiliation involves is set out in some detail. Where an employee has provided the employer, in writing, with any relevant information about himself, then the employer is allowed (for the purposes of preparing a monitoring return) to treat that employee as belonging to the community with which the information tends to show he or she has a connection, or (if the information tends to show a connection with both communities) treat the employee as belonging to the community with which, in general, it tends to show he or she has the stronger connection. The following qualifies as relevant information: surname and other names; address; schools attended by the employee (whether in Northern Ireland or elsewhere); any course that the employee has

---

[47] See, in particular, the speeches of Mr McNamara, Shadow Secretary of State for Northern Ireland, Fair Employment Bill, Standing Committee B, 21 February 1898, Cols 149–52.

[48] See, in particular, the acceptance of the Opposition arguments by the Minister, Mr Viggers, Official Report, 25 May 1989, Cols 1189–92.

[49] Fair Employment (Monitoring) Regulations (Northern Ireland) 1999, SRNI No. 148, as amended by the Fair Employment (Monitoring) (Amendment) Regulations (Northern Ireland) 2000, SR 2000 No. 228. Employees whose designation was arrived at by an employer under equivalent regulations made under the Fair Employment (Northern Ireland) Act 1989 (Fair Employment (Monitoring) Regulations (Northern Ireland) 1989, SR 1989 No. 436, as amended by the Fair Employment (Monitoring) (Amendment) Regulations (Northern Ireland) 1991) continue to be so designated and the 1999 Regulations do not apply. The main difference between the old and new monitoring regulations as regards determining community affiliation is that the 'principal method' in the old regulations allowed designation by virtue of school attended or direct question, whereas the new regulations permit only direct question as a 'principal method', but do allow school attended to be taken into account in the application of the residuary method.   [50] 1999 SR, Arts 8, 9.

[51] 1999 SR, Art. 11.

undertaken in preparation for any recognized award or any examination conducted by the Department of Education for Northern Ireland; the employee's sporting or other leisure pursuits or interests; the clubs, societies or other organizations to which he or she belongs; or the occupation as a clergyman or minister of a particular religious denomination or as a teacher in a particular school, of any referee nominated by the employee when he or she applied for the job. These are all generally reliable ways of 'telling' religio-political origin in Northern Ireland. They provide reasonable methods of establishing identity that facilitates the implementation of the legislation.

Before sending in the monitoring return to the Commission the employer must give each employee a written notice telling him or her the community to which he or she is regarded as belonging for the purposes of the return (or that the employee's community affiliation could not be determined).[52] If an employee believes that such a notice contains inaccurate information, he or she should tell the employer about this within seven days of receiving the notice. Where it appears to the employee that the employer has incorrectly designated the employee and draws this to the employer's attention, the employer is then obliged to correct the monitoring return to reflect this response.[53] The law preserves the confidentiality of monitoring information under the main methods of monitoring.[54] It does, however, allow the disclosure of otherwise confidential information to the Equality Commission, the Labour Relations Agency, the Fair Employment Tribunal, the courts, and the employment tribunals. Nor is disclosure precluded to trade union officials and consultants assisting employers to develop equal opportunity policies. Anyone who supplies false information to someone filling in a monitoring return or who knowingly includes such false information in a return can be fined.

Employment in the Police Service and the 'Patten Quota'

The third major relevant issue in the Agreement was that of police recruitment. The issue of policing was one of the central issues in the negotiations leading to the Agreement.[55] An Independent Commission was proposed in the Agreement to make recommendations for future policing arrangements in Northern Ireland, including means of encouraging widespread community support for these arrangements within the agreed framework principles. An Independent Commission on Policing in Northern Ireland (the Patten Commission) was subsequently established to advise on the measures necessary to achieve 'a police service that

---

[52] ibid, Art. 12.   [53] ibid, Art. 13.   [54] ibid, Art. 16.

[55] The judgment of Kerr J in *Re the Matter of an Application by Mark Parsons for Judicial Review* (High Court of Justice in Northern Ireland, QBD (Judicial Review), 23 July 2002) is particularly helpful. The following summary borrows heavily from this source.

can enjoy widespread support from, and is seen to be an integral part of, the community as a whole'.[56] The Commission confirmed that only about 8 per cent of the existing police force (the Royal Ulster Constabulary) was Catholic, although more than 40 per cent of Northern Ireland's population was, at the time of the Commission's report, Catholic. Despite various initiatives since 1922, it had never proved possible to increase the number of Catholics in the force above 21 per cent. The imbalance of representation was considered by the Commission to be 'the most striking problem in the composition of the RUC'. The Commission recommended that the new intake of police officers should comprise 50 per cent Catholics and 50 per cent non-Catholics, all to be selected from a pool of candidates considered to meet specified qualifications, and that this pattern of recruitment should continue for at least 10 years so as to redress the imbalance.

Following the publication of the Patten Commission report in September 1999, a Police (Northern Ireland) Bill was drafted and received Royal Assent on 23 November 2000. The sponsoring department, the Northern Ireland Office, obtained advice from the Equality Commission for Northern Ireland, which publicly supported the recruitment measures. A human rights evaluation of the contents of the Bill was conducted and this enabled the Minister in charge of the Bill to confirm the government's belief that the Bill was consistent with the Human Rights Act 1998. The 2000 Act provides that the Chief Constable is responsible for the appointment of police trainees.[57] The legislation provides: 'In making [such] appointments . . . , the Chief Constable shall appoint from the pool of qualified applicants formed for that purpose . . . an even number of persons of whom (a) one half shall be persons who are treated as Roman Catholic; and (b) one half shall be persons who are not so treated.'[58] The Secretary of State, in making regulations prescribing the arrangements for the recruitment of persons to be appointed to the police service, is required to make provision for the selection of qualified applicants to form a pool of applicants for these purposes.[59] The temporary nature of these arrangements is made clear by requiring that the system should be subject to renewal every three years.[60]

Because the Police (Northern Ireland) Act 2000 introduced more extensive affirmative action provisions relating to appointments to the police force for three years from the commencement of the legislation, the FETO 1998 was amended to ensure that such affirmative action was also protected from being unlawfully discriminatory.[61] In addition, in order to ensure that the recruitment measures did not contravene the EC Employment Discrimination Directive, the UK negotiated an exemption from its provisions. The Directive provides that: 'in order to tackle the under-representation of one of the major religious communities in the police service in Northern Ireland, differences in treatment regarding recruitment

[56] Terms of Reference of the Independent Commission on Policing for Northern Ireland (as set out in the Agreement of 10 April 1998).   [57] Police (Northern Ireland) Act 2000, s 39.
[58] ibid, s 46(1)(a).   [59] ibid, s 44(5).   [60] ibid, s 47 (2).   [61] Art. 71A.

into that service, including support staff, shall not constitute discrimination insofar as those differences in treatment are expressly authorised by national legislation'.[62] There was no discussion whether the provisions might contravene the Framework Convention.

Northern Ireland Human Rights Commission, the Bill of Rights, and the OSCE High Commissioner on National Minorities

The OSCE, the Framework Convention, and Northern Ireland prior to the Agreement

The ways in which the CSCE/OSCE and its standards relating to national minorities might play a role in Northern Ireland had been discussed at least from the mid-1990s. At least from 1991, representatives of the Ulster Unionist Party (then the largest political party representing Protestants/unionists) also began expressing the view that the Framework Convention should be included in political negotiations.[63]

The enthusiasm of the Ulster Unionists for the Framework Convention appeared to be based on two aspects of the Convention. First, as interpreted by them, the Convention guaranteed minority rights but these guarantees had a quid pro quo: that existing national borders should be guaranteed and that advocacy for minority rights should always be peaceful.[64] Second, placing the Northern Ireland discussions in the Convention context strengthened the UUP argument that Northern Ireland was not unique, could be dealt with using existing methods of minority rights protections, and therefore did not need to have extraordinary methods applied to it, such as joint sovereignty between the United Kingdom and Ireland. The UUP has rarely relied upon international or European human rights standards to this degree, so it is particularly noteworthy that the Party found the Framework Convention to be something it could comfortably support and, indeed, promote.

This enthusiasm led the Party to bring the Convention into the political negotiations that eventually culminated in the Belfast Agreement. Shortly before the Agreement was concluded, the British Government ratified the Convention. In the Agreement, the Irish Government agreed to proceed with arrangements to ratify the Convention, thus (from the UUP perspective) accepting the sanctity of the existing national borders. UUP representatives subsequently claimed that

---

[62] In November 2000, Directive 2000/78 establishing a general framework for equal treatment in employment and occupation was adopted. This includes a prohibition of discrimination in employment on grounds of religious belief. This prohibition came into force on 2 December 2003.

[63] 'Ulster Unionist Party blueprint calls for a devolved assembly', The Irish Times, 1 March 1994, 6.

[64] Art. 21.

they had been responsible for ensuring that the Convention was included in the Agreement.[65] After the Agreement, UUP politicians urged their supporters to get behind the Agreement, in part because of its inclusion of references to the Convention.[66]

There was an additional constituency of support for the Framework Convention, prior to the Agreement. In 1996, the Irish Government-sponsored forum established to consider peaceful ways forward in Northern Ireland received several submissions emphasizing the relevance of the OSCE minority rights standards to Northern Ireland. One of the most noteworthy was that by a group of law professors, amongst whom was Professor Tom Hadden, who was appointed to the NIHRC when it was established and was particularly associated with advocating a role for the Framework Convention in the Commission.[67] In addition, those who considered that the Northern Ireland problem would benefit from a more European perspective saw the Convention as an opportunity to situate discussion of minority–majority relations in Northern Ireland within a broader frame of reference.[68] Neither prior to the Agreement, nor in the negotiations (so far as I am aware) was there any opposition from nationalists, nor from human rights NGOs contributing to these negotiations from outside, to including references to the Convention in the Agreement. Indeed, one of the most innovative equality provisions in the Agreement, the public sector equality duty, which had the strong support of those groups, had been partly justified prior to the Agreement as reflecting the aims and purposes of the Convention. The apparent degree of consensus around the Convention may have led Professor Hadden to say in February 1998, referring to several international human rights conventions, including the Framework Convention, that it 'would be relatively easy for the parties to select the most relevant provisions out of these for inclusion in a special Northern Ireland Bill of Rights'.[69]

The Framework Convention and the Agreement-Positive Assessment

Indeed, more broadly, the arrangements discussed above (fair employment monitoring, the Patten quota, and the cross-community voting arrangements), are to

[65] Lord Laird, 'Wanted: a rights commission for the whole NI community', The Irish Times, 11 August 2003, 14.

[66] Dermot Nesbitt, 'European avenue can protect Unionist rights', Belfast NewsLetter, 27 February 1998; Dermot Nesbitt, 'An assessment of the Belfast Agreement, (1991) 8 Accord, available at http://www.c-r.org/accord/ ireland/accord8/assess.shtml.

[67] Kevin Boyle, Colin Campbell, and Tom Hadden, 'The protection of Human Rights in the Context of Peace and Reconciliation in Ireland' in *Forum for Peace and Reconciliation, Consultancy Study* (1996).

[68] Richard Kearney and Robin Wilson, 'Bridge over the troubles' *New Stateman and Society*, 19 February 1993, 16.

[69] Tom Hadden, 'We can't leave it to the lawyers', The Belfast Telegraph, 10 February 1998.

the external observer paradigmatic examples of the types of measures that the Framework Convention was intended to promote.[70]

The fair employment legislation, taken as a whole, partly fulfils the requirements of Article 4.[71] The purpose of this provision is to ensure the applicability of the principles of equality and non-discrimination for persons belonging to national minorities. This is reflected in the provisions of FETO prohibiting discrimination on the grounds of religion and politics. These provisions are also supported by the obligation on States who are parties to the Convention to promote 'full and effective equality between persons belonging to a national minority and those belonging to the majority' and that this may require the parties to adopt 'special measures' that take into account the specific conditions of the persons concerned. This is reflected in the provisions of the FETO regulatory scheme dealing with equality of opportunity, monitoring, affirmative action, and Equality Commission enforcement actions. In several opinions and resolutions, the monitoring bodies of the Framework Convention have pointed in the case of other States parties to the type of socio-economic problems for minorities that the FETO was explicitly designed to address.[72]

As we have seen, monitoring is an essential element in this scheme, as is the specific element of the residual method discussed above. These monitoring requirements under the fair employment legislation also appear to conform with both the letter of the Framework Convention and the advice of the Advisory Committee of the Framework Convention.[73] As the EU Network of Independent

[70] In addition, the Lund Recommendations on the Effective Participation of National Minorities in Public Life, which the HCNM supports, also provide strong support for such arrangements, see www.osce.org/documents/hcnm/1999/09/2698_en.pdf.

[71] Article 4 provides: '1. The Parties undertake to guarantee to persons belonging to national minorities the right of equality before the law and of equal protection of the law. In this respect, any discrimination based on belonging to a national minority shall be prohibited. 2. The Parties undertake to adopt, where necessary, adequate measures in order to promote, in all areas of economic, social, political and cultural life, full and effective equality between persons belonging to a national minority and those belonging to the majority. In this respect, they shall take due account of the specific conditions of the persons belonging to national minorities. 3. The measures adopted in accordance with paragraph 2 shall not be considered to be an act of discrimination.'

[72] Advisory Committee on the Framework Convention for the Protection of National Minorities, Opinion on Finland, Adopted on 22 September 2000, ACFC/INF/OP/I(2001)2. 'Despite special measures to promote equality, the Advisory Committee notes that, as is recognised in the Report, the socio-economic differences between the majority population and the Roma remain considerable (see also comments under Article 15). Surveys conducted in this field suggest, inter alia, that the unemployment rate amongst the Roma is considerably higher than the average rate in the country, and their housing situation remains far from satisfactory' Council of Europe, Committee of Ministers, Resolution ResCMN(2001)3 on the implementation of the Framework Convention for the Protection of National Minorities by Finland (Adopted by the Committee of Ministers on 31 October 2001 at the 771st meeting of the Ministers' Deputies): 'There is also reason for concern about the *de facto* discrimination suffered by Roma as well as the existing socio-economic differences between some of the Roma and the majority population.'

[73] As well as the recommendations of ECRI, see the Third report on Hungary, 5 December 2003, CRI (2004) 25, para 93; and Third report on the Czech Republic, 5 December 2003, CRI (2004) 22, para 86. See also ECRI General Policy Recommendation No.1 on combating racism, xenophobia, anti-Semitism and intolerance, 4 October 1996, CRI (96) 43 rev.

Experts on Fundamental Rights has helpfully set out in a recent report surveying the opinions of the Advisory Committee on the issue,[74] the Advisory Committee has often stressed the need for States to collect data regarding the situation of minorities, in order to combat discrimination more effectively.[75] The data collected should be both accurate and updated on a regular basis, to ensure that the State is able to protect minorities in an effective way.[76] There must also be adequate legal safeguards applied to the collection and dissemination of such data. Protections accorded private and family life must be respected but, in addition, Article 3(1) of the Framework Convention must also be complied with. This provides that every person shall have the right freely to choose to be treated or not to be treated as belonging to a national minority and that no disadvantage shall result from this choice, implying (in the view of the Advisory Committee) that each person shall be able to request to not be treated as belonging to a minority.[77] Nor may answering a question relating to minority affiliation be made compulsory:[78] an obligation to reply to a question relating to the affiliation with a minority is not compatible with Article 3(1) of the Framework Convention on National Minorities, which protects the right not to be treated as a person belonging to a minority.[79] All these conditions appear, at first sight at least, to have been reflected appropriately in the monitoring requirements under Northern Ireland fair employment legislation, as described above. Indeed, they appear to reflect a growing consensus on the need for accurate statistical monitoring in this area.[80]

The Patten quota and the cross-community voting arrangements advance the aims of Article 15, which states: 'The Parties shall create the conditions necessary for the effective participation of persons belonging to national minorities in cultural, social, and economic life and in public affairs, in particular those affecting them.' The Advisory Committee Opinion on the United Kingdom, adopted on 30 November 2001, specifically drew attention to the Patten quota, recognized the problem that it was designed to deal with, and urged further

[74] EU Network of Independent Experts on Fundamental Rights, Thematic Comment No. 3: The Protection of Minorities in the European Union, 25 April 2005, from which this paragraph draws extensively.

[75] Advisory Committee on the Framework Convention for the Protection of National Minorities, Outline for reports to be submitted pursuant to Art. 25, para 1 of the Framework Convention for the protection of national minorities. Adopted by the Committee of Ministers on 30 September 1998. See also Opinion on Slovakia, 22 September 2000, ACFC/OP/I(2000)001, para.21; Opinion on Croatia, 6 April 2001, ACFC/OP/I(2002)003, para 29; Opinion on the Czech Republic, 6 April 2001, ACFC/OP/I(2002)002, para 28.

[76] See Opinion on Croatia, 6 May 2001, ACFC/OP/I(2002)003, para 29.

[77] See Opinion on Cyprus, 6 April 2001, ACFC/OP/I(2002)004, para 18.

[78] See Opinion on Azerbaijan, 22 May 2003, ACFC/OP/I(2004)001, para 21; and Opinion on Ukraine, 1 March 2002, ACFC/OP/I(2002)010, para 22.

[79] Opinion on Estonia, 14 September 2001, ACFC/INF/OP/I(2002)005, para 19; Opinion on Poland, 27 November 2003, ACFC/INF/OP/I(2004)005, para 24.

[80] See, in general, Timo Makkonen, *Statistics and Equality: Data Collection, Data Protection and Anti-Discrimination Law* (2006, forthcoming).

action:[81] 'The Advisory Committee recognises the importance of reaching this objective, noting at the same time the difficulties that the Government faces in achieving this. The Advisory Committee considers that the Government should continue to take measures to ensure the necessary reforms in recruitment and retention are made to reach this target as soon as possible.'

More generally, the Committee of Ministers of the Council of Europe has also praised the 'Commendable efforts [that] have been made through the devolution process in (...) Northern Ireland, to create the conditions necessary for persons belonging to national minorities to participate effectively in affairs concerning them.'[82] Finally, the Belfast Agreement, which as we have seen underpins each of these provisions, is a fulfilment of Article 18(1) which provides that: 'The Parties shall endeavour to conclude, where necessary, bilateral and multilateral agreements with other States, in particular neighbouring States, in order to ensure the protection of persons belonging to the national minorities concerned.' The Opinion on the United Kingdom of the Advisory Committee on the Framework Convention for the Protection of National Minorities, adopted on 30 November 2001,[83] specifically recognized this: 'The Advisory Committee takes note of the importance of the Belfast (Good Friday) Agreement (1998) as a contribution towards peace and stability and the protection of human rights in the region.'

Enter the Human Rights Commission

So, in light of this, it may seem strange that, for a period of time, the Framework Convention came to be interpreted by some as an obstacle to these initiatives, and more broadly as in opposition to a vision of group or communal accommodation envisaged by the Agreement. Concerns had been raised relatively early as to the desirability of the 'self-declaration' mechanism on which cross-community voting in the Assembly is based. Gilbert, a prominent academic writing in the area of minority rights, discussing the Agreement in 1998, observed that: '... the method of assessing cross-community support is crude. Self-declaration is open to abuse and, even if this does not arise, then it has been assumed that nationalism and unionism are monolithic, static and homogeneous. (...) As for the non-aligned Alliance Party, if its members declare themselves to be "other" they will have no direct influence on cross-community matters.'[84] This implied criticism was

[81] ACFC/INF/OP/I(2002)006, para 99. The response by the UK Government is: Advisory Committee on the Framework Convention for the Protection of National Minorities, Comments of the Government of the United Kingdom on the Opinion of the Advisory Committee on the Implementation of the Framework Convention for the Protection of National Minorities in the United Kingdom, GVT/COM/INF/OP/I(2002)006, 18 April 2002, para 129.

[82] Council of Europe, Committee of Ministers, Resolution ResCMN(2002)9 on the implementation of the Framework Convention for the Protection of National Minorities by the United Kingdom (Adopted by the Committee of Ministers on 13 June 2002 at the 799th meeting of the Ministers' Deputies).   [83] ACFC/INF/OP/I(2002)006, para 103.

[84] Geoff Gilbert, 'The Northern Ireland Peace Agreement, Minority Rights and Self-Determination' (1998) *47* International and Comparative Law Quarterly 943, 948.

picked up by Pentassuglia in his otherwise complimentary remarks on the Agreement in his 2002 study of minorities in international law, published by the Council of Europe.[85]

Although it had been a party to the negotiations and the Belfast Agreement, the Alliance Party was at the forefront of the political 'liberal' critique of the Agreement, frequently using the Framework Convention's provision recognizing a person's right to choose not to be treated as a member of a national minority as an important legal basis for their argument that particular aspects of the Agreement were flawed.[86] In particular, it argued that the voting system in the Assembly based on designation, was contrary to the Convention.[87] In adopting this 'liberal' critique of the Agreement, it was joined by Democratic Dialogue, a political think-tank,[88] and several academics.[89] Prominent among these critics was Professor Tom Hadden, by this time a member of the NIHRC, who argued that 'a balance should be maintained between the protection of the rights of both main communities, of other minorities and of individuals who do not wish to be treated as such'.[90] He argued that 'it was undesirable to maximize the competition and political confrontation between the two main communities and that providing space for those in between to move away from exclusive communal identities is the best way of avoiding future conflict'. On this basis, he considered that 'some aspects of the Agreement go too far in promoting an exclusive two communities approach to Northern Ireland'.

Such criticisms might have remained party political and academic but for the NIHRC. The NIHRC was given the task, *inter alia*, of advising on a Bill of Rights for Northern Ireland. The Commission decided that it would establish several Working Groups on particular topics. These groups included individuals from outside the Commission as well as Commissioners. One such group was established to consider issues of culture and identity, and it saw itself as considering in particular the Agreement's requirement that any Bill of Rights should 'reflect the principles of mutual respect for the identity and ethos of both communities and parity of esteem'.[91] The report, drafted by a noted 'liberal' critic of the Agreement, Robin Wilson of Democratic Dialogue, included a discussion of

---

[85] Gaetano Pentassuglia, *Minorities in International Law: An Introductory Study* (2002) 240.

[86] eg David Ford (Alliance Party leader at the time), 'Rights are for individual people—not for 'isms', Irish News, 12 August 2003.

[87] Alliance Party of Northern Ireland, Review of Member Designations and Voting System at the Northern Ireland Assembly, November 2001, para 2.2.7.

[88] Robin Wilson, 'Reshaping a skewed vision of "reality"', The Irish News, 22 September 2003.

[89] See eg Katy Hayward and Claire Mitchell, 'Discourses of equality in post-Agreement Northern Ireland' (2003) 9(3) Contemporary Politics 293; Ian O'Flynn, 'The Problem of Recognizing Individual and National Identities: A Liberal Critique of the Belfast Agreement' (2003) 6(3) Critical Review of International Social and Political Philosophy 129.

[90] Personal communication, 16 October 2005.

[91] The Belfast Agreement, s 6(3), available at http://archive.ofmdfmni.gov.uk/publications/ba.htm.

whether the 'subject of the additional rights to be enshrined in the bill [of rights] should be individuals or groups'.[92] It reported that the group:

'…benefited considerably in this regard from a presentation by the legal adviser to the Organisation for Security and Co-operation in Europe (OSCE) high commissioner for (sic) national minorities, John Packer. Mr. Packer said that in recent international instruments on minority rights "the idea of the community is that it is composed of persons belonging to it." He emphasizes that in the context of regional integration, globalization and migration identities were multiple and changing, and he warned against the "two big communal groups here" being allowed to "dictate what is going to happen." The working group concurred with this.'

The report went on to adopt what it termed an 'individualistic, "persons belonging" approach' and 'noted with approbation the provision in the Council of Europe Framework Convention allowing any "person belonging" the right to choose not to be so designated'.[93] It considered whether protections should be given to particular groups, but opposed this on the ground that this 'would fix identities, lead to arbitrary exclusions and not allow for change'.[94] Instead, it proposed that a 'generic reference to "persons belonging to national, ethnic, religious, linguistic, cultural or other communities"' should be included. It preferred the word 'communities' rather than 'minorities', given the 'negative and potentially restrictive connotations of the latter. The intention was to guarantee the rights of all.'[95] No special recognition should be accorded to Protestants or Catholics, 'in line with the individualistic resolution of the rights-holder dilemma'. It recommended the incorporation into domestic law of the Framework Convention but with an additional provision that 'made clear that the bill explicitly embraced ethnic, religious, linguistic, cultural and other, as well as narrowly "national", minorities'.[96]

The NIHRC produced draft guidance in the form of a consultation paper in September 2001. In this document, the NIHRC addressed the question of the relationship between individuals and communities. The Commission considered that one of the 'principal issues for the Commission in making recommendations for a Bill of Rights is the balance between two objectives: on the one hand recognising and protecting the two main communities and on the other hand protecting the rights of all on an equal basis'.[97] The Bill of Rights should 'include some specific guarantees for the two communities along the lines of the commitments already undertaken by the two governments. But the main emphasis…should be on the incorporation of relevant provisions of the Framework Convention for the Protection of National Minorities, with a view to guaranteeing the rights of members of *all* communities.'[98] The implication was that the majority (unionist) community should also be able to claim protection as well as the minority (nationalist, ethnic, racial, etc) communities.

---

[92] Report of the Bill of Rights Culture and Identity Working Group, available at www.nihrc.org/documents/culture_identity_working_group.doc.   [93] ibid, 1–2.
[94] ibid, 2.   [95] ibid.   [96] ibid, 3.
[97] Consultation, 24. available at: http://www.nihrc.org/documents/pubs/bor/bor_consultation01.pdf.   [98] ibid, 25.

The Commission introduced two controversial interpretations of the Framework Convention. The first was that the Commission decided, over the dissent of some unnamed Commissioners, 'that in the particular circumstances of Northern Ireland it would be desirable to avoid the use of the term "minority" and to replace it with the term "community". This would help to avoid complaints that one or other community is being given preference over others and should help to reassure members of the current majority community that recognising the rights of other communities does not involve any reduction of their own rights.'[99] The NIHRC supported its recommendations regarding the interpretation of 'community' in the Framework Convention 'in the light of advice from experts in the field, notably the legal adviser of the High Commissioner for Minorities at the OSCE (Organisation for Security and Co-operation in Europe),'[100] Mr Packer.

Second, there was a set of provisions in the consultation document considering the relationship between the protection of identities and the existing provisions regarding voting in the Assembly and the fair employment legislation. Although the Commission proposed that a provision be included that specified that nothing in the Framework Convention 'shall be used to negate equality commitments, including positive action provisions, in this Bill of Rights or in legislation', it recommended that the Bill of Rights should include the right of individuals not to be treated as members of a minority against their will. It recognized that the 'conferring of a right freely to choose not to be treated as a member of a particular community would obviously have implications for existing monitoring requirements in Northern Ireland. The Commission does not want to undermine the rationale for such requirements and would therefore welcome comments on whether, and if so how, such a right might be conferred.'[101] A majority of Commissioners did not consider that the proposals would provide a basis 'on which to challenge what is said in the Belfast (Good Friday) Agreement about voting mechanisms in Northern Ireland' although 'some Commissioners wanted this to be made explicit'.[102]

Much of the response to these aspects of the Commission's document was critical, both substantively and in terms of the procedures adopted.[103] As regards the latter, the relationship between the NIHRC and the High Commissioner's office came in for intense scrutiny, with allegations that the NIHRC was acting unprofessionally and engaging in 'forum shopping', asking the body that would provide the answer it wanted, rather the body with the primary jurisdiction, which would have been the Advisory Committee within the Council of Europe that the Framework Convention itself established. It is difficult to establish the validity of these allegations,[104] but why, if it was not forum shopping, was the Office of the

---

[99] Report of the Bill of Rights Culture and Identity Working Group, available at www.nihrc.org/documents/culture_identity_working_group.doc, 27.   [100] ibid.

[101] ibid.   [102] ibid, 28.

[103] For a general, if partial, overview of submissions on the issues, see Northern Ireland Human Rights Commission, *Summary of Submissions on a Bill of Rights* (July 2003) 30–34.

[104] The NIHRC has responded that 'these remain "allegations" since they were not recorded in Commission minutes nor were there any discussions as to what the "right answer" might comprise. It appears that the OSCE was considered at the time to be an appropriate body for the Commission to

High Commissioner on National Minorities the main port of call for an interpretation of the Framework Convention, when it has no authoritative jurisdiction under the Framework Convention? Worse, given its importance in the debate, it emerged that the 'advice' the Commission had relied on consisted simply of an oral reply by Mr Packer, the then legal adviser to the HCNM, to a question at a seminar with the Commission's working group in November 2000. There was no transcript of the seminar. There was no formal statement from the HCNM.

Other objections concentrated, not on the procedure adopted, but on the political consequences of the intervention. Some saw raising the issue of monitoring under the fair employment legislation in the context of the Bill of Rights debate as needlessly provocative. In particular, it risked reopening issues that had been subject to long and serious debate during the 1980s but which had largely been resolved and generated little controversy amongst employers or on the shop floor. Going back to the debates of the 1970s and the 1980s on fair employment was not something that was clearly in the public interest. For a public body whose function is the protection of human rights and which is under a statutory duty to have due regard to the need to promote equality of opportunity on the basis of religion, it seemed close to irresponsible.

It looked as if the Commission, or at least a majority of its members, were pursuing an agenda that had several elements. First, it was antagonistic to policies that relied on group identification as the basis on which to pursue consociational and equality policies. Secondly, it sought to support that position on the basis of legally based international human rights arguments. Thirdly, despite the fact that there was already underway a full-scale review of equality legislation commissioned by the Northern Ireland Executive, to determine whether there should be a Single Equality Bill, to bring together the existing scattered pieces of equality legislation, including the fair employment legislation, the NIHRC wanted to raise these detailed issues concerning equality law in the Bill of Rights context.

The Equality Commission, the statutory body with responsibility for overseeing the effectiveness of equality legislation in Northern Ireland, commented unfavourably on the proposals. It had 'reservations' with regard to the approach adopted by the NIHRC for two reasons.

First, it regarded the Framework Convention as:

'designed to require states to take measures to empower minority ethnic, religious or linguistic communities that face assimilation and extinction by the dominant culture. However by substituting "community" for minority the state in Northern Ireland would be required to offer support equally to already powerful ethnic and religious communities. It is difficult to see how this could be done without further marginalizing already vulnerable groups.'[105]

---

contact and it was also willing to contact the Council of Europe when it was suggested that they do so.' (Personal communication from the Chief Commissioner, Monica McWilliams, 20 December 2005).

[105] Equality Commission for Northern Ireland, *Northern Ireland Human Rights Commission Proposed Bill of Rights for Northern Ireland: Response*, March 2002, para 16.1.

Secondly, the Equality Commission considered that the right not to be treated as a member of a particular community 'would appear to pose a threat to some aspects of current equality legislation'.[106] Although it noted that the draft stated that the proposals should not undermine existing equality legislation, 'it is difficult to believe that it would not be used to challenge current monitoring provisions or requirements as to representativeness in public bodies'.[107] It continued to raise these issues periodically with the NIHRC during 2002 and 2003.

Enter the Office of the High Commissioner on National Minorities

When challenged after the publication of the consultation document, the Human Rights Commission wrote to the HCNM asking for a formal opinion on the following question: 'Whether as a matter of international law it is necessary to use the term "minority" in the process of incorporating into domestic law international standards for the protection of minorities?' The HCNM was under no legal or other obligation to respond. Indeed, becoming involved in Northern Ireland was not uncontroversial. During the negotiations leading up to the establishment of the post of High Commissioner, the British Government (and Turkey) had been concerned that the High Commissioner would become involved in Northern Ireland (and Kurdistan) and sought explicitly to ensure his exclusion from this jurisdiction by means of a provision that prevented the High Commissioner intervening in 'situations involving organized acts of terrorism'.[108] Given that ceasefires had been in (periodic) effect since before the Agreement, the High Commissioner was not legally forbidden from intervening under this provision, but it was legitimate to ask why, at this time and on this issue, the HCNM was willing to become involved in Northern Ireland for the first time.

From a broader political perspective, intervention was also controversial. The Russian Government had, for several years, been vociferously complaining at what it regarded as the biased behaviour of the OSCE in general, especially its activities in Chechnya. It had frequently questioned why the OSCE was not involved in equivalent problem areas in Western Europe, in particular in Spain and Northern Ireland.[109] Indeed, these complaints continue and have led to formal requests that a fact-finding mission should be sent by the OSCE as

---

[106] Equality Commission for Northern Ireland, *Northern Ireland Human Rights Commission Proposed Bill of Rights for Northern Ireland: Response*, March 2002, para 16.2   [107] ibid, 6.2.

[108] Mandate of the CSCE High Commissioner on National Minorities, reprinted in Arie Bloed (ed.), *The Conference on Security and Cooperation in Europe: Analysis and Basic Documents 1972–1993* (1993), para 5(b), 716.

[109] See 'Lack of time', What the Papers Say (Russia), 6 November 2002; 'Russia Praises Ireland's Disarmament Initiative', *BBC Monitoring International reports*, 25 October 2001; 'OSCE still wants to go to Chechnya', *Current Digest of the Post-Soviet Press*, 27 December 2000; 'Moscow calls for OSCE involvement in Northern Ireland', *Interfax Russia News*, 17 February 2000; 'The West is set to revive the Cold War', What the Papers Say (Russia), 18 November 1999; 'Lebed hints that the OSCE has no role in Chechen conflict', *BBC Summary of World Broadcasts*, 17 August 1996.

recently as February 2005.[110] These proposals have always been met with the response that such involvement would not be helpful.

Of greater concern, in my view, is the interpretative role that the NIHRC appears to have envisaged the HCNM to have. The caution expressed by Judge Higgins of the International Court of Justice in the *Wall* case is surely a wiser approach. After considering whether the ICJ should be interpreting and applying the International Covenants on civil and political, and economic, social, and cultural rights in the context of that case, she 'wonder[ed] about the appropriateness of asking for advisory opinions from the Court on compliance by States parties with such obligations, which are monitored, in much greater detail, by a treaty body established for that purpose'.[111] This is not to say that international or regional human rights bodies should not be asked for their interpretative help but it does mean that such bodies should be cautious and (in particular) that they should be fully informed.

The High Commissioner formally responded (in January 2003) to this invitation from the NIHRC. Not surprisingly, perhaps, the HCNM replied that international law:

'does not require States, when implementing their minority rights obligations, to use any particular term, such as "national minority" or, simply "minority". Indeed, in practice some States have found it desirable and effective exactly not to use the term "national minority", "minority" or similar terms. International law requires only that States give effect, at every jurisdictional level, to their obligations to protect the rights of persons belonging to national or ethnic, linguistic or religious groups who are in a minority position vis-à-vis a specifically stipulated object of protection and right.'[112]

Behind the scenes, however, things were somewhat less straightforward and the events leading up to the publication of the HCNM Note in January 2003 gave rise to concerns. After considerable delay, in September 2002, the Office of the HCNM had produced a draft note for the High Commissioner, together with a memorandum on the consociational voting arrangements under the Agreement. The September 2002 draft had advanced the view that aspects of the fair employment legislation were in breach of the Convention. Interestingly, after discussion between Mr Packer and several others, the formally approved version emanating from the HCNM did not include these views. One must assume that this change in stance within the approvals process in HCNM reflected disagreement, or the expression of different points of view, and that the final note was the

---

[110] Diplomatic Panorama, *Interfax News Agency*, 15 February 2005. The acting Russian envoy to the OSCE, Boris Timokhov, was reported as saying: 'Taking part in the Northern Ireland settlement would be good for the OSCE, which as a pan-European organization, should not settle only conflicts located "to the east of Vienna".'

[111] Advisory Opinion on the Legal Consequences of the Construction of a Wall in the Occupied Palestinian Territory, 9 July 2004, Judge Higgins, concurring opinion, para 27.

[112] Office of the OSCE HCNM, *Note on the Possible Use of Terminology in the Process of Incorporating into Domestic Law International Standards for the Protection of Minorities*, 31 January 2003.

settled opinion of the institution. Indeed, if the arguments made in the draft note had been confirmed, it would imply that the Framework Convention is antagonistic to particular aspects of consociational arrangements such as those pertaining to Northern Ireland. Unsurprisingly, since this would have meant a problematic reading of the Convention on a number of grounds, the reservations expressed in the initial note were either not shared or simply not pursued by the High Commissioner.

However, in correspondence with the Commission, Mr Packer indicated that the broader advice in the initial draft had been excluded only because he was persuaded that the original question put by the Commission was narrow and that it had been agreed that the note should respond only to that narrow question. He indicated further, however, that if he were asked more specific questions regarding the implications of the Framework Convention he would advise the High Commissioner that in his view aspects of the fair employment legislation, notably the arrangements for monitoring in the fair employment legislation, were in breach of the Convention. It is not clear if these remarks by Mr Packer were offered gratuitously, or solicited, or what authority he had to make them, given that they did not emanate from the High Commissioner.

On what basis might such a view be based? There were several problems with the approach adopted in the preliminary advice emanating from staff. The first element was the assumption that the Framework Convention was essentially about protecting cultural identity; but this required ignoring the emphasis elsewhere in the Convention on substantive equality. Only such a partial reading of the Convention could lead one to underestimate the proposed shift from 'minority' to 'community', with the implication that they were inter-changeable terms. Secondly, the initial draft amounted to an essentially out-dated view of the relationship between equality and non-discrimination, in which the non-discrimination principle limits any stronger concept of equality. But this view underestimates the importance of Article 4 of the Convention, which explicitly provides that measures pursuing full and effective equality should not be considered acts of discrimination (as well as the increasingly sophisticated European and international understandings of equality). Thirdly, the draft seemed to suggest that FETO monitoring provisions could be incompatible with international standards, but this conclusion relies on a highly selective view of international standards. The interpretation by the Committee on the Elimination of Racial Discrimination of its Convention, for example, specifies that although self-identification is the preferable basis for ethnic monitoring, this is so only if no justification exists to the contrary.[113] Fourthly, an international human rights body might be expected to emphasize language and principles that have some common definitions and shared understandings. So, while there is an emerging understanding in international practice of the meaning of 'minority', and it is a term

_____

[113] CERD Recommendation VII (1990).

used in a number of international treaties, the term 'community' is based on no developing international usage, and appears to have no place in any of the sub-stantive protections in existing international human rights law. Local adaptation is of course possible, and sometimes to be encouraged, but is not wisely engaged in by international standard-setting institutions. It is this latter viewpoint that pre-vailed in the final response from the HCNM. In summary, in the final note the HCNM noted the largely self-evident point that the exact terminology used was less important than the underlying principle, and did not adopt the controversial views in the staff memorandum.

This experience highlights some problems of process. Sufficient information about these exchanges between the NIHRC and HCNM entered into the public domain to allow for appropriate challenging and clarification along the lines indicated above, but the process leaves a lot to be desired. In this situation, despite the fact that the exchanges could, if they had been determined differently by the High Commissioner, have had a potentially destabilizing impact, all the contacts between the NIHRC and the Office of the HCNM discussed above took place in private. It is by no means clear what information or briefings the NIHRC had or had not given to the OHCNM. It was only a few weeks before the Opinion was finally given that others were informally consulted and it was apparent that the OHCNM had very significant gaps in its knowledge of the relevant domestic legislation. So far as I am aware, for example, neither the British Government, nor the Equality Commission provided briefings. More broadly, it raises critical issues about the appropriateness of international bodies drawing conclusions on issues, the political, legal, and cultural context of which are much more complex than the apparently bland question asked of them suggests. The flawed process, of course, may be due in part to the fact that the role that the HCNM was requested to play was one that it was never intended to play in the first place.

After receiving the more limited opinion in early February 2003, the NIHRC set out several further questions to the HCNM in August 2003.[114] This, in turn,

---

[114] Letter from NIHRC to the OSCE HCNM, 12 August 2003. Two separate questions were asked by the NIHRC, each with several separate sub-questions.

'1(a) Could the Office of the OSCE HCNM please clarify whether the advice proffered to this Commission on 31 January 2003 means that if, for example, Protestants or Unionists in Northern Ireland could show that they were a national, ethnic, religious, linguistic or cultural minority within the UK as a whole, they could invoke the protection within Northern Ireland of particular Articles in the European Framework Convention for the Protection of National Minorities?

1(b) Whatever the answer to the previous question, does the advice mean that if, for example, Protestants or Unionists could show that they were a national, ethnic, religious, linguistic or cultural minority within a particular region or locality in Northern Ireland, they could invoke the protection of the European Framework Convention?

1(c) Some members of the Northern Ireland Human Rights Commission feel that, by using the word "communities" rather than the word "minorities" in its proposals for protecting rights to group identity, ethos and esteem in a Bill of Rights for Northern Ireland, the Commission is in danger of undermining the protection of minorities in Northern Ireland as required by the European Framework Convention. Could the Office of the OSCE HCNM please advice (sic) on this?

led to further protests, not least from the (former) Deputy First Minister, Mark Durkan, leader of the Social Democratic and Labour Party (SDLP), which receives support predominantly from Nationalists/Catholics. The SDLP called in September 2003 for the NIHRC to withdraw its further request for advice from the HCNM, and requested the British and Irish Governments to ensure instead 'that the request for advice is handled through the Committee of Experts (sic) [of the Council of Europe]'.[115] As a result, the High Commissioner's Office may, at this stage, have come under diplomatic pressure not to proceed further with this issue. Or, perhaps, it realized the paradoxical situation in which it had been placed—a body whose mandate is to prevent or limit tensions was now in the position of potentially exacerbating them. Whatever the reason, the High Commissioner delayed responding until March 2004. The response, when it came, effectively indicated that he had withdrawn from further consideration of this particular issue. Before considering this response, however, an intervening series of events must be set out.

Council of Europe Ad Hoc Group Response

Possibly in response to criticisms that the Commission had been involved in 'forum shopping', the NIHRC also asked the UK Government to send the same or equivalent questions that it had asked the HCNM to consider to the Council of Europe, and this request was transmitted to the Council of Europe Secretariat in March 2003, together with a broader set of requests for assistance regarding other aspects of the Bill of Rights proposals, in particular regarding the appropriate inclusion of economic and social rights. The Secretariat of the Council of Europe regarded this as a request by the NIHRC for expert assistance and, in April 2003, indicated the readiness of the Council of Europe to provide this assistance. An Ad Hoc group was established by the Council of Europe, consisting of Professor Aalt Willem Heringa, Professor Giorgio Malinverni (a member of the Venice Commission), and Professor Joseph Marko (a former member of the Advisory Committee on the Framework Convention). The Secretariat included Mr Mark

2(a) Are the Fair Employment (Monitoring) Regulations (Northern Ireland) 1999 (SR 148) as amended in 2000 (by SR 228), in any way in breach of the rights protected by the European Framework Convention?
   2(b) If the Commission were to abide by its provisional advice that "everyone has the right freely to choose to be treated or not to be treated as a member of what might otherwise be perceived to be their national, ethnic, religious or linguistic community and no disadvantage shall result from this choice or from the exercise of the rights which are connected to this choice", what would be the implications for the Monitoring Regulations mentioned above?
   2(c) Article 3(1) of the Framework Convention states that "Every person belonging to a national minority shall have the right freely to choose to be treated or not to be treated as such and no disadvantage shall result from this choice or from the exercise of the rights which are connected to that choice". Could the Office of the OSCE HCNM please clarify whether there are two distinct rights contained in this provision—the right to choose and the right not to be disadvantaged?'

115 SDLP, *Rescuing the Human Rights Agenda*, September 2003, para 6.

Neville, the Secretary of the Framework Convention. The Ad Hoc Group visited Northern Ireland for three days in October 2003, despite the reservations of various individuals, human rights NGOs, and political parties about the purpose of the visit and its motivation. The Ad Hoc Group issued a paper in response to the request in February 2004.[116]

By the time the Ad Hoc Group considered the issue, the proposals of the NIHRC on identity and community rights had undergone some changes. The earlier provision protecting existing equality provisions was now omitted. Despite the concern that the NIHRC's original proposal might undermine equality protections, its potential saving grace was that the specific provision proposed alluded to the importance of protecting current equality protections. The new proposals did not even propose this limit. Instead, the Framework Convention's text was retained, without any recognition that there might be some tensions between this stance and already existing equality legislation. The Framework Convention was now explicitly to be incorporated into domestic law, and the right freely to choose not to be treated as a member of a community was explicitly and repeatedly retained.

In light of that, the Group considered whether or not the domestic law of Northern Ireland should give effect to the Framework Convention, as the NIHRC had recommended. In this context, the Ad Hoc Group considered who may be considered to belong to a national minority in the context of a law to give effect to the Framework Convention. Their response was that the Group did 'not consider it necessary to provide a set answer to this question',[117] and pointed instead to the desirability of adopting an 'article by article' approach, with some having a wide personal scope and others having a narrower personal scope. If, however, 'a full discussion on the personal scope of application is to take place, the experts consider that it is important that this discussion takes place with all groups concerned and that a rigid definition is avoided'. Such a discussion would require an examination of several questions, and '*it may be preferable to examine these outside of the context of the Bill or Rights project . . .*'.[118] The significance of this position was that it was in the context of the Bill of Rights project that the Commission had located the discussion. The Ad Hoc Group thus appeared to call into question an important part of the Commission's approach to the Bill of Rights.

Turning to the issue of the right to self-identification and the implications of the right freely to choose to be treated or not to be treated as a person belonging to a national minority and that no disadvantage shall result from this choice, the Ad Hoc Group noted that the concerns raised were 'primarily that the inclusion of such a clause could open the way for challenges to be made to current equality provisions that would undermine recent gains in equality over past years'.[119] After an extensive discussion, in a footnote,[120] of the practice of the Advisory

---

[116] Aalt Willem Heringa, Giorgio Malvinverni, and Joseph Marko, *Comments by Council of Europe experts on certain aspects of a future Bill of Rights for Northern Ireland* (2004).
[117] ibid, para 58.   [118] ibid, para 59 (emphasis added).   [119] ibid, para 63.
[120] ibid, fn 19.

Committee, the Ad Hoc Group concluded that 'the experts see that there *may* be an issue concerning the compatibility of certain equality provisions with the right to self-identification'.[121] This tentative view was set in the context of a discussion which demonstrates clearly that the *theoretical* opposition of the Advisory Committee to restrictions on the right to self-identification by persons belonging to national minorities, has been combined with a significant degree of tolerance *in practice* for such restrictions where they were part of consociational arrangements.

Its reason for side-stepping the issue, however, was that the Group considered '*that this is not a matter that should be definitively solved in a bill of rights*, but rather be addressed in ordinary legislation'.[122] The Group considered that 'a bill of rights should be the product of a broad societal consensus. From the discussions held in Belfast it is clear that there is no such broad societal consensus concerning the inclusion of this provision. Furthermore, it can be said that it is rare for a bill of rights or for a constitution to treat such matters.'[123] The Group noted that the issue was also connected to the appropriateness of affirmative action measures to ensure equality, and that 'there could well be a clash of rights, for example between the right of self-identification on the one hand and the need to ensure equality on the other'.[124] The Group considered that this issue 'could be better and more fully discussed or advanced, inter alia, in the context of discussions concerning the reform of the equality legislation and proposals to have a single equality act'. There may be other forums in which the issue may be raised, 'including the Advisory Committee on the Framework Convention for the Protection of National Minorities'.[125] In conclusion, the experts advised 'that the issue of self-identification *should not be examined in the context of the Bill of Rights project*, but rather outside of the project in a more appropriate forum'.[126]

Re-enter the High Commissioner on National Minorities

As pointed out above, the Office of the HCNM responded to the equivalent set of questions (set out above in footnote 114) in March 2004, after the Ad Hoc Group had reported. Unlike the Ad Hoc Group of the Council of Europe, the OHCNM responded to each of the questions put. Essentially, the first question as a whole is designed to elicit a view as to whether 'Protestants or Unionists' (to quote the question) are able to assert rights under the Framework Convention,[127]

---

[121] Aalt Heringa, Giorgio Malvinverni, and Joseph Marko, *Comments by Council of Europe experts on certain aspects of a future Bill of Rights for Northern Ireland* (2004), para 64 (emphasis added).

[122] ibid, para 64 (emphasis added).   [123] ibid, para 65.   [124] ibid, para 67.

[125] ibid, para 68.   [126] ibid, para 69 (emphasis added).

[127] There are several provisions of the FCNM, additional to those considered previously, of particular importance in addressing these issues:

Article 1

The protection of national minorities and of the rights and freedoms of persons belonging to those minorities forms an integral part of the international protection of human rights, and as such falls within the scope of international co-operation.

and whether this would undermine the protection of other minorities in Northern Ireland. If the respective answers are 'yes' and 'no', then this would provide considerable extra weight to the second group of questions set out in question 2, regarding the monitoring arrangements under the fair employment legislation. If 'Protestants or Unionists' are able to assert rights under the Framework Convention, then there is more opportunity for Protestants/Unionists to use the answers to challenge parts of the fair employment legislation, for example.

The three separate parts of the NIHRC's question explore three different grounds on which 'Protestants or Unionists' might be regarded as able to assert rights under the FCNM. If any one of these is accepted, then this would provide a legal basis for the assertion of 'Protestant or Unionist' rights under the Framework Convention. The focus of question 1(a) is to question whether this can be achieved by claiming that 'Protestants or Unionists' are a national minority within the UK as a whole. The purpose of question 1(b) is to question whether a similar result can be achieved by claiming that 'Protestants or Unionists' might be a minority within a particular locality within Northern Ireland. The purpose of question 1(c) is to question further whether the use of 'community' rather than 'minority' is a suitable way of interpreting the Convention, thus (again) enabling 'Protestants or Unionists' to claim to be a 'community' for the purposes of the Convention.

The OHCNM was prepared to answer the question in general terms but was unwilling to venture an opinion on the implications of its views for Northern Ireland specifically. Consistent with its earlier note, the issue of who constituted a minority should be 'established on a case-by-case basis in application of each stipulated right, article-by-article, and at each level (i.e. division of jurisdiction— national, regional or local levels) within the State'. The new note made clear, and this was uncontroversial, that 'even persons belonging to groups which may constitute a majority in the State as a whole, but may be in the position of a minority vis-à-vis the particular power of the authority at regional or local level, are entitled to protection'. If Protestants could satisfy the test, then they could invoke the protection of the Convention, if they could not satisfy the test, then they could not invoke the protection of the Convention.

Article 5
1. The Parties undertake to promote the conditions necessary for persons belonging to national minorities to maintain and develop their culture, and to preserve the essential elements of their identity, namely their religion, language, traditions and cultural heritage.
2. Without prejudice to measures taken in pursuance of their general integration policy, the Parties shall refrain from policies or practices aimed at assimilation of persons belonging to national minorities against their will and shall protect these persons from any action aimed at such assimilation.

Article 6
1. The Parties shall encourage a spirit of tolerance and intercultural dialogue and take effective measures to promote mutual respect and understanding and co-operation among all persons living on their territory, irrespective of those persons' ethnic, cultural, linguistic or religious identity, in particular in the fields of education, culture and the media.

Beyond that, however, the HCNM was unwilling to go. In particular, the attempt to re-engage the Commission in estimating whether there were negative consequences in the use of the word 'community' rather than 'minority' was handled with considerable care. There was, said the HCNM, no general 'necessary negative consequences' from the use of the word 'community', but OHCNM could not determine whether there might be negative consequences in the specific context of Northern Ireland. 'It is not possible for the Office of the OSCE HCNM to interpret the NIHRC's own draft [Bill of Rights] in the absence of a full understanding of the intentions of the drafters and the context of the situation, including appreciation of the wishes of those concerned and the implications which may flow from a particular choice and use of words. This seems better done by the NIHRC itself, or by a competent authority acting independently and impartially.'

Question 2 was even more specific in its terms, seeking the opinion of the OHCNM on whether the fair employment monitoring requirements were in breach of the Framework Convention. Again, the OHCNM was unwilling to be drawn: 'In the absence of a full appreciation of the situation, including its specific context, facts and effects, it is difficult to respond to such a question which seeks a definitive and complete answer.' In particular, since the relationship between monitoring and 'special measures' (ie affirmative action) was clear, the questions asked by the NIHRC 'can only fully and prudently be answered subsequent to a careful examination'. This examination, the note continued (echoing the view of the Ad Hoc group), 'would seem best done in the context of a broader discussion relating to special measures, as might be the case in the event of an overall reform of equality law and practice in Northern Ireland and in light of existing proposals for a single equality act'. The effect of incorporating a right not to be treated as a member of a minority on the fair employment monitoring provisions 'invites speculation' and 'requires to be assessed by a competent authority taking full account of the specific situation'.

The implications of the third part of question 2 were more important. Part 2(c) asks whether the very fact of attribution to a community under the monitoring provisions, irrespective of the fact that no individual is disadvantaged by such attribution, is enough in itself to amount to a breach. In terms of textual interpertation of the Convention, the issue is whether, for an attributed identification with a national minority to be in breach of Article 3(1) of the Framework Convention, the word 'treated' should be interpreted as requiring an act directed at the individual and involving a personal effect on the individual resulting from the unwelcome (from the point of view of the person complaining) identification of the status of national minority. This is an important issue because, as far as the fair employment monitoring regulations are concerned, there is no effect on the *individual* of being attributed to the status of a Catholic or a non-Catholic. As discussed above, the effect is on the *employer* because it may give rise to enforcement action if the Commission considers the statistics demonstrate a problem.

Under the fair employment provisions, to reiterate, there is no effect on the individual employee, no more than there is on an individual citizen attributed a status after a National Census, where the purpose is to devise policies for the provision of services to that group.

Although it has clear implications for the issue of monitoring under the Fair Employment and Treatment Order 1998, the implications of the questions are broader and essentially raise the issue of attributed community identification more generally in Northern Ireland, a practice which occurs in the context of the census, and the Patten quota in recruitment to the police service. Indeed, the third sub-question has potential implications beyond attributed community identification and raises issues concerning the use of community identification more broadly, which would have implications for the Assembly voting arrangements under the Belfast Agreement. Perhaps sensing the danger, the OHCNM was prepared neither to give a view as to whether Article 3(1) of the Convention provided for two distinct rights, the right to choose and the right not to be disadvantaged, nor to give an interpretation to the word 'treated' in Article 3(1), merely referring the NIHRC to the need to interpret the Convention according to the Vienna Convention on the Law of Treaties and the Explanatory Report to the Framework Convention for guidance.

Northern Ireland Human Rights Commission Response

Both the Ad Hoc Group and the OHCNM essentially adopted a cautious legal response, but one which left little room for doubt as to what approach it considered the NIHRC should now adopt on the issues, viz that the Bill of Rights was not the appropriate place to consider the issues of self-identification. Having asked the questions but received a response that was clearly not to its liking, it proceeded, apparently, to ignore the advice provided. Within weeks of the delivery of the Group's views, the Commission had published a revised set of proposals for a Bill of Rights.[128] It no longer relied on legal advice that it would be desirable to broaden the definition of 'minorities' to include all 'communities'. Apart from that, however, the proposals were very similar to those in the original consultation in September 2001, and the revised proposals in July 2003. The Commission mentioned the existence of the Ad Hoc Group's comments, and stated that the document was available from the Commission on request and that open to further representations on the issues raised, but did not discuss them. The existence of the March 2004 note from the OHCNM was not even mentioned. The NIHRC then proceeded to offer almost exactly the same proposals as it had in July 2003. The only significant change in the April 2004 proposals was the omission of any reference to a person's right not to be treated as a member of a minority, but only because the Commission's proposal to incorporate the Convention into domestic

---

[128] NIHRC, *Progressing a Bill of Rights for Northern Ireland: An Update* (2004).

law rendered this provision unnecessary. In an interesting discussion on the impact of incorporation of the Convention (including the right not to be treated as a member of a minority), the Commission set out its revised views:

'The Commission understands that incorporation of Article 3(1) of the Framework Convention will not mean that the current requirements on employers in Northern Ireland to monitor the community background of their workforce, or of applicants for their workforce, will become unlawful. It will simply mean that employees and applicants, when being monitored, will be able to insist that their *chosen* community affiliation will be recorded, as well as any perceived community background. Under the existing Monitoring Regulations employees and applicants cannot be absolutely sure that the reality of their current community background is accurately recorded by the employer.'[129]

No explanation is given as to the basis on which the Commission arrived at this 'understanding'. In its response to these renewed proposals, the Committee on the Administration of Justice, the Northern Ireland human rights NGO, was 'not reassured that the incorporation [of the Convention] will not undermine current fair employment protections'.[130]

The issue of the role of identity and community in the Bill of Rights was only one of several controversial issues swirling around the Human Rights Commission during this period. The details of the controversies are convincingly set out in Stephen Livingstone and Rachel Murray's study of the NIHRC, funded by the Nuffield Foundation, and published in January 2005.[131] We can see from this study, however, how the issue of identity and its potentially antagonistic relationship to issues of equality in Northern Ireland contributed to the general withdrawal of support for the NIHRC by key political and NGO actors, leading to the multiple resignations of Commissioners, and the appointment of an almost entirely new NIHRC in 2005. The substantive and procedural issues will not go away, of course, because one of the new Commission's tasks will be to determine what its relationship should be to the Bill of Rights project. The NIHRC has made it clear that the newly constituted NIHRC is not committed to either the format or the content of the last draft Bill of Rights published by the NIHRC in April 2004.[132] In addition, the issue of the relationship between the fair employment legislation and the implementation of the Framework Convention has been announced as one of the questions to be examined by the Advisory Committee on the Convention in the second monitoring cycle of the Convention in relation to the UK.[133]

---

[129] NIHRC, *Progressing a Bill of Rights for Northern Ireland: An Update* (2004), 34.

[130] Committee on the Administration of Justice, *Progressing a Bill of Rights for Northern Ireland—An Update* (2004) 4.

[131] Professor Stephen Livingstone and Dr Rachel Murray, *Evaluating the Effectiveness of National Human Rights Institutions: The Northern Ireland Human Rights Commission* (2005).

[132] Personal communication from the Chief Commissioner, Monica McWilliams, 20 December 2005.

[133] See http://www.coe.int/T/E/human_rights/minorities/2._FRAMEWORK_CONVEN...vo_Report/2._Second_cycle/NGO_questionnaire_2nd_United_Kingdom.asp.

Conclusion

This essay has discussed the extent to which the Framework Convention has been considered by quasi-authoritative international bodies to have implications for consociational arrangements in Northern Ireland that use group identification as part of their implementation mechanisms, particularly voting arrangements in the legislative body and measures promoting the more equal distribution of employment. The disputes that emerged were essentially (legitimate) political disagreements about the future governance of Northern Ireland and the methods of structural change that are appropriate. These essentially political disputes were, however, fought out in an inappropriate legal context—the content of a Bill of Rights in Northern Ireland, and the interpretative jurisdiction of the HCNM. The case study illustrates how there is a strong tendency, even among those operating in good faith, to convert political preferences into existing human rights requirements of a dubious type, not least because of the moral punch that human rights and legal rhetoric can deliver. There is a danger in over-egging the human rights legal pudding, a risk that over time we undermine the moral punch of existing human rights law by claiming that too much is covered by it.

This essay has also discussed the implications of what we might call the 'fragmentation' of human rights interpretation. 'Fragmentation' may not, of course, be quite the right word if it is taken as meaning that previously there was something intact and unified that has fractured. By 'fragmentation', I mean, rather, that a multiplicity of different systems, using many different mechanisms of addressing disputes, has grown up pragmatically in response to changing circumstances. We have seen that, despite the growth of judicial bodies at the regional and international levels, much human rights interpretation still takes place outside formal judicial processes, using informal processes, making human rights interpretation both more dynamic and more uncertain than human rights ideology sometimes seems to suppose. On the plus side, fragmentation has allowed for the operationalization of abstract international human rights principles in real-life situations. Indeed, legal expertise from the Council of Europe and other bodies is frequently sought on such issues. But, if this is to prove useful and prudent, these interpretative functions must be seen to be conducted with integrity. A good example of this is illustrated by the role of the Council of Europe Ad Hoc Group that reported on Northern Ireland.

In the case of the OHCNM, readers may well take different views on whether what happened was problematic. On the one hand, when the HCNM officially responded, it was restrained. International institutions are composed of human beings and the actions of the staff were undoubtedly intended to be benign. Nothing horrible happened in the end. On the other hand, readers may see instead how the appearance (at least) of being a party to forum shopping sucked a primarily conflict prevention and resolution body into a dispute that it was ill-equipped to handle.

On this alternative view, readers may see the OHCNM, a respected human rights body, blundering into a complex situation initially supporting those that it perceived to be on the 'right' side, but failing to appreciate the significance of the local context, and then effectively having to withdraw after political pressure is brought to bear. But even taking this alternative view, there may well be differences of view as to what went wrong. On one view, the problem that the story told here exposes may be that a body which prizes informality, operates on the basis of political negotiation and behind-the-scenes advice giving, relies on its own legitimacy to secure the acceptance of 'soft law' norms, and is primarily oriented to state security and the avoidance of conflict, was never likely to be able to deal effectively with a complex legal dispute on the interpretation of a (relatively) hard law instrument. A somewhat different analysis of the problem would, instead, credit the OHCNM with dealing effectively with complex legal—and highly political and ideological—issues all over Eastern Europe and see the problem discussed here as indicating that the HCNM is likely to be ineffective where he does not have a clear track record, and where significant actors inside and outside the relevant polity do not consider the organization to have any legitimacy in dealing with the dispute in contention.

Few would disagree, however, that the OHCNM's intervention, whatever the original motivation, reduced constructive dialogue among the relevant actors, and weakened respect for the legal norms themselves. The effective withdrawal of the OHCNM from the fray, and the sensitivity and good sense of the Council of Europe Ad Hoc Group, when combined with a new NIHRC that appears likely to take the new advice, has lowered the political temperature in Northern Ireland considerably on this issue; but the dangers of equivalent interventions elsewhere arising from fragmentation need to be appreciated and lessons learned more generally.

PART III
HUMAN RIGHTS

16

The Relationship Between Parliaments and National Human Rights Institutions

Rachel Murray *

Introduction

Increased attention has been paid to the establishment of National Human Rights Institutions (NHRI) in many jurisdictions.[1] Much of the debate on these institutions has focused on their compliance with the Paris Principles, guidelines adopted by the UN General Assembly in 1993 and which have come to be seen as the starting point against which NHRIs are assessed.[2] They imply that a key issue in the effectiveness of NHRIs is their independence. How a NHRI is funded, how its members are appointed, and who it is answerable to, are all-important considerations. In this regard the role of Parliament is seen as key.[3] There is a presumption that Parliaments and NHRIs have a natural complimentary relationship[4] and

* I would like to thank Judith Cohen and Leon Wessels from the South African Human Rights Commission; Maurice Manning and Alpha Connelly from the Irish Human Rights Commission; Francesca Klug from the LSE; and the editors of this collection for their comments. Where reference is made to interviews held, these were conducted in respect of the research carried out by Stephen Livingstone and myself on the Northern Ireland Human Rights Commission, see n 22 below.

[1] L.C. Reif, 'Building Democratic Institutions: The Role of National Human Rights Institutions in Good Governance and Human Rights Protection' (2000) 13 Harvard Human Rights Journal 1; International Council on Human Rights Policy, *Performance and Legitimacy: National Human Rights Institutions* (2000); Human Rights Watch, *Protectors or Pretenders? Government Human Rights Commissions in Africa* (2001). See, however, Inter-Parliamentary Union, *Strengthening National Structures, Institutions and Organisations of Society which Play a Role in Promoting and Safeguarding Human Rights*, Adopted by 92nd Inter-Parliamentary Conference, Copenhagen, 17 September 1994, available at www.ipu.org/conf-e/92-1.htm.

[2] Principles Relating to the Status of National Institutions, General Assembly Resolution 48/134, 20 December 1993, Annex. These Paris Principles outline how NHRIs should be composed, the breadth of their mandate, how they should operate and provide guidance on their composition and the manner of appointment.

[3] Inter-Parliamentary Union, Strengthening National Structures, n 1 above, para 25.

[4] On the role of Parliament in protecting human rights, see eg Danny Nicol, 'Are Convention rights a no-go zone for Parliament?' (2002) PL 438; Conor Gearty, 'Civil Liberties and Human Rights', in Nicholas Bamforth and Peter Leyland (eds), *Public Law in a Multi-Layered Constitution* (2003); Conor Gearty, 'Reconciling Parliamentary Democracy and Human Rights' (2002) 118 LQR 248.

that greater involvement of Parliament in the various aspects of the life of the NHRI will contribute to its independence and thereby enhance its legitimacy and its credibility. Consequently, Parliaments have been encouraged to 'develop a special working relationship with NHRIs'.[5] There has, however, been limited attention to this issue in the literature on NHRIs.

Recent developments in the UK illustrate the importance of this debate. The Westminster Parliament debating the Equality Bill establishing a Commission on Equality and Human Rights for the UK,[6] and the Scottish Parliament examining the Scottish Human Rights Commissioner Bill,[7] illustrate the role of legislatures in not only defining the remit and mandate of any future NHRI in those jurisdictions, but also require closer analysis of what role they each see themselves playing in the operalization of those institutions.

This essay seeks to examine what role the legislature can play with respect to NHRIs. While I will advocate that Parliamentary involvement is a useful and indeed necessary tool in ensuring the accountability and contributing to the effectiveness of a NHRI, the relationship should be considered in more detail. How effective it will be depends on the political and constitutional context in which the NHRI finds itself. In considering the best way to formalise this relationship, the NHRI must itself develop a strategy on how it will engage effectively with the legislature, and it may also be appropriate to channel scrutiny of a NHRI's work through one specialist committee.

There are a number of points worth considering. First, the ability of legislatures to ensure accountability in practice has come under debate in recent years. This has been attributed to a range of factors including: a rise in loyalty to party politics, an increase in the scope of tasks taken on by government, a decline in the ability of Parliaments to take leadership, and a loss of power by the legislatures not only to government but also to other external bodies including the media.[8]

[5] *National Human Rights Institutions and Legislatures: Building an Effective Relationship: The Abuja Guidelines. Report on an International Workshop, Abuja, Nigeria, 23–25 March 2004*, www.britishcouncil.org (hereinafter 'The Abuja Guidelines').

[6] Equality Bill [HL] 99. See also House of Lords, House of Commons, Joint Committee on Human Rights, The Case for a Human Rights Commission, Sixth Report of Session 2002–2003, HL Paper 67-I, HC 489-I, 19 March 2003; White Paper, *Fairness for All: A New Commission for Equality and Human Rights*, Cm 6185, 12 May 2004.

[7] Scottish Commissioner for Human Rights Bill, SP Bill 48, introduced 2005. See Scottish Executive, *Protecting our Rights. A Human Rights Commission for Scotland?* (2001), available at: http://www.scotland.gov.uk/consultations/justice/porhr00.asp; Scottish Executive, *Analysis—Protecting our Rights. A Human Rights Commission for Scotland?* (2001), available at: http://www.scotland.gov.uk/library3/justice/hrcs00.asp; Scottish Executive, *The Scottish Human Rights Commission* (2003), available at: http://www.scotland.gov.uk/consultations/justice/shrs-00.asp; Scottish Executive, *The Scottish Human Rights Commission. Analysis of Consultation Responses* (2004), available at: http://www.scotland.gov.uk/library5/social/hrcacr-00.asp.

[8] G.P. Thomas, 'The Prime Minister and Parliament' (2001) 10(2/3) Journal of Legislative Studies 4, 5–6. See also Hansard Society, *The Challenge for Parliament. Making Government Accountable* (2001); Dawn Oliver, 'The Challenge for Parliament' (2001) PL 666; Jack Hayward, 'Parliament and the French Government's Domination of the Legislative Process' (2004) 10(2/3) Journal of Legislative Studies 79.

Secondly, despite its independence a NHRI must operate in a political field. It is essential, if an NHRI is to have any influence, that it uses its contacts and political relationships with both those within and outside government, Parliament and political parties to its advantage and not be afraid of doing so. Engagement with Parliament, an institution composed of political representatives, therefore, can be a difficult role to play for an institution that ideally wishes to be seen as impartial. Although not statutory or constitutionally -created bodies, non-governmental organizations (NGOs) have also had to grapple with their relationship with political actors. In order to be able to operate comfortably within a political environment and influence direction of policy, the experience of NGOs has shown that institutions have to build up a presence over a period of time,[9] be able to form networks and identify the powerful actors, and make use of political allies.[10] Even if access is denied to meetings and formal negotiations, participation and lobbying informally can be very influential in getting a message across.[11]

Will Parliament Ensure a NHRI's Accountability?

Increased involvement of Parliament in the life of a NHRI is encouraged by many. The relationship with Parliament is tied in with the institution's accountability and, in this respect, with its independence.[12] NHRIs not only assist Parliament in their oversight of government, but they are also an alternative source of information for the legislature.[13]

---

[9] Lisa Jordan and Peter Van Tuijl, 'Political Responsibility in Transnational NGO Advocacy' (2000) 28(12) World Development 2051, 2054.

[10] Margaret. E. Keck and Kathryn Sikkink, 'Transnational Advocacy Networks in International and Regional Politics' (1999) 159 International Social Science Journal 89, 97.

[11] Daniel Berlin, 'The Key to Green Power—Explaining NGO Influence in Global Environmental Governance Structure', prepared for NISA-NOPSA Conference, Reykjavik, 11–13 August 2005, Workshop Globalization as Individualization and Destabilization.

[12] eg the Irish Human Rights Commission recommended 'that the best way of ensuring the effectiveness of the Commission and its independence would be to have no formal link between the Commission and any government department. Rather, in so far as the Commission is to be made accountable to another organ of the State, the Commission should be accountable to the Oireachtas', Irish Human Rights Commission, *Report to the Government under Section 24 of the Human Rights Commission Act 2000* (2003), available at http://www.ihrc.ie/_fileupload/publications/Reports-Section_24_21-07-2003_Final.pdf, 9.

[13] 'Firstly they should be seen as complementary to Parliament's oversight function: *together* with Parliament they act as watch-dog bodies over the government and organs of state. Secondly, they support and aid Parliament in its oversight function by providing it with information that is not derived from the executive . . . . one of the constitutional functions of Parliament is to be an oversight body to provide a check on the arbitrary use of power by the executive. . . . Thus Parliament's oversight function can be enhanced by ensuring the effective functioning of state institutions supporting constitutional democracy', Hugh Corder, Sara Jagwanth, and Fred Soltau, *Report on Parliamentary Oversight and Accountability* (1999) 56.

Accountability can encompass, however, a range of perspectives.[14] On the one hand it could 'simply require that the performance of a service is no more than the sum of the actions performed, and if these are done conscientiously and competently, then all is well with the service as a whole'.[15] Accountability can also be both political and managerial. Political accountability requires the institution to justify what it has been done and for transparent and open mechanisms to be put in place to do so. Managerial accountability requires the institution to answer for how tasks have been carried out in line with specific goals set, how money has been spent and whether the result hoped for was achieved.[16] One of the difficulties of ensuring accountability of an institution such as an NHRI is that those being held accountable may see their responsibilities differently from those that are assessing their performance.[17] This may be the case particularly with institutions like NHRIs, who are operating in a context in which other factors and the role of other institutions also play a part in achieving results. In addition, applying 'value-for-money' approaches can be seen as inappropriate for NHRIs whose aim is to promote human rights.[18]

Given the complexity of the concept and the political make-up of Parliament, some caution needs to be exercised when considering how best Parliament may contribute to ensuring the accountability of a NHRI. The following sections will examine the various ways in which Parliaments have become involved in the life of a NHRI.

Role of Parliament in Creating a NHRI

It is clear that many advocate, and many examples exist, of Parliament having some role in the creation and establishment of a NHRI.[19] First, this may arise

[14] As the House of Lords noted, 'accountability is a generic term, the precise definition of which depends on the circumstances, including the relationship between the interested party to the regulator. In practice, there are multiple accountabilities', House of Lords Select Committee on the Constitution, *The Regulatory State: Ensuring its Accountability*, 6th Report of Session 2003–2004, HL Paper 68-I, 6 May 2004, para 48.

[15] Patricia Day and Rudolf Klein, *Accountabilities. Five Public Services* (1987) 236.

[16] ibid, 27.

[17] Day and Klein's research found that those interviewed saw 'accountability, answerability, or responsibility as being direct to the "community" at large, rather than following the lines of constitutional accountability', ibid, 229.

[18] ibid, 235. 'Should independent bodies be accountable for their own policies and performance; or is the degree of control implicit in such a requirement likely to restrain their independence? In broad terms, watchdogs should be accountable only for matters of performance . . . rather than for the merits of their recommendations, policies or goals. In most cases, accountability should be after the fact, rather than the sort of pre-accountability that involves seeking consent prior to a course of action, through a business plan or structuring the action by prescribing the rules', Nicole Smith, 'Policing the Constitution' (1997) PL 234, 237–38.

[19] The Inter-Parliamentary Union resolution on strengthening national institutions which play a role in human rights noted that 'parliaments play a unique and important role in helping governments by adopting legislation to establish national institutions and enhance the operation of such

with the passage of legislation creating the NHRI, if it is done through statute. The Paris Principles certainly propose the creation of NHRIs in this way, hoping that it will give them a degree of stability: 'A national institution shall be given as broad a mandate as possible, which shall be clearly set forth in a constitutional or legislative text, specifying its composition and its sphere of competence.'[20] In addition, it is presumed that accountability entails the ability of the legislature to change the founding legislation of the NHRI if necessary.[21]

However, the content of legislation can play a key role in the future institution's effectiveness. Decisions taken at this level can set in stone restrictions and difficulties that a NHRI will then have to face in its operation.[22] While some of these may be deliberate and reflect the political context in which an institution is established, others may be less obvious and reflect either procedures in drafting, common practices, or oversights.

Some of these problems can be avoided by extensive consultation and allowing comments on draft legislation. For example, the background to the Equality Act providing for the establishment of the Commission on Equality and Human Rights in Great Britain, reflects extensive consultation.[23] Some Parliaments, however, may not be as removed from executive influence as one may wish, even if they are not quite the 'elective dictatorship'[24] that is suggested exists in some jurisdictions. If the government holds a strong majority in the legislature, legislation will be subject to its approval in practice: 'Parliament is supreme, but a government with a secure majority can be expected . . . in the long run to secure the enactment of its programme of legislation.'[25] Furthermore, political alliances may also be more determinative than a desire to improve respect for human rights or to enhance the position of the NHRI. As has been noted in respect of the Human Rights Act in the UK:

'. . . others are sceptical of the ability or willingness of Parliament to act as a constitutional watchdog. Members of the House of Commons will find it difficult, when undertaking the scrutiny of legislation for compatibility with Convention rights under the Human Rights Act, to set aside their party political allegiances and reach objective decisions as to whether proposals breach Convention rights . . .'[26]

---

institutions where they already exist', Inter-Parliamentary Union, *Strengthening National Structures*, n 1 above. In addition, see *Abuja Guidelines*, n 5 above; UNDP, *Primer on Parliaments and Human Rights*, available at www.undp.org/governance/docshurist/040825Human%20Rights%20Paper%20Final2.doc. See also Commonwealth Secretariat, *National Human Rights Institutions. Best Practice*, (2001), available at http://www.thecommonwealth.org/, 15.

[20] Paris Principles, n 2 above, para A.2.
[21] House of Lords Select Committee on the Constitution, *The Regulatory State*, n 14 above, para 35.
[22] See report from the Nuffield-funded project, Stephen Livingstone and Rachel Murray, *Evaluating the Effectiveness of National Human Rights Institutions. The Northern Ireland Human Rights Commission*, February 2005, on file with author.   [23] See n 6 above.
[24] Lord Hailsham, *The Dilemma of Democracy* (1978) 126.
[25] Lord Steyn, 'Deference: A Tangled Story' (2005) PL 346, 347.
[26] Dawn Oliver, 'Democracy, Parliament and Constitutional Watchdogs' (2000) PL 553, 553.

In India, where the government appeared to rush to get legislation establishing the NHRI through Parliament there was 'indifferent Parliamentary discussion' and a lack of broad consultation leading to what has been seen as a weak piece of legislation.[27] Clearly, when drafting or amending legislation establishing a NHRI, political considerations as well as the extent of government influence and drafting procedures all have a decisive impact on the ultimate functions and composition of a NHRI.

Parliament can also play a role in the creation of a NHRI through the appointment of its members.[28] Much criticism is directed towards governments who choose to appoint the members of NHRIs, this being seen as fundamentally undermining the principle of independence. The Paris Principles advocate the involvement of a variety of actors in the appointment process:

'The composition of the national institution and the appointment of its members, whether by means of an election or otherwise, shall be established in accordance with a procedure which affords all necessary guarantees to ensure the pluralist representation of the social forces (of civilian society) involved in the protection and promotion of human rights, particularly by powers which will enable effective cooperation to be established with, or through the presence of, representatives of: Non-governmental organizations responsible for human rights and efforts to combat racial discrimination, trade unions, concerned social and professional organizations, for example, associations of lawyers, doctors, journalists and eminent scientists; Trends in philosophical or religious thought; Universities and qualified experts; Parliament; . . . '[29]

Through Parliament having some role in appointing members of the Commission,[30] it is hoped that the appointments process itself will be transparent and that this will enhance the independence of the institution.[31] Furthermore, appointment with the involvement of or by Parliament is seen as a stamp of approval of the NHRI. As a member of one NHRI said: 'I don't have any difficulties with Parliament actually appointing us, because I think that what you want to do is you want to say to any political parties that causes difficulties that you're approved by Parliament and you have this mandate that comes from the peoples' representatives.'[32] If, as may well be the case where Parliament is involved, the

---

[27] Reenu Paul, *The National Human Rights Commission of India. A Human Rights Evaluation* (2003), available at www.nhri.net, 20–21.   [28] See *Abuja Guidelines*, n 5 above.

[29] Paris Principles, n 2 above, para B.1. Further, para B.3: 'In order to ensure a stable mandate for the members of the institution, without which there can be no real independence, their appointment shall be effected by an official act which shall establish the specific duration of the mandate. This mandate may be renewable, provided that the pluralism of the institution's membership is ensured.'

[30] Some have favoured the approach whereby there is a duty to consult Parliament, as the JCHR note: 'On the whole we would tend to favour a form which requires a duty to consult Parliament on the appointment of commissioners as a guarantee of independence and democratic accountability, so long as this was a statutory duty', House of Lords, House of Commons, Joint Committee on Human Rights, *The Case for a Human Rights Commission*, Sixth Report of the Session 2002–2003, HL Paper 67-I, HC 489–1, 19 March 2003, para 223.

[31] The JCHR noted that some of those who responded to its consultation on a human rights commission felt that a Commission for the UK should be responsible to Parliament, ibid, para 222.

[32] Interview held on 14 August 2002.

appointments process is the first point of contact for a legislature with the NHRI, a relationship which must then be developed in other ways, it is essential that this initial contact is a positive and informed experience.

Yet simply allocating the responsibility of appointment to Parliament will not necessarily ensure transparency, create a more independent institution, or a better relationship with the institution itself. Part of the appointment role of Parliament is to ensure that a NHRI is accountable. However, there is research to suggest that electing individuals to a public institution may not necessarily ensure accountability. Accountability may have more to do with the individual's own sense of their responsibility.[33] The members of the South African Human Rights Commission are recommended by Parliament under sections 193 and 194 of the Constitution and then this is subject to their appointment by the President.[34] Civil society may be involved in the recommendation process but this is not obligatory. The interviews are held in public. Whilst on the face of it, Parliamentary involvement in the appointments suggests that this part of the procedure is ideal, in practice it has not been without its difficulties. For example, a Parliamentary committee may not be as neutral or disinterested a body as one might initially imagine undertaking this role. Parliamentarians may carry their political viewpoints with them to the interview process and questioning may reflect more of a concern towards political leanings than knowledge of human rights or the potential contribution to the Commission. During the first round of appointments to the South African Human Rights Commission some candidates were dissatisfied with the capacity of the committee that was doing the interviewing to make a really wise selection:

'a major difficulty is that making a Parliamentary committee responsible for nominations inevitably means that the nominations will reflect the party political make-up of the committee. The danger is that party political considerations consequently overshadow criteria more germane to the nature of the body for which nominations are being considered.'[35]

This does not necessarily mean that those who are appointed may not be the best people for the job, but more that ' . . . it was just a sense that it was luck that got the Commissioners',[36] and that the process by which it was achieved risks undermining the NHRI's legitimacy from the start.

---

[33] Day and Klein, *Accountabilities*, n 15 above, 240.

[34] See s 115 of the Interim Constitution. In the first round of appointments in 1995, Commissioners were appointed by a two-thirds majority of the members of the National Assembly, although subsequent rounds have been conducted on a majority basis.

[35] Alison Tilley, 'Process Problems May Haunt the HRC' (1995) Democracy in Action 8, as quoted in Jeremy Sarkin, 'The Development of a Human Rights Culture in South Africa' (1998) 20 Human Rights Quarterly 628. See Livingstone and Murray, n 22 above, 41. As was said about the Zambian Human Rights Commission, 'although the appointments were ratified by Parliament, there was an uproar over the haste and lack of transparency that characterized the appointment and parliamentary process. It remains a matter of debate in Zambia whether the creation of the Permanent Human Rights Commission was a consistent step in line with the stated MMD manifesto or a donor-driven public relations ploy to offset international criticism over the MMD's controversial record during the 1996 general elections', Human Rights Watch, *Protectors or Pretenders*, n 1 above, 381.

[36] Interview held on 6 August 2002.

Secondly, as with any interview process, it is essential that those interviewing candidates are informed about those individuals before them, about the issues and about the mandate of the NHRI. Whereas an independent body which appoints members of a NHRI may itself be carefully selected to ensure that it has the necessary expertise and background, the same may not be said of a Parliamentary committee, who may be chosen on the basis of ensuring equal party representation rather than their knowledge of human rights of the institution they are about to appoint.

Furthermore, the appointments process in itself is a great opportunity for human rights awareness raising and to increase the profile of the NHRI. However, in order to do so it must be vibrant, informed, and publicized. This appeared to have been the case with respect to the appointments of members of the Truth and Reconciliation Commission in South Africa:

'we had documents coming from various sources, some anonymous, with regard to a press statement that had been issued by one of the candidates five years back and could put that to them. So I think, because that's part of the independence as well, it's part of the testing.'[37]

NHRIs, however, may not tend to generate as much political or public interest. For example, when it came to nomination of Commissioners to the South African Human Rights Commission for their second term of office, Parliament 'missed that opportunity by keeping it very low key',[38] not only in the run up to the appointments but in the interviews themselves: 'one or two of the interviews were wonderful exchanges on human rights. It could have made like a wonderful little insert on the news or something. It really could have been used to promote the Commission. They missed that opportunity again.'[39] Parliament could have used the process to increase human rights awareness and knowledge of the constitutional bodies.

Discussion about how the appointments process can ensure independence and integrity of the resulting institution are not unique to NHRIs and have been discussed extensively in relation to the judiciary, for example.[40] As institutions take on an increasingly political role, so calls have been made for a more independent and accountable appointment process.[41] Whether appointments are carried out by Parliament or a separate appointments commission, the process is still not without difficulties.

In order for Parliament to act effectively in ensuring the accountability of the NHRI and (through the activities the NHRI brings to its attention) of government, the legislature must have the capacity to effect change over the statutory functions, composition or otherwise, of the institution if necessary. For example, if Parliament has some role over appointment of members of the NHRI, it may

---

[37] Interview held on 14 August 2002.   [38] Interview held on 6 August 2002.
[39] Interview held on 6 August 2002.
[40] eg Kate Malleson, *The New Judiciary. The Effects of Expansion and Activism* (1999).
[41] ibid.

well have a role in their removal and re-appointment. Here it is again essential that parliamentarians are informed and take this task seriously. This has not always been the case in practice. As one member of a NHRI who was interviewed by a parliamentary committee with a view to his re-appointment said:

'I thought that was a waste of the committee's time and my time, it wasn't a test . . . . I really thought that having served on the Commission for five years I would have been put on the spot in quite a significant way, you know, about these issues . . . and it was quite a breeze, in part because I don't think the committee members were prepared for it. I'm not sure they knew what they were looking for in terms of commissioners. So I think for all those reasons . . . at that level, the role of parliament and its relationship with the Commission is something that concerns me deeply. I mean starting from the interview process but also its ongoing relationship with the Commission.'[42]

Deciding the extent of Parliament's role in appointments, therefore, will require an honest consideration of the environment in which that particular NHRI operates. If appointments are to be carried out by a parliamentary committee, then this should be done by a committee which is informed, experienced in appointing members of such institutions, and which has the necessary resources to carry out this task effectively. The issue of which committee this should be will be discussed further below.

A final consideration with respect to Parliament's role in appointments arises when one considers whether parliamentarians themselves should be members of a NHRI. Some NHRIs do involve parliamentarians on their bodies,[43] or indeed those who used to sit in the legislature.[44] It has been suggested that this can in fact improve the relationship with Parliament: 'because you know at that time parliamentarians could really view what the Commission is doing or is not doing and the national Commission could really address and transmit the message from the representative of the Parliament and to us directly. . . . So that could create an exchange, direct exchange, between the National Commission and the Parliament.'[45] In addition, those with a working knowledge of the legislature may have contacts or experience they can exploit with respect to lobbying on the activities of the NHRI. However, it is submitted that having members of a NHRI who are also parliamentarians, particularly those who hold the positions simultaneously, is also fraught with difficulties. For example, the work of a NHRI can mean that it may conflict with policies of political parties and having their representatives sat on this institution could cause tensions in determining a NHRI's approach. Further, tensions among political parties outside the NHRI risk being played out within it. Again, to whom a member of a NHRI feels

---

[42] Interview held on 15 August 2002.

[43] eg the Sudan Advisory Council for Human Rights. See Human Rights Watch, *Protectors or Pretenders*, n 1 above, 319–30.

[44] For eg, the President of the Irish Human Rights Commission, Maurice Manning, was a member of the Irish legislature, the Oireachtas, for 21 years, serving in both the Dáil and the Seanad.

[45] Interview held on 27 November 2002.

accountable may not sit easily with political representatives' notions of accountability to their constituents.[46]

Role in Monitoring Performance

In order to ensure accountability, it is often advocated that Parliament should
have several opportunities to monitor government activities, with the assistance of
a NHRI, and to monitor a NHRI's own performance.

Legislative Scrutiny

Many NHRIs have a mandate to review legislation in terms of its compatibility
with human rights and to make recommendations to the government and
Parliament. Indeed, the Paris Principles envisage such a role for a NHRI.[47] NHRIs
may be involved, formally or informally, in making comments on draft legislation
and making recommendations for amendments to existing legislation. There is
some evidence, however, that the less contentious the legislation, or the more it is
proofed for human rights within the legislature, the less likely the NHRI will be
able to interact with Parliament. As has been said in the past with respect to the
Northern Ireland Human Rights Commission, 'There has probably been less than
I expected, to be quite frank, and I think that is because most of the legislation
has been relatively carefully crafted to not be contentious in that regard.'[48] If this
happens, although the formal opportunity for a NHRI to engage with Parliament
is potentially removed, it is still possible to interact with it in reviewing legislation. For example, the Commission for Equality and Human Rights for Great
Britain has not been given the power to review legislation, the function already
being carried out effectively by the Parliamentary Joint Committee on Human
Rights (JCHR). This does not mean, however, that there will not be some role
for the Commission in commenting on draft legislation if it wished to do so,

---

[46] Livingstone and Murray, n 22 above, 41.

[47] 'A national institution shall, *inter alia*, have the following responsibilities: To submit to the
government, parliament and any other competent body, on an advisory basis either at the request of
the authorities concerned or through the exercise of its power to hear a matter without higher referral,
opinions, recommendations, proposals and reports on any matters concerning the protection and
promotion of human rights. The national institution may decide to publicize them. These opinions,
recommendations, proposals and reports, as well as any prerogative of the national institution, shall
relate to the following areas: (i) Any legislative or administrative provisions, as well as provisions relating to judicial organization, intended to preserve and extend the protection of human rights. In that
connection, the national institution shall examine the legislation and administrative provisions in
force, as well as bills and proposals, and shall make such recommendations as it deems appropriate in
order to ensure that these provisions conform to the fundamental principles of human rights. It shall,
if necessary, recommend the adoption of new legislation, the amendment of legislation in force and
the adoption or amendment of administrative measures', Paris Principles, n 2 above, para A.3.a.

[48] Interview held on 15 October 2002.

in the same way that other organizations or individuals can do so.[49] The specific mandate of each NHRI should be matched to the particular jurisdiction in which it is to operate.

Reviewing legislation, whether on a formal or informal basis, enables the NHRI to assist Parliament in its oversight over government activities with respect to human rights. The NHRI can assist the legislature in commenting on the human rights compatibility of draft and existing legislation and provide informed recommendations to Parliament in this respect. However, it is not always clear the extent to which a NHRI's recommendations are taken on board by either Parliament or government. As noted above, the nature of the work of a NHRI can be difficult to measure in terms of its impact, given that other forces are likely to have a role to play in the outcome of legislation. However, the lack of reference to a NHRI's views can result in feelings of frustration and despondency among staff and members of the NHRI and to them questioning the worth of engaging with the legislature at all.[50]

It is important, however, that NHRI see their role in legislative scrutiny as fulfilling other functions. From Parliament's point of view or from the point of view of others outside of the NHRI, however, it may not undermine the latter's credibility if its advice is not followed. This point was raised in the *New National Party* case before the South African Constitutional Court where it was argued, among other things, that Parliament's failure to follow the Independent Electoral Commission's advice undermined the Commission's independence. The Court disagreed and stressed that it was for Parliament to legislate and the Electoral Commission could make its views known in a variety of other ways such as publishing a report on the issue.[51]

The NHRI should therefore see its commentary on legislation from a broader perspective, as providing it with an opportunity to engage regularly with Parliament across a range of fields and with its various committees. If a NHRI does not carry out this function there is a suggestion that it may be more difficult for it to interact with the local legislature, an important element in its ability to influence

---

[49] House of Lords, House of Commons, Joint Committee on Human Rights, *The Case for a Human Rights Commission*, n 30 above, paras 132–133.

[50] As a member of staff of one NHRI stated: 'it depends entirely on the attitude of the Government, we can give advice to the government but at the end of the day, they can ignore it and that can be frustrating, putting a lot of effort in overseeing a combination of responses and maybe even following that through with lobbying ministers and briefings during parliamentary debates but at the end of the day the Act that comes out doesn't contain any of the advice and sometimes you do feel that you are wasting your time'. Interview held on 2 April 2003.

[51] 'It does not follow that Parliament's failure to follow the advice of the Commission constituted an impairment of the independence of the Commission. The competence to legislate in this area is for Parliament and Parliament alone. By legislating against the advice of the Commission, Parliament cannot be said to impair the independence of the Commission whose primary function lies in managing the elections and ensuring that they are free and fair. If the Commission considers that parliamentary regulation will prevent the possibility of elections being free and fair, it has a range of remedies to pursue', *New National Party of South Africa v Government of the Republic of South Africa*, CCT9/99, 13 April 1999; 1999 (3) SA 191 (CC); 1999 (5) BCLR 489 (CC), para 163, *per* O'Regan J.

policy and legislation. So, for example, when the Northern Ireland Assembly was suspended, the Northern Ireland Human Rights Commission lost its chance to engage with local MLAs. It had worked well with Assembly committees and whilst it maintained a link with Westminster in London, this suspension gave it one less opportunity to work with local politicians and political parties, so key to its success and legitimacy.[52]

Funding

Part of the managerial accountability of an institution is that it should account for whether money has been spent as it should have been.[53] The Paris Principles advocate that NHRIs:

'shall have an infrastructure which is suited to the smooth conduct of its activities, in particular adequate funding. The purpose of this funding should be to enable it to have its own staff and premises, in order to be independent of the government and not be subject to financial control which might affect this independence.'[54]

There is a general belief that ideally the budget of an NHRI should be determined, or at least vetted, by Parliament.[55] This, it is believed, would ensure greater transparency and the NHRI, as a watchdog of government, is not then having to compete with other bodies that it is supposed to be monitoring.[56] However, even

[52] See Livingstone and Murray, n 22 above.
[53] Day and Klein, *Accountabilities*, n 15 above, 27.   [54] Paris Principles, n 2 above, para B.2.
[55] 'We recommend that, as a guarantee of independence and in accordance with the comments we make below on accountability, Parliament should be directly involved in the setting of any commission's budget', House of Lords, House of Commons, Joint Committee on Human Rights, *The Case for a Human Rights Commission*, n 30 above, para 225. As the JCHR said in relation to the Northern Ireland Human Rights Commission, 'Consideration should be given to establishing a mechanism for an independent assessment of the NIHRC's needs. We recommend that, in its response to this report, the NIO sets out clear criteria against which it proposes to assess the core funding of the NIHRC in future years', JCHR, *Work of the Northern Ireland Human Rights Commission, Fourteenth Report of Session 2002–2003*, HL Paper 132, HC 142, 30 June 2003, para 43. See also Corder, n 13 above, 57. Further, 'Members should be able to rely on a specific allocation from Parliament at a level sufficient to ensure an active and professional NHRI', Commonwealth Secretariat, *National Human Rights Institutions*, n 19 above, 19. Further, 'It is equally important that the parliament debate the budget of the NHRI in order to ensure input from various constituencies regarding the level of resources appropriated for the NHRI', ibid, 32.
[56] With respect to accountability of NDPBs, the JCHR note that the usual model is to fund them by their parent department and they are required to make a report to their minister which is then laid before parliament. They note that 'It is not an entirely satisfactory model from the point of view of independence or accountability. In negotiating their budgets, such bodies have little leverage against their parent department—a very central concern of the Commonwealth commissions which we visited. Ministers will have very varied levels of interest in the work of a particular body, and may on occasions even be hostile. There is often little sustained engagement between a commission and its government sponsor. The level of formal parliamentary accountability is generally low, reliant on the intermittent attention of select committees with very crowded agenda or of individual members using questions or adjournment debates either to probe or support their work. The level of informal engagement in Parliament is often also poor', House of Lords, House of Commons, Joint Committee on Human Rights, *The Case for a Human Rights Commission*, n 30 above, paras 227–30.

for those institutions who do receive their funding in this way or where their accountability over their funds is questioned in Parliament, problems can still arise. Competition for funding is still going to be evident in Parliament. In addition, there is a need for a balance between Parliament having to consider 'what is reasonably required by the Commission and deal with requests for funding rationally, in the light of other national interests',[57] and the NHRI having been 'afforded an adequate opportunity to defend its budgetary requirements before Parliament or its relevant committees'.[58] This can cause tension: 'it could not say that it was independent on the one hand and then ask for resources from Parliament and not be required to give comments on how they are spending it'.[59]

While having its funding determined or vetted by Parliament may enhance a NHRI's perceived independence, it may not always help towards developing a positive relationship with the legislature. Thus, just as there are likely to be tensions between a sponsoring government department and a NHRI with respect to its funding, so there may be between Parliament and a NHRI. In South Africa, for example, in the past the Portfolio Committee for Justice has questioned the South African Human Rights Commission on its use of funds and was known to criticize its expensive offices in an elite area of the city. This caused resentment among Commissioners and between the members of the Committee and the Commission, doing little to develop a positive relationship between the two.[60] If the possibility of such tensions were recognized, however, it should be possible to work around them:

'It is however incumbent upon the parties to make every effort to resolve that tension and to reach agreement by negotiation in good faith. This would no doubt entail considerable meaningful discussion, exchange of relevant information, a genuine attempt by each party to understand the needs and constraints of the other and the mutual desire to reach a reasonable conclusion.'[61]

Reporting

It is hoped that Parliament can ensure the accountability of a NHRI through the requirement that the institution report to the legislature. The founding legislation of a NHRI or the constitution often either require that the NHRI reports directly to Parliament, or reports to the government department which lays the report before the Parliament.[62] The involvement of Parliament in the reporting process is believed to enhance the accountability of the NHRI by ensuring some discussion by parliamentarians of the institution's work. However, simply laying the report before Parliament, particularly if this is done only once a year, is not going to be

---

[57] *New National Party of South Africa v Government of the Republic of South Africa*, n 51 above, paras 98–100, *per* Langa DP. [58] ibid.
[59] Interview held on 5 August 2002. [60] Interview held on 8 August 2002.
[61] *New National Party of South Africa v Government of the Republic of South Africa*, n 51 above, para 97.
[62] Although the latter in reality may mean little more than placing the report in the library.

enough to ensure true accountability. Accountability through reporting must be a coherent process that will scrutinize the report in its entirety. There is evidence that parliamentarians may not read the report, may not take it seriously, or may not look at it in detail. As one member of a NHRI said:

'I am a little bit concerned about you know when you do your presentation, you take your annual report and you do your presentation in Parliament, and people haven't read it ahead of time. I'm not sure what's picked up and what's not picked up. I'm not sure what falls through the cracks. I could stand there as Commissioner and highlight all the wonderful things I have done and that could be accepted at Parliament. Whether that's accountability I don't think so.... So I have this difficulty of a group of people both interested and disinterested people, who because it's a formality that the Commissions must report to Parliament, sit there listening to the reports, pick up on pieces of information and then question around it and maybe take cognisance of an issue that's raised. And that's about it. I'm not sure that that's accountability. I don't think the hard questions get asked by Parliament and partly I think it is because no one has the time to read this sort of stuff.'[63]

More fundamentally, as the former Speaker of the National Assembly in Zimbabwe said, 'I do not think the calibre of members is very good; that is why Parliament is meaningless... I wonder if some MPs read newspapers and books or even discuss with friends before coming to Parliament.'[64]

Consequently, the focus of the questioning may not be a true test of the NHRI's work. Indeed, members and the staff of the NHRI often want to have more of an engaging and challenging examination of their report as this would add to their sense of worth, the sense of seriousness with which their institution was taken and their confidence as a result. It seems to be important that Parliament make the NHRI *feel* accountable by taking it seriously and challenging the Commission's activities and questioning what it has done:

'I certainly haven't had the sense that we feel that we are accountable, we are made to feel accountable.... So we don't have a sense that you are engaging with those to whom you are accountable in terms of what you set as priorities.'[65]

If Parliament is the only body to question a NHRI's work, its accountability is potentially undermined if Parliament does not engage fully with the NHRI and does not go beyond simply asking for a description of its activities to interrogate what it has done.[66] If accountability is to be perceived as more than simply asking for a justification of what has been done by the institution, Parliament must engage more meaningfully with its work. This is important not only from the perspective of those examining the institution from the outside but also internally, in terms of how the members and staff of the NHRI perceive their responsibilities.

[63] Interview held on 15 August 2002.   [64] *The Abuja Guidelines*, n 5 above, 14.
[65] Interview held on 15 August 2002.
[66] As one member of staff of a NHRI said, 'personally it's disappointing, it's taken up about what we are doing instead of asking us whether we are actually doing our job properly'. Interview held on 14 August 2002.

Where parliamentarians have engaged, the outcome can be positive. As Barney Pityana noted with respect to the South African Human Rights Commission when he was chair:

'Because we are not satisfied that there is no real debate on our report in the National Assembly, this year we asked the Portfolio Committee on Justice to hold public hearings on our report which they did on 17 March 1998. The hearings were open to the press and members of the public. They allowed parliamentarians to ask the Commission probing questions about our activities, our budget, our strategies for the development of a culture of human rights. By so doing we believe that we increased the level of understanding of the work of the Commission in Parliament. Members of the Commission also found the exercise very valuable.'[67]

There is a further risk that any examination of the NHRI's work may also be directed towards political interests rather than a desire by parliamentarians to better educate themselves with the work of the NHRI or ensure its effective operation. Here a NHRI may itself need to have a sophisticated understanding of the political background of those questioning it and attempt to use this to its advantage. There may be tension if Parliament is dominated by the ruling party and 'there are political needs of that ruling party and an executive that is governed which may conflict with a human rights commission's obligations under the constitution'.[68] Further and consequently, political interests can sometimes result in inconsistency in the reporting process: 'Sometimes I get the feeling that they ignore the reports, and other times they take the issue really seriously, so there's always like a dual response depending on where the interest lies and what is important.'[69] In other jurisdictions the timing of the examination of the report before Parliament has rendered its content outdated.[70] It is essential that those examining the report of the NHRI are sufficiently versed in its content and the work of the institution and that they have the time to peruse it in detail.

Role in Ensuring the Credibility and Visibility of a NHRI

While the statutory or constitutional functions of Parliament with respect to a NHRI may be key to its independence and accountability, Parliament can enhance the institution's credibility in other ways.

---

[67] Barney Pityana, 'National Institutions at Work: The Case of the South African Human Rights Commission', in Kamel Hossain, Leonard F.M. Besselink, Haile Selassie Gebre Selassie, and Edmond Volker (eds), *Human Rights Commissions and Ombudsman Offices. National Experiences Throughout the World* (2000) 627, 636.   [68] Interview held on 5 August 2002.

[69] Interview held on 14 August 2002. See also commentary by Amnesty International that 'frequently parliamentary time is not made available for this purpose. Therefore the NHRI is effectively silenced', Amnesty International, *National Human Rights Institutions. Recommendations for Effective Protection and Promotion of Human Rights*, AI Index: IOR 40/007/2001 (2001), para 8.2.

[70] This has been the case with Sri Lanka's Human Rights Commission, see *Human Rights Features. Special Edition for the 10th Annual Meeting of the Asia Pacific Forum of National Human Rights Institutions*, (2005), available at http://www.hrdc.net/sahrdc/hrfquarterly/apf10/html/special_issue.htm.

It is apparent that a regular supportive relationship with Parliament can increase a NHRI's visibility and in turn its credibility. There is a presumption that the stronger the relationship with Parliament the greater the credibility of the NHRI. A NHRI may in fact be perceived as more independent if it reports to Parliament, as one person working for a statutory commission in the UK said: 'We are very much identified with our sponsoring ministry, we are very much identified with the Home Office as they sponsor us. It would probably give for greater independence... if it was an all-party parliamentary grouping that we were linked into.'[71]

In addition, the work of a NHRI that is debated in Parliament may make that institution more visible to the public, may get it more media attention and may enable it to gain more credibility for its work as a semi-official body: 'it would be through Parliament in many ways that due credit could be given to the Commission for these kind of interventions'.[72] In the same vein, Parliament can potentially give a more balanced view of the work of the NHRI: 'in some ways given perhaps the wrong impression of valuable work that may have been done on the ground and one of the ways that should be acknowledged would be through Parliament I would think'.[73] Discussion in Parliament of a NHRI's work can help to improve the image of the institution and counteract, in an informed forum, comments that MPs may have picked up from the media.[74]

However, this has not always been the case and the visibility of a debate in Parliament can actually undermine the image and legitimacy of a NHRI if it is one-sided or if parliamentary privilege is abused to give an unbalanced view of an institution. For example, Lord Laird in the House of Lords has waged a consistent vehement campaign against the Northern Ireland Human Rights Commission, raising sectarian questions about its performance.[75] He has often been the most vocal commentary on the Commission in the House of Lords and because his comments have often not been met by equally forceful viewpoints from supporters of the Commission, or the government in its defence, the impression left to many listening to or reading the debates is likely to be heavily skewed.

As noted at the outset, a NHRI who is keen on maintaining its independence, and its image of independence, may find it difficult to exploit contacts within a political environment. The experience of NGOs in managing these political relationships suggests that influencing politicians and debate informally, rather than just formally through participation at meetings, can be powerful.[76] Thus, defining the terms used and giving information to those involved in the formal processes

---

[71] Interview held on 11 November 2002.   [72] Interview held on 7 August 2002.
[73] Interview held on 7 August 2002.   [74] Interview held on 14 August 2002.
[75] For eg, as he commented on one occasion, 'the problem is that the Commission itself does not reflect society; rather, it has a perceived republican bias and slant, and thus is part of the cold house for Unionists to which the Secretary of State for Northern Ireland has referred', House of Lords, 3 May 2002, Col. 958.
[76] Michael Edwards, David Hulme, and Tina Wallace, 'NGOs in a Global Future: Marrying Local Delivery to Worldwide Leverage' (1999) 19 Public Administration and Development 117, 131.

has considerable impact.[77] Those organizations that acquire expertise in particular areas and provide an alternative source of information to policy makers are also more likely to be taken seriously.[78] However, institutions, whether NGOs or NHRIs, engaging in this type of political activity 'must know to whom, in what way, with what focus and at which level of detail to present this information. Successful participation...takes a certain level of political ingeniousness or sophistication.'[79]

What is hoped is that creating a relationship with Parliament will provide the NHRI with another source of support, and ideally a champion of the work of the NHRI if necessary: 'I think we rely at the moment on parliamentarians effectively and parliamentarians are quite important because they are not as defensive of government processes and government actions as people inside government are'.[80] As a non-executive body, Parliament can defend the NHRI's position and support it in its challenges to government. But balancing this with Parliament's role in ensuring the NHRI's accountability can be a difficult balance to achieve. It is not insurmountable, however:

'...we need a different relationship in the sense that these bodies must each have a committee and its chairman with whom they are really quite closely in touch. We would respect their independence but we are also there too, we are the body that appoints them, the president just has to sign on the dotted line. We are the body that recommends their removal, should that ever happen, and I don't myself see it as at all having a difficulty with having a supportive relationship but that has to come to greater maturity.'[81]

Conclusion: Enhancing the Relationship with Parliament: a Strategy for Engagement and a Single Committee?

The discussion above indicates that simply placing the establishment, appointments, budget, and accountability of a NHRI in the hands of Parliament will not necessarily ensure the legitimacy and credibility of the institution. This will depend on the constitutional context, the extent to which government has control over the legislature, and the political environment in which the NHRI operates. Further, one must also look at the capacity of Parliament itself. As Smith notes:

'At first sight the notion of direct accountability to Parliament seems attractive, as a means of bolstering the watchdogs' independence. On the other hand, Parliament lacks the

---

[77] J. A. Scholte, 'Civil Society and Democracy in Global Governance' (2002) 8 Global Governance 281.   [78] Berlin, 'The Key to Green Power', n 11 above.

[79] ibid, 11. Thus, Berlin talks about the organization's 'informational capacity (to produce relevant fact contributions to the process), another is the tactical ingeniousness (knowing whom to approach when and how), yet another being the communicative proficiency (capacity to frame issues in a winning manner). Together this parcel of resources makes up an organization's political skill', 12.

[80] Interview held on 7 August 2002.

[81] Interview with member of South African Parliament, 7 August 2002.

resources that Ministers possess: it has many fewer staff, limited time, comparatively little expertise.... Moreover, the mechanisms that can be used by Parliament to call Ministers to account for the bodies for which they are responsible—Parliamentary questions, debates, and so on—would be lost if their accountability was direct to Parliament. What this suggests is that if accountability to Parliament is desirable as a means of signalling detachment from the executive, then Parliament must devise new arrangements for securing that accountability.'[82]

If an NHRI is to have a structured and positive relationship with Parliament this will require more than just an annual appearance of the NHRI before it.[83] It needs to develop a strategy for how it will engage with Parliament which will be specific to that particular jurisdiction. While parliamentarians themselves must be familiar with a NHRI's work and with the subtleties of its relationship with government,[84] the NHRI itself needs to think practically and proactively about how best to engage with and be accessible to, often, busy parliamentarians. Thus, any reports it submits to Parliament should be user-friendly, with an executive summary and limited in length.[85] In addition, more regular interaction is desirable,[86] which can be facilitated by putting opportunities in the founding legislation for the NHRI to appear before Parliament on a regular basis. A NHRI needs to do more than just send its reports to parliament,[87] however, and should consider not only the formal, but also the informal ways in which it can engage with the legislature[88] from providing training or briefings on human rights issues to parliamentarians to keep them up-to-date,[89] to holding an annual informal social gathering. The relationship with Parliament needs to be seen as a long-term and on-going one and one which builds upon personal contacts: 'because a lot of it's got to do with personal relationships. You've got to go over to parliament, meeting among the committees, going to their workshops, chatting to individual members, engaging with them, being aware of what's going on in Parliament to get opportunities for us to go and speak to individuals who are dealing with issues that we are going to deal with. And that's the kind of thing that doesn't happen overnight. It takes a long time to build up.'[90]

There is a need to convince members of a NHRI of the value of strengthening their relationship with Parliament. In the past in South Africa, for example, 'I think that there has been a lack of appreciation within the Commission for the

---

[82] Smith, 'Policing the Constitution', n 18 above, 239.

[83] Interview with member of South African Parliament, 7 August 2002.

[84] For eg, it should be 'particularly familiar with their financial difficulties, with the line department which determines what attacks on them and so forth', Interview with member of South African Parliament, 7 August 2002.   [85] Interview held on 5 August 2002.

[86] *Abuja Guidelines*, n 5 above.

[87] 'The Commission must drive the process', Interview with member of South African Parliament, 5 August 2002.   [88] Interview held on 15 October 2002.

[89] Interviews held on 14 August 2002 and 15 October 2002.

[90] Interview held on 6 August 2002.

importance of the parliamentary role we could have',[91] and elsewhere some parliamentarians have felt that the NHRIs have not focused sufficient energies on engaging with them, spending more time on looking at the executive.[92] However, over time, as in South Africa, NHRIs have recognized the importance of this relationship, as reflected through, for example, the creation of specific posts on their staff to work with Parliament.[93] It is essential that such initiatives be commended but also matched with adequate resources and that the work of these staff feed into all other aspects of the NHRI's remit.

It has been suggested that one way of ensuring a more coherent and comprehensive approach to the relationship between a NHRI and Parliament is to set up a specialist all-party parliamentary committee.[94] This, it is argued, could enable a relationship to be built up with that particular committee and for more in-depth knowledge of the NHRI and its functions and of the concept of their accountability role to be acquired by those parliamentarians. However, some caution needs to be exercised. First, there may be a tendency for a NHRI to engage only with this one committee and not with other committees to whom the NHRI's work may be equally relevant: 'our work around socio economic rights, for example, has relevance to the health committee, the social welfare committee, regional services . . . our socio economic rights reports for example simply go to Parliament and get lost'.[95] It is submitted, however, that if the committee carries out its mandate effectively and seriously, it can enhance the opportunities of the NHRI to engage with other committees in Parliament. The responsibility must also fall on the NHRI itself to recognize the important role that Parliament can play in its work. More practically, the NHRI needs to develop relationships across the parliamentary committee spectrum, and do so in a manner which will

---

[91] Interview with staff member of South African Human Rights Commission, 6 August 2002: 'I am not sure if the Commission is sufficiently proactive there. Especially if we accept that Parliament is the only body we are accountable to.' Interview with member of NHRI held on 14 August 2002.

[92] Interview held on 15 October 2002.

[93] For eg, the South African Human Rights Commission appointed a parliamentary officer based in Cape Town to interact with Parliament there. There is a Parliamentary Unit within the Research Department.

[94] See eg, Smith, 'Policing the Constitution', n 18 above, 239; *Abuja Guidelines*, n 5 above. Corder *et al*, recommend a Standing Committee on Constitutional Institutions, Corder, *Report on Parliamentary Oversight and Accountability*, n 13 above, para 7.4. With respect to the Northern Ireland Assembly, Lord Alderdice favoured the establishment of a human rights committee within the Assembly which could encourage other committees to see the human rights elements of their work, rather than proofing every piece of legislation on human rights grounds. It could also build up a general expertise on human rights in the Assembly. Interview held on 15 October 2002. See also House of Lords Select Committee on the Constitution, *The Regulatory State*, n 14 above, para 176. The Inter-Parliamentary Union 'affirms that parliamentary activities in support of human rights can be enhanced through parliamentary committees or sub-committees with a mandate to ensure that human rights are promoted and respected and urges parliament to establish such bodies where they do not exist', Inter-Parliamentary Union, *Strengthening National Structures*, n 1 above, para 25.

[95] Interview held on 14 August 2002.

appeal to those committees. Thus, sending separate reports to separate committees with the extracts of relevance to them may assist.[96]

Having one committee which has responsibility for all regulatory or similar
statutory or constitutional bodies may solve some of the concerns that Parliament
'suffers—not unlike government—from a structural inability to exercise a consistent and overarching scrutiny of the regulatory state. Because regulators fall under
different departments, they fall under different parliamentary committees....
Although there are a few committees with cross-cutting responsibilities, there is
none with responsibility for the regulatory state as a whole.'[97] This committee
could then be properly briefed and have an appropriate length of time to discuss
the contents of an annual report: 'maybe that would be more of a sense of satisfaction because there's a huge gripe around getting a portrait and representing it'.[98]

In order to ensure that this committee acts as an effective watchdog not only
over government activities that are highlighted to it by a NHRI, but also over the
accountability of the NHRI itself, drawing upon the UK's House of Lords' work
on regulatory agencies, several proposals need to be made with respect to its functioning. First, the 'capacity' of the committee should be addressed.[99] This includes
examining the skills available to it and its members and what resources it has
including staff, time, and expertise. Human rights expertise on the committee
would be an important consideration, whether sufficient time could be allocated
to its ability to question the NHRI and how much staff and other financial
resources are put at its disposal is going to be key to its ability to be successful in
ensuring accountability of the NHRI. Secondly, the 'consistency' of this parliamentary committee should be considered, namely, how regularly it meets, how
regularly it engages with the NHRI, and how in-depth its analysis of the NHRI's
work can be.[100] Lastly, one must address the committee's 'co-ordination'. This
entails consideration of factors such as its ability to be responsible for all similar
bodies to enable it to develop expertise in assessing these types of institutions and
to ensure some degree of best practice and consistency in its approach among
them.[101] Parliament could consider revising its standing orders where necessary to
facilitate an improved relationship with an NHRI.[102]

While Parliament can play a crucial role in ensuring the independence and
legitimacy of a NHRI, this essay has sought to demonstrate that the relationship
may not be as straightforward as initially envisaged. A more in-depth consideration of how Parliament operates in a particular political context and how a NHRI
itself engages with the legislature is necessary to ensure the accountability of government for its promotion and protection of human rights and the accountability
of the NHRI itself.

[96] Interview held on 14 August 2002.
[97] Philip Norton, 'Regulating the Regulatory State' (2004) 57(4) Parliamentary Affairs 785, 796.
[98] Interview held on 14 August 2002.
[99] House of Lords Select Committee on the Constitution, *The Regulatory State*, n 14 above, paras
184–94.   [100] ibid.
[101] ibid.   [102] *Abuja Guidelines*, n 5 above.

17

A View From the Coal Face:
Northern Ireland, Human Rights
Activism, and the War on Terror

Maggie Beirne and Angela Hegarty

Introduction

In the focus on the need for security at the beginning of the twenty-first century, much rhetoric is expended on the importance of freedom and the defence of human rights; indeed the promotion of such values has served as the rationale for war, in Afghanistan and Iraq and in the wider 'War on Terror'.[1] Paradoxically, the exigencies of such wars have been used to enact laws which limit cherished freedoms,[2] in order, it is argued, to preserve those self-same freedoms. Such a contradictory rationale may be in part because much of the discussion on the need for a response to the 'War on Terror' has been characterized by an historical focus upon the uniqueness of the contemporary threat.[3] Allied to that has been a 'security first' attitude which denies the importance of human rights protections and, at its most extreme, characterizes those who defend such protections as either naive or as apologists for terrorists.[4] Despite the rhetoric of freedom, that which

---

[1] There are numerous assertions of this by leading politicians, amongst them UK Prime Minister, Tony Blair. See eg, 'PM Thanks UK Armed Forces In Basra Visit' (Speech on 4 January 2004); Speech on the threat of global terrorism (5 March 2004); Prime Minister's Speech to TUC Conference in Blackpool (10 September 2002), available at http://www.pm.gov.uk/output/Page5.asp (accessed 14 March 2006). See also Richard W. Leeman, *The Rhetoric of Terrorism and Counterterrorism* (1991).

[2] See Phil Thomas, 'Emergency and anti-terrorist powers' (2003) 36 Fordham International Law Journal 1193; Conor Gearty, '11 September 2001, Counter-terrorism, and the Human Rights Act' (2005) 32 Journal of Law and Society 18; David Cole, 'The New McCarthyism: Repeating History in the War on Terrorism' (2003) 38 Harvard Civil Rights Civil Liberties Law Review 1.

[3] 'Today's war on terrorism has already demonstrated our government's remarkable ability to evolve its tactics in ways that allow it simultaneously to repeat history and to insist that it is not repeating history.' Cole, op cit, 1–2. See also M. Cherif Bassiouni, 'Legal Control of International Terrorism: A Policy-Oriented Assessment' (2002) 43 Harvard International Law Journal 83.

[4] Neil Hicks, 'The Impact Of Counter Terror On The Promotion And Protection Of Human Rights: A Global Perspective' in Richard Ashby Wilson, (ed.) *Human Rights in the 'War on Terror'* (2005).

drives much of security policy and law-making is not the guiding principles and ideals of international human rights law, but the demands of the police and the security community. This approach privileges military intelligence and operations above substantive rights and the procedural safeguards necessary for their protection. Human rights are consequently often portrayed as an impediment to security, a nuisance which undermines the effectiveness of the response of the security forces but not as one of the fundamental prerequisites necessary to achieve *real* security.[5]

Whilst the attacks of September 11 2001 were the first domestic experience the United States have had of foreign terrorism, the experience of the British government in Northern Ireland can offer instructive parallels. Throughout the course of the conflict in Northern Ireland, a similar discourse operated between various security-driven governments and a due process-oriented rights community.[6] Many of the lessons which governments might have learned about the futility of a draconian security policy which sidelined the concerns of human rights activists and eroded rights are relevant to the current debate about the so-called 'War on Terror'. In this essay we argue that human rights protections are crucial as part of an effective counter-terrorism strategy and that individuals and vulnerable groups need safeguards supplied by human rights norms when confronted with the might of the state. Our case is a straightforward one. *Real* security is best obtained by upholding rather than undermining human rights. In making this case, we draw on the work and experience of human rights activists in the context of the political conflict in Northern Ireland. The Committee on the Administration of Justice (CAJ) was founded in 1981, and has worked continuously since then across a broad range of human rights concerns. In 1998, CAJ was honoured with the Council of Europe Human Rights Prize for its work to mainstream human rights provisions into the Good Friday Agreement.[7]

We contend that the experience in Northern Ireland of emergency laws, internment without trial, the creation of 'suspect communities',[8] coercive treatment of suspects and prisoners, and a range of other tried and failed tactics demonstrates that such policies are not just wrong but counter-productive. Our argument is that it was only when the centrality of human rights became part of the mainstream

---

[5] See Paul Hoffman, "Human Rights and Terrorism" (2004) 26 Human Rights Quarterly 932.

[6] See, eg, Kevin Boyle, Tom Hadden, and Paddy Hillyard, *Ten Years on in Northern Ireland: The legal control of political violence* (1980); Dermot Walsh, *The use and abuse of emergency legislation in Northern Ireland* (1983); Stephen C. Greer and Anthony White, *Abolishing the Diplock Courts: the case for restoring jury trial to scheduled offences in Northern Ireland* (1986); Anthony Jennings (ed.), *Justice Under Fire—The abuse of civil liberties in Northern Ireland* (1988); *Upholding the Rule of Law? Northern Ireland: Criminal Justice under the "emergency powers" in the 1990s* (1992); Committee on the Administration of Justice, *No Emergency, No Emergency Law* (1994); Lawyers Committee for Human Rights, *At the Crossroads: Human Rights and the Northern Ireland Peace Process* (1996); Committee on the Administration of Justice, *No Emergency, No Emergency Law* (1994).

[7] Paul Mageean and Martin O'Brien, n 9, supra.

[8] Paddy Hillyard, *Suspect Community: People's Experience of the Prevention of Terrorism Acts in Britain* (1993).

of political negotiations that an effective transition towards peace was assured.[9] We note that a particularly effective strategy utilized by human rights organizations in Northern Ireland was to draw upon the international human rights organizations and treaty bodies, the opprobrium of which were often the most effective check on state security policy. Finally, we argue that many of the lessons from Northern Ireland are germane to the current debate on human rights and the 'War on Terror' and that other human rights organizations, and indeed governments, can and should learn from those experiences.

The War on Terror is Not New

As noted above, much official discourse in the current War on Terror focuses on the apparently 'unprecedented' nature of the terrorist threat which, it is argued, must be met with a similarly 'exceptional' response.[10] In fact, whilst there may be some unique aspects of the current global situation, very few of the 'exceptional' responses either proposed or implemented have not already been experimented with in Northern Ireland. Indeed, throughout the conflict, the policy articulated by successive UK governments was that the violence presented an unprecedented security threat which required a robust response. Introducing the Prevention of Terrorism Bill in 1974, the then Home Secretary, Roy Jenkins said, '[t]hese powers are draconian. In combination, they are unprecedented in peacetime. I believe they are fully justified to meet the clear and present danger.'[11] The political and legal power of the state was to be brought to bear upon those whom the state regarded as responsible for the conflict, a group often distinguished from the 'ordinary decent law abiding people' of Northern Ireland.[12] Such an analysis ignored the fact that the state itself was an actor in the conflict and that its use of its power in this fashion only enmeshed it further in that conflict.[13] In an added irony, the 'exceptional' nature of the terrorist threat and required response in Northern Ireland largely ignored the fact that the jurisdiction had relied upon draconian emergency laws and a related security infrastructure since its inception.[14] Nevertheless, the consequences in terms of alienating sections of the community, embedding cultures of violence and impunity in the security forces, and corroding the rule of law in other areas of the criminal justice system soon became

[9] Paul Mageean and Martin O'Brien, 'From the Margins to the Mainstream: Human Rights and the Good Friday Agreement' (1999) 22 Fordham International Law Journal 1499.

[10] See, eg, Measures to Combat Terrorism, Charles Clarke's statement to the House (*Hansard*, HOC Deb, 26 Jan 2005 Cols. 306–9).

[11] Hansard HC Debs Vol. 882, Col. 35, 25 November 1974.

[12] See Aogán Mulcahy, *Policing Northern Ireland: Conflict, Legitimacy and Reform* (2006).

[13] See Brendan O'Leary and John McGarry, *The Politics Of Antagonism: Understanding Northern Ireland* (1993) 22–28.

[14] See Fionnuala Ni Aolain, *The Politics of Force: Conflict Management and State Violence in Northern Ireland* (2000) 12–15, 20–30.

obvious. The deployment by the state of wide and arbitrary powers thus led to further abuses, which in turn fed the conflict. While this cycle might have been countered with robust checks and balances against the power of the state, such safeguards as were introduced were often ineffective or flawed.[15]

Human rights advocates in Northern Ireland such as CAJ emphasized the circular nature of the violence/repression relationship and the ineffectiveness of such safeguards as were in place. It argued repeatedly that control by and under the law, accountability, and the principle of due process were essential bulwarks against these excessive powers. Then as now, there was a regrettable tendency amongst some advocates of the 'security-first' approach to assume that 'terrorists'—whether detained without charge, certified as such in special courts with skewed rules of evidence, or otherwise—were not as entitled to the same rights as others.[16] Then as now, much of the official discourse concerned not only that it was acceptable to do whatever was necessary to apprehend and imprison supposed 'terrorists'[17] but further, that anyone who objects to this attitude, must be—whether intentionally or naively—sympathetic to the tactics of the people whose rights they defend.[18] Such a mindset led to the villification in some quarters of human rights activists in Northern Ireland and, as discussed by McEvoy and Rebouche in this volume, culminated in the murder of two human rights lawyers.[19]

On the face of it, the position of human rights activists is generally modest. They tend to assert that legally binding human rights standards which have been entered into freely by governments should be respected in relation to all. They

[15] See Amnesty International, United Kingdom: *Human Rights Concerns* (1991); Human Rights Watch/Helsinki, *Children in Northern Ireland: Abused by Security Forces and Paramilitaries* (1992); Amnesty International, *Political Killings in Northern Ireland* (1994); British Irish Rights Watch, *Conditions in Detention in Castlereagh* (1995); British Irish Rights Watch, *Intimidation of Defence Lawyers in Northern Ireland* (1996); CAJ, *Submission to the United Nations Committee Against Torture* (1996); Lawyers Committee For Human Rights, *At the Crossroads: Human Rights and the Northern Ireland Peace Process* (1996); Julia Hall, *To Serve Without Fear Or Favor: Policing, Human Rights and Accountability in Northern Ireland* (1997), 14–24; and CAJ *Submission to the United Nations Committee Torture (Comments on the Third Periodic Report by the United Kingdom to the Committee Against Torture) 1998*, (available from http://www.caj.org.uk/keydocs/CAT.htm).

[16] For recent examples, see Ewen MacAskill, Julian Glover, and Vikram Dodd, 'Expulsions illegal, UN tells Clarke' The Guardian, August 25, 2005, quoting UK Home Secretary Charles Clarke as responding to UN criticism of UK human rights practices by saying, 'I wish the UN would look at human rights in the round, rather than simply focusing all the time on the terrorist'; See also Alan Travis, 'Clarke Rounds On 'Poisoners' Among Liberal Media Critics' The Guardian 25 April 2001.

[17] See Andrew Blick and Stuart Weir, *The Rules of the Game: The Government's Counter Terrorism Laws And Strategy* (2005).

[18] See Irene Kahn, Preface, *Amnesty International Annual Report 2002* (AI, 2003); and 'Critics Aid Terrorists, AG Argues', The Boston Globe, 7 December 2001, quoting US Attorney-General John Ashcroft responding to criticisms by civil libertarians by saying, 'To those who pit Americans against immigrants and citizens against non-citizens, to those who scare peace-loving people with phantoms of lost liberty, my message is this: Your tactics aid terrorists, for they erode our national unity and diminish our resolve . . . [t]hey give ammunition to America's enemies, and pause to America's friends.'

[19] See Peter Cory, *Cory Collusion Inquiry Report: Pat Finucane* (2003); Peter Cory, *Cory Collusion Inquiry Report: Rosemary Nelson* (2004).

contend that criminal charges should be brought openly, with due regard to the strictures of the law, that evidence be adduced to the extent that an individual defendant can properly explore the evidence against him or her, and in a manner that allows such evidence to be challenged and contested.[20] They argue not that the observation of human rights standards are the goal of the criminal justice process, but rather that such observance reduces the risks of miscarriages of justice, underpins due process, and reduces the likelihood of the draining of public confidence in the justice system, particularly in communities who are more likely to be the targets of its attention.[21] The difficulty is that an increasingly intelligence-driven policy agenda is not particularly interested in these concerns, which means that the protections of due process are given minimal weighting in the legislative equation. As Conor Gearty observed pithily, '[t]he intelligence services have never understood the need for a criminal process: their ideal world would be one in which official suspicion led straight to incarceration'.[22] All too often politicians appear swayed by the special pleading of the intelligence services that due process is an enemy of effectiveness in tackling political violence:

'If people want us to tackle the new types of crime today, international terrorism, this very brutal violent organized crime, antisocial behaviour, which I think is in every respect these types of crimes are qualitatively different from certainly when I was growing up, you can't do it by the rules of the game we have at the moment, you just can't. People can write articles about it yes but you go through this process or that process, you can't do it, it is too complicated, too laborious, the police end up being completely hide-bound by a whole series of restrictions and difficulties, it doesn't work.'[23]

The discourse around current counter-terrorism policies is strikingly similar to the debate about security policy in Northern Ireland in that the security services and the police and their concerns are the drivers of those policies.[24] The demands and concerns of those interested in the upholding of human rights standards appeared to feature little with regard to government policy formulation in Northern Ireland (other than as a source of nuisance), nor do they feature much in the formulation of the UK's current counter-terrorism strategy, which does not refer to human rights standards at all.[25] Instead the key aim of the UK's

---

[20] See Joint Committee On Human Rights Second Report (2001) and Twelfth Report (2006).

[21] See Andrew Ashworth and Ben Emmerson, *Human Rights and Criminal Justice* (2001) and Farkhanda Zia Mansoor, 'Reassessing Packer in the Light of International Human Rights Norms' (2005) 4 Connecticut Public Interest Law Journal 288.

[22] Conor Gearty, 'Short Cuts' (17 March 2005) 27 LRB, (http://www.lrb.co.uk/v27/n06/gear01_.html accessed 10th January 2006)

[23] Tony Blair, MP, *Transcript of UK Prime Minister Tony Blair's Monthly Press Conference* 10 Downing Street, 11 October 2005.

[24] See Kevin Boyle and Tom Hadden, *Northern Ireland: The Choice* (1994) 97–98: 'It is hard to resist the conclusion that it is often the views of the security authorities on what should be permitted under emergency and related legislation that determine the law, rather than the law that sets effective limits on what the security forces are permitted to do.'

[25] Hazel Blears, Home Office Minister for Minister for Policing, Security and Community Safety laid out the UK's counter-terrorism strategy for the UK (CONTEST) in a speech to the Royal United

counter-terrorism strategy is said to be the reduction of 'risk from international terrorism so that people can go about their business freely and with confidence'.[26] It is said that this strategy is 'delivered working with stakeholders who include government departments, the emergency services, voluntary organisations, the business sector and with partners from across the world'. Whilst the dangers of alienating certain groups is acknowledged, instead of benchmarking measures against human rights law, the policy speaks about 'good community relations', thus '[c]ountering the terrorist threat and ensuring good community relations are interdependent and we are continuing to work closely with communities to reassure them that law enforcement is appropriate and proportionate'.[27]

One by-product of the dominance of police[28] and intelligence agencies in the making of UK security policies is that the latter in particular have a culture of secrecy which is extremely hard to penetrate[29] and which obscures public scrutiny of their acts.[30] This was also a feature of the counter-insurgency tactics adopted by the state in Northern Ireland,[31] just as it had been a feature of other states' policies in other conflicts around the world.[32] The consequences of this for the rule of law are explained by one commentator thus:

'Using criminal law envisages the prosecution of defendants before an independent court and the presentation of admissible evidence against them to demonstrate their responsibility for offences of such particularity as to satisfy the notion of "criminal offence". The strategy and resources of the security forces are thus directed to the gathering of evidence which will go to the securing of convictions, however hard that might be in the context of

Services Institute, *The Tools to Combat Terrorism*, (available at http://press.homeoffice.gov.uk/Speeches/02–05-sp-tools-combat-terrorism, accessed 1 May 2006). See also *Counter Terrorism, Progress Report, Statement from The Secretary of State for the Home Department (Mr. Charles Clarke)* laid before Parliament on 15 December 2005 (available at http://press.homeoffice.gov.uk/Speeches/15-12-05-st-ct-progress-report, accessed 1 May 2006). See also *Security, Terrorism and the UK* ISP/NSC Briefing Paper 05/01 (available at http://www.chathamhouse.org.uk/pdf/research/niis/BPsecurity.pdf, accessed 6 May 2006).

[26] The Home Office, *About the Counter-Terrorism Strategy* (available at http://security.homeoffice.gov.uk/counter-terrorism-strategy/counter-terrorism-strategy/, accessed 1 May 2006.

[27] The Home Office, *Working with Partners* (available at http://security.homeoffice.gov.uk/working-with-partners/communities1/) accessed on 1 May 2006.

[28] 'The Police have set out why they need these powers. I think it would be irresponsible of me if I think that the fears of the Police are well grounded about the existing law and the problems with it, I think it would be irresponsible of me not to take this forward, and that is why I am doing it.' UK Prime Minister, Tony Blair explaining why he was introducing new anti-terrorist legislation, *Transcript of Monthly Press Conference*, 11 October 2005 (available at http://www.number10.gov.uk/output/Page8294.asp, accessed 12 May 2006).

[29] See Ian Leigh and Laurence Lustgarten, *In from the Cold: National Security and Parliamentary Democracy* (1994).

[30] For eg in the case of controversial killings, see Lawyers Committee for Human Rights, *Beyond Collusion: The UK security Forces and the Murder of Pat Finucane*, (2002); see also Peter Cory, *Cory Collusion Inquiry Report: Pat Finucane*, (2003); Peter Cory, *Cory Collusion Inquiry Report: Rosemary Nelson* (2004).

[31] See Brice Dickson, 'Northern Ireland's Emergency Legislation—The Wrong Medicine' (1992) Public Law 609.

[32] See Graham Ellison, *The Crowned Harp, Policing Northern Ireland* (2000) 73–78.

terrorism. The military are not concerned about process but about action, information is not "evidence" for a trial but "intelligence" for operations. Intelligence needs assessment and that assessment is not made by an independent adjudicator but by those who play the decisive part in initiating the use of military force.'[33]

As noted above, a number of the measures pursued to address the current threat from terrorism in Britain have been tried already in Northern Ireland, generating significant criticism.[34] These measures include, for example, the shooting dead of suspects in controversial circumstances; detention without trial; coercive interrogation techniques; limitations on freedom of expression; the exclusion and deportation of suspect persons; increased surveillance, and and the use of informants. In this chapter we examine the first four of these measures, focusing in particular on their relevance for the contemporary context.

Shoot to Kill

In Northern Ireland more than 3,500 people have been killed in the conflict, out of a population of around a million and a half.[35] Of these, around 900 were members of state security forces and the remainder either civilians or members of paramilitary organizations.[36] There have been very few prosecutions of state actors, that is, police officers and members of the British Army,[37] although they have been responsible for at least 10 per cent of the deaths in the conflict (a figure which does not take into account the clear evidence of state collusion with both

[33] Warbrick n 14, supra 991.

[34] For eg, in Amnesty International, *Report of allegations of ill-treatment made by persons arrested under Special Powers Act after 8 August 1971* (1971); *Report of an Amnesty International mission to Northern Ireland (28 November-6 December 1977)*, (1978); Amnesty International, *United Kingdom: Allegations of ill-treatment in Northern Ireland* (1991); Amnesty International, *United Kingdom (Northern Ireland): Alleged coerced confessions during ill-treatment at Castlereagh Holding Centre of eight youths from Ballymurphy, Northern Ireland* (1993); Committee for the Prevention of Torture and Inhuman or Degrading Treatment or Punishment, *Report to the Government of the United Kingdom on the visit to Northern Ireland carried out by the European Committee for the Prevention of Torture and Inhuman or Degrading Treatment or Punishment from 20 to 29 July 1993* (1994); Committee on the Administration of Justice, *Allegations of Psychological Ill-treatment of Detainees held under Emergency Legislation in Northern Ireland* (1994); Committee on the Administration of Justice, *No Emergency, No Emergency Law* (1995); Amnesty International, *Cruel Inhuman or Degrading Treatment: Detention of Róisín McAliskey* (1997); Amnesty International, *Special Security Units: Cruel, Inhuman or Degrading Treatment* (1997); Param Cumaraswamy, *Question of human rights of all persons subjected to any form of detention or imprisonment: Report of the Special Rapporteur on the independence of judges and lawyers* (1998).

[35] See David McKittrick, Seamus Kelters, Brian Feeney, and Chris Thornton, *Lost Lives: The stories of the men, women and children who died as a result of the Northern Ireland Troubles* (1999); Other databases produce varying numbers, see http://cain.ulst.ac.uk/issues/violence/deaths.htm, accessed 12 May 2006.

[36] Police Service of Northern Ireland *Deaths due to the Security Situation in Northern Ireland 1969–2003 (By Calendar Year)* (2003).

[37] Throughout the conflict there have been only 24 prosecutions (and 8 convictions) of police officers and soldiers for the use of force whilst on duty. Fionnuala Ni Aolain, *The Politics of Force: Conflict Management and State Violence in Northern Ireland* (2000) 73.

loyalist and republican paramilitaries[38]). Consequently, in the past 30 years, there have been numerous calls for independent investigations into the many controversial events involving the state and the practices that gave rise to them.[39] Such demands have multiplied as the failure of the existing legal processes to hold the state to account for its role in the conflict have become apparent.[40] Furthermore, as discussed by Anthony and Mageean in this collection (Chapter 10), a series of judgments in the European Court of Human Rights has provided further legal imperatives for independent inquiries into state killings.[41]

It is argued that the inadequate response of successive governments to calls for enquiries has inculcated a sense of state impunity. For example, of the deaths directly or indirectly at the hands of the state, none has been openly acknowledged as part of a formal 'shoot-to-kill' policy, yet few credibly dispute that such a policy did in fact operate in Northern Ireland in the 1980s.[42] It is worth emphasizing that, contrary to more recent developments in Britain, the government never suggested that it was engaged in a 'shoot-to-kill-to-protect' policy, nor that it had authorized any of its agents to step outside the rule of law and use lethal force in countering supposedly armed attackers. The state strategy in this regard in Northern Ireland has been, in the words of Stan Cohen, literal rather than interpretative denial.[43]

It is possible to suggest a number of reasons as to why such a steadfast denial has been maintained. First, a contemporaneous acknowledgement would have exposed a major contradiction at the heart of government policy. At that time, the Thatcher government was intent on portraying republicans and loyalists as criminals rather than armed combatants, and wanted to undermine any claim that the parties were engaged in a war.[44] This was entirely in keeping with British policy throughout the conflict, in which the state sought to portray itself as a neutral

[38] See eg British Irish Rights Watch, *Deadly Intelligence: State Collusion With Loyalist Violence In Northern Ireland* (February 1999). Sir John Stevens, *Stevens Enquiry 3: Overview & Recommendations* (2003).

[39] The persistent allegations of collusion were so serious that in May 2002, the UK and Irish governments appointed retired Canadian judge Peter Corry to carry out an investigation into seven key cases, including those of Pat Finucane and Rosemary Nelson, human rights lawyers who were murdered, it is alleged, by loyalist paramilitaries in collusion with the state. Judge Cory's reports were later published in part by the British Government and led the establishment of a number of inquiries, although not, despite his recommendations, in the case of Patrick Finucane.

[40] See Angela Hegarty, 'The Government of Memory: Public Inquiries and the Limits of Justice in Northern Ireland' (2003) 26 Fordham International Law Journal 1148, 1178–1181.

[41] *Jordan v UK* (2003) 37 EHRR 52, para 105, *Kelly and others v UK*, para 91, *McKerr v UK* Series A 2001-III (2002) 34 EHRR 553, para 108, *Shanaghan v UK*, Judgment of 4 May 2001 No. 37715/97, para 85.

[42] See John Stalker, *Stalker* (1988); Anthony Jennings, 'Shoot to Kill: The Final Courts of Justice' in Anthony Jennings (ed), *Justice Under Fire—The abuse of civil liberties in Northern Ireland* (1988).

[43] See Stan Cohen, *States of Denial: Knowing About Atrocities and Suffering* (2001).

[44] 'Crime is crime is crime; it is not political', Margaret Thatcher's famous comment on the demand of Irish republican hunger strikers for political status, Press Conference, Saudi Arabia, 21 April 1981 (see CAIN *Chronology of the Conflict, 1981* (available at http://cain.ulst.ac.uk/othelem/chron/ch81.htm, accessed on 16 January 2006).

arbitrator between 'two warring tribes'.[45] Such a framework was not 'novel':[46] the British state had done the same in other conflicts in which it was involved. However, this putative neutrality had direct implications for security policy. Even though the state was manifestly involved in a conflict, which had at the very least political underpinnings, it could not afford to acknowledge that openly. The paradox for the state was that if the Northern Ireland conflict was little other than an extended crime wave, logic dictated that suspected wrongdoers should be arrested, tried, and prosecuted through the normal criminal justice system and not executed extra-judicially. Accordingly, the logic of government's stance on criminalization required it to forego certain tactics, or at least to ringfence their usage and to deny publicly that such strategies were being deployed.

A second problem is that the extra judicial killings clearly fell foul of the British government's international human rights commitments. While such concern may be of secondary importance to a government facing a violent challenge to its status, the support of the international community in countering any threat is always valued. Criticism by European and UN bodies, and cases taken in the domestic and international courts which demonstrate illegal behaviour on the part of government, are not relished by sovereign governments claiming democratic credentials. We would argue that one of the key reasons why the most egregious aspects of state security policy began to dissipate in the 1980s was because of the sustained and critical external scrutiny was brought to bear, not least when the European Court found repeatedly that the UK government had failed to adequately uphold and safeguard the right to life.[47]

Further problems arose when the policy itself was seen to have unintended side-effects. The families of those victims who were subsequently shown to have had no paramilitary involvement naturally elicited widespread public sympathy, and questions began to be asked about the risk of an overly enthusiastic pursuit of 'security'.[48] Such questions arose despite, or sometimes because of, propaganda initiatives seeking to portray the vast majority of those killed by the state as in some way implicated in the conflict.[49]

The experiences of the 'shoot to kill' era in Northern Ireland illustrate the corrosive consequences of the illegal actions of the security forces upon the wider administration of criminal justice. Such a policy led to the creation of a 'force within a force' with consequences that inevitably become difficult to manage.[50] In

---

[45] See Roy Greenslade, *The Damien Walsh Memorial Lecture*, 4 August 1998, available on http://cain.ulst.ac.uk/othelem/media/greenslade.htm (accessed 10 January 2006).

[46] Brendan O'Leary, and John McGarry, above n 13, 183.

[47] See *McCann and others v United Kingdom* Series A No 324 (1996) 21 EHRR 97; *Jordan v UK* (2003) 37 EHRR 52, para 105, *Kelly and others v UK*, para 91, *McKerr v UK*, Series A 2001-III (2002) 34 EHRR 553, para 108, *Shanaghan v UK*, Judgement of 4 May 2001, No. 37715/97, para 85; *Finucane v UK* (2003) 37 EHRR 29.

[48] See CAJ, *Plastic Bullets and the Law* (1990); *Plastic Bullets-a briefing paper* (June 1998).

[49] See David Miller, *Don't Mention the War: Northern Ireland, Propaganda and the Media* (1994).

[50] The RUC Special Branch was frequently described as a 'force within a force'. See Patten Commission, *Independent Commission on Policing in Northern Ireland. A New Beginning: Policing in*

effect a group of front-line 'specialists' within the security forces emerged who saw themselves as above the law and able to act with impunity.[51] Apart from the consequences of such a unit to police culture generally and the undermining of the normal investigation functions carried out by other police officers, the measures taken to cover up the existence of such a policy also have a pernicious effect on the rule of law as other officers of the court appear to be compromised by the political need to cover up for such groups—two cases in point being Bloody Sunday and the murder of Pat Finucane.[52]

Contemporary efforts to reframe a 'shoot to kill' policy as a 'shoot-to-kill-to-protect' are noteworthy. This new characterization was announced to the media to explain the killing of Brazilian Jean Charles de Menezes on an underground train in London by police officers who allegedly believed that he posed an imminent threat as a suicide bomber.[53] This case differs from many earlier Northern Ireland cases in two obvious ways. First, the authorities quickly acknowledged the existence of a 'shoot to kill' policy.[54] Secondly, a striking difference has been the willingness of the mainstream media in Britain to question the official version of events.[55] Such scrutiny may result from the shooting having taken place in London rather than far away (in journalists' terms) Belfast. It may also be that years of a denied but much believed 'shoot to kill' policy in Northern Ireland has made the British media less willing to accept the received version promulgated by the state. It is also to be hoped that decades of human rights campaigning, seeking to hold the police and security forces to account for their actions, and an increased awareness of the danger of any 'shoot to kill' policy, contributed to that scrutiny.

Detention without Trial

In reviewing the the parliamentary debates and public discourse on responses to threats from international terrorist groups, it appears that 'internment' is

Northern Ireland—The Report of the Independent Commission on Policing in Northern Ireland (1999), para 12.10.

[51] See Ruth Jamiesion and Kieran McEvoy, 'State Crime by Proxy and Juridical Othering' (2005) 45 British Journal of Criminology 504.

[52] The former reference is to 30 January 1972, when 13 unarmed civilians were shot dead by the British Army in Derry. Patrick Finucane, a human rights lawyer, was shot dead by loyalist paramilitaries in front of his family on 12 February 1989. His family and many others contended consistently that the UK State was involved in his murder, a finding confirmed by the Cory Report (above n 19).

[53] See 'Yard Officer Admits "Shoot To Kill" Error', The Times, 27 October 2005. The circumstances of the case were initially disputed and are currently under investigation. See Rosie Cowan, Duncan Campbell, and Vikram Dodd, 'New Claims Emerge Over Menezes Death' The Guardian, Wednesday 17 August 2005.

[54] See The Guardian, 25 July 2005—'But (Sir Ian Blair, Metropolitan Police Chief) admitted more people could die at the hands of police marksmen in the escalating battle against terrorism. Openly discussing the shift in police tactics for the first time, Sir Ian defended the policy of "shoot to kill in order to protect", saying it was necessary to shoot suspects in the head if it was feared they might trigger devices on their body.'

[55] ibid. See also BBC Online News, Debate rages over 'shoot-to-kill', http://news.bbc.co.uk/1/hi/uk/4711769.stm (accessed 5 May 2006).

unacceptable for many politicians[56] but that 'detention without trial' remains on the agenda as a potential response to the War on Terror. Parliament's recent rejection of a 90-day period of detention without trial in favour of a 28-day limit was depicted as an honourable compromise in favour of civil liberties.[57] It is unclear what the supposed distinction between detention without trial and internment is. Many will conclude that the new nomenclature of detention without trial has been created merely to avoid parallels being drawn with the failed policies of the past.

Internment, or detention without trial, was a policy exercised in Northern Ireland in the early stages of the conflict and remained on the statute books for years after it had been discredited as a security tactic.[58] The seminal House of Lords decision on the legality of the continued detention of the Belmarsh internees under the current policy acknowledged this, stating that '[e]xperience in Northern Ireland showed that (in conditions of internal sectarian violence rather than international war) internment was also a major obstacle to political progress and reconciliation.'[59] The court went on to say, however, that the Northern Ireland context and the current 'War on Terror' were entirely different sets of circumstances.[60]

In coming to its conclusion on the failure of internment in Northern Ireland the House of Lords was merely drawing on well-publicized criticisms made by a variety of commentators in relation to the conflict. One army officer, for example, noted that internment:

'... was a complete disaster. It turned a large number of the nationalist population, who at that time had been firmly on our side and very sensibly so, against us. To my simple mind, as a regimental soldier, it was lunacy. What it did was put a few people inside who probably didn't matter very much and it didn't intern the people who did matter. It also meant that what little information we were getting at that time just totally dried up. The nationalist population didn't trust the security forces any more and, to my mind, in any internal security operation—and that's what Northern Ireland was—hearts and minds are the most important part of it. And internment destroyed it.'[61]

In the same vein, Sir Robert Andrew, who later became Permanent Under-Secretary at the Northern Ireland Office, and was Private Secretary to then Defence Secretary, Lord Carrington at the time of internment, raised a very pragmatic concern:

'The biggest problem was what do you do with these people once you've arrested them. By definition, you haven't got evidence which would stand up in a court of law, so you can't

---

[56] Such as the UK Conservative Spokesperson on Home Affairs, David Davis. See Matthew Tempest, 'Blair defeated on terror bill', The Guardian, 9 November 2005.

[57] Philippe Naughton and Simon Freeman, 'Blair Humiliated In Terror Bill Vote', The Times, 9 November 2005.

[58] It was finally removed by the Northern Ireland (Emergency Provisions) Act 1998.

[59] *A and others v Secretary of State for the Home Department* [2004] UKHL 56, *per* Lord Walker, para 202.   [60] ibid, *per* Lord Hoffman, para 93.

[61] Lt Colonel Commander Brian, of the 1st Battalion Gloucestershire Regiment, in Peter Taylor, *Brits: the War against the IRA* (2001), 67.

bring them to trial. You either have to keep them inside indefinitely, which would be the subject of much criticism, or eventually you have to let them go, as they had to do in the end. So I think the policy was a failure.'[62]

Informed observers noted that the failed policy:

'justified the claim by nationalist critics that internment was the best recruiting sergeant the IRA could ever have hoped for . . . internment turned out to be a disastrous and defining episode with far-reaching political and security consequences . . . more importantly, the introduction of internment sowed the seeds for an even more debilitating conflict that would turn the prisons into universities of terrorism and heavily influence the turbulent events of the next quarter of a century.'[63]

Unless intelligence is of very good quality, the authorities are likely to arrest a large number of innocent people, and the unfairness in the operation of the policy will antagonize the very community relied upon to provide intelligence.[64] Modern-day proponents of internment tend to argue that the policy in Northern Ireland was simply badly implemented, and these failures in intelligence could and would be avoided in any new internment policy.[65] However, it is difficult to know how any policy of detention without trial could be implemented in a way that would not fall disproportionately on some sections of the community rather than others. This in turn creates a very high risk of the appearance if not the reality of the creation of what Paddy Hillyard refers to as 'suspect communities' and inevitably discriminatory treatment by virtue of perceived national, ethnic, or religious origins. The experience of internment in Northern Ireland underlines the dangers of a counter-terrorist policy that is driven primarily by the intelligence community and the police. The safeguards and standards demanded by human rights strictures are often portrayed as impediments, yet, had they been applied in Northern Ireland, such safeguards and strictures would have mitigated many of the excesses of the state's security approach.

Coercive Interrogation Techniques

The Northern Ireland practice of detention without trial led to the use of ill-treatment and prefigured some of the coercive techniques which it is now alleged are being used in the 'War on Terror' in places such as Guantanamo, Abu Ghraib,

---

[62] Lt Colonel Commander Brian, of the 1st Battalion Gloucestershire Regiment, in Peter Taylor, *Brits: the War against the IRA* (2001), 68.   [63] Chris Ryder, *Inside the Maze* (2000).

[64] Of the 1,981 individuals interned throughout the entire period, 107 were Protestant/loyalist (cited in CAJ Preliminary submission to Eminent Jurists Panel, April 2006, available at http://www.caj.org.uk/enewsletter/april2006/icj/cajpresub1.doc, accessed 5 June 2006).

[65] Frank Kitson, counter-terrorism expert, was said to support the theory of internment on the grounds that, 'it took bad men who could not be charged off the streets, but he believed that it had to be carried out with extreme care and precision'. Taylor commented that alienating the whole nationalist community by taking away their fathers and sons in the small hours of the morning and locking them up without charge did not fit in with Kitson's strategy (Taylor, n 61, supra).

and elsewhere.[66] The use on detainees in Northern Ireland of such methods as isolation, hooding, standing for long periods, and the constant application of white noise subsequently became the cause of legal action before the European Court of Human Rights. At the preliminary phase, the European Commission found that the five techniques amounted *prima facie* to torture, but the Court subsequently determined that the UK government was culpable only of exerting cruel, inhuman, and degrading treatment.[67] Both torture and cruel, inhuman, and degrading treatment are expressly outlawed under international human rights law. Since the passage of the UN Declaration Against Torture in 1975, regardless of the fact that it continues to be practised in many parts of the world, the international legal consensus has been that no justification is ever allowed for such behaviour.[68]

While terrorist acts experienced around the world in the past 30 years have been rightly deplored, until recently, with the possible exception of Israel at different junctures, few have attempted (publicly at least) to argue that state-condoned torture is an acceptable response. Now, for the first time in recent years, the international consensus that torture is unacceptable[69] has come under sustained criticism by virtue of the 'War on Terror'. Leading academics now earnestly discuss how to regulate rather than outlaw torture.[70] The publication of the so-called 'torture memos' in the US[71] has fed into wider public debates, raising subjects that would have previously been considered almost taboo, such as the supposed distinction to be drawn between 'torture' (never acceptable) and 'cruel, inhuman and

[66] See eg, Amnesty International Annual Report 2006, Chapter on USA: 'Evidence continued to emerge of the torture and ill-treatment of detainees in Guantánamo, Afghanistan and Iraq, before and after the abuses in Abu Ghraib prison, Iraq, which came to light in April 2004. Further information was published describing interrogation techniques officially approved at various periods for "war on terror" detainees, which included the use of dogs to inspire fear, stress positions, exposure to extremes of heat or cold, sleep deprivation and isolation.' (Available at http://web.amnesty.org/report2006/usa-summary-eng, accessed 4 June 2006). [67] *Ireland v UK* (1978) 2 EHRR 25.

[68] UN Declaration on the Protection of all Persons from being subjected to Torture and other Cruel, Inhuman or Degrading treatment or punishment (Resolution 3452 of 9 December 1975). 'No state may permit or tolerate torture or other cruel, inhuman or degrading treatment or punishment. Exceptional circumstances such as a state of war or a threat of war, internal political instability or any other public emergency may not be invoked as a justification of torture or other cruel, inhuman or degrading treatment or punishment' (Article 3).

[69] The 1975 Declaration was complemented by the passage of the UN Convention Against Torture and Other Cruel, Inhuman or Degrading Treatment or Punishment in 1984, which has binding status.

[70] See Philip B. Heymann and Juliette N. Kayyem, *Protecting Liberty In An Age Of Terror* (2005); Philip B. Heymann and Juliette N. Kayyem, *The Long-Term Legal Strategy Project for Preserving Security and Democratic Freedoms in the War on Terrorism* (2004), which, *inter alia*, makes clear distinctions between 'torture' and 'cruel, inhuman and degrading treatment' and recommends that 'a list of permissible highly coercive techniques . . . be promulgated by the President . . . such techniques should be used in an individual case only when the factual basis for the need, the exceptional importance of information sought, and the likelihood that the individual has that information is certified in writing by a senior government official . . . ' (Executive Summary, pp 2–3).

[71] See Karen J. Greenberg and Joshua L. Dratel (eds), *The Torture Papers: The Road to Abu Ghraib* (2005).

degrading treatment' (sometimes acceptable). Thus, the public debate is engaging with questions such as what circumstances could justify some form of coercion and what level might be acceptable.

There are very good reasons why torture is one of the few non-derogable articles in the international human rights treaties: first, it is wrong and secondly, it is counter-productive. Human rights activists, committed as they must be to recognizing the 'inherent dignity and the equal and inalienable rights of all members of the human family',[72] are obviously going to claim that it is wrong to abuse human beings, even for the supposed good of others. Those who make the case that torture is wrong because it is counter-productive often come from the ranks of serving and former security officers. Such doubts as to the efficacy of torture from security professionals are also nothing new. In a letter to *The Times* in November 1971, senior British intelligence officers, citing service both in World War II and the Malayan conflict, commented on allegations of ill-treatment in Northern Ireland, 'If the RUC, or indeed the army, is using the methods reported, they are being singularly stupid and unimaginative.'[73] Human rights groups such as Human Rights First have harnessed such authoritative support to great political effect. The publicly expressed misgivings of senior military and former intelligence officers at the use of torture, the denigration of the Geneva Conventions and a range of other illegal tactics deployed by the Bush administration have arguably been amongst the most politically significant critiques in recent times.[74]

The recent House of Lords ruling that evidence obtained through torture is not admissible in UK courts[75] goes some way to resisting the advance towards the creeping acceptability of torture, although the test set by the court places the

[72] Preamble to the Universal Declaration of Human Rights, General Assembly Resolution 217 A (III), 10 December 1948.

[73] Amnesty International, *Report of an Enquiry into Allegations of Ill-Treatment in Northern Ireland*, (1972) 46.

[74] See eg Human Rights Trust *Letter from Retired Military to the President Endorsing Senator McCain Amendment on Treatment of Detainees in US Custody*, 18 January 2006, http://www.humanrightsfirst.info/pdf/06118-etn-ltr-bush-from-military.pdf. In 2005, in an Open Letter to the US Senate Judiciary Committee regarding the confirmation hearings of Mr Gonzalez as the new Attorney-General, a similar range of high-ranking US retired military wrote that: 'A series of memos that were prepared at his direction in 2002 recommended official authorization of harsh interrogation methods, including waterboarding, feigned suffocation, and sleep deprivation. As with the recommendations on the Geneva Conventions, these memos ignored established U.S. military policy, including doctrine prohibiting "threats, insults, or exposure to inhumane treatment as a means of or aid to interrogation." Indeed, the August 1, 2002 Justice Department memo . . . never once cites the U.S. Army Field Manual on interrogation. The Manual was the product of decades of experience— experience that had shown, among other things, that such interrogation methods produce unreliable results and often impede further intelligence collection. Discounting the Manual's wisdom on this central point shows a disturbing disregard for the decades of hard-won knowledge of the professional American military.' (Open letter to the Senate Judiciary Committee by Retired US General Brahms and others, available at http://www.humanrightsfirst.org/us_law/etn/gonzales/statements/gonz_military_010405.pdf).

[75] *A and others v Secretary of State for the Home Department* [2005] UKHL 71.

burden of proof on the individual to show that the disputed evidence has not been obtained by torture.[76] Yet the experience in Northern Ireland is that ill-treatment of suspects failed legally, morally, and practically as an appropriate response to violence. Torture and ill-treatment secures information which is often unreliable, leads to false confessions and miscarriages of justice. Further, torture creates alienation amongst the wider community from which the recipients of such behaviour are drawn; and it corrupts the principles that supposedly distinguish between the terrorist and those seeking to protect society against acts of terror. In times of desperation, governments may resort to such methods in an attempt to be seen to be doing something. It is incumbent upon human rights activists to remind governments of lessons from recent history that demonstrate that resort to such methods can only damage their cause.

Demonising Dissent—the Silencing of Opposition

Shoot-to-kill, arbitrary detention, and coercive interrogation are obvious techniques deployed by the state in response to political violence. Arguably more pernicious however, is the range of techniques deployed to silence or undermine opposition to such policies. Sometimes the processes of silencing are deliberate, in other instances they are a a by-product of a culture of fear and intimidation provoked by political violence and the state's response to that violence. Again there are strong parallels between contemporary experience and the Northern Ireland conflict. For example, there is currently a debate about using the law to prevent people advocating or 'glorifying' terrorism.[77] For many years in Northern Ireland, this was a predominant view and there was for some period the practice of refusing to allow spokespersons for proscribed organizations access to the airwaves across the UK.[78]

The practical difficulties presented to the British government of trying to put into law an intuitive distaste for the views of those who supported or advocated political violence was illustrated by the fact that many in the media, whilst not necessarily sympathetic to the views espoused, objected to such censorship and the policy was subverted by the employment of actors to do 'voice-overs' whenever certain individuals appeared on television (the Act banned only their spoken words, not the accompanying pictures). This led to the often surreal sight of senior Republicans being deliberately badly dubbed in order to demonstrate that they were being censored.

---

[76] ibid, *per* Lord Hope for the majority at para 121. Lord Bingham for the minority dismisses this as 'a test which, in the real world, can never be satisfied. The foreign torturer does not boast of his trade'. (at para 59).   [77] See s 1 of the Terrorism Act 2006 'Encouragement of terrorism'.

[78] Restrictions on broadcasting were announced on 19 October 1988 by the then UK Home Secretary, Douglas Hurd, utilizing the relevant sections of the Broadcasting Act 1981. See Ed Maloney, 'Closing Down the Airwaves: the story of the Broadcasting Ban', in Bill Rolston (ed.) *The Media and Northern Ireland* (1991).

As a means of expressing abhorrence at the actions of such groups, such a policy may be considered quite a successful tactic but it is doubtful whether it facilitated the engagement necessary to bring an end to violence or that it in any way diminished the violence. It failed also to consider what message such a policy conveyed to those who understood even if they did not condone paramilitary violence.

Our argument is not that all limitations on one's liberty are unacceptable. For years people in Belfast thought nothing of opening their bags on the way into stores or their car boots when using car parks. The legal argument in New York, for example, that people should not be randomly stopped before getting on the subway[79] seems to us to underplay the fact that the state not only has a right, but also has a duty to protect people travelling on its public transport systems.[80] Rather, our view is that any such policy must be shown to comply with the international human rights principles of necessity, proportionality, and non-discrimination.

We would reject the oftmade criticism that human rights advocates are so concerned about the rights of suspects that they ignore entirely the rights of victims.[81] As discussed above, many of the criticisms made by human rights activists relate to the inefficacy of security policies or their prejudicial use against certain sections of society. In the Northern Ireland context, republican violence was at its height in the early and mid-1970s and decreased from the early 1980s onwards.[82] It is unlikely to be coincidental that this diminution of violence started to take place alongside a more political policy of outreach and influence seeking. Any move to close down dialogue and political organization is unwise, and any move in that direction in the present climate of tension in Britain should be resisted very strongly. Freedom of expression may not have the near sacrosanct status of the right to life and freedom from torture, but it can be an important tool in the arsenal of engaging with and robustly challenging those who would advocate violence in the same way as one would challenge abrogations to the rule of law.

It is a primary concern of human rights activists that states ensure everyone's security by complying with the human rights standards that they have freely submitted to in both domestic and international law. Accordingly, when the state fails to comply with these obligations, its failure needs to be challenged and countered. Furthermore, as cases such as the Birmingham Six[83] and the Guildford Four[84] graphically illustrate, suspects can also be victims. In a society where the legal, political and economic might of the state is focused on apprehending those engaged in terrorist activity, and where the clamour for quick-fix security results

---

[79] NYCLU Sues New York City Over Subway Bag Search Policy ACLU Press Release, 4 August 2005 (available from http://www.aclu.org/police/searchseizure/20054prs20050804.html, (accessed 16 January 2006).

[80] Where there is a positive duty on the State to actively take steps to prevent the loss of life. See eg *Osman v UK* (2000) 29 EHRR 245.   [81] See nn s 16 and 17, supra.

[82] See David McKittrick, Seamus Kelters, Brian Feeney, and Chris Thornton, *Lost Lives*, (1999) at Table 2, 'Responsibility For Deaths'.   [83] *R v McIlkenny and Others* [1992] 2 All ER 417.

[84] *R v Hill and others* (1989) *The Times*, 20 October 1989.

can become deafening, it is imperative that human rights activists and NGOs remind us all of the need for clear and rational judgement based on international legal standards.

Protecting Human Rights in Conflicts—Learning from Northern Ireland

It is clear that the origins of conflicts often have human rights abuses as a cause or a contributory factor, and that the violence which ensues inflames the situation. Responses by a state to that violence frequently include further violations of human rights that fuel the conflict. Political violence can only be resolved by addressing those abuses, and by mainstreaming human rights protections in transition and post-conflict arrangements.[85] There are many lessons to learn from Northern Ireland that are relevant to the current debate about the 'War on Terror', from legislative encroachments upon civil liberties to possible routes out of the conflict.

In times of crisis, governments often seek 'extraordinary' powers to respond to an understandable public demand on government to 'do something' in response to a particular atrocity or acceleration of violence. Northern Ireland demonstrates the risk that such 'temporary' powers taken on by states in response to an 'emergency' or 'short term' crisis, often become normalized or lead to further extensions of power (the 'thin end of the wedge'). Once legislation is enacted however, there is limited external objective assessment of either the level of threat posed or its duration, with a view to repealing emergency powers. Absent such rigorous scrutiny, the powers justified to the general public and to the wider world on the grounds of a specific and very serious threat become routinized and thus distort the non-emergency criminal justice system. In Northern Ireland, the Special Powers Act, maintained since 1922, was replaced by the Emergency Provisions Act 1973, and supplemented by a variety of additional legislation aimed at preventing terrorism throughout the 1970s and 1980s. These measures stayed on the statute book until the passage of the UK-wide Terrorism Act 2000, and indeed several still remain in force. This means that the jurisdiction has had to wait more than 80 years, and nine years after the passage of a comprehensive peace agreement, to see the removal of measures that were justified on the grounds of an urgent and extraordinary 'threat to the life of the nation'. In practice, however, even if the measures are ended in 2007,[86] relatively little will change since the Terrorism Acts 2000 and 2006 have incorporated many of the elements of the security responses previously limited only to Northern Ireland. In other words, many of those extraordinary powers are now permanent and UK-wide—the ultimate example of normalization of emergency law.

[85] See CAJ Preliminary submission to Eminent Jurists Panel, April 2006; and press release from Eminent Jurists Panel on Terrorism, Counter-Terrorism and Human Rights, 21 April 2006, n 64 above.   [86] Northern Ireland Office Press Release, 1 August 2005.

Northern Ireland also confirms the experience elsewhere that the very existence of emergency powers facilitates the abuse of human rights. Draconian security measures, such as a shoot-to-kill policy—even if supposedly instituted to protect society from particular individuals perceived to pose a direct threat—have been proved to be counter-productive. They deny the suspect basic rights, corrupt those engaged in implementing the policy, and undermine the rule of law and democratic decision-making. Detention without trial poses the risk of coercive interrogation techniques, denies the suspects due process, risks creating suspect communities, alienating those communities, and leads to miscarriages of justice. Coercive interrogation techniques are both wrong *per se* and counter-productive in that whilst they undermine the state's moral stance, they rarely secure accurate intelligence, and strengthen the resolve of the opposition. Whilst privations on liberty may be necessary precisely because the state has a duty to protect its citizens, those privations must be necessary, proportionate, and applied impartially if they are not to polarize and alienate communities.

The lessons from Northern Ireland are not, however, all negative ones. Recent progress highlights the importance of addressing grievances and tackling the root causes of disaffection if patterns of spiralling violence and human rights abuses are to be broken. Seeking to understand and engage with those seen to be posing a threat is a sign of strength not weakness and is a better means of understanding the genesis of the conflict and developing lasting solutions. As Northern Ireland has moved from very high levels of conflict, it has begun to move away from anti-terrorist measures that have been seen to be counter-productive. Many of these recent initiatives would have been important bulwarks in ensuring both security and human rights if they had been introduced earlier and demonstrate that procedural safeguards are not an impediment to security and may in fact strengthen the ability of the state to protect itself.

The audio and video recording of interviews, for example, protects not only suspects but also their interrogators who might otherwise have little protection against false allegations of torture or ill-treatment.[87] Early and frequent access to medical examinations, and to independent legal advice, prevents miscarriages of justice and ensures that later stages in the process of bringing alleged perpetrators to justice do not fail because of earlier impropriety. External oversight of the police and the various criminal justice agencies, including independent complaints systems; a clear legal framework for their activities with professional codes of conduct and strong disciplinary mechanisms; transparency in the process of appointments and a workforce broadly representative of society as a whole; and effective legal and democratic accountability—all contribute to the creation of a policing and criminal justice system that is human rights compliant and works equally and

---

[87] Silent video-taping was introduced under the Northern Ireland (Emergency Provisions) Act 1996 and audio taping followed soon thereafter.

fairly for all.[88] Painful experience has shown that the torture and ill-treatment of detainees can only be prevented if there is sufficient scrutiny and oversight of the conditions of detention. Communities believed to shelter anti-state forces can only be expected to co-operate with the authorities if they believe that they will be treated fairly, and are not made to bear the brunt of discriminatory police and army actions. Due process safeguards ensure that wrongdoing can be effectively investigated and punished. Policing by consent is a complex concept but crucial to upholding the rule of law and the best possible form of security in a society otherwise under violent attack, something acknowledged by the Good Friday Agreement itself.[89]

One of the crucial lessons from Northern Ireland is the value of international and domestic agencies working in close co-ordination with each other to tackle the challenge of human rights protection. Domestic governments have the primary responsibility in international law for upholding human rights, but they need the support of an active civil society, a free and independent press, and an efficient and effective public sector answerable for their actions in law. In democratic societies, the interplay of the legislature, executive, and judiciary normally provide the necessary checks and balances. However, it is at times of great pressure—of real and perceived danger—that the normal safeguards can and often do buckle. In Northern Ireland, local political structures collapsed entirely, and central government was neither able nor willing to engage effectively with its critics. Violent conflict can often exacerbate societal divisions and made constructive critical debate difficult if not impossible. In the Northern Ireland conflict, external agencies, the United Nations, the European Court of Human Rights, respected international NGOs, all contributed to the debate regarding the appropriate balance to be struck between the security of society and the security of the individual. Having no partisan political agenda, such agencies brought a particular expertise to the debate and reminded domestic actors that security of the person requires the protection of human rights—security and human rights are complementary, not contradictory.

Lessons for Human Rights Organizations

Human rights activism is never easy, but it is especially difficult at times of violent political conflict. The Northern Ireland Civil Rights Association (NICRA) was largely destroyed very early in the conflict in the wake of the events of Bloody

---

[88] See Mary O'Rawe, and Linda Moore, *Human Rights on Duty: Principles for better policing—international lessons for Northern Ireland* (1997), summarizing the developments in policing and security regulation and oversight.

[89] Agreement reached in the multi-party negotiations, Belfast, 10 April 1998, section 9 Policing.

Sunday.[90] One immediate reason for its demise was that it had been at the forefront of trying to develop a cross-community alliance around civil rights
demands, and had relied very much on the medium of public action. This tool
was effectively destroyed with the deaths of so many innocent demonstrators. The
polarization of communities in the wake of these actions by the state also made
cross-community platforms more difficult to mobilize.[91] This collapse of political
space was exacerbated by the state's security policy after Bloody Sunday. It was to
be a further decade before another cross-community effort was launched to
address issues of civil liberties and human rights when the Committee on the
Administration of Justice was founded in 1981. The lessons learnt in 25 years of
working, both at the height of political violence, and in the slow transition to
peace, are not all applicable in other jurisdictions. Nevertheless, some of them
including the political stance of such groups, their approach to non-state actors,
may prove useful for human rights activists working to counter the current
climate of the 'War on Terror'.

One early decision by CAJ was that in a highly conflicted and politically contested space, it should focus on human rights and seek to avoid being drawn into
politically partisan positions. Thus, for example, CAJ chose explicitly not to take a
position on the constitutional status of Northern Ireland.[92] Those who founded
the group wanted to be able to draw support from across all political shades of
opinion and focus on what united rather than what divided people—that is,
that everyone, whatever their political beliefs, had basic rights that should be
respected.

Another difficult early decision was to focus on the primary responsibility of
government to ensure the highest standards in the administration of justice.[93]
Although CAJ was opposed to the use of violence for political ends, it did not
make paramilitary groups its focus, but rather sought to influence how the state
could uphold human rights even when itself under attack. This stance, quite a
traditional one for human rights groups in the early 1980s, was re-visited several
times when international practice began to change in this regard, but was a crucial
element in maintaining the organization's impartiality.[94]

In a situation of very serious violence, community division, and politicization
of debate, CAJ found that the elaboration of a clear mandate helped ensure

[90] See Bob Purdie, Politics on the Streets, *The Origins of the Civil Rights Movement in Northern
Ireland* (1990); Niall O'Dochartaigh; *From Civil Rights to Armalites: Derry and the Birth of the Irish
Troubles* (1997).
[91] See Angela Hegarty, 'Truth, Law and Official Denial: The Case of Bloody Sunday', in William
A Schabas (ed.), *Truth Commissions And Courts: The Tension Between Criminal Justice And The Search
For Truth* (2005), 2214.
[92] See CAJ *The Administration Of Justice In Northern Ireland-Proceedings Of A Conference Held In
Belfast On June 13 1981* (1981).   [93] ibid.
[94] See CAJ's Newsletter, 21st Anniversary Edition, 'CAJ and its critics' (October 2002) *Just News*,
2; Eitan Felner *Human Rights Leaders in Conflict Zones: A Case Study of the Politics of "Moral
Entrepreneurs"* (2004), available at http://www.ksg.harvard.edu/cchrp/pdf/Felner.2004.pdf, accessed
24 July 2006.

consistency and impartiality. This helped in turn protect the human rights agenda against unfair attack, or indeed—on occasion—attempts at co-option by political interests. In particular, the reliance on clear international human rights standards allowed the organization to assure itself, and those it was seeking to influence, that its demands were genuinely rooted in objective human rights standards, and in no way predicated on local particularities or prejudices. Whether formulating a position on emergency powers, the release of paramilitary prisoners, or the right to march, reference to international standards, including European Court jurisprudence, and to the stance taken by independent academics and human rights activists in other jurisdictions allowed the organization to routinely test its own bona fides, and demonstrate its legitimacy to domestic and international actors.[95]

Another lesson that CAJ found invaluable in promoting human rights as a common standard for all was the value of broad alliance building. When human rights and civil liberties groups are working on unpopular causes, it is important to work closely with broader domestic networks of support and avoid the isolation of individuals and groups who challenge the *status quo*. Coalition building is both an important safety net and is also important in countering the 'divide and rule' strategy often employed by the state. Strategizing together with other groups and sharing information, whilst maintaining one's own remit and distinctiveness, prevents the isolation of a human rights NGO on the one hand, or its assimilation into political agendas on the other.[96] Coalitions should be more than domestic and horizontal. NGOs groups have a particular contribution to make to internationalizing conflict mediation and the defence of human rights. It was the recognition by CAJ in the early 1990s of the necessity for external support from the US, the UN, and European human rights bodies that facilitated the first serious human rights policy advances in Northern Ireland. Governments that do not respond to their domestic critics are sometimes obliged to respond to those same criticisms when voiced in international fora, and by friendly governments.[97]

The experience of Northern Ireland therefore suggests a number of lessons for human rights activists elsewhere to consider. The notion of human rights activism as controversial is embedded in the dominant public and social dialogues to the extent that human rights activists are sometimes depicted as suspicious, controversial, and dangerous.[98] Moreover, activists articulate a paradox between a claim to defend freedom and policies which continually curtail freedom,[99] so that human rights advocates who disagree with the security-driven government agenda

---

[95] ibid.

[96] See CAJ Annual Reports 1998-present, with descriptions of growing coalitions and formalization of such work by way of the Equality Coalition and the Human Rights Consortium.

[97] *CAJ in The Wider World*, n 95, supra.

[98] The Carter Center Atlanta, Conference Report *Human Rights Defenders On The Frontlines Of Freedom: Protecting Human Rights in The Context Of The War On Terror*, (11–12 November 2003).

[99] See Observatory for the Protection of Human Rights Defenders / FIDH and OMCT, Human Rights Defenders In A "Security First" Environment (Annual Report 2003).

can very easily come to be viewed as part of a suspect community.[100] Such a portrayal is often encouraged by media coverage and partisan attacks.[101] Certainly it was the experience in Northern Ireland throughout the conflict that advocates for human rights were frequently criticized for, variously, being 'naive', 'ill-advised' and even 'subversive'.[102] A similar process is at work today in the so-called 'War on Terror'.[103]

Yet, when people chide activists for defending human rights and arguing that basic international standards be observed, they are dismissing the need for those elements of accountability and control that those standards bring. If it is accepted that there will always be a role for intelligence in counter-terrorism and in policing, then it must also be accepted that there is a need for the rule of law to apply to these functions of the state, since neither the state nor its agents should be above the law. The rules should be scrutinized more, not less closely when the state increases the powers it exercises against the individual.

Conclusion

The Northern Ireland experience serves as a warning as to what happens when the demands of the security community prevail over human rights in state policy and law. Further, whilst there is sometimes an understandable and even genuine tension between protecting the security of all and the liberties of the individual, these should not be considered to be contradictory goals. On the contrary, those advocating the 'security-first' approach seem not to have noticed that those freedoms they say they are defending are those very freedoms that are removed by the introduction of ever more draconian powers.

In fact human rights standards guarantee security: it may be blindingly obvious, but it is important to articulate it—in order to defend the rule of law it is necessary to defend the rule of law. Human rights standards, in their focus on the demands of accountability and safeguards, actually underpin the rule of law and thereby contribute directly to everyone's security. Human rights promotion and protection are an indispensable element of any democratic society—they are not

---

[100] See Paul Hoffman, 'Human Rights and Terrorism' (2004) 26 Human Rights Quarterly 932; Julie A. Mertus, *Bait and Switch: Human Rights and U.S. Foreign Policy* (2004).

[101] See Hina Jilani, *Third Annual Report by the Special Representative for Human Rights Defenders to the UN General Assembly* (A/58/380) (2003).

[102] See Clem McCartney, 'The Role of Civil Society', in Clem McCartney (ed.), *Striking a balance: The Northern Ireland Peace Process* (Accord—An International Review of Peace Initiatives, Issue 89 (Conciliation Resources, London: 1999); Kieran McEvoy, 'Beyond the Metaphor: Political Violence, Human Rights and "New" Peacemaking Criminology' (2003) 7 Theoretical Criminology 319, 324; CAJ and its Critics' JustNews, October 2002, 2.

[103] See eg, Stephen Zunes, 'Bush Administration Attacks on Amnesty International: Old Wine, New Bottles', 6 June 2005; *Foreign Policy in Focus*; Carole Malone, 31 July 2005 'How About Our Rights, Cherie?' Sunday Mirror.

an optional extra to be dispensed with in times of emergency. In fact, it is particularly in times of perceived public threat that there is a need for public scrutiny of state action by an independent arbitrator, such as a human rights organization, employing the normative, rational standards offered by human rights treaties, which apply equally to all. The government does not always do what is right and democracy might be much better served in some instances by challenging rather than conforming to the views of those elected or appointed to positions of authority.

This is crucial where the powers of the state are vastly increased in an emergency and where minority groups are targeted or vilified. This was true in Northern Ireland throughout the conflict and is increasingly true of Britain today. Human rights norms prevent the state victimizing individuals and communities, even if it sometimes seems as if all they are capable of doing is reacting and providing a remedy when rights are transgressed. Human rights activists are an essential part of democracy—a vibrant activist community is one way of ensuring that the state does not exceed or abuse its great power. Their role is, as Edward Said put it:

'to speak the truth to power, to reject the official discourse of orthodoxy and authority, and to exist through irony and scepticism, mixed in with the languages of the media, government and dissent, trying to articulate the silent testimony of lived suffering and stifled experience'.[104]

---

[104] *From Silence to Sound and Back Again: Music, Literature, and History, in* Reflections on Exile and Other Essays (2000), 526.

18

Linking Human Rights and Other Goals

Kevin Boyle

Introduction

'[w]*ithout development there can be no security and without security there can be no development, and without human rights and the rule of law we can have neither security nor development*'.

It was one of the major objectives of the 2005 World Summit held in New York to have the 191 Member States of the United Nations register agreement with the conceptual linkage in this quotation from Kofi Annan, the UN Secretary General.[1] That much at least was achieved at the Summit, even if other objectives were not.[2] World leaders declared:

'We acknowledge that peace and security, development and human rights are the pillars of the United Nations system and the foundations for collective security and well-being. We recognise that development, peace and security and human rights are interlinked and mutually reinforcing.'[3]

The focus of this essay is neither the Summit's agenda on world poverty and the Millennium Development Goals (MDGs) as such, nor the institutional reforms of the UN that are underway following the event. It is rather to focus on the thinking that gave rise to this conference and the implications of the renewed emphasis on the interconnectedness of UN objectives from a human rights standpoint. How open are human rights advocates to building bridges to development and

---

[1] The Summit was convened in New York from 14–16 September 2005 to review achievements on the Millennium Development Goals (Millennium + 5) and to agree a package of reforms for the UN on the 60th anniversary of its creation. The best source at this date on the aims and achievements of the Summit is to be found at the UN website: www.un.org/summit2005/; www.un.org/reform; www.un.org/millenniumgoals/. See also UNA-UK, *In Larger Freedom in the UK, An Agenda for Action following the 2005 UN World Summit* (2005).

[2] Major failures included lack of progress on non-proliferation of nuclear weapons and disarmament, and on Security Council enlargement.

[3] 2005 World Summit Outcome, UN DOC A/60/l (2005), para 9.

security goals? How open are development and security specialists to reciprocal bridge building? What has been the experience so far of efforts to do so?

The call for connectedness was propounded in the two core documents prepared for the World Summit. The first, *A More Secure World: Our Shared Responsibility* was the report of an independent High Level Panel of experts appointed by the Secretary General to review new and existing threats to international peace and security.[4] The second, *In Larger Freedom: Towards Development, Security and Human Rights For All*, was Kofi Annan's own follow-up report. It endorsed the High Level Panel's analysis and prescriptions on global security and set out proposals for action to be considered by Member States in the September conference.[5] A major theme of both reports is that future policies for human betterment and even survival must reflect the complexity of the challenges that face a globalized and increasingly unequal world.

A More Secure World

The High Level Panel report has been described by its British member, as 'the single most far-reaching review of the UN's role in particular in the fields of peace and security, since the founding fathers met in San Francisco in 1945 and signed the UN Charter'.[6] In part the Report represents a UN response to the new radical doctrine on national security adopted by the US after 9/11, which asserted that country's right of pre-emption in the use of force.[7] The Panel rebuffed that doctrine and declared that the UN Charter rules on use of force did not require revision.[8] But its principal contribution was to promote an enlarged idea of security to challenge the traditional State-centred concept of military security.

In a post-9/11 era the proliferation of weapons of mass destruction, international terrorism and organized crime are properly identified as major concerns for the future. But the High Level Panel also highlights poverty, food insecurity, infectious disease, civil wars, and conflicts, environmental degradation and climate change, as neglected and connected sources of threat and insecurity affecting the human rights of millions on the planet. The international community should urgently recognize these threats and above all their interconnectedness.[9]

---

[4] Report of the High Level Panel on Threats, Challenges and Change, *A More Secure World: Our Shared Responsibility*, UN DOC A/59/565 (2004).
[5] Report of the Secretary General, *In Larger Freedom: Towards Development, Security and Human Rights For All*, UN DOCA/59/2005.
[6] Lord Hannay, Discussion Meeting, European Parliament Office, London, 1 February 2005.
[7] Pre-emption is now proposed to include the use of nuclear weapons. See 'Pentagon Revises Nuclear Strike Plan', Washington Post, 11 September 2005.
[8] A position confirmed at the 2005 World Summit, n 3 above, para 77.
[9] See Report of the High Level Panel on Threats, Challenges and Change, *A More Secure World: Our Shared Responsibility*, n 4 above, especially 111, 'Security, infectious disease and environmental degradation'.

In Larger Freedom

The title of the Annan Report is taken from the Preamble of the UN Charter. Concepts deployed in the report, including freedom from fear and freedom from want, explicitly invoke the Atlantic Charter Four Freedoms speech of Franklin D. Roosevelt in 1941.[10] In so doing Kofi Annan was no doubt reminding the people of the US, in particular that the world organization launched at San Francisco 60 years ago was largely their creation. But he was also reminding them and the world that freedoms are interrelated. The three components of *In Larger Freedom*—security, development, and human rights—are a re-packaging of the purposes of the UN as expressed in the Charter.[11] The thrust of the Annan report is to urge renewed commitment by Member States to these linked purposes. A significant legal development that flowed from such advocacy came with the World Summit's endorsement of the Secretary General's proposal on 'the responsibility to protect'. States agreed that there was an international collective duty to be exercised, through enforcement action if necessary, by the Security Council in order to protect populations from genocide, war crimes, ethnic cleansing, and crimes against humanity where individual States failed to do so.[12]

Human Rights and Interconnectedness

Three points might be made about the argumentation in these documents. The first, already noted, is the recognition of the complexities of a globalized world and the emphasis placed on articulating the connections between previously divorced goals, challenges, and threats facing human kind. The second is that the relationship between development, security and rights is a necessary starting-point for international co-operation if the cause which the UN was established to achieve, a just and peaceful world order, is to be realized. The third striking feature is the centrality of human rights to both the analysis and the prescriptions proposed. Thus, the High Level Panel stresses the need for the international community to join up strategies and programmes, now so often pursued separately, including those on poverty, conflict prevention, infectious disease, climate change, and natural disasters. The need for greater emphasis on human rights as both ends in themselves and as a bridge to link these challenges is reflected in the recommendation that the UN High Commissioner for Human Rights should be more involved in the deliberations of the Security Council.

As a follow up to *In Larger Freedom*, the UN High Commissioner for Human Rights, Louise Arbour, was asked to develop an action plan in anticipation of the

---

[10] Franklin Delano Roosevelt, State of the Union Address, 6 January 1941.
[11] See United Nations Charter, Arts 1, 55 and 56.
[12] 2005 World Summit Outcome, n 3 above, paras 138–39. For the origins of the principle, see International Commission on Intervention and State Sovereignty, *The Responsibility to Protect* (2001).

larger responsibilities envisaged for her Office. The action plan is an ambitious one that seeks to bind the international human rights system more closely to national action over human security, tackling impunity, poverty elimination, and development.[13] This essay will explore these two trends—the remarkable journey of human rights from the periphery of international relations and politics to its centre; and the emphasis on multi-sectoral or multi-dimensional analysis and policy in addressing global problems and global goals. What are the implications of these trends for human rights in terms of future research, policy, and practice? One implication must surely be the firm acceptance that human rights do not and indeed have never stood alone. They are shorthand for much more. Implementation of universal rights requires a deeper understanding of their linkage with other norms, values and institutions than has been achieved to date. There is a stark contrast, acknowledged in the OHCHR Plan of Action, between the shift of the human rights idea and ideals over half a century from the periphery of global affairs to the centre ground, and the scale of the failure of the international human rights system to deliver on the promises of universal protection and human rights guarantees. To explain, and as important to change that contrast, requires deeper awareness of the complexity of the social, economic, and political changes which are necessarily required at local, national, and international levels if human rights are to be universally achieved. It requires the pursuit of a range of both short- and long-term multi-dimensional policies to surmount the forces and conditions that negate the effectiveness of human rights protection systems in many parts of the world. The characteristics of human rights as legal norms certainly needs to be retained in any such analysis, but the *dependency* of these norms on other factors and conditions needs to be better articulated. That requires better theories of implementation which take as their premise the *interdependency* of rights and a range of other policies, values, institutions, and goals such as are articulated in the United Nations documents under discussion.

The UN Charter and UN Purposes

The UN was an effort to envisage a new collective world security framework in which, through international co-operation operating under international law, a world order based on peace and justice could be secured thereby 'saving successive generations for the scourge of war'.

The original UN vision required not alone the co-operation of Member States in building international institutions to achieve these purposes, but equally co-operation to ensure that they were pursued within States. The transformation of the world order implicit in the Charter's purposes included disarmament,

---

[13] *The OHCHR Plan of Action: Protection and Empowerment* (2005) available at www.ohchr.org. The Action Plan was noted by the 2005 World Summit Outcome, n 3 above, para 124.

securing the self-determination of peoples, universal human rights, ending poverty, and building democratic societies that entrench the rule of law. The Millennium Declaration of Heads of States and Governments in September 2000, confirmed that vision.[14] The UN 2000–2015 campaign to implement the MDGs, the Global Call to Action against Poverty launched by worldwide civil society organizations,[15] and initiatives such as the recent British Commission for Africa,[16] are all fresh attempts to return the world community to the collective pursuit of such goals.

The Cold War

It was the geo-political environment generated by the Cold War that for a half century distorted the prospects of effective and co-ordinated progress on the linked purposes of the new UN body. Part of that environment was the emergence of nuclear weapons and the virtual paralysis of the UN in the arms race and nuclear stand-off between the Soviet Union and the US. The efforts to take up again the goals of the UN Charter began only after the end of the Cold War, encouraged by a series of World Conferences that sought to address many of the global challenges left in its wake.[17] One such was the Vienna World Conference on Human Rights in 1993.[18] Sufficient consensus emerged at Vienna to affirm the principle of universal rights and that their promotion and protection was a priority for the international community. But there was also for the first time explicit recognition of the links between the promotion and protection of all human rights and other values and goals. States declared that:

'democracy, development and respect for human rights and fundamental freedoms are interdependent and mutually reinforcing.... The international community should support the strengthening and promotion of democracy, development and respect for human rights and fundamental freedoms in the entire world.'[19]

These principles were reiterated in the Millennium Declaration when world leaders committed themselves to:

'spare no effort to promote democracy and strengthen the rule of law as well as respect for all internationally recognised human rights and fundamental freedoms including the right to development'.[20]

---

[14] UN General Assembly Resolution, A/RES/55/2 (2000).

[15] The Global Call to Action against Poverty is a worldwide alliance of groups that sprung up in 2005. Its affiliate in the UK and Ireland is Make Poverty History, see http://www.whiteband.org and www.makepovertyhistory.org.

[16] Report of the Commission for Africa, *Our Common Interest*, (2005), available at www.commissionforafrica.org.

[17] Michael G. Schechter (ed.), *United Nations-sponsored World Conferences: Focus on Impact and Follow-up* (2001).

[18] Declaration and Programme of Action, World Conference on Human Rights, UN DOC A/CONF/157/24.   [19] ibid, para 8.

[20] UN Millennium Declaration, A/res/55/2, para 24.

The High Level Panel report and *In Larger Freedom* expands these understandings by conceptualizing their relationship to human security as well as to nature.

Exploring Interconnectedness

The remainder of this essay will explore the efforts that have been made to date to articulate connections between human rights, as legal norms standards or principles, and other norms concerned with human welfare. These are the sectors of equality, development, democracy, environment, peace, and security as well as the rule of law. Such an exercise can be little more than an initial sketch given the confines of space and the complexity of the relationships involved. Nevertheless, it should serve to introduce the broader framework of analysis of rights that is emerging as the linkages are pursued at the level of theory, advocacy, and policy.[21]

As the relationships between human rights and other goals, values and institutions have come to be asserted, common features have emerged in many of the discourses that have carried the debates. First, there has been a phase in which a relationship is expressed through subsuming the subject into the corpus of human rights law as a rights claim. Thus, we have had the advocacy and promotion of the right to development, the right to peace, the right to a sustainable environment, and more recently the right to democracy. These processes have been characterized as the emergence of 'third generation' human rights, a mode of analysis that has little current purchase.[22] But the articulation of rights claims in respect of these areas over the last decades has had undoubted influence on the recognition of the independent importance of human rights as legal norms that import duties on States and on other actors (international organizations and multi-national corporations). Connecting the normative dimension of these fields to human rights and obligations has helped shape both the policies and programmes of international organizations as well as governments, and has provided a basis for civil society demands for accountability in the pursuit of such policies and programmes.[23]

---

[21] An excellent example is the work of the first ever coalition of development and environment groups highlighting the impact already of global warming on Africa. *Up in Smoke* warns of the reversal of development achievements through the uncertainties and weather extremes resulting from global warming. Over 70 per cent of employment in Africa comes from small-scale farming, which is dependent on direct rainfall and means that the continent is vulnerable to the weather extremes associated with global warming. Recurrent droughts and floods combine with widespread poverty, daily dependence on natural resources and biodiversity, and the deep impact of diseases and numerous conflicts to undermine poverty reduction programmes. Thus, climate change directly exacerbates the denial of human rights and efforts to build democratic institutions. The critical vulnerability of Africa is compounded by the burden of debt and an unjust international trade system. See The Working Group on Climate Change and Development, New Economic Foundation *Up in Smoke* (2004 and 2006) available at www.neweconomics.org.   [22] Philip Alston (ed.), *People's Rights* (2001) 1–6.

[23] eg, the Global Accountability Project launched by One World Trust in 2001 to encourage and measure the accountability of international organizations, multi-national companies and Ngos to the publics they serve. See Hetty Kovak, Caroline Nelligan, and Simon Burall, *The Global Accountability Report 2003, Power without Accountability?* (2003). A parallel initiative promoted

A second result of the recognition of affinities between human rights and other sectors has been the rise of so-called 'rights-based approaches'. In essence, rights-based approaches are methodologies for incorporating human rights norms and concepts into the pursuit of other goals. Human rights do not thereby subsume or subordinate those goals but, it is argued, add a dimension which helps achieve them. Human rights norms can also act as the connector that brings the different goals into a coherent relationship. Such thinking has had the most impact to date on development theory and practice. Development with a human rights component has been recast as human development and later under the influence of environmental knowledge as sustainable human development. In a parallel way the goals of peace and security have been broadened through a human rights perspective into the concept of human security, a concept which underlies the High Level Panel Report.[24] There have been efforts equally to integrate human rights legal principles and norms with environment. Most recently, international statements defining democracy and good governance have incorporated human rights and the rule of law as integral elements.

Each of these areas of linkage with human rights has generated considerable interest, even enthusiasm from States, scholars, professionals, and civil society activists. Nevertheless, it will become clear that it has proved easier so far to express such linkages at a conceptual level in the form of statements, declarations or judicial dicta, than it has to generate concrete policies that give effect to them.

Human Rights and Equality

The Annan report, *In Larger Freedom*, is subtitled, '*Security Development and Human Rights For All*'. The universal character of rights is an inherent characteristic and its corollary is that of equality. The first and the most important links for human rights are to the principles of universalism and non-discrimination. The vision of equal human dignity for all, articulated in the UN Charter, represented the first international commitment to the overcoming of historical practices, found in most if not all societies and cultures, of differentiation and hierarchy based on human characteristics, including those of race or ethnicity, colour, gender, language, and religion.

Equality as the Ideal that Drove Human Rights

It has been concrete struggles to achieve goals of equal human dignity and equal human treatment that have proved the most important global force for the

by the NGO, Article 19 has been on freedom of information and the monitoring of information disclosure policies of the World Bank and the other international financial institutions. See also Toby Mendel, *Freedom of Information: A Comparative Legal Survey* (2003).

[24] Report of the High Level Panel on Threats, Challenges and Change, *A More Secure World: Our Shared Responsibility*, n 4 above.

advancement of human rights over the last century. The truly transformative language of Article 1 of the UN Charter was not the limited commitment of States to the promotion and encouragement of respect for human rights but the rider 'without distinction as to race language gender or religion'. The link between equality and human rights is the most distinctive and modern idea in the International Bill of Human Rights.[25]

It was not envisaged at the outset that the UN might take action over human rights. The domestic jurisdiction clause in Article 2(7) was intended to prevent scrutiny or criticism of national practices, in particular, over colonialism and racial discrimination.[26] But the struggle against racial discrimination, first in South Africa and then the US, broke through the carefully crafted exclusion of human rights by the dominant powers.[27] In a world polarized between the superpowers and in thrall to the nuclear threat, it was the demands for equality and self-determination that made limited progress on international human rights standards possible. The legislative initiatives taken within the UN on self-determination and on discrimination and inequality—from the Genocide Convention to the instruments on racial, religious, and sex discrimination—truly marked the onset of the human rights era.[28]

Equality Between Rights

A further aspect of equality as a component of understanding human rights arises from the classification of human rights. The agreement on a classification of rights and the inclusion of all categories—civil, political, economic, social, and cultural in the Universal Declaration of Human Rights—disguised ideological disagreement over their nature and relationships.[29] The Cold War stimulated competing views over priorities between rights and the ultimate rejection by Western States of the claim to equal status of all categories. Disagreement over the equal status of rights entailed also the rejection of the interdependence between each category of rights. The decision to proceed with the drafting of two and not a single Covenant to implement the Universal Declaration was also a by-product of the Cold War, as was the ideological objections in the US to the idea of economic, social, and cultural rights.[30]

[25] Bertrand G.Ramcharan, 'Equality and non-discrimination constitute the single dominant theme of the Covenant', in Louis Henkin (ed.) *The International Bill of Rights: The Covenant on Civil and Political Rights* (1981) 24.

[26] A. W. Brian Simpson, *Human Rights and the End of Empire, Britain and the Genesis of the European Convention* (2001) 276–322.

[27] Paul Lauren 'First Principles of Racial Equality: History and the Politics and Diplomacy of Human Rights Provisions in the United Nations Charter' (1983) 5 Human Rights Quarterly 1.

[28] Johannes Morsink, *The Universal Declaration of Human Rights Origins Drafting & Intent* (1998) 92–116.   [29] ibid, 190–238

[30] Sally Morphet, 'Economic, Social and Cultural Rights: The Development of Governments' Views 1941–88', in Ralph Beddard and Dilys M. Hill (eds), *Economic, Social and Cultural Rights: Progress and Achievement* (1992) 43.

The revision of thinking on economic, social, and cultural rights, begun at the Vienna World Conference, has been advanced by the struggle for equal treatment in respect of these rights. Each of the international instruments drafted to address inequality and discrimination extend duties on ratifying States to prevent discriminatory treatment and provide remedies in respect of each category of rights, whether it be political rights, such as the right to vote, or the social and economic rights such as education, housing, or health. Thus, the nexus between the norm of equality of treatment and human rights has served to integrate all human rights and to establish their interdependence in practice.

The Continuing Power of Equality and Inequality

Equality as a value and inequality as a reality remain the most powerful vehicles for the reception of human rights analysis into other fields, such as development, global poverty, and the environment. Gender and gender discrimination provide a further prominent example.[31]

Successive reports published since the MDGs were launched have brought out continuing inequalities experienced by the poor—men, women, and children—in every aspect of life, including health care, education, and life expectancy.[32] Thus, the 2005 Human Development Report which focuses on global social inequality, documents the ever-increasing inequalities in the enjoyment of basic human rights that exist between regions, between countries, and within countries.[33] Everywhere the poor are being left behind. Poverty itself has become a human rights concept.[34]

Human Rights and Development

The current focus of the relationship between poverty and human rights is on the implementation of the MDGs which integrate certain international human rights within a set of targets to half extreme poverty and advance other development goals by 2015.[35] But the links forged between human rights and development

---

[31] See United Nations Development Fund for Women, *Progress of the World's Women 2005: Women, Work and Poverty* (2005) and the essay by Elizabeth Meehan in this volume.

[32] UN Department of Economic and Social Affairs, *The Inequality Predicament, Report of the World Social Situation 2005* (2005); The World Commission on the Social Dimension of Globalization, *A Fair Globalization: Creating Opportunities for All* (2004).

[33] Human Development Report 2005, *International Co-Operation at a crossroads, aid, trade and security in an unequal world* (2005).

[34] See OHCHR, *Draft Human Rights Guidelines for Poverty Reduction Strategies* (2002), available at www.ohchr.org.

[35] Philip Alston, 'A Human Rights Perspective on the Millennium Development Goals' (2002), Paper prepared as a contribution to the work of the Millennium Project Task Force on Poverty and Economic Development. Available at www.ohchr.org/issues/millennium-development /docs.

required as a precondition the implementation of the principle of 'equal rights and self-determination of peoples'. The Declaration on the Granting of Independence of Colonial Countries and Peoples of 1960 invoked the human rights principles of the UN Charter, including that of the equal rights and self-determination of all peoples, the only collective right expressed in the Charter.[36] The ending of imperialism and colonialism was the most important transformation of global order that the UN has overseen. Its first phase was the decolonization struggle of the south of the world to dislodge Western empires, and its second resulted in the 1990s when the Soviet Union disintegrated and the nations of Eastern and Central Europe as well as Central Asia achieved independence.

However, the achievement of political independence and membership of the UN was but a foundation for progress for the bulk of humanity. Most of the newly independent States were poor and their efforts to end poverty and the role that the rich world, which had built its own wealth on the natural resources and people of these countries, should play in that struggle is a central theme in the story of development.

The Declaration on the Right to Development

On taking up membership of the UN and the General Assembly, the newly independent countries first sought the recognition in international law of full sovereignty over their natural resources and confirmation of the right to self-determination. General Assembly Resolution No. 1803 (XV11) of 14 December 1962 on 'Permanent sovereignty over natural resources' was also inserted in substance as the common Article 1 of the International Covenants on Human Rights.[37]

Article 2 of the International Covenant on Economic Social and Cultural Rights included a provision that sought to obligate the States that ratify to assist 'through international assistance and co-operation' the progressive realization of economic, social, and cultural rights in poorer countries. The efforts to link human rights and development, including the obligations of the international community to assist development culminated in the General Assembly Declaration on the Right to Development of 1986.[38] The Declaration defined the right as:

'an inalienable human right by virtue of which every human person and all peoples are entitled to participate in, contribute to, and enjoy economic social, cultural and political development in which all human rights and fundamental freedoms can be fully realized.'[39]

It further declares that States have a duty to co-operate with each other in achieving development, including through the promotion of 'a new international

---

[36] General Assembly Resolution 1514 (XV) 14 December 1960.
[37] International Covenant on Economic, Social and Cultural Rights and International Covenant on Civil and Political Rights, both adopted by GA Resolution A (XXI) 1966.
[38] UN Doc. A/RES/41/128 (1986).   [39] ibid, Art. 1.

economic order based on sovereign equality, interdependence, mutual interest and co-operation among all States, as well as the observance of and realization of human rights'.[40]

The Declaration was passed with only one vote cast against, that of the US. Although the US subsequently affirmed the existence of the right to development in the Declaration of the Vienna World Conference on Human Rights and in the Millennium Declaration, the right to development remains one of weak consensus in principle and even less in implementation.[41] Considerable energies have been invested in giving content and policy substance to the right within the UN Human Rights Commission, which cannot be examined here.[42] But what should be noted is that the right to development was a contribution from the developing world to the understanding of the relationship between the universal aspiration for human rights, and global poverty. The conceptualization of the right as agreed in the 1986 Declaration, which links all rights—civil, political, economic, social, and cultural—and includes the right of all to participate in shaping development, has been the seed bed of much current thinking about the integration of human rights within development policies and programmes of both donor and recipient countries. The Declaration links development as a process in which all human rights are to be fulfilled within a democratic framework based on the rule of law. Its call for a different global economic order was an essential step in the recovery of the link between the vision of the world that respects human rights and one committed to the elimination of poverty. Equally, its linkage of poverty and lack of resources for development to global expenditure on armaments and its call for disarmament became a staple of development and peace campaigning in the ensuing years. The Declaration's holistic approach was far-seeing but unrealistic in the conditions of Cold War confrontation. However, much of its holistic thinking was adopted in the Millennium Declaration, from which the MDGs are drawn.[43]

Rights-Based Approaches to Development

Efforts to give content to the implementation of the right to development over several decades have also had a major influence on the emergence of so-called rights-based approaches to development. The confirmation of the links between development and human rights and democracy in the Vienna World Conference was followed by the reform agenda for the UN by the new Secretary General

---

[40] ibid, Art. 3.
[41] On the right to development, see Koen de Feyter, *World Development Law: Sharing Responsibility for Development* (2001); Margot Soloman, 'The Right to Development and the Search for Global Justice' in Bard A. Andreessen and Stephen Marks (eds), *Processes of Expanding Freedom: The Right to Development and Human Rights in Development* (2005).
[42] Arjun Sengupta, 'On the Theory and Practice of the Right to Development' (2002) 24 Human Rights Quarterly 837; Stephen Marks, 'The Human Rights to Development, Between Rhetoric and Reality' (2004) 17 Harvard Human Rights Journal 137.   [43] UN Doc. A/RES/55/2 (2000).

Kofi Annan.[44] This entailed the integration or 'mainstreaming' of human rights across the other activities of the UN, including development. Beginning with UNICEF, which adopted the Convention on the Rights of the Child as its policy framework and followed by UNDP, efforts to operationalize human rights in development began.[45] The most comprehensive and influential effort to examine the relationship between fields that had grown up separately, was the 2000 Human Development Report.[46] That Report argued for a convergence of strategies in which human rights could advance development and development in turn advance human rights:

'Poverty eradication is a major human rights challenge of the 21st Century. A decent standard of living, adequate nutrition, health care, education, decent work and protection against calamities are not just development goals—they are also human rights.'[47]

The Report called also for the poor to have guarantees of their civil and political rights to pursue their economic and social rights. Its first chapter was written by development economist Armatya Sen, whose theory of development, which sees all human rights being both the ends and the means of development, has had major influence on bilateral and multilateral policies and programmes of development.[48] Development assistance, it is now recognized, should not only be directed at economic development, its traditional focus, but should also be concerned with the expansion of human capabilities and choices. Securing peoples human rights including guarantees of civil rights and political freedoms enables them to take control of their own development and secures the democratic empowerment of women and men.[49]

Human rights bodies have contributed to the pursuit of these ideas by seeking to distil specific normative concepts from the corpus of international human rights law that can be applied in the development policies of all development actors. Such principles identified include those of non-discrimination, equity, accountability, empowerment, and participation.[50]

[44] *Renewing the United Nations: A Programme for Reform*, UN Doc. A/51/950 (1997).
[45] UNDP, *Integrating Human Rights with Sustainable Human Development, A UNDP Policy Document* (1998).
[46] UNDP, *Human Development Report 2000, Human Rights and Human Development* (2000).
[47] ibid, 8.
[48] Amartya Sen, *Development as Freedom* (1999). For an excellent overview of Sen's work, see Polly Vizard, 'Economic Theory, Freedom and Human Rights: The Work of Amartya Sen' (2001), available at www.odi.org.uk.
[49] Sen's research has demonstrated that no famine has ever occurred in a democratic country with a free press and regular elections. He has also championed the empowerment of women, citing the irrefutable evidence that securing the right to education for women has far-reaching effects on the lives of all, through the reduction of child mortality as well as fertility rates, and in increasing the effectiveness of public participation. See Amartya Sen, Commencement Day Address, 8 June 2000, 'Global Doubts'. Available at www.harvard.edu.
[50] OHCHR, 'Human Rights in Development: What, How and Why?' Available at www.ohchr./development. See also Mary Robinson, 'Bridging the Gap between Human Rights and Development: From Normative Principles to Operational Relevance', World Bank Presidential Lecture December 2001, in Kevin Boyle (ed.) *Mary Robinson: A Voice for Human Rights* (2006) 299.

The integration of human rights in development programmes has not, however, proved straightforward. The UN has secured the incorporation of States' human rights international treaty commitments in the core tools of its development work, the Common Country Assessment (CCA) and country-specific development frameworks (UNDAF).[51] The OHCHR and UNDP continue to operate a joint project to encourage collaborative planning between development and human rights workers (HURIST).[52] At the bilateral level more donor countries have pursued rights-based approaches.[53] But a leading expert reviewing the experience of linking human rights and the MDGs offers a verdict of virtual failure.[54] The integration of human rights into development work, to which the 2000 Human Development Report looked forward, remains to be achieved.[55]

Human Rights and the Environment

It has been argued that a substantive right to a 'secure, healthy and ecologically sound environment' has emerged in international law.[56] However, that seems a premature assertion.[57] There are norms at the regional international level linking human rights to the environment, as there are in many constitutions.[58] Courts have confirmed links between the environment and rights to life, health, and information.[59] But there has been no international declaration such as the Declaration on the Right to Development in respect of environment and rights. The opportunity to endorse such a right arose at the UN Earth Summit held in Rio de Janeiro in 1992.[60] It was not taken.[61] The Rio Declaration proclaimed:

'Man has the fundamental right to freedom equality and adequate conditions of life, in an environment of quality that permits a life of dignity and well being.'

But it otherwise made limited reference to human rights. The Summit did, however, recognize the need to promote sustainable economic and social development

---

[51] For details, see United Nations Development Group, available at www.undg.org.

[52] See www.undp.org/cso/areas/human.html.

[53] See eg, German Foreign Ministry for Economic Co-operation and Development, 'Every person has a right to development', Development policy action plan on human rights 2004–2007 (2004). Available at www.bmz.de.

[54] Alston, 'A Human Rights Perspective on the Millennium Development Goals', n 35 above.

[55] For a thorough and an optimistic assessment of progress, see Philip Alston and Mary Robinson, *Human Rights and Development, Towards Mutual Reinforcement* (2005).

[56] Fatma Zohra Ksentini, *Human Rights and the Environment*, Special Rapporteur's Final Report (1994) UN DOC E/CN.4/Sub.2/1994/9. See also UN GA res. 45/94 (1990).

[57] Alan E. Boyle and Michael. R. Anderson (eds), *Human Rights Approaches to Environmental Protection* (1996).

[58] For a good survey, see UNEP/OHCHR Expert Seminar (2002) E/CN.4 /2002/WP7.

[59] ibid, and Philippe Sands, *Principles of International Environmental Law* (2003).

[60] United Nations Conference on Environment and Development (UNCED) Report, (1992) UNDOCA/CONF.151/2.

[61] Dinah Shelton, 'What Happened in Rio to Human Rights?' (1992) 3 Yearbook of International Environmental Law 75.

such that would secure a proper standard of living for the current generation without prejudicing environmental and natural resources of the generations yet to be born.[62] It adopted a set of principles that included Principle 10 on the right of individuals to information, participation, and effective national remedies on environmental concerns.[63] This has proved the spur to a range of measures expanding political rights into environmental policies. A leading example is the 1998 Aarhus Convention on Access to Information Participation and Access to Justice in Environmental Matters.[64]

The Earth Summit's Principles and Plan of Action (Agenda 21) were reviewed and endorsed at the World Summit on Sustainable Development (WSSD), the Johannesburg Summit, in 2002.[65] At that Summit the Partnership for Principle 10 (PP10) was launched as a forum involving governments, international organizations, and civil society groups committed to promote public participation and access to information at national level on environmental decision-making.[66] The UK, for example, has pursued its commitments at Johannesburg through adopting a national sustainable development strategy. That includes continued exploration of the relationship between the environment and human rights.[67]

High Level Panel

The UN High Level Panel Report on *Threats, Challenges and Change* offered a gloomy assessment of the lack of preparedness of the world community to face up to challenges facing sustainable development and nature:

'International institutions and States have not organized themselves to address the problems of development in a coherent, integrated way, and instead continue to treat poverty, infectious disease and environmental degradation as stand-alone threats.... Rarely are environmental concerns factored into security, development or humanitarian strategies. Nor is there coherence in environmental protection efforts at the global level. Most attempts to create governance structures to tackle the problems of global environmental degradation have not effectively addressed climate change, deforestation and desertification. Regional and global multilateral treaties on the environment are undermined by inadequate implementation and enforcement by the Member States.'[68]

---

[62] The foundations of this approach had been laid in the 1972 Stockholm Conference on Protection of the Biosphere; UN Conference on the Human Environment, Stockholm, UN DOC A/CONF.48/14/Rev.1.

[63] UNCED Report, UN DOC A/CONF.151/26/Rev.1, Vol.1 (1993).

[64] 1998 UN-ECE Convention, ECE/CEP/43. Robert McCracken and Gregory Jones, 'The Aarhus Convention' (2003*)* Journal of Planning & Environment Law 802.

[65] *Report of the World Summit on Sustainable Development*, Res. 1, Annex: Johannesburg Declaration on Sustainable Development, A/CONF.199/20 (2002).

[66] See http://www.pp10.org/PP10_govt_52005.pdf.

[67] See *Securing the Future* (2005), available at www.sustainable-development.gov.uk, and the Foreign and Commonwealth Human Rights Annual Report 2005, FCO Cm.6606, 17–171.

[68] ibid, and the Report of the High Level Panel on Threats, Challenges and Change, *A More Secure World: Our Shared Responsibility*, n 4 above, para 54.

Despite the major achievement of the coming into force of the Kyoto Protocol, this background of crisis in international co-operation, bodes poorly, at least at the global level, for the impact of human rights approaches to environmental protection.[69]

Human Rights and Democracy

In no relationship did the Cold War do more to suppress thinking than in respect of the interface between the goal of universal human rights protection and democracy. Thus, the Universal Declaration's 'democracy' clause (article 25) manages not to use the word. The explanation lay in the developing Cold War clash between the East and West. The idea of communist democracy meant that the people, through the supremacy of the Communist Party, had no need for pluralism. The view of western societies was that democracy was precisely defined as pluralism and competition between political parties. Failing agreement, the word was left out.[70]

There was literally nothing written nor policy pursued on democracy at the global level until the 1990s. The Statute of the Council of Europe 1949 had set down its core values as 'genuine democracy, human rights and the rule of law'. But these values and, in particular, the idea of democracy were too contentious for assertion at global level.

The importance of the Declaration on the Right to Development 1986 in offering a foundation for the idea of democracy and its linkage to human rights and development has already been noted. But it took the Cold War to end before either academic or diplomatic language could address squarely the relationship. The 1993 Vienna World Conference spoke for the first time of the relationship between democracy, human rights, and development. The linkage between democracy, human rights, and the rule of law became an important basis for East–West dialogue within the Helsinki Process and the Conference on Security and Co-Operation in Europe during the 1990s.[71] Tom Frank broke new ground with his article on 'democratic entitlement'.[72] During that decade democracy came to be linked as a goal and often as a condition in development aid policies of States, including the EU.[73] But it was 1999 before democracy and its meaning

[69] The Kyoto Protocol to the UN Framework Convention on Climate Change, on reducing greenhouse gases came into force on 16 February 2005 and a regime of implementation was adopted at the Montreal Conference on Climate Change, December 2005, see http://unfccc.int.

[70] Morsink, *The Universal Declaration of Human Rights Origins Drafting & Intent*, n 28 above, 60–65.

[71] See Charter of Paris 1990 and the Document of the Copenhagen Meeting of the Conference for Security and Co-operation in Europe (CSCE), available at www.osce.org.

[72] Thomas M. Frank, 'The Emerging Right to Democratic Governance' (1992) 86 American Journal of International Law 46. Gregory Fox,' The Right to Political Participation in International Law' (1992) 17 Yale Journal of International Law 539.

[73] Commission of the European Communities, *Inclusion of Respect for Democratic Principles and Human Rights in Agreements between the Community and Third Countries*, COM (95) 216 final.

was broached at the UN when the US Secretary of State, Harold Koh, declared that the US would introduce a resolution in the Commission on Human Rights on the right to democracy and its relationship with human rights:

'We are in the second fifty years of the Universal Declaration and one thing we have come to recognize is that democracy is not just an experiment, it is a right in itself.'[74]

Resolution 1999/57 on the *Promotion of the Right to Democracy* was certainly a land mark. It declared that 'democracy fostered all rights and vice versa'. After considerable negotiation with other States it specified certain rights including freedom of opinion and expression, the right to participate freely in government, and the rule of law as being included in the definition of 'the right to democratic governance'. However, it also acknowledged that:

'the realization of all human rights civil, cultural, economic, political and social, including the right to development are indispensable to human dignity and the full development of human potential and are also integral to democratic society.'

The resolution was carried with no votes against.[75]

It is perhaps necessary to note that this initiative came from the Clinton Administration. After 9/11, the US advocacy of democracy has suffered from its invasions of Iraq and Afghanistan. Nevertheless, the spread of democracy has been one of the most significant benefits of the post-Cold War era. Other important initiatives have included the Inter-American Charter on Democracy,[76] the New Partnership for African Development (NEPAD),[77] and the emergence in 1999 of a new group of States to promote democracy, led by the US, the Community of Democracies.[78] Following a proposal by President George Bush, a Democracy Fund has been created by the UN, to support new and consolidated democracies.[79]

The new context of democracy for human rights work has been established through the spread of democratic societies in little more than a decade. But there remain many governments which hold power without democratic legitimacy, notably the world's most populous State, China. Nevertheless, the paths of human rights protection and that of democracies are now connected in principle and increasingly in practice.[80] The prospect of human rights being fulfilled depends on the consolidation of democratic systems and their capacity to fulfil expectations of their peoples. Those expectations in many poorer regions include

---

[74] Press conference, Geneva, 31 March 1999, http://usembassy-australia.state.gov.

[75] Promotion of the right to democracy, Commission on Human Rights resolution 1999/57, adopted by a roll call vote of 51 votes to none, with 2 abstentions.

[76] Adopted by the General Assembly of American States, 11 September 2001. The Declaration, *inter alia*, declares that 'democracy and social and economic development are interdependent and are mutually reinforcing'.   [77] OAU Declaration 1(XXXV11) July 2001.

[78] Towards a Community of Democracies Ministerial Conference, Final Warsaw Declaration, 27 June 2000, available at www.ccd21.org.   [79] UN press release, 5 July 2005.

[80] See the recommendations and papers prepared for the OHCHR expert seminars: The Interdependence of Democracy and Human Rights, UN DOC E/CN.4/2003/59, and Democracy and the Rule of Law Geneva, UN DOC E/CN.4/2005/58.

a better standard of living, education, health care, and employment—in other words, economic and social rights.[81] The Inter-American Democratic Charter, in specifying the rights constitutive of democracy, is explicit on the role of economic and social rights in democratic societies.[82] The Warsaw Declaration is less so and seeks to steer a course between models of liberal and social democracy.[83] The increasing consensus that democracy is the only political system which can secure human rights has not yet extended to the full acceptance of all human rights as being of equal value and being equally necessary for democratic legitimacy.[84]

International Democracy and International Social Democracy

The question of the relationship between democracy and human rights has a further dimension in an era of globalization that is beyond national boundaries.[85] The next horizon for democratic ideas is the international order and the economic and social ideologies promoted through globalization.[86] Although there is no space to develop the subject here, that debate has focused on the accountability of international organizations, including the World Bank, the International Monetary Fund, the World Trade Organization, as well as the increasingly dominant multi-national enterprises.[87] In that debate, international human rights standards are increasingly providing a framework of values principles and rules as the demand for democratic accountability grows.[88] But the debate mirrors the challenge for democracy at national level: under what constraints, predicated on human welfare and social justice, should the market operate?[89]

Security and Human Rights

Perhaps the most challenging context in which international human rights can be placed is that of promoting a link with the pursuit of peace and security. The UN as a body established to maintain international peace and security has consistently

[81] UNDP, *Democracy in Latin America: Towards a Citizens' Democracy* (2004).
[82] See n 76 above. [83] See n 78 above.
[84] David Beetham, 'What Future for Economic and Social Rights?' in David Beetham, *Democracy and Human Rights* (1999) 115.
[85] David Held and Anthony McGrew (eds), *Globalization /Anti-Globalisation* (2002).
[86] The World Commission on the Social Dimension of Globalization, *A Fair Globalization: Creating Opportunities for All* (2004).
[87] Sigrun Skogly, *The Human Rights Obligations of the World Bank and the International Monetary Fund* (2001); Marc Darrow, *Between Light and Shadow: The World Bank, the International Monetary Fund and International Human Rights Law* (2003): Office of the United Nations High Commission for Human Rights, *Globalization-Trade and Investment* (2004), available at *www.ohchr.org*.
[88] See eg 'The norms on the responsibilities of transnational corporations and other business enterprises with regard to human rights', Sub Commission resolution 2003/12, UN DOC CN.4 / Sub.2/2003/12/Rev.2.
[89] David Held, 'Globalisation: the dangers and the answers' (2004), available at www.opendemocracy. net. David Beetham, 'Market Economy and Democratic Polity' in Beetham, *Democracy and Human Rights*, n 84 above.

failed to make significant progress on disarmament, nuclear or conventional. On disarmament, the High Level Panel had recommended that the nuclear weapon States 'must honour their commitments under Article VI of the Treaty on the Non-Proliferation of Nuclear Weapons to move towards disarmament and be ready to take specific measures in fulfillment of those commitments'.[90] Following the World Summit in September 2005, Kofi Annan condemned as 'a disgrace' the dropping entirely from the final Declaration the issues of disarmament and non-proliferation of nuclear weapons.[91]

The Right to Peace

There had been efforts over the years of the Cold War to promote a right to peace. These have not prospered.[92] The General Assembly approved a Declaration on the Right of Peoples to Peace in 1984, a right proclaimed as belonging to 'the peoples of our planet'.[93] The Declaration called for nuclear disarmament, a call repeated to no avail in many later resolutions. The issue of the possession and use of nuclear weapons was referred by the General Assembly to the International Court of Justice, which produced a complex and confusing opinion.[94]

The post-Cold War World Conferences sought to link peace conflict prevention, military expenditures, and disarmament to development and human rights.[95] The impasse over disarmament has not stopped a transformation in the international concern over the persistence of conflict, particularly the effects on civilian victims.[96] The growth in the role of the UN in conflict prevention, peacekeeping, peace building and reconstruction is too large a subject to develop here, but it has been accompanied with an increasing focus on the violations of human rights that are legion in armed conflicts and in which civilians, generally children and women, are invariably the primary victims.[97] Human rights protection and the presence of human rights personnel have become an integral part of all international peacekeeping operations, reflecting the mainstreaming initiatives of Kofi Annan.[98]

[90] Report of the High Level Panel on Threats, Challenges and Change, *A More Secure World: Our Shared Responsibility*, n 4 above, para 120.   [91] UN press release, 14 September 2005.
[92] Alston, *People's Rights*, n 22 above, 279.   [93] GA Res. 39/11, 12 November 2004.
[94] *Legality of the Threat or Use of Nuclear Weapons by a States in Armed Conflict*, ICJ Advisory Opinion, 8 July 1996. But the Court did confirm that, '[t]here exists an obligation to pursue in good faith and bring to a conclusion negotiations leading to nuclear disarmament in all its aspects under strict and effective international control', 226, para 105.
[95] See the Report of the World Summit for Social Development, A/Conf.166/9 (1995) para 70; Beijing Declaration, Fourth World Conference on Women, A/Conf.177/20 (1995) paras 18 and 28.
[96] Carnegie Commission, *Preventing Deadly Conflict, Final Report* (1998).
[97] Impact of Armed Conflict on Children: Report of the Expert of the Secretary General Gracha Machel, UN DOC.A/51/3036 (1996). Report of the Secretary General to the Security Council on the Protection of Civilians in Armed Conflict, UN DOC S/1999/957 (1999).
[98] UNDP, *Human Development Report 2000, Human Rights and Human Development*, n 47 above, and see Michael O'Flaherty, 'Human Rights Monitoring and Armed Conflict: Challenges for the UN' (2004) *Disarmament Forum*, United Nations Institute for Disarmament Research, 47.

Human Security

National security is about the military security of the State from external attack. The traditional belief was that if the State is secure so are those who live within it.[99] This notion gave exaggerated emphasis to national sovereignty and ignored the insecurities and injustices afflicting populations. The emergence of the call for people-centered security came with the concept of human security, which reflects the infusion of human rights values into security thinking. First laid out in the 1994 Human Development Report, it has proved an immensely powerful insight into the limitations of the traditional focus on military security.[100] A more detailed study of the requirements of human security resulted from the work of the Human Security Commission established in 2003, chaired by Armatya Sen and Sadako Ogata.[101] Human security is defined in terms of protection of human lives from critical and pervasive threats. Such threats include environmental, economic, food, health, personal, and political threats. Thus, people need protection from poverty, natural disasters, conflict and disease. Gross and severe violations of human rights are a part of the experience of human insecurity. Protection from such abuses is part of the requirements of human security. A world awash with weapons of mass destruction and one experiencing international terrorism is equally without human security.

The infusion of human rights into thinking and policy proposals on security represents an important contribution of international human rights law. It establishes a positive link between the search for conditions for peace and the search for universal protection of human rights. Human security is equally a valuable connector between development, gender equality, democracy, and human rights. Its future challenge, however, will be in confronting large issues such as disarmament and the arms trade.[102] While existing nuclear powers set their face against accepting the link between their divesting themselves of such weapons and effective control over proliferation, there can be little progress on either human security or a right to peace.

Human Rights and the Rule of Law

In this exploration of the connections and affinities between human rights and other concepts it seemed appropriate to conclude with the most intimate of such relationships as expressed in the concept of the rule of law.[103] Indeed the values

---

[99] Taylor Owen, 'Challenges and Opportunities for defining and measuring human security' (2004) *Disarmament Forum*, United Nations Institute for Disarmament Research, 15.

[100] UNDP, *New Dimensions of Human Security, Human Development Report 1994* (1994).

[101] Commission on Human Security, *Human Security Now* (2003).

[102] Programme of Action to Prevent, Combat and Eradicate the Illicit Trade in Small Arms and Light Weapons in All Its Aspects, UN DOC A/CONF.192/15, available at www.geneva-forum.org.

[103] Richard Bellamy (ed.), *The Rule of Law and the Separation of Powers* (2005).

and the institutions that are contained within the idea of the supremacy of the rule of law, at national and international level, constitute the thread that more obviously holds together all the fields that have been discussed. Kofi Annan has offered a useful definition: 'a principle of governance in which all persons, institutions, entities, public and private, including the State itself are accountable to laws that are publicly promulgated, equally enforced, and independently adjudicated, laws which are consistent with international human rights norms and standards'.[104]

The challenge is to make that principle of governance meaningful in a world where it is largely absent. In an important recent open letter the NGO, Asia Forum, put the issues starkly:

'Today there is a widening gap within the global human rights community. It is a gap between the persons promoting human rights in established democracies, and those in the rest of the world, where people may have learnt the language of human rights, but are still very far away from the reality. It is a gap between those persons articulating and propagating its normative structure, most of whom have spent their lives in relatively stable countries where the rule of law and independence of the judiciary are taken for granted, and those concerned with the day-to-day obstacles that deny basic human rights. The normative structure in which most human rights have been articulated and enshrined as universal can be realised only where the rudiments of the rule of law are in place. These rudiments are alien to vast numbers of people around the world. Worse still, in many places where they once existed, they have been removed. In their stead, we find arbitrary governance and non-functioning legal systems. Those articulating its normative structure fail to grasp the scale of the obstacles before persons engaged in the day-to-day struggle.'[105]

To engage more effectively with this scale of failure of the rule of law human rights, advocates need to embrace the expanded and interconnected analysis discussed in this chapter of what the implementation of universal human rights requires.[106]

Conclusion

This sketch of the linkages between human rights and other fields may immediately prompt the response—so what? Human rights are about human beings and it is hardy surprising that connections flow from that fact to potentially everything. But the limited, if complex, relationships identified here concern more than aphorism. They are also more than observations about context and multiple perspectives. Essentially the linkages discussed are insights about social change.

---

[104] Rule of Law and Transitional Justice in conflict and post conflict societies. Report of the Secretary General to the Security Council, S/2004/616 (2004).

[105] The Asian Legal Resource Centre 'Open letter to the global human rights community: Let us rise to article 2 of the ICCPR', available at www.article2.org/mainfile.php/0101/3.

[106] See papers and recommendations of the OHCHR Seminar on Democracy and the Rule of Law, n 80 above.

The goals of change are those proclaimed in the UN Charter and restated in Kofi Annan's *In Larger Freedom*. The elements that constitute that vision of a just world order require all of the values and institutions which have been discussed. The perspective of this essay has been on human rights norms and their relationships with other elements, including development, democracy, and security. Other starting points on these relationships are also possible, for example, the relationship between development and democracy.[107]

The implication of the linkages between rights and other fields is primarily about implementation. Progress on delivering the promise of universal rights is dependent on parallel progress on other goals. But these goals are not sequential. They are interdependent and reinforcing.

This approach is caught effectively in the OHCHR Action Plan 2005. It identifies six global human rights challenges: poverty, discrimination, conflict, impunity, democratic deficits, and institutional weaknesses. Significantly, it also locates these challenges within structural challenges: 'arising from general situations, patterns or contexts that contribute to abuse'.[108]

How this more connected analysis will affect practice and programming remains to be seen. But the overall approach reflects an advance. However, if there are advances in recognition of multi-dimensional challenges from human rights agencies, it is not clear that it is reciprocated in the approach of others. The Africa Commission established by the British prime minister resulted in a much praised report that is silent on human rights.[109] The suggestion for example that national and regional systems of human rights protection might have a central role to play in Africa's development is not part of the analysis.

Thus, we confront the major constraint on joined-up analysis urged by the UN studies that have been discussed. World views continue to be shaped by national interest, reinforced by the disciplinary divisions that mark knowledge and expertise. With few exceptions human rights discourse is shunned by social scientists including economists. It is seen as the preserve of the diplomats and lawyers. A similar critique has been made of the gulf between the perspectives of the political scientists and legal specialists on study of democracy and the rule of law.[110] Despite the 'mainstreaming' of human rights, practitioners in development and humanitarian work, in democracy building, and the rule of law, remain disconnected. The boundaries of academic disciplines and the lack of communication between them inhibit progress towards integration in practice.

If a different approach is to emerge then it is likely to result from initiatives by global civil society. There is a need to build a common platform between different social movements working on areas such as the environment, human

---

[107] Boutros Boutros-Ghali, *The Interaction between Democracy and Development* (2002).
[108] OHCHR, *Plan of Action: Protection and Empowerment* (2005) paras 6–9.
[109] Commission for Africa, *Our Common Interest* (2005).
[110] Julio Faundez, 'The Rule of Law Enterprise: Promoting a Dialogue between Practitioners and Academics' (2005) 12/4 Democratization 568.

rights, women's empowerment, fair trade, peace, development, and democracy.[111] Human rights groups, given the increased salience of human rights thinking, are well placed to push for a common approach. The increased focus on education for global citizenship and grass roots sustainable development and democracy education can also stimulate greater convergence.[112] Pressure for accountability of business and international financial institutions is another stimulus. The new engagement of civil society with the private sector on sustainability is a hopeful sign,[113] but integrated thinking needs constant encouragement if the scale of human rights denial and failure in much of the world is to be reversed. Human rights educators, including those at university level, can contribute by rethinking their educational programmes so that they embrace different disciplinary perspectives, work to establish common ground within those perspectives, and tackle the challenges of linking the implantation of equal human rights to the goals of security and development for all.

[111] The Global Call to Action against Poverty (GCAP) is an encouraging example of what is possible, see n 15 above.
[112] See eg the educational work of the Irish NGO, 80:20, *Educating and Acting for a More Just World*, www.8020.ie, and the Development Education Association, London, http://www.dea.org.uk/.
[113] Seb Beloe, 'The 21st Century NGO: In the Market for Change', available at www.sustainabilitity.com.

19

Corporations, Human Rights, and Social Inequality

Sally Wheeler

Introduction

'The third industrial revolution—characterized by the intensive application of information and communications technology, flexible production systems and organizational structures, market segmentation, and globalization—also has profoundly altered the way that the structure of goods and assets themselves is shaped. Differentiation within production processes and the segmentation of markets have contributed to this newer shift, as has the globalization of finance, which increasingly has divorced finance capital from the state. Institutional capacities for political control, stabilization, regulation, promotion, and facilitation of economic activities have therefore become increasingly fragmented . . . new circuits of power are emerging.'[1]

The quote above I think sums up the situation that we find ourselves in. Cerny is describing economic globalization in all its glory. To his description we could add that the collapse of the possibility of a socialist transformation and the failure of the right to win all remaining ground has resulted in a politics that is rooted in the middle ground. Debate is no longer polarized between right and left positions, ideas that were once considered partners only in opposition are now paired together.[2] Interest in the position of the 'State' as one of the binding forces of political discourse has largely given way to a focus on the winners and losers in globalization.[3] Political economy is now about more than national issues. As

---

[1] Philip Cerny, 'Globalization and the Changing Logic of Collective Action' (1995) 49 International Organization 595, 607.

[2] Anthony Giddens, *The Third Way* (1998) 26; Anthony Giddens and Chris Pierson, *Conversations with Anthony Giddens* (1998) Interview 6.

[3] Globalization must be one of the most discussed, described, and disputed phenomena in the universe. Most of the debates can be accessed through perusal of James Petras and Henry Veltmeyer, *Globalization Unmasked* (2001) 31–56; and Vidya Kumar, 'A Critical Methodology of Globalization: Politics of the 21st Century' (2003) 10 Indiana Journal of Global Legal Sudies 87.

Bourdieu points out the site of the economy is moving to supra-national bodies such as the EU. These bodies now decide what were once key economic issues for the nation State, such as currency exchange rates and interest rates. Consequently, this requires the exploration of different issues such as the role of ethics.[4] Of central importance to this essay is the form that this 'turn to ethics' could take in relation to multinational enterprise (MNE). The key point as I explain below is that there are no mechanisms by which nation States can exert legal controls over the behaviour of MNE. The emerging circuits of power are markets[5] and the multinational corporations[6] that make and dominate markets for production and consumption.

We all 'know' about the internationalization of business in terms of the sites of production being spread across the globe and corporations constantly searching for host economies that can provide lower cost institutional environments for production.

- Foreign-owned multinationals employ one worker in every five in European manufacturing.
- Foreign-owned multinationals employ one worker in every seven in the US.
- Foreign-owned multinationals sell one euro in every four of manufactured goods in Europe.
- Foreign-owned multinationals sell one dollar in five in the US.[7]
- There are 61,000 TNCs with 900,000 foreign affiliates.[8]

What are less well-known 'facts' of globalization are why corporations behave in this way and the response of national governments to attempts at the supra-national level to regulate low-cost production environments, in other words a contest between protectionism and so-called free enterprise. A question that is often asked of MNE is whether its physical presence in a particular locale contributes to or inhibits the development of human rights in that host economy. I explore these issues in the first section of the essay. In the second section of the essay I focus on measurable social inequalities and the strategies that could be used to re-engineer

    [4] Pierre Bourdieu, *Acts of Resistance* (1998) 61–64.
    [5] Philip Cerny, 'Globalization and other Stories: The Search for a New Paradigm for International Relations' (1996) 51 Int J 617. Markets are of course not the 'circuits of power' that Cerny refers to.
    [6] There is, amazingly, no agreed definition of the term 'multinational'. Most commentators would agree that it refers to firms that control income-generating activity in more than one nation State. UNCTAD defines a MNE as a parent corporation and its foreign affiliates. An equity stake of 10% is sufficient. Just as globalization itself is a disputed concept so too is the position of multinational enterprise within globalization. See the arguments of Paul Doremus *et al* in *The Myth of the Global Corporation* (1998) and Paul Hirst and Grahame Thompson, *Globalization in Question* (1996) 186–187.
    [7] Figures taken from Giorgio Navaretti and Anthony Venables, *Multinational Firms in the World Economy* (2005).
    [8] Figures taken from Yair Aharoni, 'World Investment Report 2004: The Shift Towards Services' (2005) 14 Transnational Corporations 158.

capitalism to address these. I hope to offer suggestions for a model or models of personal political responsibility that encourage engagement with the issues in the essay.

Multinational Enterprise and Human Rights

In this essay I take as a given an understanding that politics asks questions about values within the polity, questions about identity, and issues around inclusion.[9] It is around these issues that global civil society has coalesced and new social movements have emerged to challenge the relentless march of capitalism.[10] These questions have pushed discussions of human rights, by which what is generally meant Western-style democratic political rights, into discourses within and between developed societies.[11] 'Human rights language'[12] is often the language in which States clothe military action and intervention against each other. The universality of human rights results as Beck puts it, '[in] a permanent battlefield of political power between or within states, in which the rich "good guys" interfere in the affairs of the poor "bad guys"'.[13] Indices of democracy as evidenced by the ability of individuals to exercise political rights are the central factor in determining debt relief to some 38 of the world's poorest countries.[14] This essay will not examine the events that have resulted in the rise of this 'new politics';[15] there are numerous accounts available elsewhere. The rise of ethics and values as subjects for discussion are not without detractors. Those on the left see it as promoting 'a sort of moralizing liberalism . . . filling the void left by the collapse of any project of real political transformation'[16] or signalling the beginning of a post-political age in

---

[9]   See the themes explored in Andrew Gamble, *Politics and Fate* (2000).

[10]   Fiona Robinson, 'Human Rights and the Global Politics of Resistance: Feminist Perspectives' (2003) 29 Rev of Int Studies 161, 165.

[11]   Robert McCorquodale and Richard Fairbrother, 'Globalization and Human Rights' (1995) 21 Human Rights Quart 735, 739 and Hakan Johansson and Bjorn Hvinden, 'Welfare Governance and the remaking of citizenship' in Janet Newman (ed.), *Remaking Governance* (2005), 101.

[12]   See the comments of Tim Murphy in reviewing Niklas Luhmann's *Law as a Social System* (2005) 25 JLS 520, 522: 'A mish-mash of human rights, morality and legal technicalities is offered, vociferously and voluminously, as the solution to our troubles and as the new *regles de jeu* for politics, international finance and so on.' I am grateful to Thérèse Murphy and Noel Whitty for drawing this point to my attention.   [13]   Ulrich Beck, *Power in the Global Age* (2005) 66.

[14]   Standards of political governance were agreed as one of the indicators for debt relief by the G8 in Edinburgh in the summer of 2005. For a predictive model on the likely success of this initiative, see Jakob Svensson, 'Why Conditional Aid does not Work and What Can Be Done About It' (2003) 70 J of Develop Econ 381. For the involvement of pan-African bodies, see John Akokpari, 'The AU, NEPAD and the Promotion of Good Governance in Africa' (2004) 13 Nordic J of African Studies 13.

[15]   The most persuasive account comes from Eric Hobsbawm, *Age of Extremes* (1994).

[16]   Chantal Mouffe, 'Which Ethics for Democracy' in Majorie Garber *et al*, *The Turn to Ethics* (2000) 85, 86. This critique is directed in part against those who offer a consensus-based politics derived from deliberative democracy (88–89). To assess the extent to which Habermas in particular

which the existence of a tolerant democracy structured around global capitalism allows 'elementary social decisions [to be] no longer discussed as political decisions [but as] simple decisions of gesture and of administration'.[17] While this argument is not without merit, the emergence of ethics within politics is very useful in respect of MNE; it allows a discussion around the practices of enterprise to take place without such discussion being immediately confounded by the argument that any notion of a redistributive function within the corporation can be framed only as a fundamental question of macro political economy.

There is a distinct lack of synergy between the globalization of human rights discourse and the realities of economic globalization. Both the scholarship provided by those in the field of human rights gazing at MNE and the scholarship offered by those gazing back the other way from MNE to human rights is startling in its positivistic approach. The starting point for their inquiries[18] is that the legal responsibilities that underpin human rights observance are imposed on States by internationally agreed norms and not on corporations. MNEs are treated very much as private actors in the sense that it is only States through the use of national laws that can curb their activities. This leads usually to an examination of the plethora of corporate codes of conduct suggested by, *inter alia*, the ILO, the UN and the OECD, codes that come from the MNE sector itself and legislative intervention from national governments.[19] It is worth noting that in the main these codes are composed in very broad general terms and demand an inoffensively low level of commitment from MNE.[20] This is something that I have explored more extensively elsewhere[21] and to which I return to for a brief while in the text below. The plea is often for resources for enforcement or sanctions. The problem for these pleas is that they fail to take into account what Teubner calls the regulatory 'trilemma' of 'circumvention, perversity and negative feedback'[22] or what McBarnet

might answer the criticisms levelled at him through his most recent work, see Deborah Cook, 'The Talking Cure in Habermas's Republic' (2001) 12 New Left Review 135.

[17] Slavoj Žižek Internet interview with Spiked magazine, see also *Contingency, Hegemony, Universality* (with Judith Butler and Ernesto Laclau) (2000) 93–101; Gillian Rose, *Mourning Becomes the Law* (1996) 15–39; and Carl Boggs, *The End of Politics* (2000) 243f.

[18] The best of these is Steven Ratner, 'Corporations and Human Rights: A Theory of Legal Responsibility' (2001) 111 Yale LJ 443. See also Beth Stephens, 'The Amorality of Profit: Transnational Corporations and Human Rights' (2002) Berkeley J of Int Law 45; and David Weissbrodt and Muria Kruger, 'Norms on the Responsibilities of Transnational Corporations and Other Business Enterprises with Regard to Human Rights' (2003) 97 AMJIL 901.

[19] See the examples given in Claire Moore Dickerson, 'Human Rights: The Emerging Norm of Corporate Social Responsibility' (2002) 76 Tulane LR 1431; Jack Kaikati *et al*, 'The Price of International Business Morality. 20 Years under the Foreign Corrupt Practices Act' (2000) 26 J of Bus Eth 213; Aseem Prakash 'Responsible Care: An Assessment' (2000) 39 Bus and Soc 183.

[20] Ans Kolk *et al*, 'International Codes of Conduct and Corporate Social Responsibility: Can Transnational Corporations Regulate Themselves?' (1999) 8 Transnational Corporations 143, 161.

[21] Sally Wheeler, *Corporations and the Third Way* (2001).

[22] Gunther Teubner, 'Juridification—Concepts, Aspects, Limits Solutions' in Gunther Teubner (ed.), *Juridification of Social Spheres: A Comparative Analysis of the Areas of Labour, Antitrust and Social Welfare Law* (1987) 3.

describes as the culture of creative compliance.[23] These are standard responses to those who call for enforcement of regulation against capitalist enterprise.[24] A rather more damning criticism is the failure to explore what is meant by 'rights' or 'a right'—can these concepts simply be extended from States to MNE and whether, if this prior question is answered in the affirmative, in the absence of legal structures of responsibility corporations can bear moral responsibility for human rights. This leads into two philosophical debates; one around the nature of rights and the second around the nature of moral responsibility. The traditional position is that rights obligations fall only upon governments as possession of a human right is dependant upon social recognition and maintenance by government action.[25] Another weaker variation on this is that rights are moral rights if they are validated by moral principles.[26] My answer to Martin is that his focus on governments comes from a belief that governments are the most powerful sovereign actors. While governments may be sovereign actors they do not possess the tools to tackle the networks and mobility of MNE.

If we turn to look at the issue of corporate responsibility then our resting point is again philosophy rather than law. Legal debates are concerned almost solely with the question of liability within the criminal law—how to make an individualized criminal law speak to a collective entity.[27] Liability-driven models of responsibility are something that I examine in more detail at the end of this essay. The most detailed discussion within philosophy occurs in the work of Peter French.[28] As a result the position taken by other commentators coalesces around agreement or not with French's position.[29] French examines the internal decision-making structure of the corporation. For him the internal decision-making structure makes it not only possible to recognize the individuality of corporations as distinct from decision-making individuals but also to assert that corporations are moral actors in their own right capable of intentionality. He illustrates his position thus:

'[a]lthough X voted to support the joining of the cartel because he was bribed to do so, X did not join the cartel, Gulf Oil Corporation joined the cartel. Consequently, we may say that X did something for which he should be held morally responsible, yet whether or

---

[23] Doreen McBarnet and Christopher Whelan, 'The Elusive Spirit of the Law: Formalism and the Struggle for Legal Control' (1991) 54 MLR 848.

[24] Julia Black, 'Decentring Regulation: Understanding the Role of Regulation and Self Regulation in a "Post-Regulatory" ' World' (2001) 54 Current Legal Problems 103.

[25] Rex Martin, 'Human Rights and Civil Rights' (1980) 37 Phil Studies 391, cf the position taken by M Cranston, that human rights are claims 'against all men' in Maurice Cranston, *What Are Human Rights?* (1973).

[26] Joel Feinberg, 'The Nature and Value of Rights' reprinted in *Rights, Justice and the Bounds of Liberty, Essays in Social Philosophy* (1980) 143.

[27] CMV Clarkson, 'Kicking Corporate Bodies and Damning Their Souls' (1996) 59 MLR 557.

[28] Peter French, *Collective and Corporate Responsibility* (1984); 'The Corporation as a Moral Person' (1979) 16 Am Phil Quart 207; 'Responsibility and the Moral Role of Corporate Entities' in Thomas Donaldson and R. Edward Freeman (eds), *Business as a Humanity* (1994) 88.

[29] There are a range of criticisms to which the following references provide a fairly comprehensive overview: John Ladd, 'Corporate Mythology and Individual Responsibility' (1984) 2 Int J of Applied

not Gulf Oil Corporation should be held morally responsible for joining the cartel is a question that turns on issues that may be unrelated to X's having accepted a bribe.'[30]

While this example would not command universal approval for the idea of a corporation having sufficient metaphysical standing to be considered as a unit possessing moral responsibility,[31] there is one point on which I think French makes an unassailable case. It is one he shares with Robert Solomon: that 'business is a social practice'.[32] By this both Solomon and French are drawing attention to the cultural embeddiness that corporations, particularly large ones, enjoy within current societal structures. To this we can add O'Neill's observation[33] that institutions have greater skills in predicting consequences, more accurate and systemic memories, greater ability to carry through plans and power to influence others' decisions. All these factors apply to corporations. Furthermore, work practices and structures dictate to those in work and their families the shape of their lives.[34] To those out of work corporations dictate quality of life through product pricing and the location of sales outlets and contribution to community infrastructure. If we look at corporations in this way then it becomes an issue within ideas of democracy that we should see them as morally responsible and so morally accountable. The idea that corporations are purely private actors required only to pay taxes and comply with other legal regulations implies tolerance of a large deficit of power.

I would add to this, in support of both French's and Solomon's position, the way in which our mental picture of corporate activity is drawn. We refer to corporations as forming and pursuing policies, as taking positions on issues and, for example, having the ability to sponsor events. The larger corporations enjoy almost iconoclastic status, becoming synonymous with particular phrases such as 'Never Knowingly Undersold', particular products and particular logos and colour arrangements. We know that corporations are vulnerable to adverse publicity in some circumstances and that past events can colour corporate policy for years to come.[35] This idea of reputational bargaining is something that I return to

Philosophy; Rita Manning, 'Corporate Responsibility and Corporate Personhood' (1984) 3 J of Bus Ethics 77 and Elizabeth Wolgast, *Ethics of an Artificial Person* (1992) 79–95.

[30] Peter French, 'The Corporation as a Moral Person', n 28 above, 214.

[31] I used to be of the view that it was impossible to reconcile the French position with the classic Strawsonian account of moral responsibility which also draws on social practices to formulate a definition of moral responsibility. Strawson defines a morally responsible actor as one which members of any given society react to with a set of attitudes that demonstrate interpersonal human relationships. These reactive attitudes can be contrasted with our ones to non-human and so non-moral actors. Non-human actors can be exploited or enjoyed whereas human ones experience reactions such as gratitude or respect. I now think that this is more of an open question. See John Martin Fischer, 'Recent Work on Moral Responsibility' (1999) 110 Ethics 93.

[32] Robert Solomon, 'Business and the Humanities: An Aristotelian Approach to Business Ethics' in Donaldson and Freeman, n 28 above, 64.   [33] Onora O'Neill, *Faces of Hunger* (1986) 37–38.

[34] Dorothy Smith, 'Women, the Family and Corporate Capitalism' in Marylee Stephenson (ed.), *Women in Canada* (1977) 1, 17.

[35] Almost exactly the contrary view is expressed by Thomas Donaldson in *Corporations and Morality* (1982) 20. For Donaldson the fact that corporations share some characteristics with human

later in this essay. As the corporate investment base becomes ever wider through the growth of institutional investment and, with the exception of family-held corporations and small incorporated partnerships, shareholders and directors are separate individuals, corporations have a case that they should be seen in a political sense as individual actors.[36] This must be the next stage in the analysis begun by Berle and Means.[37] They identified a separation between ownership and control and as a result charged corporate managers with creating responsible corporations. In an era of flexibility, technological advancement and job mobility, corporations themselves bear this responsibility[38] as individuals.

The fact that we can construct rights as applying to corporations, and corporations as morally if not legally responsible to observe human rights standards, does not mean that we necessarily wish to hold MNE to these standards. The role that MNE plays in nascent economies is a highly contested one and a highly complex one at the level of macro-economics. However, it is in a very generalized way possible to see it as one of the few remaining areas in which there is a straight knockdown contest between the political left and the political right.[39] On the right there are those that see development as coming to poorer countries through contact with richer ones. The argument put crudely is that we all lived at subsistence level once[40] and in this context MNE is seen a tool of development. On the opposing side there are those who see richer countries as manipulators of the trade institutions of the world such as the WTO, which they then impose on poorer countries in order to maintain their comparative advantage.[41] Here MNE is seen as a tool of oppression. These debates have been turned over endlessly within International Business scholarship from the 1960s onwards,[42] in the work of scholars such as Stephen Hymer and Peter Buckley, although there they are characterized more as the Marxist-inspired under-development position[43] versus

---

beings 'is inadequate to establish moral agency'. My point is that irrespective of this, corporations are too large and significant not to be in some sense moral actors.

[36] Mark Bovens, 'The Corporate Republic: Complex Organizations and Citizenship' in Emilios Christodoulidis (ed.), *Communitarianism and Citizenship* (1998) 158, 160–62.

[37] Adolph Berle and Gardiner Means, *The Modern Corporation and Private Property* (1932).

[38] The question of corporations bearing responsibility as individuals has provoked some interesting discussions of what sanctions could accompany a failure to take responsibility. An interesting discussion of this and a review of the literature can be found in Louise Dunford and Ann Ridley, 'No Soul to be Damned, No Body to be Kicked: Responsibility, Blame and Corporate Punishment' (1996) 24 Int J of Soc of Law 1, 8.

[39] Leif Wenar, 'Contractualism and Global Economic Justice' (2001) 32 Metaphilosophy 79.

[40] Peter Bauer, *From Subsistence to Exchange* (2000).

[41] Thomas Pogge, *World Poverty and Human Rights: Cosmopolitan Responsibilities and Reforms* (2002). It is Pogge's neo Rawlsian account of institutions and institutional activities that is adopted by Janet Dine in *Companies, International Trade and Human Rights* (2004). In the same genre see Mathias Risse, 'How Does the Global Order Harm the Poor' (2005) 33 Phil and Public Affs 349.

[42] The most useful guide to this whole debate can be found in Bjorn Letnes, 'Transnational Corporations and Human Rights: Silencing the Ontological Controversy' (2004) 4 Public Organization Review 259.

[43] Robert Gilpin, *The Political Economy of International Relations* (1987).

neo-liberal statements of trade policy.[44] The mirror nature of this debate can be seen by looking at the policies of then US President Bill Clinton in relation to labour standards adopted in December 1999. President Clinton announced in the face of protests at the WTO talks in Seattle USA that he supported the creation of core labour standards within the WTO and trade sanctions against those countries who breached the standards. The net effect of this was to protect home-produced (ie US-produced) goods from competition with goods produced in lower cost foreign labour markets. President Clinton was supporting not protection of the US market but the right to a living wage for overseas workers. Howls of protest from governments of countries involved in the garment trade such as Indonesia and the Philippines greeted this announcement. There protests were based upon the denial to them of the right to development.[45]

It is relatively easy for both sides of this debate to marshal evidence in support of their positions. Those on the 'tools of oppression' side are able to point to documented examples of human rights abuses by MNE such as the provision of low-waged, low-skill labour, child labour, unsafe working conditions, the outlawing of unionization, and general environmental degradation caused by the location of MNE. The bringing of employment to areas where there previously was no employment is not per se a good thing if the quality of that working environment is such that it is replete with human rights abuses.[46] There is also a significant gender dimension which is frequently ignored. The recipients of MNE employment in developing economies are frequently women. Women are seen as having two employment advantages over men; greater manual dexterity and a greater capacity for repetitive and monotonous work. Women to a greater extent than men apparently lend themselves to domination and supervision thus excluding the possibility of organized resistance.[47] The counter-position to this, if one wishes to ignore the moral argument, is that economists generally agree that MNEs and their affiliates pay more than local employers.[48] The internet is full of emotive pieces such as Jim Keady's account of living on the wages of an Indonesian working for Nike.[49] MNE is powerful enough to force States to lower taxation rates to either attract them in or persuade them to stay. This lowers the revenue available to be

---

[44] Grazia Ietto-Gillies, 'Hymer, the Nation-State and the Determinants of Multinational Corporations' Activities' (2002) 21 Contributions to Political Economy 43.

[45] Clyde Summers, 'The Battle in Seattle: Free Trade, Labor Rights and Societal Values' (2001) 22 U Pa J Int Econ Law 61.

[46] For a review of the debates around labour conditions see Denis Arnold and Laura Hartman, 'Beyond Sweatshops: positive deviancy and global labour practices' (2005) 14 *Business Ethics: A European Review* 206 and Richard Rothstein, 'Defending Sweatshops' (2005) Dissent Spring 41.

[47] Juanita Elias, 'The Gendered Political Economy of Control and Resistance on the Shop Floor of the Multinational Firm: A Case-study from Malaysia' (2005) 10 New Pol Econ 203 and Christine Ward Gailey, 'Rethinking Child Labor in an Age of Capitalist Restructuring' (1999) 19 Crit of Anthro 115.

[48] Benjamin Powell and David Skarbek, 'Sweatshops and Third World Living Standards: Are the Jobs Worth the Sweat? (2004) Independent Institute Working Paper No 53, www.independent.org.

[49] www.nikewages.org.

spent on enhancing infrastructure. Other more macro issues are the question of uneven development—for example, sub-Saharan Africa receives very little foreign direct investment or portfolio investment as the figures below show and the mobility of capital which leaves northern hemisphere workers jobless as production relocates to the cheaper south. Portfolio investment is the most mobile of all capital interventions. The depth of the decline of the East Asian economy in the 1990s and its current re-rise can be attributed to the withdrawal and subsequent return of portfolio investment. That capital mobility on this scale causes devastating economic problems goes almost without saying.

Those on the 'engines of development' side point to the promotion of first generation civil and political human rights through the presence of MNE which promote the growth of second generation economic and social rights. Economic development is enhanced by the transfer of capital requiring the development of a more robust domestic finance regime and commercial law, making the host economy more efficient and the fertilization of host economies with technical know-how. The arrival of foreign direct investment or the colonization of supply chain partnerships brings employee benefits such as health care and training. While this might seem to present a rather utopian picture of MNE activity and conjures up pictures of Indian call centres in Bangalore[50] rather than garment factories in China, Meyer presents a convincing argument that, notwithstanding the existence of documented bad practices, it is true. The essence of Meyer's argument is that different levels of analysis are used by the two sides, allowing each one to assert the correctness of their position.[51] This side of the argument is looking at the rise in literacy rates and the drop in infant mortality for example.

MNE does much to muddy the waters of this debate by engaging in the practice of 'greenwashing'. 'Greenwashing' refers to the emergence of an unofficial competition in social responsibility agendas.[52] In addition to competing in areas such as product development, production costs and ultimately price, corporations compete over their social awareness and responsiveness by making low-cost but high-impact interventions in society. Corporations have increasingly described themselves as 'citizens' or as being interested in 'being responsible citizens'. This maps onto the notion of 'ethical consumer'.[53] For example, Diageo, after taking the decision to sell alcohol in India, assured the world that they would also be

---

[50] The latest Gartner report highlights the problem of capital mobility and labour immobility under economic globalization and points to the effects of collective organization among developing country workers. Wage costs have risen from a maximum of 6,000 rupees a month to 9,000 rupees a month. The prediction is that India could lose as much as 40% of its share of the business process outsourcing by 2007. If this economic capacity in labour terms is not taken up by other inward investment activity then it will herald economic decline/slower economic growth for India.

[51] William Meyer, *Human Rights and International Political Economy in Third World Nations* (1998) 197–201.

[52] C Smith, 'The New Corporate Philanthropy' (1994) Harv Bus Rev 105.

[53] Peter Muchlinski, 'Human Rights and Multinationals: Is there a problem?' (2001) 77 International Affairs 31.

placing advertisements in India about the importance of 'responsible drinking'. Corporations worldwide engage in ethical audits carried out by management consultants.[54] A growing number of corporations voluntarily produce annual social reports.[55] In 1999 the Institute of Social and Ethical Accountability and the Association of Chartered Certified Accountants set up an award scheme to recognize this voluntary reporting.[56] Somewhat ironically the joint recipient of this first award was Shell. However, it is important to remember that the awards were set up to encourage reporting and transparency, not to influence conduct.[57] The claims made in these voluntary social reports of positive community outputs are not tested against any particular standard.

Greenwashing is often used as a way for MNE to draw attention away from environmental damage or as a method of disguising other activities which are the antithesis of responsible behaviour or observance of human rights standards. The question of whether ethical profile and assertions of corporate social responsibility have a positive impact on corporate financial performance is a hotly debated issue. There are numerous studies, mainly based on US data, which give conflicting answers.[58] There are methodological difficulties in both conducting this type of research and comparing the results. The type of conduct studied varies, as does the approach to measuring financial performance. All the studies are firmly locked into the stakeholder paradigm, which creates further difficulties as there is no standard to determine which groups are included and excluded from the 'better off or not' calculation.[59] The general view is that the worst that can be said about these activities is that they do not appear to depress financial performance.[60] In the text below I look at the rise of ethical investment and the conclusions that are drawn in that context about the presence of corporate social responsibility agendas in listed corporations. Activities carried out as a result of greenwashing can rarely put right earlier environmental damage. Often there is little local level consultation carried out on what is actually required, leading to what can only be described as imperialistic development. A current example of greenwashing is the announcement by Coca-Cola on 8 March 2006 that it had joined the UN Global Compact. The

---

[54] Ariel Colonomos and Javier Santiso, 'Vive la France! French Multinationals and Human Rights' (2005) 27 HRQ 1307, 1327.

[55] A recent PIRC survey revealed that 79 of the top 350 corporations had a separate environmental report and 40 a separate social report.   [56] http://www.accountability.org.uk.

[57] Alan Dignam and Michael Galanis, 'OECD Corporate Governance Principles' (2000) Euro Bus Law Rev 396 and Reggy Hooghiemstra, 'Corporate Communication and Impression Management—New Perspectives Why Companies Engage in Corporate Social Reporting' (2000) 27 J of Bus Ethics 55, 61f. These pieces give details of some of the social dumping that Shell and other multinationals have engaged in.

[58] For a review of the literature and an indication of the answers provided by numerous different studies, see Curtis Verschoor, 'A Study of the Link Between a Corporation's Financial Performance and Its Commitment to Ethics' (1998) 17 J of Bus Ethics 1509.

[59] For a detailed review of methodological problems, see Sandra Waddock and Samuel Graves, 'Quality of Management and Quality of Stakeholder Relations: Are They Synonymous' (1997) 36 Business and Society 250.

[60] Ronald Roman *et al*, 'The Relationship Between Social and Financial Performance: Repainting a Portrait' (1999) 38 Business and Society 109, 121.

Compact sets out 10 core principles around workplace standards, environmental standards, anti-corruption, and human rights. Yet Coca-Cola is the subject of a long-running campaign by environmental activists because of its interference with local water supplies in Kerala and by trade union and labour activists around allegations of persecution and violent intimidation of workers attempting union-ization in Columbia.[61]

Social Inequality

MNE carries on business in this way because it is driven by the goal of profit maxi-mization for shareholders. This means in practice it produces goods at the lowest possible price to be bought with the highest profit margin the market can bear by the section of the world's population that can afford them. MNE is extremely effi-cient at doing this as the figures below demonstrate. Competition of itself, even competition around social responsibility, does not create sustainable progress and development. However, the response of MNE to this may well be that the goals of States and the goals of corporations are different. States exist to improve the well-being of their inhabitants by stimulating economic growth to provide infrastruc-ture and other benefits.[62] Corporations on the other hand exist to provide an investment return to those who have gambled on its success. Where the interests of the two coincide then there is scope for mutual benefit but there is no absolute necessity for the two to coincide. The garment trade in Cambodia provides a use-ful example of this. In 1995 the Multi-Fibre Agreement (MFA) came into force. The essence of this agreement was protectionism; industrialized countries gained a 10-year window to bring down production costs in their home-based garment industry. This was achieved by forcing the large producers of low-cost economies such as India and China to pay export premiums on their garments entering developed economies. Cambodia was not then a large enough producer to be sub-ject to the MFA. Additionally, Cambodia decided to try to boost its market share by appealing to MNE taste for non-sweated labour. While Cambodia is not a workers' paradise it is ranked more highly by both the ILO and the World Bank in terms of worker rights and treatment. During the MFA, retailers such as Gap and Levi sourced their products through Cambodia citing their preference for better labour conditions even though Cambodia's weaker infrastructure meant that pro-duction costs were higher than those in the large producing countries caught by the MFA. The MFA ended in January 2005. Since then there has been a surge in the relocation of garment production to China and this has resulted in factory

---

[61] www.columbiaactionnetwork.org and www.columbiasolidarity.org.uk. On the difficulties inherent in labour organization in developing economies, see Mancur Olsen, *The Logic of Collective Action* (1971).

[62] For an argument that spending on welfare provision in developing economies is in decline despite development through globalization, see Nita Rudra, 'Globalization and the Decline of the Welfare State in Less-Developed Countries' (2002) 56 International Organization 411.

closures and job losses in Cambodia numbering 20,000. The obvious inference is that product price trumps product production conditions.[63]

Whether it is acceptable to allow MNE to maintain the position that it is at best an 'accidental agent of development' depends upon whether one is prepared to live in a world that is characterized by yawning and increasing gaps in social inequality. Social inequality is measurable through the Human Development Index (HDI) which is a composite indicator that takes three dimensions of welfare: income, health, and education.[64] Looking at measurable social inequality has a certain attraction as it allows one to argue for a redistributive goal without pulling one into difficult discussions of the merits of particular rights and problems of moral relativism and cultural imperialism.[65] It also prevents MNE disengagement by forestalling the argument about which human rights MNE should engage with and how that engagement should occur; questions such as social and economic rights or political rights, should the same rights be chosen across all countries and cultures in which the MNE operates, and what groups should be engaged with in the choice process.[66] A snapshot of the HDI index produces a very depressing picture:

- 18 countries have lower HDI scores in 2003 than 1990;
- 12 of those countries are in sub-Saharan Africa and six in the former Soviet block;
- just over 33 per cent of the sub-Saharan population live in countries with declining HDI scores;
- the adult literacy rate in the top 20 HDI countries is 99 per cent. In Sierra Leone (no 173 on HDI score) the adult literacy rate is 36 per cent; and
- a child born in Sweden has a life expectancy of 79.7 years, in Sierra Leone it is 38.9 years.[67]

Development theorists from Rawls to Sen and Nussbaum[68] concentrate their attention on institutions and how institutions exacerbate unequal development. MNE is a more significant actor than they think in terms of size and as I explain below a fruitful site for encouraging redistribution than governments and supranational bodies. Comparing GDP with MNE turnover is not the most favoured method of economists for measuring comparative economic power.[69] Their

[63] www.csmonitor.com.
[64] The debate around inequality trends is rather more complex and nuanced than I have space to discuss in this essay, see Branko Milanovic, *Worlds Apart: Measuring International and Global Inequality* (2005).
[65] Thomas Donaldson, 'Values in Tension: Ethics Away from Home' (1996) 74 Harv Bus Rev 48.
[66] Thomas Donaldson, *The Ethics of International Business* (1989) 8, 1f.
[67] Figures taken from the Human Development Reports for 2002 and 2003. The 2003 report contains the most recent data available.
[68] For an overview of the positions adopted, see Martha Nussbaum, 'Beyond the Social Contract: Capabilities and Global Justice' (2004) 32 Oxford Development Studies 3 and John Dunning, 'Is Global Capitalism Morally Defensible?' (2005) 24 Contributions to Political Economy 135.
[69] Wesley Milner *et al*, 'Security Rights, Subsistence Rights and Liberties: A Theoretical Survey of the Empirical Landscape' (1999) Human Rights Quarterly 403 and Alfred Chandler and Bruce Mazlish (eds), *Leviathans* (2005).

chosen methodology involves a series of more complex comparisons of data but it would still throw up the fairly stark contrasts shown below:

Country GDP versus Fortune 500 revenue figures ($mill)

Ranking	Country/Company	GDP/ Revenue ($ Millions)
1	United States	11,667,515
2	Japan	4,623,398
3	Germany	2,714,418
4	United Kingdom	2,140,898
5	France	2,002,582
6	Italy	1,672,302
7	People's Republic of China (mainland only)	1,649,329
21	Austria	290,109
22	Wal-Mart Stores	287,989
23	BP	285,059
24	Exxon Mobil	270,772
25	Royal Dutch/Shell Group	268,690
26	Indonesia	257,641
27	Saudi Arabia	250,557

The preferred method of measuring the economic power of MNE is to look at foreign direct investment (FDI) flows. In 2003 the flow of FDI to developing countries rose by 9 per cent and within that figure Africa recorded an increase of 28 per cent.[70] This apparently reflects the perception that the continent is rich in minerals and other natural resources.[71] Setting these figures alongside the HDI presents a far from an encouraging scenario. This view is reinforced by looking at comparisons of foreign assets held by MNEs in developed and developing countries:

The World's Top 7 non-financial MNE, ranked by foreign assets, 2003

Ranking	Corporation	Home Economy	Industry	Foreign Assets (mil $)	Total Assets (mil $)
1	General Electric	US	Electrics	258, 900	647, 483
2	Vodafone	UK	Telecoms	243, 839	262, 581
3	Ford Motor	US	Vehicles	173, 882	304, 594
4	General Motors	US	Vehicles	154, 466	304, 594
5	BP PLC	UK	Petroleum	141, 551	448, 507
6	Exxon Mobil	US	Petroleum	116, 853	177, 572
7	Shell Group	UK/N'Lands	Petroleum	112, 587	174, 278

[70] UNCTAD World Investment Report 2004. This is the most recent available.
[71] Enrico Tanuwidjaja, 'United Nations Conference on Trade and Development' (2005) 50 Sing Econ Rev 293 and Peter Veit (ed.), *Africa's Valuable Assets: A Reader in Natural Resource Management* (1998).

The World's Top 7 non-financial MNE, from developing economies, ranked by foreign assets, 2003

Ranking	Corporation	Home Economy	Industry	Foreign Assets (mil $)	Total Assets (mil $)
1	Hutchinson Whampoa	HK China	General	59, 141	80, 340
2	Singtel Ltd	Singapore	Telecomms	17, 911	21, 668
3	Petronas	Malaysia	Petroleum	16, 114	53, 457
4	Samsung	Rep of Korea	Electrics	12, 387	56, 524
5	Cemex SA	Mexico	Construction Materials	11, 054	16, 021
6	América Móvil	Mexico	Telecomms	8, 676	13, 348
7	China Ocean Shipping	China	Transport	8, 457	18, 007

There are two points to note here; the disparity in size of MNE asset base between developed and developing economies and the uneven pattern of development. A glance at the top 50 MNEs in developing economies replicates this pattern—13 are located in China, eight in Singapore and four in Mexico.

In addressing our concerns around social inequality to MNE we are recognizing the corporation for what it is—an empty signifier.[72] Corporations are what we want them to be. The corporate drive for profits is created by shareholders both individual and institutional. Institutional shareholders are simply individuals standing at one step removed. Even if we are not shareholders—and many of us unwittingly are through pension funds, life assurance, and endowment mortgages—we are consumers. If cheap products made in sweatshop conditions are what the consumer wants, demonstrated by sales figures, then that is what corporations will produce. If instead of this relentless pursuit of profit we want an agenda of caring capitalism then we have to look at adopting strategies that make this clear to the corporate sector. One such strategy is supplied by socially responsible investment (SRI). This consists of three interlinked ideas: community investing, screening, and shareholder activism—the mirror image of 'greenwash'.[73]

In the US the total value of all assets consciously invested as 'responsible investments' is $2.29 trillion.[74] In the UK the figure is put at in excess of £4.5 billion for consumer investment alone, ie ignoring the activities of institutional investors, and can be compared with a figure of £500 million in 1995.[75] Obviously there are debates about what constitutes ethical investment; not every investment fund has

---

[72] Douglas Litowitz, 'The Corporation as God' (2005) 30 J Corp Law 501, 508.
[73] Particularly apt as fund criteria on screening are known as dark green, medium green, and light green depending on the strictness of the criteria they apply.
[74] This is the 2005 figure, *Report on Responsible Investing Trends* (1997) Social Investment Forum, Washington, www.socialivest.org.   [75] EIRIS Feb 2000, www.eiris.org.

the same view on issues such as tobacco production, road building, and intensive farming. The screen filters to SRI are applied by the funds themselves. Not all funds apply all the available screens and there is no information on how they are applied. What is starting to emerge is a pyramid effect with individuals delegating ethical choices and assessments to fund managers who are promoting a range of ethical funds within a portfolio of 'socially responsible investing'. The oldest of these funds are the Stewardship funds launched by Friends Provident in 1984. These particular funds account for about 50 per cent of the market share. About 20 other financial institutions have joined Friends Provident in the market for the money of the ethical investor.[76] It seems that an ethical profile is constructed from assessing positive corporate activity such as conservation and resource management against negative corporate activity such as the production of greenhouse gasses.

There are clear difficulties with this approach such as the lack of mechanisms to test the veracity of corporate statements and the inherent bias towards clean hands corporations such as those engaged in the telecoms industry. Socially responsible investing, while it can refocus the interest of corporate managers away from sole pursuit of profit maximization, does not have the same popular appeal as consumer boycotts and lobbying, which are open to all regardless of their ability or desire to become shareholders. Ethical investing does not necessarily involve moving corporate strategy away from Milton Friedman's assertion that all responsible corporations should do is care for shareholders.[77] Shareholders in this instance have demanded 'responsible' policies be pursued to obtain return upon their investment. These demands can be satisfied without the corporations involved being forced to consider those outside the corporate property matrix. A point which slightly softens this observation is that the effect of the marketization of pension provision in the UK through the move away from support through the welfare state to occupational pension is to create a new class of investor, albeit one that is at one step removed from the market—the employee.

Pension fund trustees in the UK are estimated to hold on behalf of employees £800 billion of assets in both defined contribution and defined benefit schemes or 16 per cent of institutional investment. From 3 July 2000,[78] occupational pension funds in the UK have been obliged to disclose in their statements of investment principles 'the extent to which, if at all, social, environmental or ethical considerations are taken into account in the selection, retention and realisation of investments'.[79] 'Just Pensions' an offshoot of the UK Social Investment Forum predict that this will have a considerable impact on SRI in the next 5 years. However, this optimism should be tempered by the observation that the legislation does not

---

[76] Alan Lewis and Craig Mackenzie, 'Morals, Money, Ethical investing and economic psychology' (2000) 53 Human Relations 179.   [77] Milton Friedman, *Capitalism and Freedom* (1962) 126.

[78] Occupational Pension Schemes (Investment) Regulations of 1996, as amended in 1998.

[79] Similar regulation has been adopted in Australia, France, Germany, and Belgium.

require SRI to take place only a declaration as to the type of investments made. This is typical of the UK model of corporate regulation—generally termed comply or explain—the idea is that the market should decide whether the trustees decisions are the right ones or not.

Shareholder activism has a long history, its highwater mark being the disinvestment campaign waged against the Apartheid regime in South Africa. Since then other notable highs include 17 per cent of shareholders in Shell voting for greater social and environmental responsibility in 1997. The Myners review[80] recommended that there should be greater use of voting rights by institutional investors. Evidence from the US is that shareholder advocacy is on the increase but the figures are still very low—shareholder resolutions increased from 299 proposals in 2003 to 348 in 2005. SRI is a relatively blunt tool with which to try and address social inequality or human rights enhancement. The absence of principles, even very general ones, makes progress difficult to measure. It is impossible to know what the market value is of reputation in this context.

The re-engineering of capitalism does not have to be confined to those who have a proprietary stake in the corporation. The availability of information through media such as the internet[81] and television makes social dumping harder to hide. The same access to information makes it easier for representative consumer groups or less formal 'activist' groupings to organize product and producer boycotts. Pressure groups, both single and multi-issue NGOs, act as informers and co-ordinators of consumer feeling using these methods for knowledge acquisition, information transmission, and co-ordination of action.[82] The position of Nestlé is illustrative of this. From 1974 to 1984 consumers were urged by activists to boycott Nestlé products as a demonstration of their feeling against Nestlé's practice of distributing Infant Milk Formula in the developing world. This boycott was re-introduced in 1988 due to Nestlé's alleged non-compliance with the World Health Organisation Code on the Advertising of Milk Substitute. Individuals can participate in the debate around the boycott or consult lists of Nestlé products using information posted on the Internet. Contributions to the formal policy process around consumer issues are also co-ordinated through bodies such as the Transatlantic Consumer Dialogue. This was launched in 1998 as a

---

[80] Myners Report, *Review of Institutional Investment*, 6 March 2001, commissioned by the UK Chancellor, Gordon Brown. For an interesting and novel stance on shareholder activism see Andrew Fraser, *Reinventing Aristocracy: The Constitutional Reformation of Corporate Governance* (1998).

[81] David Crowther, 'Corporate Reporting, Stakeholders and the Internet: Mapping the New Corporate Landscape' (2000) 37 Urban Studies 1837. Crowther makes a very interesting point here; the development of internet technology, while obviously empowering individuals, is nevertheless subsumed at one level into the architecture of corporate reporting. Thus, individuals still remain in a relationship of inequality with corporations.

[82] John Rosthorn, 'Business Ethics Auditing—More than a Stakeholders' Toy' (2000) 27 J of Bus Ethics 9 and Jesper Grolin, 'Corporate Legitimacy in Risk Society: The Case of Brent Spar' (1998) 7 Business Strat and Enviro 213.

mechanism for US and EU consumer groups to make representations to the US Government and the EU Commission. The availability of global information, the ease of global communications and the decline in the importance of physical place and presence have made this easier.[83]

However, just as we have begun to feel comfortable about handing over our social conscience to the NGO movement a growing critique of them based upon diverse ideas such as capture by the corporate sector, lack of accountability, lack of adversarial engagement, has begun to gain currency. In 1997 William Fisher produced a very influential piece[84] reprising the role that had been assigned to NGOs at events like the Rio Conference in 1992.[85] Then the issue for NGOs was whether they could gain acceptance from the development industry. They were idolized as everything governments were not—flexible, responsive, and not over-burdened with bureaucracy. Since 1997, however, there has been something of a *volte face*. The core role of NGOs has moved from an advocacy of humanitarian issues to one of participating in policy development and implementation and service provision. Activities such as formal and informal linkages with each other and the development of strategic partnerships with governments and their agencies and the corporate sector which might be seen as the natural progression of maturing organizations[86] are instead viewed with suspicion. NGOs carry the scars of years of interacting with neo-liberal economic reforms. They have joined the rush for 'efficiency' through creating technical and bureaucratic structures rather than continuing to debate values.[87] They have become increasingly similar to the enemy rather than sustaining a radical alternative.[88] More specifically in relation to the material in this essay they are accused of crowding out union involvement and delaying legal regulation for workplaces through their own involvement in workers' rights.[89]

The development literature saw NGOs as evidencing the flowering of civil society,[90] which itself was the essential 'harbinger of political and economic reforms in the 3rd world',[91] the solution for everything from conflict to establishing

---

[83] N.Craig Smith, *Morality and the Market: Consumer Pressure for Corporate Accountability* (1990).

[84] William Fisher, 'DOING GOOD? The Politics and Antipolitics of Practices' (1997) 26 Ann Rev of Anthrop 439.

[85] Paul Little, 'Ritual, power and ethnography' (1995) 15 Critique of Anthropology 265.

[86] Martin Shaw, 'Global Society and Global Responsibility: the theoretical, historical and political limits of international society' (1992) 21 Millennium 421.

[87] Richard Holloway cited in Jenny Pearce, 'Development, NGOs and Civil Society: the debate and its future' in Deborah Eade (ed.), *Development, NGOs and Civil Society* (2000).

[88] Simon Zadek, *The Civil Corporation: The New Economy of Corporate Citizenship* (2001).

[89] Niklas Egels-Zandén and Peter Hyllman, 'Exploring the Effects of Union-NGO Relationships on Corporate Responsibility: The Case of the Swedish Clean Clothes Campaign' (2006) 64 J of Bus Ethics 303.

[90] For the links between NGOs and markets through civil society see John Keane, 'Global Civil Society' in Helmut Anheier *et al* (eds), *Global Civil Society 2001* (2001) 31–35.

[91] Balakrishnan Rajagopal, *Int Law from Below* (2003) 259.

440   *Human Rights*

democracy.[92] It was the ultimate tool of anti-statism.[93] Civil society is now viewed
with more caution. It is caught between the jaws of individualism and communitarianism. Composed of individuals with multiple identities and interests it is
seen as a concept that is driven with different ideas as to composition and
agenda.[94] Are NGOs, for example, any more than the mouthpiece of those members of 'civil society' who have access to education, information and computers? If
this is the case then they merely serve to deepen the digital divide.

    Once we ask this question of NGOs then the floodgates open with regard to
questions about their legitimacy and accountability. In respect of legitimacy the
key question is one of authority and representation[95] in both procedural and
substantive fields. The more established NGOs become the more the structures
they adapt and become subjected to the same criticisms that are made of governments[96] and to a lesser extent corporations in this regard. Who gives NGOs
the authority to act? The level of democratic deficit within NGOs depends to a
certain extent on the model of legitimacy that is used,[97] but whatever the model it
is hard to be certain that the individuals that NGOs make claims on behalf of have
been consulted, have participated in agenda-setting and are at ease with being
represented in this way.[98] Criticisms at a level below this are concerned with the
construction of claims based on unverifiable data and the aggregation of diverse
individuals into 'interest groups'. There are no easy answers to any of the questions raised about NGOs. Demands for greater accountability cannot be met by
the provision of a simple matrix or feedback loop. Instead what occurs is another
set of questions about accountability to whom, for what, and how? The crisis that
NGOs are suffering is in part attributable to the general reconfiguring of global
patterns of governance in a post-Westphalian world;[99] however, this is sufficient
to provoke the individual liberal conscience into wondering if anything else can
be done.

    By way of conclusion to this essay I want to examine a possible answer to this
question offered by Iris Marion Young; a model of political responsibility based on
what she describes as social connection.[100] The labels 'political' and 'responsibility'

    [92] Sheelagh Stewart, 'Happy Ever After in the Marketplace: NGOs and Uncivil Society' (1997) 71
Rev of African Pol Econ 11, 16.
    [93] Axel Hadenius and Fredick Uggla, 'Making Civil Society Work, Promoting Democratic
Development: What Can States and Donors Do?' (1996) 24 World Development 1621.
    [94] Petras and Velymeyer, *Globalization Unmasked*, n 3 above, 129–30.
    [95] Sarah Lister, 'NGO Legitimacy' (2003) 23 Crit of Anthro 175.
    [96] Vivien Collingwood and Louis Logister, 'State of the Art: Addressing the INGO 'Legitimacy
Deficit' (2005) 3 Political Studies Review 175.
    [97] Compare for example Michael Edwards, 'Legitimacy and Values in NGOs and Voluntary
Organizations: Some Sceptical Thoughts' in David Lewis (ed.), *International Perspectives on
Voluntary Action* (1999) 258 with Jurgen Habermas, *The Postnational Constellation* (2001) 201.
    [98] Neera Chandhoke, 'The Limits of Global Civil Society' in Mary Kaldor *et al* (eds), *Global Civil
Society* (2002) 35, 46–47.
    [99] Ian Clark, 'Legitimacy in a Global Order' (2003) 29 Review of Int Studies 75.
    [100] Iris Marion Young, 'Responsibility and Global Labor Justice' (2004) 12 J of Pol Phil 365 and
'Responsibility and Global Justice: A Social Connection Model' (2006) 23 Soc Phil and Policy 102.

need definitions as they are both being used in a rather novel way.[101] Young's idea of political is a broad one that exceeds government and statehood to be the act of reorganizing or reordering some aspect of collective life and persuading others to do the same. The definition of responsibility is one that is grounded not in fault, blame or liability or based upon some clarion call to care in a moral sense about people less well off than ourselves in a faraway country but on the act of connection; by using products that are produced in a way that involves environmental degradation, for example, we are connected to but not responsible for that degradation.[102]

Political responsibility is forward looking in that it leaves blame and fault[103] in the past and centres instead on a recognition that structural injustice is not acceptable. It asks that outcomes be sought which try to alter these inequalities. To take up that responsibility an individual needs to reflect on, and persuade others to reflect on, structural inequalities and the causes of that inequality and then be prepared to think through how means can be designed to change that inequality. Young acknowledges that responsibility may be discharged through engagement with the State but is more in favour of the promulgation of a public discourse at the level of individuals. Political responsibility for her translates into a model of political action based around the parameters of connection, power, and privilege. Connection involves working to remove the anonymity of inequality by asking questions of importers and retailers, for example about the sourcing and manufacture of their products. The power to challenge inequality varies depending on one's location in the process but even end-of-chain consumers have the power to make corporations change their practices if they choose to use it. The notion of privilege in Young's model is more difficult as those who benefit from cheap products may not be in a position to afford others available at a higher price.[104] This should not detract from the basic point, however, that in the main those who benefit from the sweated labours of others are privileged and should recognize that.

For all their apparent power, corporations are merely instruments of the will of the wider public in which they are situated. Political commitment at the level of the individual has the potential to change corporate behaviour in respect of human rights and social inequality. Calling time on corporate profits and cheap products does not end the march of development, nor will it end all the pain of development but it would make it slightly more palatable.

---

[101] Young's ideas for this are drawn from a wide range of sources but perhaps the most influential is the work of Hannah Arendt, ibid (2004) 375–77.

[102] Iris Marion Young, 'From Guilt to Solidarity: Sweatshops and Political Responsibility' (2003) Dissent 39, 40.

[103] For Young's view in a rather different context of the futility of blame, see Iris Marion Young, 'Katrina: Too Much Blame, Not Enough Responsibility' (2006) Dissent 41.

[104] This is a gloss on the points made in the now iconic volume by David Caplovitz, *The Poor Pay More* (1967).

20

Constitutionalism, Deliberative Democracy, and Human Rights

*David Feldman**

Introduction

This essay explores the relationships between constitutionalism, democracy, and human rights. These are the subject of keen debates, which are most intense when politicians and political theorists seek to use them to reshape a State or region to overcome the causes or legacies of conflict, as in Northern Ireland.[1]

At the level of international law theory, the work of Thomas Franck,[2] Philip Allott,[3] Susan Marks,[4] and others[5] suggests that adherence to certain values may be a litmus test for the legitimacy of States and their constitutions. In particular, it has been argued that the right of peoples to self-determination, recognized in a number of international treaties[6] and as a principle of customary international law in relation to de-colonization,[7] is accompanied by a right of the inhabitants of political units to enjoy some form of democratic governance.[8] Alongside this,

---

* The views expressed in this essay are those of the author and should not be taken to represent the opinions of any other person or institution.

[1] See eg John Morison and Stephen Livingstone, *Reshaping Public Power: Northern Ireland and the British Constitutional Crisis* (1995).

[2] Thomas M. Franck, 'The emerging right to democratic governance' (1992) 86 American Journal of International Law 46.

[3] Philip Allott, *Eunomia: New Order for a New World* (2001).

[4] Susan Marks, *The Riddle of All Constitutions: Law, Democracy, and the Critique of Ideology* (2000).

[5] See the essays collected in Gregory H. Fox and Brad R. Roth (eds), *Democratic Governance and International Law* (2000).

[6] See eg International Covenant on Civil and Political Rights, Art. 1 (and note the minority rights in Art. 27), and International Covenant on Economic, Social and Cultural Rights, Art. 1.

[7] See James Crawford, *The Creation of Statehood in International Law* (2nd ed., 2006), and the discussions in the *South-West Africa Cases* ICJ Reports, 1966, p 6, (1966) 37 ILR 243, the *Namibia Case*, ICJ Reports 1971, 16; (1971) 49 ILR 2, 3, and the *Western Sahara Case*, ICJ Reports, 1975, 12, 121–22, (1975) 59 ILR 30, 138 *per* Judge Dillard.

[8] See Franck, 'The emerging right to democratic governance', n 2 above; Marks, *The Riddle of All Constitutions: Law, Democracy, and the Critique of Ideology*, n 4 above.

other commentators have suggested that a commitment to some form of constitutionalism is so widespread that one can speak of it as a developing global norm,[9] or
have asserted that the late twentieth century was the era of human rights, even if
they attack the value and coherence of the very notion of human rights.[10]
Discussion of the nature of citizenship has become tied up with these ideas. The
civic republican tradition gives particular weight to the public, political role of
citizens and to those rights that help to make it possible for them to perform it.
For example, in the US, Cass Sunstein has argued that (some) human rights are
part of an inner morality of deliberative democracy.[11]

Claims that constitutionalism, deliberative democracy, or human rights should
be accepted as fundamental to the international legal order has led to confusion,
because even those who accept their potential usefulness as sources of constitutional guidance hold competing conceptions of them. Some people assume them
to be so closely related as to be merely different aspects of a single normative
framework. Others, seeing a tension or even potential opposition between them,
try to resolve it by defining one or more of democracy, constitutionalism, and
human rights in such a way as to make them accommodate each other. I will
suggest that these approaches obscure rather than address the problems facing
constitutional drafters, interpreters, and officials.

Constitutionalism

Let us consider two general conceptions of 'constitutionalism'. The first sees it as a
politico-legal process. The second portrays it as a limitation of political power.
There are other formulations, such as a recognition that an entrenched constitutional text has supra-legal authority, or that judicial review of legislation by reference to constitutional standards is legitimate; but these are essentially more
concrete examples of one of the two general conceptions outlined above, or an
attempt to combine elements of each within a working constitutional structure.

Constitutionalism as Politico-Legal Process

The first conception of constitutionalism, and the one which I prefer, is a state of
mind in which all the participants in the process of government and a predominant part of the citizenry accept, or at least are prepared to behave as if they accept,

---

[9] eg Bruce Ackerman, 'The rise of world constitutionalism' (1997) 83 Virginia law Review 771.
[10] For eg, Adam Tomkins regrets that in the last half-century human rights 'have played a central
role in the rhetoric (if not the reality) of international relations' and 'have additionally come to enjoy
an ever more dominant position in national constitutional or public law': 'Introduction: On being
sceptical about human rights', in Tom Campbell, K. D. Ewing, and Adam Tomkins (eds), *Sceptical
Essays on Human Rights* (2001), 1. See also Onora O'Neill, *A Question of Trust: the BBC Reith Lectures
2002.*   [11] Cass R. Sunstein, *Designing Democracy: What Constitutions Do* (2001).

four propositions: (a) that conflicts concerning the organization and use of state power must be worked out through a combination of political and legal processes; (b) that the solutions they advance must be justified by reference to a fair reading of principles that command a significant degree of consensus among the institutions of the State at an abstract level, even if there are differences as to their concrete application; (c) that those principles must be capable of fitting, more or less, the observable regularities of behaviour in both the political and the legal institutions of government; and (d) that they must be justified publicly by reference to a normative vision of the good State.

This conception of constitutionalism has two characteristics. One is an aspect of social psychology: people participating in public life must share a subjective commitment to or acceptance of the need to conduct debates and disputes about the organization and use of public power as a process of arguing about and attempting to agree on principled solutions to problems. The debaters will argue by reference to a notion of the constitution as a normative structure for allocating, controlling, and securing accountability for the use of public power. The second characteristic relates to social institutions: there must be institutions and procedures into and through which disputes can be channelled, and they must be used in practice. Sometimes they will lead to an authoritative solution, especially when the institution which has the last word on an issue is adjudicative and makes decisions of acknowledged (albeit provisional and temporary) authority. At other times there will be no authoritative solution. In either case, the debate about values will continue indefinitely, and the accepted solution may change over time. The debates in the US about the constitutional status of a woman's right to reproductive liberty and the right to engage in homosexual anal intercourse continue to swirl around and within the Supreme Court, despite a number of supposedly authoritative but in reality temporary and provisional judicial decisions on each side of both debates.[12]

In certain ways this is a very demanding conception of constitutionalism. It requires people to relate their proposed solutions to constitutional disputes to a notion of the proper role and functions of the State. At the same time it demands that they fit their preferred vision within a tenable account of current institutional practices and understandings of the constitution. In other words, this conception of constitutionalism involves a commitment to making the best of the current constitution. It does not rule out the possibility of starting afresh, but that course is usually justified only if the preferred normative vision is considered to be very

---

[12] See eg the debates around two particularly controversial lines of cases on sexual and reproductive liberty: *Roe v Wade* 410 US 113 (1973) and *Planned Parenthood of South-Eastern Pennsylvania v Casey* 505 US 833 (1992) on abortion, and *Bowers v Hardwick* 478 US 186 (1986) reversed in *Lawrence v Texas* 539 US 558 (2003). Both these issues may well be given further consideration by the Supreme Court in its more conservative aspect following the appointment of John G. Roberts Jr as Chief Justice following the death of Rehnquist CJ in 2005, and the appointment of Samuel Alito Jr as Associate Justice in 2006 to replace Justice Sandra Day O'Connor. See further below.

weighty, cannot be realized within existing constitutional constraints, and offers benefits sufficient to outweigh the advantages flowing from maintaining existing constitutional norms and processes. But at the same time, this conception does not assume that it will be possible to achieve consensus as to what is the best answer (even at a single moment in history), or that any consensus will be more than temporary, or that it is logically necessary that there should be a single correct answer to the problem.

Constitutionalism as Limitation on the use of Political Power

Comparative constitutional scholars increasingly see a trend among States towards adopting constitutions characterized by what Nevil Johnson calls 'modern liberal constitutionalism in the sense of a body of ideas justifying limited government by consent and the rule of law'.[13] The twentieth century saw a growth of interest in constitutions and limited government in many parts of the world. The development was not universal, and even in individual States it could ebb and flow. In Germany, for example, the Weimar Constitution (the German Constitution of 11 August 1919) introduced following World War I contained guarantees of freedoms, including freedom of religion, and provided, 'Enjoyment of civil and political rights and eligibility for public office shall be independent of religious denomination.'[14] However, during the 1930s the National Socialist government was able to subvert the guarantees of the Constitution. In 1949 a *Grundgesetz* or Basic Law for the Federal Republic of Germany (FRG) was adopted,[15] initially as a temporary measure until such time as a 'constitution adopted by a free decision of the German people comes into force'.[16] It has so far survived for well over half a century, accommodating the reunification of Germany in 1990 and acquiring great moral and political authority. In the process it has provided the basis for judicial as well as political controls on the exercise of political power through legislation and administration, using standards derived from the federal character of the FRG, the guaranteed rights, and restrictions on the competencies and procedures of state and *Länder* institutions. These arrangements have enabled the FRG, notably through the Federal Constitutional Court (*Bundesverfassungsgericht*), to develop a practical example of a *Rechtstaat* incorporating federal safeguards for distinctive regional interests and values as well as democracy and human rights, thereby ensuring that fundamental rights have acquired a prominent place in the structure of the EU.

---

[13] Nevil Johnson, *Reshaping the British Constitution: Essays in Political Interpretation* (2004) 9–10. See also Douglas Greenberg, Stanley N. Katz, Melanie Beth Oliviero, and Steven C. Wheatley (eds), *Constitutionalism and Democracy: Transitions in the Contemporary World* (1993).

[14] Art. 136(2) of the Weimar Constitution, translated in S. E. Finer, Vernon Bogdanor, and Bernard Rudden, *Comparing Constitutions* (1995) 206.

[15] Official translation of 1991 with authors' translations of later amendments in Finer *et al*, *Comparing Constitutions*, n 14 above, 127–205.   [16] GG, Art. 146.

The FRG is a particularly successful example of constitutionalism and other values, but many States have treated constitutional design seriously, and have shown a commitment to constitutional checks on State institutions (both through the diffusion of political power among institutions and groups—federalism, devolution and consociation,[17] for example—and through the creation of institutions with a checking function, such as constitutional courts). States in transition from one form of government or set of fundamental values to another have given expression to this view of constitutionalism when seeking to instantiate the conditions for justice and stability. Constitutional law in these situations is founded on the ideals which have stimulated change. This has become a hallmark of legitimacy in new States and reinvented States, and a criterion for the acceptability of a State's eligibility to be considered for accession to the EU. But useful as it is, the idea of limiting political power can set up tensions with certain models of democracy, a possibility to which we will return below.

The Relationship Between the Two Models

There is no necessary conflict between the idea that constitutions should facilitate debate about the values that ought to shape the allocation of power and the notion that they should provide limits on political power. A debate about constitutional values may lead to an outcome in which the participants accept, either temporarily or permanently, limits on political power. However, there may be a tension between some constitutional values and the idea of limitations on political power. For example, popular sovereignty might imply that a legislature or executive body elected on a popular franchise should be free to develop law and policy without constraint, except for ultimate accountability to the populus, which is itself unconstrained in its power of selection.

The constitution of the UK can be seen as being loosely based on this model. The characteristic feature of what Paul Craig has called its 'unitary, self-correcting democracy'[18] is the idea that political power should be concentrated on a single, presumptively appropriate institution (the Queen in Parliament) and that any limitations on that power require special and very compelling justification if they are to be regarded as legitimate. Sometimes the operation of political processes (internationally or domestically) produces agreement on an allocation of power which seems to limit the practical political authority of the Queen in Parliament. For example, accession on 1 January 1973 to the EEC (now the EU) might be thought to have had that effect in view of the doctrine of the primacy of

---

[17] For our purposes, 'consociation' can be understood as a system in which power is shared between groups of people defined by reference to their distinctive ethnic, national, political, or religious adherences, each group being protected by special arrangements in the constitution or relevant legislation against domination by a combination of other groups.

[18] P. P. Craig, *Public Law and Democracy in the United Kingdom and the United States of America* (1990), ch 2.

Community law; and devolution arrangements within the UK can be regarded in a similar light.

Yet there is no consensus within the UK as to whether even pre-EEC parliamentary sovereignty was absolute[19] or had always been limited without it having been necessary to define the limits.[20] In relation to devolution, the legislation establishing the new structures of devolved authority in Scotland, Northern Ireland, and Wales makes it clear that their powers are subordinate to those of the Westminster Parliament.[21] Any conflict between the powers of the devolved institutions and those of the UK executive and legislature are resolved by 'concordats' negotiated between the different agencies, having political force but no legal authority.[22] As to whether membership of the EEC in 1973 or later has resulted in a constitutional limitation of the political power of the key institution, the Queen in Parliament, the ideological battle lines remain even more entrenched: there are at least two different views of the effect of accession on the doctrine of parliamentary sovereignty in the UK's prior constitution. One view is that the effect of Community law on municipal law depends on the operation of (pre-1973) parliamentary sovereignty and is therefore subject to it and cannot restrict or derogate from it.[23] The other view is that sovereignty has been restricted, providing the UK with a constitution which embodies the second (limitation of political power) conception of constitutionalism, at any rate unless and until the UK withdraws from the EU.[24] The latter view is probably in the ascendant at present,[25] although it has been sustained in part through the elaboration of an idea that some statutes are superior to others, having at common law a 'constitutional' status, in a way

[19] See eg Jeffrey Goldsworthy, *Sovereignty of Parliament: History and Philosophy* (1999), and Lord Bingham of Cornhill in *R. (Jackson) v Attorney General* [2005] UKHL 56, [2005] 3 WLR 733, [2005] 4 All ER 1253, HL, para [9], offering an essentially Anglo-centric view of the nature and powers of the Westminster Parliament.

[20] See eg J. D. B. Mitchell, *Constitutional Law* (2nd ed., 1968) ch 4; *McCormick v Lord Advocate*, 1953 SC 396; T. R. S. Allan, 'Legislative Supremacy and the Rule of Law: Democracy and Constitutionalism' (1985) 44(1) Cambridge Law Journal 111; Lord Hope of Craighead in *R. (Jackson) v Attorney General*, n 19 above, paras 104–6, who offer a more nuanced and in some instances a more Scottish perspective.

[21] See Scotland Act 1998, s 28 (especially subs (7)) and ss 29 and 30; Northern Ireland Act 1998, s 5 (especially subs (6)) and ss 6 to 8). The National Assembly for Wales is an executive body acting on behalf of the Crown, is subject to judicial review and sometimes to reversal by a Minister of the Crown, and has limited functions and powers: see Government of Wales Act 1998, ss 1(3), 106–10.

[22] See Richard Rawlings, 'Concordats and the constitution' (2000) 116 Law Quarterly Review 257. The concordats are available on the UK Government Departments' websites: see eg http://www.dca.gov.uk/concordat/concord_scot.htm.

[23] See eg O. Hood Phillips and Paul Jackson, *O. Hood Phillips' Constitutional and Administrative Law* (7th ed., 1987) 80–82.

[24] See eg P. Craig, 'Parliamentary sovereignty of the United Kingdom Parliament after *Factortame*' (1991) 11 Yearbook of European Law 221.

[25] *R. v Secretary of State for Transport ex parte Factortame (No. 2)* [1991] 1 AC 603, [1991] 1 All ER 70, ECJ and HL; Craig, 'Parliamentary sovereignty of the United Kingdom Parliament after *Factortame*', n 24 above; Sir William Wade 'Sovereignty—revolution or evolution?' (1996) 112 LQR 568.

that arguably undermines the core of the idea of absolute parliamentary sovereignty generally.[26] The issue of limitation of political power is, in the UK, itself one of the controversial questions of constitutional debate, to be debated as part of the process of constitutionalism rather than being pre-empted by a specific set of values about the limitation of power, stipulated as a large part of the definition of constitutionalism.

While the idea of constitutionalism as a commitment to the limitation of political power is likely to be important at the stage of drafting a constitution, constitutionalism as a process, combining an attitude of mind with the availability of social and political channels for undertaking debate about values, is a *sine qua non* for the effective operation of a constitution once it has been drafted and approved, regardless of the values included in or supporting the constitution. But constitutionalism as process demands that people who participate in drafting and operating a constitution should see themselves as obligated to elaborate their positions to others and defend them publicly against counter-arguments. The number and characteristics of the people to whom they owe the obligations of elaboration and defence may vary. At some times and in some places it will be a specialized elite or privileged oligarchy. At other times and places it may be the whole of society. It depends on what type of political ethos is dominant in the society, and the nature of any principles which are held to flow from it. Constitutionalism as process always requires both that institutional arrangements for debate exist and that constitutional actors be committed to using them.

Both at the stage of negotiating and drafting a constitution and when operating it, the requirement to articulate and justify constitutional viewpoints to the public is closely linked to democracy. Citizens can contribute fully to (or deliberate deeply on) constitutional debates only if other participants are prepared to justify their positions publicly, rather than merely advance them privately.

On the other hand, the public, deliberative process that forms part of the notion of constitutionalism does not entail that the authoritative choice of a solution for the time being to constitutional controversies should be left in the hands of the citizenry at large. Public justification for a decision helps to legitimate it even if it is taken by a specialized group within society such as a legal or political elite, whether or not the elite is in some sense representative. It is an important element in the professional disciplines of both lawyers (especially judges) and politicians and a vital condition of the legitimacy of their decisions that they should have to explain and justify decisions, actions, and (in the case of politicians) policy proposals within a reasonably principled framework of argument and in a form that is accessible to the public. Nevertheless, the forms of justification are different. Judges must use rational argument to justify their decisions by reference

---

[26] See *Thoburn v Sunderland City Council* [2002] 3 WLR 247, paras 50–51, 59–66, 68–70; Mark Elliott, 'Embracing "Constitutional" Legislation: Towards Fundamental Law?' (2003) 54 NILQ 25.

to expressly articulated, authoritative, normative criteria. Politicians have greater freedom to appeal to goal-directed arguments and the popular will as justifications for policies and decisions, although judges may impose limits on that freedom in the constant tug-of-war between rule-of-law standards and popular sovereignty, especially where decisions directly affect identifiable individuals.[27]

Democracy

By the 1990s, as we have noted, Thomas Franck could argue that a human right to democratic participation formed part of customary international law.[28] That proposition is not incontestable, depending as it does on an interpretation of a mass of international treaties and evidence of State practice in support of and against it. Yet there is undoubtedly an assumption now that new constitutions should enable democratic institutions to function effectively, and that the legitimacy of State constitutions depends in part on their democratic pedigree (the people as the constituent body and the source of the power, which is allocated and controlled through the constitution) and on the democratic credentials of the arrangements put in place under the constitution. There is thus a strong link between constitutionalism and democracy.[29]

Yet democracy is a highly contested concept, and people tend to feed into it whatever values they favour from the point of view of political or constitutional morality. As John Morison has shown, this has produced a variety of 'thick' and 'thin' conceptions incorporating a range of values derived from many sources.[30] Some models of democracy involve consultation by an elite with 'the people', or that part of the people which is regarded as having political weight under the form of political morality prevailing at that place and time (hereafter described as 'the *demos*'). Other models treat politics as a process in which elites compete for election by, and are accountable after the event to, the *demos*; yet others regard politics as a struggle between a plurality of groups to advance their interests in government, allowing people outside the elites to participate actively in decision-making (or some kinds of decision-making), although not necessarily with the right to the last word. Relatively few forms of democracy—one thinks of the initiative and referendum systems of Switzerland and some states of the US—allow the *demos* to

---

[27] See eg *R. v Secretary of State for the Home Department, ex p. Venables and Thompson* [1998] AC 407, HL.

[28] See the collection of papers in Fox and Roth, *Democratic Governance and International Law*, n 5 above.

[29] See Douglas Greenberg *et al, Constitutionalism and Democracy: Transitions in the Contemporary World*, n 13 above, Introduction.

[30] John Morison, 'Models of democracy: from representation to participation?' in Jeffrey Jowell and Dawn Oliver (eds), *The Changing Constitution* (5th ed., 2005) ch 6, 145–49.

have a direct and decisive say on policy choices or immediate control of the process of decision-making.[31]

Morison[32] distinguishes illuminatingly between process models and framework models of democracy. In crude terms, the former consist of rules about how decision-makers are to be chosen and decisions are to be made, and draw the legitimacy of democratic institutions from the normative value of the manner in which those steps are taken. Framework models provide constraints on what can be done by institutions, and derive legitimacy from the match between outcomes of the process and values which are regarded as particularly important. There are links between different forms or models of democracy and constitutionalism. They may reinforce each other to some degree, but sometimes there is a tension, if not a conflict, between them. For example, process models of democracy tend to be more in tune with the process model of constitutionalism than with the limits-on-political-power model, which has a better fit with framework models of democracy based on substantive constraints and output values. There is a tension between the 'limitations-on-political-power' form of constitutionalism and the brand of democracy founded on the idea of popular self-determination, according to which the central requirement is not that political power be limited, but rather that it be used for the purposes approved by the *demos*, which in this case can be taken to mean the people as a whole. For these democrats, the central issues for democratic theory are how to delimit membership of the *demos*, how best to discover the wishes of the *demos*, and how to translate those wishes into action by an appropriately responsive (and usually in some sense representative) set of State institutions.

The dominant political model at present usually treats the *demos* as being composed of a large number of individuals whose views, when taken into account, are presumptively to be given equal weight as nearly as can be achieved in practice, although they may combine to advance shared interests. This approach is compatible with both liberalism and utilitarianism, but can produce profoundly illiberal effects, particularly if one is a member of a minority with common interests distinct from those of the majority on many matters. Rights may be introduced to utilitarianism to counter this potentially repressive effect of individualist majoritarianism.[33] They may help to balance the interests of individuals and of the collectivity, particularly by guaranteeing that all can participate in the political decision-making process and (perhaps) some minimal protection for the citizenship rights and other interests of members of minority groupings. However, the

---

[31] See David Held, *Models of Democracy* (1987); S. Arnstein, 'A ladder of citizen participation' (1969) J. American Institute of Planning 216, cited by Morison, 'Models of democracy: from representation to participation?' n 30 above, 165–66.

[32] Morison, 'Models of democracy: from representation to participation?' n 30 above.

[33] J. S. Mill, 'On Utilitarianism', in Mary Warnock (ed.), *Utilitarianism* (1962) 251.

stronger the protection is for other rights, the less democratic the State is, and the more the State's legitimacy relies on other values.

But whatever form democracy takes, limiting ordinary political power means limiting democracy. For this reason democrats traditionally tend to be suspicious of constitutionalism. New democrats have had to attempt to reconcile democracy with constitutionalism by reinventing democracy with limits, including those derived from constitutional settlements and human rights. The *demos* controls decision-makers, but the range of possible decisions is limited.

The tension reflects a specific way of looking at the relationship between the *demos* and the State. One may see the *demos* as separate from the State (even if it is in theory the constituent power within it): the State and its constitution is a set of constraints, some procedural and others substantive, imposed (as if by some external agency) on the *demos*. Competing individuals within the *demos* struggle to achieve objectives that seem good for them by exercising control over the use of State power. Limiting ordinary political power through constitutionalism interferes with that pursuit. This model accurately encapsulates the real experience of many individuals when attempting to achieve political or constitutional change within the structures of a modern State. State institutions tend to become cut-off from the *demos* even in a democracy, developing autonomous sets of values and objectives through a combination of technical expertise and bureaucratic professionalism. Occasionally a constitution is indeed imposed on an entire *demos* against, or without regard to, the will of the *demos*, as in the case of Bosnia and Herzegovina by the Dayton/Paris Agreement which ended the war there in 1995. In such circumstances individuals and groups can feel disempowered by a dislocation between them and their political decision-making powers on the one hand and the State and its institutions on the other.

In other circumstances, the State and its political institutions may be viewed as an expression of the will of its citizens. On this view, the *demos* is continually reconstituting the State through decisions and choices on political matters. This model sees constitutional structures and substantive rules as reflecting an accommodation achieved by the *demos* through an exercise of political authority, but does not regard them as final solutions (it is not the end of constitutional history). Instead, the *demos* remains free to develop new ways of organizing and channelling its authority. What is more, the constitutional structures—including restrictions on 'ordinary' political power—are seen as expressions of, rather than limitations on, democratic authority. A constitutional settlement is most likely to enjoy respect among the *demos* if it is truly a result of the exercise of popular participation and sovereignty, as in South Africa in 1993 and 1996.[34]

But in either case majoritarian forms of democracy may sometimes be unacceptable, because, for example, they would fail to protect adequately vital interests of certain groups within society. A model of democracy which entrenches rights

---

[34] See the essay by Hugh Corder in this collection (ch 6).

may then be adopted which entrenches the rights of certain groups to participate in and to some extent to control the political process. Consociation (in which particular social groups are given special representation in institutions) is such a model, and can be seen operating in different forms in Bosnia and Herzegovina, South Africa, and Northern Ireland. It usually involves the sharing of political power between representatives of the different groups, with the collective equality of peoples being regarded as fundamental. An example is provided by Northern Ireland, where the Good Friday Agreement and the Northern Ireland Act 1998 established a power-sharing arrangement (which has only been partially and fitfully successful) between parties representing broadly Protestant/Unionist interests and those representing generally Roman Catholic/Republican interests.[35] In Bosnia and Herzegovina (hereafter 'BiH') a similar but more complex and far-reaching form of consociation was put in place under the Constitution of BiH, forming Annex 4 to the General Framework Agreement for Peace in BiH (the Dayton/Paris Agreement) between parties broadly representing the three 'constituent peoples': Croats, Serbs, and Bosniacs (Muslims).

Consociation within a democratic constitutional system presents a number of problems. First, it is likely to entrench divisions rather than produce a common commitment to the welfare of the *demos* as a whole, because it penalizes people who do not define their identities by reference to one of the separate constituent peoples. Secondly, since it rewards constituent peoples rather than cross-community political platforms, it is likely to encourage politicians to seek support within single social groups rather than to try to build inter-group consensus or build on an overlapping consensus so far as one exists.[36] Thirdly, it tends to legitimate a system in which there are in reality several separate peoples rather than a single people which can be regarded as the sovereign *demos*. Fourthly, the power of the various peoples need not correspond to the level of popular support for the parties claiming to represent them or the size of the populations they claim to represent.

These problems can sometimes be alleviated to some extent by adopting an electoral system which rewards those people who express preferences for candidates across the ethnic spectrum. Typically the best strategy for achieving this will involve a multiple transferable preference voting system in which votes for party lists can be combined with votes for individual candidates within and across party lists.[37] This has a reasonable chance of achieving a situation in which parties, in

---

[35] This is the subject of the essay by Professor Christopher McCrudden in this volume.

[36] On the role of 'overlapping consensus' in building a liberal democracy, see John Rawls, *Political Liberalism* (1993) 133–72.

[37] See Arend Lijphart, 'Electoral systems, party systems and conflict management in segmented societies', in Robert A. Schrire (ed.), *Critical Choices for South Africa: an Agenda for the 1990s* (1990) ch 1; Arend Lijphart, 'Self-determination versus pre-determination of ethnic minorities in power-sharing systems', in Will Kymlicka (ed.), *The Rights of Minority Cultures* (1995) 275–87; Sumantra Bose, *Bosnia after Dayton: Nationalist Partition and International Intervention* (2002) ch 5.

order to succeed, must obtain support from all groups or a range of groups in society, thus forcing them towards moderation in their ethnic or nationalist policies.

However, it will have that effect only if a large enough proportion of individual electors have a sufficiently strong desire for moderation and understand how to use the system tactically in order to elect politicians who will share that desire and regard adherence to such policies as being in their long-term interests. There must also be either parties and candidates standing for election on the basis of moderate policies, or such a low chance of any one party or political grouping achieving an overall majority in the elections for legislatures and/or executives that it is virtually inevitable that the party commanding a plurality of votes will be forced to compromise with other parties holding opposed viewpoints in order to govern. If these conditions are not satisfied naturally, it might be possible to produce them artificially.

For example, in BiH the Constitutional Court has held that all parties must include in their party lists candidates drawn from all three constituent peoples in order to make possible the working of the protections for the vital interests of the constituent peoples in the legislative process.[38] The objective of protecting those vital interests cannot entirely override the principle, embodied in the Preamble to, and Article 1 of, Constitution of BiH, that the country is a democratic State. The Constitutional Court has refused to strike down laws of the Parliament of the Federation of Bosnia and Herzegovina (FBiH)[39] passed when the Serb caucus in the House of Peoples[40] had only nine Serb Delegates instead of the 17 required by the Constitution. Although this effectively prevented the Serb caucus from exercising its constitutional right to delay or impose a special-majority requirement on proposed legislation that they held to be destructive of a vital interest of the Serb people, the Constitutional Court held, *inter alia*, that: (i) the laws were not destructive of any vital Serb interest; (ii) the procedure for passing the laws by a simple majority in the absence had been complied with; and (iii) as the limited number of Serb delegates was the result of the operation of the democratic electoral process in the cantons, the principle of respect for electoral democracy in that case made the laws valid, notwithstanding the size of the Serb caucus being smaller than had been contemplated by the FBiH Constitution.[41]

[38] See Case No. U-35/03, decision of 28 January 2005, Constitutional Court of Bosnia and Herzegovina, available at http://www.ccbh.ba/?lang=en&page=decisions/byyear/2005.

[39] Bosnia and Herzegovina is a federation of two entities. One, the FBiH, is itself a federation of 10 cantons with a significant degree of self-government. The other entity, the Republika Srpska, is unitary.

[40] The Parliament of FBiH is bicameral, as the Constitutional Court held in Case No. U-5/98 (the 'constituent peoples case') that a unicameral Parliament offered insufficient protection for the vital interests of the three constituent peoples (Bosniacs [Muslims], Croats, and Serbs) in the territory. According to the Constitution of FBiH, the Delegates to the House of Peoples are to consist of 17 members from each of the constituent peoples, selected by cantonal legislatures from among their own members.

[41] Case No. U-5/05, decision of 27 January 2006, Constitutional Court of Bosnia and Herzegovina. The decision is available on the Court's website, http://www.ustavnisud.ba.

At the same time, the Constitutional Court reminded the political parties in the FBiH of the requirement, flowing from its earlier decision,[42] that parties must include members of all constituent peoples among their candidates. Where the electoral law allows voters to pick and choose among the candidates put forward by parties, this makes it impossible for a party's ruling clique to guarantee that only candidates from one constituent people will be elected on its ticket by manipulating the order in which candidates appear in the party list. It offers a chance of increasing the number of successful Serb candidates in cantonal elections in the FBiH, and hence the number of Serb delegates to the FBiH House of Peoples. Nevertheless, the evidence so far in BiH is that voters tend to vote for candidates from their own constituent people, or for entire party lists, reducing the practical efficacy of the mechanism in both the entities of BiH.[43]

BiH also illustrates a fifth problem for democratic consociation flowing from the need to protect the interests of each of the constituent peoples in BiH against the nationalisms of the others. This has been achieved largely by giving special representation to the peoples in executive and legislative bodies within BiH, and allowing the caucuses representing each constituent people in the various legislative bodies in the country to exercise what is in practical terms a veto over legislative proposals which the caucus considers to be destructive of the vital interests of their people. The State's Parliamentary Assembly includes a House of Peoples in which the delegates represent the constituent peoples.[44] The caucus of a people's delegates can delay or entirely block legislation by declaring it to be destructive of that people's vital interests, subject to a power of review by the Constitutional Court of the regularity of that declaration.[45] This arrangement, included in the Dayton Agreement as a means of safeguarding each of the constituent peoples against domination by the others, produces a legislature which is far better at blocking initiatives than approving them. It tends to emasculate the supreme and democratically- elected legislative body. What is more, the Constitutional Court in its decision in the *Constituent Peoples*[46] case has itself insisted that such arrangements are constitutionally required at the level of the entities by the structure of the Dayton constitution in order to advance the goal of the collective equality of peoples,[47] and equivalent provisions have been made at the level of the cantons in the FBiH and in municipality legislatures in the Republika Srpska.

There are similar power-sharing arrangements in executive bodies in BiH, with a multi-member Presidency of the State, the chairmanship of which rotates

---

[42] Case No. U-35/03, n 38 above.

[43] See Bose, *Bosnia after Dayton: Nationalist Partition and International Intervention*, n 37 above. The position in Northern Ireland is a little different: see the essay by Christopher McCrudden in this volume (ch 15).   [44] Constitution of Bosnia and Herzegovina, Art. IV.1.

[45] ibid, Art. IV.3(d)–(f); Decision of the Constitutional Court in Case U-4/05 of July 2005, available at http://www.ccbh.ba/?lang=en&page=decisions/byyear/2005.

[46] Third Partial Decision in Case No. U-5/98, decision of 1 July 2000, available at http://www.ccbh.ba/?lang=en&page=decisions/byyear/2000.

[47] See Decision of the Constitutional Court in the Third Partial Decision in Case U-5/98, ibid.

among the members representing the various constituent peoples.[48] Similar principles with their attendant potential problems govern appointments of staff to most public bodies in BiH. These arrangements present a danger that professionalism will take second place to ethnic representation. The idea of equality of peoples has become so entrenched in the national psyche that legislation to establish a new structure for broadcasting in BiH was said by the Croat Caucus in the House of Peoples of the Parliamentary Assembly of BiH to be destructive of the vital interests of the Croat people, partly because the proposed law did not guarantee an equal balance between the constituent peoples on the Boards which were to run the broadcasting services. If upheld, this would have imposed a super-majoritarian requirement before the legislation could have been passed by the House of Peoples. It was very unlikely that the super-majority could have been achieved. This is an example of the way in which the principle of equal protection for the vital interests of each of the constituent peoples, imposed by the Constitutional Court in 2000 in its decision in the *Constituent Peoples*[49] case, can effectively derail necessary legislation if applied formulaically. In the event, the Constitutional Court decided that the legislation was not destructive of a vital interest. Although the equal representation of the constituent peoples was legitimately regarded as a vital interest in relation to legislation and some executive functions, that principle did not apply with equal strength to the organization of bodies with merely administrative or regulatory functions. It would be for the Boards to ensure that they organized their work and the broadcasting schedules to give equal weight to the interests of all three constituent peoples.[50]

The result of these complex systems for consociation may be effective in protecting sectoral interests within the State, and democratic in the narrow sense that the membership of legislatures and executives is the outcome of an electoral process based on the idea of universal adult suffrage. However, it is a highly qualified form of democracy, and seems calculated to produce inaction rather than action. This need not be a bad thing. In the US the constitutional system of checks and balances was designed to limit the capacity of federal authorities to interfere with the decision-making competence of the States. In Bosnia and Herzegovina it is designed to ensure that the political leaderships of the constituent peoples cannot achieve by political means the dominance that escaped them despite military action and genocide in the early 1990s. But the method of pursuing this laudable objective has often produced a state of democratic stalemate, in which essential

---

[48] At the time of finalizing the text of this essay (December 2006) a case is pending before the Constitutional Court of Bosnia and Herzegovina by which one member of the Presidency is seeking to test the compatibility with the Constitution of BiH of the decision by a majority of the Presidency to continue the long-running litigation before the International Court of Justice between Bosnia and Herzegovina and Serbia and Montenegro. A decision on this is expected in 2007, but the next round of hearings in The Hague took place in February 2006, and judgment is awaited.

[49] See n 46 above.

[50] See Case U-10/05, decision of 22 July 2005, Constitutional Court of Bosnia and Herzegovina, available at http://www.ccbh.ba/?lang=en&page=decisions/byyear/2005.

decisions cannot be taken. Occasionally, the Constitutional Court can help to break the deadlock, but too frequently it has been left to the High Representative to intervene, as a kind of *deus ex machina*, to impose legislation and other reforms necessary for the stability of the State, for example to establish a State border service and to reform important State institutions.[51] When the Constitutional Court has taken the exceptional step of unblocking the legislative logjam, as in the case relating to the draft broadcasting law mentioned above, it has had to restrict the operation of the principle of collective equality of the constituent peoples in the legislative process in order to do so. The principle of collective equality, articulated by the Court for very good reasons in its *Constituent Peoples* case in 2000, is beginning to seem to many observers of and participants in the constitutional and political systems of BiH as part of the problem rather than the cure.

The effect of giving great constitutional weight to this ethnic political pluralism in BiH, and also in Northern Ireland, is to qualify ordinary notions of electoral democracy very significantly. It is not necessarily non-democratic on that account; a system may be more or less democratic, and there is always a tension between the pursuit of democracy in one form or another and the pursuit of other valuable standards or objectives. Furthermore, democracy is only one of many virtues a constitution can display, and the job of the constitutional drafter or operator is to hold the ring as satisfactorily as possible in the circumstances between the various values in play. We can show this by considering the link between democracy and popular sovereignty.

Democracy and Popular Sovereignty

At its most fundamental democracy is linked to the idea of popular sovereignty (power residing ultimately in 'the people', or *demos*, who authorize particular actors to exercise it on their behalves). This popular sovereignty may be of two kinds. The people may be sovereign in the constitutive sense: their approval (actual or notional) provides the State with its initial identity and authority, without the need for them to do anything in particular once the State is operational. Alternatively, or in addition, the people may exercise continuing, active sovereignty, manifested in their choice of governors, the accountability of the governors to them for the use of political power, and/or a role as collective decision-makers on controversial questions of policy or constitutional change.

The latter form of popular sovereignty may be expressed in forms of democracy which allow for limits on the acquisition or use of political power, as some limits on institutions and those who inhabit them (or even, perhaps, on the collective decision-making competence of the people as a whole) are needed to ensure that they do not wrest continuing sovereign power from the people. However, the

---

[51] See David Feldman, 'European human rights and constitution-building in a post-conflict society: the case of Bosnia and Herzegovina' (2005) 7 Cambridge Yearbook of European Legal Studies 101.

former type of popular sovereignty does not necessarily entail such controls. Even a belief that all power ultimately derives from the people can be coupled with arrangements to allow elected officers to make decisions after consultation with, rather than under day-to-day control of, the *demos*.

The same seems to me to be true of the specific form of democracy which has been called 'deliberative' democracy. In Cass Sunstein's model of democracy,[52] the key requirements are for a body of politically active citizens, a responsive legislature and executive, and the time and space for dialogue (between institutions, within institutions, and between citizens and institutions) during which deliberation can occur. However, decision-making institutions consisting of members chosen by and/or accountable to the people retain both the power to make final decisions and responsibility for doing so. This means that deliberative democracy can be pursued within a wide variety of political structures. Parliamentary responsible government or presidential government can accommodate it equally; so can unitary or federal structures, confederal or consociational arrangements, different kinds of separation of powers, and so on. The principle of deliberation only requires the members to open their institutions and processes to a public (but not open-ended) debate to which all citizens can have access. Moreover, deliberative democracy does not necessarily require that each individual citizen can participate in the debate on every issue. It demands a process for ensuring that all relevant information and points of view are taken into account, so the debate must encompass the widest possible diversity of approaches, not universal participation.

This is an uncomfortable conclusion for many people, and they have come up with various ways round the problem.

Attempts to Make Deliberative Democracy Incorporate Some Form of Popular Sovereignty and Constitutionalism as Limitations on Political Power

Deliberative democracy and the idea of pre-commitment

One can adopt a model of democracy which incorporates some form of restriction or conditions on the freedom of the majority to get its way. Cass Sunstein is one of those who advance a model of deliberative democracy which allows for serious, persistent disagreement to be accommodated within a framework which allows for decision-making in an informed way and does not entrench outcomes.[53] In Sunstein's view, constitutions should foster the conditions needed to ensure that the widest possible range of views and options is available as a way of moderating group dynamics which would tend towards extremism and ensuring respect for disagreement. Judges have a role in keeping the debate open, not in closing it off. The exception, allowing (for example) for the enforcement of rights going beyond

---

[52] Sunstein, *Designing Democracy: What Constitutions Do*, n 11 above.   [53] ibid, 1–66.

those necessary for deliberation, is that judges may legitimately uphold other rights (such as a right to privacy) if that is part of a 'pre-commitment' by members of society to a view of the relationship between people in that society at the time the constitution was negotiated.[54] If a society commits itself to this view, Sunstein argues, there is no conflict between constitutionalism and democracy. Instead, the constitution will uphold the inner morality of a deliberative democracy.

However, it is difficult to sustain the idea that a pre-commitment does not exclude continuing popular sovereignty. Even a pre-commitment to constitution-alism as process limits the extent to which a popular sovereign can impose views on future political societies. Any pre-commitment is likely to give rise to questions as to the justification for treating a pre-commitment as having continuing force over generations. John Rawls faced such a problem when developing his idea of justice as incorporating a pre-commitment to certain rights and to the difference principle from the idea of a notional agreement in an artificial 'original position'. He concluded that the essence of political liberalism is that it is a system of fair co-operation over time; but it is not clear why this should make the pre-commitment binding on those who were not parties to the negotiation leading to it.[55]

Redefining democracy to include other values

Other people want to write other special restrictions into the definition of democ-racy so as to argue that their preferred view of the proper limitations on political power is consistent with a right to democracy. Arguments of this kind present many different values, including the rule of law or the protection of human rights, as intrinsic to democracy.[56] The desire to stretch the idea of democracy is particu-larly strong when social divisions in a society lead political actors to design a form of political structure which requires different social, nationalistic, or ethnic groups to share power.

The example of BiH indicates the practical problems facing any attempt to make a form of democracy work in a divided society. It shows the tensions which arise between different objectives and values. Protecting the interests of particular groups, limiting power, protecting human rights: these are all legitimate object-ives of a politico-legal system, and do not necessarily pull in the same direction as a drive towards a model of democracy. We should not define democracy in such as way as to accommodate other values which are essential to the legitimacy of a con-stitutional settlement at a particular time and place but are in reality in tension with the ideal of democracy as the sovereignty of and rule by one cohesive *demos*. Seeking to incorporate other values (for example, security and collective equality

---

[54] ibid, 96–99.

[55] See John Rawls, *A Theory of Justice* (revised ed., 1999) ch III; John Rawls, *Political Liberalism*, n 36 above, lecture I; Ronald Dworkin, 'The original position', in Norman Daniels (ed.), *Reading Rawls* (1975) ch 2, on reasons why the agreement reached in the original position might not bind people once they emerge from it.

[56] See Morison, 'Models of democracy: from representation to participation?', n 30 above.

of constituent peoples, or human rights, including the right of refugees and displaced persons to return to their homes of origin) into democracy obscures the diversity and complexity of the ideals and values which must be given effect in the constitution of any State which is not socially, ethnically, religiously, economically, and culturally homogeneous. A willingness to debate the proper constitutional balance between the pursuit of different values is an essential part of constitutionalism; indeed, it underpins any worthwhile view of the good State. The concept of democracy offers guidance as to the fairest way of conducting that debate, but it does not follow that the values being debated are intrinsically or continently necessary elements of democracy. Pretending that the values form part of democracy hides the need for that debate, and may even prevent it from occurring by making it seem that, by accepting democracy, people have also necessarily accepted that there is only one possible resolution for the tension between the other values.

Human Rights

Using human rights to shape political systems has been criticized on a variety of grounds. It is sometimes said that human rights are anti-democratic, in that they restrict the freedom of decision of the sovereign *demos*. In this section we examine the relationship between human rights, constitutionalism, and democracy. Human rights first interact with constitutional principles of all kinds. The status within a municipal legal system of rights in international law will depend on the extent to which the municipal constitutional order is receptive to international legal norms (which is likely to be influenced by the place of monist or dualist theories within the constitutional order), and on the willingness and constitutional competence of officials of the system to legislate for or incorporate the right within the municipal system.[57] If a right is institutionalized within a municipal legal system, there may still be difficulties relating to the availability of remedies (for example, in respect of primary legislation or constitutional provisions which violate the right) under particular constitutional regimes. For example, in the UK the Human Rights Act 1998 embodies a compromise between parliamentary sovereignty and human rights which is not always satisfactory from the point of view of either of them. These compromises reflect the relationship between human rights and constitutionalism.

Scholars and judges such as Professor T. R. S. Allan, Professor Ronald Dworkin, and Sir John Laws have advanced a model of what, in common-law countries, has come to be known as 'common-law constitutionalism', although it has echoes in many constitutional systems. The idea is that certain principles, including particularly (in common-law systems) equal concern and respect and procedural

---

[57] See David Feldman, 'The internationalisation of public law and its impact on the United Kingdom', in Jeffrey Jowell and Dawn Oliver (eds), *The Changing Constitution* (6th ed., 2007) ch 5.

fairness, and respect for rights as moral imperatives, are inherent in the constitution and form the basis for the legitimacy of both the constitutional and legal systems and, hence, for the validity of laws. They have therefore argued that some fundamental rights are part and parcel of constitutionalism generally and the rule of law in particular, and should shape all judicial decision-making. They point out that certain rights, such as the right to a fair hearing and the right to be free of retrospective legislation, are hallmarks of any rational system of adjudication and constitutional law. The rule of law would be impossible without them.[58] Some have also argued that the right to participate in decisions affecting one's interests is valuable because it respects the dignity of the person affected as a participant in decision-making, and so is inherently important.[59] It is undeniable that fair procedures and the capacity to predict with reasonable confidence how the law and judicial decisions will affect one's interests are fundamentally important to the ability of a legal system to perform its role. It is equally true that giving affected parties the right to participate in proceedings both helps to secure the accuracy of decisions—that is why Professor Lon Fuller regarded such guarantees as part of the 'inner morality of law'[60]—and recognizes people's moral significance.

However, one must be aware of the limits of this. A broad range of human rights is not necessary for constitutionalism in either of the senses outlined above. One form of constitutionalism requires limitations on political power, but they need not be legally enforceable (for example, they might take the form of tinkering with electoral systems) and, if they do have legal force, they need not take the form of rights or derive from the common law: distribution of power through federalism and consociation are equally likely to limit the use of that political power, and to do so in systems far removed from the common law tradition.[61] Constitution as process may need some rights, or equivalent norms, but only those which are necessary to establish and protect the process of discourse among the relevant interpretative or decision-making community. The idea of democracy cannot provide the philosophical basis for the institutionalization of wide-ranging human rights, beyond those actually needed in order to make a particular model of democracy work.[62] At the national level it is possible that, empirically, States with some form of democratic politics are more likely to respect human rights

---

[58] See T. R. S. Allan, 'The Limits of Parliamentary Sovereignty' [1985] PL 614; Sir John Laws, 'Law and Democracy' [1995] PL 72; Mark Elliott, 'Reconciling Constitutional Rights and Constitutional Orthodoxy' [1997] Cambridge Law Journal 474; Ronald Dworkin, *Law's Empire* (1986); Jeffrey Jowell, 'The Rule of Law today', in Jeffrey Jowell and Dawn Oliver (eds), *The Changing Constitution* (6th ed., 2007) ch 1.

[59] For discussion, see Denis Galligan, *Due Process and Fair Procedures: A Study of Administrative Procedures* (1996) 75–82.

[60] Lon L. Fuller, *The Morality of Law* (revised ed., 1969), Lecture II.

[61] In civilian systems, the values tend to be seen as being either supra-constitutional (as in France) or inherent in the Constitution but with higher authority than other provisions in the Constitution (as in the Federal Republic of Germany).

[62] John Hart Ely, *Democracy and Distrust: a Theory of Judicial Review* (1980).

than other States, although I do not have evidence at hand to evaluate that hypothesis; but at the international level there is no general link between democracy and the protection of human rights, because so few international institutions are in any way democratized.

On the other hand, constitutionalism in both the senses outlined above—as a commitment to a form of discourse for resolving disputes, and as a set of limitations on political power—is an essential precondition for the effective protection of human rights in either international or municipal law. Human rights in the form of fundamental rights and obligations flowing from legal norms depend on the rule of law if they are to receive appropriate weight in either political or legal discourses. Unless parties to a discourse agree that legal norms are entitled to respect (albeit not unqualified respect) and that they should be identified in accordance with criteria or procedures legitimated by constitutional norms, there will never be authoritative means of settling disagreements as to which norms, rights and obligations are authoritative, or as to their formulations and any qualifications. The rule of law—as a commitment to respect for and fair adjudication on and enforcement of legal norms—is needed for human rights norms to be given appropriate weight, and is one of the ingredients in the attitude of mind which makes up constitutionalism. Indeed, the UN General Assembly asserted in the third paragraph of the Preamble to the Universal Declaration of Human Rights in 1948 that, 'it is essential, if man is not to be compelled to have recourse, as a last resort, to rebellion against tyranny and oppression, that human rights should be protected by the rule of law'.

The dependence of human rights on constitutionalism extends beyond the field of legal enforceability. It applies equally to the political process. If people want to make human rights part of political discourse they depend on finding common ground for understanding the rights and debating the weights to be attached to them, both in relation to each other and as against other social interests and constitutional values such as democracy. For this to happen, participants in the democratic and constitutional process, including politicians, must be willing to debate the place of human rights and their identities in the context of the framework of values, procedures, and purposes that constitute the constitution. We must share a commitment to thinking about human rights issues in constitutional terms. The conclusion may be that such rights form no part, or only a limited part, of the constitution, but without the attitude of mind which I have called constitutionalism there is no point even discussing the matter. One of the advantages flowing from incorporating human rights standards in a constitutional system is that it provides a focus for discussing those issues and their implications within the political system.[63]

This does not mean that the arguments will have a single authoritative conclusion. Finality is a feature of adjudication within the structure of a system of

---

[63] David Feldman, 'Injecting law into politics and politics into law: legislative and judicial perspectives on constitutional human rights' (2005) 35 Common Law World Review 103.

authoritative and, for the parties, final decision-makers, although the outcome is always likely to be open to further political or legal discussion and reconsideration. Finality is not a characteristic of political debate. In politics the participants have to strive for an outcome or acceptance of a principle knowing that any success they achieve will continue to be contested, and will only ever be provisional and temporary. In States where core constitutional rules are to some degree entrenched against amendment or repeal, it is plausible to regard those rules as being more settled and likely to retain their authority for longer than similar rules in other States. However, it is very rare to find a constitution in which rights, norms or values are permanently protected against amendment or repeal. There are some express examples. For instance, Article 79(3) of the *Grundgesetz* of the FRG provides: 'Amendments of this Basic Law affecting the division of the Federation into *Länder*, the participation on principle of the *Länder* in legislation, or the basic principles laid down in Articles 1 and 20 shall be inadmissible.'[64] In BiH, Article X.2 of the Constitution provides: '*Human Rights and Fundamental Freedoms*. No amendment to this Constitution may eliminate or diminish any of the rights and freedoms referred to in Article II of this Constitution or alter the present paragraph'. The drafters of any constitution can decide that some provisions or values are too important, given the historical and social circumstances in which the constitution is being prepared, to be subject to amendment.

There are also a few cases in which courts have interpreted constitutions as making it impossible for constitutive or legislative bodies to amend or repeal the constitution in ways that are (regarded by the courts as being) incompatible with the fundamental structure of the pre-existing constitution. In India, the Supreme Court has developed two doctrines of non-amendability, despite the absence of any express constitutional provision preventing amendment of the Constitution. In *Golak Nath v State of Punjab*[65] the court held that fundamental rights in the Constitution are not amendable, despite the absence of any provision in the Constitution expressly protecting them. In *Kesavananda Bhurathi v State of Kerala*[66] the court developed a different principle: fundamental features of the Constitution, rather than fundamental rights, cannot be amended.

Hegde and Mukherjea JJ in the Supreme Court wrote:

'Our constitution is not a mere political document. It is essentially a social document. It is based on a social philosophy and every social philosophy like every religion has two main features, namely, basic and circumstantial. The former remains constant but the latter is subject to change. The core of a religion always remains constant but the practices associated with it may change. Likewise, a constitution like ours contains certain features which are so essential that they cannot be changed or destroyed. In any event, it cannot be destroyed from within. In other words, one cannot legally use the Constitution to destroy itself.'[67]

---

[64] Translation in Finer *et al*, *Comparing Constitutions*, n 14 above, 164.
[65] AIR 1967 SC 1643.   [66] AIR 1973 SC 1461.
[67] ibid, 1624, para 667. See to the same effect *Smt. Indira Gandhi v Raj Narain* AIR 1975 SC 2299 and *Minerva Mills v Union of India* AIR 1980 SC 1789, and the discussion by Burt

These examples illustrate the special needs of particular polities, and judicial action to create a bar to amending the constitution is always politically controversial and likely to be the subject of continued political constitutional debate and possibly alteration. Generally conclusions to constitutional debates about values and norms settle issues for the time being, but also provide the focus for a renewed debate about change either through constitutional amendments or in future adjudication. The US's constitution illustrates this. The decision of the Supreme Court in the *Dred Scott* case on the status of slaves was reversed by a constitutional amendment following the Civil War.[68] The decision of the Supreme Court that State legislation outlawing buggery was constitutionally valid[69] was reversed by the Supreme Court itself in *Lawrence v Texas*,[70] holding that the controlling constitutional value at stake was liberty. The method of appointment of Justices of the Supreme Court, life appointment by the choice of the US President with approval by the Senate on grounds of political sympathy as much as legal acumen, makes it very likely that there will be significant changes in the political balance of the Court and, perhaps, in the judicial philosophies of its Justices at least once in every generation. We are likely to be embarking on such a period, with John Roberts CJ succeeding Rehnquist CJ, and O'Connor J being replaced on her retirement.

It follows that the place of human rights in constitutional processes depends heavily on the actors in the system adopting the attitude to debate that I have called 'constitutionalism'. The connection between the two is practical, not logical: from a practical point of view, constitutionalism is a precondition for the effectiveness of human rights as instruments of constitutional discourse, either in courts or in political processes.

But one can go further. Experience in BiH, Afghanistan, Kosovo, and elsewhere makes it clear that it is essential to establish the rule of law if democracy is to have a chance of becoming established. Democracy requires a certain level of social order and stability and a guarantee that decisions democratically reached will be fairly implemented. Democrats ask people to commit themselves to a system which severely limits their free choice of methods to advance their political beliefs and interests, in exchange for a right to participate in and have their points of view considered in the course of decision-making. People will not rationally be prepared to accept this unless they are confident that decisions will be fairly implemented. This requires a fair and reasonably effective police and prosecutorial system, and judges who are appointed on the basis of ability and are given enough security (in terms of salary, protection against removal, and protection against intimidation) to free them from pressures to act in a partisan or corrupt way. The

Neuborne, 'The Supreme Court of India' (2003) 1 *International Journal of Constitutional Law* 476–510, 485–95.

[68] See *Scott v Sandford* 60 US 393 (1857), and Fourteenth Amendment to the Constitution of the USA.   [69] *Bowers v Hardwick* 478 US 186 (1986).
[70] 539 US 558 (2003).

normative power of the rule of law may be in need of re-theorization after being compromised by its abuse by international actors in transitional States,[71] but without these practical manifestations of the rule of law, democracy has no practical chance of flourishing.

Conclusion

There is widespread international support for developing new and old constitutions in the direction of maximizing the incidence of some model of constitutional democracy (in other words, the use of constitutional standards which recognize elements of popular sovereignty while at the same time limiting the extent to which political actors can wield power conferred on them from the *demos*). However, the ideals of constitutionalism and democracy are both contested, and there is no general agreement on the kind of constitutionalism or the model of democracy which should be adopted, or on a common set of values that are to guide the making and operation of constitutions. Nor is there even consensus as to the criteria for deciding which model of constitutionalism or democracy should guide the drafting of constitutions in any given set of social, political, economic, or military circumstances. Even a leading proponent of world constitutionalism, Bruce Ackerman,[72] has argued for law and the constitution to be excluded from the field of executive action to combat a perceived state of emergency caused by a threat of terrorism against the US.[73]

Nevertheless, there is a feature common to all these positions: namely, a commitment to addressing areas of profound disagreement through rule-based procedures for dialogue, and sometimes (where there is sufficient agreement) to formalizing the outcome of conflict over values in rules which may be enforceable at the expense (usually only temporarily) of further political conflict. Debate over the appropriate models is one of the engines of constitutional change and legitimation. A good constitution is the outcome of an often difficult process of negotiation and debate over the relative importance of the values and the best ways of giving effect to them in prevailing circumstances. The more difficult the circumstances (for example, in States in transition), the more debate should be required.[74]

A State's constitution may, for good reasons, put certain values or commitments beyond the scope of ordinary, democratic, political processes. A decision to this may be legitimated by values or objectives such as human rights, individual or

---

[71] See the essay by Christine Bell, Colm Campbell, and Fionnuala Ní Aoláin in this volume.
[72] See Bruce Ackerman, 'The rise of world constitutionalism' (1997) 83 Virginia Law Review 771.
[73] See Bruce Ackerman, 'The Emergency Constitution' (2004) 113 Yale Law Journal 1029.
[74] See Heinz Klug, *Constituting Democracy: Law, Globalism and South Africa's Political Reconstruction* (2000), esp. ch 6.

collective equality, or the need to protect society from violence. It does not make those values and objectives part of democracy. Indeed, it restricts the field within which democratic methods of decision-making operate (whatever model of democracy operates in that place at that time). However, it need not be inimical to all models of democracy. For example, protecting constituent peoples' interests in BiH allows them all to play a fuller part in the democratic process if we see democracy as a process in which a plurality of groups battle to advance their interests through national or local governance. In any case, a State may be more or less democratic, and being less democratic may be no bad thing if as a result other important values can be better protected.

For these reasons, we should recognize that a good State, and hence a good constitution, draws its legitimacy from a number of normative sources. It is naïve to suppose that there is only one supreme criterion for the legitimacy of constitutions, whether democracy, human rights, the rule of law, or public safety, and that any other criteria must be disregarded if they cannot be shown to be consistent with, and preferably part of, it. Many values and objectives have a proper role in making constitutions and States legitimate and effective, and each can properly be the basis for a governing norm in relation to different kinds of activity or circumstances. They pull in different directions, and there will be more or less compelling arguments for giving one or another greater weight in relation to particular questions. Constitutional designers and actors (including politicians and judges) have to use political and moral, as well as legal, judgement to make sensible decisions about the relative weights of the values in specific contexts.

21

Reshaping Constitutionalism

*Murray Hunt**

Introduction

Traditional ideas of constitutionalism in the UK have been shaped and constrained by the concept and language of parliamentary sovereignty. This essay seeks to contribute to the debate about the need for a radically reshaped notion of constitutionalism which distances itself from the doctrine of sovereignty and which reflects the changing nature and locus of power in the modern polity. In so doing, it takes as its starting point the powerful critique of orthodox constitutional thinking put forward by Morison and Livingstone in their 1995 book, *Reshaping Public Power*.[1] The central theme of this work was that even those interested in reforming the constitution had failed to appreciate the fundamental nature of the changes which had been taking place: the emergence of new forms of international and supra-national legal order, the leakage of public power to new and diffuse sites, and the extent to which power formerly exercised by the State was now in the hands of private entities regulated only by the contractual terms on which they happened to be engaged. The challenge thrown down for public law scholarship was that, to revive democratic and constitutional values, it was now necessary to move beyond the traditional narrow focus on curbing a domestic executive by traditional parliamentary mechanisms, and to undertake a more radical rethinking of constitutional premises. This essay aims to offer a partial snapshot of how well our public law has responded to this challenge.

The essay is in four parts. First, it argues that the very concept of 'sovereignty' has continued to be the biggest obstacle to any reshaping of our notions of constitutionalism. Secondly, it considers the concept of a 'culture of justification' as an alternative to sovereignty as an organizing concept in contemporary discussions

---

* The views expressed in this essay are personal to the author and do not purport to represent the views of any other person or institution.

[1] John Morison and Stephen Livingstone, *Reshaping Public Power: Northern Ireland and the British Constitutional Crisis* (1995).

about constitutionalism, and what progress has been made towards such a culture of justification in the UK in the last few years, in particular since the coming into force of the Human Rights Act (HRA) in 2000. Thirdly, it considers what role can be played by Parliament's Joint Committee on Human Rights (JCHR) in that shift. Finally, it briefly considers what should be the role of parliamentary debates about fundamental rights in a culture of justification.

The 'Sovereignty' Problem

In my view it has been the very idea of 'sovereignty' which has been the central obstacle to progress towards the radical reshaping of constitutionalism envisaged in Morison and Livingstone's work. English lawyers have shown a persistent weakness for the alluring idea of 'sovereignty' as a foundational concept. The conceptual neatness of sovereignty-derived thinking too readily seduces us into a conceptualization of public law in terms of competing supremacies, which in fact bears little relation to the way in which public power is now dispersed and shared between several layers of constitutional actors, all of which profess an identical commitment to a set of values which can loosely be termed democratic constitutionalism. The very language of our constitutional discourse therefore permits the co-existence of what should be the radically opposed narratives of democratic positivism (rooted in the sovereignty of Parliament) and liberal constitutionalism (rooted in the sovereignty of the individual and the courts' task in protecting that sphere).

A review of both the literature and of court judgments concerning the HRA reveals a mixture of utterances from a democratic positivist's perspective on the one hand, with its formalistic notion of the separation of powers and romantic attachment to the idea of parliamentary sovereignty, and a liberal constitutionalist's perspective on the other, with its equally romantic judicial supremacism about the priority of individual rights and the sovereignty of the courts as their ultimate guardian. From the democratic positivist's perspective, Parliament remains the supreme law-giver in our constitutional arrangements and is therefore the final arbiter of the meaning of Convention rights, and can exercise its sovereignty by defining what those rights mean in particular contexts.[2] For the democratic positivist it is only an expression of the same foundational premise that in this legal universe Parliament can also delegate to executive and administrative decision-makers a zone of decision-making which is beyond the reach of judicial review because it is within some irreducible core of discretionary judgment. From

---

[2] See eg K. Ewing, 'The Human Rights Act and Parliamentary Democracy' (1999) MLR 79; J.A.G. Griffith, 'The Common Law and the Political Constitution' (2001) LQR 43.

the liberal constitutionalist's perspective, on the other hand, the courts are the final arbiter of whether a Convention right has been or is being violated, as they are the guardians of the area of inviolability into which public authorities cannot step, and there is therefore no room for judicial deference to democratic decision-makers, including Parliament.[3]

More interesting by far, however, than the existence of this spectrum of views is the fact that, despite their radically different theoretical underpinnings, the two views are often espoused by the same judge or commentator, depending on the issue they are addressing or whether they are seeking to justify judicial interference or abstention in a particular case. Many examples could be cited, but for present purposes it suffices to contrast Lord Hoffmann's invocation of liberal constitutionalism in his robust defence of the sovereign role of the courts in defending the individual's personal sovereignty against invasion by the majority,[4] and his invocation of, amongst other things, democratic positivism as a justification for treating as non-justiciable by the courts certain decisions 'entrusted by Parliament' to executive or administrative decision-makers.[5] Although Jowell does not agree with Lord Hoffmann's view that courts should defer on democratic grounds to the legislature on matters of public policy, the reliance on both democratic positivism and liberal constitutionalism is also evident in his account, in which the courts' constitutional role is said to be derived not from the very nature of democracy itself but from an exercise of Parliament's sovereign will in enacting the Human Rights Act.[6]

This is the contemporary manifestation of our Diceyan inheritance: a constitutional discourse which selectively invokes democratic positivism and liberal constitutionalism in order to justify or explain a particular decision, but which lacks an overarching coherent vision of democratic constitutionalism in which the apparent contradiction of these foundational commitments is explicitly confronted and an attempt made to reconcile them without resort to the language of sovereignty. So long as we are dependent on crude notions of sovereignty and authority for our underlying conceptions of law and legality, our public law will remain condemned to this perpetual lurching between democratic positivism and liberal constitutionalism.

---

[3] See eg R. Clayton, 'Regaining a Sense of Proportion: The Human Rights Act and the Proportionality Principle' (2001) EHRLR 504; I. Leigh, 'Taking Rights Proportionately: Judicial Review, the Human Rights Act and Strasbourg' (2002) PL 265.

[4] See eg *R v Secretary of State for the Home Dept., ex p. Simms and O'Brien* [2000] 2 AC 115; 'The Separation of Powers' (2002) JR 137, paras 12, 13 and 17.

[5] See eg *Secretary of State for the Home Department v Rehman* [2001] UKHL 47, [2001] 3 WLR 877; *Alconbury Developments Ltd v Secretary of State for the Environment, Transport and the Regions* [2001] 2 WLR 1389; 'The Separation of Powers', n 5 above, paras 9–11.

[6] Jeffrey Jowell, 'Beyond the Rule of Law: Towards Constitutional Judicial Review' (2000) PL 672.

A 'Culture of Justification'

It is clear that both the Government and Parliament in 1998 intended the HRA to bring about change of the order of a cultural transformation. But what type of 'human rights culture' did the HRA envisage?

The HRA is an experiment in combining both judicial and legislative models of rights protection, aiming to escape the confines of either legislative supremacy on the one hand or judicial supremacy on the other. One of the most important features of the HRA is that it begins from the premise that in today's conditions both the courts and the political branches share a commitment both to representative democracy and to certain rights, freedoms and basic values, including those which are enshrined in the ECHR. The important role accorded to Parliament in the scheme of the Act is an important feature of the Government's chosen model for giving effective protection to Convention rights and is a significant indicator of the type of human rights culture which the Act contemplates.

The Act therefore has the potential to be the foundation for a more coherent vision of constitutionalism, one which combines an important role for courts in articulating and furthering the fundamental values to which society is committed at the same time as giving a meaningful role to the democratic branches and the administration in the definition and furtherance of those values. Obviously, change of the order of a cultural shift can only take place over time. What signs are there that the Act has begun to bring about such a shift?

In my view probably the greatest success which can be claimed for the HRA is the enormous progress which has been made towards what I will describe (following David Dyzenhaus) as a 'culture of justification'—a legal culture in which all exercises of power which impinge upon fundamental rights, interests or values require public justification by reference to reasons, that is, rational explanations for why a particular action or decision has been taken, or why there has been an omission to act. The HRA has the potential to accelerate a long overdue reconfiguration of our public law around this important concept of justification, reconceiving our conceptions of law and legality away from formalistic concepts such as the historic will of Parliament, the separation of powers and ultra vires towards more substantive concepts of value and reason.[7] Such a shift could equally well be described as the embrace of an attitude of 'constitutionalism'—or what Lord Steyn has described as 'our country becoming a true constitutional state'.

The first important step towards such a culture of justification was taken by the House of Lords in *Daly*.[8] Superficially, the decision in *Daly* merely established the

---

[7] See the work of David Dyzenhaus, and in particular his efforts to build on Etienne Mureinik's conception of legality as 'a culture of justification': see eg Dyzenhaus, 'Law as Justification: Etienne Mureinik's Conception of Legal Culture' (1998) 14 SAJHR 11.

[8] *Daly v Secretary of State for the Home Department* [2001] 2 WLR 1622.

relatively unremarkable proposition that under the HRA courts reviewing the legality of executive or administrative interferences with Convention rights must apply a proportionality test and not the traditional, deferential *Wednesbury* approach or even the more recent higher intensity 'anxious scrutiny'. This was unremarkable because so much had been obvious since the decision of the European Court of Human Rights in *Smith and Grady v UK*,[9] holding that the inadequacy of judicial review for the purposes of determining the applicants' Article 8 claim in *Smith v MOD*[10] was in breach of the right to an effective remedy under Article 13 ECHR. But the real insights in *Daly*, I would argue, are twofold and are crucially interrelated.

First, Lord Steyn explicitly recognized that, although applying the proportionality approach may only make a difference to the outcome in a handful of cases, it will not be possible to identify those cases unless the approach itself is properly applied. It is therefore crucial to the effective protection of Convention rights that the highly structured proportionality approach is properly understood and applied by both decision-makers and reviewing courts wherever Convention rights are in play.[11] The real point is, as Lord Steyn makes clear, that proportionality is not so much a 'test' or a 'standard' as a new type of approach to adjudication which subjects the justification for decisions to rigorous scrutiny in order to determine their legality. Understood in this way, *Daly* is a major landmark on the road to the development of a true 'culture of justification'.

The second insight in *Daly* is in the crucial observation that there is nevertheless still a difference between a proportionality approach and a full 'merits review'. This is of the utmost significance, because it preserves the very basis on which the legitimacy of both constitutional and administrative review depend in a democratic state: the recognition by judges that on judicial review they do not have primary responsibility, but a secondary responsibility to ensure that the primary decision-maker has acted in accordance with the requirements of legality.[12] *Daly* delivers this crucial insight, but leaves entirely open the question of how it should be worked out in practice. Public law's big task for the next few years will be how to give practical effect to this second insight in *Daly*, in a way which does not forfeit the first.

There is, in my view, one other towering landmark in this progress towards a culture of justification: the House of Lords decision in the derogation case.[13] The House of Lords held, by a majority of 8:1, that the UK's derogation from the right to liberty in Article 5 ECHR, and the power in section 23 of the Anti-terrorism

---

[9] (2000) 29 EHRR 493.   [10] [1996] QB 517.

[11] Para 28: 'It is therefore important that cases involving Convention rights must be analysed in the correct way.'

[12] See Dyzenhaus, n 7 above, 24–25 for a salutary reminder, from a South African perspective, that an instrumentalist approach to the justification for judicial review (contingent on whether the legislature or executive are good or bad at a particular point in time) will lead to inconsistency on this point.   [13] *A v Secretary of State for the Home Department* [2005] 2 AC 68.

Crime and Security Act 2001 to detain without trial foreign nationals who were suspected international terrorists, were incompatible with the Convention. It upheld the Government's claim that there is a 'public emergency threatening the life of the nation',[14] but held that the indefinite detention without trial of foreign nationals who were suspected international terrorists was not justified for two reasons. First, the measures were not 'strictly required by the exigencies of the situation', as required by Article 15(1) ECHR—they were disproportionate because they restricted the right to personal liberty more than was necessary to achieve the legislative objective of protecting security. Secondly, the measures were discriminatory because they only permitted detention of suspected international terrorists who are foreign nationals.[15]

The great significance of the case for present purposes lies in the majority's response to the Government's argument that the courts had no business judicially reviewing its anti-terrorism measures. The Attorney-General argued that as it was for Parliament and the Executive to assess the threat facing the nation, so it was for those bodies and not the courts to judge the response necessary to protect the security of the public; these were matters of a political character calling for an exercise of political and not judicial judgment; and it was not for the courts to usurp authority properly belonging elsewhere. Had that argument succeeded, it would have struck a serious blow to the development of a culture of justification. But it was roundly rejected by the majority. Lord Bingham did not accept the distinction drawn between democratic institutions and the courts. But most significantly of all, he did not invoke the HRA as being the source of the court's authority to review the legality of the measures. Rather, he relied on the very nature of democracy itself. He said:

'... the function of independent judges charged to interpret and apply the law is universally recognised as a cardinal feature of the modern democratic state, a cornerstone of the rule of law itself'.

This response was therefore impeccable in its articulation of a non-sovereignty-derived justification for the legitimacy of the judicial role in testing the justification offered for a measure with a drastic impact on individual liberty.

Only a few years ago it would have been unthinkable that courts would subject the Government's response to a threat to national security to such a rigorous process of public justification. Although in my view (and it appears Lord Bingham's) the jurisdiction to do so does not derive from the HRA, let us be in no doubt that the

[14] By 8 votes to 1, Lord Hoffmann holding that the threat of serious terrorist outrages did not constitute a threat 'to the life of the nation'.
[15] It is important to note that, although disproportionality and discrimination were distinct grounds on which the House of Lords found the derogation to be incompatible with the Convention, the different treatment of British nationals was treated by the House of Lords as one of the indicators of disproportionality—the fact that British nationals who were suspected international terrorists could not be detained suggested that indefinite detention without trial was not strictly required in order to meet the threat of terrorism.

Act has accelerated the arrival of the day when our highest court feels sufficiently confident in its own legitimacy to take this important step towards a proper culture of justification.

The Role of the JCHR in Bringing about a Culture of Justification

Parliament's Joint Committee on Human Rights has a potentially important role to play in bringing about the desired transformation to a culture of justification.

As part of its work, the JCHR examines every Government Bill presented to Parliament. As is well known, the HRA requires Ministers to certify to Parliament in respect of every Government Bill they introduce that they are satisfied that its provisions are compatible with the Convention rights. There was widespread disappointment at the time of the Act's passage that this provision did not go further and require Ministers to give their reasons for their view that the Bill is compatible with Convention rights. This was compounded when, to begin with, the standard form certificate of compatibility was accompanied in the Explanatory Notes to a Bill by a formulaic statement that the Minister had considered the implications for Convention rights and signed a statement of compatibility.

In practice, the JCHR has succeeded in going behind section 19 statements of compatibility in two ways. First, by asking carefully targeted questions of the Minister as to the reasons why a particular measure is considered to be compatible. Secondly, by persuading the Government to issue guidance to departments encouraging much fuller disclosure of views about Convention compatibility in the Explanatory Notes which accompany a Bill. But what evidence is there that the JCHR's legislative scrutiny work has made any contribution to the realization of a culture of justification?

Government departments do sometimes accept that there is a human rights compatibility problem when they respond to a letter from the Chair of the Committee about a Bill. This usually results in an undertaking to introduce an amendment to the Bill or, more frequently, to introduce further procedural safeguards in regulations, codes of practice or other guidance which the Bill in questions empowers the Minister to make. Occasionally amendments have been introduced to Bills as a direct result of questioning from the JCHR or criticism in its reports.

But measuring the success of the JCHR in helping to bring about a culture of justification by reference to concrete examples of Government measures having been dropped or amended would be too narrow. Two other, less tangible, criteria are surely relevant to judging the impact of the JCHR's work. First, to what extent has its work influenced the policy-making process within Government departments, thereby preventing measures being brought forward which raise serious compatibility issues? Secondly, to what extent has the work of the JCHR succeeded in flushing into the open the justifications relied on by the Government for inter-fering with human rights, thereby improving the quality of parliamentary debate of measures which engage human rights, and taking an important step towards the culture of public justification on which the effective protection of human rights ultimately depends?

On both these scores the evidence suggests that the JCHR has already made a significant impact on the greater protection of human rights. On the first meas-ure, David Feldman, writing recently in the Statute Law Review, argues that Government departments are now more sensitive to human rights standards than they were previously, and that as a result the number of legislative measures raising significant issues of compatibility with human rights has reduced.[16] On the second, it is certainly the case that the JCHR's reports are increasingly referred to in parliamentary debates on Bills, and there is now an expectation that the Government should respond to criticisms by the JCHR and that the response should be available to Parliament when it is debating the Bill. There are some signs that more members are now prepared to take up human rights compatibil-ity questions, with the assistance of JCHR reports, and less deterred by the mis-conception that human rights compatibility is a highly technical legal question on which only lawyers can speak with authority.

But one of the real constraints on the contribution so far made by the JCHR towards a culture of justification has been the very limited extent to which its reports are used in the course of litigation concerning the human rights compati-bility of legislation on which it has reported, or of executive or administrative action taken under such legislation. It remains the case that reports of the JCHR are only rarely referred to in cases in the higher courts. Greater use of JCHR reports by both lawyers and judges, where relevant to compatibility issues, could make a significant contribution towards a culture of justification. It is not that the views of the Committee necessarily have any great claim to deference from the courts, although as the product of careful deliberation amongst a group of parlia-mentarians with extensive experience and expertise in human rights they are cer-tainly worthy of *some* respect. But the reports and their appendices contain an extensive record of the Government's public justifications for interferences with Convention rights, as well as a human rights analysis of the adequacy of those jus-tifications. This is material that might well be of use when courts are determining compatibility questions.

However, this raises a tricky question for those who would advocate reshaping constitutionalism around the notion of a culture of justification: what is the rela-tionship between judicial and legislative scrutiny of the human rights compatibil-ity of legislation in such a culture of justification?

---

[16] David Feldman, 'The Impact of Human Rights on the UK Legislative Process' (2004) 25 Statute Law Review 91.

The Role of Parliamentary Debates in a Culture of Justification

Should a court which is considering the human rights compatibility of legislation regard reports of scrutiny committees and subsequent parliamentary debates about compatibility as being of any legal relevance to the issues it has to determine? In particular, are such debates and reports relevant to the question of whether the court should defer to the judgment of the legislature, and if so, how? In my view, parliamentary materials such as Committee Reports and parliamentary debates about compatibility must be relevant to courts when they are assessing the human rights compatibility of legislative measures.

The issue was considered by the House of Lords in *Wilson*.[17] It held that when determining the ECHR compatibility of legislation it would be permissible for a court to have regard to matters stated in Parliament, as recorded in Hansard, as a source of background information to enable the court, for example, to understand the nature and extent of the social problem at which the legislation is aimed. However, such legitimate reference to parliamentary materials was to be distinguished from reference to such debates in order to ascertain the reasons which led Parliament to enact a particular statutory provision. Lord Nicholls said:

'Beyond this use of Hansard as a source of background information, the content of parliamentary debates has no direct relevance to the issues the court is called upon to decide in compatibility cases and, hence, these debates are not a proper matter for investigation or consideration by the courts. In particular, it is a cardinal constitutional principle that the will of Parliament is expressed in the language used by it in its enactments. The proportionality of legislation is to be judged on that basis. The courts are to have due regard to the legislation as an expression of the will of Parliament. The proportionality of a statutory measure is not to be judged by the quality of the reasons advanced in support of it in the course of parliamentary debate, or by the subjective state of mind of individual ministers or other members. Different members may well have different reasons, not expressed in debates, for approving particular statutory provisions. They may have different perceptions of the desirability or likely effect of the legislation. Ministerial statements, especially if made ex tempore in response to questions, may sometimes lack clarity or be misdirected. Lack of cogent justification in the course of parliamentary debate is not a matter which 'counts against' the legislation on issues of proportionality. The court is called upon to evaluate the proportionality of the legislation, not the adequacy of the minister's exploration of the policy options or of his explanations to Parliament. The latter would contravene article 9 of the Bill of Rights. The court would then be presuming to evaluate the sufficiency of the legislative process leading up to the enactment of the statute.'[18]

To a human rights lawyer, this has an air of unreality about it. Much human rights adjudication is about evaluating in a principled way the cogency of the

---

[17]   *Wilson v First County Trust Ltd. (No. 2)* [2003] UKHL 40, [2004] 1 AC 816.
[18]   ibid, para 67.

justifications offered for interfering with rights. The ECHR frequently considers the quality of the reasoning relied on in support of a legislative measure when deciding compatibility questions. In *Hirst v UK*, for example, the ECHR considered the compatibility of the UK's blanket disenfranchisement of convicted prisoners with the right to vote guaranteed by Article 3 of Protocol 1 ECHR.[19] The UK Government argued that a wide margin of appreciation was to be allowed to Contracting States in determining the conditions under which the right to vote was exercised, and that the policy of a blanket ban on convicted prisoners had been adhered to over many years with the explicit approval of Parliament. The Court rejected this argument:

'As to the weight to be attached to the position adopted by the legislature . . . in the United Kingdom, there is no evidence that Parliament has ever sought to weigh the competing interests or to assess the proportionality of a blanket ban on the right of a convicted prisoner to vote . . . . It may perhaps be said that, by voting the way they did to exempt unconvicted prisoners from the restriction on voting, Parliament implicitly affirmed the need for continued restrictions on the voting rights of convicted prisoners. Nonetheless it cannot be said that there was any substantive debate by members of the legislature on the continued justification in light of modern day penal policy and of current human rights standards for maintaining such a general restriction on the right of prisoners to vote.'[20]

In my view the approach of the Court in *Hirst* is to be preferred to the approach of the House of Lords in *Wilson*. In a culture of justification, Parliament should be required to earn judicial deference from the courts on human rights questions, by demonstrating the quality of its reasoned judgments on compatibility, not entitled to expect it by virtue of its sovereign position in the constitution. But courts, for their part, must entertain the possibility of giving due deference to Parliament's legislative decision because of the quality of those reasons.

Conclusion

That brings me to consider briefly why all this matters. What harm is there in conducting our constitutional discourse in the apparently respectful language of competing sovereignties? Three recent examples of why it matters should suffice. The first was the proposal to oust the jurisdiction of the higher courts in asylum and immigration matters brought forward by the Government in 2003. The second was the proposal to legislate to require judges to follow the approach of the minority in the ECHR in *Chahal v UK*, which presupposes a willingness to deport on grounds of national security even where there is a real risk of torture. The third was the suggestion that the HRA may need amending to make clear that public safety is the paramount consideration and trumps any reliance on human rights.

[19] (2006) 42 EHRR 41. [20] ibid, para 79.

Would such proposals ever have been brought forward by the Government in any version of constitutionalism worthy of the name? By continuing to use the language of parliamentary sovereignty and the entire doctrinal edifice constructed upon it, the courts encourage the Government, and to some extent Parliament also, to believe that fundamentals such as access to court, or the prohibition on deportation to torture, are in their gift, and that judges can be required by legislation to act incompatibly with fundamental values. In this way we condemn ourselves to repeated constitutional crises and unnecessary confrontations between the courts and the political branches.

I have argued in this essay that the considerable progress which has been made towards a culture of justification in this country in the last five years is a genuine cause for celebration. However, I have also argued that the deeper lesson of the operation of the HRA in practice is that our constitutional and administrative law is built on inherently unstable foundations which condemn it to lurch perpetually between parliamentary supremacy on the one hand and judicial supremacy on the other. The reshaping of our received ideas of constitutionalism is blighted in particular by the continuing grip of the idea of 'sovereignty'. The very idea of sovereignty, I have argued, is inimical to true constitutionalism. The achievement of a reshaped constitutionalism of the kind envisaged in the work of Morison and Livngstone requires reconfiguring our public law around the concept of public justification, and away from sovereignty and all its related doctrines. The price to pay for not doing this is to condemn ourselves to repeated constitutional crises such as that over the ouster clause in recent years, and currently being witnessed in the arguments about deportation to torture. Finally, I have argued that the JCHR, although inescapably a piece of Westminster constitutional machinery, nevertheless has a potentially important role in this reconfiguration. For this role to be fully realized, however, courts must overcome their traditional reticence about evaluating the quality of the reasoning advanced in support of legislation, and make more use of the Committee's reports when determining the human rights compatibility of legislation on which it has reported, or of executive or administrative action taken under such legislation.

22

Human Rights and Women's Rights: The Appeal to an International Agenda in the Promotion of Women's Equal Citizenship

*Elizabeth Meehan**

Introduction

The human rights agenda has become used extensively by women's movements. International norms and standards are deployed in the pursuit of claims for better representation at the domestic or regional levels. There are difficulties in making such a linkage, as indicated later in discussion of the risk of 'false universalism'. At the same time, the essay argues that, with some effect, women activists have enmeshed discourse on human rights and equality at two regional, as opposed to international, levels of governance. These are the European Union (EU) and the devolved administrations in the United Kingdom (UK).

The continental region, the EU, plays a complex role in these developments. It is both influenced by the international agenda and seeks, similarly to governmental and non-governmental organizations (NGOs), to maintain the international momentum. At the same time, it, too, is used as a resource by activists to promote changes at the domestic level. In dealing with the regional, in the sense of sub-state, level within the UK, the essay, in deference to Stephen Livingstone's major role in the promotion of equality in Northern Ireland and his respected membership of the Equality Commission, places more emphasis on Northern Ireland than Scotland and Wales. EU and UN policy opportunities have been, and are, critical to the efforts of women in Northern Ireland to bring about gender equality in representation and policy-making.

* Some of this essay is drawn from a research project, *Gender and Constitutional Change*, funded by the ESRC under its 'Devolution and Constitutional Change Programme'. The principal investigator is Dr Fiona Mackay of Edinburgh University. In addition to this author, other members of the research team are or were Alice Brown, formerly Edinburgh University; Tahnya Donaghy, formerly Queen's University Belfast; and Paul Chaney, Cardiff University. The author is also grateful to the Political Theory Group at Manchester University (MANCEPT) whose annual conference in 2005, which honoured the work of Ursula Vogel, introduced her to new work by Diane Elson upon which this essay draws heavily.

The first main part of this essay discusses why women have used the human rights agenda, despite potential risks in using a discourse of 'false universalism' arrived at in 'male' institutions. One reason is either frustration with inadequate domestic policy or an absence altogether of attention at this level to issues of gender equality—either in terms of human rights or citizens' rights or both. The legitimacy accorded to international human rights standards provides an opportunity for a form of 'naming and shaming'.[1]

The second section deals with the EU. For similar reasons, it has also been seen as a means of tackling national situations from a different direction. At the same time, women have attempted to secure stronger EU policy by imbuing their appeals for this with a human rights-inspired legitimacy. That is, women have not only used the EU as a lever on domestic governments but have used international standards to demonstrate the gender deficits of the EU's own decision-making structures and decisions.

The third main section shows how both the EU and the international human rights agenda have contributed to women's activism in efforts to influence the design of devolved institutions in the UK, with, as noted, particular reference to Northern Ireland. The wider influence takes two forms. One is the networks of communication required for social movements to transform symbolic gains into tangible improvements.[2] The other is the actual standards invoked by the claimants of rights. Here, the essay illustrates this by reference to the calls by women to be involved in the development of what became known as the Belfast, or Good Friday, Agreement. Thereafter, the essay deals briefly with a campaign in Northern Ireland that would not be possible in Scotland and Wales (as they are not countries emerging from violent conflict); that is, the application to Northern Ireland of Resolution 1325—a Resolution that specifically addresses the impact and aftermath of conflict on 'women as women' rather than 'women as half of humanity'.[3]

In conclusion, the essay revisits the risks of universalism by adding to them a reference to a critique of the gender equality content of new arrangements in Northern Ireland.[4] Nevertheless, it is suggested that experience in Northern Ireland confirms that treating women's rights as human rights can contribute to 'breaks-through' in circumstances that are hostile to women's interests. The

[1] Diane Elson, ' "Women's rights are human rights": campaigns and concepts', in Lydia Morris (ed.), *Rights: Sociological Perspectives* (Routledge, 2006).
[2] Jo Freeman, *The Politics of Women's Liberation* (1975).
[3] See Sylvia Walby, 'Feminism in a Global Era' (2002) 31(4) Economy and Society 533, 541. The phrase 'half of humanity' should not be taken to imply that, if women did *not* constitute half the population, the justification for parity would fall. This is a slogan that reflects that women *are*, and always have been, about half the population (see also the chapter's later discussion of parity democracy and the notion of the interdependence of women and men *vis a vis* citizenship). It calls for all human beings to count as humans in human rights discourse and practice.
[4] Transitional Justice Institute, *Women and the Implementation of the Good Friday/Belfast Agreement*. Working Report (2005). Report written by Barbara O'Shea with foreword by Christine Bell and Fionnuala Ní Aoláin.

conclusion also suggests that the Resolution 1325 campaign confirms the view in much of the literature that women activists can negotiate the nuances between the universal and the particular, and develop strategies that reflect a 'dynamic synergy'[5] between the two.

Resort to the Human Rights Agenda

A number of writers[6] have demonstrated a re-framing of feminist discourse and women's activism that appeals to human rights rhetoric and engages with international and regional institutions in which that rhetoric is embedded. From a more legal starting point, Loudes[7] argues that developments in human rights mean that 'women's rights are increasingly regarded as an integral part of human rights law by mainstream human rights bodies' and that this has, indeed, provided a basis for improved laws in, for example, the sphere of standing for office.

In their re-framing, feminists are using international norms, institutions, and networks to apply pressure to policy regimes at the international, regional, and domestic levels to promote equality.[8] In so doing, they seemingly depart from previous feminist approaches and understandings in which rights systems were judged to be irredeemably androcentric and States often seen as part of the problem rather than the solution—notably in connection with violence against women, an issue where this new approach has been most visible.[9]

As Elson[10] points out, women *did* engage with the setting up of the UN and 'second wave' feminists took part in the calls for the Convention on the Elimination of All Discrimination Against Women (CEDAW). But, many feminists[11] saw CEDAW in its original form (and from which there were many derogations) as toothless and part of a system that could not bring about gender equality. The 'universalism' of that body of ideas neglected systematic differences in the situations of women and men and many critics suspected that its guardians did not really count women's rights as human rights. Why, then, asks Elson,[12] did so many

---

[5] Ruth Lister, *Citizenship: Feminist Perspectives* (1997) 90.

[6] eg Elson, '"Women's rights are human rights": campaigns and concepts', n 1 above; Walby, 'Feminism in a Global Era', n 3 above; and Lister, *Citizenship: Feminist Perspectives* , n 5 above.

[7] See Christine Loudes, *Increasing Women's Political Representation: Law into Politics*. Ph.D Thesis submitted in the School of Law, Queen's University Belfast, 2003.

[8] In addition to campaigns to halt violence against women, the international human rights approach also focuses on mainstreaming, a policy that is high on the UN and EU agendas; see Walby, 'Feminism in a Global Era', n 3 above, 533–57. And, as this chapter suggests, this could be said to be the main policy success of the Belfast Agreement.

[9] As is argued by Walby, 'Feminism in a Global Era', n 3 above.

[10] Elson, '"Women's rights are human rights": campaigns and concepts', n 1 above, draws upon A. Fraser, 'Becoming Human: The Origin and Development of Women's Human Rights' (1999) 21 Human Rights Quarterly 853.

[11] Notably Charlotte Bunch; see Elson, '"Women's rights are human rights": campaigns and concepts', n 1 above.   [12] ibid.

women come to agree that a system with such defects could also be so 'valuable in
the struggle to end gender-based violence against women and in other struggles to
increase women's well-being?'

At a general level, the highlighting of violence against women as a human rights
issue was critical in securing the centrality of women's rights to human rights.[13]
The reasons why women's groups and networks around the world have used this
frame of reference for particular struggles vary. Globalization in harmful forms[14]
and benign ones[15] play a part—either inciting appeals to international standards
or facilitating communication amongst new transnational alliances of women.

Another answer to Elson's question is the transformation of the politics of the
left[16] but, for the purposes of this essay emphasis on Northern Ireland, a more
persuasive explanation is provided by Elson herself. This is the existence of insuperable difficulties in achieving gender equality within some States in transition. Women in Latin America, for example, were disillusioned with the failure
of democratization to bring about gender equality and began to claim rights,
not as women, but as half of humanity. Women in Asia and Africa 'invoked a
"re-visioned" human rights system strategically to counteract the deployment
of . . . homogeneous [and falsely static] notions of "tradition" and "culture" by
male politicians keen to preserve the existing gender regime'.[17]

As Elson also points out, women who use the human rights agenda and discourse are aware of their limitations. They are alert to prevent individual or private
rights from becoming more important than collective rights[18] and to the need to
protect and promote what Lister describes as a 'critical synthesis of the universal
and particular'—or 'differentiated universalism'.[19]

International Human Rights and Rights in the EU

Hoskyns[20] draws attention to the significance of the international (UN) to the
regional (EU) spheres of policy and action. She highlights a range of UN activities
and expenditures associated with its Decade for Women (1975–85), particularly
its funding of four global conferences on women's issues, in Mexico, Copenhagen,

---

[13] Though, as Walby, 'Feminism in a Global Era', n 3 above, points out at 541, this language was
used for political reasons. A justification based on being 'half of humanity' was more strategic than
references to male oppression of women in the predominantly male UN forum.

[14] Elson, ' "Women's rights are human rights": campaigns and concepts', n 1 above, who deals
with global socio-economic inequalities.

[15] Walby, 'Feminism in a Global Era', n 3 above, who deals with networks and the exchange of
ideas.   [16] ibid.

[17] Elson, ' "Women's rights are human rights": campaigns and concepts', n 1 above.

[18] Elson, ' "Women's rights are human rights": campaigns and concepts', n 1 above, illustrates this
with reference to indigenous women in Mexico; see also Walby, 'Feminism in a Global Era', n 3
above.   [19] Lister, *Citizenship: Feminist Perspectives*, n 5 above, 90.

[20] Catherine Hoskyns, *Integrating Gender: Women Law and Politics in the European Union* (1996)
16, 86, 142.

Nairobi, and culminating in Beijing in 1995.[21] The designation by the UN of 1975 as International Women's Year contributed to the coming about of the 1975 Equal Pay Directive which extended equal pay from the 'same work' to 'work of equal value'. The designation introduced 'a sense of urgency' in the European Community in that its leaders would have to have 'something to say' at the first conference in Mexico in 1975.[22]

The NGO forums which accompanied the official meetings provided an important means of establishing information exchanges and networks. Hoskyns argues that this set 'an important frame for women's involvement in the EU'. This frame contributed to the strength of 'the women's presence at the EU' and, together with other factors, helped in the maintenance of 'a strong policy initiative' during the 1980s.

During the 1990s, attention to women's issues expanded to take in, not only socio-economic equality, but also representation on public and political bodies. While there were controversial claims that there should be quotas, another approach that attracted attention in Europe was similar to the idea that women's human rights were justified by the fact that they formed 'half of humanity'.[23] This was Eliane Vogel Polsky's[24] call for something that went beyond tinkering or treating women as though they were a specific or minority group in a dominant framework. The 'parity democracy' that she argues for is a matter that stems 'from the founding and constitutive principles of citizenship, in the same way as universal suffrage or the separation of powers'. Since women and men 'hold an equivalent position in a relationship of structurally established interdependence', this should be acknowledged in practice 'in all the legal, political, economic, social and cultural domains' and institutions.

Though institutions at the centre of the EU called upon Member States to pay attention to the equal representation of women, it cannot be said that its own house is in order.[25] However, funding was provided for the establishment in 1990 of the European Women's Lobby (EWL) as a means for the direct representation, at least in principle, of women's interests.[26] Although skewed in its inclusion of

---

[21] As noted earlier, violence against women was the first focus. This included the whole range of degrading and inhumane treatment—such as trafficking, sexual slavery, etc; see Hoskyns, *Integrating Gender: Women Law and Politics in the European Union*, ibid, 155.

[22] Thereby unblocking the stalemate experienced by Jacqueline Nonon, then in charge of the Women's Bureau in the European Commission, coming from other Community institutions; see Hoskyns, *Integrating Gender: Women Law and Politics in the European Union*, ibid, 86, 101,104.

[23] Though the protagonists of 'half of humanity' and 'parity democracy' usually refute this, both carry the risk of being interpreted as 'essentialist'. See Lister, *Citizenship: Feminist Perspectives*, n 5 above, 158–59.

[24] Eliane Vogel Polsky, 'Parity Democracy—Law and Europe' in Mariagrazia Rossilli (ed.), *Gender Policies in the European Union* (2000). For its practical application in French elections, see both Loudes, *Increasing Women's Political Representation: Law into Politics*, n 7 above, ch 4, and Joni Lovenduski, *Feminizing Politics* (2005) 130–31.

[25] See Lister, *Citizenship: Feminist Perspectives*, n 5 above, 146.

[26] See Hoskyns, *Integrating Gender: Women Law and Politics in the European Union*, n 20 above, 183.

women—biased in favour of professional women and against women in trades unions and from minority ethnic groups[27]—it was to play a significant part in embedding Lister's[28] 'dynamic synergy between the universal and the particular'. A high profile for mainstreaming was secured and, after an adverse ruling in the Court of Justice,[29] a legal basis for positive action was restored through inclusion of a provision in the Amsterdam Treaty.

The EWL, as an umbrella body and through its delegates from each of the Member States,[30] sought to influence both the process of drafting the Constitutional Treaty and its content. The EWL called for gender parity on Valery Giscard D'Éstaing's Convention which, unusually for EU treaties, did the drafting; normally treaties are drafted by the leaders of Member States at intergovernmental conferences. The EWL also lobbied for a Treaty that had gender equality in its legal framework and would both enable gender mainstreaming and permit special projects for women.[31]

Despite the efforts of the EWL, women were conspicuously absent from the composition of the Convention. Except for the UK delegation where there was parity, only 16 per cent of delegates and alternates were female. One of the UK delegates, Gisela Stuart, served on the Praesidium that assisted Giscard D'Éstaing; the other two were men. And the EWL was disappointed in the Treaty's failure to endorse steps to promote gender parity in EU institutions. For example, the Convention's proposal that Member State nominations to the Commission should comprise a list of three names including both genders was removed from the final version.[32]

While the content of the Treaty caused some disappointment, much of it provided grounds for optimism about the future of equality policy. Women activists had called for equality between men and women to be stated in the first sentence of the Treaty's Article I-2 on *Values*. But it is there in the second. And it is in the Charter of Fundamental Human Rights that forms Part 2 of the Treaty. Moreover, the Treaty states explicitly that the right to equality does not preclude the adoption

---

[27] See Hoskyns, *Integrating Gender: Women Law and Politics in the European Union*, n 20 above, 185–89, 203.   [28] See Lister, *Citizenship: Feminist Perspectives*, n 5 above, 90.

[29] Case C450/93 *Kalanke v Freie Hansestadt Bremen*, in which it was ruled that if positive action created discrimination against men in the process of selection, it was contrary to EU law; see Hoskyns, *Integrating Gender: Women Law and Politics in the European Union*, n 20 above, 11, 22, 106, 198, 201.

[30] The UK delegation to the EWL is the Joint Committee on Women and comprises of the National Alliance of Women's Organizations in England (NAWO), the Northern Ireland Women's European Platform (NIWEP), Engender (Scotland) and the Welsh Women's Equality Network.

[31] Annette Lawson, 'The UK Joint Committee on Women: Working Together—making Europe relevant, comprehensible and important to women in the UK and vice versa'. Presentation on the EWL and the Convention and Constitution made at Conference on *Gender in the New Europe—Your Voice*. National Alliance of Women's Organizations/Northern Ireland Women's European Platform, Belfast: Waterfront Hall, 20 May 2005.

[32] European Women's Lobby *EWL Briefing Document on the Treaty establishing a Constitution for Europe* (2005) 6.

of specific measures in favour of 'the under-represented sex'.[33] In other bases for policy, the Treaty retains all existing equality provisions and includes some improvements.[34] These incorporate provisions both for mainstreaming[35] and specific protections.[36] Though agreed and signed by Member State governments and ratified in a number of parliaments, the Constitutional Treaty is now in the doldrums after being rejected in ratification referendums in two founding Member States—France and the Netherlands. But the combination of women's activism at the international and European levels remains relevant to the representation of women at other levels of government. The essay turns now to the devolved administrations of the UK.

International Human Rights, the EU, and Equal Citizenship for Women in Sub-State Governance in the UK

In many ways, the ideas of both human rights and women's rights[37] have roots in the Enlightenment, a period of thought and development in which Scotland played a leading role. There, and in different ways in Wales, the securing of devolution settlements was intimately linked with the question of women's *numeric, substantive,* and *discursive* representation.[38]

The Scottish Constitutional Convention (SCC) was founded in a recommendation of the Campaign for a Scottish Assembly (CSA) in its 1988 Report, *A Claim of Right for Scotland.*[39] From 1989–95, the SCC, as in the eighteenth-century

---

[33] European Communities, *Treaty Establishing a Constitution for Europe* (2005), Art. II-83.

[34] European Women's Lobby, *EWL Briefing Document on the Treaty establishing a Constitution for Europe*, 2–5.

[35] For eg, a general mainstreaming provision and new horizontal provisions which mean that mainstreaming is now required in Foreign and Security Policy, and Justice and Home Affairs.

[36] For eg, articles that provide the bases for legal action to combat trafficking and sexual exploitation, particularly of women and children. There is also a Declaration calling upon Member States to take all necessary measures to prevent and punish domestic violence.

[37] In addition to the 'male canon', there were Mary Wollstonecraft and other feminist writers and their nineteenth-century heirs who appealed to Enlightenment ideas. Indeed, the framing of current policy to combine equality and difference, while based on modern analysis, was adumbrated in the work of Mary Wollstonecraft.

[38] In the research project noted in the first acknowledgement at the head of this essay, *numeric* representation refers to the proportions of women elected and holding parliamentary or executive office. Improved *substantive* representation refers to the achievement of policy, the content of which takes account of what women say their interests are. Improved *discursive* representation refers to a conduct and practice of politics that is inclusive.

[39] 'Claims of Right' are a 'peculiarly Scottish action' originating in the Declaration of Arbroath of 1320 and issued again in 1689 and 1842; see Owen Dudley Edwards (ed.), *A Claim of Right for Scotland* (1989) 3. The 1988 Claim of Right did not call for independence (though some of the members of the Constitutional Steering Committee of the CSA were in the Scottish National Party, which, like the Conservatives, did not take part in the SCC). For its text and commentaries, see Dudley Edwards, *A Claim of Right for Scotland.* See also Vernon Bogdanor, *Devolution in the United Kingdom* (revised ed., 2001) 196–98, 289–90.

US, brought together a range of people from political parties (but not the Scottish National Party or the Conservatives[40]), local government and civil society to draw up a new constitution for Scotland and their work extensively informed the eventual Scotland Act 1998. The nature of the new political culture that campaigners thought devolution would bring can be seen in their insistence that the Scottish understanding of sovereignty is one of popular, not parliamentary, sovereignty—inhering in citizens not subjects. In writing about the so-called 'new politics' and Scotland, Mitchell[41] points out that its nature was never defined but can be discerned from statements by senior campaigners for a Scottish Parliament; new institutions, new processes, and a new political culture. That is, new institutions would involve, not only the achievement of greater equality between the legislature and executive, but also the displacement of elitist adversarial politics by inclusiveness and popular participation. To this can be added the work of the Women's Claim of Right Group.[42] As a result of their activism, assisted by some male champions, it became accepted that for the 'new politics' to be realized through devolution would mean nothing if it did not address the gender question and equally enable women to be sovereign citizens.

In Wales[43] matters were complicated by the indifference of much of civil society to the devolution project, the weak infrastructure of the women's movement and an outlook in the Welsh Labour Party which inhibited the development of spaces for dialogue in civil society, between civil society and parties and cross-party debate—in contrast to the SCC.

However, against this unpromising backdrop, a small group of influential women managed to insert themselves and concerns about gender equality into political dialogue. These women were gender experts, femocrats, politicians, and trade union officials and, hence, were aware of or involved in the global and EU debates and networks. Many of them held positions of influence in the Labour Party and Plaid Cymru, and worked within their parties to push for positive action to promote women candidates and to link gender equality both with internal party modernization programmes and arguments about winning female votes. In the absence of a wider grassroots mobilization, the network used a short period of

---

[40] One member of the SNP carried over, in a personal capacity, into the SCC from the CSA.

[41] James Mitchell, 'New Parliament, New Politics in Scotland' (2000) 53(3) Parliamentary Affairs 605.

[42] See n 39 above. At an early stage, women were concerned that they might again be marginalized in the 'new politics' unless they organized themselves to ensure that the ideas for new arrangements addressed, from the beginning, gender equality; see Alice Brown, David McCrone, and Lindsay Paterson, *Politics and Society in Scotland* (1996) 176, 180. Though 'new institutionalism' describes an approach in political science and not an ideology of activists, Scottish women, like 'new institutionalists', recognized the force of 'path dependency' or the idea that institutions are shaped by their past history. It was important, therefore, to get the design correct from the start.

[43] The content of all of this section, and especially the material on Wales, is heavily indebted to various unpublished reports by Fiona Mackay, the leader of the project referred to at the beginning of this essay.

intense planning and campaigning between 1997 and 1999 to achieve significant gains. Both parties operated specific mechanisms to try to achieve gender balance in representation, despite opposition and controversy. They also improved their selection and recruitment procedures for candidates seeking to join the national panels of candidates.

Thus, in a process that mirrored the top-down character of the general reform project in Wales, these 'strategic women' staked a claim for women and promoted measures for their improved *numeric* and *substantive* representation. They were able to take advantage of prevailing ideas of inclusiveness and new politics which became hallmarks of the campaign as it gathered pace and support.

In Northern Ireland, but for different reasons, there was also resistance in established parties to the idea that constitutional reform entailed attention to the gender question. There, hostile political conditions, combined with social conservatism, prevented the development of pluralist coalitions like those in Scotland or co-operation amongst party women as in Wales. The legacy of divided communities and violence, combined with social conservativism, left little space in which women *as women* could mobilize at the level of 'high politics'.

Nevertheless, grassroots women worked across significant divisions in pursuit of the common purpose of playing a part in the shaping of new constitutional settlements. As a recent report puts it:

'...women found ways to deal with communal difference without requiring its prior negation or elimination... [B]uilding on this experience, women worked together with other marginalized groups to create rainbow coalitions which were significant in placing a "human rights and equality" agenda on the table.... Women worked through their own political groupings and through the establishment of a women's political party....[44]

In the absence of 'normal' domestic politics, both the international and the European spheres of action played a critical part in enabling this to happen—as is demonstrated by Hinds and Fearon.[45]

For years, women in Northern Ireland had organized successfully to promote, on a cross-community basis, spaces for dialogue, peace, community development, equality, and justice—as they made plain in documentation prepared for the 1995 UN Beijing conference.[46] But they were regularly excluded from decision-making about the future of Northern Ireland. Already 'vibrant' and having made a 'phenomenal' contribution, Northern Ireland women's groups drew upon the further

---

[44] Transitional Justice Institute, *Women and the Implementation of the Good Friday/Belfast Agreement*, n 4 above, 4.

[45] Bronagh Hinds, 'Women Working for Peace in Northern Ireland' in Yvonne Galligan, Eilis Ward, and Rick Wilford, *Contesting politics: Women in Ireland, North and South* (1999). Kate Fearon, *Women's Work: The Story of the Northern Ireland Women's Coalition* (1999).

[46] Bronagh Hinds, Anne Hope, and Robin Whitaker, 'From Margins to the Mainstream—Working Towards Equality, Development and Peace' (1997) 48.

lessons of the European and Irish models of policy-making based on social partnership between government and people.[47] In the mid-1990s, women increasingly called for an end to their exclusion and began to interact with women's
organizations elsewhere to address issues of power and decision-making at the
political level.[48]

In 1995, the Northern Ireland Women's European Platform (NIWEP) and
the National Women's Council of Ireland made a joint submission to the Forum
for Peace and Reconciliation in Dublin.[49] This, which was well received, called
for 'any new political future . . . to be built on comprehensive equality among *all*
people, including equality between men and women' and for women's experience
and talents 'to be harnessed at an early stage in Northern Ireland's unfolding
peace process'.[50] The UN, as well as the EU and Irish forums, was used for the
expression of women's demands. The first opportunity was in 1994 at the preparatory conference in Vienna for the Beijing conference and the second was at
Beijing, itself, in 1995.[51]

Thus, there was in place the domestic and international communication network of aware women that Freeman[52] argues is a necessary, but not sufficient,
condition for social movements to secure tangible correctives to their deprivation
or inequality. The final ingredient is a 'catalytic' event—something that catalyses
action.[53] In Northern Ireland, this was the imminence of an election of a Forum
from which delegates to official talks would be drawn.

The Northern Ireland Women's Coalition (NIWC) emerged from the dissatisfaction amongst the extensive network as 'one answer' to the absence of women
from politics in general and, in particular, discussion about the future of Northern
Ireland.[54] In context of a taste, brought by the ceasefires, of what life could be like,

---

[47] Hinds, *et al*, 'From Margins to the Mainstream—Working Towards Equality, Development
and Peace', ibid, 113. Here, she is also quoting from A. Pollak (ed.), *A Citizens' Enquiry—the Opsahl
Report on Northern Ireland* (1993) 115–17.

[48] Hinds, 'Women Working for Peace in Northern Ireland', n 45 above, 110.

[49] Previously they had together assisted women in the Republic of Ireland to know about the evidence being put to the Opsahl Commission by women in the north; see Hinds, 'Women Working for
Peace in Northern Ireland', n 45 above, 113. The Opsahl Commission, the edited proceedings of
which are in Pollak, *A Citizens' Enquiry—the Opsahl Report on Northern Ireland*, n 47 above, was a
civic initiative which represented 'the most detailed consultation process ever held in Northern
Ireland and one that highlighted the stark contrast between women's activism in informal politics and
their absence from formal politics; see Hinds, 'Women Working for Peace in Northern Ireland', n 45
above, 111–12. And, together, they had responded regularly to joint governmental statements, made
other presentations, and mobilized other women at major conferences; see Hinds, 'Women Working
for Peace in Northern Ireland', n 45 above, 114, 119–29.

[50] Hinds, 'Women Working for Peace in Northern Ireland', n 45 above, 109.   [51] ibid, 111.

[52] Freeman, *The Politics of Women's Liberation*, n 2 above, was writing about the women's liberation movement in the US.

[53] The sense of inequality was there amongst a network of women in general and university-based
political groups (civil rights and anti-war) and in Federal and State Commissions on the status of
women. The catalytic event that galvanized all the components into action was the passage of the
1964 Civil Rights Act but the absence of enforcement of its provision for women.

[54] Hinds, *et al*, 'From Margins to the Mainstream—Working Towards Equality, Development
and Peace', n 46 above, 45.

the 'looming election'—'the passport to participation in . . . the talks'—was unlikely to result in many women delegates. This was clear since, prior to the announcement of the election, the NIWEP had tried, but failed, to persuade the parties and British government to take measures, such as gender-proofing party lists and providing child-care assistance, to ensure gender parity in representation.

In April 1996, the government was urged to include in the enabling legislation for the election the possibility that a women's network or caucus could be registered.[55] Since the government required urgently the name of such a network or caucus, the NIWC was registered provisionally. In mid-April, at a meeting of hundreds of women to discuss this or other options, the existence of the NIWC and its name were ratified. Thus, the NIWC came into formal existence just six weeks before the 1996 elections to the Forum and, hence, the Multi-Party Talks. The NIWC won two elected Forum members and a team at the Talks. Overnight—on the face of it—the Party brought the issue of women's political representation into the public and political arenas.

During the talks, and in adverse circumstances, the NIWC delegates and support teams brought a gender perspective into the Agreement; for example, its declaration of women's right to participate in political life and its recommendation to establish a Civic Forum. The NIWC also worked with human rights organizations and other equality groupings to broaden the dominant conceptions of equality from one that was primarily about religion and political allegiance to one that includes gender and other equality groups. It and other parties—Sinn Féin and the smaller Loyalist parties—ensured the inclusion of women under the Agreement's section on Economic, Social and Cultural Issues.[56]

The research project, referred to in the first acknowledgement at the head of this essay, examines the outcomes of women's impact on the shape of the devolution settlements in terms of the *substantive* representation of their interests (policy) and whether or not devolution has brought about a new political culture (*discursive* representation). Sadly, it is easier to do this for Scotland and Wales where there have been no interruptions to devolution than for Northern Ireland, where devolution has gone from fits and starts to nothing.[57] Despite criticisms in a review of the gender aspects of the Belfast Agreement,[58] there is one area where Northern Ireland is arguably an exemplar and continues to be so even during the suspension of devolved institutions. This is in the field of mainstreaming, overseen by the new Equality Commission established in the wake of the Agreement.

Equality mainstreaming is an area of significant policy innovation, dynamism and distinctiveness in Scotland and Wales as well as in Northern Ireland. Lessons

---

[55] Hinds, 'Women Working for Peace in Northern Ireland', n 45 above, 122.

[56] Alice Brown, Tahnya Donaghy, Fiona Mackay, and Elizabeth Meehan, 'Women and Constitutional Change in Scotland and Northern Ireland' (2002) 55(1) Parliamentary Affairs 71.

[57] Though there is a provisional review of these matters in Northern Ireland; Transitional Justice Institute, *Women and the Implementation of the Good Friday/Belfast Agreement*, n 4 above.

[58] See n 53 above.

have been learned from international experience and lesson-sharing appears to operate across the three administrations, sometimes at the level of civil servants but usually through networks of equality activists and experts, and the respective statutory equality bodies. There are also similar interchanges with Ireland.

While high on all agendas, the approach in Northern Ireland is perhaps the most entrenched and sophisticated.[59] The statutory equality mainstreaming duty (Section 75 of the Northern Ireland Act 1998) means that all 150+ public bodies must produce and implement rigorous equality schemes.

The particular circumstances of Northern Ireland contributed to the strength of this duty. On the one hand, it was already advanced on tackling inequality, though domestic conditions and pressures from the US meant that religious equality was more salient than other forms of it. Secondly, however, Northern Ireland was not immune from the British government's anxiety to meet international obligations to bring about (predominantly gender) equality. Thirdly, civic groups were mobilizing around the need for a statutory duty for a wider form of mainstreaming. The methods promoted from the bottom-up, notably from the Equality Coalition, were critical in the form of mainstreaming that came to be adopted.

Elements of this 'participative-democratic' approach to mainstreaming, which focuses upon the expertise residing amongst civic actors and groups, can also be discerned in Scotland but, in Wales, a more 'expert-bureaucratic' approach appears to have been taken so far. It is too early to assess the impact of mainstreaming in producing 'better policy' and in reducing inequalities. A number of difficulties and criticisms have emerged, even in Northern Ireland. But, even so, gender mainstreaming (albeit as part of wider equality mainstreaming initiatives) has delivered improvements in the *substantive* representation of women's concerns in the policy process through improved consultation. It also has the potential to improve the *discursive* representation of women. That is, it questions presumed gender-neutrality in political and policy institutions and highlights the ways in which these institutions reproduce and contribute to gender inequality through taken-for-granted values in working practices, policy processes, and work priorities.

Northern Ireland differs from Scotland and Wales, of course, in the fact that the devolution arrangements in the former follow from decades of violent conflict. As the Transitional Justice Institute[60] notes, 'ethnic or political violence' often 'silences the experience of women'. At the same time, 'the transition away from conflict seems to provide an opportunity for re-imagining' political futures 'in which a broader array of societal issues can be addressed'. The emergence from

---

[59] Tahnya Donaghy, 'Mainstreaming: Northern Ireland's Participative-Democratic approach', Centre for the Advancement of Women in Politics, Occasional Paper 2 (2003).

[60] Transitional Justice Institute, *Women and the Implementation of the Good Friday/Belfast Agreement* n 4 above, 2.

conflict opens a lobbying possibility for women activists in Northern Ireland that is not available to their counterparts in Scotland and Wales. This is Resolution 1325, to which the essay now turns.

UN Resolution 1325 on Women and Peace Building

The Northern Ireland Women's European Platform, in addition to promoting the 'women friendly' aspects of the Constitutional Treaty, is also turning to UN Resolution 1325 on Women, Peace and Security.[61] This Resolution is less an example of 'differentiated universalism' and is gender-specific in its recognition that women have particular experiences of conflict while also having an equal right to construct the peace.

Resolution 1325 is particularly relevant to the state of limbo that currently characterizes Northern Ireland, a situation in which the main new or reformed institutions that operate are those explicitly related to peace building. These include: the Police Service for Northern Ireland (and its Board and District Policing Partnerships), the Parades Commission, the Monitoring Commissions, and the talks between the Irish and British governments and the larger parties aimed at the restoration of devolution.

But Resolution 1325 would still be relevant even if the 'normal' institutions were up and running. If the ceasefires were the beginning of peace building, it is not the case that, in itself, the establishment of new institutions is the end of it. The absence of violence is not the same as peace, as the NIWC and its supporters very well knew. The Agreement, therefore, might be said—to borrow a phrase— to have been the end of the beginning. Its institutions, as much as those existing in the current vacuum, should be required to meet international standards of peace building.

Resolution 1325 calls for:

'Participation of women in peace processes;
Gender training in peacekeeping operations;
Protection of women and girls and respect for their rights; and
Gender mainstreaming in the reporting and implementation systems of the UN relating to conflict, peace and security.'

The NIWEP notes that the British government is assiduous in insisting that women should be involved in post-conflict, peace-keeping institutions in, for example, Afghanistan and Iraq. That the government should consider the Resolution to be equally applicable to Northern Ireland has been raised in discussions about the

---

[61] Unpublished paper by Anne-Marie Gray and Bronagh Hinds, delivered by the former, at a conference on 'Women Engaging with the State: from the Local to the Supranational', University of Edinburgh, 8 June 2005; Seminar 4 of an ESRC-funded series on 'What Difference Did the Vote Make?'

implementation of the Beijing Platform for Action,[62] the 49th Session of the Commission for the Status of Women and in connection with other issues. A 'trial' was held at Stormont to address the question:

'Have the United Kingdom Government, the Northern Ireland Executive and Northern Ireland Assembly (when in being) and the Northern Ireland political parties demonstrated sufficient commitment to the implementation of Resolution 1325 in Northern Ireland?'

The 'jury' was unanimous in a 'no' verdict.[63] The NIWEP, in being involved with the UK Working Group on UNSCR 1325, has singled out two areas where standards should be required at home that match those expected of other countries. These are: increased representation of women at all decision-making levels in institutions for the prevention, management and resolution of conflict; and adopting a gender perspective when negotiating and implementing peace agreements.

Conclusion

In assessing the impact of women on constitutional change and peace building in Northern Ireland, one is faced with the inevitable problem of whether the glass is half full or half empty. The Transitional Justice Working Report[64] is sceptical in reviewing the complete range of 'normal' and peace building institutions and policies. Its findings show, perhaps, that earlier feminist misgivings about the 'false universalism' of international human rights discourse is equally relevant to *substantive* and *discursive* representation at the domestic level. In comparison to Scotland and Wales, women in Northern Ireland have not fared well in terms of *numerical* representation.[65]

On the other hand, compared to the past, women have become more visible in Northern Ireland politics. Even though the NIWC lost its Assembly and district council seats, slightly more women, from other parties, were elected in the second

[62] In preparing for the 49th Session, the NIWEP, among other activities, submitted an alternative report to the British government's response to the questionnaire on the implementation of the Platform for Action in respect of Northern Ireland. During the 49th Session, the NIWEP held a 'side event' on regionalization and marginalization' in which a great deal more information was provided about Northern Ireland than there is in the UK's country report; report by Dr Anne-Marie Gray on study visit to the Commission on the Status of Women, 26 February to 8 March 2005; available at www.niwep.org.uk. The Declaration adopted at the 49th Session is being used to lobby for the full implementation of the Platform for Action; The Commission on the Status of Women (CSW)—49th Session. Beijing Platform for Action—Gender, Equality, Development and Peace in the 21st Century; available at www.niwep.org.uk.
[63] A Report of the Trial is available at www.niwep.org.uk.
[64] Transitional Justice Institute, *Women and the Implementation of the Good Friday/Belfast Agreement*, n 4 above.
[65] Women formed around 14 per cent of elected members in the first Northern Ireland Assembly, compared to some 38–50 per cent over two elections in the other two administrations.

election—albeit to a non-existent Assembly. Unprecedentedly, two women were elected at the same election to the Westminster Parliament. And, as noted earlier in this essay, 'mainstreaming' in Northern Ireland—whatever its problems—is in the lead. At the same time, women in Northern Ireland are no less aware than counterparts elsewhere that human rights, either in the conventional universal form or gender specific as in Resolution 1325, are not a panacea for the achievement of equal citizenship.

That being said, it was not the purpose of this essay to assess the impact of women's activism in Northern Ireland. Rather, it is to show that the case of Northern Ireland confirms the findings of more general literature on the intermeshing of the international and the domestic in the strategies of women activists. The imperfections of devolution, its interrupted life, and the loss of the NIWC seats do not invalidate the claim that there are important European and international contexts to the promotion of gender equality in political representation at lower levels of governance.

23

'In the Small Places': Education and Human Rights Culture in Conflict-Affected Societies

Lesley McEvoy and Laura Lundy

Introduction

The notion of human rights as having a central role to play in both addressing the legacy of violent conflict and in building a peaceful and stable society is generally acknowledged in human rights literature.[1] Less well explored in this literature, however, is the function of education as a contributory factor in the generation, maintenance and resolution of conflict.[2] Schools provide a natural venue in which to initiate and nurture the development of a human rights culture. They provide not only an individual's first experience of community participation and therefore of democracy, but they are also one of the 'small places' where universal human rights begin.[3] This essay will therefore use the context of schools to explore the relationship between the separate yet interrelated discourses around children's rights and human rights education. The essay begins by outlining the relationship between education and conflict before considering the distinctive contribution which the effective implementation of children's rights and human rights education can bring to the development of a human rights culture in society. Using Northern Ireland as a case study, it concludes that a co-ordinated approach, which harnesses the normative and enforcing capacity of law and the persuasive potential of education, is the most strategic means by which to establish and sustain a human rights culture in conflict-affected societies.

---

[1] See eg Christine Bell, *Peace Agreements and Human Rights* (2000).

[2] The relationship between education and conflict is well explored within *educational* literature (see eg Lynn Davies, *Conflict and Education: complexity and chaos* (2004)). However, just as human rights literature pays little attention to the role of education, educational literature is often lacking in a specific human rights focus.

[3] Eleanor Roosevelt, Speech at the United Nations, 27 March 1953.

Education and Conflict

The utilitarian view of schools as merely a vehicle through which children are prepared to be technically and socially adequate to the performance of adult roles[4] is
superseded by a more sophisticated discussion as to the purpose of education.
This debate is essentially centred on the historical tension between liberal and
functionalist discourses: education for the good of the individual and education
for the cohesion of society. It is generally accepted that education has a *constructive*
role to play in both the production of social solidarity[5] and the development of the
unique potential of every individual.[6] Conversely, it has been argued that its
contribution to cultural reproduction[7] can have a detrimental effect on society
and that educational institutions can be guilty of the manipulation of children
into conforming, un-critical citizens.[8] When the debate is located in the context of
conflict-affected societies, the dialectical relationship between conflict and education
illuminates further the political, symbolic, and practical significance of education.

   The effect of conflict *on education* is well documented, with the relationship
traditionally articulated in terms of its impact on access to basic educational
provision and general educational debilitation. Conflict not only disrupts educational opportunities, but the very fabric of society through which children learn
and develop.[9] While at times such disruption may appear as a by-product of
conflict, in other instances it can be a quite deliberate and strategic element of the
broader military or political struggle. Schools and teachers are often targeted
specifically during conflict:[10] schools in part because they present a practical and
very public location; teachers in part because they are perceived as important
community members who are better educated and therefore more politicized.[11]
However, it could be argued that the targeting of these tangible manifestations of
the education system is primarily due to the perceived ideological threat posed by
education itself.

   Concomitantly education has an influence *on conflict* at an ideological, systemic,
and operational level. First, education can be utililized by State and non-State

---

[4] Talcott Parsons, *The Social System* (1952).
[5] Emile Durkheim, *Education and Society* (Translation) (1956).
[6] John Dewey, *Democracy and Education: an Introduction to the Philosophy of Education* (1953).
[7] Pierre Bourdieu and Jean-Claude Passeron, *Reproduction in Education, Society and Culture*
(1977).   [8] Ivan Illich, *De-Schooling Society* (1971).
[9] Marion Molteno, Kimberly Ogadhoh, Emma Cain, and Bridget Compton (eds) *Towards
Responsive Schools: Supporting Better Schooling for Disadvantaged Children* (1999).
[10] For example, in addition to schools as public sites for genocide in Rwanda, protest in Northern
Ireland and hostage-taking to serve a political end in Beslan, 45% of primary school networks were
deliberately destroyed during the conflict in Mozambique, school buildings and educational records
were destroyed in Somolia in the early 1990s, and universities were intentionally shelled in Kosovo.
Also two-thirds of teachers were either killed in or fled from Rwanda during the genocide. Teachers
and other well-educated members of Cambodian society were specifically targeted by the Khymer
Rouge and public expenditure on education was reduced to almost nothing under Pol Pot's rule.
[11] Graca Machel, *The Impact of Armed Conflict on Children* (1996), para 186.

actors as an ideological tool for indoctrination,[12] as a weapon of oppression, and the denial of education employed as a weapon of war.[13] Secondly, inadequate educational provision and discriminatory practices within the educational system can generate new sources of social tension and heighten division.[14] Finally, schools as microcosms of society reflect the types of conflict existing in the societies in which they are based and tend to reproduce the attitudes and social relations of dominant groups in such societies.[15] Consequently, the daily operation of education in conflict-affected societies can contribute to conflict through, for example, the content of the taught curriculum, the values transmitted in the hidden curriculum and even the political manipulation of textbooks[16] with, as Davies describes, the enemy used as a 'teaching tool for hate'.[17]

However, just as education can be a major precipitating factor in creating or exacerbating conflict, it has a crucial ameliorative and transformative role in conflict resolution. Bush and Saltarelli note that, in addition to other positive aspects of education in conflict-affected societies, education can nurture and sustain tolerance, cultivate inclusive concepts of citizenship, and 'disarm history'.[18] Further to this ameliorative role, education can also be the arena for defiance against State oppression, and a tool for liberation.[19] This transformative potential of education has particular significance in post-conflict societies in need of social and civic reconstruction[20] where particular attention must be paid to avoiding the 'replication of educational structures that may have contributed to the conflict' in the first instance.[21]

---

[12] Lyndsay Bird, *Post Conflict Education: A review of the literature and CfBAT experience* (2003).

[13] Kenneth Bush and Diana Saltarelli (eds), *The Two Faces of Education in Ethnic Conflict: Towards a Peacebuilding Education for Children* (2000).

[14] For eg, it is recognized that the roots of the Rwandan genocide lie in Belgian colonial policy which favoured the taller, more 'European' looking Tutsis over the 'stockier' Hutus. This resulted in discriminatory practices against Hutus particularly in access to the same educational opportunities as the Tutsis. In one government-funded school a minimum height was even imposed as an entrance requirement to the disadvantage of the Hutus. Such educational policies resulted in only a small fraction of Hutus having the requisite skills to access employment in the modern economy of the late 1980s, which only served to heighten division. See Catherine Newbury, *The Cohesion of Oppression: Clientship and Ethnicity in Rwanda 1860–1960* (1988); and Rodolfo Stavenhagen, *Ethnic Conflicts and the Nation State* (1996). See also Peter Buckland *Reshaping the Future: Education and Post Conflict Reconstruction* ('Reshaping the Future') (2005).

[15] See n 2 above.

[16] Alan Smith and Tony Vaux, *Education, Conflict and International Development* (2003).

[17] Davies, *Conflict and Education: complexity and chaos*, n 2 above, 64.

[18] Bush and Saltarelli, *The Two Faces of Education in Ethnic Conflict: Towards a Peacebuilding Education for Children*, n 13 above, 19.

[19] The historical role of education as a site of State defiance is well documented from opposition to segregation in Montgomery Alabama, USA to struggles against apartheid in Soweto, South Africa. Similarly, education has been recognized for its major contribution to liberation in Palestine: see Salah Azaroo and Gillain Lewando Hunt 'Education in the Context of Conflict and Instability: The Palestinian Case' (2003) 37(2) Social Policy and Administration 165–80.

[20] Sobhi Tawil and Alexandra Harley (eds), *Studies in Comparative Education: Education Conflict and Social Cohesion* (2004).

[21] UNESCO (2002) *Education for All: Is the World on Track?* 161.

In sum, while there are many factors which contribute to the generation, maintenance and resolution of conflict, the seminal role of education as a target of
conflict, as a precipitating factor of conflict and as an instrument for conflict
transformation should not be understated. As Buckland notes:

'Education does not cause wars, nor does it end them. It does, however, frequently
contribute to the factors that are underlying conflict . . . it also has the potential to play a
significant role both directly and indirectly in building peace.'[22]

Establishing a Human Rights Culture Through Law and Education: Enforcement and Persuasion

The preamble of the Universal Declaration of Human Rights (UDHR) asserts
that the 'recognition of the inherent dignity and of the equal and inalienable
rights of all members of the human family is the foundation of freedom, justice
and peace in the world'.[23] This statement places human rights as central to the
processes of conflict resolution and peace building and indicates that the development of a human rights culture is of paramount importance in societies emerging
from conflict. While such a culture is often articulated within a legal discourse the
discussion below will demonstrate the significance of the role of education.

The dominance of human rights discourse as a modern '*lingua franca*' has
become something of a truism in legal and sociological scholarship.[24] For example,
Douzinas argues that human rights have come to dominate legal philosophy and
political practice and, as such, have impacted on law, government policy, and
international relations. To this end he contends that 'we live in a human rights culture'.[25] Though this may ring true in the abstract, the realization of a human
rights culture, particularly in conflict-affected societies, is less certain. The very
term 'human rights culture' is almost axiomatically, and often unreflectively,
invoked in discussions surrounding the role of human rights in the reconstruction
of societies emerging from conflict without a consensus as to its precise meaning.
It would appear though that there is agreement upon decisive *features* of such a
culture:[26] *governments* operating within a human rights framework; the practices of *public bodies* shaped by human rights principles; human rights standards

---

[22] Buckland, *Reshaping the Future: Education and Post Conflict Reconstruction*, n 14 above, 86.
[23] Universal Declaration of Human Rights, Preamble.
[24] See eg, Michael Ignatieff, *The Rights Revolution* (2000).
[25] Costas Douzinas, *The End of Human Rights* (2000) 246.
[26] Francis Butler, 'Building a Human Rights Culture' in Colin Harvey (ed.), *Human Rights in the Community: Rights as Agents of Change* (2005) 63–80; James L. Gibson 'Truth, Reconciliation and the Creation of a Human Rights Culture in South Africa', (2004) 38 Law and Society Review 5; Joint Committee on Human Rights (2002–3) *The Case for a Human Rights Commission (6th Report)*.

popularly accepted in wider *society*; and *individuals* recognizing and valuing both their rights and the rights of others.[27]

Since this culture of human rights will not evolve on its own, the law has both a normative and enforcing role to play in its realization. Setting standards at the constitutional level alone is insufficient; a degree of judicial activity is also required. As Harvey argues:

'There are limits to the utility of parliament and legislation in promoting human rights . . . Some individuals and groups cannot rely exclusively on the legislative process to respect and promote their rights. Minority groups, particularly those who do not command significant political power, will often be forced to resort to litigation to ensure their voices are heard.'[28]

This is not to say that a culture of rights is a culture of litigation or complaint.[29] The features of a human rights culture described above resonate more closely with a communitarian notion of human rights described by Hunt as one in which 'the individual is more than the mere bearer of negative rights against the state but [is] a participative individual taking an active part in the political realm and accepting the responsibility to respect the rights of others in the community'.[30] If individuals are to 'buy into' such a culture there is clearly a need for an additional element in the construction of a human rights culture: education. Educational approaches in this context must go beyond merely informing individuals about their rights to *persuading* individuals and society in general of the intrinsic value of human rights *per se*. This clearly involves the education of a wide range of actors in society, not least of which are members of the legal community themselves. As the Joint Committee on Human Rights has observed 'agents of the state cannot be expected to embrace a human rights culture that they do not know about'.[31]

In sum, the enforcing capacity of law and the persuasive potential of education are inextricably linked components in the realization of a human rights culture. The potential of this relationship has been recognized and utilized to good effect in other contexts and could be put no more eloquently than in the words

---

[27] The Joint Committee on Human Rights reflects these features in a description of what it refers to as a 'culture of respect for human rights'. It contends that such a culture would exist when 'there was a widely-shared sense of entitlement to these rights, of personal responsibility and of respect for the rights of others, and when this influenced all our institutional polices and practices'. Further it noted that such a culture would create 'a more humane society, a more responsive government and better public services', see n 26 above, para 9.

[28] Colin Harvey 'Creating a Culture of Respect for Human Rights' in C. Harvey (ed.), *Human Rights in the Community: Rights as Agents of Change* (2005) 2.

[29] Tom Campbell, 'Human Rights: a Culture of Controversy' (1999) 26 Journal of Law and Society 6.

[30] Murray Hunt, 'The Human Rights Act and Legal Culture: the Judiciary and the Legal Profession' (1999) 26 Journal of Law and Society 86, 89.

[31] Joint Committee on Human Rights, *The Case for a Human Rights Commission*, n 26 above, 68.

of Martin Luther King Jnr when speaking about the struggle against racial segregation:

'I know there are those who say that this can't be done through the courts, it can't be done through laws, you can't legislate morals. They would say that integration must come by education not legislation. Well I choose to be dialectical at that point. It's not either legislation or education. It's both legislation and education.'[32]

As argued above education sits squarely at the intersection between discourses on conflict and on the development of a human rights culture. However, it has also been shown that the realization of a human rights culture in society in *general* is contingent upon education working in tandem with the law. In order to explore the dynamics of this relationship further the remainder of the essay will focus on an evaluation of the contribution that can be made to the development of a human rights culture in *schools* in conflict-affected societies by legal and educational discourses: specifically children's rights and human rights education.

The Potential of Legal Discourse: Children's Rights, Education, and Conflict

In a context where much of the rhetorical and aspirational aspects of transition are framed in the context of the 'next generation', children's rights are understandably portrayed as central to the 'rebirth' of societies emerging from conflict.[33] The focus of peace-building initiatives at times of transition is both retrospective and prospective: remedying past injustices and creating the conditions for a more stable future.[34] Children are likely to have been disproportionately affected by the conflict,[35] and children's rights instruments provide a set of benchmarks for determining what is necessary to redress the social, psychological, and physical impacts of violence upon children. In terms of future planning, children's rights are thought to form the basic building blocks for a human rights culture and are therefore recognized increasingly as core aspects of political settlements in societies which are emerging from conflict.[36] More pragmatically, children's rights are

[32] Speech given by Martin Luther King Jnr at NAACP Emancipation Day Rally 1 January 1957, Atlanta Georgia.
[33] Michael Freeman, ' Introduction', *Children's Rights* (2004), Volume 1, xix.
[34] See generally Rudi Teitel, *Transitional Justice* (2001).
[35] Graca Machel, *The Impact of Armed Conflict on Children* (1996) paras 186–88; Orla Muldoon 'Children of the Troubles: The Impact of Political Violence in Northern Ireland' (2004) 60(3) Journal of Social Issue 453; Paul Connolly and Julie Healy *Children and the Conflict in Northern Ireland: the experiences and perspectives of 3–11 year olds* (2004).
[36] Luis Filipe Sacramento and Ana Maria Pessoa, 'Implementation of the Rights of the Child in the Mozambican Context' in Michael Freeman (ed)., *Children's Rights: A Comparative Perspective* (1996) 145–164; Julia Sloth-Nielsen, 'The Contribution of Children's Rights to the Reconstruction of Society: Some Implications of the Constitutionalisation of Children's Rights in South Africa' (1996) 4 International Journal of Children's Rights 323.

often perceived as politically neutral territory, making it easier to garner political and popular support for initiatives which benefit children than in other more contentious spheres of engagement (such as policing or the release of prisoners).[37] Thus, not only are children's rights regarded as 'a powerful tool with which to kick-start the reconstruction of society', they provide a potential rallying point for consensus, in the early, and therefore potentially most fragile times, in the transition process.[38]

Within the broad sphere of children's rights, education rights are particularly significant. While recognition of children's rights is a relatively recent development, the right to education has long been regarded as a fundamental human right. The Universal Declaration on Human Rights, itself an attempt to build a peaceful future in the wake of violence, upholds the right to education. The right to education is not only of intrinsic value, it an 'indispensable means of realizing other human rights'.[39] The right to education can act as a 'multiplier of rights', enhancing the individual's capacity to enjoy other human rights when it is secured and undermining that potential where it is denied.[40] Moreover, the benefits of securing children's rights in the context of education are not limited to the individual child. There is a compelling public interest in guaranteeing children's right to education: the social and economic well-being of society depends upon having a well-educated citizenry and one which respects democratic values, including human rights. While this is important always, it acquires enhanced significance in societies which are making the transition from conflict to peace and democracy.[41]

Education rights are multi-faceted. Their scope and application cannot be conveyed adequately within the uni-dimensional concept of a 'right to education' in the same way as other socio-economic rights such as the right to shelter, healthcare, or an adequate standard of living. This is apparent in the most recent formulations of the rights which pertain to education set out in the United Nations Convention on the Rights of the Child (CRC). The CRC contains two separate provisions dedicated to education rights. Article 28 focuses primarily on the right of access to education or 'schooling' and Article 29 defines the nature of the education which the child is entitled to receive. Moreover, the Committee on the Rights of the Child has observed that: 'Children do not lose their human rights by

---

[37] A good example is Northern Ireland, where the one initiative which received universal support from the various political parties in the wake of the Belfast Agreement was the establishment of the post of Commissioner for Children and Young People. See Laura Lundy, 'Mainstreaming children's rights to, through and in education in a society emerging from conflict', *International Journal of Children's Rights*, (2006).

[38] Sloth-Nielsen, 'The Contribution of Children's Rights to the Reconstruction of Society: Some Implications of the Constitutionalisation of Children's Rights in South Africa', n 36 above, 328.

[39] United Nations Committee on Economic, Social and Cultural Rights, *General Comment: The Right to Education*, E/C.12/2000/4 CESCR (UN: Geneva) para 1.

[40] *Annual Report of the Special Rapporteur on the Right to Education, E/CN.4/2001/52* (2001) para 11.

[41] Susan Limber, Vahur Kask, Mati Heidemets, Natalie Hevener Kaufman, and Gary B. Melton, 'Estonian Children's Perceptions of Rights: Implications for Societies in Transition' (1999) 7 International Journal of Children's Rights 365.

virtue of passing through the school gates.'[42] All of the other rights in the CRC and other international human rights instruments apply to children while they are at school, including for example, the right to freedom of conscience, expression, and association and to be protected from inhuman and degrading treatment. Given the wide scope of the rights which are of potential application in the domain of education, children's rights are commonly categorized as rights 'to', 'in' and 'through' education. In general terms, the right 'to' education can be taken to denote children's right of equal access to education; rights 'in' education refers to their right to be treated with dignity, respect, and equality while at school; and rights 'through' education describes the content and aims of the education which they are entitled to receive in order to prepare them 'for responsible life in a free society'.[43] With respect to the latter, the Committee on the Rights of the Child has emphasized the centrality of human rights education, starting 'with the reflection of human rights values in the daily life and experiences of children'.[44] This is considered to be not only relevant for children living in zones of peace, but 'even more important for those living in situations of conflict or emergency'.[45]

The Potential of Educational Discourse: Human Rights Education and Conflict

As with the mainstreaming human rights more generally in international law,[46] discussion surrounding the need for human rights education (HRE) principally emerged in reaction to the dehumanization of peoples witnessed during the events leading up to and including World War II. As such, the initial intention of HRE was one of intervention: ensuring that people not only understood their rights, but also understood that their rights were protected by international law.[47] This need for HRE, indicated in the UN Charter, is reiterated in the UDHR which states that: 'education shall be directed to the ... strengthening of respect for human rights and fundamental freedoms'.[48] In addition, the European Convention of Human Rights (ECHR) calls upon its signatories to promote 'a

[42] Committee on the Rights of the Child, *General Comment No. 1 on the Aims of Education*, CRC/GC/20001/1 (2001) para 8. This is an echo of the oft-quoted statement of the US Supreme Court in *Tinker v Des Moines Independent Community School District* 393 US 503 (1960).
[43] Art. 29(1) of the United Nations Convention on the Rights of the Child.
[44] Committee on the Rights of the Child, *General Comment No. 1 on the Aims of Education*, n 42 above, para 15.
[45] Committee on the Rights of the Child, *General Comment No. 1 on the Aims of Education*, n 42 above, para 16.
[46] See generally, Henry Steiner and Philip Alston, *International Human Rights in Context: Law, Politics, Morals* (2nd ed., 2000).
[47] Donna Hicks, 'Conflict Resolution and Human Rights Education' in George Andreopoulus and Richard Claude (eds), *Human Rights Education for the Twenty First Century* (1997) 80–95.
[48] Universal Declaration of Human Rights, Art. 26(2).

common understanding... of human rights'.[49] This commitment of the international human rights community to HRE, emphasized and re-emphasized through numerous declarations, protocols and recommendations[50] and grounded in half a century of history, has effectively translated the *need* for HRE into an *entitlement* and ultimately into a *human right* in and of itself.

Alongside this reality that HRE is an international obligation placed upon States,[51] academic debate has identified other possibly more cogent arguments in its support: its potential to contribute to the reduction of human rights' violations; the perpetuation of stable, peaceful societies; conflict resolution and peace building and the maintenance of democracy.[52] It is generally accepted that human rights *discourse* affords a language around which conflict can be framed and addressed,[53] and is a key dynamic in the transformation of institutions shaped or marred by such conflict.[54] It therefore follows that human rights *education* is critical to ensuring that individuals are initiated into such a discourse in order to enable them to participate in the process of conflict resolution and the reconstruction of their societies. It is precisely this potential for social transformation[55] that gives HRE particular significance in conflict-affected societies.

However, merely acknowledging HRE as a tool for transformation is insufficient. Its contribution to the realization of a human rights culture is clearly contingent upon how this tool is utilized. The absence of a clear formulation of a global concept for HRE[56] has resulted in a variety of approaches being taken, each with varying degrees of success. In particular, the involvement of States, civil society, and academics in the debate has led to a wide range of definitions and models

---

[49] European Convention on Human Rights, Preamble.

[50] Provisions for HRE have been incorporated into such international human rights instruments as the International Covenant on Economic, Social and Cultural Rights (Art 13), the Convention on the Elimination of All Forms of Discrimination Against Women (Art 10), the International Convention on the Elimination of All Forms of Racial Discrimination (Art 7), the United Nations Convention on the Rights of the Child (Arts 29 and 42). In addition to these the right to human rights education has been established through both explicit references to it as a *requirement*, and implicit references to its *intrinsic value* in international and regional human rights instruments, declarations and recommendations from international, regional and national human rights organizations (see Office of the High Commission for Human Rights *The Right to Human Rights Education* (1999) for an extensive compilation of references to HRE in international and regional instruments). Following the reaffirmation of the right to HRE in the Vienna Declaration and Programme of Action (June 1991, in particular see Pt 1, paras 33–34 and Pt 2, paras 78–82) the United Nations designated 1994–2005 as the UN Decade for Human Rights Education (General Assembly Resolution 49/184 December 1994) and subsequently announced a World Programme for Human Rights Education (General Assembly Resolution 59/113 July 2005).

[51] George Andreopoulos and Richard Claude (eds), *Human Rights Education for the Twenty First Century* (1997). [52] Jagannath Mohanty, *Human Rights Education* (2000).

[53] Michael Ignatieff, *Human Rights as Politics and Idolatry* (2001).

[54] Paul Mageean and Martin O'Brien, 'From the Margins to the Mainstream: Human Rights and the Good Friday Agreement' (1999) 22 Fordham International Law Journal 499.

[55] Felissa Tibbitts, 'Understanding What We Do: Emerging Models for Human Rights Education' (2002) 48 International Review of Education 145.

[56] Claudia Lohrenscheit, 'International Approaches to Human Rights Education' (2002) 48 International Review of Education 173.

of HRE. Flowers provides a useful analysis of these differing definitions.[57] She argues that since governments tend to view HRE as a mechanism for preserving democracy, governmental definitions overtly stress the 'rights' aspect of educational programmes. NGOs, however, she contends, advocate a more transformative approach emphasizing the 'education' aspect of HRE. Finally, she contends that educational academics are more 'human' focused in their definitions, encouraging a personal and reflective approach. This has resonance with Tibbitts' taxonomy of models based on an international review of approaches to HRE.[58] She contends that the emerging models fall into three categories: *values and awareness*-based approaches which aim to transmit basic knowledge of and commitment to the normative goals laid out in key human rights instruments, through public campaigns and school curricula; *accountability* models which focus on human rights law and the protection of rights and tend to be aimed at the legal profession, police officers, community activists etc; and *transformational* models which aim to empower individuals to recognize and commit to preventing human rights abuses which are generally directed towards vulnerable populations and victims of human rights abuses.

In reviewing this and other relevant literature,[59] we would argue that approaches to HRE can be located along two continuums: a continuum of *purpose*, resonating with the purposes of education itself, from promoting individual personal change through to securing societal change; and a continuum of *process* from promoting human rights values through to ensuring human rights compliance. If HRE is to contribute effectively to the development of a human rights culture it must bring together the distinct perspectives of the State, human rights activists and educationalists, in the development of HRE programmes. Such programmes must not only harness the potential of HRE to effect *individual* change, and assure personal commitment to human rights advocacy, but also aim to secure *societal* change through maintaining a critical edge to both content and delivery. This necessitates an approach grounded in an understanding of international human rights standards, which emphasizes accountability and which is directed not merely at children in schools but also at government and public officials and wider civic society.

Pragmatically, since it is our young people who are the voters, parliamentarians, teachers, and police officers of tomorrow, educating them about human rights is conceivably one of the most valuable investments a society can make in its future.[60] Therefore, it is unsurprising that numerous statements by the

---

[57] Nancy Flowers, *A Survey of Human Rights Education* (2003).

[58] Tibbitts, 'Understanding What We Do: Emerging Models for Human Rights Education', n 55 above.

[59] For eg Audrey Osler (ed.) *Teachers, Human Rights and Diversity* (2005); Audrey Osler and Hugh Starkey, *Teacher Education and Human Rights* (1996); Norma Tarrow 'Human rights education: alternative conceptions' in James Lynch, Celia Modgil, and Sohan Modgil (eds), *Cultural Diversity and the Schools: human rights, education and global responsibility, Vol. 4* (1992).

[60] Felissa Tibbitts, 'Planning for the Future: Human Rights in Schools' in Raymond Sweenenhuis (ed.), *Handbook for the Helsinki Committees: A Guide in Monitoring and Promoting Human Rights and NGO Management* (1995).

international human rights community explicitly stress the need for specific human rights education directed at the *young* in society.[61] This brings the focus of the location for HRE to the doors of the school and the formal curriculum. Educationalists and education policy-makers have responded and significant advances have been made internationally over the last 10 years: the development of education laws and policies which reflect HRE principles; revision of curricula to include elements of HRE; re-writing of textbooks to ensuring consistency with human rights principles; development of educational materials; provision of pre-service; and in-service training in HRE.[62] HRE has also informed international debate surrounding other curricular initiatives within schools, notably peace education,[63] education for democracy and civics, and citizenship education.[64] Many children are therefore being presented with opportunities to learn the language of human rights and to explore its application in a variety of contexts. However, there is little point in schools teaching children *about* human rights if at the same time they are denying pupils their rights within the classroom. The inextricable link between the protection of children's rights within schools and human rights education is well-recognized. The view of educationalists that HRE cannot be seen in isolation from the environment in which it is executed,[65] is endorsed by the international human rights community through the Committee on the Rights of the Child which has observed that:

'Human rights education should provide information on the content of human rights treaties. But children should also learn about human rights by seeing human rights standards implemented in practice, whether at home, in school, or within the community.'[66]

---

[61] For eg, United Nations Declaration on the Promotion among Youth of Ideals of Peace, Mutual Respect and Understanding between Peoples (GA resolution 2037, 7 December 1965) principles II and III; United Nations Convention on the Rights of the Child Articles 29, 42; United Nations Guidelines for the Prevention of Juvenille Delinquency (The Riyadh Guidelines) (GA resolution 45/112 14 December 1990); Council of Europe Recommendation No. R(83)4 (1983); Council of Europe Recommendation R(85)7 on teaching and learning about human rights in schools (14 May 1985); Council of Europe Recommendation on the Teaching and Learning of Human Rights in Schools (1991): Council of Europe; Council of Europe Recommendation 2002(12) on Education for Democratic Citizenship.

[62] United Nations High Commission for Human Rights *Promotion and Protection of Human Rights: Information and Education United Nations Decade for Human Rights Report on the Achievements and Shortcomings of the Decade and on Future UN Activities in This Area* (E/CN.4/2004/93).

[63] Betty Reardon, 'Human Rights as Education for Peace' in George Andreopoulus and Richard Claude (eds), *Human Rights Education for the Twenty First Century* (1997) 21–34; Grace Feuerverger, *Oasis of dreams: teaching and learning peace in a Jewish-Palestinian Village in Israel* (2001); Gavriel Salomon and Baruch Nevo (eds), *Peace education: the concept, principles, and practices around the world* (2002).

[64] Soon-Won Kang, 'Democracy and Human Rights Education in South Korea' (2002) 38 Comparative Education 315; Alan Smith 'Citizenship Education in Northern Ireland: beyond national identity' (2003) 33 Cambridge Journal of Education 15; Peter Lemish 'Civic and Citizenship Education in Israel' (2003) 33 Cambridge Journal of Education 53; Audrey Osler and Hugh Starkey, *Changing Citizenship: Democracy and Inclusion in Education* (2005).

[65] Norma Tarrow, *Human Rights and Education* (1992).

[66] Committee on the Rights of the Child *Comment No. 1 on the Aims of Education*, n 42 above, para 15.

In sum, an effective HRE programme requires a school environment where children not only learn *about* human rights but learn *through* human rights.[67] If such conditions are met then there is the potential to educate children *for* human rights, as advocates capable of contributing to the transformation of their society.

Delivering the Promises

The human rights discourse which pertains to education is laden with promise: the implementation of children's rights within education and the delivery of human rights education, as discussed above, are portrayed as a means with which to transform not just children's lives but society itself. This is, however, inevitably contingent upon the success or otherwise of the strategies in place for *delivering* these promises, embedding the human rights principles in the fabric of school life and making the rhetoric a reality in children's lived experience.

For human rights *law* to be effective there must be a means of enforcing the legal standards. A key difficulty is that the scope for individuals to make complaints about breaches of education rights in international human rights law is very limited.[68] Although the ECHR contains a justiciable right not to be 'denied' education,[69] this lacks 'the fine-tuning required to accommodate the full range of children's educational needs'.[70] Moreover, the European Court of Human Rights has granted individual States a very wide margin of appreciation in the context of education[71] and the domestic courts throughout Europe have followed suit.[72] Given the limitations inherent with litigation, the key legal mechanism for enforcement has fallen to the periodic reports of the Committee on the Rights of the Child. The Committee has consistently highlighted breaches of school children's rights in conflict-affected education systems.[73] However, the limitations of the UN's periodic reporting system are well-documented.[74] Not only are there

---

[67] Derek Heater, *Human Rights Education in Schools: concepts, attitudes and skills* (1984).

[68] The International Covenant on Social and Economic Rights does not yet have a procedure for individual or group complaints about breaches of its provisions.

[69] Art. 2 of the First Protocol of the European Convention on Human Rights.

[70] Jane Fortin (1999), 'Rights Brought Home for Children' (1999) 62 Modern Law Review 350, 364.

[71] Anthony Bradley, 'The Convention Right to Education and the Human Rights Act 1998' (1999) 4 European Human Rights Law Review 395.

[72] Jan De Groof and Gracienne Lauwers (eds), *No-one shall be denied the right to education* (2004).

[73] See eg, the Committee on the Rights of the Child's criticism of educational provision for Palestine Children in Israel. It expressed concern about the serious deterioration of access to education of children in the occupied Palestinian territories as a result of the measures imposed by the Israeli Defence Forces, including road closures, curfews and mobility restrictions, and the destruction of school infrastructure. United Nations Committee on the Rights of the Child (2002), *Concluding Observations of the Committee on the Rights of the Child: Israel* (UN/CRC/C/15/Add.188), (2002) para 52.

[74] Dominic McGoldrick, 'The United Nations Convention on the Rights of the Child' (1991) 5 International Journal of Law and the Family 132; Michael Freeman, 'The Future of Children's Rights', (2000) 14 Children and Society 277, 289.

insufficient resources to enable adequate follow-up and monitoring of recommendations, but the reports themselves often lack sufficient detail to be meaningful.[75] An additional difficulty lies in the fact that the reports are directed towards government and there is little evidence that they are communicated to the places where children spend their time (such as school classrooms). So, for example, Michael King has observed that, although the CRC conveys the impression of a 'direct line of command (or at least strong influence) from the United Nations to nation-state to a citizen...this impression bears little relation to any realities except those created by law'.[76] The implementation mechanisms of the CRC are not, however, confined to law. Article 42 of the CRC requires States parties to make the provisions of the Convention widely known to children and adults alike. This provision, unique in human rights instruments, acknowledges that 'knowledge is power' and that one of the most effective ways of ensuring compliance is to engage the public in the application and enforcement of the Convention through effective human rights education.[77]

For human rights *education* to be effective there must be a means of securing a committed and co-ordinated approach to its implementation at both an intergovernmental and national level if it is to achieve the promise of its impact at school level. While, as outlined above, some advances have been made, the UN Decade for HRE has failed to deliver fully on the promise of HRE recognized in part by the announcement of a new 'World Programme for HRE'.[78] Essentially it appears that a lack of commitment from national governments coupled with a lack of co-ordination at an intergovernmental level has impacted on the quantity and quality of HRE programmes being established in schools. At a national level, governments have largely ignored international calls to fulfil their obligations to HRE.[79] However, blame cannot be laid solely at the door of national governments. Inadequate co-ordination between international and regional intergovernmental organizations and a lack of resources allocated to the UN Decade[80] are

[75] One example of this is the stock reference to the need to introduce human rights education, without any attempt to link this to specific breaches of children's rights within education or even the particular context and/or conflict.

[76] Michael King, 'Children's Rights as Communication: Reflections on Autopoietic Theory and The United Nations Convention' (1994) 57 Modern Law Review 385, 401.

[77] Cynthia Price-Cohen 'The United Nations Convention on the Rights of the Child: A Feminist Landmark' (1997) 3 William and Mary Journal of Women and Law 29, 56.

[78] GA resolution 59/113.

[79] United Nations High Commission for Human Rights *Report of the United Nations High Commissioner for Human Rights on the Mid-term Evaluation of the Progress Made Towards the Achievement of the Objectives of the UN Decade for Human Rights Education* ('Mid Term Report'). This report noted that 'effective national strategies [had] rarely been developed' (para 129a) for the implementation of HRE and that nationally organized activities tended to be 'one-off' events with little or no follow up (para 96c). For further critique of the UN Decade, see Nils Rosemann, 'Human Rights Education- Towards the End of the UN Decade' (2003) 4 Mennesker and Retigheter: Nordic Journal of Human Rights.

[80] The Office of the High Commission for Human Rights, whilst entrusted with the implementation of UN Decade, was not provided with specific additional resources to carry out this function, see *Mid Term Report*, n 79 above, para 128d.

symptomatic of the fact that there has been no system-wide response within the UN to the Decade.[81] For example, several international human rights instruments contain articles relevant to HRE[82] and the UN has urged their treaty bodies, when examining reports of States parties, to place emphasis on the obligations of States in the area of HRE and to reflect that emphasis in their concluding observations.[83]

However, to date comments made by treaty bodies are at best tokenistic and to this end the potential to adequately monitor HRE has not been fully exploited.[84] This indicates that HRE is perceived at best as an 'add on' rather than a crucial element of realizing the right to education. It is not surprising therefore that only one of the countries responding to the mid-term evaluation of the UN Decade HRE indicated that HRE had the status of a subject in its own right on the school curriculum.[85] In all other countries, HRE, if present at all, is a component part of other educational initiatives such as peace studies or citizenship education. This is mirrored in the growing shift within academic literature to place aspects of HRE as a component of other educational initiatives.[86] While it is accepted that a human rights dimension to such initiatives adds value, it is crucial that HRE is embedded in the framework of such educational programmes if they are to have significant impact.[87] However, merely employing human rights as value base to subjects such as Citizenship Education could result in diluted HRE programmes which are solely values orientated, providing no opportunity for young people to understand and appreciate the need for accountability.[88] Such superficial exposure to human rights is insufficient in providing children with the necessary critical tools with which to contribute to the development of a culture of rights.

Northern Ireland: A Case Study

Educational and legal discourses, while powerful in and of themselves, are presented with real challenges in their contribution to the realization of a human rights culture. However, the recognition within each discourse of a role for the other suggests that a combined approach could release the latent power of both.

---

[81] *Mid Term Report*, n 79 above, para 128c, f; 129b.   [82] See n 50 above.
[83] Further, it urges all relevant mechanisms of the Commission on Human Right (working groups, special rapporteurs etc) to include systematically in their reports a specific section on HRE and to include it as an agenda item of their annual meetings (General Assembly Resolution 48/127 1993 57/212 2003).   [84] *Mid Term Report*, n 79 above, para 171.
[85] ibid para 96e.   [86] See eg nn 63 and 64 above.
[87] See eg Lynn Davies, *Citizenship Education and Human Rights Education: Key Concepts and Debates* (2000).
[88] The *Mid Term* Report, n 79 above, cautions against a purely values orientated approach, stating that HRE should 'make reference to human rights instruments and mechanisms for protection, and to procedures for ensuring accountability', para 131. This is re-emphasized in the *Plan of Action for the First Phase of the World Programme for Human Rights Education*.

The use of a legal discourse to claim human rights within education and the separate development of human rights education in the Northern Irish curriculum provides a useful location for illustrating the potential of such a combined approach.

Northern Ireland's school system is in many ways an ideal lens through which to explore the potential of both children's rights and human rights education, not only because it is located in a jurisdiction which is characterized by conflict and religious divisions but also because schools themselves are segregated along religious lines.[89] Over 94 per cent of children receive their education in schools which are almost exclusively Catholic or exclusively Protestant. Moreover, 30 years of violent conflict and allegations of inequality have resulted in a fairly sophisticated local understanding and use of international human rights law.[90] Thus, not only is Northern Ireland a society in which there is a compelling need for an education system which respects/promotes human rights, but there has also been a readiness to deploy a range of human rights arguments in order to effect change within the school system.[91]

Human rights discourse has been deployed strategically to secure equal State funding for children attending Catholic schools within Northern Ireland.[92] The high degree of respect afforded to parental wishes, delivered through a series of equally funded school options is, arguably, a model of minority rights protection in education. The difficulty is that the successes in terms of children's right of equal access *to* education have further embedded the separatist approach to schooling, thereby bringing with them new challenges for securing children's rights *through* education. So, while the system surpasses human rights standards at a structural level, the high degree of religious segregation within the system generates new challenges for the delivery of human rights. For those who consider that integrated ('mixed religion') education is the answer, international human rights law offers little in terms of direct support.[93] In spite of this, one of the concerns which the Committee on the Rights of the Child has expressed about Northern Ireland is the high level of religious segregation and low levels of 'integration' in the education system.[94] While more needs to be done to ensure that there are places available for children who want to attend integrated schools, it could,

---

[89] See Laura Lundy, *Education Law, Policy and Practice in Northern Ireland* (2000); Tony Gallagher, *Education in Divided Societies* (2004).

[90] Brice Dickson, 'Northern Ireland and the European Convention', in Brice Dickson (ed.), *Human Rights and the European Convention* (1997).

[91] Laura Lundy, 'From Act to Order: The Metamorphosis of Education Legislation' (1998) 20(1) Liverpool Law Review 63.

[92] Laura Lundy, 'Human Rights and Equality Litigation in Northern Ireland's Schools' (2004) Education Law Journal 82.

[93] An attempt to challenge the levels of State funding for integrated schools in the European Court of Human Rights was deemed inadmissible: *X and Y* v *United Kingdom*, (1982) EHRR 293.

[94] United Nations Committee on the Rights of the Child (2002), *Concluding Observations of the Committee on the Rights of the Child: United Kingdom of Great Britain and Northern Ireland* (UN/CRC/C/15/Add.188), (2002).

however, be argued that an exclusive focus on integration over-emphasizes the physical separation that is an unfortunate but inevitable characteristic of education systems worldwide (where divisions manifest themselves in, for example, race, class, or gender) and that more attention needs to be given to what is arguably a more fundamental obligation, that is ensuring that education, wherever it takes place, is directed towards: 'the preparation of the child for responsible life in a free society, in the spirit of understanding, peace, tolerance, equality of sexes, and friendship among all peoples, ethnic, national and religious groups and persons of indigenous origin'.[95]

Attempts to deal with the reality of religious segregation in schools have been framed almost exclusively within a community relations paradigm and have taken a tripartite approach of supporting systemic change, encouraging cross-community contact schemes, and promoting curriculum initiatives.[96] Since the segregated nature of the education system persists and cross-community contact schemes have had little impact[97] it would appear that the *curriculum* holds the greatest potential for surmounting the perceived impasse outlined above. As the Committee on the Rights of the Child has observed the child's right to education is 'not only a matter of access but also of content'.[98] Early efforts were made to create a curriculum which reflected the nature of the divided community in Northern Ireland[99] by the inclusion of the statutory cross-curricular themes of Cultural Heritage and Education for Mutual Understanding.[100] The objectives of these themes resonated with the *sentiment* expressed in the aims of education articulated in the UNCRC but it is widely accepted that they had limited impact.[101] Whilst this was due in part to implementation issues such as inadequate training, the tendency for teachers to avoid controversial issues, and a lack of institutional ownership,[102] it could be suggested that the premise of the themes themselves was fundamentally flawed. A complete absence of any reference to human rights within the objectives or guidance material for the themes has meant that they failed to tap into the transformative potential of human

---

[95] CRC, Art 29(1).

[96] It is not the place of this essay to explore the development of these three strands of the educational response to segregation, since the primary focus of the essay is on curriculum. For a fuller discussion see eg of Alan Smith 'Education and the Conflict in Northern Ireland' in Seamus Dunn (ed.), *Facets of the Conflict in Northern Ireland* (1995); Department of Education Northern Ireland, *Towards a Culture of Tolerance* (1999); Tony Gallagher *Education in Divided Societies* (2004).

[97] See eg Una O'Connor, Brendan Hartop, and Alan McCully, *A Research Study of Pupil Perceptions of the Schools Community Relations Programme* (2003); Una O'Connor, Brendan Hartop, and Alan McCully, Review of Schools Community Relations Programme (2002).

[98] Committee on the Rights of the Child, *General Comment No. 1 on the Aims of Education*, n 42 above, para 3.

[99] Leslie Caul (ed.), *A Common Curriculum—The Case for Northern Ireland* (1993).

[100] Northern Ireland Curriculum Council, *Cross-Curricular Themes—Guidance Materials* (1990).

[101] Alan Smith, 'Citizenship Education in Northern Ireland: beyond national identity?' (2003) 33(1) Cambridge Journal of Education 15.

[102] Alan Smith and Alan Robinson, *Education for Mutual Understanding, The Initial Statutory Years* (1996).

rights education described above. As such they could not deliver fully on the aims of education or contribute in any meaningful way to the development of a human rights culture.

Recent developments are, however, more promising, particularly the inclusion of citizenship education as a statutory element in the curriculum.[103] While citizenship education has been described as the 'natural evolution' of past curricular initiatives[104] a growing emphasis placed on human rights has given it a distinctly different tone. In addition to the general agreement that human rights principles provide both a framework[105] and globally accepted value base[106] for the citizenship curriculum in Northern Ireland, the *specific* teaching about human rights is a fundamental requirement of the new curriculum and as such pupils are entitled to a HRE programme.[107] In particular, specific reference is made to providing pupils with opportunities to 'investigate why different rights must be limited/balanced in our society due to expressions of diversity'.[108] The framing of such issues within a human rights paradigm is a new departure within the Northern Ireland Curriculum and, given the potential for HRE outlined above, may go some way to ensuring that issues relating to the divided nature of this society can be addressed even within a segregated education system. It is precisely the strengthening of this aspect in the Northern Ireland Curriculum which offers the most potential for it to deliver on the aims articulated in Article 29 of the UNCRC.

However, significant as these developments are, there remains scope for improvement. While the 'investigation of key human rights principles' is identified as a statutory minimum entitlement, the content of specific international instruments such as the UDHR, ECHR, and in particular the UNCRC are merely included as examples and are not afforded compulsory status in the curriculum.[109] This lack of certainty in relation to the minimum entitlement coupled with a low level of knowledge of children's rights which persists in the teaching

---

[103] For an account of the development of the citizenship curriculum in Northern Ireland, see Michael Arlow 'Citizenship education in a divided society: the case of Northern Ireland' in Sobhi Tawil and Alexandra Harley (eds), *Education, Conflict and Social Cohesion* (2004).

[104] Ken Wylie, 'Citizenship, Identity and Social Inclusion: Lessons from Northern Ireland' (2004) 39(2) European Journal of Education 237.

[105] David Kerr, Alan Smith, and Stephen McCarthy, 'Citizenship Education in England, Ireland and Northern Ireland' (2002) 37 (2) European Journal of Education 179, 187.

[106] See Smith, '*Citizenship Education in Northern Ireland: beyond national identity?*' n 101 above.

[107] Statutory aspects of the revised curriculum for Northern Ireland are referred to as statements of minimum entitlement. In relation to HRE, statutory aspects of the curriculum include reference to understanding the importance of upholding human rights standards, the investigation of key human rights principles as outlined in major human rights instruments and the examination of local and global scenarios where human rights have been seriously infringed. In addition the other key themes of the citizenship curriculum are underpinned by the core principles of human rights and social responsibility and as such, issues arising from discussion of these concepts in the classroom must be addressed through the language of human rights. See Council for the Curriculum and Assessment, *Pathway: Proposals for Curriculum and Assessment at Key Stage Three Part 1: Background Rationale and Detail* (2004).   [108] ibid, 47.

[109] ibid.

profession in Northern Ireland[110] could result in the diluted approach to HRE cautioned against above. The Committee on the Rights of the Child which has observed that: 'if the adults around children, their parents and other family members, teachers and carers do not understand the implications of the Convention, and above all its confirmation of the equal status of children as the subjects of rights, it is most unlikely that the rights set out in the Convention will be realized for many children'.[111] In view of this, the Committee has recommended that initial and in-service training for teachers and others working with children should be 'systematic and ongoing', 'emphasize the status of the child as a holder of human rights', and should 'increase knowledge and understanding of the Convention and encourage active respect for all its provisions'.[112]

As argued earlier in this essay, the development of a human rights culture requires standard setting at a constitutional level, judicial activity to enforce these standards and effective educational programmes to both inform individuals about human rights and to persuade them of their intrinsic value. Although this case study has focused primarily on the latter two arenas, the proposed Bill of Rights for Northern Ireland presents an opportunity to harness the combined potential of legal and educational strategies in building a human rights culture through constitutional guarantees. While the proposed Bill has a dedicated section on education rights, the only provision which could debatably include the right to human rights education is somewhat broad:

'The State shall ensure that education in all its forms shall be directed to the promotion of human rights, equality, dignity of the person, respect for diversity and tolerance.'[113]

The Northern Ireland Human Rights Commission explains that this statement on the nature of education is based on the general provisions contained within the UDHR and the International Covenant on Economic Social and Cultural Rights (ICESR) without any reference to the most extensive and recent statement on the right to education, namely the UNCRC. The Commission further directs that section 12(6) of the proposed Bill, that 'the State shall take appropriate measures to ensure that the rights of children are widely known', should be read in conjunction with the provision outlined above. This rather diluted statement in relation to promotion of children's rights coupled with a lack of explicit reference to human rights education does little to guarantee constitutional safeguards. Moreover, the provisions within the Proposed Bill of Rights fall short of the State's existing commitments under the UNCRC.

In sum, more concerted effort to harness the synergy of children's rights and human rights education could result in the development of a culture of human

---

[110] Ciara Davey, Clare Dwyer, Siobhan McAlister, Ursula Kilkelly, Rosemary Kilpatrick, Laura Lundy, Linda Moore, and Phil Scraton, *Children's Rights in Northern Ireland (2004)*.

[111] Committee on the Rights of the Child, *General Comment No. 1 on the Aims of Education*, n 42 above, para 66.   [112] ibid, para 53.

[113] Northern Ireland Human Rights Commission, *Progressing a Bill of Rights for Northern Ireland—an update* (2004) Section 13(6).

rights which goes beyond legal and constitutional safeguards into one in which individuals are convinced of the value of human rights, conversant with international human rights standards and the need for accountability and, as such, capable of contributing to the transformation of their society. Such a culture resonates with that envisioned by Stephen Livingstone, who maintained that the task of developing a human rights culture went beyond passing laws and creating new institutions to persuading individuals in society that securing their own rights would be safeguarded through respecting the rights of others. He argued that 'if this [were to be] achieved then Northern Ireland may well move from being a case study of human rights problems to providing a model of human rights achievement'. [114]

Conclusion

The case study presented above illustrates the potential for legal and educational discourses to contribute to the development of a human rights culture in Northern Ireland. Furthermore, it underlines the necessity for educational strategies alongside the constitutional and judicial endeavours which are more traditionally seen as the focus of 'how to realise a human rights culture'. Societies affected by conflict have a profound and compelling need to create and sustain such a culture. As noted previously, in such societies educational institutions may become direct sites of political, social, or ideological conflict. They may sustain and nurture such conflicts. They may in turn become key vehicles in a process of conflict transformation. However, we would argue that, by placing education front and centre, the Northern Ireland experience speaks directly to a deeper understanding of a human rights culture in more 'settled' societies.

Such a culture requires strategies which are designed to harness both the normative and enforcing capacity of law and the persuasive potential of education. While law can set the standards with which society is expected to comply, education can convince individuals of the inherent value of doing so. Education provides the rationale behind the rules. Schools, as the interface for both the implementation of children's rights and the delivery of human rights education, are the obvious places in which to concentrate efforts to instigate and embed a culture of human rights. In particular, school-children's rights will only be realized when HRE is recognized as a central component of the strategies for enforcement and implementation; HRE will only be meaningful when it is conducted within a climate in which the adults who act as the gatekeepers to children's enjoyment of their rights are not just informed of the content of international human rights law but are persuaded of its value. Moreover, the significance of schools as a fertile site for developing an ethos of and sustaining a commitment to human rights

[114] Ivana Bacik and Stephen Livingstone, *Towards a Culture of Human Rights in Ireland* (2000) 91.

in general cannot be underplayed. As one of the architects of the Universal Declaration, Eleanor Roosevelt, observed:

'Where after all do universal human rights begin? In small places, close to home—so close and so small that they cannot be seen on any map of the world. Yet they are the world of the individual person: the neighbourhood he lives in; the school or college he attends... Such are the places where every man, woman, and child seeks equal justice, equal opportunity, equal dignity without discrimination. Unless these rights have meaning there, they have little meaning anywhere.'[115]

If we fail to engage with human rights discourse in small but potentially potent locations such as schools we shall as Eleanor Roosevelt observed 'look in vain for progress in the larger world'.[116]

---

[115] Eleanor Roosevelt, Speech at the United Nations, 27 March 1953.   [116] ibid.

24

Protecting the Marginalized?

Colin Harvey

Introduction

The title for this chapter is borrowed from an article first published in 2000 and called, 'Protecting the Marginalised: The Role of The European Court of Human Rights'.[1] In that article, which I co-authored with Stephen Livingstone, we suggested that the European Court of Human Rights could legitimately adopt a robust approach to the protection of the rights of marginalized individuals and groups. When we stressed 'legitimately' we were fully aware of the criticism of the judicial role from a progressive perspective. Our argument was that a strong rights-based approach by the Court was consistent with democratic values and could even enhance them. We urged the Court to take an assertive approach and viewed this as consistent with a firm commitment to the values of representative democracy.

The idea that rights and democracy are necessarily in tension is now frequently rejected. However, argument persists on the potential for hostility between representative democracy and the judicial role. We reached our conclusions on the basis of an understanding of the sceptical arguments. We knew the arguments, but understood from knowledge and experience that meaningful human rights protection is at the core of a functioning political democracy. A crude way of putting this is: you do not get a proper democratic culture without secure mechanisms for human rights promotion and protection. This goes beyond simply asserting that rights make democracy possible, or even the view that the adoption of rights standards tells us very much. What matters is how standards are used, who uses them, and the difference they make in practice. The underpinning assumption in this approach is that the standards are primarily there to protect and promote the rights of vulnerable and marginalized individuals and groups. Human rights law should have a transformative impact; its aim should be to change societies and communities for the better. The standards should operate as normative footholds to assist in achieving rights-based outcomes.

---

[1] Colin Harvey and Stephen Livingstone, 'Protecting the Marginalised: The Role of the European Convention on Human Rights' (2000) 51 Northern Ireland Legal Quarterly 445.

In this essay, I will examine the argument further in two steps and make a case for a particular understanding of human rights law. First, I explore what we mean when we talk about human rights law. Secondly, I will discuss attitudes towards human rights and their use in protecting vulnerable and marginalized groups. If human rights law is not making a difference for those who require the protections most what other purposes is it serving? Are practical outcomes for individuals and communities in individual cases more significant than conceptual or doctrinal coherence and consistency? Should our primary focus be on the relative utility of rights in context?

A World of Human Rights Law

The Internationalization of Human Rights

There has been a steady growth of human rights standards. We inhabit a world of human rights standards and institutions. When we discuss human rights law we are now referring primarily to a recognized body of *law*. This is distinct from other legal and political measures which do in fact protect rights but are not framed in this way. The world of human rights law co-exists with continuing, ongoing, and widespread human rights abuse in every region of the globe. Rights have found a home in law at every level: international, regional, and national, but practical implementation is often another matter. This is more than merely a rhetorical point. It raises questions about how rights function in law and politics and whether they can in fact legitimize more than they challenge. If human rights law is so significant why is its impact often limited in situations where it matters most? What is human rights law for?

There are many human rights standards in international law. Numerous international human rights conventions and soft law measures have been adopted. These protections frequently focus on the person rather than exclusively on the citizen. From the protection of refugees in the Convention relating to the Status of Refugees 1951 and its 1967 Protocol,[2] to the International Convention on the Elimination of All Forms of Racial Discrimination 1966,[3] to the International Convention on the Protection of the Rights of All Migrant Workers and Members of their Families 1990.[4] These international human rights instruments are often underpinned by treaty-monitoring mechanisms. For example, the International Convention on the Elimination of All Forms of Discrimination against Women 1979 established a committee to monitor compliance.[5] Compliance with the UN Convention against Torture 1984[6] is monitored by the UN Committee against

---

[2] 189 UNTS 137; 606 UNTS 267.   [3] 660 UNTS 195.
[4] UNGA 45/158 of 18 December 1990.   [5] 1249 UNTS 13.
[6] UNGA 39/46 of 10 December 1984.

Torture through State reporting, communications and inquiries—and implementation has been enhanced through the recent adoption of an optional protocol to the Convention.[7] Other standard-setting work is ongoing; for example, the recent adoption of the International Convention on the Rights of Persons with Disabilities and its Optional Protocol.[8] Work continues on options for an Optional Protocol to the International Covenant on Economic, Social and Cultural Rights 1966.[9] The era of standard setting has not ended. However, the focus has moved towards how compliance can be achieved, and how monitoring can be improved and conducted in more credible ways.[10]

Within the UN, the Office of the High Commissioner for Human Rights operates as a focal point for the entire UN rights regime. The High Commissioner attempts to integrate rights in the UN system as a whole, but is also subject to the reform proposals flowing from, for example, the UN Secretary General.[11] In addition to the treaty-monitoring bodies, there are the special procedures of the UN which function on a thematic and country-specific basis. There is continuing discussion of possible reform.[12] Country mandates include Sudan, Burundi, and Haiti among others, the thematic mandates include: arbitrary detention; the situation of human rights defenders; internally displaced persons; and terrorism.[13] Consideration has been given in recent years to enhancing the effectiveness of the special procedures mechanisms and a concerted effort made to improve co-ordination between the existing treaty-monitoring bodies.[14] Work is progressing on the further development of human rights indicators, for example, in relation to social and economic rights. These would assist the treaty-monitoring bodies, and others, to make meaningful assessments of State compliance. Draft Guidelines have been produced by the Office of the High Commissioner on 'A Human Rights Approach to Poverty Reduction Strategies', which are of considerable practical value.[15] In addition to all this, the infamous UN Human Rights

---

[7] UNGA A/RES/57/199 of 18 December 2002.

[8] The UN General Assembly adopted the International Convention on the Rights of Persons with Disabilities in December 2006, UNGA Res. A/RES/61/106, 13 December, 2006.

[9] The Open-ended Working Group to Consider Options Regarding the Elaboration of an Optional Protocol to the International Covenant on Economic, Social and Cultural Rights held its third session in Geneva on 6–17 February 2006.

[10] See Office of the High Commissioner for Human Rights, *Concept Paper on the High Commissioner's Proposal for a Unified Standing Treaty Body* (14 March 2006, UN HRI/MC/2006/CRP.1).

[11] See eg, UN Secretary General, *In Larger Freedom: Towards Development, Security and Human Rights for All* (21 March 2005, UNGA A/59/2005).

[12] See the Report of the Open-Ended Seminar on Enhancing and Strengthening the Effectiveness of the Special Procedures of the Commission on Human Rights (12–13 October 2005) UN ECOSOC E/CN.4/2006/116.

[13] For further details see http://www.ohchr.org/english/bodies/chr/special/themes.htm.

[14] See n 12 above.

[15] Office of the High Commissioner for Human Rights, *Draft Guidelines: A Human Rights Approach to Poverty Reduction Strategies* (September 2002). See also Office of the High Commissioner for Human Rights, *Human Rights and Poverty Reduction: A Conceptual Framework* (March 2004).

Commission has been replaced by what is hoped will be a more effective body: the UN Human Rights Council.[16]

At the regional level, the African Union in January 2006 announced the appointment of 11 judges to the new African Court of Human and Peoples' Rights.[17] There is an Inter-American Commission and Court of Human Rights,[18] and in Europe, there is the Council of Europe's Convention on Human Rights and its Protocols.[19] The European Convention system is regarded as impressive (when viewed within the general context of weak international human rights implementation mechanisms) and the substantial jurisprudence of the Court is noted beyond Europe. The Court continues to ensure the Convention is a 'living instrument'. But it is not without its difficulties and its effectiveness is also questioned. The problems it is facing are evident in the report of Lord Woolf and others published in December 2005 on the working methods of the Court.[20] At the time of completing the report there were 82,100 cases pending, and in 2004 there were over 44,000 new applications.[21] There is, of course, more to human rights protection than the European Convention on Human Rights. The Council of Europe has appointed a Commissioner for Human Rights. The first Commissioner was Alvaro Gil-Robes and the current Commissioner is Thomas Hammarberg.[22] There are other legal instruments of note: the European Social Charter (Revised) 1996[23] and the Framework Convention on National Minorities 1995, for example.[24] In addition, there is the important work of the European Commission against Racism and Intolerance[25] and the European Committee for the Prevention of Torture.[26] When discussing the European regional context, mention should also be made of the European Union (EU). Its Charter of Fundamental Rights was proclaimed in 2000, and there will be an EU Fundamental Rights Agency.[27] The Charter of Fundamental Rights found a central place in the Constitutional Treaty.[28] There is an extensive framework of human rights standards at all levels.

---

[16] See http://www.ohchr.org/engligh/bodies/hrcouncil.   [17] See http://www.achpr.org/.
[18] See http://www.corteidh.or.cr.   [19] See http://www.echr.coe.int/echr.
[20] Lord Woolf *et al, Review of the Working Methods of the European Court of Human Rights* (December 2005).   [21] ibid.
[22] See Commissioner for Human Rights, 5th Annual Report to the Committee of Ministers and Parliamentary Assembly, 29 March 2006, CommDH (2006) 16.   [23] ETS 163.
[24] ETS 157.
[25] See eg, European Commission against Racism and Intolerance, Third Report on the United Kingdom, CRI (2005) 27.
[26] See Report to the Government of the United Kingdom on the Visit to the United Kingdom carried out by the European Committee for the Prevention of Torture and Inhuman or Degrading Treatment or Punishment from 14–19 March 2004 CPT/Inf (2005) 10.
[27] European Commission 'Proposal for a Council Regulation establishing a European Union Agency for Fundamental Rights' COM (2005) 280 final.
[28] See http://www.europa.eu/constitution/.

Rights in National Legal Systems

What about rights in national law? Rights have found a home in constitutional law for some time, from the constitutional revolutions of the seventeenth and eighteenth centuries onwards.[29] These have principally been conceived as intrinsic to notions of citizenship and the social contract between the individual and the State. But the protections can often in fact extend to those who are not citizens. To give some examples of constitutional protections: Chapter two of the constitution of Afghanistan is dedicated to fundamental rights; the Kenyan constitution Chapter five deals with rights; as does Chapter five of Vietnam's constitution; the South African constitution is well known and much celebrated, with Chapter two including the South African Bill of Rights; Chapter two of the Chinese and the Ukrainian constitutions contain extensive reference to rights.[30] In other words, rights protections are present in constitutions throughout the world. In addition, national human rights institutions have also been created in many States.[31] There are now numerous national human rights commissions with a variety of functions and powers. For example, a Human Rights Commission has recently been created in Afghanistan.[32] There are also the many excellent local, national, and international non-governmental organizations, often existing, working, and achieving results in the most difficult circumstances.

Human Rights in the British and Irish Contexts

What about human rights protection and promotion on these islands? What about the British and Irish contexts? A basic starting point is that the two constitutional contexts differ. Ireland has a single documentary constitution and an established tradition of constitutional rights protection.[33] The UK does not possess a single written constitution, but does have, for example, statutes which are described by the judiciary as of 'constitutional significance'.[34] The judiciary has also developed common law conceptions of fundamental rights.

In the Irish context, the concept of rights is a foundational principle of the Belfast Agreement.[35] There are two Human Rights Commissions on the island of

---

[29] See William A. Edmundson, *An Introduction to Rights* (2004).
[30] These constitutions can be found at http://www.worldlii.org.
[31] See Bertrand G. Ramcharan (ed.), *The Protection Role of National Human Rights Institutions* (2005). For further information, see National Human Rights Institutions Forum http://www.nhri.net.
[32] http://www.aihrc.org.af/.
[33] See James Casey, *Constitutional Law in Ireland* (3rd edn, 2000) chs 12–19.
[34] See generally Jeffrey Jowell and Dawn Oliver (eds), *The Changing Constitution* (5th ed., 2004); Vernon Bogdanor (ed.), *The British Constitution in the Twentieth Century* (2003).
[35] *Agreement Reached in the Multi-Party Negotiations* (Cm 3883, 1998). The Belfast Agreement includes both the Multi-Party Agreement and the British-Irish Agreement. For analysis of the Agreement, see Brendan O'Leary, 'The Nature of the Agreement' (1999) 22 Fordham International Law

Ireland.[36] There is a Joint Committee of the two Human Rights Commissions which, among other things, is working on a Charter of Rights.[37] The European Convention on Human Rights has been given further effect, through the Human Rights Act 1998 in Northern Ireland and the European Convention on Human Rights Act 2003 in Ireland. The Bill of Rights process in Northern Ireland holds out the prospect of a new legal instrument which would contain additional rights and supplement the European Convention.[38]

In the UK, the Human Rights Act 1998 has made an impact and has generated a voluminous literature and considerable public debate.[39] There is research ongoing by the Department for Constitutional Affairs to assess the practical impact in the public sector.[40] The British Institute of Human Rights has undertaken significant research and found that problems and gaps remain.[41] The Act has attracted popular attention in the British press and is now regularly subjected to criticism.[42]

Journal 1628; Brendan O'Leary, 'The Nature of the British-Irish Agreement' (1999) 233 New Left Review 66; Brendan O'Leary, 'The Character of the 1998 Agreement: Results and Prospects', in Wilford (ed.), *Aspects of the Belfast Agreement* (2001) 49; John McGarry and Brendan O'Leary, *The Northern Ireland Conflict: Consociational Engagements* (2004); Austen Morgan, *The Belfast Agreement: a practical legal analysis* (2000); Kieran McEvoy and John Morison, 'Beyond the "Constitutional Moment": Law, Transition and Peacemaking in Northern Ireland' (2003) 26 Fordham International Law Journal 961; Gordon Anthony, 'Public Law Litigation and the Belfast Agreement' (2002) 8 European Public Law 401. For the wider context, see Brendan O'Leary and John McGarry, *The Politics of Antagonism: Understanding Northern Ireland* (2nd ed., 1996); John McGarry, ' "Democracy" in Northern Ireland: experiments in self-rule from the Protestant Ascendancy to the Good Friday Agreement' (2002) 8 Nations and Nationalism 451.

[36] The Northern Ireland Human Rights Commission was established by the Northern Ireland Act 1998 and the Irish Human Rights Commission was established by the Human Rights Commission Act 2000, see also Human Rights Commission (Amendment) Act 2001.

[37] A Joint Committee is referred to in the Belfast Agreement in the section on 'Rights, Safeguards and Equality of Opportunity' para 10: 'It is envisaged that there would be a joint committee of representatives of the two Human Rights Commissions, North and South, as a forum for consideration of human rights issues in the island of Ireland. The joint committee will consider, among other matters, the possibility of establishing a charter, open to signature by all democratic parties, reflecting and endorsing agreed measures for the protection of the fundamental rights of everyone living in the island of Ireland.'

[38] See Stephen Livingstone, 'The Need for a Bill of Rights in Northern Ireland' (2001) 52 Northern Ireland Legal Quarterly 269.

[39] There is an extensive literature on the Human Rights Act 1998, see generally Lord Lester and Lydia Clapinska, 'Human Rights and the British Constitution', in Jowell and Oliver, *The Changing Constitution*, n 34 above, ch 3; Colin Harvey (ed.), *Human Rights in the Community: Rights as Agents for Change* (2005); Lord Steyn, '2000–2005: Laying the Foundations of Human Rights Law in the United Kingdom' [2005] European Human Rights Law Review 349.

[40] Department for Constitutional Affairs, Human Rights Insight Project Draft Final Report, Theo Gavrielides, *Stage 1 Report: Consumers—reviewing the evidence on human rights awareness and experiences of consumers of public services* (June 2005). The Department for Constitutional Affairs and the Home Office conducted reviews of the Human Rights Act in 2006.

[41] British Institute of Human Rights *Something for Everyone: The Impact of the Human Rights Act and the Need for a Human Rights Commission* (December 2002). It has also tried to defend the Act against criticism, see in particular British Institute of Human Rights *Briefing on the Human Rights Act* (May 2006).

[42] *The Sun*, at the time of writing, was running a 'Scrap the Human Rights Act' campaign. It is not alone. *The Daily Telegraph* has also called for the Act to be repealed, see the Leader column of 11 May 2006. The Conservative Party has called for the Human Rights Act to be replaced by a British Bill of Rights.

It is evident that knowledge and understanding of the Human Rights Act and Convention rights generally could be improved and in the public sector, for example, work continues to explore ways in which this might be achieved.

The establishment of the Joint Committee on Human Rights at Westminster has seen more consideration within Parliament of human rights. The Joint Committee remains impressive in both its scrutiny work and the inquiries it has established and completed. There will also be a Commission for Equality and Human Rights in Britain which, among other things, will work to build a human rights culture.[43] Scotland will have its own Human Rights Commission as well.[44] The institutional picture of human rights protection is evolving.

A World of Standards and Limitations

There is a world of human rights standards and institutions. The aim here is not to suggest that the era of standard-setting has ended—it has not—or that the existence of standards necessarily reveals much about what is happening in practice—it does not. However, given the extent of human rights law, the principal focus must now be on assessing its role, measuring impact, monitoring compliance, and ensuring effective implementation of agreed standards. The correct tools are required if this is to be done thoroughly and well. And debate continues as to what this might mean. How straightforward is it to measure compliance with a generalized norm which is itself contested? How do we evaluate the practical use made of human rights standards? Given trends in the social sciences is it naïve to talk of compliance, monitoring, and a human rights culture in the ways sometimes referred to in the human rights law literature? If human rights law is not having a transformative effect hard questions must be asked about why this is the case. Can these hard questions even be answered by human rights lawyers?

While international and regional factors are of considerable importance, the national context is central. It is at national and sub-national levels that the practical impact of human rights law must be assessed and where it matters most. This is not to suggest that national contexts should be examined in isolation. In securing national human rights protection it is evident that a complex interaction between different legal orders and institutional actors comes into play. For example, international standards have on occasion an impact which transcends their formal legal status in national law. Why would this be the case? International human rights actors can have a national impact that also goes beyond any formal status they might possess in the national legal or political arenas. Again, what factors make this the case? What matters in terms of analysis is not simply the existence of the standards, but their interpretation and practical use in context. To understand

---

[43] Equality Act 2006. [44] Scottish Commission for Human Rights Act 2006.

whether they have had a practical impact (what this might mean is itself contested) we need to know not just that they exist, but how they are interpreted and used in practice with political, social, economic, and historical contexts in mind.

It is important to stress one point in relation to institutions. We should not put the judiciary on a pedestal. The courtroom is only one forum of principle among many. Human rights practice is more sophisticated and diverse than is often acknowledged. There are other institutions at the international, regional, and national levels: treaty-monitoring bodies; special rapporteurs; human rights commissioners; parliamentary committees; national human rights commissions; and extensive NGO networks. While full and effective national-level protection is the goal, transnational and international networks and institutions are there also to make this happen. Human rights activists do not have illusions about the judiciary and have demonstrated that they will use all the available institutions and mechanisms to attempt to achieve the objectives of human rights law. However, in defending the rule of law judges have a vital role in guaranteeing that legal protections are interpreted and applied correctly.

As stated earlier in this essay, human rights law properly understood must have transformative social and political potential. If this is not the case then questions need to be asked about what precisely human rights law is promoting. Why create the illusion of a rights-based and socially just society if this was never the intention or little is being done to bring it about? Human rights standards and institutions can exist for presentational purposes. States can come under pressure, or feel obliged, to adopt human rights obligations without the political will to go much further. This does raise an intriguing point. If you put such standards in place you should expect people to use them. But the public debate on rights often circles around their practical use, the type of people who want to use them and benefit from them. Contestation over rights seems to generate the fear of insecurity and instability. What is neglected is that contestation underpins, or should underpin, a healthy democratic culture.

Sceptical Perspectives on Human Rights Law

The proliferation of human rights legal standards is matched by intense academic and public debates on rights. There have traditionally been a number of concerns expressed about the subject and there is much human rights scepticism around. There is a long and distinguished history of scepticism about human rights. This scholarly unease is often reflected in popular criticism of rights. Rights are viewed as individualistic and perpetuate an atomistic approach to human relations. Rights, it is argued, protect minorities (often unpopular minorities) and do not pay due regard to the needs of the majority. Rights impede a tough approach to law and order and undermine the protection of national security. Rights give judges too much power at the expense of elected representatives and democratic institutions. Rights impoverish political discourse by reducing everything to a zero-sum game which undermines other important political values. The list could be extended, but reflects some of the concerns often heard about human rights. Many of the arguments require empirical testing in particular contexts because they are based on the alleged impact of rights. Amartya Sen has recently noted that the 'contrast between the wide use of the idea of human rights and intellectual skepticism about its conceptual soundness is not new'.[45] As he observes, following the US and French revolutions in the eighteenth century, it did not take Jeremy Bentham too long to construct his famous assault on the idea of natural rights.[46] Criticism of rights has a history of its own: from Jeremy Bentham and Edward Burke to Karl Marx.[47] Argument continues while the practice of rights flourishes.

What about modern legal scholarship? In international law, David Kennedy highlights the dark side of international human rights and lists a range of what he views as downsides.[48] He suggests that human rights crowd out other ways of understanding harm and tend to dominate reform strategies.[49] Oona Hathaway has raised the question of whether human rights treaties do make a difference in practice.[50]

In the national legal context there is considerable scepticism about rights in the literature.[51] Some of this is connected to a wider anxiety about legalism and the never-ending arguments about the judicial role in constitutional democracies. These arguments go beyond the human rights debate to question how institutions should function within democratic States. Tom Campbell wants us to think more carefully about what is done with rights in practice; and he points to the extensive empirical reality waiting to be examined.[52] Martin Loughlin argues that contemporary public discourse on notions of liberty, equality, and justice is invariably cast in terms of rights.[53] He is not impressed.[54] He suggests, as others do, that this connects to the prevalence of a more individualistic or atomistic conception of society, and with Michael Ignatieff,[55] sees human rights activism as a form of anti-politics which disguises its political commitments in the legal language of impartiality and neutrality.[56] Loughlin thinks rights adjudication is intrinsically political, with judges and lawyers masking their own political positions while sharing aristocratic disdain for what they see as the messy and compromised world

---

[45] Amartya Sen, 'Elements of a Theory of Human Rights' (2004) 32 Philosophy & Public Affairs 315. See also Amartya Sen, *Development as Freedom* (1999) ch 10.   [46] ibid (2004), 316.

[47] Jeremy Waldron (ed.), *Nonsense Upon Stilts: Bentham, Burke and Marx on the Rights of Man* (1987); Jeremy Waldron (ed.), *Theories of Rights* (1984).

[48] David Kennedy, *The Dark Side of Virtue: Reassessing International Humanitarianism* (2004).

[49] ibid.

[50] Oona Hathaway, 'Do Human Rights Treaties Make a Difference?' (2002) 111 Yale Law Journal 1935.

[51] For an overview, see Tom Campbell, K.D. Ewing, and Adam Tomkins (eds), *Sceptical Essays on Human Rights* (2001).

[52] Tom Campbell, 'Human Rights: The Shifting Boundaries' in Tom Campbell, Jeffrey Goldsworthy, and Adrienne Stone (eds), *Protecting Human Rights: Instruments and Institutions* (2003) ch 1.

[53] Martin Loughlin, *The Idea of Public Law* (2003) ch 7.   [54] ibid.

[55] Michael Ignatieff, *Human Rights as Politics and Idolatry* (2001).

[56] Loughlin, *The Idea of Public Law*, n 53 above, ch 7.

of politics.[57] Loughlin therefore appears persuaded by Alexis de Tocqueville's critique of the secretive and aristocratic habits of lawyers.[58] Mary Ann Glendon in her well-known critique argues that rights talk has distorted American political discourse and is less about human freedom and dignity than the expression of 'insistent unending desires'.[59] Richard Rorty has called for the abandonment of the idea that there are such things as 'inalienable rights'.[60] He argues that we should accept that rights are social constructions and focus on their utility and not whether they have an essential source or nature.[61] Conor Gearty, while supportive of the concept of human rights, has called for a renewed focus on civil liberties and representative democracy.[62] He understands this tradition as intimately linked to the maintenance of representative government and simply a better way of framing the debate.[63] Gearty is part of what might be termed the democratic (or even republican) tradition in UK human rights and public law scholarship along with Keith Ewing, Aileen McColgan, and others. David Dyzenhaus has labelled this branch of public law scholarship as neo-Benthamite and connected it to the rise of what he terms 'democratic legal positivism'.[64] Simon Halliday and Patrick Schmidt stress the need for more socio-legal research on human rights in national contexts if we are to understand, for example 'whether, when, how, and why human rights have been brought home'.[65] Costas Douzinas has talked of the end of human rights.[66] Jeremy Waldron has offered a right-based critique of constitutional rights and expressed dismay at the trend towards judicially enforced Bills of Rights.[67] He believes democratic life is impoverished as a result.[68] Mark Tushnet makes similar arguments in the US context and has come up with fascinating proposals on the prospects for non-judicial constitutional review as part of the project of 'taking the US constitution away from the courts'.[69] Rights have been questioned from a feminist perspective, for example, by Carol Smart,[70] as well as within other branches of critical legal scholarship.[71]

---

[57] ibid.   [58] Alexis de Tocqueville, *Democracy in America* ((1835), 2000).
[59] Mary Ann Glendon, *Rights Talk: The Impoverishment of Political Discourse* (1991).
[60] Richard Rorty, *Philosophy and Social Hope* (1999) 83.   [61] ibid, 84–87.
[62] K.D. Ewing and Conor Gearty, *The Struggle for Civil Liberties: Political Freedom and the Rule of Law in Britain 1914–1945* (2000); Noel Whitty, Thérèse Murphy, and Stephen Livingstone (eds), *Civil Liberties Law: The Human Rights Act Era* (2001).
[63] See Conor Gearty, *Principles of Human Rights Adjudication* (2004).
[64] David Dyzenhaus, 'The Genealogy of Legal Positivism' (2004) 24 Oxford Journal of Legal Studies 39.
[65] Simon Halliday and Patrick Schmidt (eds), *Human Rights Brought Home: Socio-Legal Studies of Human Rights in the National Context* (2004).
[66] Costas Douzinas, *The End of Human Rights* (2000).
[67] Jeremy Waldron, *Law and Disagreement* (1999) P III.   [68] ibid.
[69] Mark Tushnet, *Taking the Constitution Away from the Courts* (1999).
[70] Carol Smart, *Feminism and the Power of Law* (1989).
[71] Duncan Kennedy, 'The Critique of Rights in Critical Legal Studies' in Wendy Brown and Janet Halley (eds), *Left Legalism/Left Critique* (2002) 178.

What is my point? It is a basic one. There is plenty of suspicion about rights which co-exists with the continuing proliferation of human rights standards. There are of course strong advocates of rights. Ronald Dworkin is perhaps the easiest example to cite.[72] But there are others; Amartya Sen, for example, has recently advanced a theory of human rights with an important defence of social and economic rights.[73] Siobhán Mullally argues that feminism should both reshape and reclaim the universalist discourse of human rights.[74]

I will return at the end to the implications of these debates. It is important to note the existence of this extensive body of scholarship because in human rights law we are not facing a scholarly void and human rights is not an intellectually impoverished academic discipline. It remains intriguing to note just how much mistrust of rights there is in the academic literature. This scholarly scepticism is echoed in popular criticism expressed by politicians and others. Human rights do not get a 'good press'. It is possible to rebut the criticisms and sophisticated defences of rights do exist. But the body of work expresses the considerable unease within legal and political scholarship about human rights, and many of the arguments have value for those wishing to retain a critical perspective. Do these debates matter if the understanding of rights presented here is adopted? When we wrote our article in 2000 we were fully aware of the scholarly literature. But it did seem odd that it existed alongside a practice of rights which appeared to be making, or trying to make, social and political life better for individuals and communities. In other words, there continues to be a strange divergence between a global movement dedicated to the protection of rights and a progressive scholarly community determined, it sometimes seems, to find progressive law and politics elsewhere. The small victories of the human rights movement perhaps seem less impressive to those still searching for a comprehensive and unified theory of social and political change. The scholarly scepticism and hostility co-exists alongside advocacy groups and individual human rights activism at the sub-national, national, regional, and international levels which can and does make a practical difference. As noted, there are UN bodies, regional organizations, national human rights commissions, human rights NGOs, and others all trying to use human rights law to make the lives of vulnerable and marginalized groups better. This work does not appear to be aimed at undermining democracy. The practical engagement with rights in fact seems to favour an enriched conception of democratic life and is often anchored in a strong commitment on the part of individuals and communities to a vibrant democracy. Those States with emerging and established human rights cultures appear also to have healthy democratic practices. New democracies seem to see human rights protection as vital to their

---

[72] Ronald Dworkin, *Taking Rights Seriously* (1977).
[73] See Sen, 'Elements of a Theory of Human Rights', n 45 above.
[74] Siobhán Mullally, *Gender, Culture and Human Rights: Reclaiming Universalism* (2006).

new constitutional arrangements. The human rights movement is not without problems, but the intention does not appear to be to undermine representative democracy.

Protecting and Promoting the Human Rights of Refugees and Asylum Seekers

I will now turn to the law of human rights and say something about one area I have worked on in the last decade; refugee and asylum law.[75] There is some evidence that despite a generally negative picture human rights norms have been used to attempt to force practical improvements. The international refugee law regime does provide a useful case study for examining human rights law. A straightforward reason is that the forcibly displaced rely in practice on the 'human' in human rights law. Asylum seekers are not citizens of the State they are in and depend on protections which are not anchored in nationality or citizenship requirements.

International human rights law offers a specific regime of protection: the 1951 Convention relating to the Status of Refugees and its 1967 Protocol. There are several elements to be mindful of. The Convention seeks to construct an international legal concept of the 'refugee'. In other words, as Guy Goodwin-Gill and others note, it is a legal term of art only.[76] A person may be a refugee if he or she is outside his or her country of origin, has a well-founded fear of persecution for a Convention reason, lacks the protection of the State, and is unable and unwilling to return because of that fear. There are protections attached including the principle of *non-refoulement*. The refugee law regime provides both for exclusion from and cessation of refugee status. The cessation clauses suggest that it is essentially a regime of temporary protection and that the status may come to an end. The exclusion clauses indicate that some individuals should not be granted refugee status because of their actions. The status does not apply, for example, to a person for whom there are serious reasons for considering that he or she has committed a war crime, or crime against humanity, or acts contrary to the purposes and principles of the UN.[77] There are four key points to note here. First, refugee law provides a particular understanding of what it means to be a refugee in its 'inclusion clauses'. Secondly, refugee status is a route to entitlements guaranteed in the substantive sections of the Convention. Thirdly, not everyone with a 'well-founded fear of persecution' will be entitled to refugee status. A person may be excluded from the status if he or she comes within the exclusion clauses. Finally, the

[75] See Colin Harvey, *Seeking Asylum in the UK: Problems and Prospects* (2000).
[76] Guy Goodwin-Gill, *The Refugee in International Law* (2nd ed., 1996). On the rights of refugees generally see James C. Hathaway, *The Rights of Refugees under International Law* (2005).
[77] Art. 1 F 1951 Convention.

Convention provides for the cessation of status, lending weight to the argument that it is a regime of 'surrogate international protection'.

Refugee law has been subject to criticism for both being too inclusive and too exclusive. Despite weaknesses, it still has much to commend it. It is a status-granting mechanism which brings entitlements with it, including social and economic rights. This status-granting aspect of refugee law retains its significance at a time when displaced persons are often left in a state of legal limbo. However, there are also limits to the effectiveness of refugee law from a human rights perspective. The definition is restrictive and at the regional level States have gone further, for example in the African Union,[78] and in the mandates granted to the UNHCR.[79] More formalized systems of subsidiary protection have also emerged at the regional/supra-national level. The EU is, for example, in the process of constructing a Common European Asylum System.[80]

In theory at least, the refugee law regime envisages permissible *refoulement*; in other words a person might be returned even where a risk exists of ill-treatment.[81] This position is, however, challenged by the development of customary international law rules. Human rights law, through the European Convention, the International Covenant on Civil and Political Rights and the UN Convention

[78] OAU Convention Governing the Specific Aspects of Refugee Problems in Africa 1969.
[79] Michael Kagan, 'The Beleaguered Gatekeeper: Protection Challenges Posed by UNHCR Refugee Status Determination' (2006) 18 International Journal of Refugee Law 1; Michael Barutciski, 'A Critical View of UNHCR's Mandate Dilemmas' (2002) 14 International Journal of Refugee Law 365; Corinne Lewis, 'UNHCR's Contribution to the Development of International Refugee Law: Its Foundations and Evolution' (2005) 17 International Journal of Refugee Law 67.
[80] EU Presidency Conclusions 'The Hague Programme: Strengthening Freedom, Security and Justice in the European Union' (November 2004); European Commission Communication 'The Hague Programme: Ten Priorities for the next five years' COM (2005) 184 Final; Council Directive 2003/9/EC of 27 January 2003 laying down minimum standards for the reception of asylum seekers (2003) OJ L31/18; Council Directive 2001/55/EC of 20 July 2001 on minimum standards for giving temporary protection in the event of a mass influx of displaced persons and on measures promoting a balance of efforts between Member States in receiving such persons and bearing the consequences thereof (2001) OJ L212/12; ECRE 'Renewing the Promise of Protection' (October 2004); Council Directive 2005/85/EC on minimum standards on procedures in Member States for granting and withdrawing refugee status (2005) OJ L326/13; Council Directive 2004/83/EC on minimum standards for the qualification and status of third country nationals and stateless persons as refugees or as persons who otherwise need international protection and the content of the protection granted (2004) OJ L304; Council Regulation No 343/2003 establishing the criteria and mechanisms for determining the Member State responsible for examining an asylum application lodged in one of the Member States by a third-country national (2003) OJ L50/1; European Commission Communication 'On Strengthened Practical Co-operation: New Structures, New Approaches: Improving the Quality of Decision Making in the Common European Asylum System' COM (2006) 67 Final; European Council and Commission Action Plan Implementing the Hague Programme on Strengthening Freedom, Security and Justice in the EU (June 2005); EU Presidency Conclusions Tampere European Council October 1999 'Towards a Union of Freedom, Security and Justice'; ECRE 'Report on the Application of the Dublin II Regulation in Europe' (March 2006); European Commission Communication 'On the Managed Entry into the EU of Persons in Need of International Protection and the Enhancement of the Protection Capacity of the Regions of Origin: Improving Access to Durable Solutions' Com (2004) 410 Final; European Commission Communication 'On Regional Protection Programmes' COM (2005) 388 Final. [81] Art. 33(2).

against Torture remedies the gaps in refugee law to some extent by offering protection against return even if a person falls outside formal refugee status. For example, under Article 3 ECHR the European Court of Human Rights has established that if there are substantial grounds to believe there is a real risk of Article 3 ill-treatment on return there will be a violation of the Convention.[82] There is no reason of principle why other Convention provisions should not function in a similar way. In the current political climate in Europe there is considerable pressure on the Court to give a more prominent place to the security concerns of States. The European Court of Human Rights is, however, not alone in its approach. The UN Human Rights Committee and the UN Committee against Torture have largely gone in similar directions to the European Court in cases such as *Bakhtiyari v Australia*,[83] *Attia v Sweden*,[84] and *Agiza v Sweden*.[85]

International human rights law offers possible access to treaty-monitoring mechanisms. While the UNHCR does have a supervisory jurisdiction, and it has forged agreement on principles of refugee protection and ensured effective dissemination, it does not fulfil this overall treaty-monitoring role. The practical implementation of refugee law is principally left to the national level, where refugee status determination systems have emerged of varying quality in terms of the decision-making procedures as well as the treatment accorded to those awaiting a decision. Even within the EU, the experience of being a refugee or asylum seeker still depends on national contexts. Displaced persons, whether internally or externally, like other vulnerable groups, are dependent on how protections function at the national and local levels.

The right to seek and enjoy asylum from persecution was included in Article 14 of the Universal Declaration of Human Rights.[86] Unlike a number of rights to be found in the Universal Declaration it never made it into a binding universal human rights instrument. While a UN Declaration on Territorial Asylum was adopted in 1967 no binding international instrument emerged. A right to asylum was, however, included in the EU Charter of Fundamental Rights proclaimed in 2000. Given the emphasis placed on migration control, and the well-established rights of the State in international law, this reluctance is unsurprising. It reflects the prevailing mood of disillusionment with the institution of asylum among European States and others. Significant political actors have formed the view that the asylum process as traditionally understood is flawed and is being misused as a way to enter Europe. As a result, States have constructed a barrage of deterrence

---

[82] See eg, *Chahal v UK* (judgment of 15 November 1996); *D v UK* (judgment of 2 May 1997); *Jabari v Turkey* (judgment of 11 July 2000); *Hilal v UK* (judgment of 6 March 2001); *Bensaid v UK* (judgment of 6 February 2001); and *N v Finland* (judgment of 26 July 2005).

[83] *Bakhtiyari v Australia* UNHRC Comm No. 1069/2002.

[84] *Attia v Sweden* UNCAT Comm No. 199/2002.

[85] *Agiza v Sweden* UNCAT Comm No. 233/2003

[86] '1. Everyone has the right to seek and to enjoy in other countries asylum from persecution. 2. The right may not be invoked in the case of prosecutions genuinely arising from non-political crimes or from acts contrary to the purposes and principles of the United Nations.'

and deflection policies without taking the step of renouncing the institution of asylum.

The picture does not appear particularly encouraging. In countering some of the negative trends the work of human rights commissions, parliamentary committees, courts, NGOs, and others is vital. The judiciary has been prepared to take a stand on human rights principles in this context. In the UK, the examples from the Appellate Committee of the House of Lords include cases like *Adam*, [87] as well as the *European Roma Rights Centre* [88] case and to some extent *Razgar, Ullah,* and *Do*.[89] This principled stand has on occasions caused irritation. Home Secretaries have expressed frustration and individual judges have been publicly named and criticized.[90] While we should not overstate the judicial role, and judges should expect public criticism, it is evident that judicial interventions are of considerable value in the attempts to encourage a more humane asylum regime. Again, we should not get too carried away by this; and this prompts consideration of current public law debates and the implications for human rights.

It is possible to note a reasonably clear division within existing scholarship. Jeffrey Jowell, Trevor Allan, and others appear keen to encourage the judges to be ever more expansive and dynamic in their interpretations of rights. Conor Gearty, Keith Ewing, Aileen McColgan, and others continue to support the primacy of politics and Parliament with the belief that representative democracy is ultimately the best protection against human rights abuses. Adam Tomkins has talked of models of political and legal accountability,[91] and with Martin Loughlin, has constructed an argument anchored in an imaginative reconstruction of British constitutional history in support of political accountability as the normatively more persuasive account of public law.[92]

This is a simplification of complex arguments. Nevertheless, from the perspective of the treatment of vulnerable groups such as asylum seekers, who are not the citizens of the State they are in and are not well represented in the democratic process, combined with the Northern Ireland perspective and the problems experienced there with majoritarian forms of democracy, it is hard to have an overly romantic view of the merits of the current British constitution and its representative institutions; even if temptingly reconstructed along republican lines as proposed by Adam Tomkins.[93] However, those working within this democratic/republican tradition advance arguments that can be built upon. The other

---

[87] *R v Secretary of State for the Home Department, ex p. Adam* [2005] UKHL 66.

[88] *R v Immigration Officer at Prague Airport and another, ex p. European Roma Rights Centre and others* [2004] UKHL 55.

[89] *R(Ullah) v Special Adjudicator* [2004] All ER 153; *R(Razgar) v Secretary of State for the Home Department* [2004] UKHL 27.

[90] The response to the judgment of Mr Justice Sullivan in *R(S and Ors) v Secretary of State for the Home Department* [2006] EWHC 1111 (Admin.) was revealing. The Prime Minister, Tony Blair, criticized the judgment and talked of an 'abuse of common sense', see *The Times*, 11 May 2006.

[91] Adam Tomkins, *Public Law* (2003).   [92] ibid.

[93] Adam Tomkins, *Our Republican Constitution* (2005).

path is troubling. To follow Jeffrey Jowell and others down the road of a particular conception of legal accountability seems to result in excessive emphasis on adjudication and the judges. In my view, that would be a mistake. The record of the common law judges is hardly one to get too excited about, even with encouraging trends in the UK of late. Of more significance are the risks attached to leaving representative institutions and communities locked out of a culture of human rights. This does not mean abandoning a focus on adjudication. It means widening the frame to include other institutions. What is required is an approach that can mediate credibly between legal and political accountability and acknowledges 'both and' rather than 'either/or'. David Dyzenhaus has arguably done most to sketch out the theoretical basis for such a model,[94] an approach that recognizes the promotion and protection of human rights as a shared project (linked to practical outcomes) that is anchored in substantive values and shared responsibilities.[95] This can cause unease among those who adopt a rigid view of what the separation of powers means and worry about the impact on, for example, judicial independence. The dialogue envisaged is around the meaning of applicable norms and their impact. The particular model highlighted is one that judges human rights on their ability to alter the practical circumstances of those who require the protections most. It therefore departs from purely procedural notions of 'justification'.

Models anchored in dialogue—or conversational models—can provide the basis for a more inclusive research programme in human rights, one that knows that proposing constructive interpretations of human rights law matters, because the real arguments have often shifted into legal doctrine and are being fought out in that environment, but also knows that if legislatures and communities are left on the outside of the discussion, or have a peripheral role, we will not have a culture of respect for human rights.

Governing with Human Rights

In this section of the chapter I will outline some research themes under the heading 'Governing with Human Rights' which, in my view, could form part of a research programme in human rights law which takes conversational models seriously.

The Global and the Local

First, the global and the local. Human rights standards and institutions exist at the sub-national, national, regional, and international levels. We can examine each

---

[94] See eg, David Dyzenhaus, 'Aspiring to the Rule of Law', in Campbell, Goldsworthy, and Stone, *Protecting Human Rights: Instruments and Institutions*, n 52 above, ch 9.

[95] Dyzenhaus, ibid, 209: 'In short, all the institutions of legal order are to be understood as involved in a common project, one that seeks to justify exercise of public power by explicit references to the values that make it an authority rather than the "gunman writ large".' Dyzenhaus is writing about the rule of law generally but his comments apply with equal force to the area of human rights.

level in isolation, but the more rewarding project is to map the interactions between these different legal orders. What impact are international standards having? What role do international standards play in national debates? Who uses international standards in local contexts?

Human Rights Law in Context

Secondly, human rights law in context. It is vital that human rights law is located in its historical, social, political, and cultural contexts. This means paying due regard to legal doctrine, but placing it within an interdisciplinary framework. Context matters when tackling the concerns noted in this essay. For example, the arguments of Mark Tushnet and Keith Ewing may well make sense in the US and Britain, but may seem odd, as Wojciech Sadurski has pointed out, to human rights advocates in Central and Eastern Europe who applaud their activist constitutional courts and have a sound historical basis for doubting the wisdom of their law-makers on these matters.[96]

This still means winning doctrinal legal arguments. But it also means measuring the impact of human rights at the national level: understanding the role rights play in political debates; examining how judges and lawyers absorb human rights norms; exploring the work of social movements and the strategies they deploy to achieve rights-based outcomes in particular contexts.

Legal Pluralism

The third issue is legal pluralism. This is one where more work is still needed. Human rights lawyers must recognize that there are normative orders which are not State-based, whether at the sub-national or international levels. Governing is not just a State-based activity. It can be carried out by sub-national regimes, political communities, supranational bodies, as well as regional and international organizations. This goes beyond asking what sort of entity the EU is, to understanding national and transnational, communal and cultural contexts and the role of rights in them. It also means engaging seriously with private power and recognizing, as Gavin Anderson argues, that multi-national corporations have to be viewed as part of the law-production process.[97] Legal pluralism possesses a normative and explanatory force that merits further exploration in human rights law.

Mainstreaming Human Rights

The fourth topic is mainstreaming rights. There is, in my view, a particular model of rights associated with this term. It is a model which rejects US-style judicial review as the template for discussion of human rights implementation and

---

[96] Wojciech Sadurski, 'Rights-Based Constitutional Review in Central and Eastern Europe', in Campbell, Ewing, and Tomkins, *Sceptical Essays on Human Rights*, n 51 above, ch 17.
[97] Gavin Anderson, *Constitutional Rights After Globalization* (2005).

enforcement.[98] Francesca Klug and Conor Gearty have fallen, for sound reasons, for a particular view of the Human Rights Act 1998 as a model of democratic dialogue. This vision of rights under the Human Rights Act retains its persuasive value. George Williams has also, for example, talked of a community-based Bill of Rights where legislatures, courts, and communities are all engaged in an ongoing dialogue about human rights;[99] not as a way to avoid decision or to neglect substantive values, but as functionally the best way to ensure rights are made meaningful in practice. As Williams notes: 'There are many nations in which a bill of rights has proved to be little more than a symbol of the powerlessness of the law and hence nothing more than words on a page.'[100] It is in the dynamic, and at times conflictual, interactions between institutions that progress might be made.

Mainstreaming rights means more than this. It means that rights must count in practice. So, economic and social rights should be at the core of poverty-reduction strategies—when budgets are being set the human rights impact should be firmly on the agenda; human rights indicators must be developed and used for monitoring and measuring compliance; rights should be integrated into business management practices; public procurement rules should be framed with human rights principles in mind; organizations—such as the World Trade Organization—need to take rights seriously. In order to govern effectively with rights, we need tools, mechanisms, and strategies to ensure rights compliance is achieved. As I have argued in this essay, principled adjudication is essential, but if we begin and end with the courtroom then we are only getting a partial picture.

Bringing Back the Political

And finally, 'bringing back the political'. I have added this as a final theme and I refer to it in two senses. First, political conceptions underpin law-making, law interpretation, and law application. Lawyers spend a considerable amount of time denying this. They can have a negative and pessimistic view of politics and the political process. But political morality underpins particular legal positions; it seems best to acknowledge this and build a conception of rights from it, as for example Ronald Dworkin has done.[101] Secondly, behind the cases, the laws, and the international standards there is a world of human rights politics. A research programme in human rights must be able to shine a light on that world too, a programme that brings back into the research picture all those engaged in the human rights debate. Conversational/dialogue-based models can achieve this. However,

---

[98] There are differences between constitutional developments in the UK and Canada. However, democratic dialogue as an explanation of institutional relations springs from the Canadian context, see Kent Roach, *The Supreme Court on Trial: Judicial Activism or Democratic Dialogue* (2001); Janet L. Hiebert, *Charter Conflicts: What Is Parliament's Role* (2002); Janet L. Hiebert, 'Parliament and Rights', in Campbell, Goldsworthy, and Stone, *Protecting Human Rights: Instruments and Institutions*, n 52 above, ch 11.

[99] George Williams, 'Constructing a Community-Based Bill of Rights', in Campbell, Goldsworthy, and Stone, *Protecting Human Rights: Instruments and Institutions*, n 52 above, ch 12.   [100] ibid.

[101] Ronald Dworkin, *Freedom's Law: The Moral Reading of the US Constitution* (1996).

without the substantive egalitarian dimension, tied to marginalized and vulnerable groups, it would not be possible to judge the outcomes that are worthwhile.

Do human rights impoverish democratic life? I am not convinced that this is the case. They have, in the words of David Dyzenhaus, Murray Hunt, and others, promoted a 'culture of justification',[102] a culture of calling government and public administration to account, to justify their actions and treatment of all persons within their jurisdiction. On occasion this might have temporarily thwarted the ambitions of the executive, but that is distinct from an argument about representative or parliamentary democracy. Making the executive aware that it exists within a parliamentary democracy committed to the rule of law and human rights is not the same as undermining democratic life. There are ongoing problems with the way the asylum debate is framed, but it is often a more informed debate within Parliament, in the courts, and in civil society as a result of determined human rights activism and refugee advocacy work. The risk with this approach is that it sounds exclusively process driven. In my view, it must be supplemented by a practice of rights that is focused on outcomes and means engaging with richer conceptions of 'justification'.

Conclusion

Human rights law, as an academic subject, appears to be in a healthy condition; not simply because of the mountain of books, articles, journals, reports as well as the courses, training materials and academics working on it; but because the right questions are being asked and addressed. Reference has been made here to a model of 'governing with human rights'—one that is community-based and one that examines how legislatures, courts, communities and individuals make use of and are subject to human rights law. It reflects a particular conception of rights evident in some of the current literature, a model that places human rights law in context; not in order to undermine its importance, but to encourage engaged and committed scholarship with the express aim of serving those political values which human rights law is there to promote. This is a step that not all might be willing to take. However, in my view, human rights law should have an express and declared purpose, and this must be intrinsically linked to addressing the needs of vulnerable and marginalized individuals and groups. What matters ultimately is not the origins of human rights, the doctrinal coherence of human rights norms, or who gets to make the final decision, but the practical use of the standards in particular contexts and the outcomes achieved measured against the model argued for here.

---

[102] See eg, David Dyzenhaus, 'Law as Justification: Etienne Mureinik's Conception of Legal Culture' (1998) 14 South African Journal of Human Rights 11; 'The Left and the Question of Law' (2004) 17 Canadian Journal of Law and Jurisprudence 7; Murray Hunt, 'Sovereignty's Blight: Why Contemporary Public Law Needs the Concept of "Due Deference"', in Nicholas Bamforth and Peter Leyland (eds), *Public Law in a Multi-Layered Constitution* (2003) ch 13.

'Metaphysical' debates on rights matter less than realizing the universal promise of a socially just world order held out by the normative standards.[103] Rights have an intrinsic value as normative footholds which are there for particular purposes.[104]

In that earlier Northern Ireland Legal Quarterly article we stressed that a robust approach to the interpretation of Convention rights in the context of marginalized groups was not incompatible with a commitment to political democracy. In fact, we argued that it would enhance it. It keeps lines of communication open, and ensures no individual or group is rendered invisible in democratic life. Even unsuccessful legal challenges can help to shine a light on institutions and practices that need to be reformed. This theme, of rights underpinning and enhancing democratic dialogue, is a familiar one from debates in other constitutional contexts such as the US, Canada, and South Africa. The approach might well be summed up as human rights law and practice without illusions, bringing with it the recognition that human rights scholarship needs to be engaged without losing its ability to inform practice in a critical way. This essay takes an additional step, by arguing that substantive values must play a central role and that human rights law must exist for a particular purpose. The evidence suggests that human rights activism retains an enlightened and welcome idealism in cynical times. Progressive legal scholarship can acknowledge this fact, be aware of how reform is achieved, and who the agents of this change are, without losing its critical senses. The question posed in the title should always remain a question. We should judge human rights law on its ability to change the lives of vulnerable and marginalized groups and promote socially just outcomes.

We were right to insist in that article that a robust and assertive approach to human rights protection, through a range of mechanisms, is central to democratic life. So, I will conclude with a quote from the article:

'While we can argue about the legitimacy of its role, from a results-driven perspective the jurisprudence of the court has a wide-ranging impact on rights protection. What we have sought to do here is argue that the Court, through a dynamic approach, can make a vital contribution to enriching political democracy, in particular, by ensuring that those groups silenced within democratic life are accorded due concern and respect.'[105]

[103] See Michael Hardt and Antonio Negri, *Multitude: War and Democracy in the Age of Empire* (2006) 274: 'The promise of human rights is to guarantee rights universally, with the power both to counter the injustices of national legal systems and to supplement their incompleteness.'

[104] cf Alan Dershowitz, *Rights from Wrongs: A Secular Theory of the Origins of Rights* (2004) 232: 'Because human rights are a process for achieving liberty and fairness rather than an end in themselves, the struggle for rights never stays won. Because there will always be wrongs, there must always be rights.'

[105] Harvey and Livingstone, 'Protecting the Marginalised: The Role of the European Convention on Human Rights', n 1 above, 448.

25

Risk and Human Rights: Ending Slopping Out in a Scottish Prison

*Thérèse Murphy and Noel Whitty**

Introduction

In recent years, analyses of penal policy and prison law in the UK have been heavily influenced by two discourses: one of these concerns risk, the other concerns human rights. For the most part, however, the discourse of risk has been used only by criminologists and not by lawyers; equally, although human rights has featured prominently in the work of lawyers, it is rarely discussed in criminology. This divide—amongst scholars who share a common interest in prison governance—provides one of the starting points for this essay. Another starting point for us, as human rights lawyers, is concern about the role of human rights in prison governance in an era in which regulation and service delivery are increasingly organized around concepts of risk. Specifically, if risk management has become a cornerstone of prison governance in the UK, how (if at all) has this development interacted with the parallel increase in judicial scrutiny of prison administration prompted by the legal obligations placed on public authorities by the Human Rights Act 1998 and, more broadly, by the growth of prisoner rights-consciousness?[1]

In exploring these questions, we begin with a summary of the main literatures on risk. Then we discuss the widespread lack of engagement by human rights lawyers in the UK with theorizing the concept of risk or studying its uses in the fields of risk assessment and management. In Part II, our focus shifts to British criminologists and specifically to the question why the criminological focus on risk in prison governance has not generated enquiry into the relationship between

* Our thanks to the editors, Julie Stubbs and Tony Kelly (who acted as Robert Napier's solicitor), for their helpful comments on an earlier version of this essay.

[1] On the expansion of prison law, see Stephen Livingstone, Tim Owen, and Alison Macdonald, *Prison Law* (3rd ed., 2003); Noel Whitty, Thérèse Murphy, and Stephen Livingstone, *Civil Liberties Law: The Human Rights Act Era* (2001) 215–78; and Steve Foster, 'The Negligence of Prison Authorities and the Protection of Prisoners' Rights' (2005) 26 Liverpool Law Review 75.

risk and prisoners' human rights. In Part III, we aim to start a debate on the relationship between risk and human rights in UK prison governance. Our focus is on one particular legal context: the successful challenge under the Scotland Act 1998 and the Human Rights Act 1998 to the practice of 'slopping out' in Barlinnie Prison in the case of *Robert Napier v The Scottish Ministers*.[2] We argue that different types of risk knowledges played a significant role in the construction and resolution of this human rights litigation. More generally, we use *Napier* to prompt a series of questions about the *co-existence* of risk and human rights in the prison governance context.

One introductory caveat: throughout this piece, we focus on the UK experience. We make brief reference to scholarship on Canada and the US but our argument is about the UK. Also, in what follows, we draw a sharp distinction between criminologists and lawyers. We do this because it seems the best way to convey the basic point that both lawyers and criminologists have neglected the relationship between risk and rights. The downside of this sharp distinction is that we may be guilty of a degree of misrepresentation—in practice, individuals and organizations do not always map onto a 'criminology versus law' divide.[3]

Risk and the (Human Rights) Lawyers

In 1999, the sociologist Anthony Giddens writing in the Modern Law Review observed that risk 'has not figured prominently' in legal theory.[4] This omission was surprising: law is often about using expert knowledges and managing risk (consider, for example, the use of 'risk of harm' tests in child protection and environmental contexts, and 'risk of re-offending' criteria in sentencing, parole, and civil preventative order contexts). What is more surprising however is that, seven years later, Giddens' observation still holds true in several fields of legal scholarship.[5] We discuss this further below in relation to human rights law. First, however, we turn away from law in order to introduce the extensive academic literature on risk.

In terms of academic output alone, the ascent of risk has been nothing short of remarkable. As David Garland has said, 'suddenly, everyone seems to be talking about risk'. And yet, as Garland goes on to point out, it is not at all clear that

    [2] 2005 SC 229; 2005 SC 307 (IH). The main focus of the case was the compatibility of prison conditions with the standards of Art. 3 of the European Convention on Human Rights (ECHR).

    [3] For eg, the feminist reform campaigns of the Canadian Association of Elizabeth Fry Societies (CAEFS) combine the use of human rights standards and a critique of risk assessment and management in the criminal justice system: see eg 'The Risky Business of Risk Assessment' [www.elizabethfry.ca/]. See also, Kelly Hannah-Moffat, 'Moral Agent or Actuarial Subject: Risk and Canadian Women's Imprisonment' (1999) 3 Theoretical Criminology 71; and Canadian Human Rights Commission, *Protecting Their Rights: A Systemic Review of Human Rights in Correctional Services for Federally Sentenced Women* (2003).

    [4] Anthony Giddens, 'Risk and Responsibility' (1999) 62 Modern Law Review 1, 1.

    [5] For a challenge to Giddens' claim, see Jenny Steele, *Risks and Legal Theory* (2004).

everyone is talking about the same thing: indeed, if we take what is sometimes referred to as 'the risk literature' it is quickly apparent that there are in fact 'several distinct literatures, involving different projects, different forms of inquiry, and different conceptions of their subject matter, all linked tenuously together by a tantalizing four-letter word'.[6] That said, overviews of the field generally single out four different literatures for comment. The first of these is associated with the work of the anthropologist, Mary Douglas. Its core argument is that culture, as distinct from scientific knowledges, is a crucial factor in any social group's perceptions or judgements about risk.[7] Hence this approach insists that the focus must be on 'the ways in which risks are *communicated* and how they are *politicised*'.[8] The second established perspective on risk is linked to the work of Anthony Giddens and Ulrich Beck, in particular Beck's hugely influential book, *Risk Society*.[9] There are differences in the views of Giddens and Beck, but the common ground is that both argue that processes of individualization, reflexivity, and globalization in late-modern western societies, and the reality of living with constant insecurity and uncertainty, have led to risk calculation being given priority both by those who govern us and also by each and every one of us in making choices. The third major perspective on risk builds on Foucault's writings on governmentality to examine the role of risk in managing and regulating populations and individuals: its focus is on risk as a complex disciplinary tool, operating through both coercion and voluntary compliance and tending to serve neo-liberal goals.[10] The fourth and final established risk literature, found in disciplines such as medicine and economics, stands in stark contrast to the three just outlined. Its focus is technico-scientific; that is, it treats risk as a 'taken-for-granted objective phenomenon'[11] and it aims to identify, map, predict, and regulate risk according to expert criteria.

The range of literatures within 'the risk literature' can make it difficult to get a hold on risk scholarship. There are also other concerns. The first of these is that there is a general lack of engagement between exponents of the different risk perspectives. The second is that risk assessment, by contrast with risk management, is often represented as involving expert, rational criteria and exclusively scientific processes of judgement. Thirdly, it has been argued that analyses of risk can sometimes neglect the 'everyday'. For example, as regards organizations, it has been alleged that studies of risk assessment and management 'often miss the real action

[6] David Garland, 'The Rise of Risk' in Richard Ericson and Aaron Doyle (eds.), *Risk and Morality* (2003) 48–86, 49. [7] See eg Mary Douglas, *Risk and Blame: Essays in Cultural Theory* (1992).
[8] Richard Sparks, 'Risk and Blame in Criminal Justice Controversies: British Press Coverage and Official Discourse on Prison Security (1993–6)' in Mark Brown and John Pratt (eds), *Dangerous Offenders: Punishment and Social Order* (2000) 127–43, 132.
[9] See eg Ulrich Beck, *Risk Society: Towards A New Modernity* (1992); and Anthony Giddens, *Modernity and Self-Identity* (1991).
[10] See eg Nikolas Rose, *Powers of Freedom: Reframing Political Thought* (1999); and Pat O'Malley, *Risk, Uncertainty and Government* (2004).
[11] Deborah Lupton, 'Introduction' in Deborah Lupton (ed.), *Risk and Sociocultural Theory: New Directions and Perspectives* (1999), 1–11, 2.

that happens elsewhere, particularly at the delivery level' and that the crucial issue left unexplored is the *politics* of risk regulation. That is, the ways in which:

'... risk-regulation dynamics are often shaped by different institutional players—public and private—seeking to deflect blame away from themselves and direct it towards others, often the weakest links with the least lobbying power.'[12]

More generally, it has been alleged that risk perspectives which 'tend to operate at the level of grand theory' make 'little use of empirical work into the ways in which people conceptualize and experience risk as part of their everyday lives'.[13] And it has been pointed out that there is also remarkably little critical literature examining the ways in which formulations of risk vary with identities.[14] The fourth concern relates to the fact that different perspectives on risk tend to justify different regulatory approaches. So, for example, a belief in scientific definitions of risk and the importance of technical expertise is likely to lead to the view that regulatory priorities ought to be established with reference to technical criteria, whereas an understanding of risks as socially constructed will probably lead to the rather different view that 'regulatory priorities and policies cannot be left to the "objective" evaluations of experts but have to emerge from democratically legitimate processes of debate and consultation'.[15]

In this essay, we do not intend to pursue any of these problems with the academic literature on risk. We have outlined the problems in order to make the following point: one would expect that these disputes about what it means to be 'governed in the name of risk'[16] would draw the attention of UK lawyers and of public lawyers in particular. Intriguingly, however, most (though certainly not all) public lawyers seem uninterested in the risk literature. Instead they remain fascinated by 'meta-constitutional principles such as the rule of law and separation of powers':[17] in recent years, this fascination has manifested itself in an almost ubiquitous debate about the pros and cons of rights-based adjudication. Moreover, regulation scholarship—which does explore the ways in which regulatory techniques are used to assess and control risks in the public

[12] Christopher Hood, Henry Rothstein and Robert Baldwin, *The Government of Risk: Understanding Risk Regulation Regimes* (2004) viii–ix.
[13] Lupton, *Risk and Sociocultural Theory: New Directions and Perspectives*, n 11 above, 6; and John Tulloch and Deborah Lupton, *Risk and Everyday Life* (2003).
[14] See further Wendy Chan and George Rigakos, 'Risk, Crime and Gender' (2002) 42 British Journal of Criminology 743; and Ron Levi, 'The Mutuality of Risk and Community: The Adjudication of Community Notification Statutes' (2000) 29 Economy and Society 578.
[15] Robert Baldwin and Martin Cave, *Understanding Regulation: Theory, Strategy and Practice* (1999) 142. See also Dan Kahan *et al*, 'Fear *and* Democracy or Fear *of* Democracy? A Cultural Evaluation of Sunstein on Risk' (2006) 119 Harvard Law Review 1071.
[16] Pat O'Malley, 'Introduction: Configurations of Risk' (2000) 29 Economy and Society, 457, 458.
[17] Elizabeth Fisher, 'The Rise of the Risk Commonwealth and the Challenge for Administrative Law' [2003] Public Law 455, 472. Cf Damian Chalmers, 'Risk, Anxiety and the European Mediation of the Politics of Life' (2005) 30 European Law Review 649, 650 arguing that the EU is transforming, and being transformed by, the government of risk.

and private sectors[18]—continues to be treated as a specialist subset of UK public law.[19]

The general absence of risk in public law scholarship is surprising: it is even more surprising, however, that risk has not registered as a concern amongst *human rights lawyers*. We say this because, in the UK today, risk and rights co-exist—especially in the area of detention. So, for example, the statutory duty of parole boards to identify risk factors and make predictive judgements about the release of prisoners must be performed in light of the legal obligation not to act contrary to Convention rights under the Human Rights Act 1998, notably Article 5 right to liberty standards.[20] Similarly, where a person in detention is considered at risk from other prisoners, or is a known suicide risk, the procedures for assessing and managing that risk must be Convention-compliant with Article 2 right to life standards.[21] Asylum and deportation case law provides another obvious example: it foregrounds tests to assess risk of torture, or risk of threat to mental health, flowing from the Article 3 ECHR prohibition against torture and inhuman or degrading treatment.[22] In short, references to 'risk' are now common in several areas of human rights jurisprudence.

It could of course be argued that what these examples actually illustrate is the reason why human rights lawyers have *not* focused on the risk and rights dynamic—namely, there is a strong sense that risk is a non-legal knowledge. To put it crudely, although it is routine for practising lawyers and judges to work with expert evidence, the perception that 'risk' is a scientific and technical measurement means that the critique of risk (including in the context of '*law and* risk') may be seen as belonging more properly to other disciplines—such as criminology and psychology. Support for this argument can certainly be found in the case law on prisoner challenges to parole board decisions: what this jurisprudence demonstrates is that there is a longstanding judicial reluctance to become involved in adjudicating on expert opinion in relation to risk assessments of prisoners.[23]

There is, however, a small sample of human rights literature in the UK which does at least acknowledge the co-existence of risk and rights. For example, the UK Parliament Joint Committee on Human Rights has produced a report, *Deaths in*

---

[18] See Julia Black, 'The Emergence of Risk-Based Regulation and the New Public Risk Management in the United Kingdom' [2005] Public Law 512.
[19] For a critical analysis of the use of the 'precautionary principle' in the regulation of risk in environmental and other contexts, see Mike Feintuck, 'Precautionary Maybe, but What's the Principle? The Precautionary Principle, the Regulation of Risk, and the Public Domain' (2005) 32 Journal of Law and Society 371.
[20] See generally Nicola Padfield, 'The Parole Board in Transition' [2006] Criminal Law Review 3.
[21] See *Edwards v UK* (2002) 35 EHRR 19; *Kennan v UK* (2001) 33 EHRR 38; and *Van Colle v Chief Constable of Hertfordshire Police* [2006] EWHC 360.
[22] See eg *Askarov v Turkey* [2005] ECHR 64 (risk of torture); and *J v Secretary of State for the Home Department* (2005) EWCA Civ 629 (risk of harm to mental health).
[23] See *Re McLean* [2005] UKHL 46, para 26 ('There are dangers in an unduly legalistic approach to what may well be a very difficult predictive judgment'); and *R v Parole Board, ex p Watson* [1986] 1 WLR 906, 916 ('It is not for the court to second-guess the judgment of a specialist tribunal').

Custody, which contains a separate chapter on how risk assessment and management processes in detention facilities must comply with ECHR standards.[24] There has also been discussion of the compatibility of civil preventative orders (which are premised on the identification of risk of certain future behaviour) with human rights standards, not only in relation to the standard of proof to be applied and the serious restrictions of liberty and privacy rights involved, but also the potential criminal sanction of imprisonment for breach of a civil order.[25] Furthermore, recent work by Barbara Hudson argues for an explicit balancing of human rights and risk approaches in order to achieve what she describes as 'the equilibrium of justice in the risk society'.[26] Hudson does not think that rights should be used to oust risk-based approaches in criminal justice: '[t]aking rights seriously means taking risks seriously because it means providing for the full enjoyment of rights and preventing infringements'.[27] But she does see rights as the antidote to the potential excesses of risk-based approaches, as the way to promote 'a principled risk management approach' and to avoid 'rushing into no-holds-barred risk control'. Hence, as regards the probation service, she argues that:

'The best prospect of achieving [a principled approach] is by a whole-hearted embrace of the ideas of human rights: not just the legislative regulations in the Human Rights Act, but also embrace of a rights culture. Not just ensuring that probation practices are rights compliant to avoid falling foul of the Act, but adopting a "positive rights agenda" might enable the service to pursue risk management rather than risk control.'[28]

Human Rights and Criminologists

The general lack of engagement by UK human rights lawyers with 'risk and human rights' has a parallel in the discipline of criminology.[29] In criminology, however, the problem stems from the fact that only a handful of criminologists actually mention rights: as Kieran McEvoy has pointed out, the significance of human rights 'appears to have made little genuine inroads into [the] conceptual or

[24] Eleventh Report (2004–05).
[25] See Andrew Ashworth, ' "Social Control" and "Anti-Social Behaviour": The Subversion of Human Rights?' (2004) 120 Law Quarterly Review 263.
[26] Barbara Hudson, *Justice in the Risk Society* (2003) 224–25: 'Justice entails openness of discourse for claiming redress for harm done and for promulgating policies to prevent future harms, balanced by strong commitment to universal, inalienable, human rights.' See also Barbara Hudson, 'Human Rights, Public Safety and the Probation Service: Defending Justice in the Risk Society' (2001) 40 Howard Journal 103. [27] ibid (2003).
[28] Hudson, 'Human Rights, Public Safety and the Probation Service: Defending Justice in the Risk Society', n 26 above, 224–25.
[29] But, for Canada, see Mariana Valverde, 'The Harms of Sex and the Risks of Breasts: Obscenity and Indecency in Canadian Law' (1999) 8 Social & Legal Studies 181, analysing the judicial construction of the 'risk of harm' test in Canadian obscenity law.

practical frameworks' of criminology.[30] This neglect of rights is particularly surprising given British criminology's close engagement with State power; if '[f]or
most of its existence, criminology has been located, for all practical purpose,
within the institutions of the criminal justice state',[31] it seems strange that the
growth of *prisoners' rights* has been largely overlooked. Yet McEvoy's work, examining the role of law in the context of paramilitary prisoners in Northern Ireland,
remains a clear exception to the general criminological trend in the UK.[32]

It could be that criminologists (like lawyers) adhere to disciplinary boundaries.[33] Indeed some have suggested that the disciplinary closure of British criminology may relate to its widespread administrative bias: 'Born as it was to meet
the needs of governance, criminology reaffirms itself not by internal reflection
but rather by reference to the material demands of penal administration.'[34] In
the 1970s and 1980s, Home Office penal policy, and its funded-research programmes, did not factor in human rights as a relevant focus for academic inquiry.
Subsequently, even though human rights compliance has become a primary concern for the Home Office and more broadly—in light of repeated successes of
prisoner rights claims under the ECHR system, the related development of common law standards by the English courts in judicial review of decisions by Home
Secretaries (and prison governors), and the enactment of the Human Rights Act
1998—the parameters of criminological research continue to exclude human
rights.[35] Victims' rights seem to be the only aspect of human rights law and culture that has an obvious presence in recent criminological research. Moreover, the
fact that 'the vast amount of funding [for criminological work] has been directed
to positivist/administrative projects that seek answers to crime causation or aim to
improve existing apparatuses of crime control',[36] means that criminologists have
little incentive to look at human rights rather than, for example, actuarialism or
risk management—or to look at rights in relation to these discourses.[37]

[30] Kieran McEvoy, 'Beyond the Metaphor: Political Violence, Human Rights and the 'New'
Peacemaking Criminology' (2003) 7 Theoretical Criminology 319. This criticism is also made in Ruth
Jamieson, 'Genocide and the Social Production of Immortality' (1999) 3 Theoretical Criminology 131.
[31] David Garland and Richard Sparks, 'Criminology, Social Theory and the Challenge of Our
Times' (2000) 40 British Journal of Criminology 189, 201.
[32] See Kieran McEvoy, *Paramilitary Imprisonment in Northern Ireland: Resistance, Management
and Release* (2001). See also the human rights focus in work by Stanley Cohen: eg *States of Denial:
Knowing About Atrocities and Suffering* (2001); and Laura Piacentini, *Surviving Russian Prisons:
Punishment, Economy and Politics in Transition* (2004).
[33] There is, of course, the related question of how we define the boundaries of these disciplines.
[34] Mark Brown and John Pratt, 'Introduction' in Mark Brown and John Pratt (eds), *Dangerous
Offenders: Punishment and Social Order* (2000) 1–13, 3.
[35] See further Paddy Hillyard *et al*, 'Leaving a "Stain Upon the Silence": Contemporary Criminology and the Politics of Dissent' (2004) 44 British Journal of Criminology 369, at 373.
[36] Reece Walters, 'New Modes of Governance and the Commodification of Criminological Knowledge' (2003) 12 Social & Legal Studies 5, 20–21. See further, Reece Walters, *Deviant Knowledge:
Criminology, Politics and Policy* (2003).
[37] See eg the work by Hazel Kemshall, a leading government-funded researcher on risk management: *Risk, Social Policy and Welfare* (2002) and Scottish Executive, *Serious Violent and Sexual
Offenders: The Use of Risk Assessment Tools in Scotland* (2002).

It could also be that, as Michael Freeman has pointed out, human rights—not just human rights law—has generally been seen as lawyers' territory.[38] Wariness of legalism is very deep-rooted, and is often actively promoted by lawyers themselves. Indeed, as Valverde *et al* have observed, the commonplace assumption that 'scientists are the only authorized custodians of scientific information, so that if courts use scientific facts there is some kind of obligation to use these facts in a scientific manner', has a very obvious parallel in law:

'[namely,] that lawyers are the ones who authorize or deauthorize the use of legal knowledge resources such as case law and legal doctrine. Lay uses of legal doctrine and other legal resources tend to be dismissed as uninformed and inaccurate—as if lawyers owned not only the power to represent clients but also the intellectual machinery of law itself.'[39]

Of course, the paradox here is that discussion of human rights only started to feature prominently in mainstream *legal* literature in the UK in the late 1990s; prior to the Human Rights Act 1998, civil liberties, ECHR jurisprudence, and international human rights law more broadly were subjects of specialist, not general, interest within law. Relatedly, debate about human rights amongst lawyers—arguing about the pros and cons in a broad and diverse manner,[40] and not just about Ronald Dworkin's liberal rights thesis—is of even more recent vintage, and there is still a definite shortage of socio-legal perspectives on the impact of human rights in the UK, both in terms of the initiation of rights claims and the implementation of rights norms.[41]

However, the key question that arises for us is: how might more criminologists be encouraged to take account of human rights? We think that there could be a route through 'values' to rights, especially for criminologists who do research on prisons and prisoners. We say this because of Alison Liebling's recent book, *Prisons and their Moral Performance: A Study of Values, Quality and Prison Life*.[42] In this book, Liebling develops methodologies for measuring the moral and emotional climates of penal institutions, arguing that perceptions of justice, fairness, safety, order, humanity, trust, and opportunities for personal development should be treated as quantifiable features of the prison experience: hence her title, 'prisons and their moral performance'. The opportunity for this novel form of measurement is created, she argues, by the fact that humanitarian values continue to have purchase in prison governance and are linked, albeit imperfectly, to practices of audit compliance and risk management.

[38] 'Before the 1970s almost all academic work done on human rights was done by lawyers, and most articles were published in law journals', *Human Rights* (2002), 78.

[39] Mariana Valverde *et al*, 'Legal Knowledges of Risk' in Law Commission of Canada (ed.), *Law and Risk* (2005) 86–120, 88.

[40] See eg Gavin Anderson, *Constitutional Rights After Globalization* (2005).

[41] For more on this argument, see Simon Halliday and Patrick Schmidt (eds), *Human Rights Brought Home: Socio-Legal Perspectives on Human Rights in the National Context* (2004).

[42] (2004). Liebling, in the Preface to her book, thanks Kieran McEvoy for prompting her 'in particular (but not enough, I am sure) to reflect on the role of human rights discourses in our moral performance framework'. However, explicit discussion of rights is limited to 452–53, and the index has no reference to human rights, the ECHR, or law generally.

Liebling recommends the use of her methodologies to elicit information on key aspects of prison life and suggests a correlation between her predictive tools and human rights standards. She does not provide any detail on how potentially competing discourses (such as risk and rights) might interact and be negotiated in specific contexts,[43] but her overall approach demonstrates why a normative dimension including notions of equality, individual dignity, and tolerance needs to be accommodated within prison management styles. Significantly, the approach reminds us that 'it is surely important to preserve (or try to generate) a notion of citizenship even within the prison'.[44]

Arguably, however, a more obvious route to rights—and, more specifically, to an understanding of the *co-existence of risk and rights*—is provided by the work of the criminologist, Richard Sparks. Sparks' work does not engage directly with risk and rights; its value lies in the fact that it calls for inquiry into *how* risk-based knowledges and practices intersect with other structuring principles of penal systems and penal politics. Sparks argues that '[w]hatever else we may say about contemporary penality and its associated politics, it seems clear that the discourse and practice of risk management do not have the field all to themselves'. Then he asks the following key question; '[b]ut *on what terms* do they co-habit with the existing occupants of that terrain?'[45] Drawing on Mary Douglas' work on risk, Sparks emphasizes two further points: first, that the concept of risk is inherently plural and contingent, and that we should *expect* risk discourse to be a mixed discourse and to work out differently in different contexts; secondly, that 'risk' is now a cultural keyword for holding people accountable, with the result that risk controversies expose questions of the competence and legitimacy of decision-makers.[46] In explaining these points, Sparks notes that:

'To suggest that some constructions of risk in the penal realm have been unduly singular and one-dimensional is also to say that they have neglected what is most interesting about it, namely that *like the language of rights, justice and legitimacy, with which it so closely intersects*, it is a site of struggles for influence, credibility and recognition.'[47]

Not surprisingly, we are particularly interested in this latter observation. Positioning risk and human rights as 'closely intersecting', it notes obvious parallels between the language of rights and constructions of risk in penal policy and practice: both are 'sites of struggles for influence, credibility and recognition'. Furthermore, its explicit linking of risk with questions of rights, justice, and legitimacy points to the more general need, as Sparks puts it, for criminology

---

[43] Pat Carlen, in a book review, criticizes Liebling for a reformist discourse which concentrates on 'management concerns about how values should be prioritized, . . . without any explanation of which values *must* be prioritized if prisoners are to be kept in prison' (2005) 9 Theoretical Criminology 251, 253. [44] ibid, 491.

[45] Richard Sparks, 'Perspectives on Risk and Penal Politics' in Tim Hope and Richard Sparks (eds), *Crime, Risk and Insecurity* (2000) 129–45, 129–30.

[46] Richard Sparks, 'Degrees of Estrangement: The Cultural Theory of Risk and Comparative Penology' (2001) 5 *Theoretical Criminology* 159, 168–69.

[47] ibid, 162 (our emphasis).

to 'embark on the reconnection of penological research with normative moral and political reflection'[48]—a point also made by McEvoy, Liebling, and several other criminologists.

The Co-Existence of Risk and Human Rights Discourses

As emphasized at the outset, the overall aim of this essay is to argue for a new *risk and human rights* strand of academic enquiry. Risk and human rights have become dominant discourses in the UK and are likely to remain so. In the prison context, they are predominant. Hence our argument is that the rights awareness generated by the legal instruments (such as the ECHR, Human Rights Act 1998, European Prison Rules, and European Convention for the Prevention of Torture) and extensive prisoner rights' jurisprudence now impacting on prison governance must, *in some way*, co-exist alongside the vocabularies of risk assessment and management operating in the penal system and throughout the public sector generally. To develop this argument, we shall examine the case of *Napier v The Scottish Ministers*.

The background to *Napier* was as follows: Napier, who had a history of eczema, was held on remand in C Hall in Barlinnie Prison in conditions of overcrowding, poor ventilation and light, and without access to sanitary facilities in his cell (hence the need for 'slopping out'). During a 40-day period between May and June 2001, he suffered a severe outbreak of eczema and then successfully obtained an interim court order against the Scottish Ministers (the collective legal term for the Scottish administration) requiring his transfer to healthier conditions of detention. In subsequent litigation for damages, Napier sought a determination that the conditions for remand prisoners in C Hall were 'inhuman and degrading' contrary to the standards of Article 3, ECHR (and also Article 8, ECHR) and that the Scottish Executive (through the actions of the Scottish Prison Service, an executive agency) was directly responsible for the injury to his physical and mental health. The judge, Lord Bonomy, held that the Scottish Ministers made policy choices about the administration of the prison service which were unlawful: namely, that they were responsible for remand prisoners (in Napier's condition) being placed in conditions where there was an obvious risk of being subjected to 'degrading treatment' contrary to minimum human rights standards.[49]

Lord Bonomy's judgment has provoked considerable controversy, not least because of its financial implications. What interests us, however, is the level of detail on the prison environment in the judgment and the range and number of 'risk' and 'rights' knowledges assimilated into the reasoning. In what follows, we argue that *risk's relationship with human rights* is a key factor in understanding

[48] ibid, 172.
[49] See also Steve Foster, 'Prison Conditions, Human Rights and Article 3 ECHR' [2005] Public Law 35; and Anna Lawson and Amrita Mukherjee, 'Slopping Out in Scotland: The Limits of Degradation and Respect' (2004) 6 European Human Rights Law Review 645.

Napier. First, we illustrate the way that different risk knowledges and rights knowledges were introduced into legal argument by both parties and then used by Lord Bonomy to construct his findings. Secondly, we examine the *Napier* litigation through the lens of 'organizational risk': we focus in particular on the nature of 'legal risk' affecting public sector organizations in the new human rights culture in the UK. Thirdly, we draw upon the work of Mariana Valverde and others to discuss a process known as 'translation'; that is, the ways in which risk can undergo changes when it moves from one site to another (for example, from the scientific field to the legal one). We focus on the specific translation practice of 'swapping knowledges', whereby knowledges migrate between legally trained personnel and non-legal professionals. Finally, we look at the relevance of cultural context to the terms upon which risk and rights co-exist.

Risk Knowledges and Rights Knowledges in *Napier v The Scottish Ministers*

In the first half of his judgment, Lord Bonomy outlines the conditions and normal routine of prisoners detained in C Hall. Under headings such as cell size, illumination, ventilation, slopping out, mental state, and eczema, he discusses a range of expert evidence establishing the environmental, medical, and psychological risks associated with Napier's detention. These 'risk knowledges' are then compared against relevant human rights standards, such as the European Prison Rules and UN norms, in order to help to establish legal findings on the adequacy of Napier's prison environment. Thus, for example, the expert evidence on cell illumination—provided by a Professor of Building Services Design and an environmental engineer—is described as 'extremely complex' and is calculated as a percentage called the 'average daylight factor' with average illumination expressed as a number of lux. This scientific knowledge is 'translated' by the judge and assessed against human rights standards as in the following extract:

'In contrast, the average daylight factor of 0.3% provides an average illumination of 200 lux or more for just over 3 minutes per day and 100 lux or more for approximately 1 hour 45 minutes per day. The average daylight factor of 0.36% extends these periods to 20 minutes and 2 hours 24 minutes respectively. From that evidence it followed that the provision of artificial light was essential. . . . Rule 16(a) of the European Prison Rules provides that, where prisoners are required to live or work, the window shall be large enough to enable them to read or work by natural light in normal conditions. Article 11 of the United Nations Standard Minimum Rules for the Treatment of Prisoners provides that artificial light shall be provided for prisoners to read or work without injury to eyesight. Neither of these recommendations was met in [Napier's] cell.'[50]

The most detailed risk analysis in the judgment centres on the practice of slopping out, both the use of chamber pots and urine bottles in cells, and the process of

[50] paras 13–15.

emptying and cleaning these vessels in inadequate sanitation areas. Lord Bonomy first emphasizes the general risks associated with slopping out, and their exacerbation by prison overcrowding, dual-occupancy in traditional single cells without sanitation, and locking up of prisoners during daytime. Evidence from a range of 'expert' and 'non-expert' sources such as a Professor in Microbiology, a consultant medical microbiologist, prison officers, and prisoners themselves is used to create a detailed 'risk knowledge' surrounding the daily regime in C Hall in Barlinnie Prison:

'[T]here were often collisions and spillages which might contaminate the shoes, clothing or skin of a passing prisoner. . . . The main significance of Professor Goodwin's evidence was to point to features of the prison conditions which gave rise to unnecessary additional risks of infection by staphylococci aurei, diarrhoea, tuberculosis, hepatitis and HIV. . . . That risk arose because of the very process of carrying faeces to the arches and slopping them out there. The risk was increased by the practice of taking eating utensils and cutlery to be washed in the arches. The risk was further increased by features of the system which discouraged prisoners from washing their hands, which is the principal means of preventing faecal infection.'[51]

Having established the general risks of prison life, Lord Bonomy then proceeds to consider the specific impact of this environment on Napier in light of his medical condition and continued detention in C Hall (after his initial request for transfer was rejected by the Governor of Barlinnie Prison). Expert evidence from two consultant forensic psychiatrists, a clinical psychologist, an environmental psychologist, a Professor of Forensic Psychology, a general practitioner, and two dermatologists is 'translated' by the judge into a legal finding that Napier suffered psychological symptoms (shame, disgust, anxiety, and anger) as a reaction to the stressful environment in C Hall. In particular, the resurgence and persistence of Napier's eczema was found to be caused by the impact of the prison conditions on his physical health:

'Having regard to the factual evidence, the experts medical, psychological, scientific and technical evidence, the informed opinion of those with special experience of prison conditions, I am entirely satisfied that the petitioner was exposed to conditions of detention which, taken together, were such as to diminish his human dignity and to arouse in him feelings of anxiety, anguish, inferiority and humiliation.'[52]

In the second half of the judgment, Lord Bonomy sets out the legal framework for establishing the potential liability of the Scottish Prison Service and the Scottish Ministers for violating Napier's human rights. Section 6 of the Human Rights Act 1998 prohibits a public authority, and section 57(2) of the Scotland Act 1998 prohibits a member of the Scottish Executive, from acting contrary to Convention rights (in this instance, Articles 3 and 8).[53] The question as to

---

[51] para 25.   [52] paras 48 and 78.
[53] For background, see Lord Reed, 'Scotland' in Anthony Lester and David Pannick (eds), *Human Rights Law and Practice* (2004).

whether the Scottish Executive itself can be held *directly* responsible and legally accountable for causing Napier harm—as distinct from its acceptance of executive responsibility for the actions of the Scottish Prison Service in running Barlinnie Prison—is flagged up as a key issue in the dispute. Reference is then made to the range of expert rights knowledges introduced by Napier's legal team on the unacceptability of prison conditions in C Hall throughout the 1990s, in particular the condemnation of the delay in ending slopping out in Scottish prisons. The list of experts included a former Chief Inspector of Prisons for Scotland, a member of the Secretariat for the Prevention of Torture, a former governor of three Scottish prisons, the chairman of the Parole Board for Scotland and the Prison Complaints Commissioner. Their evidence is described by Lord Bonomy as 'an impressive body of consistent, informed opinion about the demeaning nature of slopping out' and the judge then proceeds to a detailed analysis of the Article 3 'inhuman and degrading treatment' jurisprudence of the European Court of Human Rights. In so doing, Lord Bonomy generates a new 'expert' rights knowledge on Article 3 in the specific context of Scottish prison governance.

The argument of the Scottish Ministers that, although Scottish prison conditions were 'unacceptable', they did not fall below the minimum threshold standard set by the Strasbourg Court, was roundly rejected. Lord Bonomy stated:

'[T]o detain a person along with another prisoner in a cramped, stuffy and gloomy cell which is inadequate for the occupation of two people, to confine them there together for at least 20 hours on average per day, to deny him overnight access to a toilet throughout the week and for extended periods at the weekend and to thus expose him to both elements of the slopping out process, to provide no structured activity other than daily walking exercise for one hour and one period of recreation lasting an hour and an half in a week, and to confine him to a 'dog box' for two hours or so each time he entered or left the prison was, in Scotland, in 2001, capable of attaining the minimum level of severity necessary to constitute degrading treatment and thus to infringe Article 3.'[54]

The final issue to be resolved was the determination where legal responsibility lay for the violation of Napier's human rights. Rejecting the Scottish Ministers' arguments that the Governor of Barlinnie Prison (by placing Napier in C Hall), or the Scottish Prison Service (by refusing to transfer Napier from C Hall) were responsible, Lord Bonomy stated that it was Scottish Executive *policy* which effectively determined where remand prisoners in Scotland were detained. Furthermore, it was a *positive choice* by the Scottish Executive in its resource allocation decisions and determination of political priorities which resulted in the continuation of slopping out in C Hall:

'[L]atter day explanations and excuses...have emerged since a positive policy decision was made to divert capital from the Prison Service to tackle other criminal justice problems, which the [Scottish Executive] regarded as priorities. The turning point was devolution

---

[54] para 75. There was also a finding that Napier's Art. 8 Convention right was infringed.

in 1999. ... Two particular facts demonstrate that the [Scottish Executive] could easily have installed integral sanitation in the cells in C Hall before 2001. The first of these was the decision...made in December 1999, to claw £13m back from the Scottish Prison Service budget. ... Secondly, ... C Hall has now been refurbished... [which only] took six months and cost either £3.6m or £4m. ... I consider that section 57(2) is engaged and that the [Scottish Executive] acted *ultra vires* by detaining the petitioner in C Hall when they were aware of the activity of his eczema.'[55]

Identifying Different Types of Organizational Risk

The first way in which we think *Napier* is useful in theorizing the relationship between risk and rights is in drawing our attention to the existence of different types of organizational risk. In what follows, we examine the litigation through this lens and focus in particular on the nature of 'legal risk'—especially the ways in which expert evidence can play a key role in predicting or establishing a causal link between harm (for example, the risk of infection) and legal liability. But we begin by highlighting other aspects of organizational risk that were clearly relevant to the *Napier* litigation. These latter risks remain largely submerged in Lord Bonomy's judgment, but they are crucial to an understanding of the events leading up to the litigation, the strategies adopted in the legal proceedings, and the social, political, and legal aftermath of the case. More generally, attention to the range of organizational risks at play in *Napier* helps to illustrate both the problem with trying to explain risk in discipline-specific terms and the more general tendency towards one-dimensionality in many existing accounts of risk—whether in the penal sector (where, as Sparks points out, risk 'refers primarily to the likelihood of reoffending by the already convicted'[56]) or more broadly (where, as Pat O'Malley has observed, there is a tendency towards models of 'the omniscient or omnicompetent state, or of an irresistible logic of risk'[57]).

Organizational risk (or 'business risk') is now claimed to be fundamental in contemporary governance: specifically, the 'handling of risk'[58] is viewed as an overarching concept of administrative governance in the UK. Hence the Scottish Executive Finance document, *Risk Management: A Self-Assessment Guide*, can be considered typical of the standard literature that permeates the public sector:

'There are broadly three kinds of business risk (although some risks may fall into more than one category): *financial risks*—which are those events and actions which have a direct financial impact on Departments leading to increased expenditure (e.g. claims for compensation) or nugatory spending (e.g. the costs of a failed project); *operational risks*—which

---

[55] paras 85–90. Damages of £2,450 were awarded to Napier for breach of the common law duty to take reasonable care for the health and safety of prisoners.

[56] Sparks, 'Degrees of Estrangement: The Cultural Theory of Risk and Comparative Penology', n 46 above, 160.   [57] Pat O'Malley, *Risk, Uncertainty and Government* (2004) 150.

[58] Strategy Unit of the Cabinet Office, *Risk: Improving Government's Capacity to Handle Risk and Uncertainty, Full Report: A Source Document* (2002) 4.

are those events or actions which could disrupt our ability to provide a service or which could result in a Department acting in a way contrary to its objectives; and *reputational risks* —which are events or actions which could cause embarrassment to Ministers, senior management or to the Scottish Executive in general.'[59]

In our opinion, *Napier* should prompt us to query the actual influence of organizational risk on the policies and practices of the Scottish administration. The judgment has imposed huge financial costs on the Scottish Executive and Scottish Prison Service: £44 million was set aside in the Scottish Prison Service accounts for 2004–05 to cover expected liability arising from *Napier* since 1999.[60] The scale of these potential damages raises interesting questions about the identification and monitoring of financial risk. To what extent do the technical procedures for risk assessment and management in Scottish prison administration actually govern practice? Does the vocabulary of risk in fact '*share* the penal field with other values, commitments, ambitions and restraints'?[61]

Until Scottish political life reveals the decision-making processes that were followed, who had input, and what factors were considered or ignored, we can only speculate on the following: Did the Scottish Executive decide to claw back £13m of the Scottish Prison Service budget confident that it did not run any organizational risk? Did anybody in the Scottish Prison Service have a contrary view and was there a calculated trade-off between different 'risky' outcomes?[62] And did political disagreement or incompetence affect the Executive's approach to slopping out and the *Napier* litigation? Opposition political parties (especially the Scottish Conservatives and the SNP) and media coverage of the litigation generally paint a picture of Executive incompetence and money-wasting: emphasizing, for example, the dispute over who was at fault when the Scottish Ministers failed to lodge an appeal in *Napier* to the Inner House of the Court of Session within the requisite 21 days (which the Court excused).

More generally, can it be claimed that genuine attempts to create a new Parliament and Scottish Executive, alongside the imposition of strict human rights obligations under section 57(2) of the 1998 Act, proved overwhelming for the

---

[59] (2005) para 4. See also, Scottish Executive, *Scottish Public Finance Manual* (2004) para 29, on ensuring that 'risk assessment is embedded into the corporate and performance management, business planning and financial reporting processes and not carried out as an isolated exercise'.

[60] See Auditor General for Scotland's Report (SE/2005/142). The Scottish Prison Service paid legal costs of £970,000 to Napier and an additional £500,000 for legal and other costs incurred by the Scottish Ministers in pursuing the litigation. Over 800 prisoner claims for damages are estimated to be pending.

[61] Sparks, 'Degrees of Estrangement: The Cultural Theory of Risk and Comparative Penology', n 46 above, 161 (our emphasis).

[62] It was argued by Napier's legal team that the implication of the evidence of Dr Andrew Coyle (an expert witness with contacts amongst Scottish prison personnel) was that 'the former chief executive of SPS, Mr Frizzell, had anticipated that the £13 million could and would be used to help end slopping out, and that his departure from office might not have been unconnected with the decision to claw it back' (Written Submissions for the Petitioner, para 3.40).

Scottish administration?[63] Or, in light of the particular 'political risks' associated with the penal realm, were the decisions of the Scottish Ministers, in particular the decision to transfer £13 million from the Scottish Prison Service budget to 'other priorities in the Justice Department such as a drug enforcement agency, tackling domestic violence, and establishing a witness support scheme for all of Scotland's sheriff courts', an example of 'populist punitiveness'? That is, did politicians believe that it was best to reach out to the alleged 'feelings and intuitions of voters and newspaper readers'?[64] If so, Lord Bonomy made it clear that he had a different view, insisting that 'people in general in Scotland' would find slopping out an 'abhorrent practice' if they had 'the misfortune to experience it'.[65]

We turn now to an examination of another type of organizational risk, *legal risk*, which may have played a decisive role in influencing these political deliberations. What we are interested in here is the extent to which the Scottish Executive— and, crucially, its law officers and advisers—fully weighed up the relevant legal framework, including making predictions about the Article 3 jurisprudence of the European Court of Human Rights and its likely influence on the Scottish judiciary. How did they go about assessing the legal risk associated with con- tinuing to detain prisoners in conditions such as C Hall in Barlinnie Prison? Was *Napier*-type litigation expected in 1999 and, when *Napier* commenced in 2003, how did they go about the task of calculating and responding to legal risk in a complex fact context, involving *slopping out* and a *remand* prisoner with a *medical condition*? Moreover (assuming Executive policy decisions *were* being assessed for human rights compliance), what type of legal knowledges (for example, ECHR case law, Committee for the Prevention of Torture reports, common law of negli- gence) were considered, and in what way, in constructing an account of legal risk?

The input of the Scottish Prison Service should have been key here as human rights auditing and organizational risk management had been priorities for the Service in preparing for devolution. One result was the Convention Rights (Compliance) (Scotland) Act 2001, which removed Ministerial control over the release of life prisoners, thereby satisfying ECHR standards on independent and impartial decision-making. Furthermore, as a result of the case of *Anderson v The Scottish Ministers*,[66] involving an unsuccessful challenge to the first Act of the Scottish Parliament, the Mental Health (Public Safety and Appeals) (Scotland) Act 1999, it seems fair to suggest that there would have been an awareness throughout the Scottish administration of the need to take seriously the legal risk of potential human rights challenges.

---

[63] See Chris Himsworth, 'The Hamebringing: Devolving Rights Seriously' in Alan Boyle *et al* (ed.), *Human Rights and Scots Law* (2002) 19–38, 38, re the 'super-imposition of a uniform and rigid human rights regime' on Scotland. On the lack of organizational planning for devolved government, see Richard Parry, 'The Scottish Executive and the Challenges of Complex Policy-Making' (2003) 74 Political Quarterly 450.

[64] Sparks, 'Risk and Blame in Criminal Justice Controversies: British Press Coverage and Official Discourse on Prison Security (1993–6)', n 8 above, 130.   [65] para 23.

[66] [2001] UKPC D5.

However, in *Napier*, Lord Bonomy is openly critical of the complacency of both the Scottish Prison Service and the Scottish Executive as to whether the conditions in Barlinnie Prison were contrary to human rights standards:

'The Chief Executive of the Prison Service wrote to the [Prison Complaints] Commissioner . . . "The Scottish Prison Service agrees that slopping is a degrading practice which has no place in the modern prison system." . . . As recently as 18 April 2002, the then Justice Minister Jim Wallace told the Parliament: "We believe that slopping out is unacceptable. . . . [T]he concession made by witnesses from the Prison Service was generally to describe the conditions as 'unacceptable' ". The witnesses appeared to be comfortable with that description as one which recognised a need for improvement but did not acknowledge any greater failure than falling short of a standard of desirability.'[67]

A number of factors may help to explain why the Scottish Executive may have felt confident that it was not running a significant legal risk and that its prison policy was actually human rights compliant. First, in the course of their legal arguments in *Napier*, there was strong reliance on the assertion that Scottish prison conditions would not fall below the Strasbourg Court's 'high threshold' test for inhuman and degrading treatment under Article 3 of the ECHR.[68] This approach to interpreting human rights norms is reminiscent of accounts of risk as '*decidable* by the perfection of technical knowledge'.[69] It also ignores the way in which national judges will sometimes use the ECHR jurisprudence as an essential, but *not determinative*, adjudicatory tool.[70] This contingency of human rights adjudication is amplified when, as in *Napier*, an extensive range of written and oral risk and rights knowledges are placed before the court.

Secondly, there may have been an element of reliance on the historical conservatism of the Scottish judiciary.[71] In particular, an assumption that the judiciary would not involve itself in detailed questions of prison governance, especially when policy choices and allocation of resources were at stake. Even if the case was to be lost, the Scottish Executive argued that only a determination that the Scottish Prison Service had violated section 6 of the Human Rights Act 1998 should be made—and not a determination under section 57(2) of the Scotland Act 1998 that the Executive itself had acted contrary to Convention rights. However, as outlined earlier, Lord Bonomy rejected such 'blame avoidance': he found section 57(2) directly engaged and he pursued the line of executive

---

[67] paras 58–59 and 64.

[68] The Scottish Ministers' argument about re-allocating resources would also lend support to this view as it could only form the basis of a possible defence under the limitation clause in Art. 8(2); the guarantee in Art. 3, by contrast, is absolute.

[69] Sparks, 'Degrees of Estrangement: The Cultural Theory of Risk and Comparative Penology', n 46 above, 163.

[70] For a discussion of different styles of legal knowledge, see Christopher McCrudden, 'A Common Law of Human Rights?: Transnational Judicial Conversations on Constitutional Rights' (2000) 20 Oxford Journal of Legal Studies 499.

[71] See generally, Stephen Tierney, 'Constitutionalising the Role of the Judge: Scotland and the New Order' in Boyle, *Human Rights and Scots Law*, n 63 above, 57–81.

accountability up to Ministerial level, closely examining the detail of the policy choices that were made.[72]

The nature of 'legal risk' in the new Scottish rights culture will have been a surprise to many, not just the Scottish Executive.[73] Lord Bonomy's account of legal risk in *Napier* illustrates a judicial journey—from an historically antagonistic view of the ECHR, in a legal culture which characterized itself as lacking a 'Scots public law', to the use of Article 3 jurisprudence to question and condemn the re-allocation of £13 million of Scottish Executive finances. It goes without saying that this journey is potentially repeatable in other contexts. One lasting effect of *Napier*, therefore, may be to force not just the Scottish administration, but the Scottish public sector generally (for example, local authorities), to conduct its organizational risk assessments in ways that now acknowledge the complexity of *legal risk in a rights culture*.[74]

Processes of Translation

The second main point that we want to draw from *Napier* is the need to focus on processes of 'translation', including 'knowledge swapping'. We have taken these terms from the work of Mariana Valverde and others.[75] The first refers to the ways in which risk and its evaluation undergo changes—how they are 'either reinforced or solidified or else contradicted or undermined'[76]—when they move from one site to another (for example, from the scientific to the legal field, and from the legal one to the scientific). The second term refers to a specific translation practice: namely, the migration of knowledges between legally trained personnel and extra-legal professionals.

In order to study translation, generalizations about law have to be put aside. This includes the assumption that legal processes are dominated by expert knowledges and, its counterpart, that expert knowledges are separate from law. The effective study of translation requires a focus on the detail of specific processes, 'asking questions about the specific role played by knowledges of extra-legal and legal provenance in particular "problematizations"'.[77] Taking *Napier* as an example of a 'problematization', the first thing to note is that a range of knowledges were

---

[72] One consequence, however, of this focus on how Executive policy decisions led to the violation of Art. 3 is the absence of any detailed information on the management and priorities of the Scottish Prison Service, a problem in regulation analysis terms as the delivery level is as relevant and interesting as the policy level.

[73] See also *Somerville v The Scottish Ministers* [2005] CSOH 24 (claims for damages under the SA 1998 are not time-barred as under the HRA 1998); and Barry K. Winetrobe, 'The Judge in the Scottish Parliament Chamber' [2005] Public Law 3.

[74] Another effect of *Napier*, arguably, has been to contribute to the political wariness about the impact of the new human rights framework: see the Scottish Parliament Justice 1 Committee Report (23 February 2006), which refused to endorse the general principles of the proposed Scottish Commissioner for Human Rights Bill and asserted that 'breaches of human rights are extremely rare' in Scotland.   [75] Valverde *et al*, 'Legal Knowledges of Risk', n 39 above.

[76] ibid, 86.   [77] ibid, 93.

present. Secondly, expert risk knowledges (environmental, medical, psychological, etc) introduced into the litigation by both parties were used by Lord Bonomy to build up a picture of the living environment and routine in Barlinnie Prison, thereby bringing the normative framework of Article 3 to life. The judge also incorporated lay or everyday knowledges, specifically those of prisoners and prison officers in C Hall. In addition, he invoked the common sense of 'people in general in Scotland':

'I was left in no doubt, by the evidence of those who experienced slopping out in C Hall around the time of [Napier's] detention, that it was an abhorrent practice, and that people in general in Scotland would have found it to be so, had they had the misfortune to experience it.'[78]

One conclusion to be drawn from the mixing of knowledges in Lord Bonomy's judgment is that we need to be careful in the assumptions we make about 'expert' evidence. There is no obvious hierarchy of knowledge or expertise in the legal reasoning in *Napier*. In formulating his definition of degrading treatment under Article 3, Lord Bonomy used not just the detail in the science-based evidence but also the detail in the evidence provided by the prisoners and prison officers. It is, therefore, not easy to identify the specific authority or role of the science-based evidence.

In order to provide an example of 'swapping knowledges', we need to draw directly on the work of Valverde *et al*. They provide a case study on the ways in which courts in New Jersey have 'translated' expert assessments of risk of re-offending under Megan's Law, a community notification statute authorizing public access to information about the identity of convicted sex offenders who are considered to present a risk of re-offending. 'Swapping knowledges' occurs in the prosecutorial and judicial practice of relying on reports of acts, or alleged acts, that have not been the subject of a conviction in order to determine the risk level of particular individuals. In short, 'despite privileging legal knowledge in the risk assessment process', courts 'then rely on non-legal paradigms to renegotiate legal practices'.[79] Hence:

'The judge may rely on documentation he or she considers relevant and trustworthy in making a determination . . . This may include but is not limited to criminal complaints not the subject of a conviction but which are supported by credible evidence, victim statements, admissions by the registrant, police reports, medical, psychological or psychiatric reports, pre-sentencing reports and Department of Corrections discharge summaries.'[80]

One final point merits mention here. In developing an account of translation in the field of risk and rights, it should not be assumed that judgment by a court marks the end of the process. As socio-legal scholars have emphasized, it is important to

---

[78] para 23. Valverde *et al* also stress the need to include the role that 'common sense' can play in processes of translation.   [79] ibid, 106.

[80] ibid, 106–7, citing *In the Matter of Registrant C.A.*, N.J. Superior Court 1995, 347–48.

go on to examine implementation, especially in a rights culture; and, in light of the fluidity and hybridity of risk, this task is arguably doubly important in a 'risk and rights' culture. Furthermore, as Valverde has argued, in her exploration of the 'risk of harm' test used by the Canadian Supreme Court in freedom of expression challenges to obscenity laws, it is not easy to predict what effects flow from judicial decisions:

'... something that makes the mapping of pragmatic effects difficult is the fact that, while discourses such as psychiatry are closely attached to enforcement machineries (with the writers of key texts often being in charge of hospital wards), judges do not have direct control over the enforcement of their own texts. Something that is often forgotten by those who stress the 'sovereign' aspect of the criminal law is that judges do not give direct orders to either prosecutors or police: their words cannot be directly contradicted by the enforcers but they can be endlessly reinterpreted, applied, or not applied.'[81]

Risks and Rights Cultures

The final point we draw from *Napier* concerns the question of culture: an understanding of risk and rights requires consideration of the specificity of particular cultural contexts.[82] As we have argued throughout, constructions of risk and rights are socially mediated; in other words, perceptions of both risk and rights are the product of politically negotiated outcomes. The understanding of a particular risk, or human right, by professional actors (as well as by the media and the public generally) will be influenced by different beliefs, values, knowledges, and practices. Thus, different cultures can produce different understandings of risk and rights.

The *Napier* litigation provides a clear illustration of this. It points, first, to the need to see the *legal cultures* of Scotland, the UK, and the European Court of Human Rights as related but also distinct: that is, to the need to reflect on the ways in which human rights norms are interpreted and articulated within, and between, these legal orders, and also how judicial self-perception varies across and within legal cultures.[83] Lord Bonomy's judgment makes use of both 'foreign' and local culture: it invokes the abolition of slopping out in England and Wales by 1996 as a comparative benchmark against which to establish the obligations of the Scottish Executive, and it also insists that 'people in general in Scotland' would find slopping out an 'abhorrent practice' if they had 'the misfortune to experience it'.[84] The significance of devolution must also be addressed. In a

---

[81] Valverde, 'The Harms of Sex and the Risks of Breasts: Obscenity and Indecency in Canadian Law' n 29 above, 184.

[82] For discussion of the different meanings of 'culture', and the relationship between rights and culture, see Jane Cowan *et al* (eds), *Culture and Rights: Anthropological Perspectives* (2001); and David Nelken, 'Using the Concept of Legal Culture' (2004) 29 Australian Journal of Legal Philosophy 1.

[83] See generally, Murray Hunt, 'The Human Rights Act and Legal Culture: The Judiciary and the Legal Profession' (1999) 26 Journal of Law & Society 86.   [84] para 23.

devolved framework, there is the obvious need to consider the political (and financial) relationship between 'London' and 'Edinburgh' in relation to risk assessment and management of litigation like *Napier*, and the influence that UK Treasury officials and Whitehall legal officers have on the Scottish decision-making process.[85] *Napier* also raises the question of the distinctiveness of legal professional cultures. The 'pioneering' litigation strategy adopted by Napier's legal team centred on a mass of expert risk and human rights knowledges. Another notable feature was the use of key professionals (such as Scottish prison inspectors) as expert witnesses and the reliance on significant legal aid backing. The success of the strategy raises questions as to whether it could work in other prisoner rights' contexts and whether, more generally, it might be adopted as standard practice for human rights litigation in Scotland. A key factor here may be whether damages are being sought as part of the human rights litigation, as distinct from other remedies such as declaratory relief, and any long-term political and financial 'fallout' from claims for compensation against public authorities.[86]

The distinctiveness of different *organizational cultures* also requires attention. Organizations involved in prison governance—for example, the Scottish Finance Department, the Scottish Prison Service, and the Scottish Women's Prison at Corton Vale[87]—will differ from one another, especially in relation to understanding and prioritizing risks, including 'legal risk'. They will also differ on rights, with some adopting a broader understanding of the value of human rights compliance.[88] Distinctive cultures will also exist within an individual organization: there will be agreement, resistance, and diversity amongst individuals (and between different groups) as to role-perception, the choices available and awareness of the politics of accountability.

[85] For critiques of devolved Scotland as a distinctive political and legal culture, see Kenneth Armstrong, 'Contesting Government, Producing Devolution: The Repeal of 'Section 28' in Scotland' (2003) 23 Legal Studies 205; and Gavin Little, 'Scotland and Parliamentary Sovereignty' (2004) 24 Legal Studies 540.

[86] See *Martin v Northern Ireland Prison Service* [2006] NIQB 1, para 42, where no damages were awarded on public interest grounds after a finding that slopping out violated the prisoner's Art. 8 right: 'Having regard to the wider public who have an interest in the continued funding of a public service one cannot lose sight of the financial consequences of even a modest award . . . to the large number of prisoners going through the prison system at Magilligan.'

[87] See Pat Carlen, 'Death and the Triumph of Governance? Lessons from the Scottish Women's Prison' (2001) 3 Punishment and Society 459. For litigation on the sanitation conditions in a women's prison, see *Carson v Northern Ireland Prison Service* [2005] NIQB 80 (arrangements did not violate Arts 3 and 8).

[88] See eg *Martin*, above n 86, para 22: 'The powerpoint documentation used at the training showed a general education on the implications of the 1998 [Human Rights] Act and the Convention. The [Northern Ireland] Prison Service witnesses, however, revealed a somewhat cursory and unparticularised knowledge of the Convention'. More generally, it has been argued that the absence of an array of audit and performance indicators associated with the HRA has affected its implementation, and relative prioritization, by local authorities: see Luke Clements and Rachel Morris, 'The Millennium Blip: The Human Rights Act 1998 and Local Government' in Halliday and Schmidt, *Human Rights Brought Home: Socio-Legal Perspectives on Human Rights in the National Context*, n 41 above, 209–29.

We would argue that regulation scholarship should be seen as a key resource in fleshing out the culture element of a risk and rights enquiry. There is a need for information on how different areas of social and economic life respond to governance by legal and non-legal rules, and the relationships between these sets of rules.[89] This is especially so in light of the twin requirements on public authorities of organizational risk management (with its origins in private sector standards of corporate governance) and human rights compliance. To date, there has been a dearth of literature addressing how these two regulatory forces combine in the public sector. That said, what we do know suggests that risk management practice is variable and that 'organisations adopt structures and follow procedures not just, or not even, to achieve goals, but to gain legitimacy in the widest sense'. As Julia Black points out, this emphasis on legitimacy has important political effects:

'The rhetoric of 'risk management' and 'risk-based' approaches combines a sense of strategy and control in a way which is politically compelling; moreover, framing one's actions as 'risk-based' is, in the current climate, a useful legitimating device. But the framing of the regulatory task in terms of risk has the potential to have more than a rhetorical effect: it imports particular conceptions of the problem at hand, and leads to the framing of a solution in a particular way.'[90]

Conclusion

In this essay, we have described how UK human rights lawyers and criminologists have mostly followed separate paths of scholarship, even in areas of common interest. We have sought to problematize this separation by pointing to the need for a new stream of academic enquiry into risk and rights in prison governance. Penal policy and practice, as well as prison law, have become enveloped by discourses of risk and of rights: what is little understood, however, is how these discourses are interacting with one another.

Using the case of *Napier*, we suggested three necessary features of a risk and rights analysis in the prisons context: first, the importance of identifying and taking account of different types of organizational risk (such as financial, legal, and political risks), and investigating how they are affected by the growth of rights consciousness. Secondly, there needs to be detailed examination of processes of 'translation'; that is, the ways in which evaluations of risk can be either fortified or weakened when they move from one site to another (for example, from the scientific field to the legal one), and also how risk knowledges migrate between legal and non-legal actors. Thirdly, account has to be taken of cultural

---

[89] See eg C. Parker *et al* (eds), *Regulating Law* (2004); and Hood *et al, The Government of Risk: Understanding Risk Regulation Regimes*, n 12 above.

[90] Black, 'The Emergence of Risk-Based Regulation and the New Public Risk Management in the United Kingdom', n 18 above, 519.

contexts: constructions of risk and rights are socially mediated and the differences within, and between, cultures need to be acknowledged.

These suggestions should not be treated as a finite list; other questions will also have to be addressed. More generally, it needs to be acknowledged that analysing the intersection of risk and rights knowledges will be genuinely complex, not least because in critiquing the processes of politicization surrounding 'human rights' and 'risk', the temptation to see one concept as more politically controversial than the other, or one as the essential constraint on the other, will have to be resisted.

Index